To my parents

*Imagination is more important
than knowledge.*

– Albert Einstein

Microsoft®

Programming Microsoft® ASP.NET 2.0 Core Reference

Dino Esposito

PUBLISHED BY
Microsoft Press
A Division of Microsoft Corporation
One Microsoft Way
Redmond, Washington 98052-6399

Library of Congress Control Number 2005933933

Printed and bound in the United States of America.

3 4 5 6 7 8 9   QWT   8 7 6

Distributed in Canada by H.B. Fenn and Company Ltd.

A CIP catalogue record for this book is available from the British Library.

Microsoft Press books are available through booksellers and distributors worldwide. For further information about international editions, contact your local Microsoft Corporation office or contact Microsoft Press International directly at fax (425) 936-7329. Visit our Web site at www.microsoft.com/mspress. Send comments to *mspinput@microsoft.com*.

Acquisitions Editor: Ben Ryan
Project Editors: Lynn Finnel
Technical Editor: Kenn Scribner
Copy Editor: Roger LeBlanc
Indexer: Lynn Armstrong

Body Part No. X11-50070

Contents at a Glance

Part I **Building an ASP.NET Page**

1　The ASP.NET Programming Model 3

2　Web Development in Microsoft Visual Studio .NET 2005 37

3　Anatomy of an ASP.NET Page 79

4　ASP.NET Core Server Controls 119

5　Working with the Page 175

6　Rich Page Composition 219

Part II **Adding Data in an ASP.NET Site**

7　ADO.NET Data Providers 263

8　ADO.NET Data Containers 319

9　The Data-Binding Model 353

10　Creating Bindable Grids of Data 413

11　Managing Views of a Record 467

Part III **ASP.NET Infrastructure**

12　The HTTP Request Context 501

13　State Management 537

14　ASP.NET Caching 591

15　ASP.NET Security 647

Table of Contents

Acknowledgments. xv
Introduction xvii

Part I   Building an ASP.NET Page

1   The ASP.NET Programming Model 3

What's ASP.NET, Anyway? 4
Programming in the Age of Web Forms 5
Event-Driven Programming over HTTP 6
The HTTP Protocol 8
Structure of an ASP.NET Page 11
The ASP.NET Component Model 15
A Model for Component Interaction 15
The *runat* Attribute 16
ASP.NET Server Controls 19
The ASP.NET Development Stack 20
The Presentation Layer 20
The Page Framework 22
The HTTP Runtime Environment 24
The ASP.NET Provider Model 27
The Rationale Behind the Provider Model 27
A Quick Look at the ASP.NET Implementation 30
Conclusion 34

2   Web Development in Microsoft Visual Studio .NET 2005 37

Introducing Visual Studio .NET 2005 38
Visual Studio .NET 2003 Common Gripes 38
Visual Studio .NET 2005 Highlights 40
Create an ASP.NET Project 45
Page Design Features 45
Adding Code to the Project 53
ASP.NET Reserved Folders 57
Build the ASP.NET Project 63

Application Deployment. 66

XCopy Deployment. 66

Site Precompilation. 69

Administering an ASP.NET Application. 72

The Web Site Administration Tool. 72

Editing ASP.NET Configuration Files. 75

Conclusion 77

3   Anatomy of an ASP.NET Page. 79

Invoking a Page 79

The Runtime Machinery. 80

Processing the Request. 86

The Processing Directives of a Page 91

The *Page* Class 99

Properties of the *Page* Class 100

Methods of the *Page* Class. 103

Events of the *Page* Class. 108

The Eventing Model 109

The Page Life Cycle 110

Page Setup 110

Handling the Postback 113

Page Finalization 114

Conclusion 116

4   ASP.NET Core Server Controls 119

Generalities of ASP.NET Server Controls. 120

Properties of the *Control* Class 121

Methods of the *Control* Class. 124

Events of the *Control* Class. 124

New Features 125

HTML Controls 129

Generalities of HTML Controls. 129

HTML Container Controls. 132

HTML Input Controls. 138

The *HtmlImage* Control 144

Web Controls 145

Generalities of Web Controls. 145

Core Web Controls 148

Miscellaneous Web Controls 154

Validation Controls. 159
 Generalities of Validation Controls 160
 Gallery of Controls. 162
 Special Capabilities. 166
Conclusion. 172

5 Working with the Page **175**
Programming with Forms. 176
 The *HtmlForm* Class. 176
 Multiple Forms 178
 Cross-Page Postings. 182
Dealing with Page Errors. 188
 Basics of Error Handling 188
 Mapping Errors to Pages. 192
ASP.NET Tracing 197
 Tracing the Execution Flow in ASP.NET. 197
 Writing Trace Messages. 199
 The Trace Viewer 201
Page Personalization 202
 Creating the User Profile. 203
 Interacting with the Page 206
 Profile Providers 212
Conclusion. 216

6 Rich Page Composition. **219**
Working with Master Pages 220
 Authoring Rich Pages in ASP.NET 1.x 220
 Writing a Master Page. 222
 Writing a Content Page. 225
 Processing Master and Content Pages 229
 Programming the Master Page 233
Working with Themes 236
 Understanding ASP.NET Themes 237
 Theming Pages and Controls 241
 Putting Themes to Work. 244
Working with Wizards 247
 An Overview of the *Wizard* Control 248
 Adding Steps to a Wizard 252
 Navigating Through the Wizard 255
Conclusion. 259

Part II   Adding Data in an ASP.NET Site

7   ADO.NET Data Providers 263

.NET Data Access Infrastructure 264

.NET Managed Data Providers 265

Data Sources You Access Through ADO.NET 268

The Provider Factory Model 271

Connecting to Data Sources 274

The *SqlConnection* Class 275

Connection Strings 280

Connection Pooling 287

Executing Commands 293

The *SqlCommand* Class 293

ADO.NET Data Readers 297

Asynchronous Commands 303

Working with Transactions 308

SQL Server 2005–Specific Enhancements 313

Conclusion 317

8   ADO.NET Data Containers 319

Data Adapters 319

The *SqlDataAdapter* Class 320

The Table-Mapping Mechanism 326

How Batch Update Works 330

In-Memory Data Container Objects 332

The *DataSet* Object 333

The *DataTable* Object 340

Data Relations 346

The *DataView* Object 348

Conclusion 351

9   The Data-Binding Model 353

Data Source–Based Data Binding 354

Feasible Data Sources 354

Data-Binding Properties 357

List Controls 362

Iterative Controls 368

Data-Binding Expressions 373
    Simple Data Binding 373
    The *DataBinder* Class 376
    Other Data-Binding Methods 378
Data Source Components 382
    Overview of Data Source Components 382
    Internals of Data Source Controls 384
    The *SqlDataSource* Control 386
    The *AccessDataSource* Class 392
    The *ObjectDataSource* Control 393
    The *SiteMapDataSource* Class 404
    The *XmlDataSource* Class 407
Conclusion 411

10   **Creating Bindable Grids of Data** **413**
The *DataGrid* Control 414
    The *DataGrid* Object Model 414
    Binding Data to the Grid 419
    Working with the *DataGrid* 423
The *GridView* Control 427
    The *GridView* Object Model 428
    Binding Data to a *GridView* Control 433
    Paging Data 442
    Sorting Data 449
    Editing Data 455
    Advanced Capabilities 459
Conclusion 464

11   **Managing Views of a Record** **467**
The *DetailsView* Control 467
    The *DetailsView* Object Model 468
    Binding Data to a *DetailsView* Control 474
    Creating Master/Detail Views 477
    Working with Data 480
The *FormView* Control 489
    The *FormView* Object Model 489
    Binding Data to a *FormView* Control 491
    Editing Data 494
Conclusion 497

Part III   ASP.NET Infrastructure

12   The HTTP Request Context. 501

Initialization of the Application 502

Properties of the *HttpApplication* Class 502

Application Modules. 503

Methods of the *HttpApplication* Class 503

Events of the *HttpApplication* Class. 504

The *global.asax* File 507

Compiling *global.asax*. 508

Syntax of *global.asax* 509

Tracking Errors and Anomalies 512

The *HttpContext* Class. 514

Properties of the *HttpContext* Class 515

Methods of the *HttpContext* Class 516

The *Server* Object. 518

Properties of the *HttpServerUtility* Class 518

Methods of the *HttpServerUtility* Class. 518

The *HttpResponse* Object 524

Properties of the *HttpResponse* Class 524

Methods of the *HttpResponse* Class 528

The *HttpRequest* Object 530

Properties of the *HttpRequest* Class 531

Methods of the *HttpRequest* Class 534

Conclusion 535

13   State Management 537

The Application's State 538

Properties of the *HttpApplicationState* Class. 539

Methods of the *HttpApplicationState* Class 539

State Synchronization 540

Tradeoffs of Application State 541

The Session's State 542

The Session-State HTTP Module 543

Properties of the *HttpSessionState* Class 548

Methods of the *HttpSessionState* Class 549

Working with Session's State. 549
  Identifying a Session 550
  Lifetime of a Session 555
  Persist Session Data to Remote Servers 557
  Persist Session Data to SQL Server. 562
Customizing Session State Management 567
  Building a Custom Session-State Provider 568
  Generating a Custom Session ID 571
The View State of a Page. 573
  The *StateBag* Class 574
  Common Issues with View State 575
  Programming Web Forms Without View State 578
  Changes in the ASP.NET 2.0 View State 581
  Keeping the View State on the Server. 586
Conclusion. 589

14   ASP.NET Caching **591**
Caching Application Data 591
  The *Cache* Class 592
  Working with the ASP.NET *Cache* 596
  Practical Issues 604
  Designing a Custom Dependency. 609
  A Cache Dependency for XML Data 612
  SQL Server Cache Dependency 616
Caching ASP.NET Pages. 624
  The *@OutputCache* Directive. 625
  The *HttpCachePolicy* Class 630
  Caching Multiple Versions of a Page. 633
  Caching Portions of ASP.NET Pages. 636
  Advanced Features in ASP.NET 2.0. 641
Conclusion. 644

15   ASP.NET Security **647**

    Where the Threats Come From 648

    The ASP.NET Security Context 648

        Who Really Runs My ASP.NET Application? 649

        Changing the Identity of the ASP.NET Process 652

        The Trust Level of ASP.NET Applications 655

        ASP.NET Authentication Methods 658

    Using Forms Authentication 660

        Forms Authentication Control Flow 661

        The *FormsAuthentication* Class 665

        Configuration of Forms Authentication 667

        Advanced Forms Authentication Features 671

    The Membership and Role Management API 675

        The *Membership* Class 676

        The Membership Provider 682

        Managing Roles 686

    Security-Related Controls 691

        The *Login* Control 691

        The *LoginName* Control 694

        The *LoginStatus* Control 694

        The *LoginView* Control 696

        The *PasswordRecovery* Control 698

        The *ChangePassword* Control 699

        The *CreateUserWizard* Control 701

    Conclusion 702

Index 705

Acknowledgments

A good ensemble of people made this book happen: Ben Ryan, Lynn Finnel, Kenn Scribner, Roger LeBlanc, Robert Lyon. To all of them I owe a monumental "thank you" for being so kind, patient, and accurate. They reviewed, edited, reworked, and tested all the text and code that makes up this book.

Other people contributed in various ways to improve the overall quality of the book that you hold in your hands. An unordered list of names certainly includes Jeff Prosise, Fernando Guerrero, Marius Constantinescu, Marco Bellinaso, and Steve Toub. I would especially like to thank Andrea Saltarello, who spent quite a few afternoons typing quickly on messenger to help me out with problematic examples and design patterns that were not very well understood, as well as with unknown Internet Information Server (IIS) features and common practices.

A bunch of other people helped me significantly, although perhaps unknowingly. Many of them just posted on their respective blogs, but Google was smart enough to catch their thoughtful remarks and comments and serve them to me. Thanks to Fritz Onion, Julia Lerman, Shawn Farkas, Scott Hanselman, Angel Saenz-Badillos, Bertrand LeRoy, Mike Pope, and Fredrik Normen.

Matthew Gibbs, Brad Millington, Nikhil Kothari, and Stefan Schackow on the Microsoft ASP.NET team provided significant help and contributed a lot to transform my hunches and hypotheses into correct statements. And thanks to Scott Guthrie for being so surprisingly quick with his answers in spite of the huge amount of work that he was doing to make ASP.NET a wonderful reality.

Bits and pieces of this book appeared in my monthly "Cutting Edge" column in *MSDN Magazine*. Writing a book is a very long process that unfolds itself in many little steps. A good chapter sometimes begins with a good article, and a good article begins with a good idea. Good ideas come more easily if there's great technology behind it. Thanks to Steve Toub, Josh Trupin, and all the great people at *MSDN Magazine*.

It was my greatest pleasure to work with all of you!

—Dino

PS: After years of practice, my wife and kids treated this nearly 1000-page book as usual business. Nothing special, just everyday work. They know me. And how to handle me.

Introduction

The beginning of Web development dates back ten years. Since then, numerous technologies have crossed our lives at different speeds, leaving a variety of memories. We had meteors like ActiveX Documents and vivid stars like Active Server Pages (ASP). ASP in particular, I believe, marked the watershed; it was introduced around 1997. ASP made it clear that real-world Web development was possible only through a rich and powerful server-side programming model.

Just as Microsoft Visual Basic did for Microsoft Windows development, ASP provided a set of server tools to build dynamic applications quickly and effectively and showed the way ahead. ASP.NET is the culmination of Web development technologies that have rapidly followed one another over the past ten years—one building on another, and each filling the gaps left by its predecessor. As a result, ASP.NET is currently the most technologically advanced, feature-rich, and powerful platform for building distributed applications transported by the HTTP protocol.

The more you work with ASP.NET, the more you realize that even more is needed. ASP.NET simplifies a number of tasks and presents itself as a sort of programming paradise, especially for developers coming from classic ASP. ASP.NET 1.1 only whetted the appetite of the developer community. Thus, after the first months of working with and assessing ASP.NET 1.1, members of the developer community started asking and wishing for more—in fact, much more.

ASP.NET 2.0 is a major upgrade to the platform, even though it doesn't introduce any new or revolutionary programming paradigm to learn. At first sight, there's no radically new approach to code design and implementation and there's no new syntax model to become familiar with. Nonetheless, ASP.NET 2.0 is a fundamental milestone in the Microsoft Web development roadmap.

Reworked and enhanced as a development platform, ASP.NET 2.0 makes new practices emerge as best practices. Its new programming techniques require attention from architects and lead developers, and its new system features provide native solutions to known issues with earlier versions.

Today, programming ASP.NET applications means becoming familiar with all techniques available and possible, no matter which version of the platform you're actually using. This book covers the state of the art in Web programming with Microsoft .NET technologies. You'll find it useful no matter which version of ASP.NET you use, with each topic covered in a top-down approach—from the broader perspective of the feature, down to the implementation and programming details of a particular ASP.NET version.

A book that attempts to detail state-of-the-art ASP.NET programming practices can't do that in fewer than 2000 pages. Therefore, we cover ASP.NET 2.0 in two books: *Programming Microsoft ASP.NET 2.0 Core Reference* and *Programming Microsoft ASP.NET 2.0 Applications: Advanced Topics*. People who buy both books will get a complete reference and programmer's guide to

ASP.NET and related technologies such as ADO.NET, mobile applications, and Web services. People who buy only one of the books get coverage of either fundamental topics or more advanced ASP.NET topics.

This book provides in-depth coverage of the ASP.NET fundamentals: the HTTP runtime, security, caching, state management, pages, controls, and data binding and data access.

Who Is This Book For?

To avoid beating around the bush, let me state clearly: this is not a book for novice developers. This is not the appropriate book if you have only a faint idea of what ASP.NET is or if you are looking for an introduction to ASP.NET technology. If you are a novice and looking for step-by-step instruction, start with *Microsoft ASP.NET 2.0 Step By Step*, by George Shepherd (Microsoft Press, 2005). Once you have grabbed hold of ASP.NET principles and features and want to apply them, this core reference is the book for you.

Here you won't find screen shots illustrating Visual Studio 2005 wizards or any mention of options to select or unselect to get a certain behavior from your code. Of course, this doesn't mean that I am against Visual Studio 2005 or that I don't recommend using Visual Studio 2005 to develop ASP.NET applications. Visual Studio 2005 is a great tool for writing ASP.NET 2.0 applications but, from an ASP.NET perspective, Visual Studio is merely a tool. This book, instead, is all about the ASP.NET technology.

If you already know Visual Studio 2005 and its wonderful set of tricks and time-saving features and feel ready to learn more about the underlying machinery, this is the right book for you.

I do recommend this book to developers who have read and digested *Microsoft ASP.NET 2.0 Step By Step* or have equivalent knowledge. This book is certainly a useful reference for your library; it's just not the book to begin with.

System Requirements

You'll need the following hardware and software to build and run the code samples for this book:

- Microsoft Windows XP with Service Pack 2, Microsoft Windows Server 2003 with Service Pack 1, or Microsoft Windows 2000 with Service Pack 4.

- Microsoft Visual Studio 2005 Standard Edition or Microsoft Visual Studio 2005 Professional Edition.

- Internet Information Services (IIS) is not strictly required, but it is helpful for testing sample applications in a realistic run-time environment.

- Microsoft SQL Server 2005 Express (included with Visual Studio 2005) or Microsoft SQL Server 2005.

- The Northwind database of Microsoft SQL Server 2000 is used in most examples in this book to demonstrate data-access techniques throughout the book.

- 766-MHz Pentium or compatible processor (1.5 GHz Pentium recommended).

- 256 MB RAM (512 MB or more recommended).

- Video (800 × 600 or higher resolution) monitor with at least 256 colors (1024 × 768 High Color 16-bit recommended).

- CD-ROM or DVD-ROM drive.

- Microsoft Mouse or compatible pointing device.

Configuring SQL Server 2005 Express Edition

Chapters 5 through 11 of this book require that you have access to SQL Server 2005 Express Edition (or SQL Server 2005) to create and use the Northwind Traders database. If you are using SQL Server 2005 Express Edition, log in as Administrator on your computer and follow these steps to grant access to the user account that you will be using for performing the exercises in these chapters:

1. On the Windows Start menu, click All Programs, click Accessories, and then click Command Prompt to open a Command Prompt window.

2. In the Command Prompt window, type the following command:

   ```
   sqlcmd -S YourServer\SQLExpress -E
   ```

   Replace *YourServer* with the name of your computer.

   You can find the name of your computer by running the *hostname* command in the Command Prompt window, before running the *sqlcmd* command.

3. At the 1> prompt, type the following command, including the square brackets, and then press Enter:

   ```
   sp_grantlogin [YourServer\UserName]
   ```

   Replace *YourServer* with the name of your computer, and replace *UserName* with the name of the user account you will be using.

4. At the 2> prompt, type the following command and then press Enter:

   ```
   go
   ```

   If you see an error message, make sure you have typed the *sp_grantlogin* command correctly, including the square brackets.

5. At the 1> prompt, type the following command, including the square brackets, and then press Enter:

   ```
   sp_addsrvrolemember [YourServer\UserName], dbcreator
   ```

6. At the 2> prompt, type the following command and then press Enter:

   go

   If you see an error message, make sure you have typed the *sp_addsrvrolemember* command correctly, including the square brackets.

7. At the 1> prompt, type the following command and then press Enter:

   exit

8. Close the Command Prompt window.

Prerelease Software

This book was reviewed and tested against the August 2005 Community Technical Preview (CTP) of Visual Studio 2005. The August CTP was the last preview before the final release of Visual Studio 2005. This book is expected to be fully compatible with the final release of Visual Studio 2005. If there are any changes or corrections for this book, they will be collected and added to a Microsoft Knowledge Base article. See the "Support for this Book" section in this Introduction for more information.

Technology Updates

As technologies related to this book are updated, links to additional information will be added to the Microsoft Press Technology Updates Web page. Visit this page periodically for updates on Visual Studio 2005 and other technologies:

http://www.microsoft.com/mspress/updates/

Code Samples

All of the code samples discussed in this book can be downloaded from the book's companion content page at the following address:

http://www.microsoft.com/mspress/companion/0-7356-2176-4/

Support for This Book

Every effort has been made to ensure the accuracy of this book and the companion content. As corrections or changes are collected, they will be added to a Microsoft Knowledge Base article. To view the list of known corrections for this book, visit the following article:

http://support.microsoft.com/kb/905045

Microsoft Press provides support for books and companion content at the following Web site:

http://www.microsoft.com/learning/support/books/

Questions and Comments

If you have comments, questions, or ideas regarding the book or the companion content, or questions that are not answered by visiting the preceding sites, please send them to Microsoft Press via e-mail to

mspinput@microsoft.com

or via postal mail to

Microsoft Press
Attn: *Programming Microsoft ASP.NET 2.0 Core Reference* Editor
One Microsoft Way
Redmond, WA 98052-6399

Please note that Microsoft software product support is not offered through the above addresses.

Part I
Building an ASP.NET Page

Chapter 1
The ASP.NET Programming Model

In this chapter:
What's ASP.NET, Anyway?. 4
The ASP.NET Component Model. 15
The ASP.NET Development Stack 20
The ASP.NET Provider Model. 27
Conclusion 34

ASP.NET is a Web development platform that provides services, a programming model, and software infrastructure necessary to build enterprise-class applications. Although largely syntax compatible with its popular predecessor—Active Server Pages (ASP)—ASP.NET is a revolutionary new programming framework designed to enable the rapid development of Web applications. As part of the Microsoft .NET platform, ASP.NET provides a component-based, extensible, and easy-to-use way to build, deploy, and run Web applications that target any browser or mobile device.

ASP.NET is the culmination of Web development technologies that rapidly followed one another in the past ten years—one building on another, and each filling the gaps of its predecessor. As a result, ASP.NET is currently the most technologically advanced, feature-rich, and powerful platform for building distributed applications transported by the HTTP protocol.

While amazingly growing in popularity and successfully being employed in thousands of real-world projects, ASP.NET 1.1 is only the first step of a clearly longer road. The more one works with ASP.NET, the more he or she realizes that even more is needed. ASP.NET simplifies a number of tasks and is sort of a programming paradise, especially for developers coming from classic ASP, Internet Server Application Programming Interface (ISAPI) programming, or other Web platforms. ASP.NET 1.1 just whetted the appetite of the developer community. Thus, after the first months of working with and assessing ASP.NET, members of this community started asking and wishing for more—well, actually much more.

ASP.NET 2.0 is a major upgrade to the platform, even though it doesn't introduce any new or revolutionary programming paradigm. At first sight, there's no radically new approach to code design and implementation, and there's no new syntax model to become familiar with. Nonetheless, ASP.NET 2.0 is a milestone on the Microsoft Web development roadmap—for application architects as well as for developers. Many of the constituent classes have been reworked, and some underwent face-lift operations. Several new controls have been added for the sake of productivity, and a bunch of new and enhanced system modules now make the run-time pipeline more customizable, flexible, robust, and secure. As a result, new practices emerge as best practices, new programming techniques are available to architects and lead developers, and new system features provide native solutions to known issues with earlier versions. To maximize the benefits of using ASP.NET, you should first look at the overall model—the components, programmability, and infrastructure.

A close look at the overall model is exactly what this chapter provides. To start out, let's examine some basic concepts of the ASP.NET platform and its programming model.

What's ASP.NET, Anyway?

Prior to the advent of ASP.NET, three main technologies and platforms were available to develop Web applications: ASP, Java Server Pages (JSP), and the open source Web platform commonly referred to as LAMP (Linux plus Apache plus MySQL plus either Perl, Python, or PHP as the programming language).

> **Note**   For completeness, we should also mention a couple of platform-specific, lower-level technologies that ASP and JSP rely on. ASP is actually an ISAPI extension, whereas JSP is implemented as a special *servlet* application. ISAPI extensions on IIS-based platforms and servlets on Java-based systems, let you create server-side, Web-deployed applications using a more classic approach. You write a module that builds and renders the page rather than declaratively design the page using a mix of markup text and embedded code.

Although each has language-specific and architecture-specific features, all these Web development platforms are designed to create interactive pages as part of a Web-based application. To some extent, all enable developers to separate programming logic from the page layout through the use of components that the page itself is responsible to call and render. Aside from this common ultimate goal, significant differences exist among those platforms, most of which relate to the programming model and languages they promote and support. For example, JSP exploits the Java framework of classes and, with JavaBeans, provides an effective extensibility model for reusing components. In addition, JSP supports tag customization and lets developers associate code with a custom tag definition. Finally, because it's a key element of the Java 2 Enterprise Edition (J2EE) platform, JSP relies on the Java language, a first-class, compiled language as opposed to the scripting languages used by both ASP and LAMP platforms. So how does ASP.NET fit in exactly?

Like ASP and other Web development environments, ASP.NET also works on top of the HTTP protocol and takes advantage of HTTP commands and policies to set up two-way, browser-to-server communication and cooperation. What really differentiates ASP.NET from the plethora of other Web development technologies is the abstract programming model it propounds, the Web Forms model. In addition, the whole ASP.NET platform comes as a native part of the Microsoft .NET Framework. To be sure you grasp the importance of this last point, let me explain. ASP.NET applications are compiled pieces of code, are made of reusable and extensible components, can be authored with first-class languages (including C#, Microsoft Visual Basic .NET, Microsoft JScript .NET, and J#), and can access the entire hierarchy of classes in the .NET Framework.

In short, ASP.NET combines the best of all worlds. It is semantically compatible (and, to some extent, also language compatible) with ASP. It provides the same object-oriented features as JSP applications (tag customization, compiled languages, components, extensibility, and reusability). And as icing on the cake, ASP.NET delivers a wealth of goodies, tools, and powerful system features that can be effectively grouped within the blanket expression *tools for abstracting the HTTP programming model*. Lots of programmer-friendly classes let you develop pages using typical desktop methods. The Web Forms model promotes an overall event-driven approach, but it is deployed over the Web.

> **Note**   ASP.NET Is supported on a variety of platforms, including Microsoft Windows 2000 with at least Service Pack 2, Windows XP Professional, and Windows Server 2003. To develop ASP.NET server applications, Internet Information Services (IIS) version 5.0 or later, is also required. Other software you need—for example, Microsoft Data Access Components (MDAC) 2.7—is automatically installed when you set up the .NET Framework. In terms of performance, robustness, and security, the ideal combination of system software for hosting ASP.NET applications appears to be Windows Server 2003 (preferably with Service Pack 1 applied) and IIS 6.0.

Programming in the Age of Web Forms

The rationale behind the ASP.NET Web Forms model is directly related to the search for a better strategy to deal with the growing demand for cheap but powerful Web interaction. As a matter of fact, the HTTP protocol represents the major strength and weakness of Web applications. The stateless nature of the HTTP protocol introduces vastly different programming concepts that are foreign to many desktop developers—first and foremost among these concepts is session state management. On the other hand, the inherent simplicity and scalability of HTTP is the key to its worldwide adoption and effectiveness—in short, we probably couldn't have the Internet as we know it without a protocol like HTTP. Yet, as demand for rich and powerful applications increases, programmers have to devise better ways of setting up easy and effective communication from the client to the server and vice versa.

Various techniques have been experimented with over time to smooth the communication across different pages and across multiple invocations of the same page. Most programmers are used to thinking in terms of a client-generated action that results in a server-side reaction. Such a basic and fundamental pattern cannot be accomplished, at least not literally, over the Web. A certain degree of abstraction and some system-provided services are needed to make smooth communication happen.

ASP, much more so than JSP, thinks declaratively and has quite a slim and scanty object model. Overall, programmers who become Web programmers are forced to adopt a different mindset and toss the familiar action/reaction paradigm out the door.

Event-Driven Programming over HTTP

ASP.NET Web Forms bring the event-driven model of interaction to the Web. Implementing an event model over the Web requires any data related to the client-side user's activity to be forwarded to the server for corresponding and *stateful* processing. The server processes the output of client actions and triggers reactions. The state of the application contains two types of information: the state of the client and the state of the session. The state of the client—mostly the contents of form input fields collectively referred to as the page state—is easily accessible through the server-side collections that store posted values. But what about the overall state of the session? The client expects that sending information to the server through one page is naturally related to any other page he or she might view later, such as when adding items to a shopping cart. Who remembers what a particular user has in the shopping cart? By itself, HTTP is incapable of keeping track of this information; that's where session state and a proper server-side infrastructure surrounding and integrating HTTP fit in.

I can't emphasize enough the importance of understanding the concepts involved with *stateless programming* when developing Web applications. As mentioned, HTTP is a stateless protocol, which means two successive requests across the same session have no knowledge of each other. They are resolved by newly instantiated environments in which no session-specific information is maintained, except all the information the application itself might have stored in global objects. In ASP, reentrant forms are a common way to work around such a system limitation. A reentrant form is an HTML *<form>* element that posts to the same page that contains it. Reentrant forms alone do not fully solve the issue. However, by combining them with code blocks and hidden fields storing state information that is critical for the page, many developers elegantly overcame the obstacle.

What was once an ASP best-practice has been standardized and integrated in the ASP.NET runtime to become the key feature that endows ASP.NET applications with automatic state maintenance. The ASP.NET runtime carries the page state back and forth across page requests. When generating HTML code for a given page, ASP.NET encodes and stuffs the state of server-side objects into a few hidden, and transparently created, fields. When the page is requested, the same ASP.NET runtime engine checks for embedded state information—the hidden fields—and uses any decoded information to set up newly created instances of server-side objects. The net effect of such a mechanism is not unlike the Windows Forms model on the desktop and is summarized in Figure 1-1.

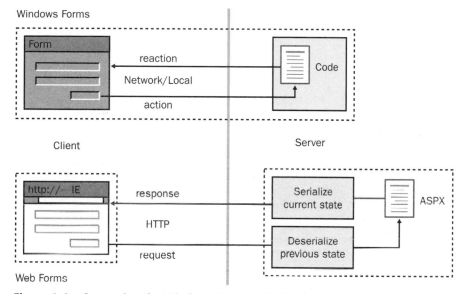

Figure 1-1   Comparing the Windows Forms and Web Forms models in the .NET Framework.

The Windows Forms model stems from the typical event-driven desktop programming style. No matter what connectivity exists between the client and server components, the server always works in reaction to the client's input. The server is aware of the overall application state and operates in a two-tier, connected manner. The Web Forms model needs some machinery to support the same event-driven programming model. In Figure 1-1, the needed *machinery* is represented by the state deserialization that occurs when the page is requested, and the state serialization performed when the HTML response is being generated.

In charge of this filtering work is the ASP.NET HTTP runtime—a piece of code that extends and specializes the overall capabilities of the hosting Web server. Reentrant forms and hidden fields are the low-level tools used to perform the trick. Such a model wouldn't be as effective without a back-end, rich object model spanning the whole content of the server page. Crucial to the building and effective working of the ASP.NET development platform is the component model.

The ASP.NET component model identifies and describes the building blocks of ASP.NET pages. It is implemented through an object model that provides a server-side counterpart to virtually any HTML page elements, such as HTML tags like <*form*> and <*input*>. In addition, the ASP.NET object model includes numerous components (called server controls or Web controls) that represent more complex elements of the user interface (UI). Some of these controls have no direct mapping with individual HTML elements but are implemented by combining multiple HTML tags. Typical examples of complex UI elements are the *Calendar* control and the *DataGrid* control.

In the end, an ASP.NET page is made of any number of server controls mixed with verbatim text, markup, and images. Sensitive data excerpted from the page and controls state is unobtrusively stored in hidden fields, and it forms the context of that page request. The association between an instance of the page and its state is unambiguous, not programmatically modifiable, and controlled by the ASP.NET HTTP runtime.

The ASP.NET component model is the first stop on the way to the full understanding of the ASP.NET platform. The component model escorts you through the whole development cycle, including the phase of page authoring and run-time system configuration, as shown in Figure 1-2.

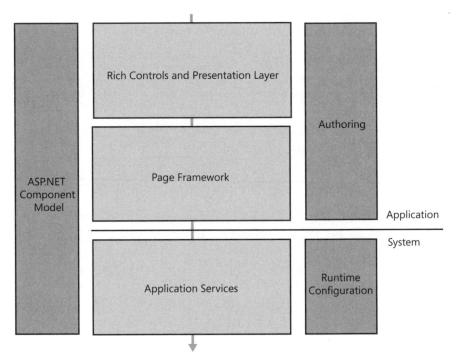

Figure 1-2   A bird's-eye view of the ASP.NET development stack. The arrow indicates the typical top-down application perspective, going down from the user interface to the system services.

Before we dive into the various elements shown in Figure 1-2, let's briefly review the basics of the HTTP protocol, which remains the foundation of Web interaction. After that, we'll move on to describe the structure of an ASP.NET page and how to write and deploy ASP.NET applications.

The HTTP Protocol

This section provides a quick overview of the way Web applications operate. If you already have a working knowledge of the Web underpinnings, feel free to jump ahead to the section "Structure of an ASP.NET Page."

The acronym *HTTP* has become so familiar to us developers that we sometimes don't remember exactly what it stands for. Actually, *HTTP* stands for Hypertext Transfer Protocol. HTTP is a text-based protocol that defines how Web browsers and Web servers communicate. The format of HTTP packets is fully described in RFC 2068 and is available for download from *http://www.w3.org/Protocols/rfc2068/rfc2068.txt*. HTTP packets travel over a Transmission Control Protocol (TCP) connection directed toward default port 80 at the target Internet Protocol (IP) address.

The HTTP Request

When you point the browser to a URL, it uses the available Domain Name System (DNS) to translate the server name you provided with the URL into an IP address. Next, the browser opens a socket and connects to port 80 at that address. The packet with the download request for *http://www.contoso.com/default.aspx* can take the following simple form:

```
GET /default.aspx HTTP/1.1
Host: www.contoso.com
```

The first line of text in a request is the *start line* of the request. It must contain the name of the HTTP command to execute (*GET* in this case), the URL of the resource, plus the version of the HTTP protocol you want to use.

An HTTP request can contain, and usually does contain, a number of headers. An HTTP header is a line of text that provides additional information about the request. In the HTTP request just shown, the line beginning with "Host:" is an HTTP header. Headers that can be found in an HTTP request include the following:

- **User-Agent.**   Identifies the type of browser that originated the request
- **Connection.**   Closes a connection or keeps a connection alive
- **If-Modified-Since.**   Provides client-side cache validation

GET and POST are the most commonly used HTTP commands or verbs. The GET verb means retrieve whatever information is identified by the request URL. The POST verb is used to request that the origin server accept the content enclosed in the request and process it. Typically, the POST verb is used to provide a block of data (that is, the result of submitting a form) to a data-handling process.

The HTTP Response

The server's response includes a *status line* made from the message's protocol version and an exit code (indicating success or that an error has occurred). The status line is followed by a bunch of headers—typically the page content type and length—and the body content. A blank line separates the body content from the rest of the message, as shown in the following response:

```
HTTP/1.1 200 OK
Server: Microsoft-IIS/5.0
Content-Type: text/html
Content-Length: 51

<html><body><h1>ASP.NET is cool!</h1></body></html>
```

The preceding code illustrates the simple HTML output returned by the Web server. Requests and responses are strings formatted according to the HTTP schema, and they travel over a TCP connection. The code *200* means that all went OK with the request. The specified Web server processes the request and returns content of a certain length expressed in the given Multipurpose Internet Mail Extensions (MIME) type (*text/html*). HTTP codes that could be returned are listed in the HTTP specification, available at the aforementioned URL. In addition, it should be noted that the blank line between the last header and the content of the HTTP response is not just formatting—the pair carriage-return and line-feed are required and are a precise part of the standard.

What happens next mostly depends on the MIME type and the local browser's capabilities. As long as the MIME type is *text/html*, the browser displays the content as HTML. If the MIME type is, say, *text/xml*, some browsers will render the content as plain text, while others (for example, Microsoft Internet Explorer 6.0) will apply a built-in style sheet.

Building a Server-Side Abstraction Layer

Every conversation between browsers and Web servers consists of an exchange of packets similar to the ones we have just examined. If the requested URL is an HTML page, the Web server typically reads the contents of the *.html* file and flushes it into the body of the response packet. If the URL is an ASP.NET page, a special IIS module gets involved. The module is an IIS ISAPI plug-in.

An ISAPI extension is a dynamic-link library (DLL) registered on a per-file extension basis. An ISAPI extension registered to handle *.aspx* files gets involved whenever a request comes in for this type of resource. The ISAPI extension analyzes the request and configures the server-side environment that will actually process the source of the page. When the state for the request has been successfully retrieved and restored completely, the page is allowed to run and produce the HTML output.

Submitting Forms

The HTML *<form>* tag is the only element authorized to transmit client-side data to the server. When the user clicks on a button of type "submit," by design the browser stuffs the current content of all the controls that belong to the form into a string. The string is then passed to the server as part of the GET or POST command.

The following HTML snippet illustrates a simple form containing a text box and submit button. As you can see, the form is associated with the POST command and the default.aspx URL:

```
<form method="post" action="default.aspx">
    <input type="text" name="EmpCode" />
    <input type="submit" value="Send" />
</form>
```

The following request shows the POST command that hits the Web server when the user clicks the submit button:

```
POST /default.aspx HTTP/1.1
Host: www.contoso.com
Content-Type: application/x-www-form-urlencoded
Content-Length: 12

EmpCode=1001
```

While processing the page request, the ISAPI extension parses the body of the request and exposes any information found through a more programmer-friendly object model. For example, instead of remaining a simple name/value string, the *EmpCode* variable is moved within an application-wide collection—the *Request.Form* collection. This represents a first level of abstraction built over the raw HTTP programming model. Objects such as *Request*, *Response*, and *Server* form the HTTP context for the call and, as such, represent the minimum set of objects you find in most Web development platforms, including JSP and ASP. In ASP.NET, though, you find much more.

Structure of an ASP.NET Page

An ASP.NET page is a server-side text file saved with the *aspx* extension. The internal structure of the page is extremely modular and comprises three distinct sections—page directives, code, and page layout:

- **Page directives**   Page directives set up the environment in which the page will run, specify how the HTTP runtime should process the page, and determine which assumptions about the page are safe to make. Directives also let you import namespaces to simplify coding, load assemblies not currently in the global assembly cache (GAC), and register new controls with custom tag names and namespace prefixes.

- **Code section**   The code section contains handlers for page and control events, plus optional helper routines. Any source code pertinent to the page can be inserted inline or attached to the page through a separate file. If inserted inline, the code goes into a tag with the misleading name of <script>. (The name <script> has been chosen for backward-compatibility reasons.) Server-side <script> tags are distinguished from client side <script> tags by the use of the *runat=server* attribute. (More on this in a moment.) Any page code is always compiled before execution. In ASP.NET 2.0, it can also be precompiled and deployed in the form of a binary assembly.

- **Page layout**   The page layout represents the skeleton of the page. It includes server controls, literal text, and HTML tags. The user interface of the server controls can be fleshed out a bit using declared attributes and control properties.

For the page to work, you don't need to specify all sections. Although real-world pages include all the sections mentioned, perfectly valid and functional pages can include only the code section or page layout. In some special cases, you can even have an ASP.NET page made of a single directive.

In Chapter 2, and even more in Chapter 3, we'll delve deep into the features of a page and its building blocks.

A Sample ASP.NET Page

It is about time we see what an ASP.NET page looks like. To start, a simple text editor will suffice; so let's open Notepad and let the sleeping giant (Microsoft Visual Studio .NET) lie. The following code implements a simple ASP.NET page that lets you enter a string and then changes it to uppercase letters after you click a button. For the sake of simplicity, we use inline code. (As you'll learn later in the book, this is *not* what you'll be doing in real-world applications and in any page with some complexity.)

```
<!-- Directives -->
<% @Page Language="C#" %>

<!-- Code Section -->
<script runat="server">
private void MakeUpper(object sender, EventArgs e)
{
    string buf = TheString.Value;
    TheResult.InnerText = buf.ToUpper();
}
</script>

<!-- Layout -->
<html>
<head><title>Pro ASP.NET (Ch 01)</title></head>
<body>
<h1>Make It Upper</h1>
<form runat="server">
    <input runat="server" id="TheString" type="text" />
    <input runat="server" id="Button1" type="submit" value="Proceed..."
        OnServerClick="MakeUpper" />
    <hr>
    <h3>Results:</h3>
    <span runat="server" id="TheResult" />
</form>
</body>
</html>
```

Blank lines and comments in the preceding listing separate the three sections—directives, code, and page layout. Notice the unsparing use of the *runat* attribute—it's one of the most important pieces of the whole ASP.NET jigsaw puzzle. In the next section, we'll discuss *runat* in more detail. For now, it suffices to say that the *runat* attribute promotes an otherwise lifeless server-side tag to the rank of a component instance.

The page layout is made of literals and HTML tags, some of which contain the aforementioned *runat* attribute. Everything flagged this way, despite the appearances, is not really an HTML element. More precisely, it is the markup placeholder of a server-side component—an ASP.NET control—that is actually responsible for the final markup served to the browser. In an ASP.NET source, every tag marked with the *runat* attribute is not output as is, but undergoes a transformation process on the server at the end of which the real markup is generated. The ASP.NET runtime is in charge of mapping tags to control instances. Let's quickly review the code.

Quick Review of the Code

Thanks to the *runat* attribute the input text field becomes an instance of the *HtmlInputControl* class when the page is processed on the server. The *Value* property of the class determines the default text to assign to the input field. When the user clicks the submit button, the page automatically posts back to itself. The magic is performed by the *runat* attribute set for the *<form>* tag. Once on the server, the posted value of the input field is read and automatically assigned to the *Value* property of a newly created instance of the *HtmlInputControl*. Next, the code associated with the *OnServerClick* event runs. This code takes the current content of the text box—the posted string—and converts it to uppercase letters. Finally, the uppercase string is assigned it to the *InnerText* property of the server-side control bound to the HTML *<span>* tag. When the *MakeUpper* event handler completes, the page is ready for rendering. At this point, updated HTML code is sent to the browser.

To test the page, copy the *.aspx* file to your Web server's root directory. Normally, this is *c:\inetpub\wwwroot*. If you want, create an ad hoc virtual directory. Let's assume the page is named *hello.aspx*. Next, point the browser to the page. Figure 1-3 shows what you get.

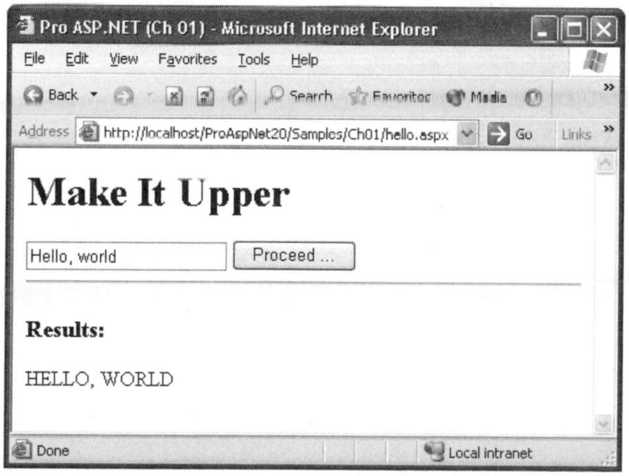

Figure 1-3   Our first (and rather simple) ASP.NET page in action

It would be useful to take a look at the HTML source of the page when it is first displayed to the user—that is, before the user clicks to make the text uppercase.

```html
<!-- Directives -->

<!-- Code Section -->

<!-- Layout -->
<html>
<head><title>Pro ASP.NET (Ch 01)</title></head>
<body>
<h1>Make It Upper</h1>
<form method="post" action="hello.aspx" id="Form1">
<div>
    <input type="hidden" name="__EVENTTARGET" value="" />
    <input type="hidden" name="__EVENTARGUMENT" value="" />
    <input type="hidden" name="__VIEWSTATE" value="/wEPDwUJNzM4N…==" />
</div>

<script type="text/javascript">
<!--
var theForm = document.forms['Form1'];
if (!theForm) {
    theForm = document.Form1;
}
function __doPostBack(eventTarget, eventArgument) {
    if (!theForm.onsubmit || (theForm.onsubmit() != false)) {
        theForm.__EVENTTARGET.value = eventTarget;
        theForm.__EVENTARGUMENT.value = eventArgument;
        theForm.submit();
    }
}
// -->
</script>

<input name="TheString" type="text" id="TheString" value="Hello, world" />
<input name="Button1" type="submit" id="Button1" value="Proceed ..." />
<hr>
<h3>Results: </h3><span id="TheResult"></span>
</form>
</body>
</html>
```

Within the *<form>* tag, a hard-coded *action* attribute has been added to force posting to the same page. This is by design and is one of the most characteristic aspects of ASP.NET. The various hidden fields you see are essential to the implementation of the postback mechanism and are generated automatically. The same can be said for the embedded script code. The *<input>* tags are nearly identical to their counterpart in the *.aspx* source—only the *runat* attribute disappeared.

Now that we've dirtied our hands with some ASP.NET code, let's step back and review the layers that actually make ASP.NET pages work in the context of an application.

The ASP.NET Component Model

ASP.NET is the key enabling technology for all Web-related functionality provided by the .NET Framework. The .NET Framework is made entirely of an object-oriented hierarchy of classes that span all programming topics for Windows operating systems. Generally speaking, a Web application is made of pages the user requests from a server and that the server processes and returns as markup code—mostly HTML. How the requested resource is processed, and therefore how the markup is generated, is server-specific. In particular, when the resource happens to have an *.aspx* extension, IIS delegates any further processing to the ASP.NET runtime system.

The ASP.NET runtime transforms the source code of the requested *.aspx* page into the living instance of a .NET Framework class that inherits from a base class named *Page*. At the end of the day, a running ASP.NET page is an object, and so it is for some of its components—the server-side controls.

A large number of new ASP.NET features are just a direct or an indirect propagation of the .NET infrastructure. ASP.NET benefits from cross-language integration and exception handling, garbage collection and code access security, deployment and configuration, and an incredibly rich class library. All these features aren't the products of a self-contained engine, they are available to you because ASP.NET applications are a special breed of a .NET application.

A Model for Component Interaction

Any element in an ASP.NET page that is marked with the *runat* attribute can be given a unique ID, allowing you to access that element from your server-side code. Accessing items by ID is a natural approach on the client (such as the use of Dynamic HTML pages), but it represents a brand new scheme for server applications. Two factors make this revolutionary approach possible:

■ The component-based architecture of the .NET platform, and the fact that ASP.NET is a constituent part of that platform

■ The ASP.NET built-in mechanism for the application's state management

The component-based design of .NET makes component interaction easy and effective in all environments including ASP.NET applications. ASP.NET components access page features and interact by calling one another's methods and setting properties.

The fact that all elements in the page are true components, and not simply parsable text, provides a flexible and powerful extensibility model. Creating new controls is as easy as deriving a new class; building a page inheritance hierarchy is as easy as specifying a parent class different from the base *Page* class.

> **Warning**   Visual Studio .NET 2005 returns a design-time error if you don't explicitly assign each ASP.NET control a unique ID. However, the page will work just fine at run time.

The *runat* Attribute

The *runat* attribute is what determines whether a piece of markup text is to be emitted verbatim at render time or transformed into a stateful instance of a particular .NET class. In the latter case, the class would make itself responsible for emitting the related markup. In an ASP.NET page, all markup elements that have the *runat* attribute set to *server* are considered server-side controls. The control class exposes methods and properties that let you configure the state of the component. The control is responsible for emitting HTML code when the page is rendered to the browser. Let's consider the following simple code that renders an anchor element in the client page:

```
Response.Write("<A id=myAnchor href=www.asp.net>Click me</A>")
```

The anchor element is created programmatically and is not defined in the page layout. In classic ASP, code blocks and the *Response.Write* method are the only ways you have to create or configure controls dynamically. In some development environments, such as Microsoft Visual InterDev, *design-time controls* provided an object-based way to output dynamically generated HTML. Design-time controls, though, were just what the name indicates—that is, controls you can use at design-time to generate markup and script code. In ASP.NET, you have a new breed of controls that we could call *run-time controls* to mark the contrast with design-time controls.

Working with Server-Side Controls

Within an ASP page, there's no way for you to code against the *myAnchor* element. It's just frozen, lifeless text, only good for sending to the browser. Once on a client, the *myAnchor* element gets back to life and can accept script instructions. Suppose now that you need to set the *href* attribute of the anchor based on run-time conditions. In classic ASP, you could first obtain the value for the *href* attribute and then call *Response.Write*:

```
strHref = "www.asp.net"
strHtml = "<A id=myAnchor "
strHtml = strHtml + "href=" + strHref
strHtml = strHtml + ">Click me</A>"
Response.Write(strHtml)
```

This code will work unchanged in an ASP.NET page but is certainly not the best you can do. By declaring the *<A>* tag with the *runat* attribute, you can give life to the anchor element on the server too:

```
<A runat="server" id="myAnchor">Click me</A>
```

When the page is loaded, the ASP.NET runtime parses the source code and creates instances of all controls marked with the *runat* attribute. Throughout the page, the *myAnchor* ID identifies an instance of the server-side control mapped to the *<A>* tag. The following code can be used to set the *href* attribute programmatically when the page loads:

```
<script runat="server" language="C#">
void Page_Load(object sender, EventArgs e)
{
    myAnchor.HRef = "http://www.asp.net";
}
</script>
```

The markup elements whose name matches an HTML element are mapped to the corresponding HTML server control. Note that not all feasible HTML tags have corresponding ASP.NET controls; for those that don't, a generic control is used. The list of tags and their associated controls is hard-coded in the ASP.NET runtime. Elements that belong to the *<asp>* namespace are mapped to Web server controls. Other markup elements are mapped to the assembly and class name declared by using an *@Register* directive.

Pagewide Tags

The *runat* attribute can be used also with pagewide tags such as *<head>* and *<body>*. These tags are represented through an instance of the *HtmlGenericControl* class. *HtmlGenericControl* is the .NET class used to represent an HTML server-side tag not directly represented by a .NET Framework class. The list of such tags also includes *<span>*, *<font>*, and *<iframe>*.

In the following page, the background color is set programmatically when the page loads:

```
<%@ Page Language="C#" %>
<script runat="server">
private void Page_Load(object sender, EventArgs e)
{
    TheBody.Style[HtmlTextWriterStyle.BackgroundColor] = "lightblue";
}
</script>
<html>
<body id="TheBody" runat="server">
   <h3>The background color of this page has been set programmatically.
       Open View|Source menu to see the source code.</h3>
</body>
</html>
The resulting HTML code is as follows:
<html>
<head><title>Pro ASP.NET (Ch 01)</title></head>
<body id="TheBody" style="background-color:lightblue;">
<form method="post" action="Body.aspx" id="Form1">
  <div>
    <input type="hidden" name="__VIEWSTATE" value="/wEPD... RVC+" />
  </div>
```

```
   <h3>The background color of this page has been set programmatically.
      Open View|Source menu to see the source code.</h3>
</form>
</body>
</html>
```

Likewise, you can set any of the attributes of the *<body>* tag, thus deciding programmatically, say, which style sheet or background image to use. You use the *HtmlGenericControl*'s *Attributes* collection to create attributes on the tag. You use the *InnerText* property to set the inner text of a tag.

```
TheBody.Attributes["Background"] = "/proaspnet20/images/body.gif";
```

We'll discuss the programming interface of the *HtmlGenericControl* class in more detail in Chapter 4.

> **Note**   In ASP.NET 2.0, the contents of the *<head>* tag can be accessed programmatically as long as it is flagged with the *runat* attribute. The *Page* class exposes a bunch of ad hoc methods and properties that we'll explore in Chapter 3.

Unknown Tags

In case of unknown tags, namely tags that are neither predefined in the current schema nor user-defined, the ASP.NET runtime can behave in two different ways. If the tag doesn't contain namespace information, ASP.NET treats it like a generic HTML control. The empty namespace, in fact, evaluates to the HTML namespace, thereby leading the ASP.NET runtime to believe the tag is really an HTML element. No exception is raised, and markup text is generated on the server. For example, let's consider the following ASP.NET page:

```
<%@ Page Language="C#" %>
<script runat="server">
void Page_Load(object sender, EventArgs e)
{
    dinoe.Attributes["FavoriteFood"] = "T-bone steak";
}
</script>
<html>
<head><title>Pro ASP.NET (Ch 01)</title></head>
<body>
<form runat="server">
  <Person id="dinoe" runat="server" />
  Click the <b>View|Source</b> menu item...
</form>
</body>
</html>
```

The *<Person>* tag is still processed as if it was a regular HTML tag, and the *FavoriteFood* attribute is added. Figure 1-4 shows what the HTML code for this page actually is. In the preceding sample, the type of the *dinoe* object is *HtmlGenericControl*.

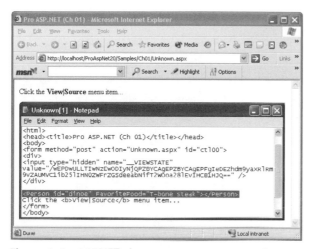

Figure 1-4   ASP.NET also processes namespace-less custom tags, mapping them to the *HtmlGenericControl* class.

If the tag does contain namespace information, it is acceptable as long as the namespace is *<asp>* or a namespace explicitly associated with the tag name using an *@Register* directive. If the namespace is unknown, a compile error occurs.

ASP.NET Server Controls

There are basically two families of ASP.NET server controls. They are HTML server controls and Web server controls. *System.Web.UI.HtmlControls* is the namespace of HTML server controls. *System.Web.UI.WebControls* groups all the Web server controls.

HTML Server Controls

HTML server controls are classes that represent a standard HTML tag supported by most browsers. The set of properties of an HTML server control matches a commonly used set of attributes of the corresponding tag. The control feature properties such as *InnerText*, *InnerHtml*, *Style*, and *Value* plus collections such as *Attributes*. Instances of HTML server controls are automatically created by the ASP.NET runtime each time the corresponding HTML tag marked with runat="server" is found in the page source.

As mentioned, the available set of HTML server controls doesn't cover all possible HTML tags of any given version of the HTML schema. Only most commonly used tags found their way to the *System.Web.UI.HtmlControls* namespace. Tags such as *<iframe>*, *<frameset>*, *<body>*, and *<hn>* have been left out as well as less frequently used tags such as *<fieldset>*, *<marquee>*, and *<pre>*.

The lack of a specialized server control, however, doesn't limit your programming power when it comes to using and configuring those tags on the server. You only have to use a more generic programming interface—the *HtmlGenericControl* class, which we looked at briefly in this section.

Web Server Controls

Web server controls are controls with more features than HTML server controls. Web server controls include not only input controls such as buttons and text boxes, but also special-purpose controls such as a calendar, an ad rotator, a drop-down list, a tree view, and a data grid. Web server controls also include components that closely resemble some HTML server controls. Web server controls, though, are more abstract than the corresponding HTML server controls in that their object model doesn't necessarily reflect the HTML syntax. For example, let's compare the HTML server text control and the Web server *TextBox* control. The HTML server text control has the following markup:

```
<input runat="server" id="FirstName" type="text" value="Dino" />
```

The Web server *TextBox* control has the following markup:

```
<asp:textbox runat="server" id="FirstName" text="Dino" />
```

Both controls generate the same HTML markup code. However, the programming interface of the HTML server text control matches closely that of the HTML *<input>* tag, while methods and properties of the Web server *TextBox* control are named in a more abstract way. For example, to set the content of an HTML server text control you must use the *Value* property because *Value* is the corresponding HTML attribute name. If you work with the Web server *TextBox* control, you must resort to *Text*. With very few exceptions (that I'll discuss in Chapter 3), using HTML server controls or Web server controls to represent HTML elements is only a matter of preference and ease of development and maintenance.

The ASP.NET Development Stack

At the highest level of abstraction, the development of an ASP.NET application passes through two phases—pages authoring and run-time configuration. You build the pages that form the application, implement its user's requirements, and then fine-tune the surrounding run-time environment to make it serve pages effectively and securely. As Figure 1-2 shows, the ASP.NET component model is the bedrock of all ASP.NET applications and their building blocks. With Figure 1-2 in mind, let's examine the various logical layers to see what they contain and why they contain it.

The Presentation Layer

An ASP.NET page is made of controls, free text, and markup. When the source code is transformed into a living instance of a page class, the ASP.NET runtime makes no further distinction between verbatim text, markup, and server controls—everything is a control, including literal text and carriage-return characters. At run time, any ASP.NET page is a mere graph of controls.

Rich Controls

The programming richness of ASP.NET springs from the wide library of server controls that covers the basic tasks of HTML interaction—for example, collecting text through input tags—as well as more advanced functionalities such as grid-based data display. The native set of controls is large enough to let you fulfill virtually any set of requirements. In addition, the latest version of ASP.NET adds a few new rich controls to take developer's productivity close to its upper limit.

In ASP.NET 2.0, you find controls to create Web wizards, collapsible views of hierarchical data, advanced data reports, commonly used forms, declarative data binding, menus, site navigation. You even find a tiny API to create portal-like pages. Availability of rich controls means reduction of development time and coding errors, more best practices implemented, and more advanced functionalities delivered to end users. We'll specifically cover controls in Chapter 4, Chapter 6, and later on in Chapter 10.

Custom Controls

ASP.NET core controls provide you with a complete set of tools to build Web functionalities. The standard set of controls can be extended and enhanced by adding custom controls. The underlying ASP.NET component model greatly simplifies the task by applying the common principles and rules of object-oriented programming.

You can build new controls by enhancing an existing control or aggregating two or more controls together to form a new one. ASP.NET 1.x comes with a small set of base classes to build brand new controls on. This set of classes has been extended in ASP.NET 2.0, in particular to simplify the development of new data-bound controls.

Adaptive Rendering

Starting with version 2.0, ASP.NET ships a new control adapter architecture that allows any server control to create alternate renderings for a variety of browsers. Note, though, that the new ASP.NET 2.0 adapter model doesn't apply to *mobile controls*. Mobile controls are a special family of Web controls designed to build applications for mobile devices. ASP.NET 2.0 mobile controls still use the old adapter model, which was available since ASP.NET 1.1, for controls that inherit from *MobileControl* and are hosted on pages that inherit from *MobilePage*. In short, if you need to write a mobile application with ASP.NET 2.0, you should use the mobile controls, as you would have done with ASP.NET 1.1.

So what's the added value of the new adapter model? With this form of adaptive rendering, you can write control adapters to customize server controls for individual browsers. For example, you can write a control adapter to generate a different HTML markup for the *Calendar* control for a given desktop browser.

The Page Framework

Any ASP.NET page works as an instance of a class that descends from the *Page* class. The *Page* class is the ending point of a pipeline of modules that process any HTTP request. The various system components that work on the original request build step by step all the information needed to locate the page object to generate the markup. The page object model sports several features and capabilities that could be grouped in terms of events, scripting, personalization, styling, and prototyping.

Page Events

The life cycle of a page in the ASP.NET runtime is marked by a series of events. By wiring their code up to these events, developers can dynamically modify the page output and the state of constituent controls. In ASP.NET 1.x, a page fires events such as *Init*, *Load*, *PreRender*, and *Unload* that punctuate the key moments in the life of the page. ASP.NET 2.0 adds quite a few new events to allow you to follow the request processing more closely and precisely. In particular, you find new events to signal the beginning and end of the initialization and loading phase. The page life cycle will be thoroughly examined in Chapter 3.

Page Scripting

The page scripting object model lets developers manage script code and hidden fields to be injected in client pages. This object model generates JavaScript code used to glue together the HTML elements generated by server controls, thus providing features otherwise impossible to program on the server. For example, in this way you can set the input focus to a particular control when the page displays in the client browser.

ASP.NET pages can be architected to issue client calls to server methods without performing a full postback and subsequently refresh the whole displayed page. This sort of remote scripting engine is implemented through a callback mechanism that offers a clear advantage to developers. When you use script callbacks, the results of the execution of a server-side method are passed directly to a JavaScript function that can then update the user interface via Dynamic HTML. A roundtrip still occurs, but the page is not fully refreshed.

Script callbacks, though, are not the only good news. Cross-page posting is another feature that the community of ASP.NET developers loudly demanded. It allows the posting of content of a form to another page. Sounds like teaching old tricks to a new dog? Maybe. As mentioned earlier in this chapter, one of the most characteristic aspects of ASP.NET is that each page contains just one *<form>* tag, which continuously posts to itself. That's the way ASP.NET has been designed, and it results in several advantages.

In previous versions of ASP.NET, cross-page posting could be implemented the same way as in classic ASP—that is, posting through an HTML pure *<form>* not marked with the *runat* attribute. This method works fine, but it leaves you far from the object-oriented and strongly typed world of ASP.NET. Cross-page posting as implemented in ASP.NET 2.0 fills the gap.

Page Personalization

In ASP.NET 2.0, you can store and retrieve user-specific information and preferences without the burden of having to write the infrastructural code. The application defines its own model of personalized data, and the ASP.NET runtime does the rest by parsing and compiling that model into a class. Each member of the personalized class data corresponds to a piece of information specific to the current user. Loading and saving personalized data is completely transparent to end users and doesn't even require the page author to know much about the internal plumbing. The user personalized information is available to the page author through a page property. Each page can consume previously saved information and save new information for further requests.

Page Styling

Much like Microsoft Windows XP themes, ASP.NET themes assign a set of styles and visual attributes to elements of the site that can be customized. These elements include control properties, page style sheets, images, and templates on the page. A theme is the union of all visual styles for all customizable elements in the pages—a sort of super CSS (cascading style sheet) file. A theme is identified by name and consists of CSS files, images, and control skins. A *control skin* is a text file that contains default control declarations in which visual properties are set for the control. With this feature enabled, if the developer adds, say, a *DataGrid* control to a page, the control is rendered with the default appearance defined in the theme.

Themes are a great new feature because they allow you to change the look and feel of pages in a single shot and, perhaps more importantly, give all pages a consistent appearance.

Page Prototyping

Almost all Web sites today contain pages with a similar layout. For some sites, the layout is as simple as a header and footer; others sites might contain sophisticated navigational menus and widgets that wrap content. In ASP.NET 1.x, the recommended approach for developers was to wrap these UI blocks in user controls and reference them in each content page. As you can imagine, this model works pretty well when the site contains only a few pages; unfortunately, it becomes unmanageable if the site contains hundreds of pages. An approach based on user controls presents several key issues for content-rich sites. For one thing, you have duplicate code in content pages to reference user controls. Next, application of new templates requires the developer to touch every page. Finally, HTML elements that span the content area are likely split between user controls.

In ASP.NET 2.0, page prototyping is greatly enhanced thanks to *master pages*. Developers working on Web sites where many pages share some layout and functionality can now author any shared functionality in one master file, instead of adding the layout information to each page or separating the layout among several user controls. Based on the shared master, developers can create any number of similar-looking *content pages* simply by referencing the master page through a new attribute. We'll cover master pages in Chapter 6.

The HTTP Runtime Environment

The process by which a Web request becomes plain HTML text for the browser is not much different in ASP.NET 2.0 than in ASP.NET 1.1. The request is picked up by IIS, given an identity token, and passed to the ASP.NET ISAPI extension (*aspnet_isapi.dll*)—the entry point for any ASP.NET-related processing. This is the general process, but a number of key details depend on the underlying version of IIS and the process model in use.

The process model is the sequence of operations needed to process a request. When the ASP.NET runtime runs on top of IIS 5.x, the process model is based on a separate worker process named *aspnet_wp.exe*. This Microsoft Win32 process receives control directly from IIS through the hosted ASP.NET ISAPI extension. The extension is passed any request for ASP.NET resources, and it hands them over to the worker process. The worker process loads the common language runtime (CLR) and starts the pipeline of managed objects that transform the original request from an HTTP payload into a full-featured page for the browser. The *aspnet_isapi* module and the worker process implement advanced features such as process recycling, page output caching, memory monitoring, and thread pooling. Each Web application runs in a distinct AppDomain within the worker process. By default, the worker process runs under a restricted, poorly privileged account named ASPNET.

> **Note**   In the CLR, an application domain (AppDomain) provides isolation, unloading, and security boundaries for executing managed code. An AppDomain is a kind of lightweight, CLR-specific process where multiple assemblies are loaded and secured to execute code. Multiple AppDomains can run in a single CPU process. There is not a one-to-one correlation between AppDomains and threads. Several threads can belong to a single AppDomain, and while a given thread is not confined to a single application domain, at any given time, a thread executes in a single AppDomain.

When ASP.NET runs under IIS 6.0, the default process model is different and the *aspnet_wp.exe* process is not used. The worker process in use is the standard IIS 6.0 worker process (*w3wp.exe*). It looks up the URL of the request and loads a specific ISAPI extension. For example, it loads aspnet_isapi.dll for ASP.NET-related requests. Under the IIS 6.0 process model, the aspnet_isapi extension is responsible for loading the CLR and starting the HTTP pipeline.

Once in the ASP.NET HTTP pipeline, the request passes through various system and user-defined components that work on it until a valid page class is found and successfully instantiated. Developers can modify and adapt the run-time environment to some extent. This can happen in three ways: changing the list of installed HTTP modules, configuration files, state and personalization providers, and other application services.

System HTTP Modules

HTTP modules are the ASP.NET counterpart of ISAPI filters. An HTTP module is a .NET Framework class that implements a particular interface. All ASP.NET applications inherit a few system HTTP modules as defined in the machine.config file. Preinstalled modules provide features such as authentication, authorization, and session-related services. Generally speaking, an HTTP module can preprocess and postprocess a request, and it intercepts and handles system events as well as events raised by other modules.

The good news is that you can write and register your own HTTP modules and make them plug into the ASP.NET runtime pipeline, handle system events, and fire their own events. In addition, you can adapt on a per-application basis the list of default HTTP modules. You can add custom modules and remove those that you don't need.

Application Configuration

The behavior of ASP.NET applications is subject to a variety of parameters; some are system-level settings, some depend on the characteristics of the application. The common set of system parameters is defined in the *machine.config* file. This file contains default and machine-specific values for all supported settings. Machine settings are normally controlled by the system administrator, and applications should not be given writing access to the *machine.config* file. The *machine.config* file is located outside the Web space of the application and, as such, cannot be reached even if an attacker succeeds in injecting malicious code in the system.

Any application can override most of the default values stored in the machine.config file by creating one or more application-specific web.config files. At a minimum, an application creates a web.config file in its root folder. The web.config file is a subset of machine.config, written according to the same XML schema. The goal of *web.config* is to override some of the default settings. Beware, however, that not all settings that are defined in machine.config can be overridden in a child configuration file. In particular, the information about the ASP.NET process model can be defined only in a machinewide manner using the machine.config file.

If the application contains child directories, it can define a web.config file for each folder. The scope of each configuration file is determined in a hierarchical, top-down manner. The settings valid for a page are determined by the sum of the changes that the various web.config files found along the way applied to the original machine configuration. Any web.config file can extend, restrict, and override any type of settings defined at an upper level, including the machine level. If no configuration file exists in an application folder, the settings that are valid at the upper level are applied.

Application Services

Authentication, state management, and caching are all examples of essential services that the ASP.NET runtime environment supplies to running applications. With ASP.NET 2.0, other services have been added to the list—including administration, membership, role management, and personalization—as shown in Figure 1-5.

Most application services must persist and retrieve some data for internal purposes. While doing so, a service chooses a data model and a storage medium, and it gets to the data through a particular sequence of steps. Applications based on these services are constrained by the design to using those settings—which usually includes a fixed data schema, a predefined storage medium, a hard-coded behavior. What if you don't like or don't want these restrictions?

Run-time configuration, as achieved through *machine.config* and *web.config* files, adds some more flexibility to your code. However, run-time configuration does not provide a definitive solution that is flexible enough to allow full customization of the service that would make it extensible and smooth to implement. A more definitive solution is provided by ASP.NET 2.0, which formalizes and integrates into the overall framework of classes a design pattern that was originally developed and used in several ASP.NET Starter Kits. Known as the *provider model*, this pattern defines a common API for a variety of operations—each known as the *provider*. At the same time, the provider's interface contains several hooks for developers to take complete control over the internal behavior of the API, data schema used, and storage medium.

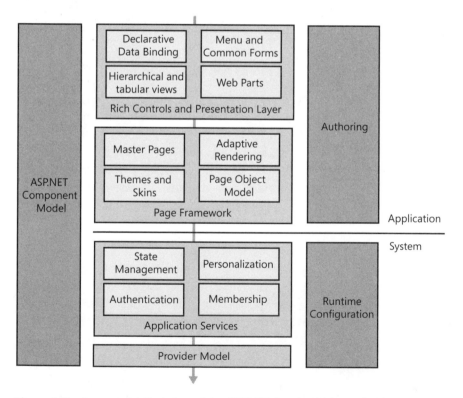

Figure 1-5   A more detailed view of the ASP.NET development stack. The arrow indicates the typical top-down application perspective, going down from the user interface to the system services.

> **Important**   The provider model is one of the most important and critical aspects of ASP.NET. A good understanding of it is crucial to conduct effective design and implementation of cutting-edge applications. The provider model is formalized in ASP.NET 2.0, but it is simply the implementation of a design pattern. As such, it is completely decoupled at its core from any platform and framework. So once you understand the basic idea, you can start using it in any application, even outside the boundaries of ASP.NET.

The ASP.NET Provider Model

There's a well-known design pattern behind the ASP.NET provider model—the *strategy* pattern. Defined, the strategy pattern indicates an expected behavior (say, sorting) that can be implemented through a variety of interchangeable algorithms (say, Quicksort, Mergesort). Each application then selects the algorithm that best fits while keeping the public, observable behavior and programming API intact.

The most notable feature of the strategy pattern is that it provides a way for an object, or an entire subsystem, to expose its internals so that a client can unplug the default implementation of a given feature and plug his own in. This is exactly what happens in ASP.NET for a number of services, including membership, roles, state management, personalization, site navigation. The ASP.NET provider model is the ASP.NET implementation of the strategy pattern.

The Rationale Behind the Provider Model

The provider model is not an application feature that end users can see with their own eyes. In itself, it doesn't make an application show a richer content, run faster, or be more responsive. The provider model is an infrastructural feature that improves an application's architecture by enabling developers and architects to operate under the hood of some system components. At the same time, it enables developers to build new components that expose hooks for clients to plug in and customize behavior and settings. Implementing the strategy pattern doesn't transform an application into an open-source project, allowing anybody to modify anything. It simply means that you have a simple, elegant, and effective pattern to make certain parts of your application customizable by clients. At the same time, the ASP.NET implementation of the pattern—the provider model—makes you capable of customizing certain parts of the ASP.NET runtime environment through special classes named providers from which you can derive your own.

Exemplifying the Provider Model

To see an example of the provider model and its major benefits, let's look at Figure 1-6. The figure outlines the classic schema for authenticating a user. The blocks of the diagram follow closely the flow of operations in ASP.NET 1.1.

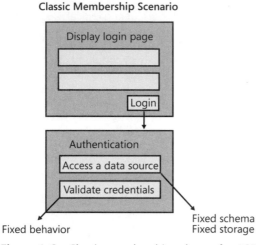

Figure 1-6   Classic membership schema for ASP.NET 1.1 applications.

The user who attempts to connect to a protected page is shown a login page and invited to type credentials. Next, the name and password are passed on to a function, which is ultimately responsible for validating the user. ASP.NET 1.x can automatically check users against Windows accounts or a list of names in the web.config file. None of these approaches work well in a realistic Web application; in most cases, developers just end up writing a custom piece of code to validate credentials against a homemade data source. The schema and storage medium of the data source are fixed and determined by the developer. Likewise, the algorithm employed to validate credentials is constrained by the design.

Is there anything wrong with this solution? Not necessarily. It works just fine, puts you in control of everything, and can be adapted to work in other applications. The rub is that there's no well-defined pattern that emerges from this solution. Sure, you can port it from one application to the next, but overall the solution relates to the adapter pattern mostly like cut-and-paste relates to object-oriented inheritance.

Let's briefly consider another scenario—session state management. In ASP.NET 1.x, you can store the session state in a process separate from the running application—be it SQL Server or a Windows service (the ASP.NET state server). If you do so, though, you're constrained to using the data schema that ASP.NET hard-codes for you. Furthermore, imagine you're not a SQL Server customer. In this case, either you abandon the idea of storing session state to a database or you buy a set of licenses for SQL Server. Finally, there's nothing you can do about the internal behavior of the ASP.NET session module. If you don't like the way it, say, serializes data to the out-of-process storage, you can't change it. Take it or leave it—there's no intermediate choice.

Can you see the big picture? There are modules in ASP.NET that force you to take (or leave) a fixed schema of data, a fixed storage medium, and a fixed internal behavior. The most that you can do is (sometimes) avoid using those modules and write your own from scratch, as we outlined in the membership example. However, rolling your own replacement is not necessarily a smart move. You end up with a proprietary and application-specific system that is not automatically portable from one application to another. In addition, if you hire new people, you have to train those people before they get accustomed to using your API. Finally, you have to put forth a lot of effort to make such a proprietary API general enough to be reusable and extensible in a variety of contexts. (Otherwise, you get to reinvent the wheel time after time.)

In which way is the provider model a better solution? In the first place, it supplies a well-documented and common programming interface to perform common tasks. In addition, you gain the ability to completely control the internal business and data access logic of each API that falls under its umbrella.

In the end, in ASP.NET 1.1 you often have no other choice than writing your own API to roll certain functions the way you want. In ASP.NET 2.0, the provider model offers a much better alternative. So much better that it's practically a crime not to use it.

Provider-based Scenario

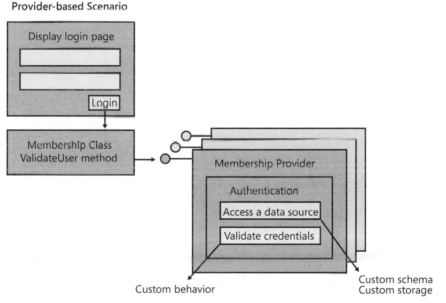

Figure 1-7   Membership revisited to use the provider model in ASP.NET 2.0.

Figure 1-7 revisits Figure 1-6 in light of the provider model. ASP.NET 2.0 makes available a bunch of static methods on a global class—*Membership*. (We'll cover the membership API in great detail in Chapter 15.) At the application level, you always invoke the same method to perform the same operation (for example, validating user credentials, creating new users, changing passwords.) Below this common API, though, you can plug in your own provider to do the job just the way you want. Writing a new provider is as easy as deriving a new class from a known base and overriding a few well-known methods. The selection of the current provider for a given task takes place in the configuration file.

Benefits of the Provider Model

In the ASP.NET implementation, the strategy pattern brings you two major benefits: extensive customization of the application's run-time environment, and code reusability. Several areas in ASP.NET are affected by the provider model. You can write providers to handle user membership and roles, persist session state, manage user profiles through personalization, and load site map information from a variety of sources. For example, by writing a provider you can change the schema of the data used to persist credentials, store this data in an Oracle or DB2 database, and store passwords hashed rather than as clear text. This level of customization of system components is unprecedented, and it opens up a new world of possibilities for application developers. At the same time, it gives you an excellent starting point for writing new providers and even extending the model to your own components.

If you look at ASP.NET 2.0 from the perspective of existing applications, the provider model gains even more technical relevance because it is the key to code reuse and subsequent preservation of investments in programming and development time. As we pointed out, a realistic membership system in ASP.NET 1.1 requires you to roll your own API as far as validation and user management are concerned. What should you do when the decision to upgrade to ASP.NET 2.0 is made? Should you drop all that code to embrace the new dazzling membership API of ASP.NET 2.0? Or would you be better sticking to the old-fashioned and proprietary API for membership?

The provider model delivers the answer (and a good answer, indeed) in its unique ability of switching the underlying algorithm while preserving the overall behavior. This ability alone wouldn't be sufficient, though. You also need to adapt your existing code to make it pluggable in the new runtime environment. Another popular pattern helps out here—the adapter pattern. The declared intent of the adapter pattern is convert a class A to an interface B that a client C understands. You wrap the existing code into a new provider class that can be seamlessly plugged into the existing ASP.NET 2.0 framework. You change the underlying implementation of the membership API, and you use your own schema and storage medium while keeping the top-level interface intact. And, more importantly, you get to fully reuse your code.

A Quick Look at the ASP.NET Implementation

The implementation of the ASP.NET provider model consists of three distinct elements—the provider class, configuration layer, and storage layer. The provider class is the component you plug into the existing framework to provide a desired functionality the way you want. The configuration layer supplies information used to identify and instantiate the actual provider. The storage layer is the physical medium where data is stored. Depending on the feature, it can be Active Directory, an Oracle or SQL Server table, an XML file, or whatever else.

The Provider Class

A provider class implements an interface known to its clients. In this way, the class provides clients with the functionality promised by that interface. Clients are not required to know anything about the implementation details of the interface. This code opacity allows for the magic of code driving other code it doesn't even know about. In the ASP.NET provider model, the only variation to the original definition of the strategy pattern is that base classes are used instead of interfaces.

In ASP.NET, a provider class can't just be any class that implements a given interface. Quite the reverse, actually. A provider class must inherit from a well-known base class. There is a base class for each supported type of provider. The base class defines the programming interface of the provider through a bunch of abstract methods.

All provider base classes derive from a common class named *ProviderBase*. This base class provides one overridable method—*Initialize*—through which the run-time environment passes any pertinent settings from configuration files. Figure 1-8 outlines the hierarchy of provider classes for membership.

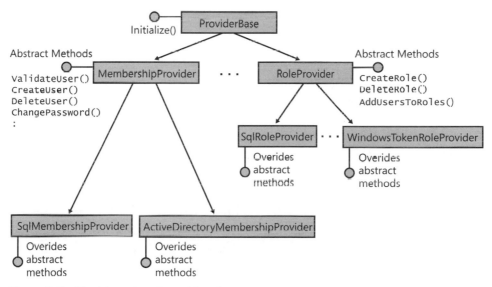

Figure 1-8 The hierarchy of provider classes.

Interfaces vs. Base Classes

Raise your hand if you are a developer who has never been involved in hours and hours of debate on the subject of interfaces versus base classes. It's a discussion that rarely comes to an end and always leave folks from different camps firmly holding to their respective positions. Should you use interfaces, or are base classes better? Which considerations is your answer based on? Consider the following fact, first.

Prebeta builds of ASP.NET 2.0 implemented the provider model literally with the definition of the strategy pattern—that is, through interfaces. In the Beta 1 timeframe, interfaces were replaced with base classes, and so it is with the released version. The ASP.NET team seemingly came to a conclusion on the issue, did it not?

An interface is a collection of logically related methods that contains only member definitions and no code. An interface type is a partial description of a type, which multiple classes can potentially support. In other words, a good interface is one that is implemented by a number of different types and encapsulates a useful, generalized piece of functionality that clients want to use. That's why many interfaces just end with the suffix "able", such as *IDisposable*, *IComparable*, and *IFormattable*. If an interface has only one useful implementing class, it is likely the offspring of a bad design choice. As a practical rule, new interfaces should be introduced sparingly and with due forethought.

A base class defines a common behavior and a common programming interface for a tree of child classes. Classes are more flexible than interfaces and support versioning. If you add a new method to version 2.0 of a class, any existing derived classes continue to function unchanged, as long as the new method is not abstract. This is untrue for interfaces.

In light of these considerations, the emerging rule is that one should use base classes instead of interfaces whenever possible (which doesn't read as, "always use base classes"). To me, base classes appear to be an excellent choice, as far as the provider model is concerned.

The Configuration Layer

Each supported provider type is assigned a section in the configuration file, which is where the default provider for the feature is set and all available providers are listed. If the provider sports public properties, default values for these properties can be specified through attributes. The contents of the section are passed as an argument to the *Initialize* method of the *ProviderBase* class—the only method that all providers have in common. Within this method, each provider uses the passed information to initialize its own state. Here's a snapshot of the configuration section for the membership provider.

```
<membership defaultProvider="AspNetSqlProvider">
   <providers>
      <add name="AspNetSqlProvider"
         type="System.Web.Security.SqlMembershipProvider, System.Web"
         connectionStringName="LocalSqlServer"
         enablePasswordRetrieval="false"
         enablePasswordReset="true"
         requiresQuestionAndAnswer="true"
         ⋮
         passwordFormat="Hashed" />
      ⋮
   </providers>
</membership>
```

The Storage Layer

All providers need to read and write information to a persistent storage medium. In many cases, two providers of the same type differ only for the storage they employ. Details of the storage medium are packed in the attributes of the provider in the *<providers>* section, as shown in the preceding code sample. For example, the preceding *AspNetSqlProvider* provider is the predefined membership provider that reads and writes to a SQL Server table. The connection string for the provider is specified through the *connectionStringName* attribute, which in turn refers to another centralized section of the configuration files that lists all available connection strings.

For the provider to work, any needed infrastructure (that is, database, tables, relationships) must exist. Setting up the working environment is a task typically accomplished at deployment time. ASP.NET makes it a breeze thanks to the Web site administration console, which is shown in Figure 1-9.

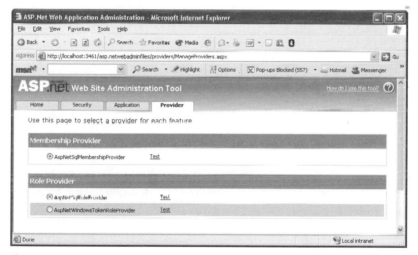

Figure 1-9   The ASP.NET Web site administration console you invoke from within Visual Studio .NET 2005.

Available Types of Providers

The provider model is used to achieve several tasks, the most important of which are as follows:

- The implementation of a read/write mechanism to persist the user profile

- The creation of a user-defined repository of user credentials that supports most common operations, such as checking a user for existence, adding and deleting users, and changing passwords

- The creation of a user-defined repository for user roles

- The definition of the site map

- The introduction of newer types of data storage for the session state

Table 1-1 shows the list of the provider classes available in ASP.NET.

Table 1-1   Available ASP.NET Provider Base Classes

Class	Description
MembershipProvider	Base class for membership providers used to manage user account information.
ProfileProvider	Base class for personalization providers used to persist and retrieve user's profile information.
RoleProvider	Base class for role providers used to manage user role information.
SessionStateStoreProviderBase	Base class for session state store providers. These providers are used to save and retrieve session state information from persistent storage media.
SiteMapProvider	Base class for managing site map information.

The classes listed in Table 1-1 define an abstract method for each aspect that's customizable in the feature they represent. For example, regarding membership management, the class *MembershipProvider* exposes methods such as *ValidateUser*, *CreateUser*, *DeleteUser*, *ChangePassword*, and so forth. Note that you'll never use *MembershipProvider* in your code just because it's an abstract class. Instead, you'll use a derived class such as *SqlMembershipProvider* or, perhaps, *ActiveDirectoryMembershipProvider*. The same holds true for other types of providers.

Finally, if you're going to write a custom membership provider that wraps your existing code, you'd create a class that inherits from *MembershipProvider* or similar classes if other provider-based features are involved.

Note   The provider architecture is one of ASP.NET 2.0's most important new features and also one of the most delicate with regard to applications. To prevent developers from producing buggy providers, the ASP.NET team supplies a made-to-measure provider toolkit that details what you can and cannot do in a provider, plus lots of sample code to serve as a guide. Writing a custom provider can be tricky for at least a couple of reasons. First, ASP.NET providers must be thread-safe. Second, their initialization step can lead you straight into a deadly reentrancy. Be sure you download the ASP.NET provider toolkit from the ASP.NET Developer Center before you leap into a new provider project.

Conclusion

As part of the .NET Framework, ASP.NET allows you to take full advantage of features of the common-language runtime (CLR), such as type safety, inheritance, language interoperability, and versioning. As the newest platform for Web applications, ASP.NET builds on the successes of a variety of other platforms, including classic ASP, JSP, and LAMP. ASP.NET promotes a programming model that, although built on top of the stateless HTTP protocol, appears to be stateful and event-driven to programmers.

In this chapter, we first analyzed the component model that backs up ASP.NET Web pages and then went through the development stack from top (presentation layer and rich controls) to bottom (infrastructure and providers). The provider model—in the end, an implementation of the strategy pattern—is a key element in the new ASP.NET architecture and a pillar of support for new applications. Extensively applied, it allows you to customize several low-level aspects of the application's run-time environment and reuse large portions of existing code. Fully understood, it gives you a way to build new components that are flexible and extensible beyond imagination and, as such, seamless to plug in to a variety of projects and easier to customize for clients.

Just the Facts

- In ASP.NET, you take full advantage of all CLR features, such as type safety, inheritance, code access security, language interoperability.

- At execution time, ASP.NET pages are represented by an instance of a class that descends from the *Page* class.

- The *Page* class is the ending point of a pipeline of modules that process any HTTP request.

- Only elements in an ASP.NET page marked with the *runat* attribute can be programmatically accessed when the page is executed on the server.

- Page elements devoid of the *runat* attribute are not processed on the server and emitted verbatim.

- The *runat* attribute applies to virtually any possible tags you can use in an ASP.NET page, including custom and unknown tags.

- The process model is the sequence of operations needed to process a request. The process model is determined by IIS and determines which worker process takes care of running ASP.NET applications and under which account.

- ASP.NET applications run under a weak account.

- The behavior of ASP.NET applications can be configured through a bunch of configuration files.

- The ASP.NET provider model is an infrastructural feature that improves an application's architecture by enabling developers and architects to operate under the hood of some system components.

- The ASP.NET provider model brings you two major benefits: extensive customization of the application's run-time environment and code reusability.

Chapter 2

Web Development in Microsoft Visual Studio .NET 2005

In this chapter:

Introducing Visual Studio .NET 2005 38

Create an ASP.NET Project 45

Application Deployment 66

Administering an ASP.NET Application 72

Conclusion 77

No matter how you design and implement a Web application, at the end of the day it always consists of a number of pages bound to a public URL. The inexorable progress of Web-related technologies has not changed this basic fact, for the simple reason that it is the natural outcome of the simplicity of the HTTP protocol. As long as HTTP remains the underlying transportation protocol, a Web application can't be anything radically different from a number of publicly accessible pages. So in this context, what's the role of Microsoft ASP.NET and Visual Studio .NET 2005?

ASP.NET provides an abstraction layer on top of HTTP with which developers build Web sites and Web-based front ends for enterprise systems. Thanks to ASP.NET, developers can work with high-level entities such as classes and components within the object-oriented paradigm. Development tools assist developers during the work and try to make the interaction with the ASP.NET framework as seamless and productive as possible. Development tools are ultimately responsible for the application or the front-end being created and deployed to users. They offer their own programming model and force developers to play by those rules.

The key development tool for building ASP.NET applications and front-ends is Visual Studio .NET 2005—the successor to Visual Studio .NET 2003. It has a lot of new features and goodies expressly designed for Web developers to overcome some of the limitations that surfaced from using Visual Studio .NET 2003.

In this chapter, we'll review the main characteristics and features of Visual Studio .NET 2005 as far as ASP.NET applications are concerned. We'll see changes made to the project, new IDE and editing features, and deployment capabilities.

Introducing Visual Studio .NET 2005

Visual Studio .NET is a container environment that integrates the functionality of multiple visual designers. You have a designer for building Windows Forms applications, one for building ASP.NET sites, one for building Web services, and so on. All items required by your work—such as references, connectors to data sources, folders, and files—are grouped at two levels: solutions and projects. A solution container contains multiple projects, whereas a project container typically stores multiple items. Using these containers, you manage settings for your solution as a whole or for individual projects. Each item in the project displays its own set of properties through a secondary window—the Properties window.

Before we meet Visual Studio .NET 2005 in person, let's briefly review the major shortcomings of its predecessor. In this way, you can enjoy the new set of features even more.

Visual Studio .NET 2003 Common Gripes

As you probably know from your own experiences, Visual Studio .NET 2003 has a single model for designing applications: the project-based approach. Real-world experience has shown this is not necessarily the best approach—at least as far as ASP.NET and Web applications are concerned.

The project is the logical entity that originates any type of .NET application—be it Windows Forms, the Web, a console, or a Web service. Developers build an application by creating a new project, configuring it, and then adding items such as pages, resources, classes, controls, and whatever else will help. For Web applications, a Visual Studio .NET project poses a few issues at two levels at least: machine and integrated development environment (IDE).

Constraints at the Machine Level

For Visual Studio .NET 2003 to run successfully on a development machine, you need to install Microsoft FrontPage Server Extensions (FPSE). FPSE are the only supported way to get to the files of the project, as Visual Studio .NET does not support FTP or even direct Internet Information Server (IIS) access. Among other things, an FPSE-equipped machine runs into trouble as soon as you try to install Windows SharePoint Services (WSS) on it. Additional setup work is required if you want Visual Studio .NET and ASP.NET to work on the same development machine along with WSS test sites.

Visual Studio .NET is dependent on IIS, which must be installed on the same development machine or on a connected server. In addition, each application you create must be tied to an IIS virtual folder. These limitations have a much greater impact on the development process than one might think at first. For example, developers need administrative privileges to create new projects, and effective corporate security policies for developer machines should be defined throughout the company. Furthermore, debugging various configurations and scenarios is definitely hard and challenging, though certainly not impossible.

Constraints at the IDE Level

All in all, the number-one issue with Visual Studio .NET–driven Web development is the tool's inability to open a single ASP.NET page outside of a project. You can open and edit an *.aspx* page, but Microsoft IntelliSense won't work on it; the same happens with other key features, such as running and debugging the page. Frankly, in this type of scenario Visual Studio .NET 2003 offers only one advantage over Notepad—HTML syntax coloring.

In Visual Studio .NET 2003, the project file is the single point of management for the constituent elements of the application. As a result, to make a file part of the project, you must explicitly add it into the project file and configure it—you can't just point at an existing virtual directory and go. The information coded in the project file counts more than the actual contents of the directory. As a result, more often than not useless files are forgotten and left around the site. Synchronizing hundreds of files in large applications is not easy; deploying projects onto other machines can be even more annoying.

This model is problematic also from the source control perspective. When managing Web projects under source control, you should perform all available source control operations using Visual Studio .NET. In addition, you shouldn't manually force a file to be under source control. All files that should be source controlled are placed there automatically when you use the appropriate menu commands. In other words, the project file ends up being the single point of contention with source control.

Visual Studio .NET also does all that it can to force you to use a code-behind class for each page added to the project. In general, keeping code (*.cs* or *.vb* file) separated from layout (*.aspx* file) is a good and highly recommended practice. However, the Visual Studio .NET 2003 implementation of this feature injects a lot of tool-generated code in the project files. This leads to a brittle model of keeping file and control references in sync. Furthermore, the contents of a project are compiled down to single assembly, with the subsequent creation of a single contention point for shared projects, an application's domain restart on every change, and a significantly expensive (and explicitly requested) compile step for large projects.

Finally, you find no support in Visual Studio .NET 2003 for declarative resources and you must perform an explicit code-generation step for adding resources such as WSDL and XSD files.

To sum it up in one sentence: although developers successfully use Visual Studio .NET 2003 for real-world applications, the tool isn't ideal for simpler projects and still has a number of shortcomings.

Visual Studio .NET 2005 Highlights

Visual Studio .NET 2005 provides a simpler and more friendly way to create ASP.NET applications. The key improvements remedy the shortcomings detailed earlier. Let's outline these features briefly. We'll go into more detail later in the chapter as we develop a start-up project.

No IIS Dependency

IIS is no longer a strict requirement for Visual Studio .NET to work. Visual Studio .NET 2005 ships, in fact, with a local Web server that makes IIS optional, at least for quick testing and debugging purposes. Figure 2-1 shows the user interface of the embedded Web server.

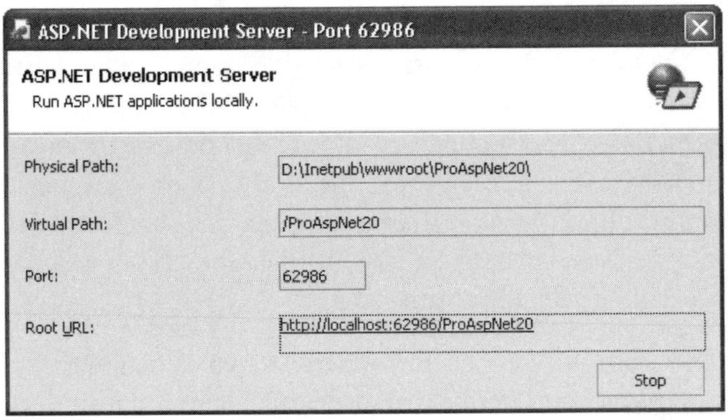

Figure 2-1 The local Web server in action in Visual Studio .NET 2005.

The embedded Web server is a revisited version of Cassini, the free mini-Web server that originally shipped with Web Matrix—a community-supported, free editor designed for ASP.NET applications. It is important to note that the local Web server represents only the default option. If you open the project from an existing IIS virtual directory, Visual Studio .NET would use IIS to test the application.

The embedded Web server is only a small piece of executable code and can't replace all the features of a full-blown Web server such as IIS. It works only with individual pages and doesn't include any of the extra features of IIS, such as the metabase.

Ways to Access Web Sites

Visual Studio .NET 2005 supports multiple ways to open Web sites. In addition to using FPSE, you can access your source files by using FTP or a direct file system path. You can also directly access the local installation of IIS, browse the existing hierarchy of virtual directories, and access existing virtual roots or create new ones. As Figure 2-2 demonstrates, you can open your Web site using a file system path or an IIS virtual directory. In the former case, the local Web server is used to test the site.

The interaction with IIS is greatly simplified, as Figure 2-3 shows. When you try to open a Web site, you are given a few options to choose from. You can locate a project by using a file system path, using the IIS hierarchy of virtual directories (only the local IIS), using FTP, or by just typing the URL of the site configured with FrontPage Server Extensions. The IIS tab also contains buttons to create new virtual roots and applications.

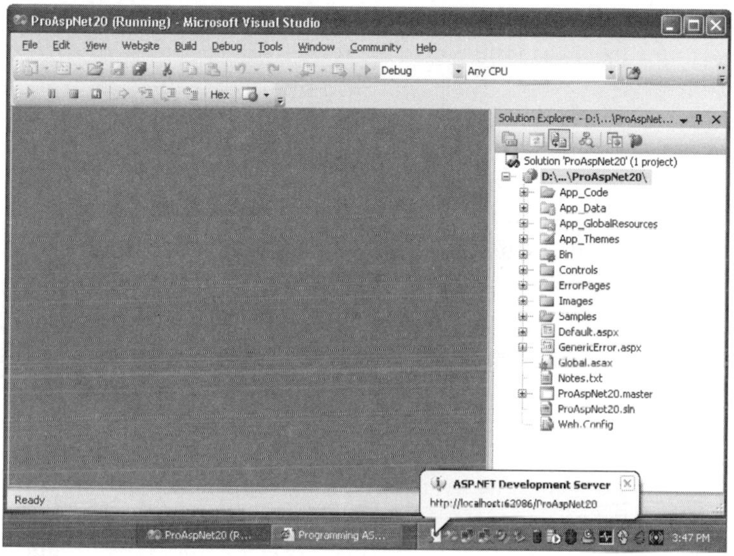

Figure 2-2   The ASP.NET application is controlled by the local Web server if the Web site is opened from a file system path.

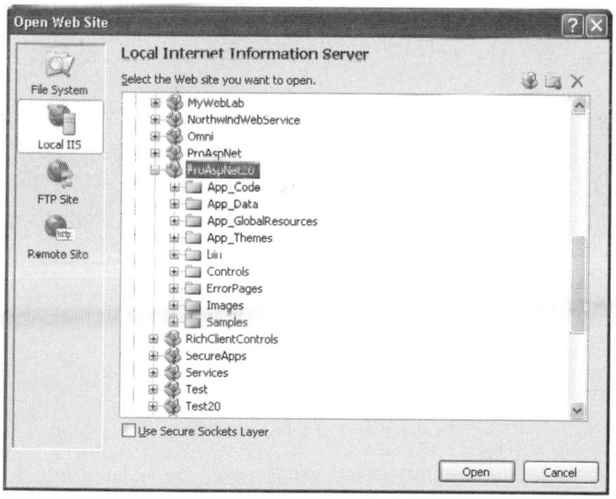

Figure 2-3   Navigating your way through the IIS hierarchy to locate an existing virtual directory to open.

> **Note**   You can open existing Web sites using the FTP protocol and then create and edit files. However, you must have access to the FTP server and read and write permissions for a particular FTP directory. The directory must already exist because Visual Studio .NET 2005 cannot create a new Web site via FTP.

Building the Project Output

Visual Studio .NET 2005 does not compile everything in the site into a single assembly, as Visual Studio .NET 2003 does. Instead, it builds on the new ASP.NET compilation model and dynamically recognizes file types based on the folder they belong to. In this way, not only are changes to *.aspx* files immediately caught, but so are those made to constituent *.cs* or *.vb* files and a variety of accessory resource files. This results in a sort of dynamic compilation for code-behind classes.

There are pros and cons about the new ASP.NET 2.0 compilation model, and some additional parameters need to be considered thoroughly before one can come to a reasonable conclusion about the model. Whatever your final assessment is, though, two facts remain set in stone. First, the ASP.NET 2.0 compilation model allows you to deploy more types of source files (for example, C# and VB.NET classes), monitors these source files for changes, and automatically recompiles. Second, this behavior is optional. If you cringe at the idea of leaving valuable C# source files on the Web potentially at the mercy of hackers, you should just stick to the old model and compile external classes into a separate assembly through an explicit compile step. Whatever your position on the matter is, ASP.NET 2.0 and Visual Studio .NET 2005 give you an alternative.

Solution files (*.sln) are supported, but they're no longer necessary for creating and managing a Web project. The root Web directory defines a Web project; you just add files to the directory and they are in the project. If a file doesn't immediately show up, you right-click on the Solution Explorer window and select Refresh Folder. Solution files are still useful to manage multiple projects, but they don't need to live in the Web directory.

Copying a Web Project

Another long-awaited feature worth a mention is the Copy Web site feature. In earlier versions of Visual Studio .NET, duplicating and synchronizing a Web project onto another machine, or simply moving it to another location within the same machine, was not a hassle-free task. Basically, it was completely up to you and to any FTP-based tool you could come up with. If your server host supported FPSE, you could go through the Visual Studio .NET 2003 integrated wizard—the Project|Copy function. Otherwise, the most viable solution was using raw File Transfer Protocol (FTP). (Moving a Web site within the same network or machine is a similar experience, except that you can use Windows Explorer.)

Sure the overall procedure was not smooth; but it was hardly a mission-impossible task because only a brute-force copy is required. But what if, with good reason, you wanted to move modified files only? Or only files that match given criteria? In these cases, you were left alone to find and copy only these files. (On the other hand, I'd say, who's better qualified than you for this kind of task?)

In Visual Studio .NET 2005, by selecting a menu item you can copy your current Web site to another local or remote location. The Copy Web Site function is a sort of integrated FTP tool that enables you to easily move files around. Figure 2-4 shows a glimpse of the feature.

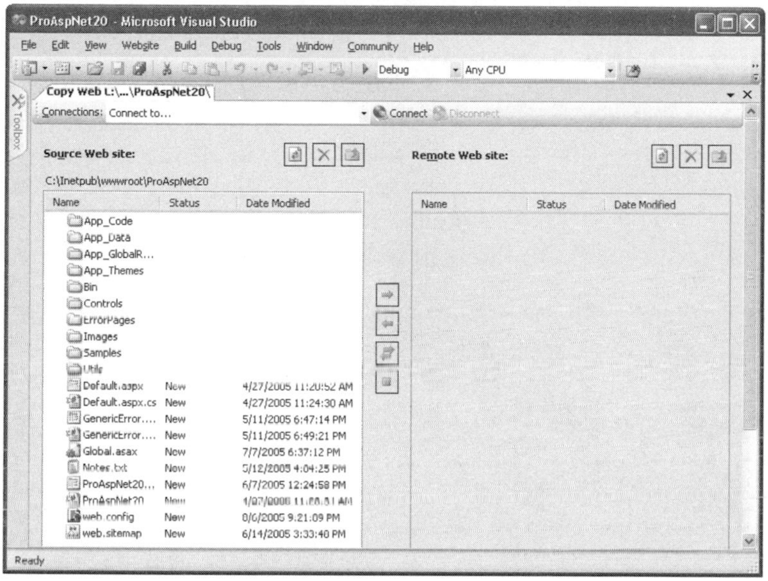

Figure 2-4   The Copy Web Site feature in action.

You connect to the target destination, select the desired copy mode—either Overwrite Source To Target Files, Target To Source Files, or Sync Up Source And Target Projects—and then proceed with the physical copying of files. As Figure 2-5 shows, you can copy files to and from virtual and physical folders, within or across the machine's boundaries.

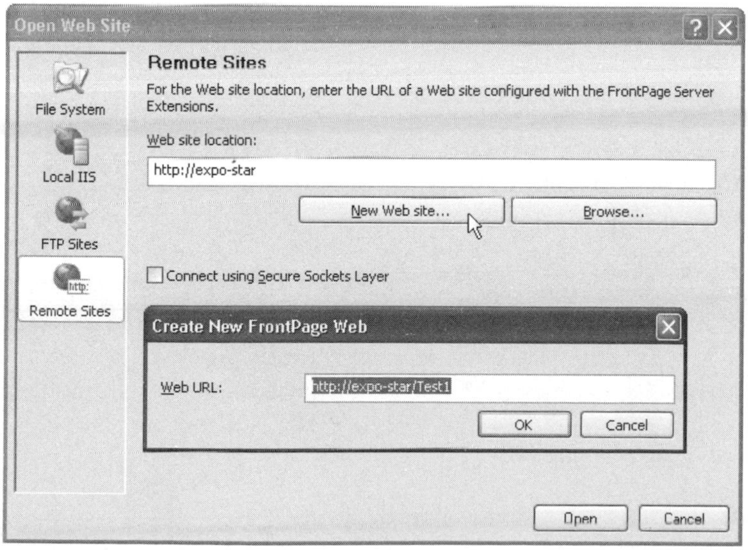

Figure 2-5   Connecting to a remote site to make a copy of the local project.

As you can see yourself, the Copy Web Site function is ideal for deployment especially in hosting environment scenarios in which you need to manage live server files. In addition, the Visual Studio .NET 2005 tool can operate as a synchronization tool, which is helpful to quickly test applications in different scenarios and configurations.

Smarter Editing with IntelliSense

Last but not least, Visual Studio .NET 2005 supports standalone file editing and doesn't require a project to edit a single file on disk. So if you double-click an *.aspx* file in Windows Explorer, Visual Studio .NET 2005 starts up and lets you edit the source code. Unlike with the previous version, IntelliSense and related syntax-coloring work effectively. The page can be viewed live in the embedded browser through the local Web server.

Note that IntelliSense now works everywhere within the source file (see Figure 2-6), including within data-binding expressions, page directives, and code inline in *.aspx* files.

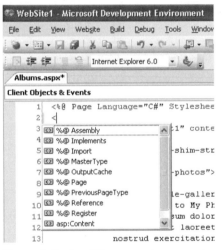

Figure 2-6   IntelliSense works everywhere around the source code of the page.

In Visual Studio .NET 2003, IntelliSense support in the HTML view of the page was hard to achieve for custom controls. Basically, you had to create an XSD file manually to describe the public interface of a control; next, you had to install that file in a particular folder and link it to the page through an *xmlns* attribute. Thankfully, you should never have to author this schema file manually in Visual Studio .NET 2005. A valid schema file is automatically generated when the page author first drops the control on the page. The schema generator does its job after looking at any metadata associated with the controls. However, no new metadata attributes are used. The schema generator grabs all that it needs out of existing attributes used for declaring expected parsing and persistence behavior for controls. (See the "Resources" section at the end of this chapter.)

> **Important**   In light of this, if you are authoring custom controls for ASP.NET 2.0 be sure to check how IntelliSense works for your control in Visual Studio .NET 2005. You can do a lot to ensure that IntelliSense works appropriately by applying the appropriate metadata to controls.

Create an ASP.NET Project

Let's go further and create a sample ASP.NET project with Visual Studio .NET 2005. You first create a new Web site by choosing the corresponding command on the File | New menu. The dialog box that appears prompts you for the type of site you want to create, as in Figure 2-7.

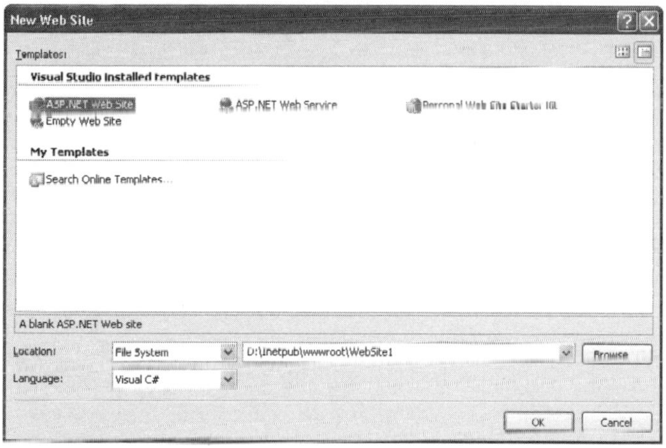

Figure 2-7   The options available for creating a new Web site with Visual Studio .NET 2005.

If you select the Web Site option, Visual Studio generates the minimum number of files for a Web site to build. Basically, it creates a default *.aspx* page and an empty Data directory. If you opt for a personal Web site, an ASP.NET starter kit is used to give you a functional Web site with several standard features built in. Let's go for a Web site. Visual Studio .NET 2005 creates a project file but doesn't use it to track all the files that form an application. The root directory of the site implicitly defines a Web project. Any file or folder added or created under the root is automatically part of the project.

Page Design Features

The ASP.NET front-end of an application can include several types of entities, the most important of which are pages. To edit a Web page, you can choose between two views—Design and Source. The Design view displays the HTML layout, lets you select and edit controls and static elements, and provides a graphical preview of the page. The Source view shows the HTML markup along with the inline code. The markup is syntax-colored and enriched by features such as IntelliSense, tips, and autocompletion.

You choose the template of the item to add to the site from the menu shown in Figure 2-8.

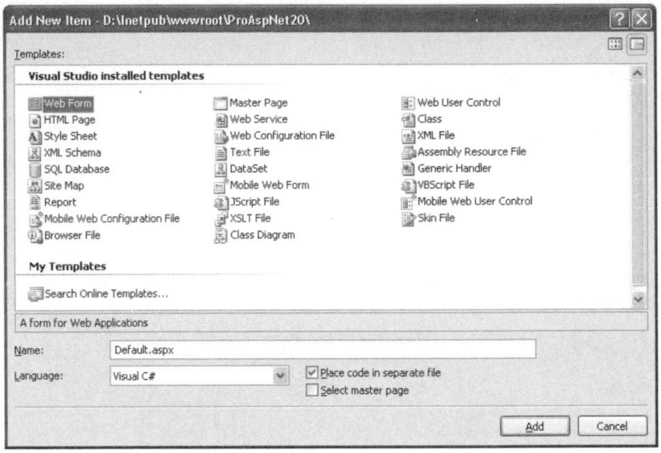

Figure 2-8   Item templates supported by Visual Studio .NET 2005.

Note the two check boxes that appear at the bottom of the window. You can choose to keep the code of the page in a separate file (similar to the code-behind model of Visual Studio .NET 2003) and can associate the current page with a master page. Master pages are a cool new feature of ASP.NET 2.0 that we'll discuss thoroughly in Chapter 6. The code-behind schema touted by Visual Studio .NET 2003 has been revised and restructured. As a result, pages built with Visual Studio .NET 2005 are not forced to use code separation (that is, the page is separated into .*aspx* and .*cs* files). Code separation is still fully supported and recommended, but it is now optional.

Before we get to add some code to build a sample page, let's review some design-time features of the page.

Master Pages

The master page is a single file that defines the template for a set of pages. Similar to an ordinary .*aspx* page, the master contains replaceable sections that are each marked with a unique ID. Pages in an application that will inherit the structure defined in the master reference the master page in their @*Page* directive or even programmatically. A page based on a master is said to be a *content page*. One master page can be bound to any number of content pages. Master pages are completely transparent to end users. When working with an application, a user sees and invokes only the URL of content pages. If a content page is requested, the ASP.NET runtime applies a different compilation algorithm and builds the dynamic class as the merge of the master and the content page.

Master pages are among the hottest new features of ASP.NET 2.0 and address one of the hottest threads in many ASP.NET 1.x newsgroups. By using master pages, a developer can create a Web site in which various physical pages share a common layout. You code the shared user interface and functionality in the master page and make the master contain named placeholders for content that the derived page will provide. The key advantage is that shared information is stored in a single place—the master page—instead of being replicated in each page.

Second, the contract between the master and content page is fixed and determined by the ASP.NET Framework. No change in the application or constituent controls can ever break the link established between master and content.

> **Important**   ASP.NET 2.0 master pages offer *one* way of building Web pages. In no way are master pages the only or preferred way of building Web sites. You should use master pages only if you need to duplicate portions of your user interface or if your application lends itself to being (re)designed in terms of master and content pages.

Content Pages

The master defines the common parts of a certain group of pages and leaves placeholders for customizable regions. Each content page, in turn, defines what the content of each region has to be for a particular *.aspx* page. A content page is a special type of ASP.NET page, as it is allowed to contain only *<asp:Content>* tags. Any classic HTML tags—including client-side *<script>* and comments—are not allowed and if used raise compile errors.

The reason for this lies in the implementation of the master page feature. Because the content regions are substituted into the master page placeholders, the destination for any literal markup (that is, comments, script, other tags) would be ambiguous, because the same kind of content is also allowed in the master.

Visual Studio .NET offers a special Design view of content pages, as Figure 2-9 demonstrates. The view contains as many drawing surfaces as there are content regions in the master. At the same time, the master layout is displayed in the background grayed out to indicate that it's there but you can't access it.

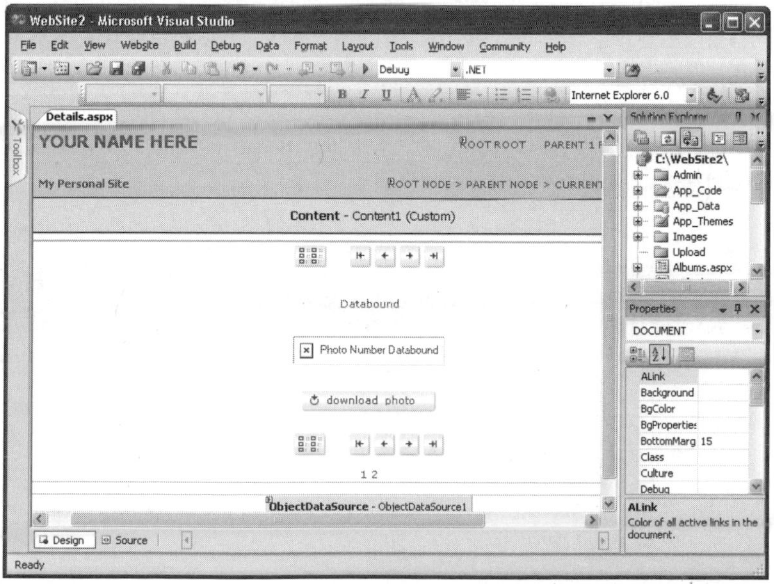

Figure 2-9   Content pages in Visual Studio .NET 2005.

> **Important**   Content pages can be used only in conjunction with master pages. A Web
> Forms page silently becomes a content page when you check the Select Master Page option in
> the dialog box shown in Figure 2-8.

Code-Behind Classes

When you add new Web Forms and require code and layout separation, a C# (or Visual
Basic .NET) class file is created along with the *.aspx* file in the same folder. The class file is
named after the *.aspx* resource simply by adding a language extension. For example, if the
Web Forms is named *WebForm1.aspx*, the corresponding code-behind class is named
WebForm1.aspx.cs. This name is just the default name, and it obeys the default naming
convention. Although it is not recommended for the sake of consistency, you should feel free
to rename the class file to whatever name you like.

Nothing bad can happen to your application if you make it use inline code instead of code and
layout separation. Nonetheless, real-world pages need a good amount of server code, and
appending all that code to the *<script>* tag of the *.aspx* file makes the file significantly hard to
read, edit, and maintain. Code-behind, on the other hand, is based on the idea that each Web
Forms page is bound to a separate class file that contains any code that is relevant to the page.
The code-behind class ends up being the basis of the dynamically generated page class that
the ASP.NET runtime creates for each requested *.aspx* resource. All the server code you need
to associate to the *.aspx* resource flows into the code-behind class. The code-behind model
promotes object-orientation, leads to modular code, and supports code and layout separation,
allowing developers and designers to work concurrently to some extent.

Visual Studio .NET 2005 delivers an improved page model even though the overall syntax
is nearly identical to that of previous versions. There are two main changes you'll notice in
Visual Studio .NET 2005. First, having the code in a separate class file is now optional. (See
Figure 2-8.) Second, thanks to *partial classes*—a .NET Framework–specific feature available
only in version 2.0—multiple developers (and designers) can work on the same page at the
same time. A *partial class* is a .NET class defined across multiple source files that the compiler sews back together.

> **Note**   You should use code-behind classes for all your project pages, except test pages
> you quickly arrange in the context of toy applications or to verify a given feature. Using the
> code-behind model along with the principle of class inheritance gives you enough program-
> ming power to create a hierarchy of classes to cut off development time and maximize code
> reusability.

The Toolbox of Controls

A Web Forms page is mostly made of controls—either predefined HTML and Web controls, user controls, or custom controls. Except for user controls (*.ascx* files), all the others are conveniently listed in the editor's toolbox. (See Figure 2-10.) The toolbox can be toggled on and off and is an easy way to pick up the control of choice and drop it onto the Web form via a drag-and-drop operation. The toolbox is visible only if *.aspx* resources are selected, either in Design or Source view.

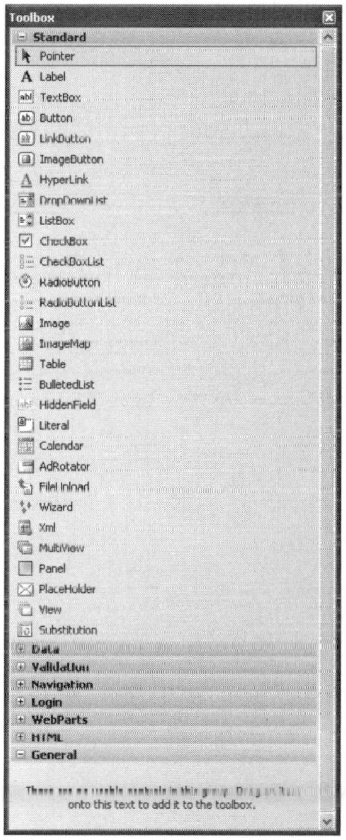

Figure 2-10 The Visual Studio .NET 2005 toolbox.

The toolbox is widely customizable and supports the addition of new controls as well as the creation of new user-defined tabs. Controls defined in a project within the current solution are automatically added to the toolbox.

Editor's Special Capabilities

The Visual Studio .NET 2005 code editor presents some interesting features that prove the team commitment to excellence and all users' satisfaction. I'd like to call your attention to four of them: check for accessibility, markup preservation, simplified tabification and indentation, and target schema validation.

A button on the HTML source editing toolbar allows you to select a few accessibility requirements and validate the page's code against them. (See Figure 2-11.)

Figure 2-11 The dialog box that allows you to select options for an accessibility check.

Note how many recommendations you get even for an empty page. Among other things, you're invited to synchronize alternatives and captions with time-based multimedia tracks, and to ensure that you don't convey information using color alone.

Visual Studio .NET 2005 preserves the formatting of your HTML edits and doesn't even attempt to reformat the source as you switch between views. At the same time, it comes with powerful features for indentation and tag formatting that you can optionally turn on. The days of the Visual Studio .NET 2003 auto-formatting features kicking in on view switching are definitely gone.

In Figure 2-12, you see the list of supported client targets. Once you select a target, the whole editing process is adapted to the features of the specified device. Want a quick example? Imagine you select Netscape Navigator 4.0 (NN4) as the client target. NN4 doesn't recognize the *<iframe>* tag; instead, it sports the *<layer>* tag with nearly the same characteristics. As Figure 2-13 shows, Visual Studio .NET detects the difference and handles it correctly. IntelliSense doesn't list *iframe* but prompts you for *layer*. If you insist and type in *<iframe>* anyway, a squiggle shows up to catch your attention.

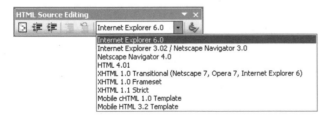

Figure 2-12 The list of client targets for which Visual Studio .NET can cross-check your markup.

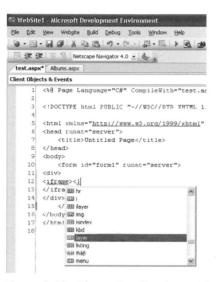

Figure 2-13   The code editor is sensitive to the selected client target schema.

Note   The number of ASP.NET client targets is significantly larger in Visual Studio .NET 2005 and ranges from Internet Explorer 6.0 to HTML 3.2 (covering Internet Explorer 3.x and Netscape Navigator 3.x). Other validation targets are mobile schemas (Compact HTML 1.0 and mobile HTML 3.2), Netscape 4.0, and the XHTML 1.0 Transitional schema. The latter schema covers browsers such as Netscape 7.0 and Opera 7.0.

Code Refactoring

When a *.vb* or a *.cs* file is open for editing in Visual Studio .NET 2005, a new menu appears on the top-most menu strip—the Refactor menu, shown in Figure 2-14.

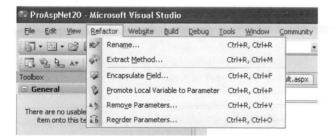

Figure 2-14   The new menu for helping developers to quickly refactor the code of classes.

As you can see, the menu provides advanced facilities for code editing. Among the other things, you can extract a block of code and transform it into a new method or rename a member all the way through. The refactor feature doesn't disappoint when it comes to managing properties. Admittedly, one of most boring tasks when writing classes is turning a field into a property with *get* and *set* accessors. Imagine you have a field like the following one:

```
private int _counters;
```

At a certain point, you might realize that a full-featured property would be better. Instead of typing code yourself, you just select the line and refactor to encapsulate the field. Needless to say, the menu item is *Refactor|Encapsulate field*. With the power of a click, the old code becomes the following:

```
public int Counters
{
    get
    {
        return _counters;
    }

    set
    {
        _counters = value;
    }
}
```

You are free to change the public name of the property and, of course, to flesh out the bodies of the get/set accessors.

Import/Export of IDE Features

It is common for developers to move a project from one machine to another. This happens for a variety of reasons. For example, you might use multiple machines for test purposes; you continually swing between the client's site and your own office; you are an absolute workaholic who just can't spend a night home without working.

Typically, the various machines have Visual Studio .NET installed with the same set of features, and although it's not necessary, they share the same set of IDE settings. To feel comfortable with the environment, you might have developed macros, reordered menus and toolbars, added new controls to the toolbox, created new project templates, and assigned preferences for colors and fonts. This wealth of information is not easy to catalog, organize, and persist if you have to do that manually.

Figure 2-15 shows the new Import/Export Settings dialog box associated with the Tools menu. You select the IDE settings you want to persist and save them to a file. The file can be created anywhere and is given a *.vssettings* extension. In spite of the extension, it is an XML file.

Figure 2-15   The wizard for importing and exporting IDE settings.

Adding Code to the Project

Adding code to the project mostly means that you added Web Forms to the project and now need to hook up some of the page events or events that controls in the form generate. In addition, you might want to add some classes to the project representing tailor-made functionalities not otherwise available.

Filling a Web Forms page is easy and intuitive. You open the form in layout mode and drag and drop controls from the toolbox onto it. Next, you move elements around and configure their properties. If needed, you can switch to the Source view and manually type the HTML markup the way you want it to be.

A pleasant surprise for many developers is that you can drag and drop controls from the toolbox directly into the Source view; instead of viewing the control graphically rendered, you see the corresponding markup code. Similarly, you can edit the properties of a server control by selecting it in the Design view or highlighting the related HTML in the Source view. In addition, each control deployed on the form can have its own design-time user interface through which you can configure properties for the run time.

Defining Event Handlers

Adding code to a Web Form page means handling some page's or control's events. How do you write an event handler for a particular page element? To try it out, place a button on a form and double-click. Visual Studio switches to the Source view and creates an empty event handler for the control's default event. For a button control, it is the *Click* event. The code you get looks similar to the following:

```
void Button1_Click(object sender, EventArgs e)
{
    ...
}
```

The HTML markup is automatically modified to contain an additional *OnClick* attribute:

```
<asp:button runat="server" id="Button1"
    text="Click"
    OnClick="Button1_Click" />
```

Notice that event binding is always done declaratively in the body of the *.aspx* page. Unlike its predecessor, Visual Studio .NET 2005 doesn't inject automatically generated code in the page for event wireup. Recall that in Visual Studio .NET 2003, double-clicking a button adds the following (C#) code to the code-behind class:

```
// VS.NET injects this code in the code-behind class of a page
// when you double-click a button to handle its default event
Button1.Click += new EventHandler(this.Button1_Click);
```

The code would obviously be different if Visual Basic .NET is your language of choice.

If you're dealing with a code-behind page, the event handler is defined in the code-behind class instead of being placed inline.

When you double-click on a control or on the body of the page, a handler for the default page or control event is generated. What if you need to write a handler for another event? You select the desired control and click on the Events icon in the Properties window. You get a view like that in Figure 2-16 and pick up the event you need.

Figure 2-16   The Events view in the Properties window.

Writing Helper Classes

Writing helper classes is as easy as adding a new class to the project, as shown in Figure 2-17.

The class file can define any number of classes, even partial class definitions, and will actually be compiled to an assembly. Where should you deploy this class file in your project? You have two options: either you create an additional project to generate a DLL component library or you drop the class file in a special folder below the application's virtual root—the *App_Code* folder.

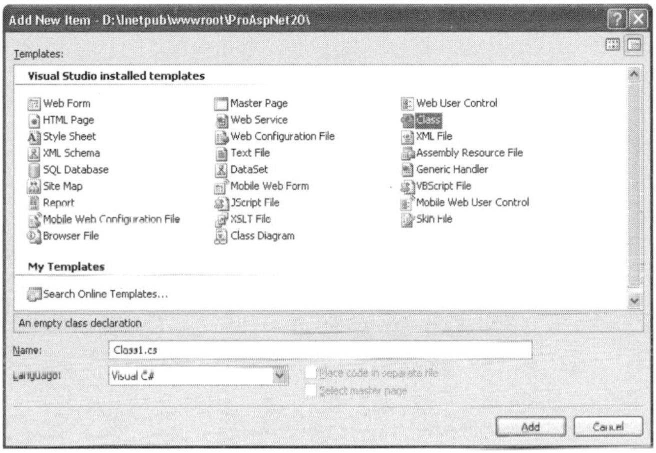

Figure 2-17   Adding a new class to an ASP.NET project

In the former case, you add another project to the solution by using the File|Add menu. From the list of available projects, you pick up a Class Library project and then add any class files to it. When you're done, you reference the library project in the Web site project and go. Pleasantly enough, IntelliSense will just detect new classes and work as expected.

What's the *App_Code* folder, then? It is an application's subdirectory that has a special meaning to the ASP.NET runtime. The *App_Code* folder is designed to contain reusable components that are automatically compiled and linked to the page code. The folder stores source class files (*.vb* or *.cs*) that the ASP.NET runtime engine dynamically compiles to an assembly upon execution. Created in a predefined path visible to all pages in the site, the resulting assembly is updated whenever any of the source files are updated. It is important to note that any file copied to the *App_Code* folder is deployed as source code on the production box. (I'll say more about special ASP.NET directories in the next section.)

Building a Sample Shared Class

To experience the advantages of reusable source components, let's design a page that makes use of a nontrivial component that would be annoying to insert inline in each page that needs it. The page looks like the one in Figure 2-18.

Many products and services available over the Web require a strong password. The definition of a "strong password" is specific to the service, but normally it addresses a password at least eight characters long with at least one character from each of the following groups: uppercase, lowercase, digits, and special characters. We'll use that definition here. The sample page you will build asks the user for the desired length of the password and suggests one built according to the rules just mentioned. You create a new file named *StrongPassword.cs* and place it in the purposely created *App_Code* subdirectory. The class outline is shown here:

```
public class StrongPassword
{
    public StrongPassword()
    {...}

    public string Generate()
    {...}
    public string Generate(int passwordLength)
    {...}
}
```

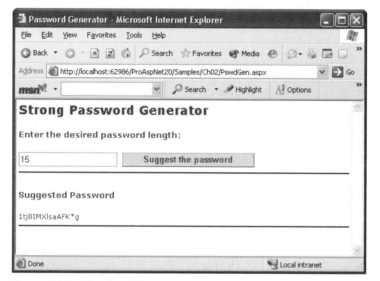

Figure 2-18   The PswdGen.aspx page to generate a new "strong" password of the specified length.

The class features one method—*Generate*—that will actually generate a new strong password. Of course, the definition of a "strong password" is arbitrary. Once placed in the *App_Code* directory, this class is compiled on demand and made available to all pages. In the sample page, the code to generate and validate a password becomes simpler and more readable:

```
void buttonGenerate_Click(Object sender, System.EventArgs e)
{
    // Gets the desired length of the password and ensures
    // it is really expressed as a number. (This is a simple but
    // effective pattern to prevent code/data injection.)
    int pswdLen = 8;
    bool result = Int32.TryParse(PswdLength.Text, out pswdLen);

    // Create and display the new password
    StrongPassword pswd = new StrongPassword();
    labelPassword.Text = pswd.Generate(pswdLen);
}
```

Figure 2-18 shows the page in action. Note that the same functionality can also be achieved by placing the code inline or packing the *StrongPassword* class in a separate assembly.

A Look at the *web.config* File

The behavior of an ASP.NET application is affected by the settings defined in various configuration files—*machine.config* and *web.config*. The *machine.config* file contains default and machine-specific values for all supported settings. Machine settings are normally controlled by the system administrator, and applications should never be given write access to it. An application can override most default values stored in the *machine.config* file by creating one or more *web.config* files.

At a minimum, an application creates a *web.config* file in its root folder. The *web.config* file is a subset of *machine.config*, written according to the same XML schema. Although *web.config* allows you to override some of the default settings, you cannot override all settings defined in *machine.config*.

If the application contains child directories, it can define a *web.config* file for each folder. The scope of each configuration file is determined in a hierarchical, top-down manner. The settings actually applied to a page are determined by the sum of the changes that the various *web.config* files on the way from *machine.config* to the page's directory carry. Any *web.config* file can locally extend, restrict, and override any type of settings defined at an upper level. If no configuration file exists in an application folder, the settings valid at the upper level are applied.

Visual Studio .NET usually generates a default *web.config* file for you. The *web.config* file is not strictly necessary for an application to run. Without a *web.config* file, though, you can't debug the application.

ASP.NET Reserved Folders

ASP.NET uses a number of special directories below the application root to maintain application content and data. In ASP.NET 1.x, only the Bin directory was used. ASP.NET 2.0 introduces seven additional protected directories. None of these directories are automatically created by ASP.NET 2.0 or Visual Studio .NET 2005, nor are the directories necessarily required to exist. Each directory needs to be created either manually by developers or on demand through Visual Studio .NET when a feature that requires it is enabled.

Additional Application Directories

Table 2-1 lists all the additional directories you can take advantage of. Note that the directories will be there only if they are required by your specific application. Don't be too worried about the number of new directories (that is, seven) you can potentially have. A reasonable estimate would be that only two or three (out of seven) additional directories will be present in an average ASP.NET application.

Table 2-1   Special Reserved Directories in ASP.NET Applications

Directory Name	Intended Goal
Bin	Contains all precompiled assemblies needed by the application.
App_Browsers	Contains browser capabilities information.
App_Code	Contains source class files (*.vb* or *.cs*) used by pages. All the files must be in the same language; you can't have both C# and VB.NET files in the folder.
App_Data	Contains data files for the application. This can include XML files and Access databases to store personalization data.
App_GlobalResources	Contains *.resx* resource files global to the application.
App_LocalResources	Contains all *.resx* resource files that are specific to a particular page.
App_Themes	Contains the definition of the themes supported by the application. (I'll say more about themes in Chapter 6.)
App_WebReferences	Contains *.wsdl* files linking Web services to the application.

The content in all the directories listed in Table 2-1 won't be accessible via HTTP requests to the server. The only exception is the content of the *App_Themes* folder.

> **Important**   The names of these folders aren't customizable. The reason lies in the way the ISAPI filter in charge of blocking HTTP requests to these folders work. For performance reasons, the ISAPI filter can't just access the *web.config* file to read about directory names to look for. That would require the filter to parse the XML file on *any* request and, as you can easily imagine, would be a major performance hit. Alternately, the names of the directories could have been written in the registry, which would make for a much faster and affordable access. Unfortunately, a registry-based approach would break XCopy deployment and introduce a major breaking change in the ASP.NET architecture. (See the "Application Deployment" section for more information on XCopy deployment.)

The contents of many folders listed in Table 2-1 are compiled to a dynamic assembly when the request is processed for the first time. This is the case for themes, code, resources, and Web references. (See the "Resources" section for more information on the ASP.NET 2.0 compilation model.)

The *App_Code* Directory

As mentioned, you can use the server *App_Code* directory to group your helper and business classes. You deploy them as source files, and the ASP.NET runtime ensures that classes will be automatically compiled on demand. Furthermore, any changes to these files will be detected, causing the involved classes to recompile. The resulting assembly is automatically referenced in the application and shared between all pages participating in the site.

You should put only components into the *App_Code* directory. Do not put pages, Web user controls, or other noncode files containing noncode elements into the subdirectory. The resulting assembly has application scope and is created in the *Temporary ASP.NET Files* folder—well outside the Web application space.

> **Note**   If you're worried about deploying valuable C# or VB.NET source files to the Web server, bear in mind that any (repeat, *any*) access to the *App_Code* folder conducted via HTTP is monitored and blocked by the aforementioned ASP.NET ISAPI filter.

Note that all class files in the *App_Code* folder must be written in the same language—be it Visual Basic .NET or C#—because they are all compiled to a single assembly and processed by a single compiler. To use different languages, you must organize your class files in folders and add some entries to the configuration file to tell build system to create distinct assemblies—one per language.

Here's an example. Suppose you have two files named source.cs and source.vb. Because they're written in different languages, they can't stay together in the *App_Code* folder. You can then create two subfolders—say, *App_Code/VB* and *App_Code/CS*—and move the files to the subfolder that matches the language. Next you can add the following entries to the *web.config* file:

```
<configuration>
<system.web>
<compilation>
    <codeSubDirectories>
        <add directoryName="VB" />
        <add directoryName="CS" />
    </codeSubDirectories>
</compilation>
</system.web>
</configuration>
```

Note that the *<codeSubDirectories>* section is valid only if it is set in the *web.config* file in the application root. Each section instructs the build system to create a distinct assembly. This means that all the files in the specified directory must be written in the same language, but different directories can target different languages.

> **Note**   The *App_Code* directory can also contain XSD files, like those generated for typed *DataSets*. An XSD file represents the strongly typed schema of a table of data. In the .NET Framework 1.1, a typed *DataSet* must be manually created using the *xsd.exe* tool. In ASP.NET 2.0, all you have to do is drop the source XSD file in the *App_Code* folder.

The Resource Directories

A localizable Web page uses resources instead of hard-coded text to flesh out the user interface of contained controls. Once a resource assembly is linked to the application, ASP.NET can select the correct property at run time according to the user's language and culture. In

ASP.NET 1.x, developers had to create satellite assemblies manually. ASP.NET 2.0, on the other hand, creates resource assemblies parsing and compiling any resource files found in the two supported folders—*App_LocalResources* and *App_GlobalResources*.

A local resource is a resource file specific to a page. A simple naming convention binds the file to the page. If the page is named *sample.aspx*, its corresponding resource file is *sample.aspx.resx*. To be precise, this resource file is language neutral and has no culture defined. To create a resource assembly for a specific culture, say Italian, you need to name the resource file as follows: *sample.aspx.it.resx*. Generally, the *it* string should be replaced with any other equivalent string that identifies a culture, such as *fr* for French or *en* for English. Figure 2-19 shows the a sample local resource folder.

Figure 2-19   The local resource directory for the *respage.aspx* page.

Local resources provide a sort of implicit localization where the page itself automatically ensures that each contained control is mapped to a particular entry in the *.resx* file. Here's how a simple page changes once you add support for local resources.

```
<%@ Page Language="C#" meta:resourcekey="PageResource1" UICulture="auto" %>

<html>
<head id="Head1" runat="server">
    <title>Pro ASP.NET (Ch 02)</title>
</head>
<body>
<h1>
    <asp:Label runat="server" id="H1" meta:resourcekey="LabelResource1" />
</h1>
<form id="Form1" runat="server">
```

```
    <asp:Button ID="btn" Runat="server" meta:resourcekey="BtnResource1" />
</form>
</body>
</html>
```

The page itself and each constituent control are given a resource key. The *.resx* file contains entries in the form *ResourceKey.PropertyName*. For example, the *Text* property of the button is implicitly bound to the *BtnResource1.Text* entry in the *.resx* file. You don't have to write a single line of code for this mapping to take place. You are only requested to populate the resource files as outlined. The *UICulture* attribute set to *auto* tells the ASP.NET runtime to use the current browser's language setting to select the right set of resources.

> **Tip**   To quickly test a page against different languages, you open the Internet Explorer Tools menu and click the Languages button. Next, you add the language of choice to the list box of supported languages and move the language of choice to the first position in the list. Click OK and exit. From now on, Internet Explorer will be sending the selected language ID with each served request.

Figure 2-20 shows how the same page looks when different languages are set.

Figure 2-20   The *respage.aspx* file in English and Italian.

Implicit localization works automatically, meaning that you don't need to specify how to read information about each property from a resource file. However, at times you need more direct control over how properties are set. For this, you turn to global resources. When you choose to add a resource file to the application, Visual Studio .NET creates the *App_GlobalResources* directory and places a new *.resx* file in it. You can rename this file at will and fill it with strings, images, sounds, and whatever else is suitable to you. (See Figure 2-21.)

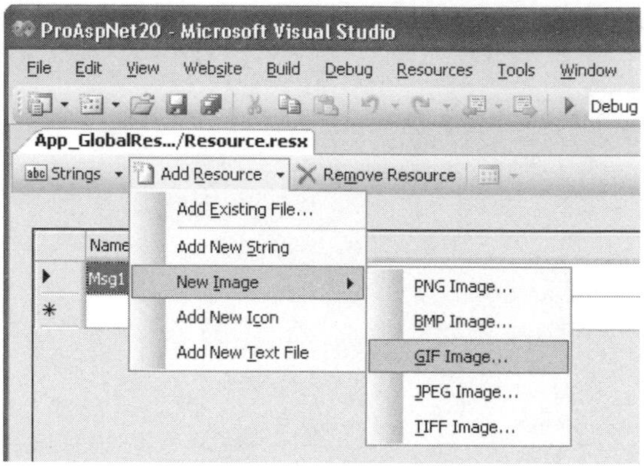

Figure 2-21 The Visual Studio .NET Resource editor in action.

Within the page or controls code, you reference resources using an expression, as in the following code:

```
<asp:Label Runat="server" Text="<%$ Resources:Resource, Msg1 %>" />
```

Resources is the namespace of the object, whereas *Resource* is the name of the *.resx* file that contains the resources. Finally, *Msg1* is the name of the entry to use. Explicit localization is useful when you have large bodies of text or custom messages you want to localize.

> **Note** The resulting resource assembly for the neutral culture has application scope and is therefore referenced from other assemblies generated in the application. All types defined in the resource assemblies belong to the *Resources* namespace and are static objects.

Linked Web Services

When you add a reference to a Web service, the *.wsdl* file for the Web service is downloaded and copied to the *App_WebReferences* directory. At runtime, any WSDL file found in the Web reference directory is dynamically compiled in a C# or Visual Basic .NET proxy class in much the same way as business classes in the *App_Code* directory are processed.

Note that in ASP.NET 1.x, you have to reference the Web service and have Visual Studio .NET 2003 to generate the proxy class explicitly. If you can obtain a WSDL file in other ways (that is, you don't download it through the Add Web Reference Wizard), you can add it manually to the *App_WebReferences* directory.

Available Themes

The *App_Themes* directory defines one or more themes for controls. A *theme* is a set of skins and associated files such as style sheets and images that can be used within an application to give a consistent user interface to controls. In the *App_Themes* directory, each theme occupies a single subdirectory, which has the same name as the theme. All related files are stored in this directory.

When a theme is loaded, the contents of the theme directory are parsed and compiled into a class that inherits from a common base class. Any theme defined outside the *App_Themes* directory is ignored by the ASP.NET build system.

Build the ASP.NET Project

To build and run the ASP.NET application, you simply click the Start button on the toolbar (or press F5) and wait for a browser window to pop up. In Visual Studio .NET 2005, no compile step takes place to incorporate code-behind and helper classes. All the dynamically generated assemblies, and all precompiled assemblies deployed into the *Bin* folder, are linked to the application as used to visit pages.

Once any needed assemblies have been successfully built, Visual Studio .NET autoattaches to the ASP.NET run-time process—typically, *w3wp.exe*—for debugging purposes. Next, it opens the start page of the application.

> **Important**   The ASP.NET run-time process might differ based on the process model in use. The process model is configurable; the default model, though, depends on the underlying operating systems and Web server settings. If your Web server runs Windows 2000 Server, or perhaps any version of Windows XP, the run-time process is *aspnet_wp.exe*. It runs under a weak user account named ASPNET and is designed to interact with IIS 5.x. If you run Windows 2003 Server and IIS 6.0 and didn't change the default process model, the run-time process is *w3wp.exe*, which is the standard worker process of IIS 6.0. The *w3wp.exe* process runs under the NETWORK SERVICE account. This process doesn't know anything about ASP.NET, but its behavior is aptly customized by a version-specific copy of the ASP.NET ISAPI extension. Under IIS 6.0, you can even switch back to the IIS 5 process model. If you do so, though, you lose a lot in performance.

When you build the project, Visual Studio .NET 2005 might complain about a missing *web.config* file, which is necessary if you want to debug the code. If you just want to run the page without debugging it, click the Run button in the message box you get. Otherwise, you let Visual Studio generate a proper *web.config* file for you. If you create your own *web.config* file, make sure it contains the following string to enable debugging:

```
<compilation debug="true" />
```

Once this is done, you can commence your debugging session.

Debugging Features

As long as you compiled the project in debug mode (which is the default indeed), you can set a few breakpoints in the sources and step into the code, as shown in Figure 2-22.

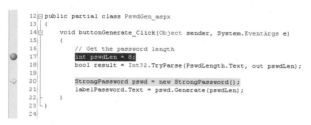

```
12 ⊟ public partial class PswdGen_aspx
13   {
14 ⊟     void buttonGenerate_Click(Object sender, System.EventArgs e)
15       {
16           // Get the password length
17           int pswdLen = 8;
18           bool result = Int32.TryParse(PswdLength.Text, out pswdLen);
19
20           StrongPassword pswd = new StrongPassword();
21           labelPassword.Text = pswd.Generate(pswdLen);
22       }
23   }
24
```

Figure 2-22   Stepping into the code of the page by using the Visual Studio .NET integrated debugger.

The Debug menu is a little richer in Visual Studio .NET 2005 than it was in the previous version. You now have more choices as far as exceptions and breakpoints are concerned. In particular, you can configure the IDE so that it automatically breaks when an exception is thrown. The feature can be fine-tuned to let you focus on any exceptions, any exceptions in a specified set, or all exceptions not handled by the current application.

Breakpoints can be set at an absolute particular location or in a more relative way when the execution reaches a given function. Braveheart debuggers also have the chance to break the code when the memory at a specified address changes.

Watch windows feature a richer user interface centered around the concept of visualizers. A visualizer is a popup window designed to present certain types of data in a more friendly and readable manner—XML, text, or *DataSets*. (See Figure 2-23.)

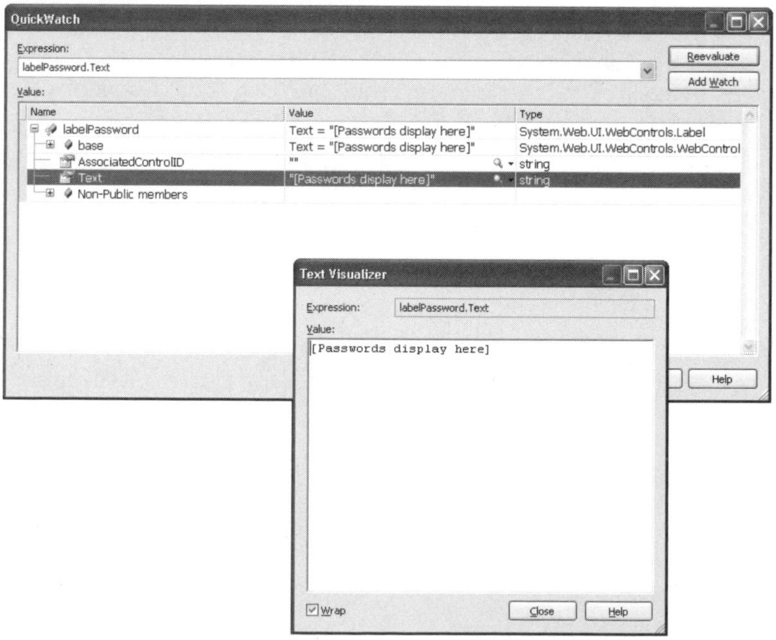

Figure 2-23   The text visualizer invoked from the quick-watch window during a debug session.

Visualizers are also active from within code tip windows. A code tip is the made-to-measure ToolTip that previews the value of variables during a debug session. (See Figure 2-24.)

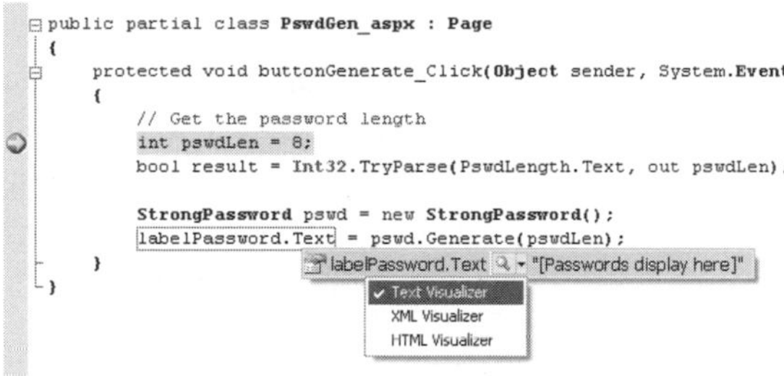

Figure 2-24   Invoking a visualizer from within a code tip.

Visualizers are defined for a few types of data. Personally, I just love the *DataSet* visualizer. Checking what's in a *DataSet* instance couldn't be easier.

Testing the Application

As mentioned, there are two ways of testing pages in Visual Studio .NET 2005. You can have pages served by IIS (if installed) or by the embedded local Web server. By default, Visual Studio .NET uses IIS if you open the project as a Web site and indicate its URL; otherwise, it defaults to the local Web server. An important point to consider about the embedded Web server concerns the security context. Under IIS, an ASP.NET application is served by a worker process running under the *real* account defined for the application—typically, a highly restricted account such as ASP.NET or NETWORK SERVICE.

In contrast, the embedded Web server takes the security token of the currently logged-on user—that is, you. This means that if the developer is currently logged on as an administrator—a much more common scenario than it should be—the application receives administrative privileges. The problem here is not a risk of being attacked; the real problem is that you are actually testing the application in a scenario significantly different from the real one. Things that work great under the local Web server might fail miserably under IIS.

For simple applications that only read and run ASP.NET pages, this problem is not that relevant. However, the results of your testing under the local server will become less reliable if you access files other than Web pages, files located on other machines, files in the Windows registry, or files on a local or remote database. In all these cases, you must make sure that the real ASP.NET account has sufficient permissions to work with those resources.

The bottom line is that even though you can use the local Web server to test pages, it sometimes doesn't offer a realistic test scenario.

Application Deployment

Installing a .NET application in general, and an ASP.NET application in particular, is a matter of performing an *XCopy*—that is, a recursive copy of all the files—to the target folder on the target machine. Aside from some inevitable emphasis and promotion, the *XCopy deployment* expression, which is often used to describe setup procedures in .NET, communicates the gist of .NET deployment: you don't need to do much more than copy files. In particular, there's no need to play with the registry, no components to set up, and no local files to create. Or, at least, nothing of the kind is needed just because the .NET Framework mandates it.

XCopy Deployment

The deployment of a Web application is a task that can be accomplished in various ways depending on the context. As far as copy is concerned, you can use any of the following: FTP transfer, any server management tools providing forms of smart replication on a remote site, or an MSI installer application. In Visual Studio .NET 2005, you can even use the Copy Web Site function that we discussed earlier in this chapter.

Each option has pros and cons, and the best fit can only be found once you know exactly the runtime host scenario and the purpose of the application is clearly delineated. Be aware that if you're going to deploy the application on an ISP host, you might be forced to play by the rules (read, "use the tools") that your host has set. If you're going to deliver a front end for an existing system to a variety of servers, you might perhaps find it easier to create a setup project. On the other hand, FTP is great for general maintenance and for applying quick fixes. Ad hoc tools, on the other hand, could give you automatic sync-up features. Guess what? Choosing the right technique is strictly application-specific and is ultimately left to you.

Copying Files

FTP gives you a lot of freedom, and it lets you modify and replace individual files. It doesn't represent a solution that is automatic, however: whatever you need to do must be accomplished manually. Assuming that you have gained full access to the remote site, using FTP is not much different than using Windows Explorer in the local network. I believe that with the Copy Web Site functionality of Visual Studio .NET 2005 in place, the need for raw FTP access is going to lessen. If nothing else, the new Copy Web Site function operates as an integrated FTP-like tool to access remote locations.

The new copy function also provides synchronization capabilities too. It is not like the set of features that a specifically designed server management tool would supply, but it can certainly work well through a number of realistic situations. At the end of the day, a site replication tool doesn't do much more than merely transfer files from end to end. Its plusses are the user interface, and the intelligence, built around and atop this basic capability. So a replication tool maintains a database of files with timestamps, attributes, properties and can sync up versions of the site in a rather automated way, minimizing the work on your end.

Building a Setup Project

Another common scenario involves using an out-of-the-box installer file. Deploying a Web application this way is a two-step operation. First, create and configure the virtual directory; next, copy the needed files. Visual Studio .NET makes creating a Web setup application a snap. You just create a new type of project—a Web Setup Project—select the files to copy, and build the project. Figure 2-25 shows the user interface of the setup project.

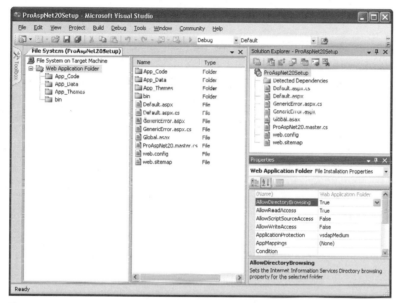

Figure 2-25   Creating a Web setup project.

The Web Application Folder node represents the virtual directory of the new application on the target machine. The Properties box lets you configure the settings of the new virtual directory. For example, the *AllowDirectoryBrowsing* property lets you assign browsing permission to the IIS virtual folder you will create. You can also control the virtual directory name, application execute permissions, level of isolation, and default page. The *Bin* subfolder is automatically created, but you can ask the setup to create and populate as many subfolders as you need.

When you build the project, you obtain a Windows Installer *.msi* file that constitutes the setup to ship to your clients. The default installer supports repairing and uninstalling the application. The setup you obtain in this way—which is the simplest you can get—does not contain the .NET Framework, which must be installed on the target machine or explicitly included in the setup project itself.

What Else Do You Need to Do?

One of the coolest features of .NET assemblies is that they are self-describing components. An application that wants to know about the internal characteristics of an assembly has only to ask! The .NET reflection of an API is the programming interface by which a client can interrogate an assembly. This fact eliminates the need of using the registry (or any other sort of centralized repository) to track paths and attributes of binary components. Another pleasant effect of the assembly's structure is that side-by-side execution is now a snap, and ASP.NET applications take advantage of it on a regular basis. In practice, whenever you update a page, two versions of the "same" assembly live side by side for awhile without interference and conflict.

So the XCopy deployment model rocks. Is there something more you need to do to finalize the deployment of your application? Sure there is. Let's detail some additional tasks.

If you use read/write files (XML files, configuration files, Access databases), you need to grant proper writing permission to the application. Likewise, if your application or control generates temporary files, you need to make accommodations for a proper folder with proper writing permissions. These tasks must be accomplished in one way or another before the application goes live. Note that in an ISP scenario you are normally given an isolated disk subtree with full write permissions granted to the ASP.NET account. You must design your applications to be flexible enough to support a configurable path for all their temporary files.

> **Note**   We're not saying anything specific about database configuration here. We're simply assuming that all required databases are in place, properly working, and entirely configured. If this is not the case, you might want to add this task to the list too. The same holds true for any remote application and network services you might need, including Web services and COM+ components.

Configuring the Runtime Environment

Another aspect to consider is runtime configuration. When you develop the ASP.NET code, you test it on a machine with its own *machine.config* file. When you deploy the application on a production box, you might not be able to restore the same settings. One possible reason is that the administrator does not want you to modify the current settings because they proved to be great for other applications. (This is especially true in an ISP host scenario.)

You can work around the issue by simply replicating any needed *machine.config* settings to the application's *web.config*. However, if you are deploying your code to a service provider, you might find that many *machine.config* settings have been locked down and cannot be overridden. In this case, you should ask (or more exactly, beg) the administrator to let you tweak the server's configuration in a way that suits you without hurting other applications. This normally entails creating an application-specific *<location>* section in the server's *machine.config* file.

Deploying an ASP.NET application in a Web-farm scenario poses a few extra configuration issues you must be aware of. All *machine.config* files in the Web farm must be synchronized to the value of a few attributes. You can achieve this in two ways, the simplest of which is packing all attribute values in the application's *web.config*. This approach greatly simplifies the deployment because you only have to run the setup on all machines and no other changes are needed. If any of the required sections are locked down (once more, this is likely to happen in an ISP scenario), you find yourself in the situation described previously, that of begging the administrator to create a new *<location>* section for you.

> **Note**   The *<location>* section can be used in both *machine.config* and *web.config* to limit Web settings to the specified application path. In a deployment scenario, the section assumes particular importance in the *machine.config* file and subsequently requires administrative privileges. The *<location>* section is normally used in a *web.config* file in case of a deployment with a main application and a bunch of subapplications.

Site Precompilation

As mentioned, dynamically created assemblies are placed in an internal folder managed by the ASP.NET runtime. Unless source files are modified, the compilation step occurs only once per page—when the page is first requested. Although in many cases the additional overhead is no big deal, removing it still is a form of optimization. Site precompilation consists of deploying the whole site functionality through assemblies. A precompiled application is still made up of source files, but all pages and resources are fictitiously accessed before deployment and compiled to assemblies. The dynamically created assemblies are then packaged and installed to the target machine. As you can see, site precompilation also saves you from deploying valuable source files, thus preserving the intellectual property.

> **Important**   Source files, like C# classes or WSDL scripts, are protected against HTTP access. However, they are at the mercy of a hacker in the case of a successful exploitation that allows the attacker to take control of the Web directories.

Site precompilation was possible in ASP.NET 1.x, but in version 2.0 it has the rank of a system tool, fully supported by the framework. In summary, site precompilation offers two main advantages:

- Requests to the site do not cause any delay because the pages and code are compiled to assemblies.

- Sites can be deployed without any source code, thus preserving and protecting the intellectual property of the solutions implemented.

Precompilation can take two forms: in-place precompilation and deployment precompilation.

> **Note**   To protect intellectual property, you can also consider obfuscation in addition to site precompilation. *Obfuscation* is a technique that nondestructively changes names in the assembly metadata, thus preventing potential code-crackers from scanning your files for sensitive strings. Obfuscation does not affect the way the code runs, except that it compacts the executable, making it load a bit faster. If decompiled, an obfuscated assembly generates a much less readable intermediate code. Although applicable to all .NET applications, there is nothing wrong with obfuscating your ASP.NET assemblies in case of hacker access for the very same reasons. Visual Studio .NET 2005 provides the community edition of a commercial tool— Dotfuscator.

In-Place Precompilation

In-place precompilation allows a developer or a site administrator to access each page in the application as if it were being used by end users. This means each page is compiled as if for ordinary use. The site is fully compiled before entering production, and no user will experience a first-hit compilation delay, as in version 1.x. In-place precompilation takes place after the site is deployed, but before it goes public. To precompile a site in-place, you use the following command, where */proaspnet20* indicates the virtual folder of the application:

```
aspnet_compiler -v /proaspnet20
```

If you precompile the site again, the compiler skips pages that are up to date and only new or changed files are processed and those with dependencies on new or changed files. Because of this compiler optimization, it is practical to compile the site after even minor updates.

Precompilation is essentially a batch compilation that generates all needed assemblies in the fixed ASP.NET directory on the server machine. If any file fails compilation, precompilation will fail on the application.

Precompilation for Deployment

Precompilation for deployment generates a file representation of the site made of assemblies, static files, and configuration files—a sort of manifest. This representation is generated on a target machine and can also be packaged as MSI and then copied and installed to a production machine. This form of precompilation doesn't require source code to be left on the target machine.

Precompilation for deployment also requires the use of the *aspnet_compiler* command-line tool:

```
aspnet_compiler -m metabasePath
                -c virtualPath
                -p physicalPath
                targetPath
```

The role of each parameter is explained in Table 2-2.

Table 2-2   Parameters of the *aspnet_compiler* Tool

Parameter	Description
metabasePath	An optional parameter that indicates the full IIS metabase path of the application
virtualPath	A required parameter that indicates the virtual path of the application
physicalPath	An optional parameter that indicates the physical path of the application
targetPath	An optional parameter that indicates the destination path for the compiled application

If no target path is specified, the precompilation takes place in the virtual path of the application, and source files are therefore preserved. If a different target is specified, only assemblies are copied, and the new application runs with no source file in the production environment. The following command line precompiles ProAspNet20 to the specified disk path:

```
aspnet_compiler -v /ProAspNet20 c:\ServerPath
```

Static files such as images, *web.config*, and HTML pages are not compiled—they are just copied to the target destination.

> **Warning**   If you don't want to deploy HTML pages as clear text, rename them to *.aspx* and compile them. A similar approach can be used for image files. Note, however, that if you hide images and HTML pages behind ASP.NET extensions, you lose in performance because IIS is used to process static files more efficiently than ASP.NET.

Precompilation for deployment comes in two slightly different forms—with or without support for updates. Sites packaged for deployment only are not sensitive to file changes. When a change is required, you modify the original files, recompile the whole site, and redeploy the new layout. The only exception is the site configuration; you can update *web.config* on the production server without having to recompile the site.

Sites precompiled for deployment and update are made of assemblies obtained from all files that normally produce assemblies, such as class and resource files. The compiler, though, doesn't touch *.aspx* page files and simply copies them as part of the final layout. In this way, you are allowed to make limited changes to the ASP.NET pages after compiling them. For example, you can change the position of controls or settings regarding colors, fonts, and other visual parameters. You can also add new controls to existing pages, as long as they do not require event handlers or other code.

In no case could new pages be added to a precompiled site without recompiling it from scratch.

Of the two approaches to precompilation for deployment, the former clearly provides the greatest degree of protection for pages and the best performance at startup. The option that provides for limited updates still requires some further compilation when the site runs the first time. In the end, opting for the deployment and update in ASP.NET 2.0 is nearly identical to the compilation and deployment model of ASP.NET 1.1, where *.aspx* files are deployed in source and all classes (including code-behind classes) are compiled to assemblies.

Administering an ASP.NET Application

In addition to working pages, well-done graphics, and back-end services and components, a real-world Web application also requires a set of administrative tools to manage users, security, and configuration. In most cases, these tools consist of a passable and quickly arranged user interface built around a bunch of database tables; application developers are ultimately responsible for building them. To save time, these tools are often created as Windows Forms applications. If the application is properly designed, some business and data access objects created for the site can be reused. Are these external and additional applications always necessary?

While an ad hoc set of utility applications might be desired in some cases, having an integrated, rich, and further customizable tool built into Visual Studio .NET would probably be helpful and sufficient in many cases. In Visual Studio .NET 2005, you find available a whole Web application to administer various aspects of the site. The application, known as the Web Site Administration Tool (WSAT), is available through the Web site menu (or the Solution Explorer toolbar) and is extensively based on the ASP.NET provider model.

The Web Site Administration Tool

Figure 2-26 presents the administration tool in its full splendor. The tool is articulated in four blocks (plus the home), each covering a particular area of administration—membership, user profiles, application settings, and providers.

As mentioned, WSAT is a distinct application that the ASP.NET 2.0 setup installs with full source. You find it under the *ASP.NETWebAdminFiles* directory, below the ASP.NET build installation path. This path is:

```
%WINDOWS%\Microsoft.NET\Framework\[version]\CONFIG\Browsers
```

You can also run the tool from outside Visual Studio .NET 2005. In this case, though, you must indicate a parameter to select the application to configure. Here's the complete URL to type in the browser's address bar for an application named ProAspNet20.

```
http://localhost:XXXX/asp.netwebadminfiles/default.aspx?applicationUrl=/ProAspNet20
```

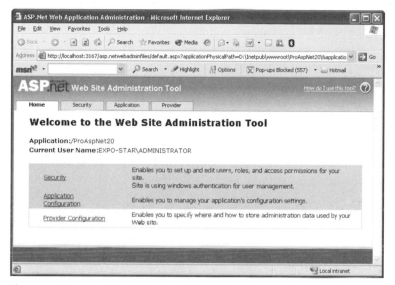

Figure 2-26   The Visual Studio .NET 2005 ASP.NET Administration Tool.

The *XXXX* indicates the port used by the local Web server. The WSAT application, in fact, is not publicly exposed through IIS for obvious security reasons. Table 2-3 details what you can expect to do with the tool.

Table 2-3   Classes of Settings Defined Through WSAT

Configuration Tab	Description
Security	Enables you to set up and edit users, roles, and access permissions for your site
Application	Enables you to manage your application's configuration settings, such as debugging and SMTP options
Provider	Enables you to select the provider to use for each ASP.NET feature that supports providers

Membership and Role Management

The Security tab of WSAT lets you manage all the security settings for your application. You can choose the authentication method, set up users and passwords, create roles and groups of users, and create rules for controlling access to specific parts of your application. A wizard will guide you throught the steps needed to set up individual users and roles. By default, membership and roles information are stored in a local SQL Server database (aspnetdb.mdf) stored in the *App_Data* folder of your Web site. If you want to store user information in a different storage medium, use the Provider tab to select a different provider.

In ASP.NET 1.1, it is fairly common to have a custom database store credentials for authorized users. The point is that this database must be filled out at some time; in addition, the site administrator must be able to manage users and especially roles. In ASP.NET 1.1, you have a few options: charge your developers with this additional task, be charged by external consultants with this extra cost, or buy a third-party product. If you can find the product that suits you to perfection in terms of functionalities and costs, you're probably better off buying this instead of building code yourself. With homebrew code, you end up with a smaller set of features, often renounce the implementation of important security guidelines (for example, force password change every *n* days), and usually spend at least as much money, if not more, for a system with less capabilities and likely less reliability.

On the other hand, a WSAT-like tool doesn't sound like a mission-impossible task. However, it is the kind of cost that you might cut out of your budget. Finding a WSAT-like tool integrated in the development environment sounds like the perfect fit. It lets you accomplish basic administration tasks at no extra cost; and if you need more features, you can always turn to third-party products or, because you have the source code, you can inject your own extensions quite seamlessly.

Application Settings Management

Sometimes ASP.NET applications consume information (UI settings, favorites, general preferences, and connection strings) that you don't want to hard-code into pages. While applications can work out their own solutions for keeping data as configurable as possible (for example, databases or XML files), still the *<appSettings>* section in the *web.config* file provides an easy way out. The *<appSettings>* section, in fact, is specifically designed to store application-specific settings that can be expressed in a simple name/value fashion. The WSAT Application tab provides a convenient way to edit this section and create or edit entries.

As you can see in Figure 2-27, you can use the Application tab also to set debugging/tracing options and manage SMTP settings. In particular, mail settings determine how your Web application sends e-mail. If your e-mail server requires you to log on before you can send messages, you'll use the page to specify the type of authentication that the server requires, and if necessary, any required credentials.

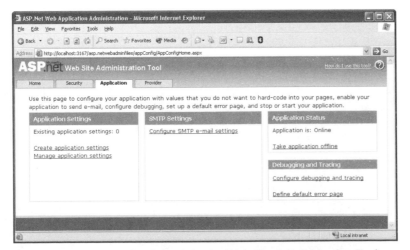

Figure 2-27   The Application tab in the Web Site Administration Tool.

The Application tab also contains a page for you to set error pages to show for particular HTTP errors.

Selecting and Configuring Providers

Profile and membership information require a persistent storage medium for user-specific data. The ASP.NET 2.0 provider model (discussed in Chapter 1) supplies a plug-in mechanism for you to choose the right support for storing data. ASP.NET 2.0 installs predefined providers for membership, roles, and personalization based on SQL Server local files. Extensibility, though, is the awesome feature of providers, and it gives you a way to write and plug in your own providers.

If you want to change the default provider for a particular feature, you use the Provider tab. You also use the same page to register a new provider, as in Figure 2-28.

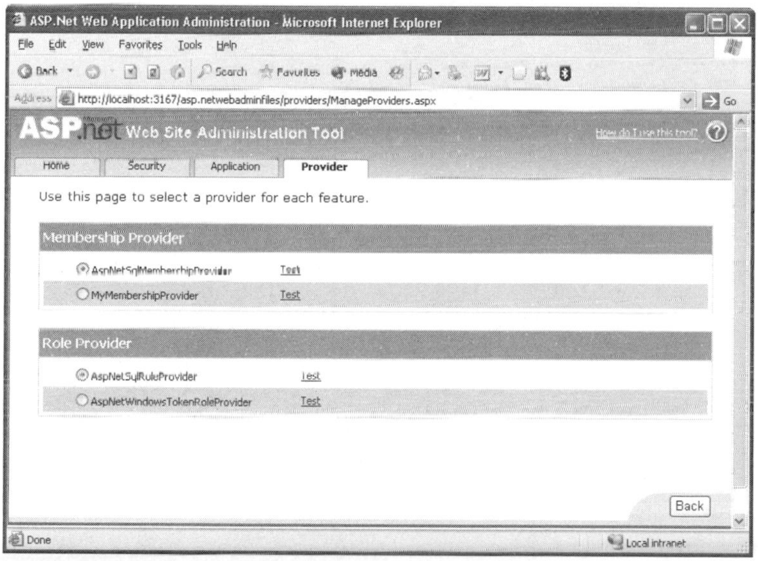

Figure 2-28   The Provider tab in the Web Site Administration Tool.

Editing ASP.NET Configuration Files

WSAT is mostly an administrative tool and, although it allows you to edit certain areas of the configuration files, you can't just consider it to be a *web.config* editor. Visual Studio .NET 2005 has improved the text editor that takes care of *web.config* files and has made it offer full IntelliSense support. Even though IntelliSense helps quite a bit, editing *web.config* through the IDE still requires a lot of tapping on the keyboard and typing many angle brackets on your own. Where else can you turn to edit *web.config* files more seamlessly?

A Visual Editor for *web.config* Files

ASP.NET 2.0 provides an interactive tool for configuring the runtime environment and ultimately editing the *web.config* file. The tool is an extension (that is, a custom property page) to the IIS Microsoft Management Console (MMC) snap-in. As a result, a new property page (named ASP.NET) is added to each Web directory node. (See Figure 2-29.)

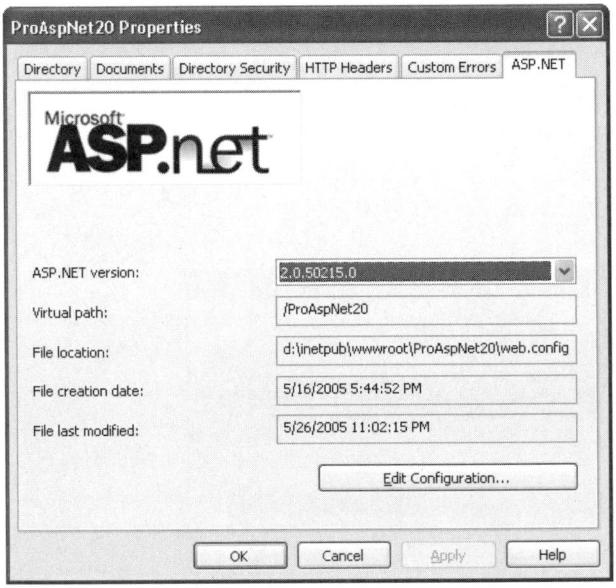

Figure 2-29 The ASP.NET MMC snap-in.

To reach the aforementioned property page, you open the IIS MMC snap-in (from the Control Panel) and select the desired Web application in the specified Web site. Next, you right-click to see the properties of this application and select the tab named ASP.NET. At this point, you should get what's presented in Figure 2-29. To start the *web.config* editor, click the Edit Configuration button. At this point, you get a new set of property pages that together supply an interactive user interface for editing the *web.config* files. The code behind this ASP.NET administrative tool leverages the new configuration API that allows you to read and write the contents of *.config* files. Figure 2-30 shows how to configure session state management for the current Web application.

The editor lets you edit virtually everything you might ever need to change in a *web.config* file. Any changes you enter are saved to a *web.config* file in the current directory—be it the application's root or the subdirectory from where you clicked. In other words, if you want to create or edit the *web.config* file of a subdirectory, locate that directory in the IIS snap-in tree, right-click to turn the editor on, and edit the local configuration.

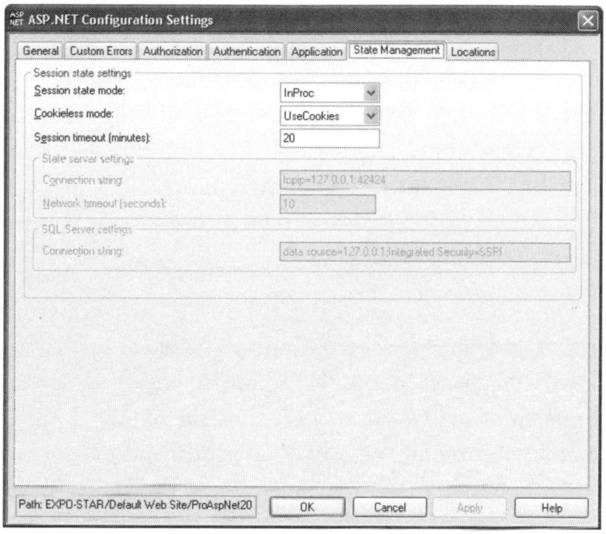

Figure 2-30   The bolted-on visual editor for *web.config* files.

When to Use the Configuration Editor

The snap-in tool works only with *web.config* files located on the local machine. You can use it to edit the *web.config* file you're concurrently editing through Visual Studio .NET, provided that you have a local installation of IIS and that you have opened the project through IIS. Aside from that, the *web.config* editor mostly remains a server-side, administrator-level tool to tweak, rather than edit/create, the *web.config* files of a site on a staging, or even production, box.

> **Note**   I love the snap-in *web.config* editor and would like to have it integrated with Visual Studio .NET, at the very minimum as an external tool. Unfortunately, there's no way to bring up the IIS MMC snap-in in a specific application using a command line. For future versions of IIS (starting with IIS 7), there are plans to provide a richer administration UI that can be integrated directly into the Visual Studio .NET shell. Let's wait and see.

Conclusion

Visual Studio .NET 2005 is the made-to-measure tool to build ASP.NET applications. Built to integrate the functionality of multiple visual designers in a common container environment, Visual Studio .NET is capable of providing a unique editing experience to Web and Windows developers. In situations where Microsoft came up short with its predecessor—Visual Studio .NET 2003—the newest version rocks. It's impressive to see how strong points in the new version overcome the shortcomings in the previous version.

In this chapter, we traversed the main phases of Web application development through Visual Studio .NET 2005—the page design, maintenance, and evolution of a Web project; and the deployment and administration of the final set of pages, files, and assemblies. The goal of this chapter was to provide the details of ASP.NET development with Visual Studio .NET 2005—what's great, what's been improved, what's new, and what you should know. If you successfully worked with previous version of Visual Studio .NET, you'll just fall in love with this one. If you had complaints about Visual Studio .NET 2003, you'll be pleased to see that most of the problems you complained about have been resolved.

I also spent some time discussing themes such as deployment and administration. Both are essential steps in finalizing a project, but both steps are often overlooked and often end up forcing developers and customers to swallow bitter pills. In some cases, deployment and administration require ad hoc tools; in as many other cases, though, a small handful of applications can let developers and administrators do their work smoothly and effectively. The point of contrast discussed in the chapter was who writes what and at what cost? Visual Studio .NET 2005 makes it easy to agree on the following points: essential tasks are cost-free, well done, and all included in the product.

Just the Facts

- IIS is no longer a strict requirement for developing ASP.NET applications, as Visual Studio .NET 2005 incorporates a local, mini Web server to be used only for testing during the development cycle.

- Visual Studio .NET 2005 supports multiple ways to open Web sites. In addition to using FPSE, you can access your source files by using FTP, IIS, and even the file system path.

- Visual Studio .NET 2005 supports standalone file editing and doesn't require a project to edit a single file on disk.

- An ASP.NET 2.0 application can be made of folders that receive special treatment from the ASP.NET runtime—for example, App_Code for classes, App_Themes for themes, and App_GlobalResources for satellite assemblies.

- Even though you can use the local Web server to test pages, be aware that it doesn't offer a realistic test scenario (such as having different accounts, different settings, and so forth). Don't rely on it to determine conclusively that your application works as expected.

- ASP.NET supports two forms of site precompilation: in-place precompilation and deployment precompilation.

- In-place precompilation applies to deployed applications and simply precompiles all pages to save the first-hit compilation delay.

- Precompilation for deployment creates a file representation of the site made of assemblies and static files. This representation can be generated on any machine, and it can be packaged to MSI and deployed.

- Precompilation for deployment doesn't leave source files on the production server, thus it preserves your intellectual property

Chapter 3
Anatomy of an ASP.NET Page

In this chapter:

Invoking a Page 79
The *Page* Class 99
The Page Life Cycle 110
Conclusion 116

ASP.NET pages are dynamically compiled on demand when first required in the context of a Web application. Dynamic compilation is not specific to ASP.NET pages alone (*.aspx* files); it also occurs with .NET Web Services (.asmx files), Web user controls (.ascx files), HTTP handlers (.ashx files), and a few more ASP.NET application files such as the *global.asax* file. A pipeline of run-time modules takes care of the incoming HTTP packet and makes it evolve from a simple protocol-specific payload up to the rank of a server-side ASP.NET object—precisely, an instance of a class derived from the system's *Page* class. The ASP.NET HTTP runtime processes the page object and causes it to generate the markup to insert in the response. The generation of the response is marked by several events handled by user code and collectively known as the *page life cycle*.

In this chapter, we'll review how an HTTP request for an *.aspx* resource is mapped to a page object, the programming interface of the *Page* class, and how to control the generation of the markup by handling events of the page life cycle.

Invoking a Page

Let's start by examining in detail how the *.aspx* page is converted into a class and then compiled into an assembly. Generating an assembly for a particular *.aspx* resource is a two-step process. First, the source code of the resource file is parsed and a corresponding class is created that inherits either from *Page* or another class that, in turn, inherits from *Page*. Second, the dynamically generated class is compiled into an assembly and cached in an ASP.NET-specific temporary directory.

The compiled page remains in use as long as no changes occur to the linked *.aspx* source file or the whole application is restarted. Any changes to the linked *.aspx* file invalidates the current page-specific assembly and forces the HTTP runtime to create a new assembly on the next request for page.

> **Note**   Editing files such as *web.config* and *global.asax* causes the whole application to restart. In this case, all the pages will be recompiled as soon as each page is requested. The same happens if a new assembly is copied or replaced in the application's *Bin* folder.

The Runtime Machinery

All resources that you can access on an Internet Information Server (IIS)–based Web server are grouped by file extension. Any incoming request is then assigned to a particular run-time module for actual processing. Modules that can handle Web resources within the context of IIS are Internet Server Application Programming Interface (ISAPI) extensions—that is, plain old Win32 dynamic-link libraries (DLLs) that expose, much like an interface, a bunch of API functions with predefined names and prototypes. IIS and ISAPI extensions use these DLL entries as a sort of private communication protocol. When IIS needs an ISAPI extension to accomplish a certain task, it simply loads the DLL and calls the appropriate function with valid arguments. Although the ISAPI documentation doesn't mention an ISAPI extension as an interface, it is just that—a module that implements a well-known programming interface.

When the request for a resource arrives, IIS first verifies the type of the resource. Static resources such as images, text files, HTML pages, and scriptless ASP pages are resolved directly by IIS without the involvement of external modules. IIS accesses the file on the local Web server and flushes its contents to the output console so that the requesting browser can get it. Resources that require server-side elaboration are passed on to the registered module. For example, ASP pages are processed by an ISAPI extension named asp.dll. In general, when the resource is associated with executable code, IIS hands the request to that executable for further processing. Files with an *.aspx* extension are assigned to an ISAPI extension named aspnet_isapi.dll, as shown in Figure 3-1.

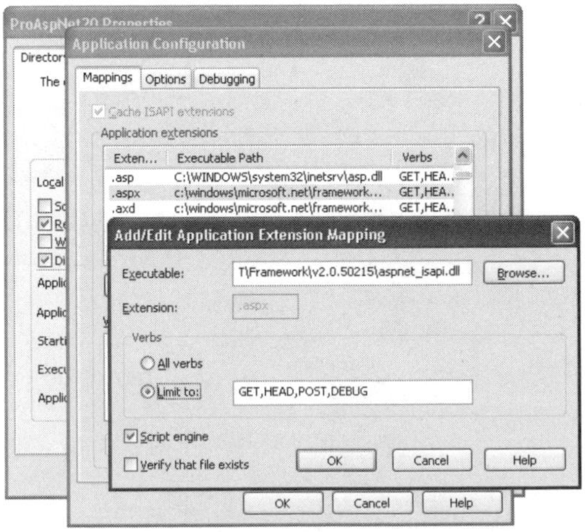

Figure 3-1   The IIS application mappings for resources with an *.aspx* extension.

Resource mappings are stored in the IIS metabase. Upon installation, ASP.NET modifies the IIS metabase to make sure that aspnet_isapi.dll can handle some typical ASP.NET resources. Table 3-1 lists some of these resources.

Table 3-1   IIS Application Mappings for aspnet_isapi.dll

Extension	Resource Type
.asax	ASP.NET application files. The typical example is *global.asax*.
.ascx	ASP.NET user control files.
.ashx	HTTP handlers, namely managed modules that interact with the low-level request and response services of IIS.
.asmx	Files that implement .NET Web services.
.aspx	Files that represent ASP.NET pages.
.axd	Extension that identifies internal HTTP handlers used to implement system features such as application-level tracing (trace.axd) or script injection (webresource.axd).

In addition, the aspnet_isapi.dll extension handles other typical Microsoft Visual Studio .NET extensions such as *.cs*, *.csproj*, *.vb*, *.vbproj*, *.config*, *.resx*.

As mentioned in Chapter 1, the exact behavior of the ASP.NET ISAPI extension depends on the process model selected for the application.

IIS 5.0 Process Model

The IIS 5.0 process model is the only option you have if you host your ASP.NET application on any version of Microsoft Windows prior to Windows 2003 Server. According to this processing model, aspnet_isapi.dll doesn't process the *.aspx* file, but instead acts as a dispatcher. It collects all the information available about the invoked URL and the underlying resource, and then it routes the request toward another distinct process—the ASP.NET worker process named *aspnet_wp.exe*. The communication between the ISAPI extension and worker process takes place through named pipes.

The whole diagram is illustrated in Figure 3-2.

A single copy of the worker process runs all the time and hosts all the active Web applications. The only exception to this situation is when you have a Web server with multiple CPUs. In this case, you can configure the ASP.NET runtime so that multiple worker processes run, one per each available CPU. For example, you might want to do this if you have multiple CPUs and need to run code that is thread safe, but not so safe as to assume it works well in a multiprocessor environment. A model in which multiple processes run on multiple CPUs in a single-server machine is known as a *Web garden* and is controlled by attributes on the *<processModel>* section in the *machine.config* file.

When a single worker process is used by all CPUs and controls all Web applications, it doesn't necessarily mean that no process isolation is achieved. Each Web application is, in fact, identified with its virtual directory and belongs to a distinct *application domain*, commonly referred to as an AppDomain. A new AppDomain is created within the ASP.NET worker process whenever a client addresses a virtual directory for the first time. After creating the new AppDomain, the ASP.NET runtime loads all the needed assemblies and passes control to the hosted HTTP pipeline to actually service the request.

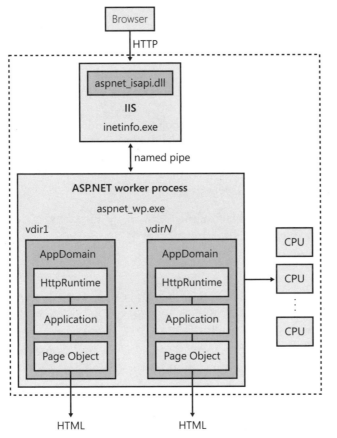

Figure 3-2   The ASP.NET runtime environment according to the IIS 5.0 process model.

If a client requests a page from an already running Web application, the ASP.NET runtime simply forwards the request to the existing AppDomain associated with that virtual directory. If the assembly needed to process the page is not loaded in the AppDomain, it will be created on the fly; otherwise, if it was already created upon the first call, it will be simply used.

IIS 6.0 Process Model

The IIS 6.0 process model is the default option for ASP.NET when the Web server operating system is Windows 2003 Server. As the name of the process model clearly suggests, this model requires IIS 6.0. However, on a Windows 2003 Server machine you can still have

ASP.NET play by the rules of the IIS 5.0 process model. If this is what you want, explicitly enable the model by tweaking the *<processModel>* section of the *machine.config* file.

```
<processModel enable="true">
```

Be aware that switching back to the old IIS 5.0 process model is not a recommended practice, although it is perfectly legal. The main reason lies in the fact that IIS 6.0 employs a different pipeline of internal modules to process an inbound request and can mimic the behavior of IIS 5.0 only if running in emulation mode. The IIS 6.0 pipeline is centered around a generic worker process named *w3wp.exe*. A copy of this executable is shared by all Web applications assigned to the same application pool. In the IIS 6.0 jargon, an application pool is a group of Web applications that share the same copy of the worker process. IIS 6.0 lets you customize the application pools to achieve the degree of isolation that you need for the various applications hosted on a Web server.

The *w3wp.exe* worker process loads aspnet_isapi.dll; the ISAPI extension, in turn, loads the common language runtime (CLR) and starts the ASP.NET runtime pipeline to process the request. When the IIS 6.0 process model is in use, the built-in ASP.NET worker process is disabled.

> **Note**   Only ASP.NET 1.1 fully takes advantage of the IIS 6.0 process model. If you install ASP.NET 1.0 on a Windows 2003 Server machine, the process model will default to the IIS 5.0 process model. This happens because only the version of aspnet_isapi.dll that ships with ASP.NET 1.1 is smart enough to recognize its host and load the CLR if needed. The aspnet_isapi.dll included in ASP.NET 1.0 is limited to forwarding requests to the ASP.NET worker process and never loads the CLR.

Figure 3-3 shows how ASP.NET applications and other Web applications are processed in IIS 6.0.

IIS 6.0 implements its HTTP listener as a kernel-level module. As a result, all incoming requests are first managed by such a driver—http.sys—and in kernel mode. No third-party code ever interacts with the listener, and no user-mode crashes will ever affect the stability of IIS. The http.sys driver listens for requests and posts them to the request queue of the appropriate application pool. A module called the Web Administration Service (WAS) reads from the IIS metabase and instructs the http.sys driver to create as many request queues as there are application pools registered in the metabase.

In summary, in the IIS 6.0 process model, ASP.NET runs even faster because no interprocess communication between *inetinfo.exe* (the IIS executable) and the worker process is required. The HTTP request is delivered directly at the worker process that hosts the CLR. Furthermore, the ASP.NET worker process is not a special process but simply a copy of the IIS worker process. This fact shifts to IIS the burden of process recycling, page output caching, and health checks.

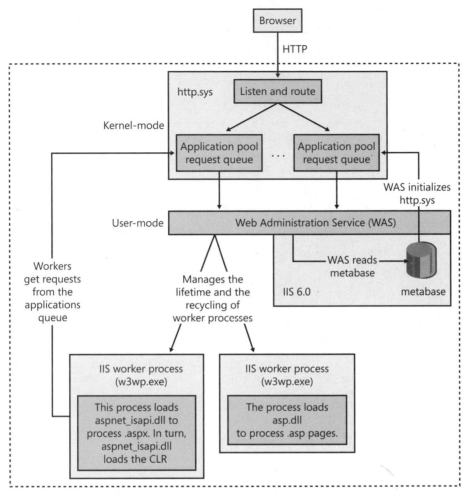

Figure 3-3 How ASP.NET and Web applications are processed in IIS 6.0.

In the IIS 6.0 process model, ASP.NET ignores most of the contents of the *<processModel>* section from the *machine.config* file. Only thread and deadlock settings are read from that section of *machine.config*. Everything else goes through the metabase and can be configured only by using the IIS Manager. (Other configuration information continues being read from .config files.)

Representing the Requested Page

Each incoming request that refers to an *.aspx* resource is mapped to, and served through, a *Page*-derived class. The ASP.NET HTTP runtime environment first determines the name of the class that will be used to serve the request. A particular naming convention links the URL of the page to the name of the class. If the requested page is, say, default.aspx, the associated class turns out to be *ASP.default_aspx*. If no class exists with that name in any of the assemblies currently loaded in the AppDomain, the HTTP runtime orders that the class be created and compiled. The source code for the class is created by parsing the source code of the .aspx resource, and it's temporarily saved in the ASP.NET temporary folder. Next, the class is compiled and loaded in memory to serve the request. When a new request for the same page arrives, the class is ready and no compile step will ever take place. (The class will be re-created and recompiled only if the timestamp of the .aspx source changes.)

The *ASP.default_aspx* class inherits from *Page* or from a class that in turn inherits from *Page*. In most cases, the base class for *ASP.default_aspx* will be a combination of the code-behind, partial class created through Visual Studio .NET and a second partial class dynamically arranged by the ASP.NET HTTP runtime. Figure 3-4 provides a graphical demonstration of how the source code of the dynamic page class is built.

Written by you in default.aspx

```
public partial class HelloWorld : Page
{
    // Any event handlers you need

    // NB: no protected members for
    //     server controls in the page
}
```

Generated by ASP.NET while compiling

```
public partial class HelloWorld : Page
{
    // Any needed protected members
    // for server controls in the page

    // This code was in VS auto-generated
    // regions in VS 2003 and ASP.NET 1.x
}
```

Compiler merges partial class definitions

```
public class HelloWorld : Page
{
    // Any event handlers you need

    // Any needed protected members
    // for server controls in the page
}
```

ASP.NET runtime parses ASPX source and dynamically
generates the page to serve the request for default.aspx

```
public class default.aspx : HelloWorld
{
    // Build the control tree
    // parsing the ASPX file in much
    // the same way as in ASP.NET 1.x
}
```

Figure 3-4   ASP.NET generates the source code for the dynamic class that will serve a request.

Partial classes are a hot feature of the new generation of .NET compilers. When partially declared, a class has its source code split over multiple source files, each of which appears to contain an ordinary class definition from beginning to end. The new keyword *partial*, though, informs the compiler that the class declaration being processed is incomplete. To get full and complete source code, the compiler must look into other files specified on the command line.

Partial Classes in ASP.NET Projects

Ideal for team development, partial classes simplify coding and avoid manual file synchronization in all situations in which a mix of user-defined and tool-generated code is used. Want an illustrious example? ASP.NET projects developed with Visual Studio .NET.

Partial classes are a compiler feature specifically designed to overcome the brittleness of tool-generated code in many Visual Studio .NET projects, including ASP.NET projects. A savvy use of partial classes allows you to eliminate all those weird, auto-generated, semi-hidden regions of code that Visual Studio .NET 2003 inserts to support page designers.

Generally, partial classes are a source-level, assembly-limited, non-object-oriented way to extend the behavior of a class. A number of advantages are derived from intensive use of partial classes. For example, you can have multiple teams at work on the same component at the same time. In addition, you have a neat and elegant way to add functionality to a class incrementally. In the end, this is just what the ASP.NET runtime does.

The ASPX markup defines server controls that will be handled by the code in the code-behind class. For this model to work, the code-behind class needs to incorporate references to these server controls as internal members—typically, protected members. In Visual Studio .NET 2003, these declarations are added by the integrated development environment (IDE) as you save your markup and stored in semi-hidden regions. In Visual Studio .NET 2005, the code-behind class is a partial class that just lacks members declaration. Missing declarations are incrementally added at run time via a second partial class created by the ASP.NET HTTP runtime. The compiler of choice (C#, Microsoft Visual Basic .NET, or whatever) will then merge the two partial classes to create the real parent of the dynamically created page class.

Processing the Request

To serve a request for a page named default.aspx, the ASP.NET runtime needs to get a reference to a class *ASP.default_aspx*. If this class doesn't exist in any of the assemblies currently loaded in the AppDomain, it will be created. Next, the HTTP runtime environment invokes the class through the methods of a well-known interface—*IHttpHandler*. The root *Page* class implements this interface, which includes a couple of members—the *ProcessRequest* method and the Boolean *IsReusable* property. Once the HTTP runtime has obtained an instance of the class that represents the requested resource, invoking the *ProcessRequest* method—a public method—gives birth to the process that culminates in the generation of the final response for the browser. As mentioned, the steps and events that execute and trigger out of the call to *ProcessRequest* are collectively known as the page life cycle.

Unlike ASP pages, ASP.NET pages are not simply parsed and served to the user. While serving pages is the ultimate goal of the ASP.NET runtime, the way in which the resultant markup code is generated is much more sophisticated than in ASP and involves many more objects. The ASP.NET worker process—be it *w3wp.exe* or *aspnet_wp.exe*—passes any incoming HTTP requests to the so-called HTTP pipeline. The HTTP pipeline is a fully extensible chain of managed objects that works according to the classic concept of a pipeline. All these objects form what is often referred to as the *ASP.NET HTTP runtime environment*.

The *HttpRuntime* Object

A page request passes through a pipeline of objects that process the original HTTP payload and, at the end of the chain, produce some markup code for the browser. The entry point in this pipeline is the *HttpRuntime* class. The ASP.NET worker process activates the HTTP pipeline by creating a new instance of the *HttpRuntime* class and then calling its *ProcessRequest* method. For the sake of clarity, note that despite the name, *HttpRuntime.ProcessRequest* has nothing to do with the *IHttpHandler* interface.

The *HttpRuntime* class contains a lot of private and internal methods and only three public static methods: *Close*, *ProcessRequest*, and *UnloadAppDomain*, as detailed in Table 3-2.

Table 3-2   Public Methods in the *HttpRuntime* Class

Method	Description
Close	Removes all items from the ASP.NET cache, and terminates the Web application. This method should be used only when your code implements its own hosting environment. There is no need to call this method in the course of normal ASP.NET request processing.
ProcessRequest	Drives all ASP.NET Web processing execution.
UnloadAppDomain	Terminates the current ASP.NET application. The application restarts the next time a request is received for it.

It is important to note that all the methods shown in Table 3-2 have a limited applicability in user applications. In particular, you're not supposed to use *ProcessRequest* in your own code, whereas *Close* is useful only if you're hosting ASP.NET in a custom application. Of the three methods in Table 3-2, only *UnloadAppDomain* can be considered for use if, under certain runtime conditions, you realize you need to restart the application. (See the sidebar "What Causes Application Restarts?" later in this chapter.)

Upon creation, the *HttpRuntime* object initializes a number of internal objects that will help carry out the page request. Helper objects include the cache manager and the file system monitor used to detect changes in the files that form the application. When the *ProcessRequest* method is called, the *HttpRuntime* object starts working to serve a page to the browser. It creates a new context for the request and initializes a specialized text writer object in which the markup code will be accumulated. A context is given by an instance of the *HttpContext* class, which encapsulates all HTTP-specific information about the request.

After that, the *HttpRuntime* object uses the context information to either locate or create a Web application object capable of handling the request. A Web application is searched using the virtual directory information contained in the URL. The object used to find or create a new

Web application is *HttpApplicationFactory*—an internal-use object responsible for returning a valid object capable of handling the request.

Before we get to discover more about the various components of the HTTP pipeline, a look at Figure 3-5 is in order.

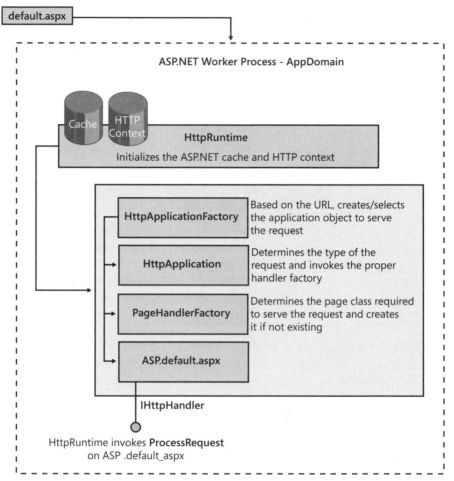

Figure 3-5   The HTTP pipeline processing for a page.

The Application Factory

During the lifetime of the application, the *HttpApplicationFactory* object maintains a pool of *HttpApplication* objects to serve incoming HTTP requests. When invoked, the application factory object verifies that an AppDomain exists for the virtual folder the request targets. If the application is already running, the factory picks an *HttpApplication* out of the pool of available objects and passes it the request. A new *HttpApplication* object is created if an existing object not be available.

If the virtual folder has not yet been called for the first time, a new *HttpApplication* object for the virtual folder is created in a new AppDomain. In this case, the creation of an *HttpApplication* object entails the compilation of the *global.asax* application file, if one is present, and the creation of the assembly that represents the actual page requested. This event is actually equivalent to the start of the application. An *HttpApplication* object is used to process a single page request at a time; multiple objects are used to serve simultaneous requests.

The *HttpApplication* Object

HttpApplication is the base class that represents a running ASP.NET application. A running ASP.NET application is represented by a dynamically created class that inherits from *HttpApplication*. The source code of the dynamically generated application class is created by parsing the contents of the *global.asax* file, if any is present. If *global.asax* is available, the application class is built and named after it: *ASP.global_asax*. Otherwise, the base *HttpApplication* class is used.

An instance of an *HttpApplication*-derived class is responsible for managing the entire lifetime of the request it is assigned to. The same instance can be reused only after the request has been completed. The *HttpApplication* maintains a list of HTTP module objects that can filter and even modify the content of the request. Registered modules are called during various moments of the elaboration as the request passes through the pipeline.

The *HttpApplication* object determines the type of object that represents the resource being requested—typically, an ASP.NET page, a Web service, or perhaps a user control. *HttpApplication* then uses the proper handler factory to get an object that represents the requested resource. The factory either instantiates the class for the requested resource from an existing assembly or dynamically creates the assembly and then an instance of the class. A handler factory object is a class that implements the *IHttpHandlerFactory* interface and is responsible for returning an instance of a managed class that can handle the HTTP request—an HTTP handler. An ASP.NET page is simply a handler object—that is, an instance of a class that implements the *IHttpHandler* interface.

The Page Factory

The *HttpApplication* class determines the type of object that must handle the request and delegates the type-specific handler factory to create an instance of that type. Let's see what happens when the resource requested is a page.

Once the *HttpApplication* object in charge of the request has figured out the proper handler, it creates an instance of the handler factory object. For a request that targets a page, the factory is a class named *PageHandlerFactory*. To find the appropriate handler, *HttpApplication* uses the information in the <httpHandlers> section of the configuration file. Table 3-3 contains a brief list of the main handlers registered.

Table 3-3 Handler Factory Classes in the .NET Framework

Handler Factory	Type	Description
HttpRemotingHandlerFactory	*.rem; *.soap	Instantiates the object that will take care of a .NET Remoting request routed through IIS. Instantiates an object of type *HttpRemotingHandler*.
PageHandlerFactory	*.aspx	Compiles and instantiates the type that represents the page. The source code for the class is built while parsing the source code of the *.aspx* file. Instantiates an object of a type that derives from *Page*.
SimpleHandlerFactory	*.ashx	Compiles and instantiates the specified HTTP handler from the source code of the .ashx file. Instantiates an object that implements the *IHttpHandler* interface.
WebServiceHandlerFactory	*.asmx	Compiles the source code of a Web service, and translates the SOAP payload into a method invocation. Instantiates an object of the type specified in the Web service file.

Bear in mind that handler factory objects do not compile the requested resource each time it is invoked. The compiled code is stored in an ASP.NET temporary directory on the Web server and used until the corresponding resource file is modified.

So the page handler factory creates an instance of an object that represents the particular page requested. As mentioned, this object inherits from the *System.Web.UI.Page* class, which in turn implements the *IHttpHandler* interface. The page object is returned to the application factory, which passes that back to the *HttpRuntime* object. The final step accomplished by the ASP.NET runtime is calling the *IHttpHandler*'s *ProcessRequest* method on the page object. This call causes the page to execute the user-defined code and generate the markup for the browser.

In Chapter 12, we'll return to the initialization of an ASP.NET application, the contents of *global.asax*, and the information stuffed into the HTTP context—a container object that, created by the *HttpRuntime* class, is populated and passed along the pipeline and finally bound to the page handler.

What Causes Application Restarts?

There are a few reasons why an ASP.NET application can be restarted. For the most part, restarts occur because the system reclaims server resources, cleans the working set, or in an attempt to prevent the long-term effect of latent bugs, makes the application irresponsive. Another reason is that too many dynamic changes to ASPX pages have caused too large a number of assemblies (typically, one per page) to be loaded in memory. An application that consumes more than a certain share of virtual memory is killed and restarted. The ASP.NET runtime environment implements a good deal of checks and automatically restarts an application if any the following scenarios occur:

■ The maximum limit of dynamic page compilations is reached.

- The physical path of the Web application has changed, or any directory under the Web application folder is renamed.

- Changes occurred in *global.asax*, *machine.config*, or *web.config* in the application root, or in the *Bin* directory or any of its subdirectories.

- Changes occurred in the code-access security policy file, if one exists.

- Too many files are changed in one of the content directories. (Typically, this happens if files are generated on the fly when requested.)

- Changes occurred to settings that control the restart/shutdown of the ASP.NET worker process. These settings are read from *machine.config* if you don't use Windows 2003 Server with the IIS 6.0 process model. If you're taking full advantage of IIS 6.0, an application is restarted if you modify properties in the *Application Pools* node of the IIS manager.

In addition to all this, in ASP.NET 1.1 and superior an application can be restarted programmatically by calling *HttpRuntime.UnloadAppDomain*.

The Processing Directives of a Page

Processing directives configure the runtime environment that will execute the page. In ASP.NET, directives can be located anywhere in the page, although it's a good and common practice to place them at the beginning of the file. In addition, the name of a directive is case-insensitive and the values of directive attributes don't need to be quoted. The most important and most frequently used directive in ASP.NET is *@Page*. The complete list of ASP.NET directives is shown in Table 3-4.

Table 3-4   Directives Supported by ASP.NET Pages

Directive	Description
@ Assembly	Links an assembly to the current page or user control.
@ Control	Defines control-specific attributes that guide the behavior of the control compiler.
@ Implements	Indicates that the page, or the user control, implements a specified .NET Framework interface.
@ Import	Indicates a namespace to import into a page or user control.
@ Master	Identifies an ASP.NET master page. (See Chapter 6.) *This directive is not available with ASP.NET 1.x.*
@ OutputCache	Controls the output caching policies of a page or user control. (See Chapter 14.)
@ Page	Defines page-specific attributes that guide the behavior of the page compiler and the language parser that will preprocess the page.
@ Reference	Links a page or user control to the current page or user control.
@ Register	Creates a custom tag in the page or the control. The new tag (prefix and name) is associated with the namespace and the code of a user-defined control.

With the exception of *@Page*, *@Master*, and *@Control*, all directives can be used both within a page and a control declaration. *@Page* and *@Control* are mutually exclusive. *@Page* can be used only in *.aspx* files, while the *@Control* directive can be used only in user control *.ascx* files. *@Master*, in turn, is used to define a very special type of page—the master page.

The syntax of a processing directive is unique and common to all supported types of directives. Multiple attributes must be separated with blanks, and no blank can be placed around the equal sign (=) that assigns a value to an attribute, as the following line of code demonstrates:

```
<%@ Directive_Name attribute="value" [attribute="value"...] %>
```

Each directive has its own closed set of typed attributes. Assigning a value of the wrong type to an attribute, or using a wrong attribute with a directive, results in a compilation error.

> **Important**   The content of directive attributes is always rendered as plain text. However, attributes are expected to contain values that can be rendered to a particular .NET Framework type. When the ASP.NET page is parsed, all the directive attributes are extracted and stored in a dictionary. The names and number of attributes must match the expected schema for the directive. The string that expresses the value of an attribute is valid as long as it can be converted into the expected type. For example, if the attribute is designed to take a Boolean value, *true* and *false* are its only feasible values.

The *@Page* Directive

The *@Page* directive can be used only in *.aspx* pages and generates a compile error if used with other types of ASP.NET pages such as controls and Web services. Each *.aspx* file is allowed to include at most one *@Page* directive. Although not strictly necessary from the syntax point of view, the directive is realistically required by all pages of some complexity.

@Page features about 30 attributes that can be logically grouped in three categories: compilation (defined in Table 3-5), overall page behavior (defined in Table 3-6), and page output (defined in Table 3-7). Each ASP.NET page is compiled upon first request, and the HTML actually served to the browser is generated by the methods of the dynamically generated class. Attributes listed in Table 3-5 let you fine-tune parameters for the compiler and choose the language to use.

Table 3-5   *@Page* Attributes for Page Compilation

Attribute	Description
ClassName	Specifies the name of the class name that will be dynamically compiled when the page is requested. Must be a class name without namespace information.
CodeFile	Indicates the path to the code-behind class for the current page. The source class file must be deployed to the Web server. *Not available with ASP.NET 1.x.*

Table 3-5   @*Page* Attributes for Page Compilation

Attribute	Description
CodeBehind	Attribute consumed by Visual Studio .NET 2003, indicates the path to the code-behind class for the current page. The source class file will be compiled to a deployable assembly.
CodeFileBaseClass	Allows you to specify the grandparent class for a page. ASP.NET uses the information in this attribute to determine the parent for the code file class. *Not available with ASP.NET 1.x.*
CompilationMode	Indicates whether the page should be compiled at run time. *Not available with ASP.NET 1.x.*
CompilerOptions	A sequence of compiler command-line switches used to compile the page.
Debug	A Boolean value that indicates whether the page should be compiled with debug symbols.
Explicit	A Boolean value that determines whether the page is compiled with the Visual Basic *Option Explicit* mode set to *On*. *Option Explicit* forces the programmer to explicitly declare all variables. The attribute is ignored if the page language is not Visual Basic .NET.
Inherits	Defines the base class for the page to inherit. It can be any class derived from the *Page* class.
Language	Indicates the language to use when compiling inline code blocks (<% ... %>) and all the code that appears in the page <script> section. Supported languages include Visual Basic .NET, C#, JScript .NET, J#. If not otherwise specified, the language defaults to Visual Basic .NET.
MasterPageFile	Indicates the master page for the current page. *Not available with ASP.NET 1.x.*
Src	Indicates the source file that contains the implementation of the base class specified with *Inherits*. The attribute is not used by Visual Studio .NET and other rapid application development (RAD) designers.
Strict	A Boolean value that determines whether the page is compiled with the Visual Basic *Option Strict* mode set to *On*. When enabled, *Option Strict* permits only type-safe conversions and prohibits implicit conversions in which loss of data is possible. (In this case, the behavior is identical to that of C#.) The attribute is ignored if the page language is not Visual Basic .NET.
Trace	A Boolean value that indicates whether tracing is enabled. If tracing is enabled, extra information is appended to the page's output. The default is *false*.
TraceMode	Indicates how trace messages are to be displayed for the page when tracing is enabled. Feasible values are *SortByTime* and *SortByCategory*. The default, when tracing is enabled, is *SortByTime*.
WarningLevel	Indicates the compiler warning level at which you want the compiler to abort compilation for the page. Possible values are *0* through *4*.

Notice that the default values of the *Explicit* and *Strict* attributes are read from the application's configuration settings. The configuration settings of an ASP.NET application are obtained by merging all machine-wide settings with application-wide and even folder-wide settings. This means you can also control what the default values for the *Explicit* and *Strict* attributes are. Unless you change the default configuration settings—the .config files are created when the .NET Framework is installed—both *Explicit* and *Strict* default to *true*. Should the related settings be removed from the configuration files, both attributes would default to *false* instead.

Attributes listed in Table 3-6 allow you to control to some extent the overall behavior of the page and the supported range of features. For example, you can set a custom error page, disable session state, and control the transactional behavior of the page.

Table 3-6 @*Page* Attributes for Page Behavior

Attribute	Description
AspCompat	A Boolean attribute that, when set to *true*, allows the page to be executed on a single-threaded apartment (STA) thread. The setting allows the page to call COM+ 1.0 components and components developed with Microsoft Visual Basic 6.0 that require access to the unmanaged ASP built-in objects. (I'll cover this topic in Chapter 12.)
Async	If set to *true*, the generated page class derives from *IHttpAsyncHandler* rather than having *IHttpHandler* adding some built-in asynchronous capabilities to the page. *Not available with ASP.NET 1.x.*
AutoEventWireup	A Boolean attribute that indicates whether page events are automatically enabled. Set to *true* by default. Pages developed with Visual Studio .NET have this attribute set to *false*, and page events are individually tied to handlers.
Buffer	A Boolean attribute that determines whether HTTP response buffering is enabled. Set to *true* by default.
Description	Provides a text description of the page. The ASP.NET page parser ignores the attribute, which subsequently has only a documentation purpose.
EnableSessionState	Defines how the page should treat session data. If set to *true*, the session state can be read and written. If set to *false*, session data is not available to the application. Finally, if set to *ReadOnly*, the session state can be read but not changed.
EnableViewState	A Boolean value that indicates whether the page *view state* is maintained across page requests. The view state is the page call context—a collection of values that retain the state of the page and are carried back and forth. View state is enabled by default. (I'll cover this topic in Chapter 13.)
EnableViewStateMac	A Boolean value that indicates ASP.NET should calculate a machine-specific authentication code and append it to the view state of the page (in addition to Base64 encoding). The *Mac* in the attribute name stands for *machine authentication check*. When the attribute is *true*, upon postbacks ASP.NET will check the authentication code of the view state to make sure that it hasn't been tampered with on the client.
ErrorPage	Defines the target URL to which users will be automatically redirected in case of unhandled page exceptions.

Table 3-6   @*Page* Attributes for Page Behavior

Attribute	Description
SmartNavigation	A Boolean value that indicates whether the page supports the Microsoft Internet Explorer 5 or later smart navigation feature. Smart navigation allows a page to be refreshed without losing scroll position and element focus.
Theme, StylesheetTheme	Indicates the name of the theme (or style-sheet theme) selected for the page. *Not available with ASP.NET 1.x.*
Transaction	Indicates whether the page supports or requires transactions. Feasible values are: *Disabled, NotSupported, Supported, Required*, and *RequiresNew*. Transaction support is disabled by default.
ValidateRequest	A Boolean value that indicates whether request validation should occur. If this value is set to *true*, ASP.NET checks all input data against a hard-coded list of potentially dangerous values. This functionality helps reduce the risk of cross-site scripting attacks for pages. The value is *true* by default. *This feature is not supported in ASP.NET 1.0.*

Attributes listed in Table 3-7 allow you to control the format of the output being generated for the page. For example, you can set the content type of the page or localize the output to the extent possible.

Table 3-7   @*Page* Directives for Page Output

Attribute	Description
ClientTarget	Indicates the target browser for which ASP.NET server controls should render content.
CodePage	Indicates the code page value for the response. Set this attribute only if you created the page using a code page other than the default code page of the Web server on which the page will run. In this case, set the attribute to the code page of your development machine. A code page is a character set that includes numbers, punctuation marks, and other glyphs. Code pages differ on a per-language basis.
ContentType	Defines the content type of the response as a standard MIME type. Supports any valid HTTP content type string.
Culture	Indicates the culture setting for the page. Culture information includes the writing and sorting system, calendar, and date and currency formats. The attribute must be set to a non-neutral culture name, which means it must contain both language and country information. For example, *en-US* is a valid value unlike *en* alone, which is considered country-neutral.
LCID	A 32-bit value that defines the locale identifier for the page. By default, ASP.NET uses the locale of the Web server.
ResponseEncoding	Indicates the character encoding of the page. The value is used to set the *CharSet* attribute on the content type HTTP header. Internally, ASP.NET handles all strings as Unicode.
UICulture	Specifies the default culture name used by the Resource Manager to look up culture-specific resources at run time.

As you can see, many attributes discussed in Table 3-7 concern the issue of page localization. Building multilanguage and international applications is a task that ASP.NET, and the .NET Framework in general, greatly simplify.

The @*Assembly* Directive

The @*Assembly* directive links an assembly to the current page so that its classes and interfaces are available for use on the page. When ASP.NET compiles the page, a few assemblies are linked by default. So you should resort to the directive only if you need linkage to a non-default assembly. Table 3-8 lists the .NET assemblies that are automatically provided to the compiler.

Table 3-8   Assemblies Linked by Default

Assembly File Name	Description
Mscorlib.dll	Provides the core functionality of the .NET Framework, including types, AppDomains, and run-time services.
System.dll	Provides another bunch of system services, including regular expressions, compilation, native methods, file I/O, and networking.
System.Configuration.dll	Defines classes to read and write configuration data. *Not included in ASP.NET 1.x.*
System.Data.dll	Defines data container and data access classes, including the whole ADO.NET framework.
System.Drawing.dll	Implements the GDI+ features.
System.EnterpriseServices.dll	Provides the classes that allow for serviced components and COM+ interaction.
System.Web.dll	The assembly implements the core ASP.NET services, controls, and classes.
System.Web.Mobile.dll	The assembly implements the core ASP.NET mobile services, controls, and classes. *Not included if version 1.0 of the .NET Framework is installed.*
System.Web.Services.dll	Contains the core code that makes Web services run.
System.Xml.dll	Implements the .NET Framework XML features.

In addition to these assemblies, the ASP.NET runtime automatically links to the page all the assemblies that reside in the Web application *Bin* subdirectory. Note that you can modify, extend, or restrict the list of default assemblies by editing the machine-wide configuration settings set in the *machine.config* file. In this case, changes apply to all ASP.NET applications run on that Web server. Alternately, you can modify the assembly list on a per-application basis by editing the application's specific *web.config* file. To prevent all assemblies found in the *Bin* directory from being linked to the page, remove the following line from the root configuration file:

```
<add assembly="*" />
```

> **Warning** For an ASP.NET application, the whole set of configuration attributes is set at the machine level. Initially, all applications hosted on a given server machine share the same settings. Then, individual applications can override some of those settings in their own *web.config* files. Each application can have a *web.config* file in the root virtual folder and other copies of it in subdirectories—not necessarily subapplications. Each page is subject to settings as determined by the configuration files found in the path from the machine to the containing folder. In ASP.NET 1.x, the *machine.config* file contains the whole tree of default settings. In ASP.NET 2.0, the configuration data that specifically refers to Web applications has been moved to a *web.config* file installed in the same system folder as *machine.config*. The folder is named CONFIG and located below the installation path of ASP.NET—that is, *%WINDOWS%\Microsoft.Net\Framework\[version]*.

To link a needed assembly to the page, use the following syntax:

```
<%@ Assembly Name="AssemblyName" %>
<%@ Assembly Src="assembly_code.cs" %>
```

The *@Assembly* directive supports two mutually exclusive attributes: *Name* and *Src*. *Name* indicates the name of the assembly to link to the page. The name cannot include the path or the extension. *Src* indicates the path to a source file to dynamically compile and link against the page. The *@Assembly* directive can appear multiple times in the body of the page. In fact, you need a new directive for each assembly to link. *Name* and *Src* cannot be used in the same *@Assembly* directive, but multiple directives defined in the same page can use either.

> **Note** In terms of performance, the difference between *Name* and *Src* is minimal, although *Name* points to an existing and ready-to-load assembly. The source file referenced by *Src* is compiled only the first time it is requested. The ASP.NET runtime maps a source file with a dynamically compiled assembly and keeps using the compiled code until the original file undergoes changes. This means that after the first application-level call the impact on the page performance is identical whether you use *Name* or *Src*.

The *@Import* Directive

The *@Import* directive links the specified namespace to the page so that all the types defined can be accessed from the page without specifying the fully qualified name. For example, to create a new instance of the ADO.NET *DataSet* class, you either import the *System.Data* namespace or resort to the following code:

```
System.Data.DataSet ds = new System.Data.DataSet();
```

Once you've imported the *System.Data* namespace into the page, you can use more natural coding, as shown here:

```
DataSet ds = new DataSet();
```

The syntax of the *@Import* directive is rather self-explanatory:

```
<%@ Import namespace="value" %>
```

@Import can be used as many times as needed in the body of the page. The *@Import* directive is the ASP.NET counterpart of the C# *using* statement and the Visual Basic .NET *Imports* statement. Looking back at unmanaged C/C++, we could say the directive plays a role nearly identical to the *#include* directive.

> **Caution**   Notice that *@Import* helps the compiler only to resolve class names; it doesn't automatically link required assemblies. Using the *@Import* directive allows you to use shorter class names, but as long as the assembly that contains the class code is not properly linked, the compiler will generate a type error. In this case, using the fully qualified class name is of no help because the compiler lacks the type definition.
>
> You might have noticed that, more often than not, assembly and namespace names coincide. Bear in mind it only happens by chance and that assemblies and namespaces are radically different entities, each requiring the proper directive.

For example, to be able to connect to a SQL Server database and grab some disconnected data, you need to import the following two namespaces:

```
<%@ Import namespace="System.Data" %>
<%@ Import namespace=" System.Data.SqlClient" %>
```

You need the *System.Data* namespace to work with the *DataSet* and *DataTable* classes, and you need the *System.Data.SqlClient* namespace to prepare and issue the command. In this case, you don't need to link against additional assemblies because the System.Data.dll assembly is linked by default.

The *@Implements* Directive

The directive indicates that the current page implements the specified .NET Framework interface. An interface is a set of signatures for a logically related group of functions. An interface is a sort of contract that shows the component's commitment to expose that group of functions. Unlike abstract classes, an interface doesn't provide code or executable functionality. When you implement an interface in an ASP.NET page, you declare any required methods and properties within the *<script>* section. The syntax of the *@Implements* directive is as follows:

```
<%@ Implements interface="InterfaceName" %>
```

The *@Implements* directive can appear multiple times in the page if the page has to implement multiple interfaces. Note that if you decide to put all the page logic in a separate class file, you can't use the directive to implement interfaces. Instead, you implement the interface in the code-behind class.

The @*Reference* Directive

The @*Reference* directive is used to establish a dynamic link between the current page and the specified page or user control. This feature has significant consequences in the way in which you set up cross-page communication. It also lets you create strongly typed instances of user controls. Let's review the syntax.

The directive can appear multiple times in the page and features two mutually exclusive attributes—*Page* and *Control*. Both attributes are expected to contain a path to a source file:

```
<%@ Reference page="source_page" %>
<%@ Reference control="source_user_control" %>
```

The *Page* attribute points to an *.aspx* source file, whereas the *Control* attribute contains the path of an *.ascx* user control. In both cases, the referenced source file will be dynamically compiled into an assembly, thus making the classes defined in the source programmatically available to the referencing page. When running, an ASP.NET page is an instance of a .NET Framework class with a specific interface made of methods and properties. When the referencing page executes, a referenced page becomes a class that represents the *.aspx* source file and can be instantiated and programmed at will. Notice that for the directive to work the referenced page must belong to the same domain as the calling page. Cross-site calls are not allowed, and both the *Page* and *Control* attributes expect to receive a relative virtual path.

> **Note**   In ASP.NET 2.0, you are better off using cross-page posting to enable communication between pages.

The *Page* Class

In the .NET Framework, the *Page* class provides the basic behavior for all objects that an ASP.NET application builds by starting from *.aspx* files. Defined in the *System.Web.UI* namespace, the class derives from *TemplateControl* and implements the *IHttpHandler* interface:

```
public class Page : TemplateControl, IHttpHandler
```

In particular, *TemplateControl* is the abstract class that provides both ASP.NET pages and user controls with a base set of functionality. At the upper level of the hierarchy, we find the *Control* class. It defines the properties, methods, and events shared by all ASP.NET server-side elements—pages, controls, and user controls.

Derived from a class—*TemplateControl*—that implements *INamingContainer*, *Page* also serves as the naming container for all its constituent controls. In the .NET Framework, the naming container for a control is the first parent control that implements the *INamingContainer* interface. For any class that implements the naming container interface, ASP.NET creates a new virtual namespace in which all child controls are guaranteed to have unique names in the overall tree of controls. (This is also a very important feature for iterative data-bound controls, such as *DataGrid*, and for user controls.)

The *Page* class also implements the methods of the *IHttpHandler* interface, thus qualifying as the handler of a particular type of HTTP requests—those for *.aspx* files. The key element of the *IHttpHandler* interface is the *ProcessRequest* method, which is the method the ASP.NET runtime calls to start the page processing that will actually serve the request.

> **Note** *INamingContainer* is a marker interface that has no methods. Its presence alone, though, forces the ASP.NET runtime to create an additional namespace for naming the child controls of the page (or the control) that implements it. The *Page* class is the naming container of all the page's controls, with the clear exception of those controls that implement the *INamingContainer* interface themselves or are children of controls that implement the interface.

Properties of the *Page* Class

The properties of the *Page* object can be classified in three distinct groups: intrinsic objects, worker properties, and page-specific properties. The tables in the following sections enumerate and describe them.

Intrinsic Objects

Table 3-9 lists all properties that return a helper object that is intrinsic to the page. In other words, objects listed here are all essential parts of the infrastructure that allows for the page execution.

Table 3-9 ASP.NET Intrinsic Objects in the *Page* Class

Property	Description
Application	Instance of the *HttpApplicationState* class; represents the state of the application. It is functionally equivalent to the ASP intrinsic *Application* object.
Cache	Instance of the *Cache* class; implements the cache for an ASP.NET application. More efficient and powerful than *Application*, it supports item priority and expiration.
Request	Instance of the *HttpRequest* class; represents the current HTTP request. It is functionally equivalent to the ASP intrinsic *Request* object.
Response	Instance of the *HttpResponse* class; sends HTTP response data to the client. It is functionally equivalent to the ASP intrinsic *Response* object.
Server	Instance of the *HttpServerUtility* class; provides helper methods for processing Web requests. It is functionally equivalent to the ASP intrinsic *Server* object.
Session	Instance of the *HttpSessionState* class; manages user-specific data. It is functionally equivalent to the ASP intrinsic *Session* object.
Trace	Instance of the *TraceContext* class; performs tracing on the page.
User	An *IPrincipal* object that represents the user making the request.

We'll cover *Request*, *Response*, and *Server* in Chapter 12; *Application* and *Session* in Chapter 13; *Cache* will be the subject of Chapter 14. Finally, *User* and security will be the subject of Chapter 15.

Worker Properties

Table 3-10 details page properties that are both informative and provide the ground for functional capabilities. You can hardly write code in the page without most of these properties.

Table 3-10   Worker Properties of the *Page* Class

Property	Description
ClientScript	Gets a *ClientScriptManager* object that contains the client script used on the page. *Not available with ASP.NET 1.x.*
Controls	Returns the collection of all the child controls contained in the current page.
ErrorPage	Gets or sets the error page to which the requesting browser is redirected in case of an unhandled page exception.
Form	Returns the current *HtmlForm* object for the page. *Not available with ASP.NET 1.x.*
Header	Returns a reference to the object that represents the page's header. The object implements *IPageHeader*. *Not available with ASP.NET 1.x.*
IsAsync	Indicates whether the page is being invoked through an asynchronous handler. *Not available with ASP.NET 1.x.*
IsCallback	Indicates whether the page is being loaded in response to a client script callback. *Not available with ASP.NET 1.x.*
IsCrossPagePostBack	Indicates whether the page is being loaded in response to a postback made from within another page. *Not available with ASP.NET 1.x.*
IsPostBack	Indicates whether the page is being loaded in response to a client postback or whether it is being loaded for the first time.
IsValid	Indicates whether page validation succeeded.
Master	Instance of the *MasterPage* class; represents the master page that determines the appearance of the current page. *Not available with ASP.NET 1.x.*
MasterPageFile	Gets and sets the master file for the current page. *Not available with ASP.NET 1.x.*
NamingContainer	Returns *null*.
Page	Returns the current *Page* object.
PageAdapter	Returns the adapter object for the current *Page* object.
Parent	Returns *null*.
PreviousPage	Returns the reference to the caller page in case of a cross-page postback. *Not available with ASP.NET 1.x.*
TemplateSourceDirectory	Gets the virtual directory of the page.
Validators	Returns the collection of all validation controls contained in the page.
ViewStateUserKey	String property that represents a user-specific identifier used to hash the view-state contents. This trick is a line of defense against one-click attacks. *Not available with ASP.NET 1.0.*

In the context of an ASP.NET application, the *Page* object is the root of the hierarchy. For this reason, inherited properties such as *NamingContainer* and *Parent* always return *null*. The *Page* property, on the other hand, returns an instance of the same object (*this* in C# and *Me* in Visual Basic .NET).

The *ViewStateUserKey* property that has been added with version 1.1 of the .NET Framework deserves a special mention. A common use for the user key would be to stuff user-specific information that would then be used to hash the contents of the view state along with other information. (See Chapter 13.) A typical value for the *ViewStateUserKey* property is the name of the authenticated user or the user's session ID. This contrivance reinforces the security level for the view state information and further lowers the likelihood of attacks. If you employ a user-specific key, an attacker can't construct a valid view state for your user account unless the attacker can also authenticate as you. With this configuration, you have another barrier against one-click attacks. This technique, though, might not be effective for Web sites that allow anonymous access, unless you have some other unique tracking device running.

Note that if you plan to set the *ViewStateUserKey* property, you must do that during the *Page_Init* event. If you attempt to do it later (for example, when *Page_Load* fires), an exception will be thrown.

Context Properties

Table 3-11 lists properties that represent visual and nonvisual attributes of the page, such as the URL's query string, the client target, the title, and the applied style sheet.

Table 3-11   Page-Specific Properties of the *Page* Class

Property	Description
ClientID	Always returns the empty string.
ClientQueryString	Gets the query string portion of the requested URL. *Not available with ASP.NET 1.x.*
ClientTarget	Set to the empty string by default; allows you to specify the type of the browser the HTML should comply with. Setting this property disables automatic detection of browser capabilities.
EnableViewState	Indicates whether the page has to manage view-state data. You can also enable or disable the view-state feature through the *EnableViewState* attribute of the *@Page* directive.
EnableViewStateMac	Indicates whether ASP.NET should calculate a machine-specific authentication code and append it to the page view state.
EnableTheming	Indicates whether the page supports themes. *Not available with ASP.NET 1.x.*
ID	Always returns the empty string.

Table 3-11   Page-Specific Properties of the *Page* Class

Property	Description
MaintainScrollPositionOnPostback	Indicates whether to return the user to the same position in the client browser after postback. *Not available with ASP.NET 1.x.*
SmartNavigation	Indicates whether smart navigation is enabled. Smart navigation exploits a bunch of browser-specific capabilities to enhance the user's experience with the page. The feature requires Internet Explorer 5.5 or newer.
StyleSheetTheme	Gets or sets the name of the style sheet applied to this page. *Not available with ASP.NET 1.x.*
Theme	Gets and sets the theme for the page. Note that themes can be programmatically set only in the *PreInit* event. *Not available with ASP.NET 1.x.*
Title	Gets or sets the title for the page. *Not available with ASP.NET 1.x.*
TraceEnabled	Toggles page tracing on and off. *Not available with ASP.NET 1.x.*
TraceModeValue	Gets or sets the trace mode. *Not available with ASP.NET 1.x.*
UniqueID	Always returns the empty string.
ViewStateEncryptionMode	Indicates if and how the view state should be encrypted.
Visible	Indicates whether ASP.NET has to render the page. If you set *Visible* to *false*, ASP.NET doesn't generate any HTML code for the page. When *Visible* is *false*, only the text explicitly written using *Response.Write* hits the client.

The three ID properties (*ID*, *ClientID*, and *UniqueID*) always return the empty string from a *Page* object. They make sense only for server controls.

Methods of the *Page* Class

The whole range of *Page* methods can be classified in a few categories based on the tasks each method accomplishes. A few methods are involved with the generation of the markup for the page; others are helper methods to build the page and manage the constituent controls. Finally, a third group collects all the methods that have to do with client-side scripting.

Rendering Methods

Table 3-12 details the methods that are directly or indirectly involved with the generation of the markup code.

Table 3-12 Methods for Markup Generation

Method	Description
DataBind	Binds all the data-bound controls contained in the page to their data sources. The *DataBind* method doesn't generate code itself but prepares the ground for the forthcoming rendering.
RenderControl	Outputs the HTML text for the page, including tracing information if tracing is enabled.
VerifyRenderingInServerForm	Controls call this method when they render to ensure that they are included in the body of a server form. The method does not return a value, but it throws an exception in case of error.

In an ASP.NET page, no control can be placed outside a *<form>* tag with the *runat* attribute set to *server*. The *VerifyRenderingInServerForm* method is used by Web and HTML controls to ensure that they are rendered correctly. In theory, custom controls should call this method during the rendering phase. In many situations, the custom control embeds or derives an existing Web or HTML control that will make the check itself.

Not directly exposed by the *Page* class, but strictly related to it, is the *GetWebResourceUrl* method on the *ClientScriptManager* class in ASP.NET 2.0. The method provides a long-awaited feature to control developers. When you develop a control, you typically need to embed static resources such as images or client script files. You can make these files be separate downloads but, even though it's effective, the solution looks poor and inelegant. Visual Studio .NET 2003 and newer versions allow you to embed resources in the control assembly, but how would you retrieve these resources programmatically and bind them to the control? For example, to bind an assembly-stored image to an <IMG> tag, you need a URL for the image. The *GetWeb-ResourceUrl* method returns a URL for the specified resource. The URL refers to a new Web Resource service (*webresource.axd*) that retrieves and returns the requested resource from an assembly.

```
// Bind the <IMG> tag to the given GIF image in the control's assembly
img.ImageUrl = Page.GetWebResourceUrl (typeof(TheControl), GifName));
```

GetWebResourceUrl requires a *Type* object, which will be used to locate the assembly that contains the resource. The assembly is identified with the assembly that contains the definition of the specified type in the current AppDomain. If you're writing a custom control, the type will likely be the control's type. As its second argument, the *GetWebResourceUrl* method requires the name of the embedded resource. The returned URL takes the following form:

```
WebResource.axd?a=assembly&r=resourceName&t=timestamp
```

The timestamp value is the current timestamp of the assembly, and it is added to make the browser download resources again should the assembly be modified.

Controls-Related Methods

Table 3-13 details a bunch of helper methods on the *Page* class architected to let you manage and validate child controls and resolve URLs.

Table 3-13 Helper Methods of the *Page* Object

Method	Description
DesignerInitialize	Initializes the instance of the *Page* class at design time, when the page is being hosted by RAD designers such as Visual Studio.
FindControl	Takes a control's ID and searches for it in the page's naming container. The search doesn't dig out child controls that are naming containers themselves.
GetTypeHashCode	Retrieves the hash code generated by *ASP.xxx_aspx* page objects at run time. In the base *Page* class, the method implementation simply returns *0*; significant numbers are returned by classes used for actual pages.
GetValidators	Returns a collection of control validators for a specified validation group. *Not available with ASP.NET 1.x.*
HasControls	Determines whether the page contains any child controls.
LoadControl	Compiles and loads a user control from an .ascx file, and returns a *Control* object. If the user control supports caching, the object returned is *PartialCachingControl*.
LoadTemplate	Compiles and loads a user control from an .ascx file, and returns it wrapped in an instance of an internal class that implements the *ITemplate* interface. The internal class is named *SimpleTemplate*.
MapPath	Retrieves the physical, fully qualified path that an absolute or relative virtual path maps to.
ParseControl	Parses a well-formed input string, and returns an instance of the control that corresponds to the specified markup text. If the string contains more controls, only the first is taken into account. The *runat* attribute can be omitted. The method returns an object of type *Control* and must be cast to a more specific type.
RegisterRequiresControlState	Registers a control as one that requires control state. *Not available with ASP.NET 1.x.*
RegisterRequiresPostBack	Registers the specified control to receive a postback handling notice, even if its ID doesn't match any ID in the collection of posted data. The control must implement the *IPostBackDataHandler* interface.
RegisterRequiresRaiseEvent	Registers the specified control to handle an incoming postback event. The control must implement the *IPostBackEventHandler* interface.
RegisterViewStateHandler	Mostly for internal use, the method sets an internal flag causing the page view state to be persisted. If this method is not called in the prerendering phase, no view state will ever be written. Typically, only the *HtmlForm* server control for the page calls this method. There's no need to call it from within user applications.

Table 3-13   Helper Methods of the *Page* Object

Method	Description
ResolveUrl	Resolves a relative URL into an absolute URL based on the value of the *TemplateSourceDirectory* property.
Validate	Instructs any validation controls included on the page to validate their assigned information. ASP.NET 2.0 supports validation groups.

The methods *LoadControl* and *LoadTemplate* share a common code infrastructure but return different objects, as the following pseudocode shows:

```
public Control LoadControl(string virtualPath) {
    Control ascx = GetCompiledUserControlType(virtualPath);
    ascx.InitializeAsUserControl();
    return ascx;
}
public ITemplate LoadTemplate(string virtualPath) {
    Control ascx = GetCompiledUserControlType(virtualPath);
    return new SimpleTemplate(ascx);
}
```

Both methods differ from *ParseControl* in that the latter never causes compilation but simply parses the string and infers control information. The information is then used to create and initialize a new instance of the control class. As mentioned, the *runat* attribute is unnecessary in this context. In ASP.NET, the *runat* attribute is key, but in practice, it has no other role than marking the surrounding markup text for parsing and instantiation. It does not contain information useful to instantiate a control, and for this reason it can be omitted from the strings you pass directly to *ParseControl*.

Script-Related Methods

Table 3-14 enumerates all the methods in the *Page* class that have to do with HTML and script code to be inserted in the client page.

Table 3-14   Script-Related Methods

Method	Description
GetCallbackEventReference	Obtains a reference to a client-side function that, when invoked, initiates a client call back to server-side events. *Not available with ASP.NET 1.x.*
GetPostBackClientEvent	Calls into *GetCallbackEventReference*.
GetPostBackClientHyperlink	Appends *javascript:* to the beginning of the return string received from *GetPostBackEventReference*. `javascript:__doPostBack('CtlID','')`
GetPostBackEventReference	Returns the prototype of the client-side script function that causes, when invoked, a postback. It takes a *Control* and an argument, and it returns a string like this: `__doPostBack('CtlID','')`

Table 3-14   Script-Related Methods

Method	Description
IsClientScriptBlockRegistered	Determines whether the specified client script is registered with the page. *Marked as obsolete.*
IsStartupScriptRegistered	Determines whether the specified client startup script is registered with the page. *Marked as obsolete.*
RegisterArrayDeclaration	Use this method to add an ECMAScript array to the client page. This method accepts the name of the array and a string that will be used verbatim as the body of the array. For example, if you call the method with arguments such as *theArray* and *"'a', 'b'"*, you get the following JavaScript code: `var theArray = new Array('a', 'b');` *Marked as obsolete.*
RegisterClientScriptBlock	An ASP.NET page uses this method to emit client-side script blocks in the client page just after the opening tag of the HTML *<form>* element. *Marked as obsolete.*
RegisterHiddenField	Use this method to automatically register a hidden field on the page. *Marked as obsolete.*
RegisterOnSubmitStatement	Use this method to emit client script code that handles the client *OnSubmit* event. The script should be a JavaScript function call to client code registered elsewhere. *Marked as obsolete.*
RegisterStartupScript	An ASP.NET page uses this method to emit client-side script blocks in the client page just before closing the HTML *<form>* element. *Marked as obsolete.*
SetFocus	Sets the browser focus to the specified control. *Not available with ASP.NET 1.x.*

As you can see, some methods in Table 3-14, which are defined and usable in ASP.NET 1.x, have been marked as obsolete. In ASP.NET 2.0 applications, you should avoid calling them and resort to methods with the same name exposed out of the *ClientScript* property. (See Table 3-10.)

```
// Avoid this in ASP.NET 2.0
Page.RegisterArrayDeclaration(…);
// Use this in ASP.NET 2.0
Page.ClientScript.RegisterArrayDeclaration(…);
```

Methods listed in Table 3-14 let you emit script in the client page—either JavaScript or VBScript. When you use any of these methods, you actually tell the page to insert that script code when the page is rendered. So when any of these methods execute, the script-related information is simply cached in internal structures and used later when the page object generates its HTML text.

> **Note**   JavaScript is the script language that virtually any available browser supports. For this reason, some of the methods in Table 3-14 default to JavaScript. However, when you register a script block, nothing really prevents you from using VBScript as long as you set the language attribute of the *<script>* tag accordingly. On the other hand, methods such as *RegisterOnSubmitStatement* and *RegisterArrayDeclaration* can be used only with JavaScript code.

Events of the *Page* Class

The *Page* class fires a few events that are notified during the page life cycle. As Table 3-15 shows, some events are orthogonal to the typical life cycle of a page (initialization, postback, rendering phases) and are fired as extra-page situations evolve. Let's briefly review the events and then attack the topic with an in-depth discussion on the page life cycle.

Table 3-15   Events That a Page Can Fire

Event	Description
AbortTransaction	Occurs for ASP.NET pages marked to participate in an automatic transaction when a transaction aborts.
CommitTransaction	Occurs for ASP.NET pages marked to participate in an automatic transaction when a transaction commits.
DataBinding	Occurs when the *DataBind* method is called on the page to bind all the child controls to their respective data sources.
Disposed	Occurs when the page is released from memory, which is the last stage of the page life cycle.
Error	Occurs when an unhandled exception is thrown.
Init	Occurs when the page is initialized, which is the first step in the page life cycle.
InitComplete	Occurs when all child controls and the page have been initialized. *Not available in ASP.NET 1.x.*
Load	Occurs when the page loads up, after being initialized.
LoadComplete	Occurs when the loading of the page is completed and server events have been raised. *Not available in ASP.NET 1.x.*
PreInit	Occurs just before the initialization phase of the page begins. *Not available in ASP.NET 1.x.*
PreLoad	Occurs just before the loading phase of the page begins. *Not available in ASP.NET 1.x.*
PreRender	Occurs when the page is about to render.
PreRenderComplete	Occurs just before the pre-rendering phase begins. *Not available in ASP.NET 1.x.*
SaveStateComplete	Occurs when the view state of the page has been saved to the persistence medium. *Not available in ASP.NET 1.x.*
Unload	Occurs when the page is unloaded from memory but not yet disposed.

The Eventing Model

When a page is requested, its class and the server controls it contains are responsible for executing the request and rendering HTML back to the client. The communication between the client and the server is stateless and disconnected because of the HTTP protocol. Real-world applications, though, need some state to be maintained between successive calls made to the same page. With ASP, and with other server-side development platforms such as Java Server Pages and LAMP, the programmer is entirely responsible for persisting the state. In contrast, ASP.NET provides a built-in infrastructure that saves and restores the state of a page in a transparent manner. In this way, and in spite of the underlying stateless protocol, the client experience appears to be that of a continuously executing process. It's just an illusion, though.

Introducing the View State

The illusion of continuity is created by the view state feature of ASP.NET pages and is based on some assumptions about how the page is designed and works. Also, server-side Web controls play a remarkable role. In brief, before rendering its contents to HTML, the page encodes and stuffs into a persistence medium (typically, a hidden field) all the state information that the page itself and its constituent controls want to save. When the page posts back, the state information is deserialized from the hidden field and used to initialize instances of the server controls declared in the page layout.

The view state is specific to each instance of the page because it is embedded in the HTML. The net effect of this is that controls are initialized with the same values they had the last time the view state was created—that is, the last time the page was rendered to the client. Furthermore, an additional step in the page life cycle merges the persisted state with any updates introduced by client-side actions. When the page executes after a postback, it finds a stateful and up-to-date context just as it is working over a continuous point-to-point connection.

Two basic assumptions are made. The first assumption is that the page always posts to itself and carries its state back and forth. The second assumption is that the server-side controls have to be declared with the *runat=server* attribute to spring to life once the page posts back.

The Single Form Model

Admittedly, for programmers whose experience is with ASP, the single form model of ASP.NET can be difficult to understand. These programmers frequently ask questions on forums and newsgroups such as, "Where's the *Action* property of the form?" and "Why can't I redirect to a particular page when a form is submitted?"

ASP.NET pages are built to support exactly one server-side *<form>* tag. The form must include all the controls you want to interact with on the server. Both the form and the controls must be marked with the *runat* attribute; otherwise, they will be considered as plain text to be output verbatim. A server-side form is an instance of the *HtmlForm* class. The *HtmlForm* class does not expose any property equivalent to the *Action* property of the HTML *<form>* tag. The reason is that an ASP.NET page always posts to itself. Unlike the *Action* property, other common form properties such as *Method* and *Target* are fully supported.

Valid ASP.NET pages are also those that have no server-side forms and those that run HTML forms—a *<form>* tag without the *runat* attribute. In an ASP.NET page, you can also have both HTML and server forms. In no case, though, can you have more than one *<form>* tag with the *runat* attribute set to *server*. HTML forms work as usual and let you post to any page in the application. The drawback is that in this case no state will be automatically restored. In other words, the ASP.NET Web Forms model works only if you use exactly one server *<form>* element. We'll return to this topic in Chapter 5.

> **Note**   ASP.NET pages are served by a HTTP handler like an instance of the *Page* class. Each request takes up a thread in the ASP.NET thread pool and releases it only when the request completes. What if a frequently requested page starts an external and particularly lengthy task? The risk is that the ASP.NET process is idle but has no free threads in the pool to serve incoming requests for other pages. This is mostly due to the fact that HTTP handlers, including page classes, work synchronously. To alleviate this issue, ASP.NET supports asynchronous handlers since version 1.0 through the *IHttpAsyncHandler* interface. In ASP.NET 2.0, creating asynchronous pages is even easier thanks to a specific support from the framework. We'll cover this topic in great detail in *Programming Microsoft ASP.NET 2.0 Applications: Advanced Topics* (Microsoft Press, 2005).

The Page Life Cycle

A page instance is created on every request from the client, and its execution causes itself and its contained controls to iterate through their life-cycle stages. Page execution begins when the HTTP runtime invokes *ProcessRequest*, which kicks off the page and control life cycles. The life cycle consists of a sequence of stages and steps. Some of these stages can be controlled through user-code events; some require a method override. Some other stages, or more exactly substages, are just not public, out of the developer's control, and mentioned here mostly for completeness.

The page life cycle is articulated in three main stages: setup, postback, and finalization. Each stage might have one or more substages and is composed of one or more steps and points where events are raised. The life cycle as described here includes all possible paths. Note that there are modifications to the process depending upon cross-page posts, script callbacks, and postbacks.

Page Setup

When the HTTP runtime instantiates the page class to serve the current request, the page constructor builds a tree of controls. The tree of controls ties into the actual class that the page parser created after looking at the ASPX source. It is important to note that when the request processing begins, all child controls and page intrinsics such as HTTP context, request objects, and response objects are set.

The very first step in the page lifetime is determining why the runtime is processing the page request. There are various possible reasons: a normal request, postback, cross-page postback, or callback. The page object configures its internal state based on the actual reason, and it prepares the collection of posted values (if any) based on the method of the request—either *GET* or *POST*. After this first step, the page is ready to fire events to the user code.

The *PreInit* Event

Introduced with ASP.NET 2.0, this event is the entry point in the page life cycle. When the event fires, no master page and no theme have been associated with the page. Furthermore, the page scroll position has been restored, posted data is available, and all page controls have been instantiated and default to the properties values defined in the ASPX source. (Note that at this time controls have no ID, unless it is explicitly set in the *.aspx* source.) Changing the master page or the theme programmatically is possible only at this time. This event is available only on the page. *IsCallback*, *IsCrossPagePostback*, and *IsPostback* are set at this time.

The *Init* Event

The master page, if one exists, and the theme have been set and can't be changed anymore. The page processor—that is, the *ProcessRequest* method on the *Page* class—proceeds and iterates over all child controls to give them a chance to initialize their state in a context-sensitive way. All child controls have their *OnInit* method invoked recursively. For each control in the control collection, the naming container and a specific ID are set, if not assigned in the source.

The *Init* event reaches child controls first and the page later. At this stage, the page and controls typically begin loading some parts of their state. At this time, the view state is not restored yet.

The *InitComplete* Event

Introduced with ASP.NET 2.0, this page-only event signals the end of the initialization sub stage. For a page, only one operation takes place in between the *Init* and *InitComplete* events: tracking of view-state changes is turned on. Tracking view state is the operation that ultimately enables controls to *really* persist in the storage medium any values that are programmatically added to the *ViewState* collection. Simply put, for controls not tracking their view state, any values added to their *ViewState* are lost across postbacks.

All controls turn on view-state tracking immediately after raising their *Init* event, and the page is no exception. (After all, isn't the page just a control?)

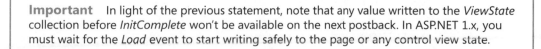

Important   In light of the previous statement, note that any value written to the *ViewState* collection before *InitComplete* won't be available on the next postback. In ASP.NET 1.x, you must wait for the *Load* event to start writing safely to the page or any control view state.

View-State Restoration

If the page is being processed because of a postback—that is, if the *IsPostBack* property is *true*—the contents of the *__VIEWSTATE* hidden field is restored. The *__VIEWSTATE* hidden field is where the view state of all controls is persisted at the end of a request. The overall view state of the page is a sort of call context and contains the state of each constituent control the last time the page was served to the browser.

At this stage, each control is given a chance to update its current state to make it identical to what it was on last request. There's no event to wire up to handle the view-state restoration. If something needs be customized here, you have to resort to overriding the *LoadViewState* method, defined as protected and virtual on the *Control* class.

Processing Posted Data

All the client data packed in the HTTP request—that is, the contents of all input fields defined with the *<form>* tag—are processed at this time. Posted data usually take the following form:

```
TextBox1=text&DropDownList1=selectedItem&Button1=Submit
```

It's an &-separated string of name/value pairs. These values are loaded into an internal-use collection. The page processor attempts to find a match between names in the posted collection and ID of controls in the page. Whenever a match is found, the processor checks whether the server control implements the *IPostBackDataHandler* interface. If it does, the methods of the interface are invoked to give the control a chance to refresh its state in light of the posted data. In particular, the page processor invokes the *LoadPostData* method on the interface. If the method returns *true*—that is, the state has been updated—the control is added to a separate collection to receive further attention later.

If a posted name doesn't match any server controls, it is left over and temporarily parked in a separate collection, ready for a second try later.

The *PreLoad* Event

Introduced with ASP.NET 2.0, the *PreLoad* event merely indicates that the page has terminated the system-level initialization phase and is going to enter the phase that gives user code in the page a chance to further configure the page for execution and rendering. This event is raised only for pages.

The *Load* Event

The *Load* event is raised for the page first and then recursively for all child controls. At this time, controls in the page tree are created and their state fully reflects both the previous state and any data posted from the client. The page is ready to execute any initialization code that has to do with the logic and behavior of the page. At this time, access to control properties and view state is absolutely safe.

Handling Dynamically Created Controls

When all controls in the page have been given a chance to complete their initialization before display, the page processor makes a second try on posted values that haven't been matched to existing controls. The behavior described earlier in the "Processing Posted Data" section is repeated on the name/value pairs that were left over previously. This apparently weird approach addresses a specific scenario—the use of dynamically created controls.

Imagine adding a control to the page tree dynamically—for example, in response to a certain user action. As mentioned, the page is rebuilt from scratch after each postback, so any information about the dynamically created control is lost. On the other hand, when the page's form is submitted, the dynamic control there is filled with legal and valid information that is regularly posted. By design, there can't be any server control to match the ID of the dynamic control the first time posted data is processed. However, the ASP.NET framework recognizes that some controls could be created in the *Load* event. For this reason, it makes sense to give it a second try to see whether a match is possible after the user code has run for a while.

If the dynamic control has been re-created in the *Load* event, a match is now possible and the control can refresh its state with posted data.

Handling the Postback

The postback mechanism is the heart of ASP.NET programming. It consists of posting form data to the same page using the view state to restore the call context—that is, the same state of controls existing when the posting page was last generated on the server.

After the page has been initialized and posted values have been taken into account, it's about time that some server-side events occur. There are two main types of events. The first type of event signals that certain controls had the state changed over the postback. The second type of event executes server code in response to the client action that caused the post.

Detecting Control State Changes

The whole ASP.NET machinery works around an implicit assumption: there must be a one-to-one correspondence between some HTML input tags that operate in the browser and some other ASP.NET controls that live and thrive in the Web server. The canonical example of this correspondence is between <input type="text"> and *TextBox* controls. To be more technically precise, the link is given by a common ID name. When the user types some new text into an input element and then posts it, the corresponding *TextBox* control—that is, a server control with the same ID as the input tag—is called to handle the posted value. I described this step in the "Processing Posted Data" section earlier in the chapter.

For all controls that had the *LoadPostData* method return *true*, it's now time to execute the second method of the *IPostBackDataHandler* interface: the *RaisePostDataChangedEvent* method. The method signals the control to notify the ASP.NET application that the state of the control has changed. The implementation of the method is up to each control. However, most controls do the same thing: raise a server event and give page authors a way to kick in and execute code to handle the situation. For example, if the *Text* property of a *TextBox* changes over a postback, the *TextBox* raises the *TextChanged* event to the host page.

Executing the Server-Side Postback Event

Any page postback starts with some client action that intends to trigger a server-side action. For example, clicking a client button posts the current contents of the displayed form to the server, thus requiring some action and a new, refreshed page output. The client button control—typically, a hyperlink or a submit button—is associated with a server control that implements the *IPostBackEventHandler* interface.

The page processor looks at the posted data and determines the control that caused the postback. If this control implements the *IPostBackEventHandler* interface, the processor invokes the *RaisePostBackEvent* method. The implementation of this method is left to the control and can vary quite a bit, at least in theory. In practice, though, any posting control raises a server event letting page authors write code in response to the postback. For example, the *Button* control raises the *onclick* event.

There are two ways a page can post back to the server—by using a submit button (that is, <input type="submit">) or through script. The markup for a submit button is generated through the *Button* server control. Instead of using *LinkButton* controls and other controls, insert some script code in the client page to bind an HTML event (for example, *onclick*) to the form's *submit* method in the browser's HTML object model. We'll return to this topic in the next chapter.

> **Note**   In ASP.NET 2.0, a new property, *UseSubmitBehavior*, exists on the *Button* class to let page developers control the client behavior of the corresponding HTML element as far as form submission is concerned. In ASP.NET 1.x, the *Button* control always outputs an *<input type="submit">* element. In ASP.NET 2.0, by setting *UseSubmitBehavior* to *false*, you can change the output to *<input type="button">*. The postback, in this case, occurs via script.

The *LoadComplete* Event

Introduced in ASP.NET 2.0, the page-only *LoadComplete* event signals the end of the page-preparation phase. It is important to note that no child controls will ever receive this event. After firing *LoadComplete*, the page enters its rendering stage.

Page Finalization

After handling the postback event, the page is ready for generating the output for the browser. The rendering stage is divided in two parts—prerendering and markup generation. The prerendering substage is in turn characterized by two events for preprocessing and postprocessing.

The *PreRender* Event

By handling this event, pages and controls can perform any updates before the output is rendered. The *PreRender* event fires for the page first and then recursively for all controls. Note that at this time the page ensures that all child controls are created. This step is important especially for composite controls.

The *PreRenderComplete* Event

Because the *PreRender* event is recursively fired for all child controls, there's no way for the page author to know when the prerendering phase has been completed. For this reason, in ASP.NET 2.0 a new event has been added and raised only for the page. This event is *PreRenderComplete*.

The *SaveStateComplete* Event

The next step before each control is rendered out to generate the markup for the page is saving the current state of the page to the view-state storage medium. It is important to note that every action taken after this point that modifies the state could affect the rendering, but it is not persisted and won't be retrieved on the next postback. Saving the page state is a recursive process in which the page processor walks its way through the whole page tree calling the *SaveViewState* method on constituent controls and the page itself. *SaveViewState* is a protected and virtual (that is, overridable) method that is responsible for persisting the content of the *ViewState* dictionary for the current control. (We'll come back to the *ViewState* dictionary in Chapter 13.)

In ASP.NET 2.0, controls provide a second type of state, known as a "control state." A control state is a sort of private view state that is not subject to the application's control. In other words, the *control state* of a control can't be programmatically disabled as is the case with the view state. The control state is persisted at this time, too.

Introduced with ASP.NET 2.0, the *SaveStateComplete* event occurs when the state of controls on the page have been completely saved to the persistence medium.

> **Note**   The view state of the page and all individual controls is accumulated in a unique memory structure and then persisted to storage medium. By default, the persistence medium is a hidden field named *__VIEWSTATE*. Serialization to, and deserialization from, the persistence medium is handled through a couple of overridable methods on the *Page* class: *SavePageStateToPersistenceMedium* and *LoadPageStateFromPersistenceMedium*. For example, by overriding these two methods you can persist the page state in a server-side database or in the session state, dramatically reducing the size of the page served to the user. (We'll talk more about this in Chapter 13.)

Generating the Markup

The generation of the markup for the browser is obtained by calling each constituent control to render its own markup, which will be accumulated into a buffer. Several overridable methods allow control developers to intervene in various steps during the markup generation—begin tag, body, and end tag. No user event is associated with the rendering phase.

The *Unload* Event

The rendering phase is followed by a recursive call that raises the *Unload* event for each control, and finally for the page itself. The *Unload* event exists to perform any final cleanup before the page object is released. Typical operations are closing files and database connections.

Note that the unload notification arrives when the page or the control is being unloaded but has not been disposed of yet. Overriding the *Dispose* method of the *Page* class, or more simply handling the page's *Disposed* event, provides the last possibility for the actual page to perform final clean up before it is released from memory. The page processor frees the page object by calling the method *Dispose*. This occurs immediately after the recursive call to the handlers of the *Unload* event has completed.

Conclusion

ASP.NET is a complex technology built on top of a substantially simple—and, fortunately, solid and stable—Web infrastructure. To provide a highly improved performance and richer programming toolset, ASP.NET builds a desktop-like abstraction model, but it still has to rely on HTTP and HTML to hit the target and meet end-user expectations.

There are two relevant aspects in the ASP.NET Web Forms model: the process model, including the Web server process model, and the page object model. Each request of a URL that ends with *.aspx* is assigned to an application object working within the CLR hosted by the worker process. The request results in a dynamically compiled class that is then instantiated and put to work. The *Page* class is the base class for all ASP.NET pages. An instance of this class runs behind any URL that ends with *.aspx*. In most cases, you won't just build your ASP.NET pages from the *Page* class directly, but you'll rely on derived classes that contain event handlers and helper methods at the very minimum. These classes are known as code-behind classes.

The class that represents the page in action implements the ASP.NET eventing based on two pillars, the single form model (page reentrancy) and server controls. The page life cycle, fully described in this chapter, details the various stages (and related substages) a page passes through on the way to generate the markup for the browser. A deep understanding of the page life cycle and eventing model is key to diagnosing possible problems and implementing advanced features quickly and efficiently.

In this chapter, we mentioned controls several times. Server controls are components that get input from the user, process the input, and output a response as HTML. In the next chapter, we'll explore various server controls, which include Web controls, HTML controls, and validation controls.

Just the Facts

- A pipeline of run-time modules receive from IIS an incoming HTTP packet and make it evolve from a protocol-specific payload up to an instance of a class derived from *Page*.

- The page class required to serve a given request is dynamically compiled on demand when first required in the context of a Web application.

- The page class compiled to an assembly remains in use as long as no changes occur to the linked *.aspx* source file or the whole application is restarted.

- Each page class is an HTTP handler—that is, a component that the run time uses to service requests of a certain type.

- The ASP.NET 2.0 code-behind model employs partial classes to generate missing declarations for protected members that represent server controls. This code was auto-generated by Visual Studio .NET 2003 and placed in regions.

- ASP.NET pages always post to themselves and use the view state to restore the state of controls existing when the page was last generated on the server.

- The view state creates the illusion of a stateful programming model in a stateless environment.

- Processing the page on the server entails handling a bunch of events that collectively form the page life cycle. A deep understanding of the page life cycle is key to diagnosing possible problems and implementing advanced features quickly and efficiently.

Chapter 4
ASP.NET Core Server Controls

In this chapter:

Generalities of ASP.NET Server Controls 120

HTML Controls 129

Web Controls 145

Validation Controls 159

Conclusion 172

ASP.NET pages are made of code, markup tags, literal text, and server controls. Based on the request, the server controls generate the right markup language. The ASP.NET runtime combines the output of all controls and serves the client a page to display in a browser. The programming richness of ASP.NET springs from the wide library of server controls that covers the basic tasks of HTML interaction—for example, collecting text through input tags—as well as more advanced functionalities such as calendaring, menus, tree views, and grid-based data display.

The *runat* attribute is key to ASP.NET control programming. If a tag in the *.aspx* source is declared without the *runat* attribute, it is considered plain text and is output verbatim. Otherwise, the contents of the tag are mapped to a server control and processed during the page life cycle. Back in Chapter 1, we identified two main families of server controls—HTML server controls and Web server controls. HTML controls map to HTML tags and are implemented through server-side classes whose programming interface faithfully represents the standard set of attributes for the corresponding HTML tag. Web controls, in turn, are a more abstract library of controls in which adherence of the proposed API to HTML syntax is much less strict. As a result, Web and HTML controls share a large common subset of functionalities and, in spite of a few exceptions, we could say that Web controls, functionally speaking, are a superset of HTML controls. Web controls also feature a richer development environment with a larger set of methods, properties, and events and participate more actively in the page life cycle.

As we'll see in more detail in the following pages, a second and more thoughtful look at the characteristics of the server controls in ASP.NET reveals the existence of more than just two families of controls. In real world ASP.NET applications, you'll end up using controls from at least the following functional categories: HTML controls, core Web controls, validation controls, data-bound controls, user controls, mobile controls, and custom controls. Validation controls are a special subset of Web controls and deserve to be treated in a separate section. Data-bound controls are not a category per se, with features that make them different from HTML or Web controls. Data binding, instead, refers to the control's capability of connecting some of its properties to particular data sources. Hence, data-bound controls fall into any of the previously listed groups of server controls, but they deserve a section of their own because of their frequent use. User controls are visual aggregates of existing Web and HTML controls that appear as individual, encapsulated, programmable controls to external callers. *Mobile controls* are used when creating Web applications that target mobile devices. *Custom controls* refer to server controls you create that derive from a base control class.

In this chapter, we'll cover HTML controls, Web controls, and validation controls. Data-bound controls will be covered in Chapter 9. User controls, mobile controls, and custom controls will find their place in my other recent book, *Programming Microsoft ASP.NET 2.0 Applications: Advanced Topics* (Microsoft Press, 2005), which is written for advanced users as a companion book to this one.

Generalities of ASP.NET Server Controls

All ASP.NET server controls, including HTML and Web controls, plus any custom controls you create or download, descend from the *Control* class. The class is defined in the *System.Web.UI* namespace and, as we discussed in Chapter 3, it is also the foundation of all ASP.NET pages. The *Control* class is declared as follows:

```
public class Control : IComponent, IDisposable, IParserAccessor,
   IUrlResolutionService, IDataBindingsAccessor,
   IControlBuilderAccessor, IControlDesignerAccessor,
   IExpressionsAccessor
```

The *IComponent* interface defines the way in which the control interacts with the other components running in the common language runtime (CLR), whereas *IDisposable* implements the common pattern for releasing managed objects deterministically. Table 4-1 explains the role of the other interfaces that the *Control* class implements.

Table 4-1   Interfaces Implemented by the *Control* Class

Interface	Goal
IControlBuilderAccessor	Internal-use interface; provides members to support the page parser in building a control and the child controls it contains. *Not available in ASP.NET 1.x.*
IControlDesignerAccessor	Internal-use interface; provides members to make the control interact with the designer. *Not available in ASP.NET 1.x.*
IDataBindingsAccessor	Makes the control capable of supporting data-binding expressions at design time.

Table 4-1 **Interfaces Implemented by the** *Control* **Class**

Interface	Goal
IExpressionsAccessor	Internal-use interface; defines the properties a class must implement to support collections of expressions. *Not available in ASP.NET 1.x.*
IParserAccessor	Enables the control to work as the container of child controls and to be notified when a block of child markup is parsed.
IUrlResolutionService	Provides members to resolve relative URLs both at run time and design time. *Not available in ASP.NET 1.x.*

The *IDataBindingsAccessor* interface defines a read-only collection—the *DataBindings* property—that contains all the data bindings for the controls available to rapid application development (RAD) designers such as Microsoft Visual Studio .NET. Note that the collection of data bindings exists only at design time and, as such, is useful only if you write a RAD designer for the control.

> **Note** Compared to ASP.NET 1.x, the base *Control* class implements many more interfaces. However, only one of them, *IExpressionsAccessor*, represents some really new functionality. The *IExpressionsAccessor* interface provides members to retrieve and process custom data binding expressions—a brand new feature of ASP.NET 2.0 that we'll cover briefly in Chapter 9 and that is covered in detail in *Programming Microsoft ASP.NET 2.0 Applications: Advanced Topics.* All the other interfaces refactor and rationalize control capabilities that exist in ASP.NET 1.x as well.

Properties of the *Control* Class

The properties of the *Control* class have no user interface–specific features. The class, in fact, represents the minimum set of functionalities expected from a server control. The list of properties for the *Control* class is shown in Table 4-2.

Table 4-2 **Properties Common to All Server Controls**

Property	Description
BindingContainer	Gets the control that represents the logical parent of the current control as far as data binding is concerned. *Not available in ASP.NET 1.x.*
ClientID	Gets the ID assigned to the control in the HTML page. The string is a slightly different version of the *UniqueID* property. *UniqueID* can contain the dollar symbol ($), but this symbol is not accepted in *ClientID* and is replaced with the underscore (_).
Controls	Gets a collection filled with references to all the child controls.
EnableTheming	Indicates whether themes apply to the control. *Not available in ASP.NET 1.x.*
EnableViewState	Gets or sets whether the control should persist its view state—and the view state of any child controls across multiple requests—to the configured medium (for example, HTML hidden field, session state, and server-side databases or files).
ID	Gets or sets the name that will be used to programmatically identify the control in the page.

Table 4-2   Properties Common to All Server Controls

Property	Description
NamingContainer	Gets a reference to the control's naming container. The naming container for a given control is the parent control above it in the hierarchy that implements the *INamingContainer* interface. If no such control exists, the naming container is the host page.
Page	Gets a reference to the *Page* instance that contains the control.
Parent	Gets a reference to the parent of the control in the page hierarchy.
Site	Gets information about the container that hosts the current control when rendered on a design surface. For example, you use this property to access the Visual Studio .NET 2005 designer when the control is being composed in a Web form.
SkinID	Gets or sets the name of the skin to apply to the control. A skin is a particular subset of attributes in a theme. *Not available in ASP.NET 1.x.*
TemplateControl	Gets a reference to the template that contains the current control. *Not available in ASP.NET 1.x.*
TemplateSourceDirectory	Gets the virtual directory of the host page.
UniqueID	Gets a hierarchically qualified ID for the control.
Visible	Gets or sets whether ASP.NET has to render the control.

The *Control* class is the ideal base class for new controls that have no user interface and don't require style information.

Identifying a Server Control

The client ID of a control is generated from the value of the *UniqueID* property—the truly server-side identifier that ASP.NET generates for each control. The contents of the *ClientID* property differ from *UniqueID* simply in that all occurrences of the dollar symbol ($), if any, are replaced with the underscore (_). Dollars in the *UniqueID* string are possible only if the control belongs to a naming container different from the page.

ASP.NET generates the value for the *UniqueID* property based on the value of the *ID* property that the programmer indicates. If no ID has been specified, ASP.NET auto-generates a name such as _ctlX, where *X* is a progressive 0-based index. If the control's naming container is the host page, *UniqueID* simply takes the value of *ID*. Otherwise, the value of *ID* is prefixed with the string representing the naming container and the result is assigned to *UniqueID*.

Naming Containers

A naming container is primarily a control that acts as a container for other controls. In doing so, the naming container generates a sort of virtual namespace so that ASP.NET roots the actual ID of contained controls in the ID of the naming container. To fully understand the role and importance of naming containers, consider the following example.

Imagine you have a composite control that includes a child control—say, a button. Entirely wrapped by the outermost control, the button is not directly accessible by the page code and can't be given a distinct and per-instance ID. In the end, the ID of the button is hard-coded in the outermost control that creates it. What happens when two or more instances of the composite control are placed on a page? Are you going to have two button child controls with the same ID? This is exactly what will happen unless you configure the composite control to be a naming container.

The importance of naming containers doesn't end here. Imagine you have two instances of the composite controls named *Control1* and *Control2*, respectively. Imagine also that the embedded button is named *Trigger*. The full name of the two child buttons will be *Control1$Trigger* and *Control2$Trigger*. Suppose you click on the first button and cause the page to post back. If the name of the posting control contains the $ symbol, the ASP.NET runtime recognizes a known pattern: tokenize the name and locate the postback control correctly, no matter its depth in the page tree.

On the other hand, if the button is contained in a control not marked to be a naming container, the ID of the clicked button is not prefixed and will simply be, say, *Trigger*. In this case, the ASP.NET runtime will look for it as a direct child of the form. The search will obviously fail—the button is a child of a top-level control—and the postback event will pass unnoticed.

> **Note**   ASP.NET 2.0 uses the dollar ($) symbol to separate the various parts to form the ID of a control rooted in a naming container. In ASP.NET 1.x, the colon symbol (:) is used for the same purpose.

Binding Containers

In ASP.NET 2.0, a new kind of container is introduced—the binding container. The binding container—the *BindingContainer* property—indicates which control in the page hierarchy represents the parent of a control as far as data binding is concerned. In other words, the binding container is the control that receives bound data from the host (typically, the page) and that passes it down to child controls.

As you can easily imagine, binding and naming containers often coincide. The only exception is when the control is part of a template. In that case, the *NamingContainer* property is generally set to the physical parent of the control, namely a control in the template. *BindingContainer*, instead, will point to the control that defines the template.

Visibility of a Server Control

If you set *Visible* to *false*, ASP.NET doesn't generate any markup code for the control. However, having *Visible* set to *false* doesn't really mean that no path in the control's code can output text. The control is still an active object that exposes methods and handles events. If a method, or an event handler, sends text directly to the output console through *Response.Write*, then this text will be displayed to the user anyway. A control with the *Visible* attribute set to *false* is still part of the page and maintains its position in the control tree.

Methods of the *Control* Class

The methods of the *Control* class are listed and described in Table 4-3.

Table 4-3   Methods of a Server Control

Method	Description
ApplyStyleSheetSkin	Applies the properties defined in the page style sheet to the control. The skin properties used depend on the *SkinID* property. *Not available in ASP.NET 1.x.*
DataBind	Fires the *OnDataBinding* event and then invokes the *DataBind* method on all child controls.
Dispose	Gives the control a chance to perform clean-up tasks before it gets released from memory.
Focus	Sets the input focus to the control. *Not available in ASP.NET 1.x.*
FindControl	Looks for the specified control in the collection of child controls. Child controls not in the *Controls* collection of the current controls—that is, not direct children—are not retrieved.
HasControls	Indicates whether the control contains any child controls.
RenderControl	Generates the HTML output for the control.
ResolveClientUrl	Use the method to return a URL suitable for use by the client to access resources on the Web server, such as image files, links to additional pages, and so on. Can return a relative path. The method is sealed and can't be overridden in derived classes.
ResolveUrl	Resolves a relative URL to an absolute URL based on the value passed to the *TemplateSourceDirectory* property.
SetRenderMethod-Delegate	Internal-use method; assigns a delegate to render the control and its content into the parent control.

Each control can have child controls. All children are stored in the *Controls* collection, an object of type *ControlCollection*. This collection class has a few peculiarities. In particular, it post-processes controls that are added to, and removed from, the collection. When a control is added, its view state is restored if needed and view-state tracking is turned on. When a control is removed, the *Unload* event is fired.

Events of the *Control* Class

The *Control* class also defines a set of base events supported by all server controls in the .NET Framework. Table 4-4 lists these events.

Table 4-4 **Events of a Server Control**

Event	Description
DataBinding	Occurs when the *DataBind* method is called on a control and the control is binding to a data source.
Disposed	Occurs when a control is released from memory—the last stage in the control life cycle.
Init	Occurs when the control is initialized—the first step in the life cycle.
Load	Occurs when the control is loaded into the page. Occurs after *Init*.
PreRender	Occurs when the control is about to render its content.
Unload	Occurs when the control is unloaded from memory.

All server controls are rendered to HTML using the *RenderControl* method and, when this happens, the *PreRender* event is fired.

New Features

In the transition from ASP.NET 1.x to ASP.NET 2.0, server controls gained some new features that are more architectural than programming-related. These new features are the offspring of significant changes that occurred in the underpinnings of the controls.

Adaptive Rendering

Adaptive rendering is the process that enables controls to generate different markup for individual browsers. This result is obtained by delegating the generation of the markup to an external component—the adapter. When each control is about to render, it figures out its current adapter and hands the request over to that adapter.

The selected adapter depends on the current browser. The adapter for a control is resolved by looking at the browser capabilities as configured in the ASP.NET browser database. If the browser record includes an adapter class for that control, the class is instantiated and used. Otherwise, the adapter for the control is an instance of the *ControlAdapter* class. The *Control-Adapter* class is a generic adapter and simply generates the markup for a control by calling the rendering methods on the control itself.

> **Note** The ASP.NET database storing browser information is not a real database. It is, instead, a list of text files with a *.browser* extension located under the ASP.NET installation folder on the Web server. The exact path is the following: %WINDOWS%\Microsoft.NET\Framework\ [version]\CONFIG\Browsers
>
> The data located in this folder is used to return browser capabilities.

A control holds a reference to the mapped adapter instance through the *Adapter* (protected) property. Each control has an associated adapter unless it is a composite control that defers to its children for rendering.

Browser-Sensitive Rendering

In ASP.NET 2.0, you can declaratively assign a browser-specific value to all control properties. Here's a quick example:

```
<asp:Button ID="Button1" runat="server" Text="I'm a Button"
    ie:Text="IE Button"
    mozilla:Text="FireFox Button" />
```

The *Text* property of the button will contain "IE button" if the page is viewed through Microsoft Internet Explorer and "FireFox button" if the page goes through Firefox. If another browser is used, the value of the unprefixed *Text* attribute is used. All properties that you can insert in a tag declaration can be flagged with a browser ID. Each supported browser has a unique ID. As in preceding code, *ie* is for Internet Explorer and *mozilla* is for Firefox. Unique IDs also exist for various versions of Netscape browsers and mobile devices.

Browser-specific filtering is also supported for master pages. We'll return to this feature in Chapter 6 and present a table with the most common browser IDs. However, browser IDs are interspersed in *.browser* files, which you can find at the following path:

```
%windows%\Microsoft.NET\Framework\[version]\CONFIG\Browsers
```

XHTML Compliance

XHTML is a World Wide Web Consortium (W3C) standard that defines Web pages as XML documents. This approach guarantees that the elements in the pages are well formed and more forward-compatible with browsers in the near future. By default, the markup produced by ASP.NET 2.0 controls conforms to the XHTML standard with very few exceptions. This compliance with standards produces a number of observable changes in the final markup served to browsers. For example, each element either includes an explicit closing tag or is self-closing (with />) and is always enclosed in a container element. For example, the view state hidden field is now surrounded by a *<div>* tag, and the *name* attribute has been removed from the *<form>* element:

```
<form method="post" action="default.aspx" id="MainForm">
<div>
    <input type="hidden" name="__VIEWSTATE" id="__VIEWSTATE" value="…" />
</div>
    ...
</form>
```

In addition, any script tags rendered into the page include an appropriate *type* attribute and are rendered in *CDATA* elements.

It's clear that some of these changes might break existing pages. What if you have a page that relies on the *name* attribute on the form? To smooth the migration of ASP.NET 1.x pages, you can add the following setting to the *web.config* file, which forces ASP.NET to render controls as in ASP.NET 1.x:

```
<system.web>
    <XHTML11Conformance enableObsoleteRendering="true" />
</system.web>
```

The option to disable XHTML rendering is provided primarily to assist you in upgrading existing pages. You should not abuse it, as it might not be supported in future versions of ASP.NET. Moreover, you should be migrating to XHTML anyway; ASP.NET 2.0 just gives you one more reason to do it now, if possible.

> **Note** The generation of XHTML-compliant output is guaranteed only for the vast majority of core ASP.NET server controls. Controls such as *HyperLink*, *BulletedList*, and *AdRotator* generate non-XHTML-compliant markup regardless of the settings you choose. *GridView* and *TreeView* controls are also at risk if they incorporate *HyperLinkColumn* and *TreeNode* components. You should avoid using these controls in pages where XHTML compliance is a strict requirement. If you make use of third-party controls, you should always check with the vendor to see whether they generate XHTML markup. Finally, note that ASP.NET is unable to fix XHTML errors that occur in the literal parts of the pages. If your page contains static text or HTML elements, the responsibility of ensuring that they are XHTML-compliant is entirely yours.

How can you make sure that a given page, or a given custom control, renders XHTML markup? You must use a service that runs the page and checks its output. For example, you can use the W3C Markup Validation Service at *http://validator.w3.org*. You can use the validator in two ways: by entering the URL of your page and having it request and check the page, or by uploading the page to the validator's site.

Themeable Controls

In the ASP.NET 2.0 jargon, a *theme* is a named collection of property settings that can be applied to controls to make them look consistent across pages. You can apply theme settings to an entire Web site, to a page and its controls, or to an individual control. A theme is identified by name and consists of cascading style sheet (CSS) files, images, and control skins. A *control skin* is a text file that contains predefined values for some control properties. Applied together, these settings contribute to change the look and feel of the control and give the whole site a consistent (and, you hope, appealing) user interface. In addition, because themes are a sort of monolithic attribute, you can easily export that look from one application to the next. With themes enabled, if the developer adds, say, a *DataGrid* control to a page, the control is rendered with the default appearance defined in the currently selected theme.

Server controls can dynamically accept or deny theming through a Boolean property named *EnableTheming*, set to *true* by default. As a general rule, themes affect only properties that relate to the control's appearance. Properties that explicitly specify a behavior or imply an action should not be made themeable. Each control has the power to state which properties are themeable and which are not. This happens at compile time through attributes—in particular, the *Themeable* attribute. We'll return to themes in Chapter 6. We'll cover custom control development in *Programming Microsoft ASP.NET 2.0 Applications: Advanced Topics*.

Control State

Some ASP.NET controls require that some state be kept across requests. Examples of this type of state information include the current page of a paged control and the current sort order of a sortable data control. In ASP.NET 1.x, there is only one container in which this data can be stored—the view state. However, the view state is mainly designed to maintain settings set by the application, and more important, it can be turned off. What would happen to control-specific state in this case? For this reason, ASP.NET 2.0 introduces the notion of the control state and keeps it separate from the view state to make clear that control state is a vital piece of the control infrastructure.

Control state is a collection of critical view-state data that controls need to function. Because of its critical role, control state data is contained in separate member variables from normal view state and is not affected when view state is disabled. Unlike view state, control state requires extra implementation steps to use.

For one thing, each control needs to signal to the page that it requires control state. Next, there's no unique container to store data, such as *ViewState*; but the data can be retrieved from any object you want—arrays, collections, or a slew of instance variables. Each control persists and loads its control state using a pair of overridable methods, as shown here:

```
protected override object SaveControlState()
protected override void LoadControlState(object state)
```

Control state works similarly to view state and is saved and loaded at the same stage of the pipeline that view state is processed. Ultimately, control state is persisted in the same hidden field as the view state.

Input Focus

A useful feature that ASP.NET 1.x lacks is the ability to quickly assign the input focus to a particular control when the page is displayed. This feature can be coded in not much time by a seasoned developer and can be easily engineered into a company-wide framework for building controls and pages.

As we saw in Chapter 3, the *Page* class of ASP.NET 2.0 provides the *SetFocus* method to assign the input focus to any control you want. The following code shows how to set the focus to a *TextBox* control named *txtLastName*:

```
void Page_Load(object sender, EventArgs e)
{
    if (!IsPostBack)
        SetFocus("txtLastName");
}
```

The *SetFocus* method caches the ID of the control and forces the *Page* class to generate ad hoc script code when the page is rendered. Each control can also reclaim the input focus for itself by calling its new *Focus* method. All controls in the ASP.NET 2.0 Framework benefit from this feature.

HTML Controls

At first sight, HTML server controls look like HTML tags except for the extra *runat=server* attribute. While it's true that they look the same, the additional *runat* attribute makes a huge difference. As mentioned, in ASP.NET by simply adding the *runat* attribute, you can bring to life otherwise dead HTML text. Once transformed into a living instance of a server-side component, the original tag can be configured programmatically using an object-oriented approach. By design, HTML controls expose a set of methods and properties that carefully reflect the HTML syntax. For example, to set the default text of an input form field, you use a property named *Value* instead of the more expressive *Text*. The name of the server control is determined by the value of the *ID* attribute. The following code snippet shows how to define a server-side input tag named *lastName*:

```
<input runat="server" id="lastName" type="text" />
```

The tag declaration does not include an explicit and static value for the *Value* attribute, which can be configured programmatically as follows:

```
void Page_Load(object sender, EventArgs e)
{
    lastName.Value = "Esposito";
}
```

After being processed by the ASP.NET runtime, the preceding declaration generates the following HTML code:

```
<input name="myName" id="myName" type="text" value="Esposito" />
```

Notice that a server-side *ID* attribute expands to a pair of HTML attributes—*Name* and *ID*. Be aware that this happens for browser compatibility. In no way does this mean that on the server *Name* and *ID* can be used interchangeably to name the server instance of the control. The name of the server control instance is given by *ID*. If you specify both *Name* and *ID* on a server-side tag, the value assigned to *Name* will be silently overridden.

Generalities of HTML Controls

The .NET Framework provides predefined server controls for commonly used HTML elements such as *<form>*, *<input>*, and *<select>*, as well as for tables, images, and hyperlinks. All the predefined HTML server controls inherit from the same base class—the *HtmlControl* class. In addition, each control then provides its own set of specific properties and its own events.

Controls typically supply properties that allow you to manipulate the HTML attributes programmatically from within server code. HTML controls integrate well with data binding and the ASP.NET state maintenance, and they also provide full support for postback events and client scripting. For example, for a button that gets clicked, you can have some JavaScript code running on the client responding to the *onclick* event, as well as some code that handles the event on the server if the page posts back as the result of that event.

HTML controls are defined in the *System.Web.UI.HtmlControls* namespace. Most, but not all, HTML tags have a direct class counterpart in the .NET Framework. HTML elements that don't map to a made-to-measure class are rendered through the *HtmlGenericControl* class and have attributes set using generic collections rather than direct properties. Generic controls include *<iframe>*, *<hr>*, *<font>*, and *<body>*. In general, you should bear in mind that every element that can appear in an HTML page can be marked as *runat="server"* and programmed and styled on the server.

The *HtmlControl* Base Class

The *HtmlControl* class inherits from *Control* and defines the methods, properties, and events common to all HTML controls. Actually, many properties and all methods and events are simply inherited from the base class. Table 4-5 shows the list of properties specific to HTML controls.

Table 4-5   Specific Properties of an HTML Control

Property	Description
Attributes	Gets a collection object representing all the attributes set on the control with the corresponding value
Disabled	Gets or sets a Boolean value, which indicates whether the HTML control is disabled
Style	Gets a collection object representing all CSS properties applied to the control
TagName	Gets the name of the HTML tag behind the control

A disabled HTML server control is visible and always gets generated as HTML code. If the *Disabled* property is set to *true*, the *disabled* HTML attribute is inserted in the HTML output for the control. As mentioned earlier, if the *Visible* property is set to *false*, HTML is not generated for the control.

Working with HTML Attributes

Each HTML control features more properties than those listed in Table 4-5. Properties of HTML server controls map to HTML attributes, and the values assigned to the properties are replicated in the HTML output. For controls that don't have an HTML direct counterpart, the *Attributes* collection is used to set attributes on the resulting HTML tag. This collection can also be used to set properties not mapped by the control's interface and, if needed, to define custom HTML attributes. Any content of the *Attributes* collection is managed as a string.

Given the following HTML code snippet, let's see how to programmatically set some attributes on the *<body>* tag:

```
<script>
function Init() {
    alert("Hello");
}
</script>

<script runat=server language="C#">
void Page_Load(object sender, EventArgs e) {
    theBody.Attributes["onload"] = "Init()";
}
</script>

<html>
<body runat="server" id="theBody">
</body>
</html>
```

You bind a JavaScript script to the *onload* attribute of the *<body>* tag. The resulting HTML code that the browser displays is as follows:

```
<script>
function Init() {
    alert("Hello");
}
</script>

<html>
<body id="theBody" onload="Init()">
</body>
</html>
```

The *Attributes* property is rendered through a special type of class named *Attribute-Collection*. In spite of the name, the content of the class is not directly enumerable using the *for...each* statement because the *IEnumerable* interface is not supported. The *AttributeCollection* class provides ad hoc methods to render attributes of a text writer object and to add and remove elements. Interestingly, if you add an attribute named *Style*, the class is smart enough to reroute the assigned content to the *Style* collection.

Hierarchy of HTML Controls

Most HTML controls can be grouped into two main categories—container and input controls. A few controls, though, cannot be easily catalogued in either of the two groups. They are *HtmlImage*, *HtmlLink*, *HtmlMeta*, and *HtmlTitle*, and they are the ASP.NET counterpart of the *<img>*, *<link>*, *<meta>*, and *<title>* tags. Figure 4-1 shows the tree of HTML controls.

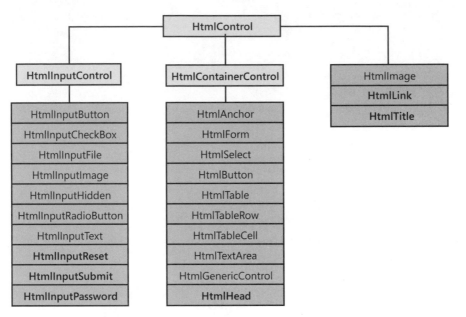

Figure 4-1   A diagram that groups all HTML controls by looking at their base class. Controls in boldface type require ASP.NET 2.0.

The input controls category includes all possible variations of the *<input>* tag, from submit buttons to check boxes and from text fields to radio buttons. The container controls category lists anchors, tables, forms, and, in general, all HTML tags that might contain child elements.

HTML Container Controls

The base class for container controls is the *HtmlContainerControl* class, which descends directly from *HtmlControl*. The HTML elements addressed by this tag are elements that must have a closing tag—that is, forms, selection boxes, and tables, as well as anchors and text areas. Compared to the *HtmlControl* class, a container control features a couple of additional string properties—*InnerHtml* and *InnerText*.

Both properties manipulate the reading and writing of literal content found between the opening and closing tags of the element. Note that you cannot get the inner content of a control if the content includes server controls. *InnerHtml* and *InnerText* work only in the presence of all literal content. The tag itself is not considered for the output. Unlike *InnerText*, though, *InnerHtml* lets you work with HTML rich text and doesn't automatically encode and decode text. In other words, *InnerText* retrieves and sets the content of the tag as plain text, whereas *InnerHtml* retrieves and sets the same content but in HTML format.

Table 4-6 lists the HTML container controls defined in ASP.NET.

Table 4-6   HTML Container Controls

Class	Description
HtmlAnchor	Represents an HTML anchor—specifically, the *<a>* tag.
HtmlButton	Represents the HTML *<button>* tag. The *<button>* element is defined in the HTML 4.0 specification and supported only in Internet Explorer version 4.0 and later.
HtmlForm	Represents the *<form>* tag, but can be used only as a container of interactive server controls on a Web page. Cannot really be used to create HTML forms programmable on the server.
HtmlGenericControl	Represents an HTML tag for which the .NET Framework does not provide a direct class. Sample tags include *<font>*, *<hr>*, and *<iframe>*. You program these controls by using the *Attributes* collection and set attributes indirectly.
HtmlHead	Represents the *<head>* tag, and allows you to control meta tags, the style sheet, and the page title programmatically. *Not available in ASP.NET 1.x.*
HtmlSelect	Represents the *<select>* tag—that is, an HTML selection box.
HtmlTable	Represents an HTML table—specifically, the *<table>* tag.
HtmlTableCell	Represents the *<td>* HTML tag—that is, a cell in a table.
HtmlTableRow	Represents the *<tr>* HTML tag—that is, a row in a table.
HtmlTextArea	Represents a multiline text box, and maps the *<textarea>* HTML tag.

Note that the *HtmlButton* control is different than *HtmlInputButton*, which represents the button variation of the *<input>* tag. The *HtmlButton* control represents the HTML 4.0–specific *<button>* tag. We'll say more about buttons in the next section while discussing the Web controls.

Server-side forms play a key role in the economy of ASP.NET applications, as they are the means for implementing postbacks and guaranteeing state maintenance. For this reason, the *HtmlForm* control is not simply a form element you can program on the server. In particular, the *HtmlForm* hides the *Action* property and cannot be used to post content to a page different than the content that generated the HTML for the browser. We will cover HTML forms in great detail in Chapter 5.

Managing Header Information

An instance of the *HtmlHead* control is automatically created if the page contains a *<head>* tag marked with the attribute *runat=server*. Note that this setting is the default when you add a new page to a Visual Studio .NET 2005 Web project, as shown in the following snippet:

```
<head runat="server">
    <title>Untitled Page</title>
</head>
```

The header of the page is returned through the new *Header* property of the *Page* class. The property returns *null* if the *<head>* tag is missing or if it is present but lacks the *runat* attribute.

The *HtmlHead* control implements the *IPageHeader* interface, which consists of three collection properties—*Metadata*, *LinkedStylesheet*, and *Stylesheet*—and a string property—*Title*. The

Metadata property is a dictionary that collects all the desired child *<meta>* tags of the header:

```
Header.Metadata.Add("CODE-LANGUAGE", "C#");
```

The code results in the following markup:

```
<meta name="CODE-LANGUAGE" content="C#" />
```

To express other common metadata such as *Http-Equiv*, you can resort to the newest *Html-Meta* control, as shown here:

```
void Page_Init(object sender, EventArgs e)
{
   HtmlMeta meta = new HtmlMeta();
   meta.HttpEquiv = "refresh";
   meta.Content = Int32.Parse(Content.Text).ToString();
   ((Control)Header).Controls.Add(meta);
}
```

The preceding code creates a *<meta>* tag dynamically and adds it to the *<head>* section of the page during the initialization phase. You can also manipulate an existing *<meta>* programmatically, as long as it is flagged with the *runat* attribute.

> **Tip** In Internet Explorer only, the *<meta>* tag can be used to smooth the transition from one page to the next, and also when you move back to a previously visited page. When navigating from page to page in the browser, the current page usually disappears all of a sudden and the new page shows up in its place. By using the following two meta tags, you can make them fade away smoothly:
>
> ```
> <meta http-equiv="Page-Enter"
>       content="progid:DXImageTransform.Microsoft.Fade(duration=.5)" />
> <meta http-equiv="Page-Exit"
>       content="progid:DXImageTransform.Microsoft.Fade(duration=.5)" />
> ```
>
> Needless to say, the tags can be created and managed programmatically in ASP.NET 2.0.

> **Note** To add a *<meta>* tag programmatically in ASP.NET 1.x, you must resort to a trick. You create the string as a literal control and add it to the *Controls* collection of the header:
>
> ```
> string meta = "<meta http-equiv='refresh' content='3' />";
> LiteralControl equiv = new LiteralControl(meta);
> Header.Controls(equiv);
> ```
>
> Header indicates the server-side *<head>* tag you're modifying.

To link a style sheet file, you use the following code:

```
Header.LinkedStyleSheets.Add("MyStyles.css");
```

Alternately, you can resort to the *HtmlLink* control. The *HtmlLink* control represents the *<link>* element. Unlike *<a>*, the *<link>* tag can appear only in the *<head>* section of a document, although it might appear any number of times.

Finally, the *HtmlHead* control features the *Title* property, through which you can retrieve and set the title of the page:

```
Header.Title = "This is the title";
```

Note that this property returns the correct page title only if the *<title>* tag is correctly placed within the *<head>* tag. Some browsers, in fact, are quite forgiving on this point and allow developers to define the title outside the header. To manipulate the *<title>* tag independently from the header, use the *HtmlTitle* control and mark the *<title>* tag with the *runat* attribute.

> **Note**   In ASP.NET 2.0, the list of HTML elements that enjoy a made-to-measure HTML control grows to include *<head>*, *<title>*, *<link>*, and *<meta>*. In addition, some special configurations of the *<input>* tag have a corresponding HTML control. These corresponding HTML controls are submit buttons, reset buttons, and password fields.

Navigating to a URL

The *HtmlAnchor* class is the programmatic way of accessing and configuring the *<a>* tag. With respect to the other container controls, the *HtmlAnchor* class provides a few extra properties such as *HRef*, *Name*, *Target*, and *Title*. The *HRef* property sets the target of the hyperlink and can be used to navigate to the specified location. The *Name* property names a section in the ASP.NET page that can be reached from anywhere on the same page through #-prefixed *HRefs*. The following code demonstrates a bookmarked anchor named *MoreInfo*:

```
<a name="MoreInfo" />
```

This anchor can be reached using the following hyperlink:

```
<a href="#MoreInfo">Get More Info</a>
```

The *Target* property identifies the target window or the frame where the linked URL will be loaded. Common values for *Target* are *_self*, *_top*, *_blank*, and *_parent*, as well as any other name that refers to a page-specific frame. Although the feature is mostly browser-dependent, you should always consider these special names as lowercase. Finally, the *Title* property contains the text that virtually all browsers display as a ToolTip when the mouse hovers over the anchor's area.

Handling Events on the Server

In addition to being used for navigating to a different page, the anchor control—as well as the *HtmlButton* control—can be used to post back the page. Key to this behavior is the *ServerClick* event, which lets you define the name of the method that will handle, on the server, the event generated when the user clicks the control. The following code demonstrates an anchor in which the click event is handled on both the client and server:

```
<a runat=server onclick="Run()" onserverclick="DoSomething">Click</a>
```

The *onclick* attribute defines the client-side event handler written using JavaScript; the *onserverclick* attribute refers to the server-side code that will run after the page posts back. Of course, if both event handlers are specified, the client-side handler executes first before the post back occurs.

The *HtmlSelect* Control

The *HtmlSelect* control represents a list of options from which you choose one or more. You control the appearance and behavior of the control by setting the *Size* and *Multiple* properties. The *Size* property specifies the number of rows to be displayed by the control, whereas the *Multiple* property indicates whether more than one item can be selected in the control. Internal items are grouped in the *Items* collection, and each element is represented by a *ListItem* object. Interestingly, the *ListItem* class is not defined in the *HtmlControls* namespace but lives instead in the *WebControls* namespace. To specify the text for each selectable item, you can either set the *Text* property of the *ListItem* or simply define a series of *<option>* tags within the opening and closing tags of the *<select>* element.

By default, the *HtmlSelect* control shows up as a drop-down list. However, if multiple selections are allowed or the height is set to more than one row, the control is displayed as a list box. The index of the selected item in a single-selection control is returned through the *SelectedIndex* property. If the multiple selection is enabled, you just loop through the *Items* collection and check the *Selected* property on individual list items.

The *HtmlSelect* control supports data binding through additional properties. The *DataSource* property lets you set the data source, which can be any .NET object that implements the *IEnumerable* interface. If the data source contains multiple bindable tables (for example, a *DataSet* object), by using the *DataMember* property you can choose a particular one. Finally, the *DataTextField* and *DataValueField* properties are used to bind the list item's *Text* and *Value* properties to columns in the data source. (We'll cover data binding in Chapter 9.)

HTML Tables

In ASP.NET, HTML tables provide a minimum set of functions when rendered using the *HtmlTable* control. In most cases, you don't need to use server-side tables because you typically rely on richer list and grid controls to do the job of displaying tables or records. So you resort to tables when you need to define a fixed layout for graphical elements of the page, but this is not a feature that requires a server-side table.

Server-side tables are not as powerful as pure HTML tables—which are created by using the *<table>* tag. The main limitation is that the *HtmlTable* class does not support HTML elements such as *<caption>*, *<col>*, *<colgroup>*, *<tbody>*, *<thead>*, and *<tfoot>*. If you use these elements in your ASP.NET code, no run-time exception or compile error is ever thrown. Nevertheless, those elements are silently removed from the HTML code being generated. For example, let's consider the following code:

```
<table runat="server">
    <thead><th>Name</th><th>Last Name</th></thead>
    <tr><td>Joe</td><td>Users</td></tr>
    <tr><td>Bob</td><td>Whosthisguy</td></tr>
</table>
```

As you can see in the following code, the HTML output that is generated by the preceding example does not include the *<thead>* element:

```
<table>
    <tr><td>Joe</td><td>Users</td></tr>
    <tr><td>Bob</td><td>Whosthisguy</td></tr>
</table>
```

By design, an *HtmlTable* control can have only children of the *HtmlTableRow* class. Any attempt to programmatically add other table elements, such as a *<thead>* or a *<tfoot>*, will generate an exception.

The behavior of *HtmlTable* doesn't change in ASP.NET 2.0. However, the newer version of ASP.NET provides a richer server-side support for tables through the *Table* control—the *Html-Table* counterpart in the *WebControls* namespace. In particular, you can associate each *Table-Row* object with a particular section, be it header, body, or footer. When the *Table* control renders out to HTML, it checks the section of each row and inserts <tbody>, <thead>, and <tfoot> as appropriate.

The *HtmlTextArea* Control

The *HtmlTextArea* control corresponds to the *<textarea>* HTML element and allows you to programmatically create and configure a multiline text box. The *HtmlTextArea* class provides the *Rows* and *Cols* properties to control the number of rows and columns of the text box. The *Value* property can be used to assign some text to display in the control area.

The *HtmlTextArea* class also provides a *ServerChange* event that fires during a postback and allows you to validate on the server the data contained in the control. Note that the *Html-TextArea* control does not fire the event itself and does not directly cause the page to post back. Rather, when the page posts back in response to a click on a link or submit button, the *HtmlTextArea* control intervenes in the server-side chain of events and gives the programmer a chance to run some code if the internal content of the control is changed between two successive postbacks.

All ASP.NET controls that, like *HtmlTextArea*, implement the *IPostBackDataHandler* interface can invoke user-defined code when the control's internal state changes. As discussed in Chapter 3, controls can fire custom events by overriding the *RaisePostDataChangedEvent* method on the aforementioned interface. The following pseudocode shows what happens in the method's implementation of *HtmlTextArea*:

```
void System.Web.UI.IPostBackDataHandler.RaisePostDataChangedEvent() {
    this.OnServerChange(EventArgs.Empty);
}
```

Finally, note that the control raises the event only if the state has changed between two successive posts. To determine whether that has happened, the control needs to track the content it had the time before. This value can be stored only in the view state. Of course, the *Server-Change* event won't fire if you disable the view state for the host page or the control.

HTML Input Controls

In HTML, the *<input>* element has several variations and can be used to provide a submit button as well as a check box or text box. In ASP.NET, each possible instance of the *<input>* element is mapped to a specific class. All input classes derive from the *HtmlInputControl* class. *HtmlInputControl* is the abstract class that defines the common programming interface for all input controls. The class inherits from *HtmlControl* and simply adds three custom properties—*Name*, *Type*, and *Value*—to the inherited interface.

The *Name* property returns the name assigned to the control. In ASP.NET, this property is peculiar because, although it's marked as read/write, it actually works as a read-only property. The *get* accessor returns the control's *UniqueID* property, while the *set* accessor is just void. As a result, whatever value you assign to the property, either programmatically or declaratively, is just ignored and no exception or compile error is ever thrown.

The *Type* property mirrors the *type* attribute of the HTML input elements. The property is read-only. Finally, the *Value* property is read/write and represents the content of the input field.

Table 4-7 lists the HTML input controls defined in ASP.NET.

Table 4-7   HTML Input Controls

Class	Description
HtmlInputButton	Represents the various flavors of a command button supported by HTML. Feasible values for the *Type* attribute are *button*, *submit*, and *reset*.
HtmlInputCheckBox	Represents an HTML check box—that is, the *<input>* tag with a type equal to *checkbox*.
HtmlInputFile	Represents the file uploader—that is, the *<input>* tag with a type equal to *file*.

Table 4-7   **HTML Input Controls**

Class	Description
HtmlInputHidden	Represents a hidden buffer of text data—that is, the *<input>* tag with a type equal to *hidden*.
HtmlInputImage	Represents a graphic button—that is, the *<input>* tag with a type equal to *image*. Note that this tag is supported by all browsers.
HtmlInputPassword	Represents a protected text field—that is, the *<input>* tag with a type of *password*. *Not available in ASP.NET 1.x.*
HtmlInputRadioButton	Represents a radio button—that is, the *<input>* tag with a type equal to *radio*.
HtmlInputReset	Represents a reset command button. *Not available in ASP.NET 1.x.*
HtmlInputSubmit	Represents a reset command button. *Not available in ASP.NET 1.x.*
HtmlInputText	Represents a text field—that is, the *<input>* tag with a type of either *password* or *text*.

The hidden and text input controls are nearly identical, and the contents of both are posted back. Essentially, they differ only in that hidden fields are not displayed and, subsequently, they don't provide some UI-related properties such as *MaxLength* and *Size*.

Command Buttons

The *HtmlInputButton* class is the most flexible button class in the .NET Framework. It differs from the *HtmlButton* class in that it renders through the *<input>* tag rather than the Internet Explorer–specific *<button>* tag. This fact ensures much wider support for the control from browsers.

The HTML input button controls support the *ServerClick* event, which allows you to set the code to run on the server after the button is clicked. Note that if you set the button type to *Button* and the *ServerClick* event handler is specified, the control automatically adds the postback script code to the *onclick* HTML attribute. In this way, any click causes the page to post back and the code to execute. Let's consider the following ASP.NET code:

```
<input runat="server" type="button" id="btn" value="Click"
    onserverclick="buttonClicked" />
```

The corresponding HTML code is as follows:

```
<input language="javascript" onclick="__doPostBack('btn','')" name="btn"
    type="button" value="Click" />
```

The client-side *__doPostBack* script function is the standard piece of code generated by ASP.NET to implement the postback. If the button type is set to *Submit*—that is, a value that would always cause a postback—no client-side script code is generated and the *onclick* attribute is not set.

In ASP.NET 2.0, more specific controls have been added to render submit and reset buttons: *HtmlInputSubmit* and *HtmlInputReset*.

> **Note**   The *HtmlInputImage* control supports a nearly identical pattern for handling server-side events and validation. The *HtmlInputImage* control features a few more properties specific to the image it shows. In particular, you can set the alternate text for the image, the border, and the alignment with respect to the rest of the page. The *ServerClick* event handler has a slightly different form and looks like the following:
>
> ```
> void ImageClickEventHandler(object sender, ImageClickEventArgs e);
> ```
>
> When an image button is clicked, the coordinates of the click are determined by using the *X* and *Y* properties of the *ImageClickEventArgs* data structure.

Controlling Validation

The *HtmlInputButton* class, as well as the *HtmlButton* class, support a Boolean property named *CausesValidation*. The property indicates whether the content of the input fields should be validated when the button is clicked. By default, the property is set to *true*, meaning the validation always takes place. We'll examine data validation later in the chapter. For now, suffice it to say that you can programmatically enable or disable the validation step by using the *CausesValidation* property.

Typically, you might want to disable validation if the button that has been clicked doesn't perform a concrete operation but simply clears the user interface or cancels an ongoing operation. By design, in fact, server-side page validation takes place just before the *ServerClick* event handler is executed. Setting the *CausesValidation* property to *false* is the only means you have to prevent an unnecessary validation.

Detecting State Changes of Controls

Earlier in this chapter, while discussing the features of the *HtmlTextArea* control, we ran into the *ServerChange* event and described it as the mechanism to detect and validate changes in the control's state between two successive postbacks. The *ServerChange* event is not an exclusive feature of the *HtmlTextArea* control but is also supported by other input controls such as *HtmlInputCheckBox*, *HtmlInputRadioButton*, *HtmlInputHidden*, and *HtmlInputText*. Let's look at an example in which we use the *ServerChange* event to detect which elements have been checked since last time the control was processed on the server.

We build a page with a list of check boxes and a button to let the user post back to the server when finished. Notice, in fact, that neither the *HtmlInputCheckBox* control nor any other input control except buttons posts back to the server when clicked. For this reason, you must provide another control on the Web page that supports posting to the server—for example, an *HtmlButton* or an *HtmlInputButton* control. The following code implements the page shown in Figure 4-2:

```
<%@ Page Language="C#" %>
<html>
<script runat="server">
```

```
public void DetectChange(object sender, EventArgs e) {
    HtmlInputCheckBox cb = (HtmlInputCheckBox) sender;
    Response.Write("Control <b>" + cb.UniqueID + "</b> changed<br>");
}
</script>

<body>
<form runat="server">
    <input runat="server" type="checkbox" id="one"
        OnServerChange="DetectChange">One<br>
    <input runat="server" type="checkbox" id="two"
        OnServerChange="DetectChange">Two<br>
    <input runat="server" type="checkbox" id="three"
        OnServerChange="DetectChange">Three<br>
    <input runat="server" type="submit" value="Submit" />
</form>
</body>
</html>
```

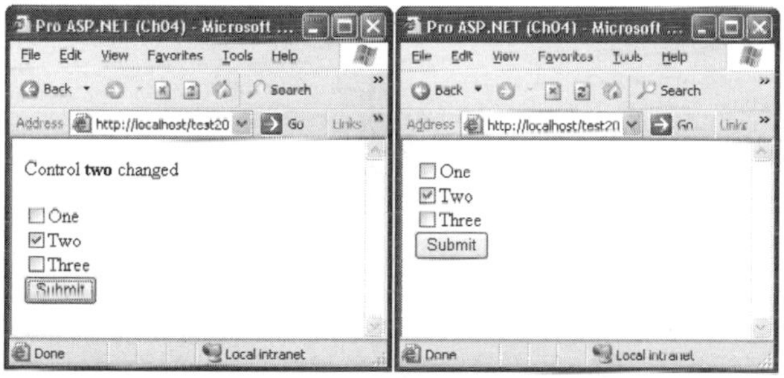

Figure 4-2 The *ServerChange* event fires only if the status of the control has changed since the last time the control was processed on the server.

The *ServerChange* event is fired only if the state of the control results changed after two post-backs. To get the first screen shot, you check the element and then submit. Next, if you submit again without checking or unchecking anything, you get the second screen shot.

As mentioned in Chapter 3, by implementing the *IPostBackDataHandler* interface, each server control gets a chance to update its current state with data posted by the client. I cover this interface in detail in *Programming Microsoft ASP.NET 2.0 Applications: Advanced Topics*.

Uploading Files

The *HtmlInputFile* control is the HTML tool for uploading files from a browser to the Web server. Note that file upload requires Internet Explorer version 3.0 or newer. To take advantage of the *HtmlInputFile* control, you should first ensure that the server form's *Enctype* property is set to *multipart/form-data*. Note, though, that in ASP.NET 2.0, the proper *EncType* is automatically set, care of the *HtmlInputFile* control, before the control's markup is rendered:

```
<form runat="server" enctype="multipart/form-data">
    <input runat="server" type="file" id="upLoader" >
    <input runat="server" type="submit" value="Upload..." />
</form>
```

The way in which the *HtmlInputFile* control is rendered to HTML is browser-specific, but it normally consists of a text box and a Browse button. The user selects a file from the local machine and then clicks the button to submit the page to the server. When this occurs, the browser uploads the selected file to the server, as shown in Figure 4-3.

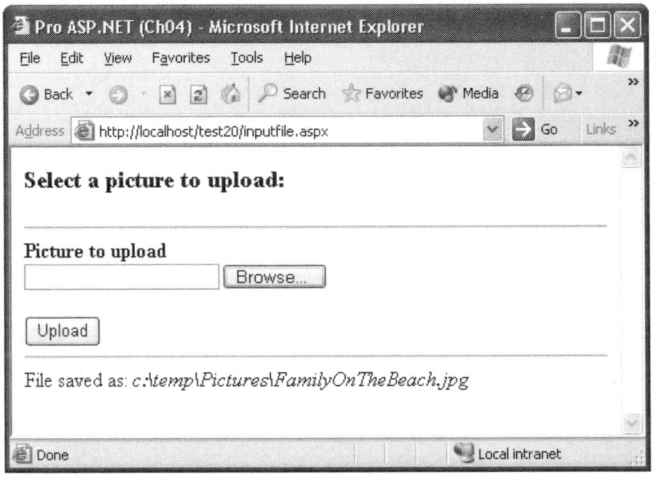

Figure 4-3 A new file has been uploaded to the Web server and copied to the destination folder.

> **Note** Prior to ASP.NET, a server-side process—the posting acceptor—was required to run in the background to handle multipart/form-data submissions. In ASP.NET the role of the posting acceptor is no longer necessary, as it is carried out by the ASP.NET runtime itself.

On the server, the file is parked in an object of type *HttpPostedFile* and stays there until explicitly processed—for example, saved to disk or to a database. The *HttpPostedFile* object provides properties and methods to get information on an individual file and to read and save the file. The following code shows how to save a posted file to a particular folder to disk:

```
<%@ Page language="C#" %>
<%@ Import Namespace="System.IO" %>

<script runat="server">
    void UploadButton_Click(object sender, EventArgs e)
    {
        // *** ASSUME THE PATH EXISTS ***
        string savePath = @"c:\temp\Pictures\";
        if (!Directory.Exists(savePath)) {
            string msg = "<h1>The upload path doesn't exist: {0}</h1>";
            Response.Write(String.Format(msg, savePath));
            Response.End();
        }

        // Verify that a file has been posted
        if (FileUpload1.PostedFile != null)
```

```
        {
            // Save the uploaded file to the specified path
            string fileName = Path.GetFileName(FileUpload1.Value);
            savePath += fileName;
            FileUpload1.PostedFile.SaveAs(savePath);

            // Notify the user of the name the file was saved under.
            UploadStatus.InnerText = "File saved as: " + savePath;
        }
        else
        {
            // Notify the user that a file was not uploaded.
            UploadStatus.InnerText = "No file specified.";
        }
    }
</script>

<html>
<head runat="server">
    <title>Pro ASP.NET (Ch04)</title>
</head>
<body>
    <form runat="server">
      <h3>Select a picture to upload:</h3>
        <hr />
        <b>Picture to upload</b><br />
        <input type="file" id="FileUpload1" runat="server" />
        <br><br>
        <input runat="server" id="UploadButton" type="submit"
            value="Upload" onserverclick="UploadButton_Click" />
        <hr />
        <span runat="server" id="UploadStatusLabel" />
    </form>
</body>
</html>
```

You can also use the *InputStream* property of the *HttpPostedFile* object to read the posted data before persisting or processing. The *HttpInputFile* control also allows you to restrict the file types that can be uploaded to the server. You do this by setting the *Accept* property with a comma-separated list of MIME types.

> **Caution**   When you use the *SaveAs* method, you should be sure to specify the full path to the output file. If a relative path is provided, ASP.NET attempts to place the file in the system directory. This practice can result in an access denied error. Furthermore, be sure to provide write permission for the account used by ASP.NET for the directory where you want to store the file.

ASP.NET exercises some control on the amount of data being uploaded. The *maxRequestLength* attribute in the <httpRuntime> section of the configuration file sets the maximum allowable file size. An error is generated in the browser when the file exceeds the specified size—4 MB by default. Uploading large files might also generate another run-time error as a result of an excessive consumption of system memory.

The *HtmlImage* Control

The *HtmlImage* class is the ASP.NET counterpart of the *<img>* tag. You can use it to configure on the server the display of an image. Possible parameters you can set are the size of the image, the border, and the alternate text. An instance of *HtmlImage* is created only when the *runat* attribute is added to the *<img>* tag. If you simply need to display an image within a page, and the image is not dynamically determined or configured, there is no need to resort to the *HtmlImage* control, which would add unnecessary overhead to the page.

The following code snippet shows how to configure a server-side *<img>* tag called to display an image whose name is determined based on run-time conditions:

```
theImg.Width = 100;
theImg.Height = 100;
theImg.Src = GetImageUrl(Request);
```

The *HtmlImage* control should be used to programmatically manipulate the image to change the source file, the width and height, or the alignment of the image relative to other page elements. The majority of properties of the *HtmlImage* control are implemented as strings, including *Src*—the URL of the image—and *Align*. Feasible values of *Align* are only a small set of words such as *left*, *right*, *top*, and so forth. These words would have been more appropriately grouped in a custom enumerated type, thus providing for a strongly typed programming model. If you think so, too, you just got the gist of the difference between HTML and Web server controls! HTML controls just mirror HTML tags; Web controls attempt to provide a more consistent and effective programming interface by exploiting the characteristics of the .NET Framework.

Literal Controls

Literal controls are a special type of server control that ASP.NET creates and uses whenever it encounters plain text that doesn't require server-side processing. In general, everything that appears in the context of an ASP.NET page is treated like a control. If a tag includes the *runat="server"* attribute, ASP.NET creates an instance of a specific class; otherwise, if no *runat* attribute has been specified, the text is compiled into a *LiteralControl* object. Literal controls are simple text holders that are added to and removed from pages using the same programming interface defined for other server controls.

Note that a literal control is created for each sequence of characters placed between two successive server controls, including carriage returns. Using a new line to separate distinct server controls and increase code readability actually affects the number of server controls being created to serve the page. Writing the page as a single string without carriage returns produces the smallest number of server controls.

Web Controls

Web controls are defined in the *System.Web.UI.WebControls* namespace and represent an alternative approach to HTML server controls. Like HTML controls, Web controls are server-side components that spring to life thanks to the *runat="server"* attribute. Unlike HTML controls, Web controls provide a programming interface that refactors the classic set of HTML attributes and events. For this reason, Web controls sometimes appear to be more consistent and abstract in the API design and richer in functionality, but they still generate valid markup. When hosted in *.aspx* pages, Web controls are characterized by the *asp* namespace prefix.

To a large degree, Web controls and HTML controls overlap and generate almost the same markup, although they do it through different programming interfaces. For example, the Web controls namespace defines the *TextBox* control and makes it available through the *<asp:textbox>* tag; similarly, the HTML controls namespace provides the *HtmlInputText* control and declares it using the *<input>* tag. Using either is mostly a matter of preference; only in a few cases will you run into slight functionality differences.

Generalities of Web Controls

The *WebControl* class is the base class from which all Web controls inherit. *WebControl* inherits from *Control*. The class defines several properties and methods that are shared, but not necessarily implemented, by derived controls. Most properties and methods are related to the look and feel of the controls (font, style, colors, CSS) and are subject to browser and HTML versions. For example, although all Web controls provide the ability to define a border, not all underlying HTML tags actually support a border.

Properties of Web Controls

Table 4-8 lists the properties available on the *WebControl* class.

Table 4-8   Specific Properties of Web Controls

Property	Description
AccessKey	Gets or sets the letter to press (together with Alt) to quickly set focus to the control in a Web form. Supported on Internet Explorer 4.0 and newer.
Attributes	Gets the collection of attributes that do not correspond to properties on the control. Attributes set in this way will be rendered as HTML attributes in the resulting page.
BackColor	Gets or sets the background color of the Web control.
BorderColor	Gets or sets the border color of the Web control.
BorderStyle	Gets or sets the border style of the Web control.
BorderWidth	Gets or sets the border width of the Web control.
ControlStyle	Gets the style of the Web server control. The style is an object of type *Style*.
ControlStyleCreated	Gets a value that indicates whether a *Style* object has been created for the *ControlStyle* property.

Table 4-8   Specific Properties of Web Controls

Property	Description
CssClass	Get or sets the name of the cascading style sheet (CSS) class associated with the client.
Enabled	Gets or sets whether the control is enabled.
Font	Gets the font properties associated with the Web control.
ForeColor	Gets or sets the foreground color of the Web control mostly used to draw text.
Height	Gets or sets the height of the control. The height is expressed as a member of type *Unit*.
Style	Gets a *CssStyleCollection* collection object made of all the attributes assigned to the outer tag of the Web control.
TabIndex	Gets or sets the tab index of the control.
ToolTip	Gets or sets the text displayed when the mouse pointer hovers over the control.
Width	Gets or sets the width of the control. The width is expressed as a member of type *Unit*.

The *ControlStyle* and *ControlStyleCreated* properties are used primarily by control developers, while the *Style* property is what application developers would typically use to set CSS attributes on the outer tag of the control. The *Style* property is implemented using an instance of the class *CssStyleCollection*. The *CssStyleCollection* class is a simple collection of strings like those you would assign to the HTML *style* attribute.

Styling Web Controls

The *ControlStyle* property evaluates to an object of type *Style*—a class that encapsulates the appearance properties of the control. The *Style* class groups together some of the properties shown in Table 4-8, and it works as the repository of the graphical and cosmetic attributes that characterize all Web controls. The grouped properties are: *BackColor*, *BorderColor*, *Border-Style*, *BorderWidth*, *CssClass*, *Font*, *ForeColor*, *Height*, and *Width*. All properties of the *Style* class are strongly typed. The properties just mentioned are not persisted to the view state individually, but benefit from the serialization machinery supported by the *Style* object.

It should be clear by now that the *Style* class is quite different from the *Style* property, whose type is *CssStyleCollection*. Note that style values set through the *Style* property are not automatically reflected by the (strongly typed) values in the *Style* object. For example, you can set the CSS *border-style* through the *Style* property, but that value won't be reflected by the value of the *BorderStyle* property:

```
// Set the border color through a CSS attribute
MyControl.Style["border-color"] = "blue";

// Set the border color through an ASP.NET style property
MyControl.BorderColor = Color.Red;
```

So what happens if you run the preceding code snippet? Which setting would win? When a control is going to render, the contents of both *ControlStyle* and *Style* properties are rendered to HTML *style* attributes. The *ControlStyle* property is processed first, so in case of overlapping settings the value stuffed in *Style*, which is processed later, would win, as shown by the following markup:

```
style="border-color:Red;border-color:blue; ..."
```

Managing the Style of Web Controls

The style properties of a Web control can be programmatically manipulated to some extent. For example, in the *Style* class, you can count on a *CopyFrom* method to duplicate the object and on the *MergeStyle* method to combine two style objects:

```
currentStyle.MergeStyle(newStyle);
```

The *MergeStyle* method joins the properties of both objects. In doing so, it does not replace any property that is already set in the base object but limits itself to defining uninitialized properties. Finally, the *Reset* method clears all current attributes in the various properties of the style object.

Methods of Web Controls

The *WebControl* class supports a few additional methods that are not part of the base *Control* class. These methods are listed in Table 4-9

Table 4-9   Specific Methods of Web Controls

Method	Description
ApplyStyle	Copies any nonempty elements of the specified style object to the control. Existing style properties are overwritten.
CopyBaseAttributes	Imports from the specified Web control the properties *AccessKey*, *Enabled*, *ToolTip*, *TabIndex*, and *Attributes*. Basically, it copies all the properties not encapsulated in the *Style* object.
MergeStyle	Like *ApplyStyle*, copies any nonempty elements of the specified style to the control. Existing style properties are *not* overwritten, though.
RenderBeginTag	Renders the HTML opening tag of the control into the specified writer. The method is called right before the control's *RenderControl* method.
RenderEndTag	Renders the HTML closing tag of the control into the specified writer. The method is called right after the control's *RenderControl* method.

All these methods are rarely of interest to application developers. They are mostly designed to support control developers.

Core Web Controls

The set of Web controls can be divided into various categories according to the provided functionality—input and button controls, validators, data-bound controls, security-related controls, grid and view controls, plus a few miscellaneous controls that provide ad hoc functions and are as common on the Web as they are hard to catalogue (for example, calendar, ad rotator, and so forth).

In this chapter, we're focused on covering the most common and essential Web controls, such as the controls for capturing and validating the user's input and posting data to the server. We'll cover the various types of data-bound controls in Chapter 9, Chapter 10, and Chapter 11. Security-related controls, on the other hand, are slated for Chapter 15. Table 4-10 details the core server controls of ASP.NET.

Table 4-10   Core Web Controls

Control	Description
Button	Implements a push button through the *<input>* tag.
CheckBox	Implements a check box through the *<input>* tag.
FileUpload	Allows users to select a file to upload to the server. *Not available in ASP.NET 1.x.*
HiddenField	Implements a hidden field. *Not available in ASP.NET 1.x.*
HyperLink	Implements an anchor *<a>* tag, and lets you specify either the location to jump to or the script code to execute.
Image	Implements a picture box through the *<img>* tag.
ImageButton	Displays an image and responds to mouse clicks on the image like a real button.
ImageMap	Displays an image and optionally defines clickable hot spots on it. *Not available in ASP.NET 1.x.*
Label	Represents a static, nonclickable piece of text. Implemented through the *<span>* tag.
LinkButton	Implements an anchor *<a>* tag that uses only the ASP.NET postback mechanism to post back. It is a special type of hyperlink where the programmer can't directly set the target URL.
MultiView	Represents a control that acts as a container for a group of child *View* controls. *Not available in ASP.NET 1.x.*
Panel	Implements an HTML container using the *<div>* block element. In ASP.NET 2.0, the container supports scrolling. Note that in down-level browsers the control renders out as a *<table>*.
RadioButton	Implements a single radio button through the *<input>* tag.
Table	Implements the outer table container. Equivalent to the HTML *<table>* element.
TableCell	A table cell; is equivalent to the HTML *<td>* element.
TableRow	A table row; is equivalent to the HTML *<tr>* element.

Table 4-10 **Core Web Controls**

Control	Description
TextBox	Implements a text box using the *<input>* or *<textarea>* tag as appropriate and according to the requested text mode. Can work in single-line, multiline, or password mode.
View	Acts as a container for a group of controls. A *View* control must always be contained within a *MultiView* control. *Not available in ASP.NET 1.x.*

Most controls in Table 4-10 look like HTML controls. Compared to HTML controls, their programming model is certainly richer and more abstract, but in the end it still generates valid and legal markup. If a given feature can't be obtained with raw HTML, there's no way a custom Web control can provide it. No matter how complex the programming model is, all Web controls must produce valid HTML for both up-level and down-level browsers.

Button Controls

In ASP.NET 2.0, controls that provide button functions are characterized by a new interface—*IButtonControl*. Core controls that implement the interface are *Button*, *ImageButton*, and *LinkButton*. In general, by implementing *IButtonControl* any custom control can act like a button on a form.

The *IButtonControl* interface is a clear example of the refactoring process that the entire ASP.NET Framework went through in the transition from 1.x to 2.0. The interface now groups a few properties that most button controls (including some HTML button controls) support since ASP.NET 1.x. In addition to this, a few new properties heralding new functions have been added, such as *PostBackUrl* and *ValidationGroup*. Table 4-11 details the *IButtonControl* interface.

Table 4-11 **The *IButtonControl* Interface**

Name	Description
CausesValidation	Boolean value, indicates whether validation is performed when the control is clicked.
CommandArgument	Gets or sets an optional parameter passed to the button's *Command* event along with the associated *CommandName*.
CommandName	Gets or sets the command name associated with the button that is passed to the *Command* event.
PostBackUrl	Indicates the URL that will handle the postback triggered through the button control. This ASP.NET 2.0–specific feature is known as cross-page postback. (We'll cover this further in Chapter 5.)
Text	Gets or sets the caption of the button.
ValidationGroup	Gets or sets the name of the validation group that the button belongs to.
Visible	Boolean value, indicates whether the button control is rendered.

In addition to the properties defined by the *IButtonControl* interface, the *Button* class features two new properties in ASP.NET 2.0—*OnClientClick* and *UseSubmitBehavior*. The former standardizes a common practice that many developers used countless times in ASP.NET 1.x projects. *OnClientClick* lets you define the name of the JavaScript function to run when the client-side *onclick* event is fired. The following two statements are perfectly legal and equivalent:

```
// New in ASP.NET 2.0
Button1.OnClientClick = "ShowMessage()";

// Equivalent in ASP.NET 1.x
Button1.Attributes["onclick"] = "ShowMessage()";
```

The *OnClientClick* property is available also on *LinkButton* and *ImageButton* controls.

By default, the *Button* class is rendered through a *<input type=submit>* tag. In this way, it takes advantage of the browser's submit mechanism to post back. The *UseSubmitBehavior* property allows you to change the default behavior. Set the *UseSubmitBehavior* property to *false* and the control will render out through an *<input type=button>* tag. Also in this case, though, the *Button* control remains a postback button. When *UseSubmitBehavior* is *false*, the control's *onclick* client event handler is bound to a piece of JavaScript code (the *__doPostBack* function) that provides the ASP.NET postback mechanism just like for *LinkButton* or *ImageButton* controls.

> **Important**   Buttons are not the only controls that can trigger a postback. Text boxes and check boxes (plus a few more data-bound list controls, which we'll see in Chapter 9) can also start a postback if their *AutoPostBack* property is set to *true*. (Note that the default setting is *false*.) When this happens, the control wires up to a client-side event—*onchange* for text boxes and *onclick* for check boxes—and initiates a postback operation via script.

HyperLinks

The *HyperLink* control creates a link to another Web page and is typically displayed through the text stored in the *Text* property. Alternatively, the hyperlink can be displayed as an image; in this case, the URL of the image is stored in the *ImageUrl* property. Note that if both the *Text* and *ImageUrl* properties are set, the *ImageUrl* property takes precedence. In this case, the content of the *Text* property is displayed as a ToolTip when the mouse hovers over the control's area.

The *NavigateUrl* property indicates the URL the hyperlink is pointing to. The *Target* property is the name of the window or frame that will contain the output of the target URL.

Images and Image Buttons

The *Image* control displays an image on the Web page. The path to the image is set through the *ImageUrl* property. Image URLs can be either relative or absolute, with most programmers showing a clear preference for relative URLs because they make a Web site inherently easier to move. You can also specify alternate text to display when the image is not available or when the browser doesn't render the image for some reason. The property to use in this case is *AlternateText*. The image alignment with respect to other elements on the page is set by using the *ImageAlign* property. Feasible values are taken from the homonymous *enum* type.

The *Image* control is not a clickable component and is simply limited to displaying an image. If you need to capture mouse clicks on the image, use the *ImageButton* control instead. The *ImageButton* class descends from *Image* and extends it with a couple of events—*Click* and *Command*—that are raised when the control is clicked. The *OnClick* event handler provides you with an *ImageClickEventArgs* data structure that contains information about the coordinates for the location at which the image is clicked.

The *OnCommand* event handler makes the *ImageButton* control behave like a command button. A command button has an associated name that you can control through the *Command-Name* property. If you have multiple *ImageButton* controls on the same page, the command name allows you to distinguish which one is actually clicked. The *CommandArgument* property can be used to pass additional information about the command and the control.

Another new entry in ASP.NET 2.0 is the *ImageMap* control. In its simplest and most commonly used form, the control displays an image on a page. However, when a hot-spot region defined within the control is clicked, the control either generates a post back to the server or navigates to a specified URL. The hot spot is a clickable region within the displayed image. The hot spot is implemented with a class that inherits from the *HotSpot* class. There are three predefined types of hot spots—polygons, circles, and rectangles.

Check Boxes and Radio Buttons

Check boxes and radio buttons are implemented through the *<input>* tag and the *type* attribute set to *checkbox* or *radio*. Unlike the HTML control versions, the Web control versions of check boxes and radio buttons let you specify the associated text as a property. The HTML elements and corresponding HTML controls lack an attribute whose content becomes the text near the check box or radio button. In HTML, to make the text near the check box or radio button clickable, you have to resort to the *<label>* tag with the *for* attribute:

```
<input type="checkbox" id="ctl" />
<label for="ctl">Check me</label>
```

Neither the *HtmlInputCheckBox* nor the *HtmlInputRadioButton* control adds a label; this is your responsibility. The counterparts to these Web controls, on the other hand, are not bound to the HTML syntax and do precisely that—they automatically add a *Text* property, which results in an appropriate *<label>* tag. For example, consider the following ASP.NET code:

```
<asp:checkbox runat="server" id="ctl" text="Check me" />
```

It results in the following HTML code:

```
<input type="checkbox" id="ctl" />
<label for="ctl">Check me</label>
```

Scrollable Panels

The *Panel* control groups controls in a *<div>* tag. It allows developers to add and remove controls, and it supports style information. In ASP.NET 2.0, panels support horizontal and vertical scrollbars implemented through the *overflow* CSS style. Here's an example that demonstrates a scrollable panel:

```
<asp:Panel ID="Panel1" runat="server" Height="80px" Width="420px"
        ScrollBars="Auto" BorderStyle="Solid">
   <h2>Choose a technology</h2>
   <asp:CheckBox ID="ChkBox1" runat="server" Text="ASP.NET" /><br />
   <asp:CheckBox ID="ChkBox2" runat="server" Text="ADO.NET" /><br />
   <asp:CheckBox ID="ChkBox3" runat="server" Text="Web Services" /><br />
   <asp:CheckBox ID="ChkBox4" runat="server" Text="XML" /><br />
   <asp:CheckBox ID="ChkBox5" runat="server" Text="SQL Server" /><br />
   <asp:CheckBox ID="ChkBox6" runat="server" Text="CLR" /><br />
</asp:Panel>
```

Figure 4-4 shows the page in action.

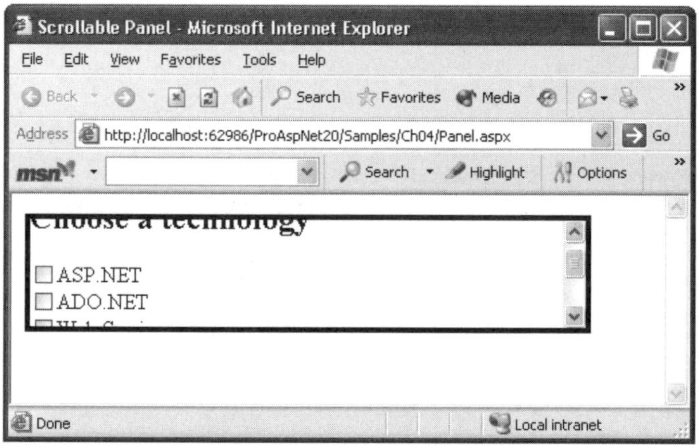

Figure 4-4   A page that uses a scrollable panel.

Text Controls

The fastest way to insert text in a Web page is through literals—that is, static text inserted directly in the *.aspx* source. This text will still be compiled to a control, but at least the number of dynamically created literal controls will be the minimum possible because any sequence of consecutive characters will be grouped into a single literal. If you need to identify and manipulate particular strings of text programmatically, you can resort to a *Literal* control or, better yet, to the richer *Label* control. Modifiable text requires a *TextBox*.

Some minor changes occurred to these controls in ASP.NET 2.0. First, a few new interfaces have been introduced to logically group capabilities. They are *ITextControl* and *IEditable-TextControl*. The former includes the sole *Text* property and is implemented by *Literal*, *Label*,

TextBox, and list controls. The latter interface defines the *TextChanged* event and is specific to *TextBox* and list controls.

It is worth mentioning a new accessibility feature of the *Label* control—the *AssociatedControlID* property. The property takes the ID of a control in the page—typically, an input control such as a *TextBox*—that you want to associate with the label. The *AssociatedControlID* changes the way the *Label* control renders out. It is a *<span>* tag if no associated control is specified; it is a *<label>* tag otherwise. Let's consider the following example:

```
<asp:Label ID="Label1" runat="server" Text="Sample text" />
<asp:TextBox ID="TextBox1" runat="server" />
```

As is, it generates the following markup:

```
<span id="Label1">Sample text</span>
<input name="TextBox1" type="text" id="TextBox1" />
```

If you set the label's *AssociatedControlID* property to *TextBox1*, the markup changes as shown here:

```
<label for="TextBox1" id="Label1">Sample text</label>
<input name="TextBox1" type="text" id="TextBox1" />
```

The run-time behavior changes a bit because now any click on the label text will be extended to the associated control. For example, clicking on the label will move the input focus to a text box, or it will select or deselect a check box.

> **Note**   *AssociatedControlID* is a feature designed to improve the accessibility of the resulting page. In Visual Studio .NET 2005, you can check any page for accessibility rules (both WCAG and Section 508) by clicking on the *Tools|Check Accessibility* menu item.

Hidden Fields and File Upload

If you're looking for a more comfortable programming interface to create hidden fields and upload files, two new Web controls in ASP.NET 2.0 might help. The *HiddenField* and *FileUpload* controls add no new functionality to the ASP.NET programmer's bag, but they have been added to the toolbox for completeness. A hidden field can be created in two other ways that work with ASP.NET 1.x, too. For example, you can use the *RegisterHiddenField* method on the *Page* class:

```
// Works in ASP.NET 1.x but declared obsolete in ASP.NET 2.0
RegisterHiddenField("HiddenField1", "Great book!");
```

Note that the *RegisterHiddenField* method has been flagged as obsolete in ASP.NET 2.0. The recommended code analogous to the previous snippet is shown next:

```
// Recommended code in ASP.NET 2.0
ClientScriptManager.RegisterHiddenField("HiddenField1", "Great book!");
```

In addition, to create a hidden field you can resort to the HTML markup, adding a *runat* attribute if you need to set the value programmatically:

```
<input runat="server" id="HiddenField1" type="hidden" value="…" />
```

Analogous considerations can be made for the *FileUpload* control, which provides the same capabilities as the *HtmlInputFile* control that we discussed earlier. In this case, though, the programming interface is slightly different and perhaps more intuitive. The *HasFile* property and *SaveAs* method hide any reference to the object that represents the posted file. Likewise, the *FileName* property provides a more immediate name for the name of the posted file. The code to upload a file can be rewritten as follows:

```
if (FileUpload1.HasFile)
{
    // Get the name of the file to upload.
    string fileName = FileUpload1.FileName;
    string targetPath = GetSavePath(fileName);
    FileUpload1.SaveAs(targetPath);
}
```

Whether you use *FileUpload* or *HtmlInputFile* is mostly a matter of preference.

Creating Tables

As you might have noticed, there are three ways to build tables in ASP.NET pages: static HTML tags, *HtmlTable* controls, and *Table* controls. Which is the best option?

Static HTML tags provide the greatest flexibility as far as the structure of the table is concerned. If you want to support all possible tags that the HTML specification allows, this is the option to take. By contrast, *HtmlTable* appears to be the least flexible option. In fact, it accepts only row tags and silently removes any additional and unsupported tags.

The *Table* control in ASP.NET 2.0 supports various row types (normal, header, footer) and dynamic manipulation of rows and cells, but it still lacks full declarative support of all possible HTML table-related tags and attributes, including *COLGROUP* and *TBODY*. Note, though, that each table row can be associated with a table section (body, footer, header) programmatically. This is possible through the *TableSection* property of the *TableRow* class.

Miscellaneous Web Controls

The *WebControls* namespace also includes a few controls that provide useful functionality that is common in Web applications. In particular, we'll examine the *AdRotator* control, which works like an advertisement banner, and the *Calendar* control, which is a flexible and highly interactive control used to specify a date.

The *AdRotator* Control

Abstractly speaking, the *AdRotator* control displays an automatically sized image button and updates both the image and the URL each time the page refreshes. The image to display and other information is read from an XML file written according to a specific schema. More concretely, you use the *AdRotator* control to create an advertisement banner on a Web Forms page. The control actually inserts an image and a hyperlink in the page and makes them point to the advertisement page selected. The image is sized by the browser to the dimensions of the *AdRotator* control, regardless of its actual size. The following code shows a typical XML advertisement file:

```
<Advertisements>
<Ad>
    <ImageUrl>6235.gif</ImageUrl>
    <NavigateUrl>www.microsoft.com/MSPress/books/6235.asp</NavigateUrl>
    <AlternateText>Applied XML Programming with .NET</AlternateText>
    <Impressions>50</Impressions>
</Ad>
<Ad>
    <ImageUrl>5727.gif</ImageUrl>
    <NavigateUrl>www.microsoft.com/MSPress/books/5727.asp</NavigateUrl>
    <AlternateText>Building Web Solutions with ASP.NET</AlternateText>
    <Impressions>50</Impressions>
</Ad>
</Advertisements>
```

The *<Advertisement>* root node contains multiple *<Ad>* elements, one per each image to show. The advertisement file must reside in the same application as the *AdRotator* control. The syntax of the *AdRotator* control is as follows:

```
<%@ Page Language="C#" %>
<html>
<head><title>Pro ASP.NET (Ch04)</title></head>
<body>
    <form runat="server">
        <h1>Dino Esposito's Books</h1>
        <asp:AdRotator runat="server" id="bookRotator"
            AdvertisementFile="MyBooks.xml" />
    </form>
</body>
</html>
```

In the XML advertisement file, you use the *<ImageUrl>* node to indicate the image to load and the *<NavigateUrl>* node to specify where to go in case of a click. The *<AlternateText>* node indicates the alternate text to use if the image is unavailable, whereas *<Impressions>* indicates how often an image should be displayed in relation to other images in the advertisement file. Each image can also be associated with a keyword through the *<Keyword>* node. Of all the elements, only *<ImageUrl>* is required.

Once per roundtrip, the *AdRotator* control fires the server-side *AdCreated* event. The event occurs before the page is rendered. The event handler receives an argument of type *AdCreated-EventArgs*, which contains information about the image, navigation URL, alternate text, and any custom properties associated with the advertisement. The *AdCreated* event can be used to select programmatically the image to show. The XML schema of the advertisement is not fixed and can be extended with custom elements. All nonstandard elements associated with the selected advertisement will be passed to the *AdCreated* event handler stuffed in the *AdProperties* dictionary member of the *AdCreatedEventArgs* class.

> **Note**   The *AdRotator* control has undergone a significant change in ASP.NET 2.0. It is derived from *WebControl* in ASP.NET 1.x, but it inherits from *DataBoundControl* in ASP.NET 2.0. Among other things, this means that the advertisement feed can also be provided through an XML or a relational data source. Image and navigation URLs, as well as the alternate text, can be read from fields belonging to the data source. The control cannot be bound to more than one data source at a time. If more than one property—*AdvertisementFile*, *DataSourceID*, or *DataSource*—is set, an exception will be thrown.

The *Calendar* Control

The *Calendar* control (shown in Figure 4-5) displays a one-month calendar and allows you to choose dates and navigate backward and forward through the months of the year. The control is highly customizable both for appearance and functionality. For example, by setting the *SelectionMode* property, you can decide what the user can select—that is, whether a single date, week, or month can be selected:

```
<asp:calendar runat="server" id="hireDate"
    SelectedDate="2005-05-04" VisibleDate="2005-05-04" />
```

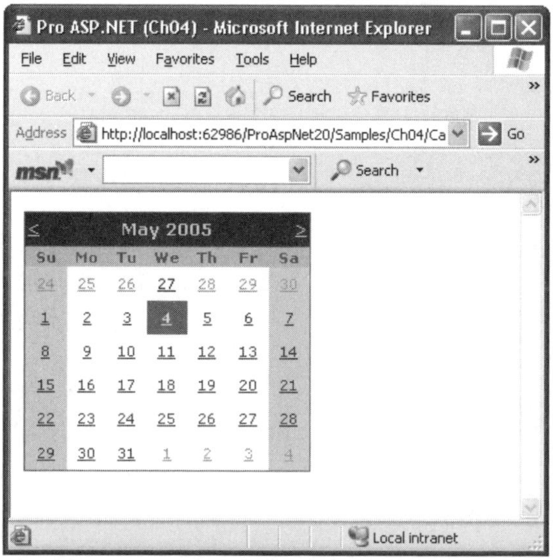

Figure 4-5   The *Calendar* control in action.

The *VisibleDate* property sets a date that must be visible in the calendar, while *SelectedDate* sets with a different style the date that is rendered as selected. The control also fires three ad hoc events: *DayRender*, *SelectionChanged*, and *VisibleMonthChanged*. The *DayRender* event signals that the control has just created a new day cell. You can hook the event if you think you need to customize the cell output. The *SelectionChanged* event fires when the selected date changes, while *VisibleMonthChanged* is raised whenever the user moves to another month using the control's selector buttons.

The *Calendar* control originates a roundtrip for each selection you make. Although it is cool and powerful on its own, for better performance you might also want to provide a plain text box for manually typing dates.

The *Xml* Control

The *Xml* control, defined by the <asp:Xml> tag, is used to output the content of an XML document directly into an ASP.NET page. The control can display the source XML as is or as the result of an XSL transformation (XSLT). The *Xml* control is a sort of declarative counterpart for the *XslTransform* class and can make use of the .NET Framework XSLT transform class internally.

You use the *Xml* control when you need to embed XML documents in a Web page. For example, the control is extremely handy when you need to create XML data islands for the client to consume. The control lets you specify a document to work with and, optionally, a transformation to apply. The XML document can be specified in a variety of formats—an XML document object model, string, or file name. The XSLT transformation can be defined through either an already configured instance of the .NET Framework *XslTransform* class or a file name:

```
<asp:xml runat="server"
    documentsource="document.xml"
    transformsource="transform.xsl" />
```

If you're going to apply some transformation to the XML data, you could also embed it inline between the opening and closing tags of the control. The control also makes it easier to accomplish a common ASP task: apply browser-dependent transformations to portions of the page expressed in an XML meta language. In this case, you exploit the programming interface of the control as follows:

```
<asp:xml runat="server" id="theXml" documentsource="document.xml" />
```

In the *Page_Load* event, you just check the browser capabilities and decide which transformation should be applied:

```
void Page_Load(object sender, EventArgs e)
{
    if (IsInternetExplorer(Request.Browser))
        theXml.TransformSource = "ie5.xsl";
    else
        theXml.TransformSource = "downlevel.xsl";
}
```

The *PlaceHolder* Control

The *PlaceHolder* control is one of the few controls in the *WebControls* namespace that isn't derived from the *WebControl* class. It inherits from *Control* and is used only as a container for other controls in the page. The *PlaceHolder* control does not produce visible output of its own and is limited to containing child controls dynamically added through the *Controls* collection. The following code shows how to embed a placeholder control in a Web page:

```
<asp:placeholder runat="server" id="theToolbar" />
```

Once you have a placeholder, you can add controls to it. As mentioned, the placeholder does not add extra functionality, but it provides for grouping and easy and direct identification of a group of related controls. The following code demonstrates how to create a new button and add it to an existing placeholder:

```
Button btn = new Button();
btn.Text = "Click me";
theToolbar.Controls.Add(btn);
```

The *PlaceHolder* control reserves a location in the control tree and can be extremely helpful in identifying specific areas of the page to customize and extend by adding controls programmatically.

> **Important**   Note that each control dynamically added to the *Controls* collection of a parent control is not restored on postback. If the control generates some input elements on the client, the client data is regularly posted but there will be no server-side control to handle that. To avoid this, you must remember that you created a certain control dynamically and re-create it while the page loads on postbacks. To remember that a certain control was added to a parent, you can create a custom entry in the view state or use a hidden field.

View Controls

ASP.NET 2.0 introduces two new related controls to create a group of interchangeable panels of child controls. The *MultiView* control defines a group of views, each represented with an instance of the *View* class. Only one view is active at a time and rendered to the client. The *View* control can't be used as a standalone component and can only be placed inside a *Multi-View* control. Here's an example:

```
<asp:MultiView runat="server" id="Tables">
    <asp:View runat="server" id="Employees">
        ...
    </asp:View>
    <asp:View runat="server" id="Products">
        ...
    </asp:View>
    <asp:View runat="server" id="Customers">
        ...
    </asp:View>
</asp:MultiView>
```

You change the active view through postback events when the user clicks buttons or links embedded in the current view. To indicate the new view, you can either set the *ActiveViewIndex* property or pass the view object to the *SetActiveView* method.

Figure 4-6 shows a sample page in action. You select the page from the drop-down list and refresh the view:

```
void Page_Load(object sender, EventArgs e)
{
    // Views is an auto-postback drop-down list
    Tables.ActiveViewIndex = Views.SelectedIndex;
}
```

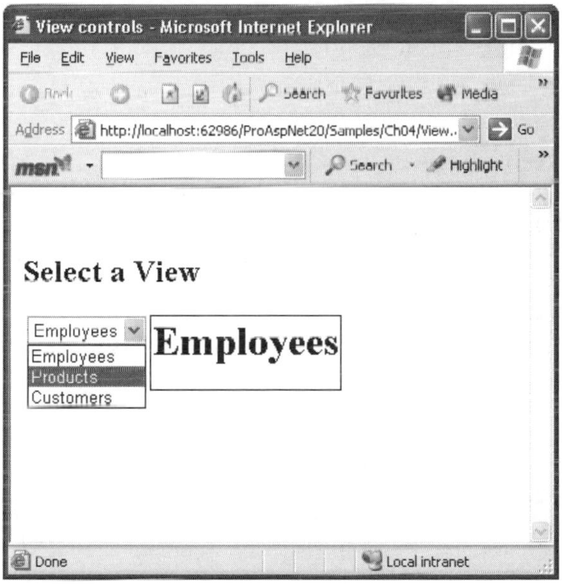

Figure 4-6   A *MultiView* control in action.

The combination of *View* and *MultiView* controls lends itself very well to implementing wizards. In fact, the new ASP.NET *Wizard* control uses a *MultiView* control internally. We'll cover the *Wizard* control in Chapter 6.

Validation Controls

A key rule for writing more secure applications is to get the data right—before you use it. Getting the data right requires you to apply a validation step to any external input. In ASP.NET, validation controls provide an easy-to-use mechanism to perform a variety of validation tasks, including testing for valid types, values within a given range, or required fields.

Validation controls inherit from the *BaseValidator* class which, in turn, descends from *Label*. All validators defined on a page are automatically grouped in the *Validators* collection of the

Page class. You can validate them all in a single shot using the *Validate* method in the page class or individually by calling the *Validate* method on each validator. The *Validate* method sets the *IsValid* property both on the page and on the individual validator. The *IsValid* property indicates whether the user's entries match the requirements of the validators. Other than explicitly using the *Validate* method, the user's entry is also automatically validated whenever the page posts back.

> **Note**   In ASP.NET 2.0, typical control members involved with input validation have been grouped in the *IValidator* interface that the *BaseValidator* class implements. The interface includes the *Validate* method and the *IsValid* and *ErrorMessage* properties.

The .NET Framework also provides complete client-side implementation for validation controls. This allows Dynamic HTML–enabled browsers (such as Internet Explorer version 4.0 and later) to perform validation on the client as soon as the user tabs out of a monitored input field.

Generalities of Validation Controls

Each validation control references an input control located elsewhere on the page. When the page is going to be submitted, the contents of the monitored server control is passed to the validator for further processing. Each validator would perform a different type of verification. Table 4-12 shows the types of validation supported by the .NET Framework.

Table 4-12   Validator Controls in the .NET Framework

Validator	Description
CompareValidator	Compares the user's entry against a fixed value by using a comparison operator such as *LessThan*, *Equal*, or *GreaterThan*. Can also compare against the value of a property in another control on the same page.
CustomValidator	Employs a programmatically defined validation logic to check the validity of the user's entry. You use this validator when the other validators cannot perform the necessary validation and you want to provide custom code that validates the input.
RangeValidator	Ensures that the user's entry falls within a specified range. Lower and upper boundaries can be expressed as numbers, strings, or dates.
RegularExpressionValidator	Validates the user's entry only if it matches a pattern defined by a regular expression.
RequiredFieldValidator	Ensures that the user specifies a value for the field.

Multiple validation controls can be used with an individual input control to validate according to different criteria. For example, you can apply multiple validation controls on a text box that is expected to contain an e-mail address. In particular, you can impose that the field is not skipped (*RequiredFieldValidator*) and that its content matches the typical format of e-mail addresses (*RegularExpressionValidator*).

Table 4-12 lacks a reference to the *ValidationSummary* control. The control does not perform validation tasks itself. It displays a label to summarize all the validation error messages found on a Web page as the effect of other validators. We'll cover the *ValidationSummary* control later in the chapter.

The *BaseValidator* Class

Table 4-13 details the specific properties of validation controls. Some properties—such as *ForeColor*, *Enabled*, and *Text*—are overridden versions of base properties on base classes.

Table 4-13   Basic Properties of Validators

Property	Description
ControlToValidate	Gets or sets the input control to validate. The control is identified by name—that is, by using the value of the *ID* attribute.
Display	If client-side validation is supported and enabled, gets or sets how the space for the error message should be allocated—either statically or dynamically. In case of server-side validation, this property is ignored. A *Static* display is possible only if the browser supports the *display* CSS style. The default is *Dynamic*.
EnableClientScript	True by default; gets or sets whether client-side validation is enabled.
Enabled	Gets or sets whether the validation control is enabled.
ErrorMessage	Gets or sets the text for the error message.
ForeColor	Gets or sets the color of the message displayed when validation fails.
IsValid	Gets or sets whether the associated input control passes validation.
SetFocusOnError	Indicates whether the focus is moved to the control where validation failed. *Not available in ASP.NET 1.x.*
Text	Gets or sets the description displayed for the validator in lieu of the error message. Note, though, this text does not replace the contents of *ErrorMessage* in the summary text.
ValidationGroup	Gets or sets the validation group that this control belongs to. *Not available in ASP.NET 1.x.*

All validation controls inherit from the *BaseValidator* class except for compare validators, for which a further intermediate class—the *BaseCompareValidator* class—exists. The *BaseCompareValidator* class serves as the foundation for validators that perform typed comparisons. An ad hoc property, named *Type*, is used to specify the data type the values are converted to before being compared. The *CanConvert* static method determines whether the user's entry can be converted to the specified data type. Supported types include string, integer, double, date, and currency. The classes acting as compare validators are *RangeValidator* and *CompareValidator*.

Associating Validators with Input Controls

The link between each validator and its associated input control is established through the *ControlToValidate* property. The property must be set to the ID of the input control. If you do not specify a valid input control, an exception will be thrown when the page is rendered. The association validator/control is between two controls within the same container—be it a page, user control, or template.

Not all server controls can be validated, only those that specify their validation property through an attribute named *[ValidationProperty]*. The attribute takes the name of the property that contains the user's entry to check. For example, the validation property for a *TextBox* is *Text* and is indicated as follows:

```
[ValidationProperty("Text")]
public class TextBox : WebControl, ITextControl
{
    ...
}
```

The list of controls that support validation includes *TextBox*, *DropDownList*, *ListBox*, *Radio-ButtonList*, *FileUpload*, plus a bunch of HTML controls such as *HtmlInputFile*, *HtmlInputText*, *HtmlInputPassword*, *HtmlTextArea*, and *HtmlSelect*. Custom controls can be validated too, as long as they are marked with the aforementioned *[ValidationProperty]* attribute.

> **Note**   If the validation property of the associated input control is left empty, all validators accept the value and pass the test. The *RequiredFieldValidator* control represents a rather natural exception to this rule as it has been specifically designed to detect fields the user skipped and left blank.

Gallery of Controls

Let's take a closer look at the various types of validation controls that you'll use in ASP.NET Web forms.

The *CompareValidator* Control

The *CompareValidator* control lets you compare the value entered by the user with a constant value or the value specified in another control in the same naming container. The behavior of the control is characterized by the following additional properties:

- **ControlToCompare.**   Represents the ID of the control to compare with the current user's entry. You should avoid setting the *ControlToCompare* and *ValueToCompare* properties at the same time. They are considered mutually exclusive; if you set both, the *Control-ToCompare* property takes precedence.

- **Operator.** Specifies the comparison operation to perform. The list of feasible operations is defined in the *ValidationCompareOperator* enumeration. The default operator is *Equal*; feasible operators are also *LessThan*, *GreaterThan*, and their variations. The *DataTypeCheck* operator is useful when you want to make sure that certain input data can be converted to a certain type. When the *DataTypeCheck* operator is specified, both *ControlToCompare* and *ValueToCompare* are ignored. In this case, the test is made on the type of the input data and succeeds if the specified data can be converted to the expected type. Supported types are expressed through the following keywords: *String*, *Integer*, *Double*, *Date*, and *Currency* (decimal).

- **ValueToCompare.** Indicates the value to compare the user's input against. If the *Type* property is set, the *ValueToCompare* property must comply with it.

The following code demonstrates the typical markup of the *CompareValidator* control when the control is called to validate an integer input from a text box representing someone's age:

```
<asp:CompareValidator runat="server" id="ageValidator"
    ControlToValidate="ageTextBox"
    ValueToCompare="18"
    Operator="GreaterThanEqual"
    Type="Integer"
    ErrorMessage="Must specify an age greater than 17." />
```

The *CustomValidator* Control

The *CustomValidator* control is a generic and totally user-defined validator that uses custom validation logic to accomplish its task. You typically resort to this control when none of the other validators seems appropriate or, more simply, when you need to execute your own code in addition to that of the standard validators.

To set up a custom validator, you can indicate a client-side function through the *ClientValidation-Function* property. If client-side validation is disabled or not supported, simply omit this setting. Alternatively, or in addition to client validation, you can define some managed code to execute on the server. You do this by defining a handler for the *ServerValidate* event. The code will be executed when the page is posted back in response to a click on a button control. The following code snippet shows how to configure a custom validator to check the value of a text box against an array of feasible values:

```
<asp:CustomValidator runat="server" id="membershipValidator"
    ControlToValidate="membership"
    ClientValidationFunction="CheckMembership"
    OnServerValidate="ServerValidation"
    ErrorMessage="Membership can be Normal, Silver, Gold, or Platinum." />
```

If specified, the client validation function takes a mandatory signature and looks like this:

```
function CheckMembership(source, arguments)
{ ... }
```

The *source* argument references the HTML tag that represents the validator control—usually, a *<span>* tag. The *arguments* parameter references an object with two properties, *IsValid* and *Value*. The *Value* property is the value stored in the input control to be validated. The *IsValid* property must be set to *false* or *true* according to the result of the validation.

The *CustomValidator* control is not associated in all cases with a single input control in the current naming container. For this type of validator, setting the *ControlToValidate* property is not mandatory. For example, if the control has to validate the contents of multiple input fields, you do not simply set the *ControlToValidate* property and the *arguments.Value* variable evaluates to the empty string. In this case, you write the validation logic so that any needed values are dynamically retrieved. With client-side script code, this can be done by accessing the members of the document's form, as shown in the following code:

```
function CheckMembership(source, arguments) {
    // Retrieve the current value of the element
    // with the specified ID
    var membership = document.forms[0]["membership"].value;
    ...
}
```

> **Warning** Setting only a client-side validation code opens a security hole because an attacker could work around the validation logic and manage to have invalid or malicious data sent to the server. By defining a server event handler, you have one more chance to validate data before applying changes to the back-end system.

To define a server-side handler for a custom validator, use the *ServerValidate* event:

```
void ServerValidation(object source, ServerValidateEventArgs e)
{
    ...
}
```

The *ServerValidateEventArgs* structure contains two properties—*IsValid* and *Value*—with the same meaning and goal as in the client validation function. If the control is not bound to a particular input field, the *Value* property is empty and you retrieve any needed value using the ASP.NET object model. For example, the following code shows how to check the status of a check box on the server:

```
void ServerValidation (object source, ServerValidateEventArgs e) {
    e.IsValid = (CheckBox1.Checked == true);
}
```

The *CustomValidator* control is the only option you have to validate controls that are not marked with the *[ValidationProperty]* attribute—for example, calendars and check-box controls.

The *RegularExpressionValidator* Control

Regular expressions are an effective way to ensure that a predictable and well-known sequence of characters form the user's entry. For example, using regular expressions, you can validate the format of Zip Codes, Social Security numbers, e-mail addresses, phone numbers, and so on. When using the *RegularExpressionValidator* control, you set the *ValidationExpression* property with the regular expression, which will be used to validate the input.

The following code snippet shows a regular expression validator that ensures the user's entry is an e-mail address:

```
<asp:RegularExpressionValidator runat="server" id="emailValidator"
    ControlToValidate="email"
    ValidationExpression="[a-zA-Z 0-9.-]+\@[a-zA Z_0-9.-]+\.\w+"
    ErrorMessage="Must be a valid email address." />
```

The regular expression just shown specifies that valid e-mail addresses are formed by two nonzero sequences of letters, digits, dashes, and dots separated by an @ symbol and followed by a dot (.) and an alphabetic string. (This might not be the perfect regular expression for e-mail addresses, but it certainly incorporates the majority of e-mail address formats.)

> **Note** The regular expression validation syntax is slightly different on the client than on the server. The *RegularExpressionValidator* control uses Microsoft JScript regular expressions on the client and the .NET Framework *Regex* object on the server. Be aware that the JScript regular expression syntax is a subset of the *Regex* model. Whenever possible, try to use the regular expression syntax supported by JScript so that the same result is obtained for both the client and server.

The *RangeValidator* Control

The *RangeValidator* control lets you verify that a given value falls within a specified range. The type of the values involved in the check is specified dynamically and picked from a short list that includes strings, numbers, and dates. The following code shows how to use a range validator control:

```
<asp:RangeValidator runat="server" id="hiredDateValidator"
    ControlToValidate="hired"
    MinimumValue="2000-1-4"
    MaximumValue="9999-12-31"
    Type="Date"
    ErrorMessage="Must be a date after <b>Jan 1, 1999</b>." />
```

The key properties are *MinimumValue* and *MaximumValue*, which together clearly denote the lower and upper boundaries of the interval. Note that an exception is thrown if the strings assigned *MinimumValue* or *MaximumValue* cannot be converted to the numbers or dates according to the value of the *Type* property.

If the type is set to *Date*, but no specific culture is set for the application, you should specify dates using a culture-neutral format, such as *yyyy-MM-dd*. If you don't do so, the chances are good that the values will not be interpreted correctly.

> **Note**   The *RangeValidator* control extends the capabilities of the more basic *CompareValidator* control by checking for a value in a fixed interval. In light of this, the *RangeValidator* control might raise an exception if either *MinimumValue* or *MaximumValue* is omitted. Whether the exception is thrown depends on the type chosen and its inherent ability to interpret the empty string. For example, an empty string on a *Date* type causes an exception. If you want to operate on an unbound interval—whether lower or upper unbound—either you resort to the *Greater-Than* (or *LessThan*) operator on the *CompareValidator* control or simply use a virtually infinite value, such as the 9999-12-31 value.

The *RequiredFieldValidator* Control

To catch when a user skips a mandatory field in an input form, you use the *RequiredFieldValidator* control to show an appropriate error message:

```
<asp:RequiredFieldValidator runat="server" id="lnameValidator"
    ControlToValidate="lname"
    ErrorMessage="Last name is mandatory" />
```

As long as you're using an up-level browser and client-side scripting is enabled for each validator, which is the default, invalid input will display error messages without performing a postback.

> **Important**   Note that just tabbing through the controls is not a condition that raises an error; the validator gets involved only if you type blanks or if the field is blank when the page is posted back.

How can you determine whether a certain field is really empty? In many cases, the empty string is sufficient, but this is not a firm rule. The *InitialValue* property specifies the initial value of the input control. The validation fails only if the value of the control equals *InitialValue* upon losing focus. By default, *InitialValue* is initialized with the empty string.

Special Capabilities

The primary reason why you place validation controls on a Web form is to catch errors and inconsistencies in the user's input. But how do you display error messages? Are you interested in client-side validation and, if so, how would you set it up? Finally, what if you want to validate only a subset of controls when a given button is clicked? Special capabilities of validation controls provide a valid answer to all these issues.

Displaying Error Information

The *ErrorMessage* property determines the static message that each validation control will display in case of error. It is important to know that if the *Text* property is also set, it would take precedence over *ErrorMessage*. *Text* is designed to display inline where the validation control is located; *ErrorMessage* is designed to display in the validation summary. (Strategies for using *Text* and *ErrorMessage* will be discussed more in the next section, "The *ValidationSummary* Control.") Because all validation controls are labels, no other support or helper controls are needed to display any message. The message will be displayed in the body of the validation controls and, subsequently, wherever the validation control is actually placed. The error message is displayed as HTML, so it can contain any HTML formatting attribute.

Validators that work in client mode can create the *<span>* tag for the message either statically or dynamically. You can control this setting by using the *Display* property of the validator. When the display mode is set to *Static* (the default), the *<span>* element is given the following style:

```
style="color:Red;visibility:hidden;"
```

The CSS *visibility* style attribute, when set to *Hidden*, causes the browser not to display the element but reserves space for it. If the *Display* property contains *Dynamic*, the style string changes as follows:

```
style="color:Red;display:none;"
```

The CSS *display* attribute, when set to *none*, simply hides the element, which will take up space on the page only if displayed. The value of the *Display* property becomes critical when you have multiple validators associated with the same input control. (See Figure 4-7.)

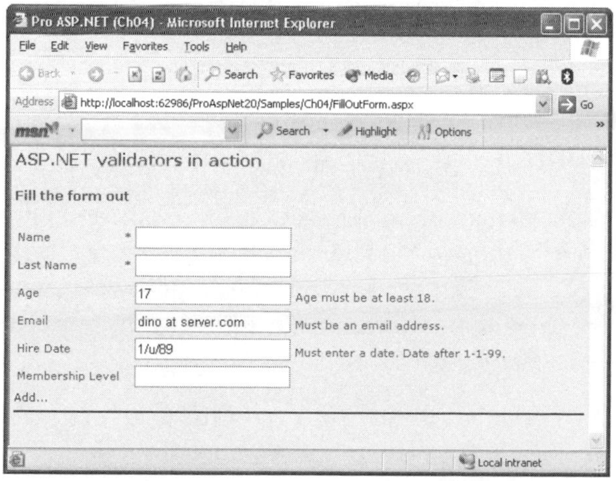

Figure 4-7   Input controls in the form are validated on the client.

As you can see, the hire text box is first validated to ensure it contains a valid date and then to verify the specified date is later than 1-1-1999. If the *Display* property is set to *Static* for the first validator, and the date is outside the specified range, you get a page like the one shown in Figure 4-8.

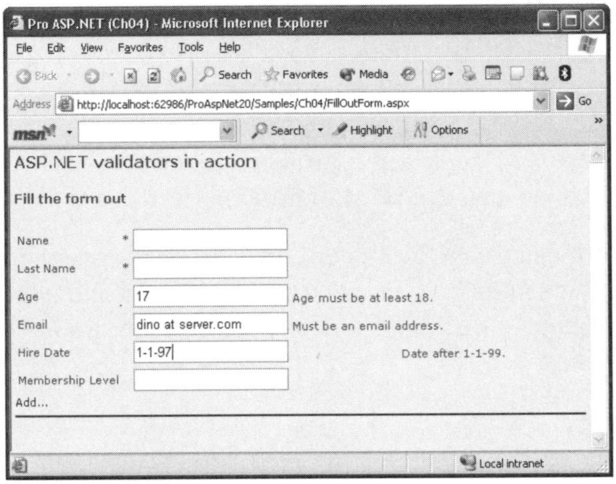

Figure 4-8   Static error messages take up space even if they're not displayed.

The full source code of the page in the figure is available on the Web at the following address: *http://www.microsoft.com/mspress/companion/0-7356-2176-4.*

> **Note**   You can associate multiple validators with a single input control. The validation takes place in order, and each validation control generates and displays its own error message. The content of the input control is considered valid if all the validators return *true*. If an input control has multiple valid patterns—for example, an ID field can take the form of a Social Security number or a VAT number—you can either validate by using custom code or regular expressions.

The *ValidationSummary* Control

The *ValidationSummary* control is a label that summarizes and displays all the validation error messages found on a Web page after a postback. The summary is displayed in a single location formatted in a variety of ways. The *DisplayMode* property sets the output format, which can be a list, a bulleted list, or a plain text paragraph. By default, it is a bulleted list. The feasible values are grouped in the *ValidationSummaryDisplayMode* enumeration.

Whatever the format is, the summary can be displayed as text in the page, in a message box, or in both. The Boolean properties *ShowSummary* and *ShowMessageBox* let you decide. The output of the *ValidationSummary* control is not displayed until the page posts back no matter what the value of the *EnableClientScript* property is. The *HeaderText* property defines the text that is displayed atop the summary:

```
<asp:ValidationSummary runat="server"
    ShowMessageBox="true"
    ShowSummary="true"
    HeaderText="The following errors occurred:"
    DisplayMode="BulletList" />
```

This code snippet originates the screen shown in Figure 4-9.

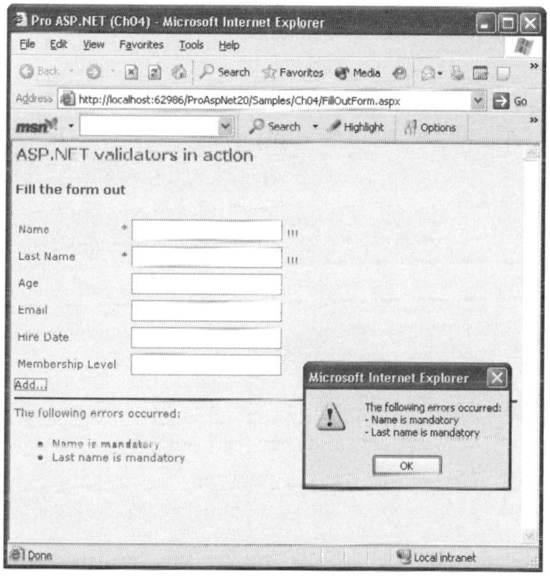

Figure 4-9 After the page posts back, the validation summary is updated and a message box pops up to inform the user.

The validation summary is displayed only if there's at least one pending error. Notice that in the default case, the labels near the input controls are updated anyway, along with the summary text. In summary, you can control the error information in the following ways:

- **Both in-place and summary information.**   This is the default scenario. Use the *ValidationSummary* control and accept all default settings on the validator controls. If you want to leverage both places to display information, a recommended approach consists of minimizing the in-place information by using the *Text* property rather than *ErrorMessage*. If you set both, *Text* is displayed in-place while *ErrorMessage* shows up in the validation summary. For example, you can set *Text* with a glyph or an exclamation mark and assign *ErrorMessage* with more detailed text.

- **Only in-place information.**   Do not use the *ValidationSummary* control, and set the *ErrorMessage* property in each validation control you use. The messages appear after the page posts back.

- **Only summary information.** Use the control, and set the *ErrorMessage* property on individual validation controls. Set the *Display* property of validators to *None* so that no in-place error message will ever be displayed.

- **Custom error information.** You don't use the *ValidationSummary* control, and you set the *Display* property of the individual validators to *None*. In addition, you collect the various error messages through the *ErrorMessage* property on the validation controls and arrange your own feedback for the user.

Enabling Client Validation

As mentioned earlier, the verification normally takes place on the server as the result of the postback event or after the *Validate* method is called. If the browser supports Dynamic HTML, though, you can also activate the validation process on the client, with a significant gain in responsiveness. To be precise, ASP.NET automatically enables client-side validation if it detects a browser with enough capabilities. While ASP.NET 1.x limits its client-side support only to Internet Explorer 4.0 or higher, in ASP.NET 2.0 validation controls also work fine on the client with Mozilla Firefox, Netscape 6.x, and Safari 1.2. Figure 4-10 shows the previous sample page in action in Mozilla Firefox.

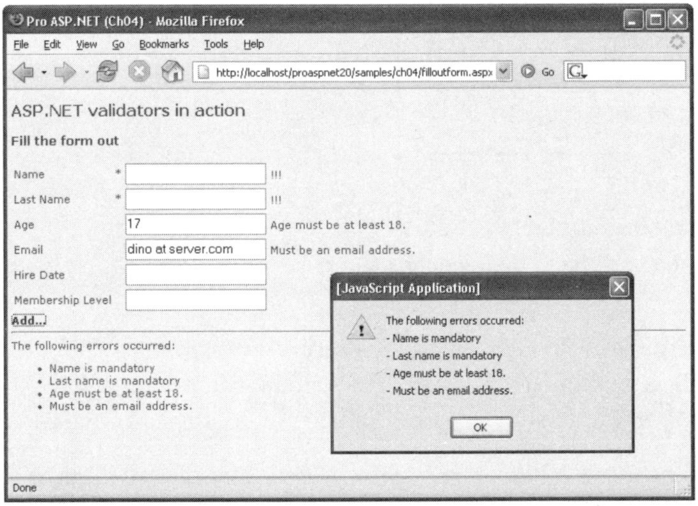

Figure 4-10 Client-side validation active also in Mozilla Firefox.

If client-side validation is turned on, the page won't post back until all the input fields contain valid data. To run secure code and prevent malicious and underhanded attacks, you might want to validate data on the server, too. Consider also that not all types of validation can be accomplished on the client. In fact, if you need to validate against a database, there's no other option than posting back to the server.

Client validation can be controlled on a per-validation control basis by using the *EnableClient-Script* Boolean property. By default, the property is set to *true*, meaning client validation is enabled as long as the browser supports it. By default, the code in the *BaseValidator* class detects the browser's capabilities through the *Request.Browser* property. If the browser is considered up-level, the client validation will be implemented. Browsers and client devices that are considered up-level support at least the following:

- ECMAScript (including JScript and JavaScript) version 1.2
- HTML version 4.0
- The Microsoft Document Object Model
- Cascading style sheets

For down-level browsers, the only requirement is HTML version 3.2. You can also control the client validation at the page level by using the *ClientTarget* attribute on the *@Page* directive. The following code disables client validation by specifying that any code in the page should target a down-level browser:

```
<% @Page ClientTarget="DownLevel" %>
```

The *ClientTarget* attribute overrides the type of browser that ASP.NET should target when generating the page. When the *ClientTarget* attribute is set, ASP.NET doesn't detect the actual browser's capabilities but instead loads the capabilities for the specified browser from the browser database.

Validation Groups

In ASP.NET 1.x, control validation occurs in an all-or-nothing kind of way. For example, if you have a set of input and validation controls and two buttons on the form, clicking either button will always validate all controls. In other words, there's no way to validate some controls when one button is clicked, and some others when the other button is clicked. The *CausesValidation* property on button controls allows you to disable validation on a button, but that is not the point here. What is missing is the ability to do validation on a group of controls. This is exactly what the *ValidationGroup* property provides in ASP.NET 2.0. The property is available on validators, input controls, and button controls.

Using the *ValidationGroup* property is simple; just define it for all the validation controls that you want to group together, and then assign the same name to the *ValidationGroup* property of the button that you want to fire the validation. Here's an example:

```
<asp:textbox runat="server" id="TextBox1"  />
<asp:RequiredFieldValidator runat="server"
    ValidationGroup="Group1"
    ControlToValidate="TextBox1"
    ErrorMessage="TextBox1 is mandatory" />
<asp:textbox runat="server" id="TextBox2"  />
<asp:RequiredFieldValidator runat="server"
    ValidationGroup="Group2"
    ControlToValidate="TextBox2"
```

```
    ErrorMessage="TextBox2 is mandatory" />
<asp:Button runat="server" Text="Check Group1" ValidationGroup="Group1" />
<asp:Button runat="server" Text="Check Group2" ValidationGroup="Group2" />
```

The two *RequiredFieldValidator* controls belong to distinct validation groups—*Group1* and *Group2*. The first button validates only the controls defined within Group1; the second button takes care of the input associated with Group2. In this way, the validation process can be made as granular as needed.

> **Important**   The *ValidationGroup* property can optionally be defined also on input controls. This is required only if you use the *CustomValidator* control as a way to check whether a given input control belongs to the right validation group.

The validation group feature becomes especially helpful when combined with cross-page postbacks—an ASP.NET 2.0 feature that we'll cover in the next chapter. Cross-page postback allows a button to post the contents of the current form to another page, in a certain way over-riding the single-form model of ASP.NET. Imagine you have a search box in your page, and you want to post its contents directly to a search page without passing through the classic post-back mechanism and an additional redirect. Validation groups allow you to check only the contents of the search text box prior to posting to the search page.

Validation groups are also reflected on the server-side where the *Validate* method of the *Page* class now features an overload that lets you select the group according to which the page must be validated.

Conclusion

In ASP.NET pages, server controls are vital components and transform the programming model of ASP.NET from a mere factory of HTML strings to a more modern and effective component-based model. ASP.NET features a long list of control classes. Looking at the namespaces involved, we should conclude that only two families of controls exist—HTML and Web controls. Controls in the former group simply mirror the set of elements in the HTML syntax. Each constituent control has as many properties as there are attributes in the corre-sponding HTML tag. Names and behavior have been kept as faithful to the originals as possi-ble. The ultimate goal of the designers of HTML controls is to make the transition from ASP to ASP.NET as seamless as possible—just add *runat="server"* and refresh the page.

The overall design of Web controls is more abstract and much less tied to HTML. In general, Web controls do not promote a strict one-to-one correspondence between controls and HTML tags. However, the capabilities of Web and HTML controls overlap. All ASP.NET server controls render in HTML, but Web controls render to more complex HTML representation than HTML controls.

In the family of core Web controls, we can identify interesting and powerful families of controls—for example, validators. Validators let you put declarative boundaries around input controls so that any user's input is filtered and validated both on the client and server. This alone is not sufficient to certify an application as secure, but it is a quantum leap in the right direction.

Just the Facts

- In ASP.NET, there are two big families of controls: HTML controls and Web controls. The former group includes controls that are in one-to-one correspondence with HTML elements. The controls in the latter group offer a more abstract programming model and richer functionalities not specifically bound to one HTML element.

- If made invisible, ASP.NET controls don't generate any markup code but are activated and processed anyway.

- Adaptive rendering is the process that enables controls to generate different markup for individual browsers.

- ASP.NET 2.0 controls let you declaratively assign a browser-specific value to properties. For example, you can use one style for Internet Explorer and another one for Mozilla Firefox.

- The vast majority of ASP.NET 2.0 controls can generate XHTML-compliant markup. Non-XHTML mode is supported for backward compatibility.

- New controls let you fully manage programmatically the *<head>* tag of a page.

- Everything you put on a page is ultimately processed as a control, including literal text, blanks, and carriage returns. Contiguous characters are conveyed to a single control instance.

- Validation controls let you test for valid types, values within a given range, regular expressions, and required fields.

- Validators let you put declarative boundaries around input controls so that any user's input is filtered and validated both on the client and server.

- In ASP.NET 2.0, group validation allows you to specify validation of only certain controls when the page posts back.

Chapter 5
Working with the Page

In this chapter:

Programming with Forms. 176

Dealing with Page Errors 188

ASP.NET Tracing 197

Page Personalization 202

Conclusion 216

Although formless pages are still accepted and correctly handled, the typical ASP.NET page contains a single *<form>* tag decorated with the *runat* attribute set to *server*. On the server, the *<form>* tag is mapped to an instance of the *HtmlForm* class. The *HtmlForm* class acts as the outermost container of all server controls and wraps them in an HTML *<form>* element when the page is rendered. The obtained HTML form posts to the same page URL and for this reason is said to be *reentrant*. The default method used to submit form data is *POST*, but *GET* can be used as well.

In most cases, the server form is the outermost tag of the page and is contained directly in *<body>*. In general, though, the server *<form>* tag can be the child of any other server container control, such as *<table>*, *<div>*, *<body>*, and any other HTML generic control. (We covered HTML controls and Web controls in Chapter 4.) If any noncontainer controls (for example, a *TextBox*) are placed outside the form tag, an exception is thrown. Notice, though, that no check is made at compile time. The exception is raised by the control itself when the host page asks to render. Noncontainer Web controls, in fact, check whether they are being rendered within the boundaries of a server form and throw an *HttpException* if they are not. A call to the *Page*'s *VerifyRenderingInServerForm* method does the job. (Be aware of this virtuous behavior when you get to write custom controls.)

In this chapter, we'll examine some aspects of form-based programming in ASP.NET, including how to use multiple forms in the same page and post data to a different page. We'll touch on personalization—a hot new feature of ASP.NET 2.0—and end by discussing tools and effective techniques to debug, trace, and handle errors.

Programming with Forms

One of the most common snags ASP developers face when they first approach the ASP.NET lifestyle is the fact that managed Web applications support the single-form interface (SFI) model.

> **Note**   If you've never heard anyone use the SFI acronym, there's no reason for you to panic. It's an acronym I've purposely created to mimic other more popular acronyms that, although used in different contexts, describe similar programming models—the single-document interface (SDI) and its opposite, the multiple-document interface (MDI).

In the SFI model, each page always posts to itself and doesn't supply any hook for developers to set the final destination of the postback. What in HTML and ASP programming was the *Action* property of the form is simply not defined on the ASP.NET *HtmlForm* class. As a result, the SFI model is a built-in feature so deeply integrated with the ASP.NET platform that you have only two choices: take it, or code the old ASP way without server forms. Note that in ASP.NET 2.0, posting data to different pages is possible, but the implementation of the feature passes through some new capabilities of button controls. Forms work in ASP.NET 2.0 the same way they do in ASP.NET 1.x.

Unlike the action URL, the HTTP method and the target frame of the post can be programmatically adjusted using ad hoc *HtmlForm* properties—*Method* and *Target*.

The *HtmlForm* Class

The *HtmlForm* class inherits from *HtmlContainerControl*, which provides the form with the capability of containing child controls. This capability is shared with other HTML control classes, such as *HtmlTable*, characterized by child elements and a closing tag.

Properties of the *HtmlForm* Class

The *HtmlForm* class provides programmatic access to the HTML *<form>* element on the server through the set of properties shown in Table 5-1. Note that the table includes only a few of the properties *HtmlForm* inherits from the root class *Control*.

Table 5-1   Form Properties

Property	Description
Attributes	Inherited from *Control*, gets a name/value collection with all the attributes declared on the tag.
ClientID	Inherited from *Control*, gets the value of *UniqueID*.
Controls	Inherited from *Control*, gets a collection object that represents the child controls of the form.

Table 5-1 Form Properties

Property	Description
DefaultButton	String property, gets or sets the button control to display as the default button on the form. *Not available in ASP.NET 1.x.*
DefaultFocus	String property, gets or sets the button control to give input focus when the form is displayed. *Not available in ASP.NET 1.x.*
Disabled	Gets or sets a value indicating whether the form is disabled. Matches the *disabled* HTML attribute.
EncType	Gets or sets the encoding type. Matches the *enctype* HTML attribute.
ID	Inherited from *Control*, gets or sets the programmatic identifier of the form.
InnerHtml	Inherited from *HtmlContainerControl*, gets or sets the markup content found between the opening and closing tags of the form.
InnerText	Inherited from *HtmlContainerControl*, gets or sets the text between the opening and closing tags of the form.
Method	Gets or sets a value that indicates how a browser posts form data to the server. The default value is *POST*. Can be set to *GET* if needed.
Name	Gets the value of *UniqueID*.
Style	Gets a collection of all cascading style sheet (CSS) properties applied to the form.
SubmitDisabledControls	Indicates whether to force controls disabled on the client to submit their values, allowing them to preserve their values after the page posts back to the server. *False* by default. *Not available in ASP.NET 1.x.*
TagName	Returns "form".
Target	Gets or sets the name of the frame or window to render the HTML generated for the page.
UniqueID	Inherited from *Control*, gets the unique, fully qualified name of the form.
Visible	Gets or sets a value that indicates whether the form is rendered. If *false*, the form is not rendered to HTML.

The form must have a unique name. If the programmer doesn't assign the name, ASP.NET generates one by using a built-in algorithm. The programmer can set the form's identifier by using either the *ID* or *Name* property. If both are set, the *ID* attribute takes precedence. (Note, though, that any reliance on the *Name* attribute compromises the XHTML compliance of the page.)

The parent object of the form is the outer container control with the *runat* attribute. If such a control doesn't exist, the page object is set as the parent. Typical containers for the server form are *<table>* and *<div>* if they are marked as server-side objects.

By default, the *Method* property is set to *POST*. The value of the property can be modified programmatically. If the form is posted through the *GET* method, all form data is passed on the URL's query string. However, if you choose the *GET* method, make sure the limited size of a *GET* request (2 KB) does not affect the integrity of your application or raise security issues.

Methods of the *HtmlForm* Class

Table 5-2 lists the methods available on the *HtmlForm* class that you'll be using most often. All the methods listed in the table are inherited from the base *System.Web.UI.Control* class.

Table 5-2 Form Methods

Method	Description
ApplyStyleSheetSkin	Applies the style properties defined in the page style sheet. *Not available in ASP.NET 1.x.*
DataBind	Calls the *DataBind* method on all child controls.
FindControl	Retrieves and returns the control that matches the specified ID.
Focus	Set input focus to a control. *Not available in ASP.NET 1.x.*
HasControls	Indicates whether the form contains any child controls.
RenderControl	Outputs the HTML code for the form. If tracing is enabled, caches tracing information to be rendered later, at the end of the page.

It is important to note that the *FindControl* method searches only among the form's direct children. Controls belonging to an inner naming container, or that are a child of a form's child control, are not found.

Multiple Forms

As mentioned, the SFI model is the default in ASP.NET and plays a key role in the automatic view state management mechanism we described in Chapter 3. Generally speaking, the ASP.NET enforcement of the SFI model does not significantly limit the programming power, and all things considered, doing without multiple forms is not a big sacrifice. Some pages, though, would have a more consistent and natural design if they could define multiple *logical* forms. In this context, a *logical* form is a logically related group of input controls. For example, think of a page that provides some information to users but also needs to supply an additional form such as a search or a login box.

You can incorporate search and login capabilities in ad hoc classes and call those classes from within the page the user is displayed. This might or might not be the right way to factorize your code, though. Especially if you're porting some old code to ASP.NET, you might find easier to insulate login or search code in a dedicated page. Well, to take advantage of form-based login, how do you post input data to this page?

Using HTML Forms

As mentioned, ASP.NET prevents you from having multiple *<form>* tags flagged with the *runat* attribute. However, nothing prevents you from having one server-side *<form>* tag and multiple client HTML *<form>* elements in the body of the same Web form. Here's an example:

```
<body>
    <table><tr><td>
        <form id="form1" runat="server">
        <h2>Ordinary contents for an ASP.NET page</h2>
        </form>
    </td>
    <td>
        <form method="post" action="search.aspx">
            <table><tr>
                <td>Keyword</td>
                <td><input type="text" id="Keyword" name="Keyword" /></td>
            </tr><tr>
                <td><input type="submit" id="Go" value="Search" /></td>
            </tr></table>
        </form>
    </td>
    </tr></table>
</body>
```

The page contains two forms, one of which is a classic HTML form devoid of the *runat* attribute and, as such, is completely ignored by ASP.NET. The markup served to the browser simply contains two *<form>* elements, each pointing to a different action URL.

This code works just fine but has a major drawback: you can't use the ASP.NET programming model to retrieve posted data in the action page of the client form. When writing *search.aspx*, in fact, you can't rely on view state to retrieve posted values. To know what's been posted, you must resort to the old-fashioned but still effective ASP model, as shown in the following code sample:

```
public partial class Search : System.Web.UI.Page
{
    protected void Page_Load(object sender, EventArgs e)
    {
        // Use the Request object to retrieve posted data
        string textToSearch = Request.Form["Keyword"].ToString();
        ...

        // Use standard ASP.NET programming model to populate the page UI
        KeywordBeingUsed.Text = textToSearch;
    }
}
```

You use the protocol-specific collections of the *Request* object to retrieve posted data—*Form* if *POST* is used and *QueryString* in case of *GET*. In addition, you have to use the *name* attribute to identify input elements. Overall, this is perhaps not a recommended approach, but it definitely works. Figure 5-1 shows the page in action.

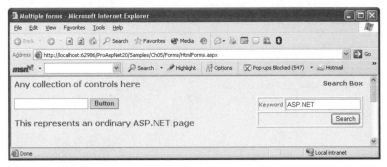

Figure 5-1   A server form control and a client HTML form working together.

When the user clicks the search button, the *search.aspx* page is invoked. It receives only the values posted through the HTML form, and it uses them to proceed.

Multiple *<form>* Tags on a Page

The preceding code works because we have only one server form control at a time. If multiple server forms are declared in the same Web form, an exception is thrown. A little-known fact is that a Web form can actually contain as many server-side forms as needed as long as only one at a time is visible. For example, a page with three *<form runat=server>* tags is allowed, but only one form can actually be rendered. Given the dynamics of page rendering, an exception is thrown if more than one *HtmlForm* control attempts to render. By playing with the *Visible* property of the *HtmlForm* class, you can change the active server form during the page lifetime. This trick doesn't really solve the problem of having multiple active forms, but it can be helpful sometimes.

Let's consider the following ASP.NET page:

```
<body>
    <form id="step0" runat="server" visible="true">
        <h1>Welcome</h1>
        <asp:textbox runat="server" id="Textbox1" />
        <asp:button ID="Button1" runat="server" text="Step #1"
            OnClick="Button1_Click" />
    </form>

    <form id="step1" runat="server" visible="false">
        <h1>Step #1</h1>
        <asp:textbox runat="server" id="Textbox2" />
```

```
    <asp:button ID="Button2" runat="server" text="Previous step"
        OnClick="Button2_Click" />
    <asp:button ID="Button3" runat="server" text="Step #2"
        OnClick="Button3_Click" />
</form>

<form id="step2" runat="server" visible="false">
    <h1>Finalizing</h1>
    <asp:button ID="Button4" runat="server" text="Finish"
        OnClick="Button4_Click" />
</form>
</body>
```

As you can see, all *<form>* tags are marked as *runat*, but only the first one is visible. Mutually exclusive forms are great at implementing wizards in ASP.NET 1.x. By toggling a form's visibility in button event handlers, you can obtain wizard-like behavior, as shown in Figure 5-2.

```
public partial class MultipleForms : System.Web.UI.Page
{
    protected void Page_Load(object sender, EventArgs e)
    {
        Title = "Welcome";
    }
    protected void Button1_Click(object sender, EventArgs e)
    {
        Title = "Step 1";
        step0.Visible = false;
        step1.Visible = true;
    }
    protected void Button2_Click(object sender, EventArgs e)
    {
        step0.Visible = true;
        step1.Visible = false;
    }
    protected void Button3_Click(object sender, EventArgs e)
    {
        Title = "Finalizing";
        step1.Visible = false;
        step2.Visible = true;
    }
    protected void Button4_Click(object sender, EventArgs e)
    {
        Title = "Done";
        step2.Visible = false;
        Response.Write("<h1>Successfully done.</h1>");
    }
}
```

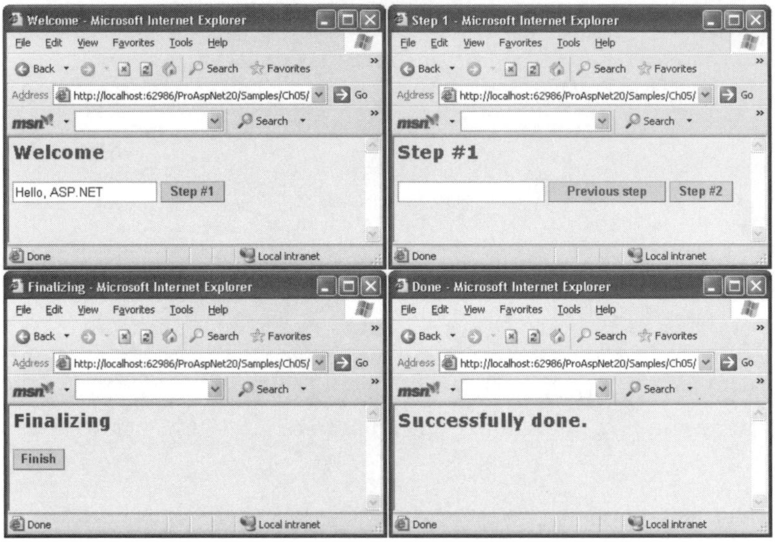

Figure 5-2 Mutually exclusive forms used to implement wizards in ASP.NET 1.x.

Multiple View and Wizards in ASP.NET 2.0

If you're writing an ASP.NET 2.0 application, you don't need to resort to the preceding trick. You find two new controls—*MultiView* and *Wizard*—ready for the job. The *MultiView* control employs logic nearly identical to that of multiple exclusive forms, except that it relies on panels rather than full forms.

The *MultiView* control allows you to define multiple and mutually exclusive HTML panels. The control provides an application programming interface (API) for you to toggle the visibility of the various panels and ensure that exactly one is active and visible at a time. The *MultiView* control doesn't provide a built-in user interface. The *Wizard* control is just that—a *MultiView* control plus some wizard-like predefined user interface (UI) blocks. We'll cover the *Wizard* control in great detail in the next chapter.

Cross-Page Postings

ASP.NET 2.0 offers a built-in mechanism to override the normal processing cycle and prevent the page from posting back to itself. Postbacks occur in one of two ways—either through a submit button or via script. The client browser usually takes on any post conducted through a button and automatically points to the page that the *action* attribute of the posting form indicates. More flexibility is possible when the post occurs via script. In ASP.NET 2.0, you can configure certain page controls—in particular, those that implement the *IButtonControl* interface—to post to a different target page. This is referred to as cross-page posting.

Posting Data to Another Page

Authoring a Web page that can post data to another page requires only a couple of steps. First, you choose the controls that can cause postback and set their *PostBackUrl* property. A page can include one or more button controls and, generally, any combination of button controls and submit buttons. Notice that in this context a button control is any server control that implements *IButtonControl*. (We fully covered the *IButtonControl* interface in Chapter 4.) The following code snippet shows how to proceed:

```
<form runat="server">
    <asp:textbox runat="server" id="Data" />
    <asp:button runat="server" id="buttonPost"
            Text="Click"
            PostBackUrl="target.aspx" />
</form>
```

When the *PostBackUrl* property is set, the ASP.NET runtime binds the corresponding HTML element of the button control to a new JavaScript function. Instead of using our old acquaintance __*doPostback*, it uses the new *WebForm_DoPostBackWithOptions* function. The button renders the following markup:

```
<input type="submit" name="buttonPost" id="buttonPost"
    value="Click"
    onclick="javascript:WebForm_DoPostBackWithOptions(
        new WebForm_PostBackOptions("buttonPost", "",
            false, "", "target.aspx", false, false))" />
```

As a result, when the user clicks the button, the current form posts its content to the specified target page. What about the view state? When the page contains a control that does cross-page posting, a new hidden field is also created: __*PREVIOUSPAGE*. The field contains the view state information to be used to serve the request. This view state information is transparently used in lieu of the original view state of the page being posted to.

You use the *PreviousPage* property to reference the posting page and all of its controls. Here's the code behind a sample target page that retrieves the content of a text box defined in the form:

```
protected void Page_Load(object sender, EventArgs e)
{
    // Retrieves posted data
    TextBox txt = (TextBox) PreviousPage.FindControl("TextBox1");
    ...
}
```

By using the *PreviousPage* property on the *Page* class, you can access any input control defined on the posting page. Access to input controls is weakly typed and occurs indirectly through the services of the *FindControl* method. The problem here lies in the fact that the target page doesn't know anything about the type of the posting page. *PreviousPage* is declared as a property of type *Page* and, as such, it can't provide access to members specific to a derived page class.

Furthermore, note that *FindControl* looks up controls only in the current naming container. If the control you are looking for lives inside another control (say, a template), you must first get a reference to the container, and then search the container to find the control. To avoid using *FindControl* altogether, a different approach is required.

The *@PreviousPageType* Directive

Let's say it up front. To retrieve values on the posting page, *FindControl* is your only safe option if you don't know in advance which page will be invoking your target. However, when using cross-page posting in the context of an application, the chances are good that you know exactly who will be calling the page and how. In this case, you can take advantage of the *@PreviousPageType* directive to cause the target page's *PreviousPage* property to be typed to the source page class.

In the target page, you add the following directive:

```
<%@ PreviousPageType VirtualPath="crosspostpage.aspx" %>
```

The directive can accept either of two attributes—*VirtualPath* or *TypeName*. The former points to the URL of the posting page; the latter indicates the type of the calling page. The directive just shown makes the *PreviousPage* property on the target page class be of the same type as the page at the given path (or the specified type). This fact alone, though, is not sufficient to let you access input controls directly. In Chapter 2 and Chapter 3, we pointed out that each page class contains protected members that represent child controls; unfortunately, you can't call a protected member of a class from an external class. (Only derived classes can access protected members of the parent class.)

To work around the issue, you must add public properties in the caller page that expose any information you want posted pages to access. For example, imagine that *crosspostpage.aspx* contains a *TextBox* named *_textBox1*. To make it accessible from within a target page, you add the following code to the code-behind class:

```
public TextBox TextBox1
{
    get { return _textBox1; }
}
```

The new *TextBox1* property on the page class wraps and exposes the internal text-box control. In light of this code, the target page can now execute the following code:

```
Response.Write(PreviousPage.TextBox1.Text);
```

Detecting Cross-Page Postings

Being the potential target of a cross-page call doesn't automatically make a target page a different kind of page all of a sudden. There's always the possibility that the target page is invoked on its own—for example, via hyperlinking. When this happens, the *PreviousPage* property returns *null* and other postback-related properties, such as *IsPostBack*, assume the usual values.

If you have such a dual page, you should insert some extra code to discern the page behavior. The following example shows a page that allows only cross-page access:

```
if (PreviousPage == null)
{
    Response.Write("Sorry, that's the wrong way to invoke me.");
    Response.End();
    return;
}
```

The *IsCrossPagePostBack* property on the *Page* class deserves a bit of attention. The property returns *true* if the current page has called another ASP.NET page. It goes without saying that *IsCrossPagePostBack* on the target page always returns *false*. Therefore, the following code is *not* equivalent to the previous code:

```
if (!IsCrossPagePostBack)
{
    ...
}
```

To know whether the current page is being called from another page, you have to test the value of *IsCrossPagePostBack* on the page object returned by *PreviousPage*.

```
// PreviousPage is null in case of a normal request
if (!PreviousPage.IsCrossPagePostBack)
{
    ...
}
```

However, this code will inevitably throw an exception if the page is invoked in a normal way (that is, from the address bar or via hyperlinking). In the end, the simplest and most effective way to see whether a page is being invoked through cross-page postbacks is by checking *PreviousPage* against *null*.

Dealing with Validation

What if the original page contains validators? Imagine a page with a text box whose value is to be posted to another page. You don't want the post to occur if the text box is empty. To obtain the preferred result, you add a *RequiredFieldValidator* control and bind it to the text box:

```
<asp:TextBox ID="TextBox1" runat="server"></asp:TextBox>
<asp:RequiredFieldValidator ID="Validator1" runat="server"
```

```
       ControlToValidate="TextBox1" Text="*" />
<asp:Button ID="Button1" runat="server" Text="Apply request..."
    OnClick="Button1_Click" PostBackUrl="targetpage.aspx" />
```

As expected, when you click the button the page won't post if the text box is empty; a red asterisk (plus an optional message) is displayed to mark the error. This is because by default button controls validate the input controls before proceeding with the post. Is that all, or is there more to dig out?

In most cases, the *RequiredFieldValidator* benefits the client-side capabilities of the browser. This means that, in the case of empty text boxes, the button doesn't even attempt to make the post. Let's work with a *CustomValidator* control, which instead requires that some server-side code be run to check the condition. Can you imagine the scenario? You're on, say, *post.aspx* and want to reach *target.aspx*; to make sure you post only under valid conditions, though, you first need a trip to *post.aspx* to perform some validation. Add this control, write the server validation handler, and put a breakpoint in its code:

```
<asp:CustomValidator ID="CustomValidator1" runat="server" Text="*"
    ControlToValidate="TextBox1" OnServerValidate="ServerValidate" />
```

Debugging this sample page reveals that posting to another page is a two-step operation. First, a classic postback is made to run any server-side code registered with the original page (for example, server-side validation code or code associated with the click of the button). Next, the cross-page call is made to reach the desired page:

```
void ServerValidate(object source, ServerValidateEventArgs args)
{
    args.IsValid = false;
    if (String.Equals(args.Value, "Dino"))
        args.IsValid = true;
}
```

The preceding code sets the page's *IsValid* property to *false* if the text box contains anything other than "Dino." However, this fact alone doesn't prevent the transition to the target page. In other words, you could have invalid input data posted to the target page.

Fortunately, this issue has an easy workaround, as shown in the following code:

```
if (!PreviousPage.IsValid)
{
    Response.Write("Sorry, the original page contains invalid input.");
    Response.End();
    return;
}
```

In the target page, you test the *IsValid* property on the *PreviousPage* property and terminate the request in the case of a negative answer.

Redirecting Users to Another Page

In addition to the *PostBackUrl* property of button controls, ASP.NET provides another mechanism for transferring control and values from one page to another—the *Server.Transfer* method.

The URL of the new page is not reflected by the browser's address bar because the transfer takes place entirely on the server. The following code shows how to use the method to direct a user to another page:

```
protected void Button1_Click(object sender, EventArgs e)
{
    Server.Transfer("targetpage.aspx");
}
```

Note that all the code that might be following the call to *Transfer* in the page is never executed. In the end, *Transfer* is just a page-redirect method. However, it is particularly efficient for two reasons. First, no roundtrip to the client is requested as is the case, for example, with *Response.Redirect*. Second, the same *HttpApplication* that was serving the caller request is reused, thus limiting the impact on the ASP.NET infrastructure.

In ASP.NET 1.x, the spawned page can access the page object representing its caller by using the *Handler* property of the HTTP context, as follows:

```
Page caller = (Page) Context.Handler;
```

Because *Handler* returns a valid instance of the referrer page object, the spawned page can access all of its properties and methods. It cannot directly access the controls because of the protection level, though. This programming model also works in ASP.NET 2.0.

In ASP.NET 2.0, things are simplified; using *Handler* is no longer necessary. You can use the same programming model of cross-page postings and rely on a non-null *PreviousPage* property and the *@PreviousPageType* directive for strongly typed access to input fields. How can a page detect whether it's being called through a server transfer or through a cross-page postback? In both cases, *PreviousPage* is not null but the *IsCrossPagePostBack* on the *PreviousPage* object is *true* for a cross-page posting and *false* in the case of a server transfer. (This and all other techniques related to form posting are demonstrated in great detail in the sample companion code.)

> **Important** Passing values from one page to another is a task that can be accomplished in a variety of ways—using cross-page posting, server transfer, HTML forms, or query strings. Which one is the most effective? In ASP.NET 2.0, cross-page posting and server transfer offer a familiar programming model but potentially move a significant chunk of data through the *__PREVIOUSPAGE* field. Whether this information is really needed depends on the characteristics of the target page. In many cases, the target page just needs to receive a few parameters to start working. If this is the case, HTML client forms might be more effective in terms of data being moved. HTML forms, though, require an ASP-like programming model.

Dealing with Page Errors

Just like other .NET applications, ASP.NET applications can take advantage of exceptions to catch and handle run-time errors that occur in the code. Exceptions, though, should be just what their name suggests—exceptional events in the life of the application, raised when something happens that violates an assumption. A typical bad programming practice is to rely on exceptions to catch any possible error resulting from an operation. Admittedly, wrapping a piece of code with a *try/catch* block makes programming much simpler while offering a single point of control for errors. However, employing this technique on a large scale can result in a dramatic loss of performance. Exceptions are meant to target exceptional events that aren't predictable in other ways. Exceptions should not be used to control the normal flow of the program. If there is a way to detect possible inconsistent situations, by all means use that other method and keep exceptions as the last resort.

This said, bear in mind that exceptions are the official tool to handle errors in .NET applications. They're not lightweight and should not be overused, but they provide a solid, modern, and effective way of catching errors and recovering from them.

When an exception occurs in an ASP.NET application, the common language runtime (CLR) tries to find a block of code willing to catch it. Exceptions walk their way up the stack until the root of the current application is reached. If no proper handler shows up along the way, the exception gains the rank of unhandled exception and causes the CLR to throw a system-level exception. Users are shown a standard error page that some developers familiarly call YSOD (Yellow Screen of Death), which is a spin-off of the just as illustrious BSOD (Blue Screen of Death) that we all have come to know after years of experience with the Microsoft Windows operating system.

An unhandled exception originates an error and stops the application. As a developer, how should you deal with unhandled exceptions in ASP.NET applications?

Basics of Error Handling

Any ASP.NET application can incur various types of errors. There are configuration errors caused by some invalid syntax or structure in one of the application's *web.config* files and parser errors that occur when the syntax on a page is malformed. In addition, you can run into compilation errors when statements in the page's code-behind class are incorrect. Finally, there are run-time errors that show up during the page's execution.

Default Error Pages

When an unrecoverable error occurs in an ASP.NET page, the user always receives a page that (more or less) nicely informs him or her that something went wrong at a certain point. ASP.NET catches any unhandled exception and transforms it into a page for the user, as shown in Figure 5-3.

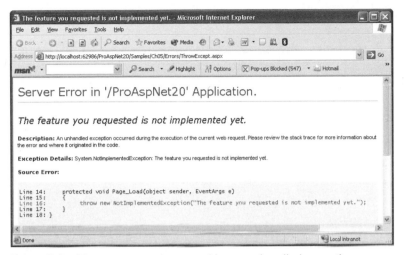

Figure 5-3 The error page generated by an unhandled exception.

The typical error page differs for local and remote users. By default, local users—namely, any user accessing the application through the local host—receive the page shown in Figure 5-3. The page includes the call stack—the chain of method calls leading up to the exception—and a brief description of the error. Additional source code information is added if the page runs in debug mode. For security reasons, remote users receive a less detailed page, like the one shown in Figure 5-4.

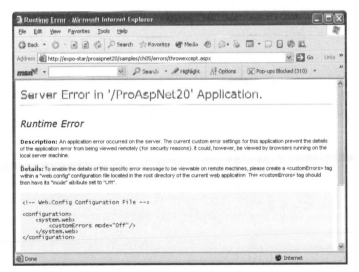

Figure 5-4 A run-time error occurred on the server. The page does not provide information about the error, but it still can't be called a user-friendly page!

Exception handling is a powerful mechanism used to trap code anomalies and recover or degrade gracefully. By design, though, exception handling requires you to know exactly the points in the code where a given exception, or a given set of exceptions, can occur. Exceptions raised outside any interception points you might have arranged become unhandled exceptions and originate YSOD.

ASP.NET provides a couple of global interception points for you to handle errors programmatically, at either the page level or the application level. As mentioned in Chapter 3, the *Page* base class exposes an *Error* event, which you can override in your pages to catch any unhandled exceptions raised during the execution of the page. Likewise, an *Error* event exists on the *HttpApplication* class, too, to catch any unhandled exception thrown within the application.

Page-Level Error Handling

To catch any unhandled exceptions wandering around a particular page, you define a handler for the *Error* event. Here's an example:

```
protected void Page_Error(object sender, EventArgs e)
{
    // Capture the error
    Exception ex = Server.GetLastError();

    // Resolve the error page based on the exception that occurred
    // and redirect to the appropriate page
    if (ex is NotImplementedException)
        Server.Transfer("/errorpages/notimplementedexception.aspx");
    else
        Server.Transfer("/errorpages/apperror.aspx");

    // Clear the error
    Server.ClearError();
}
```

You know about the raised exception through the *GetLastError* method of the *Server* object. In the *Error* handler, you can transfer control to a particular page and show a personalized and exception-specific message to the user. The control is transferred to the error page, and the URL in the address bar of the browser doesn't change. If you use *Server.Transfer* to pass control, the exception information is maintained and the error page itself can call into *GetLastError* and display more detailed information. Finally, once the exception is fully handled, you clear the error by calling *ClearError*.

> **Important**   When displaying error messages, take care not to hand out sensitive information that a malicious user might use against your system. Sensitive data includes user names, file system paths, connection strings, and password-related information. You can make error pages smart enough to determine whether the user is local, or whether a custom header is defined, and display more details that can be helpful to diagnose errors:
>
> ```
> if (Request.UserHostAddress == "127.0.0.1") {
>     ...
> }
> ```
>
> You can also use the *Request.Headers* collection to check for custom headers added only by a particular Web server machine. To add a custom header, you open the Properties dialog box of the application's Internet Information Server (IIS) virtual folder and click the HTTP Headers tab.

Global Error Handling

A page *Error* handler catches only errors that occur within a particular page. This means that each page that requires error handling must point to a common piece of code or define its own handler. Such a fine-grained approach is not desirable when you want to share the same generic error handler for all the pages that make up the application. In this case, you can create a global error handler at the application level that catches all unhandled exceptions and routes them to the specified error page.

The implementation is nearly identical to page-level error handlers except that you will be handling the *Error* event on the *HttpApplication* object that represents your application. To do that, you add a *global.asax* file to your application and write code in the predefined *Application_Error* stub:

```
void Application_Error(Object sender, EventArgs e) {
    ...
}
```

In Microsoft Visual Studio .NET 2005, to generate the *global.asax* file, you select Add New Item and then pick up a Global Application Class item.

> **Note**   You can have at most one *global.asax* file per ASP.NET application. In Visual Studio .NET 2003, an empty *global.asax* file is generated when you create a Web application project. In Visual Studio .NET 2005, if your Web site project already contains a *global.asax* file, the corresponding selection is removed from the list of available items when you click the Add New Item menu.

You could do something useful in this event handler, such as sending an e-mail to the site administrator or writing to the Windows event log to say that the page failed to execute properly. ASP.NET 2.0 provides a set of classes in the *System.Net.Mail* namespace for just this purpose. (Note that a similar set of classes exist for ASP.NET 1.x in the *System.Web.Mail* namespace, which is obsolete in ASP.NET 2.0.)

```
MailMessage mail = new MailMessage();
mail.From = new MailAddress("automated@contoso.com");
mail.To.Add(new MailAddress("administrator@contoso.com"));
mail.Subject = "Site Error at " + DateTime.Now;
mail.Body = "Error Description: " + ex.Message;
SmtpClient server = new SmtpClient();
server.Host = outgoingMailServerHost;
server.Send(mail);
```

The code to use for ASP.NET 1.x is slightly different, doesn't require you to explicitly set the host, and uses the *SmtpMail* class.

Robust Error Handling

A good strategy for a robust and effective error handling is based on the following three guidelines:

1. Anticipate problems by wrapping all blocks of code that might fail in *try/catch/finally* blocks. This alone doesn't guarantee that no exceptions will ever show up, but at least you'll correctly handle the most common ones.

2. Don't leave any exceptions unhandled. By following this guideline, even if you did not anticipate a problem, at least users won't see an exception page. You can do this both at the page and application level. Needless to say, an application-level error handler takes precedence over page-level handlers.

3. Make sure that error pages don't give away any sensitive information. If necessary, distinguish between local and remote users and show detailed messages only to the former. A local user is defined as the user that accesses the application from the Web server machine.

Outlined in this way, error handling is mostly a matter of writing the right code in the right place. However, ASP.NET provides developers with a built-in mechanism to automatically redirect users to error-specific pages. This mechanism is entirely declarative and can be controlled through the *web.config* file.

> **Warning**   As we delve deeper into the various topics of ASP.NET, we'll be making extensive use of the information stored in configuration files. Configuration files were briefly introduced in Chapter 1, but you won't find in this book a chapter expressly dedicated to them. For appropriate coverage, you might want to take a look at *Programming Microsoft ASP.NET 2.0 Applications: Advanced Topics* (Microsoft Press, 2005).

Mapping Errors to Pages

When an unhandled exception reaches the root of the stack, ASP.NET renders a default page, displaying the previously mentioned yellow screen of death. Developers can customize this aspect of ASP.NET to a large extent through the *<customErrors>* section in the application's *web.config* file.

The *<customErrors>* Section

You turn on custom error messages for an ASP.NET application acting on the *<customErrors>* section. Here's an example:

```
<configuration>
    <system.web>
        ...
        <customErrors mode="RemoteOnly" />
    </system.web>
</configuration>
```

The *mode* attribute specifies whether custom errors are enabled, disabled, or shown only to remote clients. The attribute is required. When the *mode* attribute is set to *RemoteOnly* (the default setting) remote users receive a generic error page that informs them that something went wrong on the server. (See Figure 5-4.) Local users, on the other hand, receive pages that show lots of details about the ASP.NET error. (See Figure 5-3.)

The error handling policy can be changed at will. In particular, ASP.NET can be instructed to display detailed pages to all local and remote users. To activate this functionality, you change the value of the *mode* attribute to *Off*. For obvious security reasons, *Off* should not be used in production environments—it might reveal critical information to potential attackers.

Using Custom Error Pages

Overall, whatever your choice is for the *mode* attribute, all users have a good chance to be served a rather inexpressive and uninformative error page. To display a more professional, friendly, and apologetic page that has a look and feel consistent with the site, you set *web.config* as follows. Figure 5-5 gives an idea of the results you can get.

```
<configuration>
    <system.web>
        <customErrors mode="On"
            defaultRedirect="/GenericError.aspx" />
    </system.web>
</configuration>
```

Figure 5-5   A nicer-looking, friendlier error page.

Whatever the error is, ASP.NET now redirects the user to the *GenericError.aspx* page, whose contents and layout are completely under your control. This look is obtained by adding an optional attribute such as *defaultRedirect*, which indicates the error page to use to notify users. If *mode* is set to *On*, the default redirect takes on the standard error pages for all local and remote users. If *mode* is set to *RemoteOnly*, remote users will receive the custom error page while local users (typically, the developers) still receive the default page with the ASP.NET error information.

In most cases, the custom error page is made of plain HTML so that no error could recursively be raised. However, should the error page, in turn, originate another error, the default generic page of ASP.NET will be shown.

> **Note**   When a default redirect is used, the browser receives an HTTP 302 status code and is invited to issue a new request to the specified error page. This fact has a key consequence: any information about the original exception is lost and *GetLastError*, which is called from within the custom error page, returns *null*.

Handling Common HTTP Errors

A generic error page invoked for each unhandled exception can hardly be context-sensitive—especially if you consider that there's no immediate way for the page author to access the original exception. We'll return to this point in a moment.

In addition to redirecting users to a common page for all errors, ASP.NET enables you to customize pages to show when certain HTTP errors occur. The mapping between error pages and specific HTTP status codes is defined in the *web.config* file. The *<customErrors>* section supports an inner *<error>* tag, which you can use to associate HTTP status codes with custom error pages:

```
<configuration>
  <system.web>
    <customErrors mode="RemoteOnly" defaultRedirect="/GenericError.aspx">
        <error statusCode="404" redirect="/ErrorPages/Error404.aspx" />
        <error statusCode="500" redirect="/ErrorPages/Error500.aspx" />
    </customErrors>
  </system.web>
</configuration>
```

The *<error>* element indicates the page to redirect the user to when the specified HTTP error occurs. The attribute *statusCode* denotes the HTTP error. Figure 5-6 shows what happens when the user mistypes the name of the URL and the error HTTP 404 (resource not found) is generated.

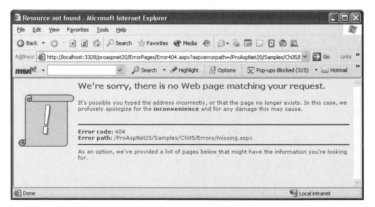

Figure 5-6   A custom page for the popular HTTP 404 error.

When invoked by the ASP.NET infrastructure, pages are passed the URL that caused the error on the query string. The following code shows the code-behind of a sample HTTP 404 error page:

```
public partial class Error404 : System.Web.UI.Page
{
    protected void Page_Load(object sender, EventArgs e)
    {
        string errPath = "<i>No error path information is available.</i>";
        object o = Request.QueryString["AspxErrorPath"];
        if (o != null)
            errPath = (string) o;

        // Update the UI
        ErrorPath.InnerHtml = errPath;
    }
}
```

Getting Information About the Exception

As mentioned, when you configure ASP.NET to redirect to a particular set of error pages, you lose any information about the internal exception that might have caused the error. Needless to say, no internal exception is involved in an HTTP 404 or HTTP 302 error. Unhandled exceptions are the typical cause of HTTP 500 internal errors. How do you make the page show context-sensitive information, at least to local users?

You get access to the exception in the *Error* event both at the page and application level. One thing you can do is this: write a page-level error handler, capture the exception, and store the exception (or only the properties you're interested in) to the session state. The default redirect will then retrieve any context information from the session state.

```
protected void Page_Error(object sender, EventArgs e)
{
    // Capture the error and stores exception data
    Exception ex = Server.GetLastError();

    // Distinguish local and remote users
    if (Request.UserHostAddress == "127.0.0.1")
        Session["LastErrorMessage"] = ex.Message;
    else
        Session["LastErrorMessage"] = "Internal error.";

    // Clear the error
    Server.ClearError();
}
```

The preceding code checks the host address and stores exception-related information (limited to the message for simplicity) only for local users. The following code should be added to the *Page_Load* method of the page that handles the HTTP 500 error:

```
string msg = "No additional information available.";
object extraInfo = Session["LastErrorMessage"];
```

```
if (extraInfo != null)
    msg = (string) extraInfo;
ExtraInfo.InnerHtml = msg;
Session["LastErrorMessage"] = null;
```

Figure 5-7 shows the final result.

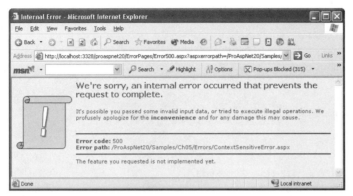

Figure 5-7   A context-sensitive error page for the HTTP 500 status code.

Writing context-sensitive error pages requires a page-level *Error* handler to cache the original exception. This means that you should write the same handler for every page that requires context-sensitive errors. You can either resort to a global error handler or write a new *Page*-derived class that incorporates the default *Error* handler. All the pages that require that functionality will derive their code file from this class instead of *Page*.

> **Note**   What takes precedence if you have an application-level error handler, a page-level handler, and a bunch of redirects? The application-level handler takes precedence over the others. The page-level code runs later, followed by any code that handles HTTP 500 internal errors. Note that HTTP errors other than 500 are not caught by *Error* page and application events because they're handled by the Web server and don't go through the ASP.NET error-handling mechanism described here.

Debugging Options

Debugging an ASP.NET page is possible only if the page is compiled in debug mode. An assembly compiled in debug mode incorporates additional information for a debugger tool to step through the code. You can enable debug mode on individual pages as well as for all the pages in a given application. The *<compilation>* section in the *web.config* file controls this setting. In particular, you set the *Debug* attribute to *true* to enable debug activity for all pages in the application. The default is *false*. To enable debug on a single page, you add the *Debug* attribute to the *@Page* directive:

```
<% @Page Debug="true" %>
```

ASP.NET compiles the contents of any *.aspx* resource before execution. The contents of the *.aspx* resource is parsed to obtain a C# (or Microsoft Visual Basic .NET) class file, which is then handed out to the language compiler. When a page is flagged with the *Debug* attribute, ASP.NET doesn't delete the temporary class file used to generate the page assembly. This file is available on the Web server for you to peruse and investigate. The file is located under the Windows folder at the following path: Microsoft.NET\ Framework\[version]\Temporary ASP.NET Files.

Debug mode is important for testing applications and diagnosing their problems. Note, though, that running applications in debug mode has a significant performance overhead. You should make sure that an application has debugging disabled before deploying it on a production server.

ASP.NET Tracing

Error handling and tool-assisted debugging are essential instruments to make an application run without anomalies and recover gracefully from unexpected exceptions. Tools for tracing complete the kit. *Tracing* refers to the ability to output messages commenting on the execution of the code. This feature is extremely useful for tracking data inconsistencies, monitoring the flow, asserting conditions, and even gathering profiling information.

The .NET Framework comes with a rather feature-rich set of tools for tracing applications. In particular, the *Systems.Diagnostics* namespace defines two classes, named *Trace* and *Debug*, whose methods can be used to trace the code. The *Trace* and *Debug* classes are essentially identical and work on top of more specialized modules known as "listeners." The listener acts like a driver, collects tracing messages, and stores the messages in a particular medium such as the Windows event log, an application window, or a text file. Each application can have its own set of listeners, which will receive all emitted messages. The ASP.NET support for tracing is different and fairly disjointed, at least in ASP.NET 1.x.

ASP.NET comes with a made-to-measure subsystem to provide applications with diagnostic information about individual requests. The tracing subsystem is part of the infrastructure, and all that an application or a page has to do is enable it.

Tracing the Execution Flow in ASP.NET

Tracing lets developers write and leave debug statements in the code and turn them on and off through an attribute, and they can even do this once the application is deployed to a production server. When tracing for a page is enabled, ASP.NET appends diagnostic information to the page's output or sends it to a trace viewer application. For the most part, trace information has a fixed layout and fixed content, but page and control authors can customize it to some extent.

Enabling Page Tracing

Although a *<trace>* configuration section does exist in the *web.config* file to let you configure tracing at the application level, you typically want to control tracing on a per-page basis. However, for large projects you can toggle on and off the trace attribute by using the following code in the application's *web.config* file:

```
<configuration>
    <system.web>
        <trace enabled="true" pageOutput="true" />
    </system.web>
</configuration>
```

The *enabled* attribute enables tracing on the application, while the *pageOutput* attribute permits output to appear in the page. If *pageOutput* is set to *false* (the default setting), the tracing output is automatically routed to the ASP.NET tracer tool— *trace.axd*. At the end of the project, you simply drop the *<trace>* element from the *web.config* file or set both attributes to *false*. In this way, you eliminate at the root the risk of inadvertently leaving tracing enabled on one of the application pages.

The *trace* attribute in the *@Page* directive defaults to *false*; if set to *true*, it enables tracing information to appear at the bottom of pages, as shown in Figure 5-8.

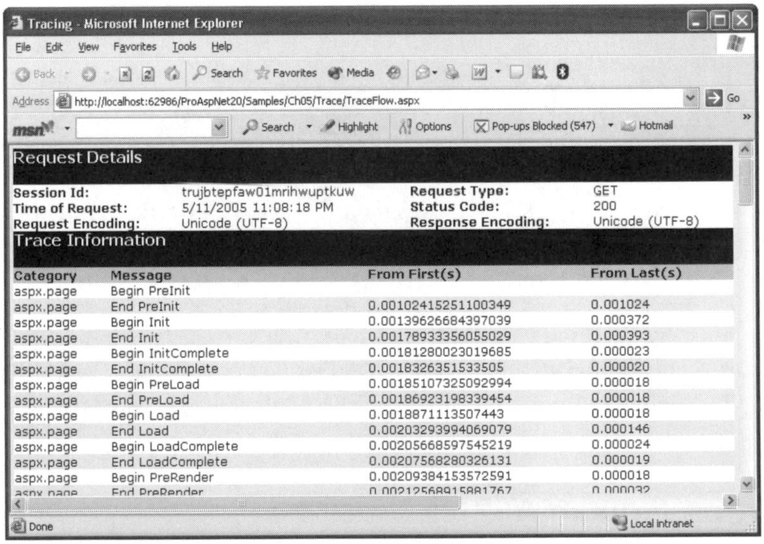

Figure 5-8   ASP.NET tracing in action.

The trace information is part of the page and, as such, displays through any type of browser that accesses the page. Several tables of information show up along with the trace information generated by the page. Additional tables display request details, the control tree, and some useful collections such as cookies, headers, form values, and server variables. If the session and the application state are not empty, the contents of the *Session* and *Application* intrinsic properties are also included in the view.

The *@Page* directive also supplies the *TraceMode* attribute to let you choose the order in which the information should be displayed. Feasible values are *SortByCategory* and *SortByTime*. By default, the trace messages appear in the order in which they are emitted. If you set the *TraceMode* attribute to the *SortByCategory* value, the rows appearing in the Trace Information section are sorted by category name. The category to which each row belongs is determined by the method used to emit the message.

Enabling Tracing Programmatically

The *Page* class provides two properties to control tracing programmatically. They are *TraceModeValue* and *TraceEnabled*. As the names suggest, both are the programmatic counterpart of the aforementioned *@Page* directive attributes. *TraceEnabled* is a read/write Boolean property that turns tracing on and off for the specified page. *TraceModeValue* gets and sets a value in the *TraceMode* enumeration to indicate the desired tracing mode of the page—either sort by category or by time.

To be honest, enabling and disabling output trace programmatically is not a feature that many applications require in a production scenario. The feature, though, might be valuable during the development cycle.

Writing Trace Messages

A third property on the *Page* class that is relevant to tracing is *Trace*—an instance of the *TraceContext* class. An ASP.NET page populates its trace log using methods on the *TraceContext* class. An instance of this class is created when the HTTP request is set up for execution. The trace object is then exposed through the *Trace* property of the *HttpContext* class and is mirrored by the *Trace* property on the *Page* class.

The *TraceContext* Class

The *TraceContext* class has a simple interface and features a couple of properties and as many methods. The properties are *IsEnabled* and *TraceMode*. The *IsEnabled* property is a read-only Boolean property that indicates whether tracing is enabled. The value that this property returns is affected by the *trace* attribute on the *@Page* directive as well as the *enabled* attribute in the *<trace>* section of the *web.config* file. The *TraceMode* property gets and sets the order in which the traced rows will be displayed in the page. The property is of type *TraceMode*—an enumeration that includes values such as *SortByCategory* and *SortByTime*.

Emitting Trace Messages

To emit messages, you can use either of two methods: *Write* or *Warn*. Both methods have three overloads, which all behave in the same way. *Write* and *Warn* are nearly identical methods— the only visible difference is that *Warn* always outputs messages in red:

```
public void Write(string);
public void Write(string, string);
public void Write(string, string, Exception);
```

The simplest overload just emits the specified text in the Message column. (See Figure 5-8.) In the second overload, the first string argument represents the name of the category you want to use for the message—the second argument. The category name can be used to sort trace information and is any name that makes sense to the application to better qualify the message. Finally, the third overload adds an extra *Exception* object in case the message is tracing an error. In this case, the text in the Message column is the concatenation of the specified text and the exception's message.

> **Note** Although the text being passed to both *Write* and *Warn* methods is meant to be displayed in HTML pages, no HTML formatting tag is ever processed. The text is written as plain text so that if you attempt to use boldface characters, your only result is having a trace message with ** and ** substrings.

Tracing from External Classes

The ASP.NET *Trace* object is accessible without a fully qualified name from the source code of the page or from the code file class. Custom controls embedded in the page, and their code file classes, can also access the tracing subsystem directly. Other classes don't have the same possibility, though.

Suppose your code-behind class delegates an external class to accomplish some tasks. How can the worker class trace in the ASP.NET page? In the context of the worker class, the *Trace* object is unavailable, or at least not in its unqualified form. External classes that want to emit text in the trace log of the current HTTP request can do that using the following expression:

```
System.Web.HttpContext.Current.Trace.Write(category, msg);
```

In ASP.NET 2.0, you can configure the tracing subsystem to automatically forward messages to the .NET Framework tracing infrastructure, for any listeners registered to display diagnostic messages. To enable this, you add the following code to the *web.config* file:

```
<system.web>
    <trace enabled="true" writeToDiagnosticsTrace="true" />
</system.web>
```

New to ASP.NET 2.0, the *writeToDiagnosticsTrace* attribute defaults to *false*. Listeners that can receive any messages output to the ASP.NET trace context are those listed in the <trace> section under the <system.diagnostics> section.

The Trace Viewer

ASP.NET also supports application-level tracing through the trace viewer tool. Once tracing has been enabled for the application, each page request routes all the page-specific trace information to the viewer. You can view the trace viewer by requesting *trace.axd* from the root application directory. The trace viewer is shown in Figure 5-9.

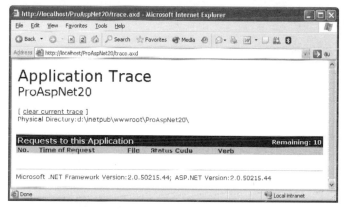

Figure 5-9 The trace viewer ready for action.

To enable the viewer, you need to have a <trace> section in your application *web.config* file—that is, the configuration file deployed in the root folder:

```
<configuration>
    <system.web>
        <trace enabled="true" />
    </system.web>
</configuration>
```

The <trace> section supports a few attributes. The *pageOutput* attribute, for example, indicates whether the trace output should be visible to the individual pages too or accessible only through the viewer. By default, *pageOutput* is *false* and only the viewer receives trace information. However, each page can individually override this setting by using the *Trace* attribute on the @Page directive. The trace viewer caches no more than the number of requests specified by the *requestLimit* attribute (which is 10 by default).

In short, the ASP.NET trace viewer acts as a centralized console and gathers all the trace information generated by the pages in a certain application. Each request, up to the maximum number fixed by *requestLimit*, is identified by a row in the viewer's interface and can be consulted until the viewer's cache is cleared, as shown in Figure 5-10.

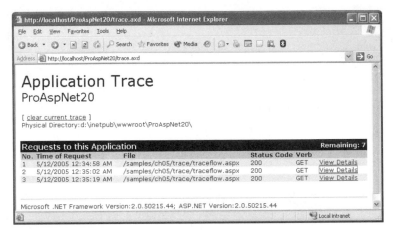

Figure 5-10   The trace viewer in action.

The trace viewer automatically tracks all requests and caches the full trace for each. When the request limit is reached, no other request will be cached until the log is manually cleared.

Page Personalization

ASP.NET pages do not necessarily require a rich set of personalization features. However, if you can build an effective personalization layer into your Web application, final pages will be friendlier, more functional, and more appealing to use. For some applications (such as portals and shopping centers), though, personalization is crucial. For others, it is mostly a way to improve visual appearance. In ASP.NET 2.0, personalization comes in two complementary forms: user profiles and themes.

The user profile is designed for persistent storage of structured data using a friendly and type-safe API. The application defines its own model of personalized data, and the ASP.NET runtime does the rest by parsing and compiling that model into a class. Each member of the personalized class data corresponds to a piece of information specific to the current user. Loading and saving personalized data is completely transparent to end users and doesn't even require the page author to know much about the internal plumbing.

Themes assign a set of styles and visual attributes to elements of the site that can be customized. These elements include control properties, page style sheets, images, and templates on the page. A theme is the union of all visual styles for all customizable elements in the pages—a sort of super-CSS file. We'll work on themes in the next chapter.

Important   No personalization facilities are available in ASP.NET 1.x. I discussed how to build a similar infrastructure in the March 2004 issue of *MSDN Magazine*. The article is online at *http://msdn.microsoft.com/msdnmag/issues/04/03/CuttingEdge*.

Creating the User Profile

At the highest level of abstraction, a user profile is a collection of properties that the ASP.NET 2.0 runtime groups into a dynamically generated class. Any profile data is persisted on a per-user basis and is permanently stored until someone with administrative privileges deletes it. When the application runs and a page is displayed, ASP.NET dynamically creates a profile object that contains, properly typed, the properties you have defined in the data model. The object is then added to the current *HttpContext* object and is available to pages through the *Profile* property.

The data storage is hidden from the user and, to some extent, from the programmers. The user doesn't need to know how and where the data is stored; the programmer simply needs to indicate what type of profile provider he wants to use. The profile provider determines the database to use—typically, a Microsoft SQL Server database—but custom providers and custom data storage models can also be used.

> **Note**   In ASP.NET 2.0, the default profile provider is based on SQL Express, a lightweight version of SQL Server 2005. The physical storage medium is a local file named *aspnetdb.mdf*, which is located in the *App_Data* folder of the Web application.

Definition of the Data Model

To use the ASP.NET 2.0 profile API, you first decide on the structure of the data model you want to use. Then you attach the data model to the page through the configuration file. The layout of the user profile is defined in the *web.config* file and consists of a list of properties that can take any of the .NET common language runtime (CLR) types. The data model is a block of XML data that describe properties and related .NET Framework types.

The simplest way to add properties to the profile storage medium is through name/value pairs. You define each pair by adding a new property tag to the *<properties>* section of the configuration file. The *<properties>* section is itself part of the larger *<profile>* section, which also includes provider information. The *<profile>* section is located under *<system.web>*. Here's an example of a user profile section:

```
<profile>
    <properties>
        <add name="BackColor" type="string" />
        <add name="ForeColor" type="string" />
    </properties>
</profile>
```

All the properties defined through an *<add>* tag become members of a dynamically created class that is exposed as part of the HTTP context of each page. The *type* attribute indicates the type of the property. If no type information is set, the type defaults to *System.String*. Any valid

CLR type is acceptable. Table 5-3 lists the valid attributes for the *<add>* element. Only *name* is mandatory.

Table 5-3   Attributes of the *<add>* Element

Attribute	Description
allowAnonymous	Allows storing values for anonymous users. *False* by default.
defaultValue	Indicates the default value of the property.
customProviderData	Contains data for a custom profile provider.
Name	Name of the property.
Provider	Name of the provider to use to read and write the property.
readOnly	Specifies whether the property value is read-only. *False* by default.
serializeAs	Indicates how to serialize the value of the property. Possible values are *Xml*, *Binary*, *String*, and *ProviderSpecific*.
Type	The .NET Framework type of property. It is a string object by default.

The User Profile Class Representation

As a programmer, you don't need to know how data is stored or retrieved from the personalization store. However, you must create and configure the store. We skirted this step, but we'll discuss it in detail shortly. The following code snippet gives you an idea of the class being generated to represent the profile's data model:

```
namespace ASP
{
    public class ProfileCommon : ProfileBase
    {
        public virtual string BackColor
        {
            get {(string) GetPropertyValue("BackColor");}
            set {SetPropertyValue("BackColor", value);}
        }
        public virtual string ForeColor
        {
            get {(string) GetPropertyValue("ForeColor");}
            set {SetPropertyValue("ForeColor", value);}
        }
        public virtual ProfileCommon GetProfile(string username)
        {
            object o = ProfileBase.Create(username);
            return (ProfileCommon) o;
        }
        ...
    }
}
```

An instance of this class is associated with the *Profile* property of the page class and is accessed programmatically as follows:

```
// Use the BackColor property to paint the page background
theBody.Attributes["bgcolor"] = Profile.BackColor;
```

There's a tight relationship between user accounts and profile information. We'll investigate this in a moment—for now, you need to notice this because anonymous users are supported as well.

Using Collection Types

In the previous example, we worked with single, scalar values. However, the personalization engine fully supports more advanced scenarios, such as using collections or custom types. Let's tackle collections first. The following code demonstrates a property *Links* that is a collection of strings:

```
<properties>
    <add name="Links"
        type="System.Collections.Specialized.StringCollection" />
</properties>
```

Nonscalar values such as collections and arrays must be serialized to fit in a data storage medium. The *serializeAs* attribute simply specifies how. As mentioned, acceptable values are *String*, *Xml*, *Binary*, and *ProviderSpecific*. If the *serializeAs* attribute is not present on the *<properties>* definition, the *String* type is assumed. A collection is normally serialized as XML or in a binary format.

Using Custom Types

You can use a custom type with the ASP.NET personalization layer as long as you mark it as a serializable type. You simply author a class and compile it down to an assembly. The name of the assembly is added to the type information for the profile property:

```
<properties>
    <add name="ShoppingCart"
        type="My.Namespace.DataContainer, MyAssem"
        serializeAs="Binary" />
</properties>
```

The assembly that contains the custom type must be available to the ASP.NET application. You obtain this custom type by placing the assembly in the application's *Bin* directory or by registering it within the global assembly cache (GAC).

Grouping Properties

The *<properties>* section can also accept the *<group>* element. The *<group>* element allows you to group a few related properties as if they are properties of an intermediate object. The following code snippet shows an example of grouping:

```
<properties>
    ...
    <group name="Font">
        <add name="Name" type="string" defaultValue="verdana" />
```

```
        <add name="SizeInPoints" type="int" defaultValue="8" />
    </group>
</properties>
```

The font properties have been declared children of the *Font* group. This means that from now on any access to *Name* or *SizeInPoints* passes through the *Font* name, as shown here:

```
string fontName = Profile.Font.Name;
```

> **Note** Default values are not saved to the persistence layer. Properties declared with a default value make their debut in the storage medium only when the application assigns them a value different from the default one.

Interacting with the Page

To enable or disable profile support, you set the *enabled* attribute of the *<profile>* element in the *web.config* file. If the property is *true* (the default), personalization features are enabled for all pages. If personalization is disabled, the *Profile* property isn't available to pages.

Creating the Profile Database

As mentioned earlier, profile works strictly on a per-user basis and is permanently stored. Enabling the feature simply turns any functionality on, but it doesn't create the needed infrastructure for user membership and data storage.

ASP.NET 2.0 comes with an administrative tool—the ASP.NET Web Site Administration Tool (WSAT)—that is fully integrated in Visual Studio .NET 2005. (See Figure 5-11.) You invoke the tool by choosing ASP.NET Configuration from the Web site menu.

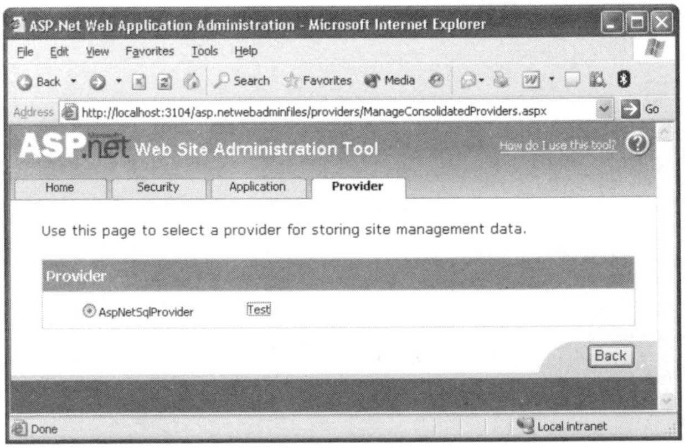

Figure 5-11 The ASP.NET Web Site Administration Tool, which is used to select the profile provider.

You can use this tool to create a default database to store profile data. The default database is a SQL Server 2005 file named *aspnetdb.mdf*, which is located in the *App_Data* special folder of the ASP.NET application. Tables and schema of the database are fixed. The same database contains tables to hold membership and roles information. The use of a membership database with users and roles is important because personalization is designed to be user-specific and because a user ID—either a local Windows account or an application-specific logon—is necessary to index data.

Profile data has no predefined duration and is permanently stored. It is up to the Web site administrator to delete the information when convenient.

Needless to say, WSAT is just one option—not the only one—for setting up the profile infrastructure. For example, if you're using a custom provider, the setup of your application is responsible for preparing any required storage infrastructure—be it a SQL Server table, an Oracle database, or whatever else. We'll cover the setup of profile providers in the next section.

Working with Anonymous Users

Although user profiles are designed primarily for authenticated users, anonymous users can also store profile data. In this case, though, a few extra requirements must be fulfilled. In particular, you have to turn on the *anonymousIdentification* feature, which is disabled by default:

```
<anonymousIdentification enabled="true" />
```

Anonymous identification is a new feature of ASP.NET 2.0. Its purpose is to assign a unique identity to users who are not authenticated and to recognize and treat each of them as an additional registered user.

> **Note** Anonymous identification in no way affects the identity of the account that is processing the request. Nor does it affect any other aspects of security and user authentication. Anonymous identification is simply a way to give a "regular" ID to unauthenticated users so that they can be tracked as authenticated, "regular" users.

In addition, to support anonymous identification you must mark properties in the data model with the special Boolean attribute named *allowAnonymous*. Properties not marked with the attribute are not made available to anonymous users:

```
<anonymousIdentification enabled="true" />
<profile enabled="true">
    <properties>
        <add name="BackColor"
            type="System.Drawing.Color"
            allowAnonymous="true" />
```

```
    <add name="Links"
        type="System.Collections.Specialized.StringCollection"
        serializeAs="Xml" />
    </properties>
</profile>
```

In the preceding code snippet, anonymous users can set the background color but not add new links.

Accessing Profile Properties

Before the request begins its processing cycle, the *Profile* property of the page is set with an instance of a dynamically created class that was created after the user profile defined in the *web.config* file. When the page first loads, the profile properties are set with their default values (if any) or are empty objects. They are never null. When custom or collection types are used to define properties, assigning default values might be hard. The code just shown defines a string collection object—the property *Links*—but giving that a default value expressed as a string is virtually impossible. At run time, though, the *Links* property won't be null—it will equal an empty collection. So how can you manage default values for these properties?

Properties that don't have a default value can be initialized in the *Page_Load* event when the page is not posting back. Here's how you can do that:

```
    if (!IsPostBack)
    {
        // Add some default links to the Links property
        if (Profile.Links.Count == 0) {
            Profile.Links.Add("http://www.contoso.com");
            Profile.Links.Add("http://www.northwind.com");
        }
    }
```

Let's consider some sample code. Imagine a page like the one in Figure 5-12 that displays a list of favorite links in a panel. Users can customize the links as well as a few other visual attributes, such as colors and font.

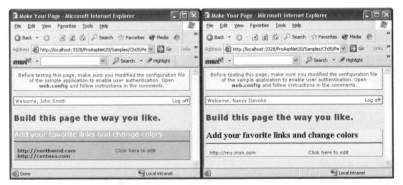

Figure 5-12   Profile information makes the same page display differently for different users.

The profile data is expressed by the following XML:

```
<profile enabled="true">
    <properties>
        <add name="BackColor" type="string" />
        <add name="ForeColor" type="string" />
        <add name="Links"
            type="System.Collections.Specialized.StringCollection"/>
        <group name="Font">
            <add name="Name" type="string" />
            <add name="SizeInPoints" type="int" defaultValue="12" />
        </group>
    </properties>
</profile>
```

The page uses the profile data to adjust its own user interface, as shown in the following code:

```
private void ApplyPagePersonalization()
{
    // Set colors in the panel
    InfoPanel.ForeColor = ColorTranslator.FromHtml(Profile.ForeColor);
    InfoPanel.BackColor = ColorTranslator.FromHtml(Profile.BackColor);

    // Set font properties in panel
    InfoPanel.Font.Name = Profile.Font.Name;
    InfoPanel.Font.Size = FontUnit.Point(Profile.Font.SizeInPoints);

    // Create links
    Favorites.Controls.Clear();
    if(Profile.Links.Count == 0)
        Favorites.Controls.Add(new LiteralControl("No links available."));
    else
        foreach (object o in Profile.Links) {
            HyperLink h = new HyperLink ();
            h.Text = o.ToString ();
            h.NavigateUrl = o.ToString ();
            Favorites.Controls.Add(h);
            Favorites.Controls.Add(new LiteralControl("<br />"));
        }
}
```

The *ApplyPagePersonalization* method is invoked from *Page_Load*:

```
protected void Page_Load(object sender, EventArgs e)
{
    if (!IsPostBack) {
        // Initialize profile properties as needed
    }
    ApplyPagePersonalization();
}
```

Initialization is an important phase, but it's strictly application-specific. For example, the first time a user requests the page, no colors are set and no links are defined. Because we enumerate the contents of the collections, an empty collection is just fine and there's no need to further initialize it. (Note that the framework guarantees that reference objects are always instantiated.) What about color properties? If you specify a default value in the *web.config* file, the framework uses that value to initialize the corresponding property the first time a user requests the page; otherwise, you take care of finding a good default value in *Page_Load*.

At the end of the request, the contents of the profile object are flushed into the profile storage medium and retrieved the next time the page is invoked. When this happens, no properties result that are uninitialized unless the site administrator has deleted some data offline.

Note that pages that make intensive use of personalization should also provide a user inter-face to let users modify settings and personalize the visual appearance of the page. The sample page in Figure 5-12 uses a *MultiView* control to switch between the menu-like view that invites you to edit and the editor-like view shown in Figure 5-13.

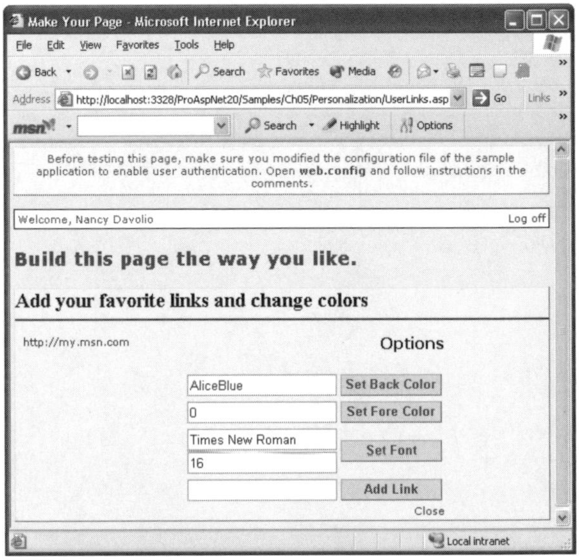

Figure 5-13 The page incorporates a little editor to let users personalize the page's look and feel.

The full source code for the page is available online.

> **Note** The personalization data of a page is all set when the *Page_Init* event fires. ASP.NET 2.0 also defines a *Page_PreInit* event. When this event arrives, no operation has been accomplished yet on the page, not even the loading of personalization data.

Personalization Events

As mentioned, the personalization data is added to the HTTP context of a request before the request begins its processing route. But which system component is in charge of loading personalization data? ASP.NET 2.0 employs a new HTTP module for this purpose named *ProfileModule*.

The module attaches itself to a couple of HTTP events and gets involved after a request has been authorized and when the request is about to end. If the personalization feature is off, the module returns immediately. Otherwise, it fires the *Personalize* event to the application and then loads personalization data from the current user profile. When the *Personalize* event fires, the personalization data hasn't been loaded yet. Handlers for events fired by an HTTP module must be written to the *global.asax* file:

```
void Profile_Personalize(object sender, ProfileEventArgs e)
{
    ProfileCommon profile = null;

    // Exit if it is the anonymous user
    if (User == null) return;

    // Determine the profile based on the role. The profile database
    // contains a specific entry for a given role.
    if (User.IsInRole("Administrators"))
        profile = (ProfileCommon) ProfileBase.Create("Administrator");
    else if (User.IsInRole("Users"))
        profile = (ProfileCommon) ProfileBase.Create("User");
    else if (User.IsInRole("Guests"))
        profile = (ProfileCommon) ProfileBase.Create("Guest");

    // Make the HTTP profile module use THIS profile object
    if (profile != null)
        e.Profile = profile;
}
```

The personalization layer is not necessarily there for the end user's fun. You should look at it as a general-purpose tool to carry user-specific information. User-specific information, though, indicates information that applies to the user, not necessarily information entered by the user.

The personalization layer employs the identity of the current user as an index to retrieve the proper set of data, but what about roles? What if you have hundreds of users with different names but who share the same set of profile data (such as menu items, links, and UI settings)? Maintaining hundreds of nearly identical database entries is out of the question. But the standard profile engine doesn't know how to handle roles. That's why you sometimes need to handle the *Personalize* event or perhaps roll your own profile provider.

The code shown previously overrides the process that creates the user profile object and ensures that the returned object is filled with user-specific information accessed through the user role. The static method *Create* on the *ProfileBase* class takes the user name and creates an instance of the profile object specific to that user. *ProfileCommon* is the common name of the dynamically created class that contains the user profile.

The handler of the *Personalize* event receives data through the *ProfileEventArgs* class. The class has a read/write member named *Profile*. When the event handler returns, the profile HTTP module checks this member. If it is *null*, the module proceeds as usual and creates a profile object based on the user's identity. If not, it simply binds the current value of the *Profile* member as the profile object of the page.

Migrating Anonymous Data

As mentioned, anonymous users can store and retrieve settings that are persisted using an anonymous unique ID. However, if at a certain point a hitherto anonymous user decides to create an account with the Web site, you might need to migrate to her account all the settings that she made as an anonymous user. This migration doesn't occur automatically.

When a user who has been using your application anonymously logs in, the personalization module fires an event—*MigrateAnonymous*. Properly handled, this global event allows you to import anonymous settings into the profile of an authenticated user. The following pseudocode demonstrates how to handle the migration of an anonymous profile:

```
void Profile_MigrateAnonymous(object sender, ProfileMigrateEventArgs e)
{
    // Load the profile of the anonymous user
    ProfileCommon anonProfile;
    anonProfile = Profile.GetProfile(e.AnonymousId);

    // Migrate the properties to the new profile
    Profile.BackColor = anonProfile.BackColor;
    ...
}
```

You get the profile for the anonymous user and extract the value of any property you want to import. Next, you copy the value to the profile of the currently logged-on user.

Profile Providers

In ASP.NET 2.0, the profile API is composed of two distinct elements—the access layer and the storage layer.

The access layer provides a strongly typed model to get and set property values and also manages user identities. It guarantees that the data is retrieved and stored on behalf of the currently logged-on user.

The second element of the profile system is the data storage. The system uses ad hoc providers to perform any tasks involved with the storage and retrieval of values. ASP.NET 2.0 comes with a profile provider that uses SQL Server 2005 Express as the data engine. If necessary, you can also write custom providers. The profile provider writes data into the storage medium of choice and is responsible for the final schema of the data. A profile provider must be able to either serialize the type (by using XML serialization and binary object serialization, for example) or know how to extract significant information from it.

Important   As discussed in Chapter 1, an ASP.NET 2.0 provider is defined as a pluggable component that extends or replaces a given system functionality. The profile provider is just one implementation of the ASP.NET 2.0 provider model. Other examples of providers are the membership provider and role manager provider, both of which we'll discuss in Chapter 15. At its core, the provider infrastructure allows customers to change the underlying implementation of some out-of-the-box system functionalities while keeping the top-level interface intact. Providers are relatively simple components with as few methods and properties as possible. Only one instance of the provider exists per application domain.

Configuring Profile Providers

All features, such as user profiling, that have providers should have a default provider. Normally, the default provider is indicated via a *defaultProvider* attribute in the section of the configuration file that describes the specific feature. By default, if a preferred provider is not specified, the first item in the collection is considered the default.

The default profile provider is named *AspNetSqlProfileProvider* and uses SQL Server 2005 Express for data storage. Providers are registered in the *<providers>* section of the configuration file under the main node *<profile>*, as shown here:

```
<profile>
    <providers>
        <add name="AspNetSqlProfileProvider"
            connectionStringName="LocalSqlServer" applicationName="/"
            type="System.Web.Profile.SqlProfileProvider" />
    </providers>
</profile>
```

The *<add>* nodes within the *<providers>* section list all the currently registered providers. The previous code is an excerpt from the *machine.config* file. Attributes such as *name* and *type* are common to all types of providers. Other properties are part of the provider's specific configuration mechanism. Tightly connected with this custom interface is the set of extra properties—in this case, *connectionStringName* and *description*. The *description* attribute is simply text that describes what the provider does.

The *connectionStringName* attribute defines the information needed to set up a connection with the underlying database engine of choice. However, instead of being a plain connection string, the attribute contains the name of a previously registered connection string. For example, *LocalSqlServer* is certainly not the connection string to use for a local or remote connection to an instance of SQL Server. Instead, it is the name of an entry in the new *<connectionStrings>* section of the configuration file. That entry contains any concrete information needed to connect to the database.

The *LocalSqlServer* connection string placeholder is defined in *machine.config* as follows:

```
<connectionStrings>
    <add name="LocalSqlServer"
```

```
        connectionString="data source=.\SQLEXPRESS;
                        Integrated Security=SSPI;
                        AttachDBFilename=|DataDirectory|aspnetdb.mdf;
                        User Instance=true"
        providerName="System.Data.SqlClient" />
</connectionStrings>
```

As you can see, the connection strings refers to an instance of SQL Server named SQLEXPRESS and attaches to the *aspnetdb.mdf* database located in the application's data directory—the *App_Data* folder.

Structure of *AspNetDb.mdf*

As a developer, you don't need to know much about the layout of the table and the logic that governs it—instead, you're responsible for ensuring that any needed infrastructure is created. To do so, you use the Website menu in Visual Studio .NET 2005 to start the ASP.NET site administration tool.

A view of the tables in the database is shown in Figure 5-14.

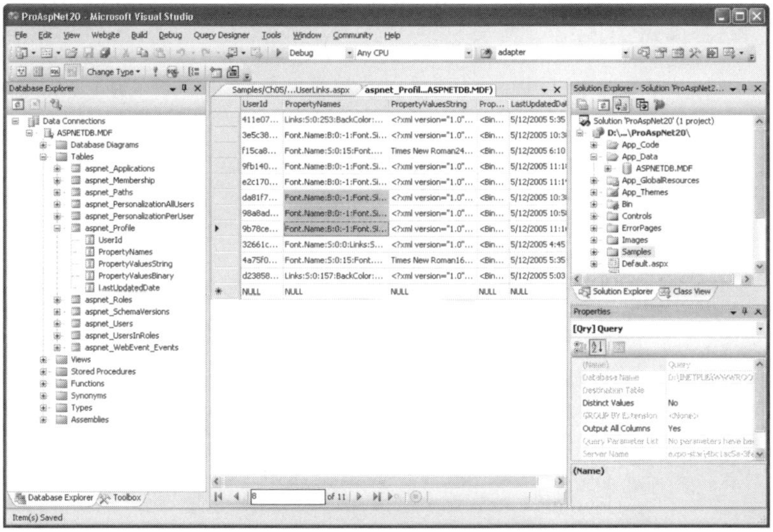

Figure 5-14   A view of the interior of the *AspNetDb* database and the profile table.

Note that the *ASPNetDB* database isn't specific to the personalization infrastructure. As you can see in the figure, it groups all provider-related tables, including those for membership, roles, and users. The internal structure of each database is specific to the mission of the underlying provider.

To view and edit the contents of the *AspNetDb* database (and other databases bound to the application), you can use Server Explorer. You create a new connection to the specified data source and use the menu commands to get what appears in Figure 5-14. The Server Explorer view is integrated with Visual Studio .NET and requires the IDE to be available in the production box. As an alternative for first-aid maintenance, you can consider the add-on tool SQL Server Express Manager—a separate download from *http://msdn.microsoft.com/vs2005*. The tool is a lightweight version of Enterprise Manager and Query Analyzer together. It lets you attach databases and work against them through SQL commands. Note that SQL Server Express Manager lacks UI facilities to attach and detach databases. Use the following command to attach your *AspNetDb.mdf* file:

```
CREATE DATABASE AspNetDb
ON (FILENAME = 'C:\Inetpub\wwwroot\ProAspNet20\App_Data\aspnetdb.mdf')
FOR ATTACH;
```

To detach a database, you use the *sp_detach* built-in stored procedure.

> **Important** The default profile provider uses the ADO.NET managed provider for SQL Server and is in no way limited to SQL Express. By changing the connection string, you can make it work with a database handled by the full version of SQL Server 2000 and SQL Server 2005. Using SQL Express is recommended for small applications in Internet scenarios or if you simply want to experiment with the functionality.

Custom Profile Providers

The SQL Server profile provider is good at building new applications and is useful for profile data that is inherently tabular. In many cases, though, you won't start an ASP.NET 2.0 application from scratch but will instead migrate an existing ASP or ASP.NET application. You often already have data to integrate with the ASP.NET profile layer. If this data doesn't get along with the relational model, or if it is already stored in a storage medium other than SQL Server, you can write a custom profile provider.

Profile providers push the idea that existing data stores can be integrated with the personalization engine using a thin layer of code. This layer of code abstracts the physical characteristics of the data store and exposes its content through a common set of methods and properties. A custom personalization provider is a class that inherits *ProfileProvider*.

> **Note** A custom provider can be bound to one or more profile properties through the property's *provider* attribute:
>
> ```
> <properties>
>     <add name="BackColor" type="string" provider="MyProvider" />
>     ...
> </properties>
> ```
>
> As shown in the preceding code, the *BackColor* property is read and written through the *MyProvider* provider. It goes without saying that the provider name must correspond to one of the entries in the *<providers>* section.

Conclusion

In this chapter, we examined three issues you might face when building pages and interacting with them—forms, errors, and user profiles.

Form-based programming is fundamental in Web applications because it's the only way to have users and applications interact. ASP.NET pages can have only one server-side form with a fixed *action* property. While you can still change the *action* property on the fly with a bit of client script code, this often results in a view state corruption error. ASP.NET 2.0 introduces cross-page posting as a way to let users post data from one page to another.

Often, good programs do bad things and raise errors. In the Web world, handling errors is a task architecturally left to the runtime environment that is running the application. The ASP.NET runtime is capable of providing two types of error pages, both of which are not very practical for serious and professional applications, although for different reasons. When a user who is locally connected to the application does something that originates an error, by default ASP.NET returns a "geek" page with the stack trace and the full transcript of the exception that occurred. The remote user, on the other hand, receives a less compromising page, but certainly not a user-friendly one. Fortunately, though, the ASP.NET framework is flexible enough to let you change the error pages, even to the point of distinguishing between HTTP errors.

The third aspect that relates to users and pages that we covered in this chapter is personalization. Personalization allows you to write pages that persist user preferences and parametric data from a permanent medium in a totally automated way. As a programmer, you're in charge of setting up the personalization infrastructure, but you need not know anything about the internal details of storage. All you do is call a provider component using the methods of a well-known interface. Personalization is an ASP.NET 2.0–only feature.

In the next chapter, we'll take page authoring to the next level by exploring powerful and effective ways to build pages, including master pages, themes, and wizards.

Just the Facts

- The typical ASP.NET page contains a single *<form>* tag with the *runat* attribute set. Multiple server-side forms are not allowed to be visible at the same time.

- In ASP.NET 2.0, controls that implement the *IButtonControl* interface are allowed to post to a different target page. The runtime takes care of posting the view state and arranges the post.

- Exceptions remain the official .NET way to handle anomalies, but exceptions should be kept to handling exceptional events in the life of the application—namely, those that are raised when something happens that violates an assumption.

- When an unrecoverable error occurs in an ASP.NET page, the user receives a different message, based on its local or remote location. Remote users will get a generic error message; local users get details and the call stack.

■   As a developer, you can customize the page being displayed both programmatically and declaratively. In the latter case, you can automatically bind a custom page to the HTTP status code.

■   ASP.NET 2.0 pages can be attached to an additional context property—the profile object. The profile is an instance of a class dynamically built around the data model specified in the configuration file.

■   When the profile is active, pages persist user preferences and parametric data to and from a permanent medium in a totally automated way. Developers have no need to know where and how this happens.

■   A common profile is available for anonymous users that provides the possibility of migrating data to the real profile object when the user logs in.

■   Pages that take advantage of the user profile object should consider adding some UI blocks to let end users modify parameters on the fly.

■   Page personalization is tightly coupled with membership.

Chapter 6
Rich Page Composition

In this chapter:

Working with Master Pages 220
Working with Themes 236
Working with Wizards 247
Conclusion 259

A large number of Web sites these days contain similar-looking, rich pages that share the same graphics, appearance, user interface (UI) widgets, and perhaps some navigational menus or search forms. These pages are rich in content and functionality, are visually appealing, and, more important, have an overall look and feel that abides by the golden rule of Web usability: be consistent. What's the recommended approach for building such pages and Web sites?

One possibility is wrapping these UI elements in user controls and referencing them in each page. Although such a model is extremely powerful and produces modular code, when you have hundreds of pages to work with, it soon becomes unmanageable. Both classic ASP and ASP.NET 1.x provide some workarounds for this type of issue, but neither tackles such a scenario openly and provides a definitive, optimal solution. ASP.NET 2.0 faces up to the task through a new technology—*master pages*—and basically benefits from the ASP.NET Framework's ability to merge a "supertemplate" with user-defined content replacements.

With themes, you can easily give the whole site a consistent (and, you hope, appealing) user interface and easily export that look from one application to the next. Much like Microsoft Windows XP themes, ASP.NET themes assign a set of styles and visual attributes to the customizable elements of the site. Themes are a superset of cascading style sheets (CSS) and are supported only in ASP.NET 2.0.

A recurring task in Web development is collecting user input by using forms. When the input to collect is large and pretty much articulated (in other words, easy to categorize), multiple forms are typically used to accomplish the task. The whole procedure is divided into various steps, each of which takes care of collecting and validating a particular subset of the expected data. This multistep procedure is often called a *wizard*. ASP.NET 2.0 introduces a new view control that makes building wizards a snap.

Overall, building rich pages is a much more approachable task in ASP.NET today than it was with previous versions. With master pages, you build pages based on an existing template of code and markup; with themes, you use skins to control pages and achieve visual consistency as well as profile capabilities. Finally, with wizards, you add rich functionality to pages.

Working with Master Pages

As a matter of fact, ASP.NET and Microsoft Visual Studio .NET greatly simplified the process of authoring Web pages and Web sites and made it affordable to a wide range of people with different skills. However, after a few months of real-world experience, many developers recognized that something was missing in the ASP.NET approach to page authoring. While building simple sites is easy, architecting real-world sites with hundreds of complex and rich pages still requires additional work and, more important, key decisions to be made without guidance.

Almost all Web sites use a similar graphical layout for all their pages. This doesn't happen by chance—it grows out of accepted guidelines for design and usability. A consistent layout is characteristic of all cutting-edge Web sites, no matter how complex. For some Web sites, the layout consists of the header, body, and footer; for others, it is a more sophisticated aggregation of navigational menus, buttons, and panels that contain and render the actual content. Needless to say, manual duplication of code and HTML elements is simply out of the question. Making code automatically reusable clearly represents a better approach, but how do you implement it *in practice*?

Authoring Rich Pages in ASP.NET 1.x

In ASP.NET 1.x, the best approach to authoring pages with a common layout is to employ *user controls*. User controls are aggregates of ASP.NET server controls, literal text, and code. (We'll cover user controls in my other recent book, *Programming Microsoft ASP.NET 2.0 Applications: Advanced Topics* [Microsoft Press, 2005], which is published as a companion volume to this book.) The ASP.NET runtime exposes user controls to the outside world as programmable components. The idea is that you employ user controls to tailor your own user interface components and share them among the pages of the Web site. For example, all the pages that need a navigational menu can reference and configure the user control that provides that feature.

What's Good About User Controls

User controls are like embeddable pages. Turning an existing ASP.NET page into a user control requires only a few minor changes. User controls can be easily linked to any page that needs their services. Furthermore, changes to a user control's implementation do not affect the referencing page and only require you (or the runtime) to recompile the user control into an assembly.

> **Note** In ASP.NET, user controls make the use of classic ASP include files obsolete. A typical ASP include file contains either static or dynamic content for the portion of the page it represents. There's no object orientation in this approach, making thoughtful design and easy maintainability very difficult, if not impossible, for very large Web sites. In addition, include file tags opened in one file are frequently closed in another file. This situation makes WYSIWYG designer support virtually impossible.

What's Bad About User Controls

If you change the *internal* implementation of the user control, no referencing page will be affected. However, if you alter any aspect of the control's *public* interface (such as the class name, properties, methods, or events), all the pages that reference the control must be updated. This means you must manually retouch all the pages in the application that use the control. Then you must recompile these pages and deploy the assemblies. In addition, the next time a user views each page, the ASP.NET runtime will take a while to respond because the dynamic assembly for the page must be re-created.

Architecturally speaking, the solution based on user controls works just fine. In practice, though, it is not a very manageable model for large-scale applications—its effectiveness decreases as the complexity of the application (the number of pages involved) increases. If your site contains hundreds of pages, handling common elements through user controls can quickly become inefficient and unmanageable.

Visual Inheritance

ASP.NET pages are built as instances of special classes—code-behind or code file classes. Because pages are ultimately classes, what happens if you stuff part of the common UI in some base class and inherit new pages from there? This approach resembles the visual inheritance feature that Windows Forms developers have been familiar with for a long time.

Pure visual inheritance *a là* Windows Forms is impractical in ASP.NET. This is because ASP.NET pages are made of code *and* markup. The markup determines the position of the controls, while code adds logic and functionality. Building predefined graphic templates in the base class doesn't pose issues, but how would you import those standard UI blocks in derived pages, and, more important, how would you merge those with controls local to the derived page?

In Windows Forms, controls have an absolute position that the designer reproduces, making it easy for developers to insert new controls anywhere. Web Forms, though, typically use relative positioning, which leads to either of the next two design choices. Option one is to supply predefined and named UI blocks in base classes and have derived classes load them in matching placeholders. Option two involves using master pages as defined in ASP.NET 2.0. To implement the former technique do the following:

1. Derive your page from a base class that knows how to create special UI blocks such as toolbars, headers, and footers. Each of these UI blocks has a unique name.

2. Add *<asp:placeholder>* controls to the derived page whose ID matches any of the predefined names. The base class contains the code to explore the control's tree and expand placeholders with predefined UI blocks.

This approach exploits inheritance but provides no WYSIWYG facilities and forces you to create UI blocks in code-only mode with no markup. This option is demonstrated in the companion code, but it should be considered only for ASP.NET 1.x applications. The second option mentioned—using master pages—is described in the following section.

Writing a Master Page

In ASP.NET 2.0, a master page is a distinct file referenced at both the application level and the page level that contains the static layout of the page. Regions that each derived page can customize are referenced in the master page with a special placeholder control. A *derived* page is simply a collection of blocks the runtime will use to fill the holes in the master. True visual inheritance *à la* Windows Forms is not a goal of ASP.NET 2.0 master pages. The contents of a master page are merged into the content page, and they dynamically produce a new page class that is served to the user upon request. The merge process takes place at compile time and only once. In no way do the contents of the master serve as a base class for the content page.

What's a Master Page, Anyway?

A master page is similar to an ordinary ASP.NET page except for the top *@Master* directive and the presence of one or more *ContentPlaceHolder* server controls. A *ContentPlaceHolder* control defines a region in the master page that can be customized in a derived page. A master page without content placeholders is technically correct and will be processed correctly by the ASP.NET runtime. However, a placeholderless master fails in its primary goal—to be the super-template of multiple pages that look alike. A master page devoid of placeholders works like an ordinary Web page but with the extra burden required to process master pages. Here is a simple master page:

```
<%@ Master Language="C#" CodeFile="Simple.master.cs" Inherits="Simple" %>
<html>
<head runat="server">
    <title>Hello, master pages</title>
</head>
<body>
    <form id="form1" runat="server">
        <asp:Panel ID="HeaderPanel" runat="server"
            BackImageUrl="Images/SkyBkgnd.png" Width="100%">
```

```
        <asp:Label ID="TitleBox" runat="server"
            Text="Programming ASP.NET 2.0" />
    </asp:Panel>
    <asp:contentplaceholder id="PageBody" runat="server">
     <!-- derived pages will define content for this placeholder -->
    </asp:contentplaceholder>
    <asp:Panel ID="FooterPanel" runat="server"
        BackImageUrl="Images/SeaBkgnd.png">
        <asp:Label ID="SubTitleBox" runat="server"
            Text="Dino Esposito" />
    </asp:Panel>
  </form>
</body>
</html>
```

As you can see, the master page looks like a standard ASP.NET page. Aside from the identifying @Master directive, the only key differences are ContentPlaceHolder controls. A page bound to this master automatically inherits all the contents of the master (the header and footer, in this case) and can attach custom markup and server controls to each defined placeholder. The content placeholder element is fully identified by its ID property and normally doesn't require other attributes.

The @*Master* Directive

The @*Master* directive distinguishes master pages from content pages and allows the ASP.NET runtime to properly handle each. A master page file is compiled to a class that derives from the *MasterPage* class. The *MasterPage* class, in turn, inherits *UserControl*. So, at the end of the day, a master page is treated as a special kind of ASP.NET user control.

The @*Master* supports quite a few attributes. For the most part, though, they are the same attributes that we reviewed in Chapter 3 for the @*Page* directive. Table 6-1 details the attributes that have a special meaning to master pages.

Table 6-1   Attributes of the @*Master* Directive

Attribute	Description
ClassName	Specifies the name for the class that will be created to render the master page. This value can be any valid class name but should not include a namespace. By default, the class name for simple.master is *ASP.simple_master*.
CodeFile	Indicates the URL to the file that contains any source code associated with the master page.
Inherits	Specifies a code-behind class for the master page to inherit. This can be any class derived from *MasterPage*.
MasterPageFile	Specifies the name of the master page file that this master refers to. A master can refer to another master through the same mechanisms a page uses to attach to a master. If this attribute is set, you will have nested masters.

The master page is associated with a code file that looks like the following:

```
public partial class Simple : System.Web.UI.MasterPage {
    protected void Page_Load(object sender, EventArgs e) {
        ...
    }
    §
}
```

The *@Master* directive doesn't override attributes set at the *@Page* directive level. For example, you can have the master set the language to Visual Basic .NET and one of the content pages can use C#. The language set at the master page level never influences the choice of the language at the content page level. You can use other ASP.NET directives in a master page—for example, *@Import*. However, the scope of these directives is limited to the master file and does not extend to child pages generated from the master.

> **Note**   You can create master pages programmatically. You build your own class and make it inherit *MasterPage*. Then you create *.master* files in which the *Inherits* attribute points to the fully qualified name of your class. Rapid application development (RAD) designers such as the one embedded in Microsoft Visual Studio .NET 2005 use this approach to create master pages.

The *ContentPlaceHolder* Container Control

The *ContentPlaceHolder* control acts as a container placed in a master page. It marks places in the master where related pages can insert custom content. A content placeholder is uniquely identified by an ID. Here's an example:

```
<asp:contentplaceholder runat="server" ID="PageBody" />
```

A content page is an ASP.NET page that contains only *<asp:Content>* server tags. This element corresponds to an instance of the *Content* class that provides the actual content for a particular placeholder in the master. The link between placeholders and content is established through the ID of the placeholder. The content of a particular instance of the *Content* server control is written to the placeholder whose ID matches the value of the *ContentPlaceHolderID* property, as shown here:

```
<asp:Content runat="server" contentplaceholderID="PageBody">
    ...
</asp:Content>
```

In a master page, you define as many content placeholders as there are customizable regions in the page. A content page doesn't have to fill all the placeholders defined in the bound master. However, a content page can't do more than just fill placeholders defined in the master.

> **Note**   A placeholder can't be bound to more than one content region in a single content page. If you have multiple *<asp:Content>* server tags in a content page, each must point to a distinct placeholder in the master.

Specifying Default Content

A content placeholder can be assigned default content that will show up if the content page fails to provide a replacement. Each *ContentPlaceHolder* control in the master page can contain default content. If a content page does not reference a given placeholder in the master, the default content will be used. The following code snippet shows how to define default content:

```
<asp:contentplaceholder runat="server" ID="PageBody">
    <!-- Use the following markup if no custom
        content is provided by the content page -->
    ...
</asp:contentplaceholder>
```

The default content is completely ignored if the content page populates the placeholder. The default content is never merged with the custom markup provided by the content page.

> **Note**   A *ContentPlaceHolder* control can be used only in a master page. Content placeholders are not valid on regular ASP.NET pages. If such a control is found in an ordinary Web page, a parser error occurs.

Writing a Content Page

The master page defines the skeleton of the resulting page. If you need to share layout or any UI block among all the pages, placing it in a master page will greatly simplify management of the pages in the application. You create the master and then think of your pages in terms of a delta from the master. The master defines the common parts of a certain group of pages and leaves placeholders for customizable regions. Each *content page*, in turn, defines what the content of each region has to be for a particular ASP.NET page. Figure 6-1 shows how to create a content page in Visual Studio .NET 2005.

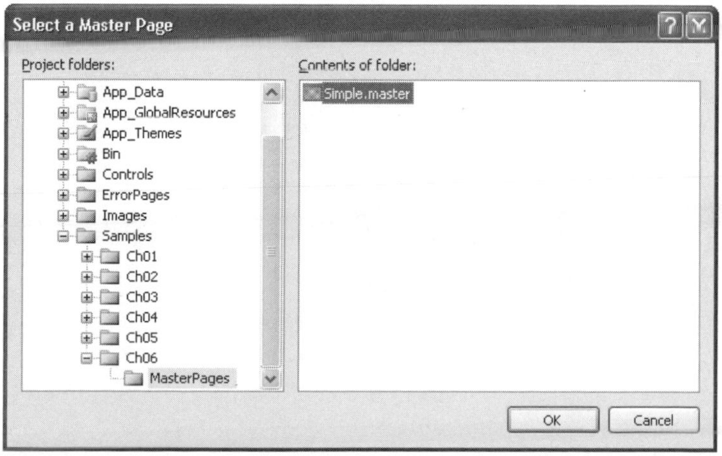

![Select a Master Page dialog box showing Project folders tree with App_Data, App_GlobalResources, App_Themes, Bin, Controls, ErrorPages, Images, Samples (expanded with Ch01–Ch06, and MasterPages under Ch06). Contents of folder pane shows Simple.master. OK and Cancel buttons at bottom.]

Figure 6-1   Adding a content page to a Visual Studio .NET 2005 project.

The *Content* Control

The key part of a content page is the *Content* control—a mere container for other controls. The *Content* control is used only in conjunction with a corresponding *ContentPlaceHolder* and is not a standalone control. The master file that we considered earlier defines a single placeholder named *PageBody*. This placeholder represents the body of the page and is placed right below an HTML table that provides the page's header. Figure 6-2 shows a sample content page based on the aforementioned master page.

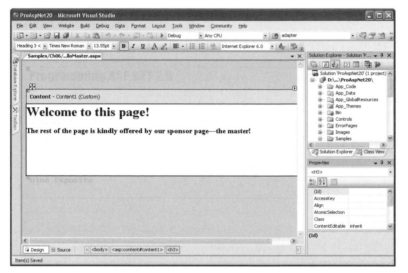

Figure 6-2   A preview of the content page. Notice the layout of the master page grayed out in the background.

Let's take a look at the source code of the content page:

```
<%@ Page Language="C#" MasterPageFile="Simple.master"
        CodeFile="HelloMaster.aspx.cs" Inherits="HelloMaster" %>

<asp:Content ID="Content1" ContentPlaceHolderID="PageBody" Runat="Server">
    <h1>Welcome to this page!</h1>
    <h3>The rest of the page is kindly offered by our sponsor
        page-the master!</h3>
</asp:Content>
```

The content page is the resource that users invoke through the browser. When the user points her or his browser to this page, the output in Figure 6-3 is shown.

The replaceable part of the master is filled with the corresponding content section defined in the derived pages. A content page—that is, a page bound to a master—is a special breed of page in that it can *only* contain *<asp:Content>* controls. A content page is not permitted to host server controls outside of an *<asp:Content>* tag.

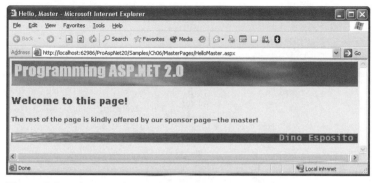

Figure 6-3   The sample page in action.

Let's explore the attachment of pages to masters in a bit more detail.

Attaching Pages to a Master

In the previous example, the content page is bound to the master by using the *MasterPageFile* attribute in the *@Page* directive. The attribute points to a string representing the path to the master page. Page-level binding is just one possibility—although it is the most common one.

You can also set the binding between the master and the content at the application or folder level. Application-level binding means that you link all the pages of an application to the same master. You configure this behavior by setting the *Master* attribute in the *<pages>* element of the principal *web.config* file:

```
<configuration>
    <system.web>
        <pages master="MyApp.master" />
    </system.web>
</configuration>
```

If the same setting is expressed in a child *web.config* file—a *web.config* file stored in a site subdirectory—all ASP.NET pages in the folder are bound to a specified master page.

Note that if you define binding at the application or folder level, all the Web pages in the application (or the folder) must have *Content* controls mapped to one or more placeholders in the master page. In other words, application-level binding prevents you from having (or later adding) a page to the site that is not configured as a content page. Any classic ASP.NET page in the application (or folder) that contains server controls will throw an exception.

Device-Specific Masters

Like all ASP.NET pages and controls, master pages can detect the capabilities of the underlying browser and adapt their output to the specific device in use. ASP.NET 2.0 makes choosing a device-specific master easier than ever. If you want to control how certain pages of your site appear on a particular browser, you can build them from a common master and design the master to address the specific features of the browser. In other words, you can create multiple versions of the same master, each targeting a different type of browser.

How do you associate a particular version of the master and a particular browser? In the content page, you define multiple bindings using the same *MasterPageFile* attribute, but you prefix it with the identifier of the device. For example, suppose you want to provide ad hoc support for Microsoft Internet Explorer and Netscape browsers and use a generic master for any other browsers that users employ to visit the site. You use the following syntax:

```
<%@ Page masterpagefile="Base.master"
    ie:masterpagefile="ieBase.master"
    netscape6to9:masterpagefile="nsBase.master" %>
```

The ieBase.master file will be used for Internet Explorer; the nsBase.master, on the other hand, will be used if the browser belongs to the Netscape family, versions 6.x to 9.0. In any other case, a device-independent master (Base.master) will be used. When the page runs, the ASP.NET runtime automatically determines which browser or device the user is using and selects the corresponding master page, as shown in Figure 6-4.

Figure 6-4 Browser-specific master pages.

The prefixes you can use to indicate a particular type of browser are those defined in the ASP.NET configuration files for browsers. Table 6-2 lists the most commonly used Brower IDs.

Table 6-2 ID of Most Common Browsers

Browser ID	Browser Name
IE	Any version of Internet Explorer
Netscape3	Netscape Navigator 3.x
Netscape4	Netscape Communicator 4.x
Netscape6to9	Any version of Netscape higher than 6.0
Mozilla	Firefox
Opera	Opera
Up	Openwave-powered devices

It goes without saying that you can distinguish not only between up-level and down-level browsers but also between browsers and other devices, such as cellular phones and personal digital assistants (PDAs). If you use device-specific masters, you must also indicate a device-independent master.

> **Warning**   Browser information is stored differently in ASP.NET 1.x and ASP.NET 2.0. In ASP.NET 1.x, you find it in the *<browserCaps>* section of the *machine.config* file. In ASP.NET 2.0, it is stored in text files with a *.browser* extension located in the *Browsers* folder under the ASP.NET installation path on the Web server: WINDOWS%\Microsoft.NET\Framework\ [**version**]\Config\Browsers.

Setting the Title of a Page

As a collection of *<asp:Content>* tags, a content page is not allowed to include any markup that can specify the title of the page. Using the *<title>* tag is possible in the master page, but the master page—by design—works as the base for a variety of pages, each requiring its own title. The trick to setting the title is in using the *Title* property of the *@Page* directive in the content page:

```
<@Page MasterPageFile="simple.master" Title="Hello, master" %>
```

Note, though, the setting of the title of the page is possible only if the *<title>* or the *<head>* tag in the master is flagged as *runat=server*.

Processing Master and Content Pages

The use of master pages slightly changes how pages are processed and compiled. For one thing, a page based on a master has a double dependency—on the *.aspx* source file (the content page) and on the *.master* file (the master page). If either of these pages changes, the dynamic page assembly will be re-created. Although the URL that users need is the URL of the content page, the page served to the browser results from the master page fleshed out with any replacement provided by the content page.

Compiling Master Pages

When the user requests an *.aspx* resource mapped to a content page—that is, a page that references a master—the ASP.NET runtime begins its job by tracking the dependency between the source *.aspx* file and its master. This information is persisted in a local file created in the ASP.NET temporary files folder. Next, the runtime parses the master page source code and creates a Visual Basic .NET or C# class, depending on the language set in the master page. The class inherits *MasterPage*, or the master's code file, and is then compiled to an assembly.

If multiple *.master* files are found in the same directory, they are all processed at the same time. Thus a dynamic assembly is generated for any master files found, even if only one of them is used by the ASP.NET page whose request triggered the compilation process. Therefore, don't leave unused master files in your Web space—they will be compiled anyway. Also note that the compilation tax is paid only the first time a content page is accessed within the application. When a user accesses another page that requires the second master, the response is faster because the previously compiled master is cached.

Serving the Page to Users

As mentioned, any ASP.NET page bound to a master page must have a certain structure—no server controls or literal text are allowed outside the *<asp:Content>* tag. As a result, the layout of the page looks like a plain collection of content elements, each bound to a particular placeholder in the master. The connection is established through the ID property. The *<asp:Content>* element works like a control container, much like the *Panel* control of ASP.NET or the HTML *<div>* tag. All the markup text is compiled to a template and associated with the corresponding placeholder property on the master class.

The master page is a special kind of user control with some templated regions. It's not coincidental, in fact, that the *MasterPage* class inherits from the *UserControl* class. Once instantiated as a user control, the master page is completed with templates generated from the markup defined in the content page. Next, the resulting control is added to the control tree of the current page. No other controls are present in the final page except those brought in by the master. Figure 6-5 shows the skeleton of the final page served to the user.

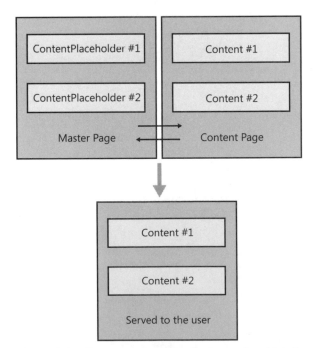

Figure 6-5   The structure of the final page in which the master page and the content page are merged.

Nested Master Pages

So far we've seen a pretty simple relationship between a master and a collection of content pages. However, the topology of the relationship can be made as complex and sophisticated as needed. A master can, in fact, be associated with another master and form a hierarchical, nested structure. When nested masters are used, any child master is seen and implemented as a plain content page in which extra *ContentPlaceHolder* controls are defined for an extra level of content pages. Put another way, a child master is a kind of content page that contains a combination of *<asp:Content>* and *<asp:ContentPlaceHolder>* elements. Like any other content page, a child master points to a master page and provides content blocks for its parent's placeholders. At the same time, it makes available new placeholders for its child pages.

> **Note**   There's no architectural limitation in the number of nesting levels you can implement in your Web sites. Performance-wise, the depth of the nesting has a negligible impact on the overall functionality and scalability of the solution. The final page served to the user is always compiled on demand and never modified as long as dependent files are not touched.

Let's expand on the previous example to add an intermediate master page. The root master page—named *parent.master*—defines the header, the footer, and a replaceable region. Except for the class names, the source code is identical to the example we considered earlier. Let's have a closer look at the intermediate master—named *content.master*:

```
<%@ Master Language="C#" MasterPageFile="Parent.master"
    CodeFile="Content.master.cs" Inherits="ContentMaster" %>

<asp:Content Runat="Server" ContentPlaceHolderID="ContentOfThePage" >
    <table width="100%"><tr>
        <td>
            <h1>Welcome to this page!</h1>
            <h3>The rest of the page is kindly offered by our
                sponsor page-the master!</h3>
        </td>
        <td align="center">
            <h2>Select Your Favorite Chapter</h2>
            <asp:ContentPlaceHolder runat="server" ID="ChapterMenu" />
        </td>
    </tr></table>
</asp:Content>
```

As you can see, the master contains both a collection of *<asp:Content>* and *<asp:ContentPlaceHolder>* tags. The top directive is that of a master but contains the *MasterPageFile* attribute, which typically characterizes a content page.

The *content.master* resource is not directly viewable because it contains a virtual region. If you're familiar with object-oriented programming (OOP) terminology, I'd say that an intermediate master class is much like an intermediate virtual class that overrides some methods on the parent but leaves other abstract methods to be implemented by another derived class. Just as abstract classes can't be instantiated, nested master pages can't be viewed through a browser. In any case, the *content.master* resource is undoubtedly a master class, and its code file contains a class that inherits from *MasterPage*.

> **Warning** Because Visual Studio .NET 2005 doesn't support visual editing of nested master pages, you have to create an intermediate master page as a content page, change the top directive to *@Master*, remove the *Title* attribute and, last but not least, change the base class of the code file to *MasterPage*.

The following code illustrates a content page that builds on two masters:

```
<%@ Page Language="C#" MasterPageFile="Content.master"
        CodeFile="ViewBook.aspx.cs" Inherits="ViewBook"
        Title="Book Viewer" %>

<asp:Content ContentPlaceHolderID="ChapterMenu" Runat="Server">
    <asp:DropDownList runat="server">
        ...
    </asp:DropDownList><br />
    <asp:Button runat="server" Text="Read ..." />
</asp:Content>
```

Figure 6-6 shows the final results.

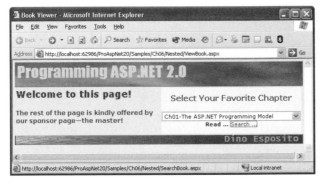

Figure 6-6 The page results from the combination of two master pages.

Admittedly, there's nothing in the figure that clearly indicates the existence of two masters; for your information, the innermost master controls the leftmost area where the drop-down list is laid out. This means that writing another page that offers an alternative technique to find a chapter is particularly easy. Have a look at the code and Figure 6-7:

```
<%@ Page Language="C#" MasterPageFile="Content.master"
    CodeFile="SearchBook.aspx.cs" Inherits="SearchBook" %>

<asp:Content ContentPlaceHolderID="ChapterMenu" Runat="Server">
    <asp:TextBox runat="server" Text="[Enter keywords]" />
    <asp:LinkButton runat="server" Text="Search ..." />
</asp:Content>
```

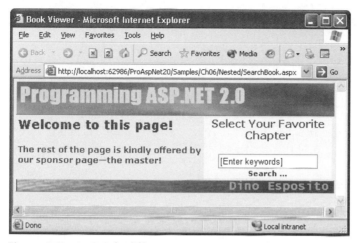

Figure 6-7   A slightly different page requires slightly different code!

A sapient use of master and content pages leads straight to an obvious conclusion: slightly different pages require slightly different code.

Programming the Master Page

You can use code in content pages to reference properties, methods, and controls in the master page, with some restrictions. The rule for properties and methods is that you can reference them if they are declared as public members of the master page. This includes public page-scope variables, public properties, and public methods.

Exposing Master Properties

To give an identity to a control in the master, you simply set the *runat* attribute and give the control an ID. Can you then access the control from within a content page? Not directly. The only way to access the master page object model is through the *Master* property. Note, though, that the *Master* property of the *Page* class references the master page object for the content page. This means that only public properties and methods defined on the master page class are accessible.

The following code enhances the previous master page to make it expose the text of the header as a public property:

```
public partial class SimpleWithProp : System.Web.UI.MasterPage
{
    protected void Page_Load(object sender, EventArgs e)
    {
    }

    public string TitleBoxText
    {
```

```
        get { return TitleBox.Text; }
        set { TitleBox.Text = value; }
    }
}
```

The header text of Figure 6-3 (shown earlier) is represented by a *Label* control named *TitleBox*. The control's protection level makes it inaccessible from the outside world, but the public property *TitleBoxText* defined in the preceding code represents a public wrapper around the *Label*'s Text property. In the end, the master page has an extra public property through which programmers can set the text of the header.

Invoking Properties on the Master

The *Master* property is the only point of contact between the content page and its master. The bad news is that the *Master* property is defined to be of type *MasterPage*; as such, it doesn't know anything about any property or method definition specific to the master you're really working with. In other words, the following code wouldn't compile because no *TitleBoxText* property is defined on the *MasterPage* class:

```
public partial class HelloMaster : System.Web.UI.Page
{
    protected void Page_Load(object sender, EventArgs e)
    {
        Master.TitleBoxText = "Programming ASP.NET—version 2.0";
    }
}
```

What's the real type behind the *Master* property?

The *Master* property represents the master page object as compiled by the ASP.NET run-time engine. This class follows the same naming convention as regular pages—*ASP.XXX_master*, where *XXX* is the name of the master file. Developers can override the default class name by setting the *ClassName* attribute on the *@Master* directive. The attribute lets you assign a user-defined name to the master page class:

```
<%@ Master Inherits="SimpleWithProp" … Classname="MyMaster" %>
```

In light of this, to be able to call custom properties or methods, you must first cast the object returned by the *Master* property to the actual type:

```
((ASP.MyMaster)Master).TitleBoxText = "Programming ASP.NET—version 2.0";
```

Interestingly enough, Visual Studio .NET 2005 provides some facilities to let you identify the right dynamically generated type already at design time. (See Figure 6-8.)

The *ASP* namespace is the system namespace that all system dynamically defined types belong to. In Visual Studio .NET 2005, that namespace is properly recognized and handled by Microsoft IntelliSense. That was not the case with the previous version of Visual Studio .NET.

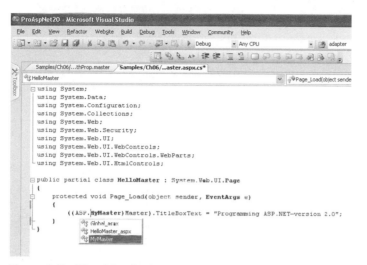

Figure 6-8   Visual Studio .NET 2005 pops up names of classes that will be created only during the page execution.

The @*MasterType* Directive

By adding the @*MasterType* directive in the content page, you can avoid all the casting just shown. The @*MasterType* informs the compiler about the real type of the *Master* property. The *Master* property is declared of the right type in the dynamically created page class, and this allows you to write strong-typed code, as follows:

```
<%@ Page Language="C#" MasterPageFile="SimpleWithProp.master"
    CodeFile="HelloMasterType.aspx.cs" Inherits="HelloMasterType" %>
<%@ MasterType VirtualPath="SimpleWithProp.master" %>
```

In the code file, you can have the following statements:

```
protected void Page_Load(object sender, EventArgs e)
{
    Master.TitleBoxText = "Programming ASP.NET-version 2.0";
}
```

The @*MasterType* directive supports two mutually exclusive attributes—*VirtualPath* and *Type-Name*. Both serve to identify the master class to use. The former does it by URL; the latter does it by type name.

Changing the Master Page Dynamically

To associate an ASP.NET content page with a master page—keeping in mind that in no case can you associate a classic ASP.NET page with a master—you use the *MasterPageFile* attribute of the @*Page* directive. *MasterPageFile*, though, is also a read/write property on the *Page* class that points to the name of the master page file. Can you dynamically select the master page via code and based on run-time conditions?

Using a dynamically changing master page is definitely possible in ASP.NET 2.0 and is suitable, for example, for applications that can present themselves to users through different skins. However, programmatically selecting the master page is not a task that you can accomplish at any time. To be precise, you can set the *MasterPageFile* property only during the *PreInit* page event—that is, before the runtime begins working on the request:

```
protected void Page_PreInit(object sender, EventArgs e)
{
    MasterPageFile = "simple2.master";
}
```

If you try to set the *MasterPageFile* property in *Init* or *Load* event handlers, an exception is raised.

> **Note**   The *Master* property represents the current instance of the master page object, is a read-only property, and can't be set programmatically. The *Master* property is set by the runtime after loading the content of the file referenced by the *MasterPageFile* property.

Working with Themes

For years, CSS styles have helped site developers to easily and efficiently design pages with a common and consistent look and feel. Although page developers can select the CSS file programmatically on the server, at its core CSS remains an inherent client-side technology, devised and implemented to apply skins to HTML elements. When you build ASP.NET pages, though, you mostly work with server controls.

CSS styles can be used to style server controls, but they're not the right tool for the job. The main issue here is that ASP.NET controls can have properties that are not the direct emanation of a CSS style property. The appearance of an ASP.NET control can be affected by an array of resources—images, strings, templates, markup, combinations of various CSS styles. To properly apply skins to ASP.NET server controls, CSS files are necessary but not sufficient. Enter ASP.NET themes.

ASP.NET themes are closely related to Windows XP themes. Setting a theme is as simple as setting a property, and all the settings the theme contains are applied in a single shot. Themes can be applied to individual controls and also to a page or an entire Web site.

> **Warning**   Themes are a specific feature of ASP.NET 2.0. There's no built-in support for themes in ASP.NET 1.x. I discussed how to build a theme infrastructure for ASP.NET 1.x in the June 2004 issue of *MSDN Magazine*. The article is online at *http://msdn.microsoft.com/msdnmag/issues/04/06/CuttingEdge*.

Understanding ASP.NET Themes

In ASP.NET 1.x, when you author a page you don't just focus on the tasks a certain set of controls must be able to accomplish. You also consider their appearance. Most of the time, you end up setting visual attributes such as colors, font, borders, and images. The more sophisticated the control, the more time you spend making it look nice rather than just functional.

In ASP.NET 1.x, the *DataGrid* control—one of the most popular and customizable controls—provides a gallery of predefined styles from which you choose the most appealing. This gallery of predefined styles is the *DataGrid*'s auto-format feature. *DataGrid*'s built-in styles are implemented through a set of predefined settings that Visual Studio .NET 2003 applies to the control at design time. The auto-format feature saves testing and typing and lets you choose the style visually. Added as a time-saving feature, auto-format addresses the issue only partially, as it has two main drawbacks. First, a lot of visual attributes are still persisted to the *.aspx* source file, making rich pages hard to read and maintain. Second, the list of available formats is closed and can't be further extended or personalized.

Wouldn't it be great if you could compose your pages just by picking controls off the toolbox and connecting them, without even bothering about their final look? Wouldn't it be nice if you could then simply create an additional file in the project to define visual attributes for each type of control? In this way, the *.aspx* source file would be free of verbose visual attributes, and you could change the style of controls at will while performing few or no modifications to the original page. ASP.NET themes provide exactly this capability.

What's a Theme, Anyway?

A *theme* is a set of skins and associated files such as style sheets and images—a sort of super CSS file. Once enabled, the theme determines the appearance of all controls under its jurisdiction. Consider the following simple markup:

```
<asp:Calendar ID="Calendar1" runat="server" />
```

Without themes, the calendar will look spare and spartan. With a theme added, the same markup renders a more colorful and appealing calendar. As you can see, a neat separation exists between the page contents and formatting rules. Look at Figure 6-9. Which do you think is the unthemed calendar?

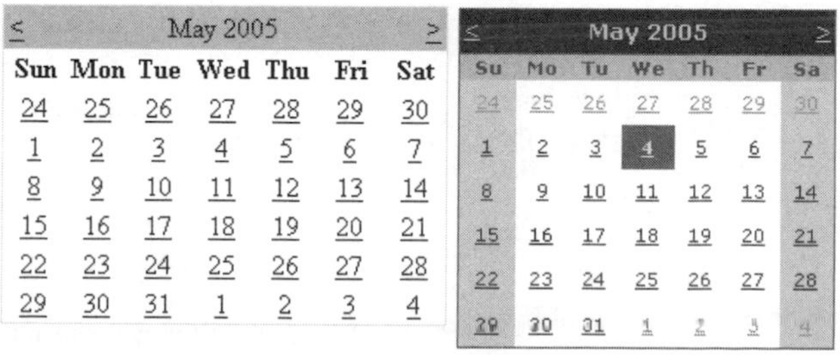

Figure 6-9   The same controls, with and without themes.

To fully understand ASP.NET themes, you must be familiar with a few terms, which are detailed in Table 6-3.

Table 6-3   ASP.NET Themes Terminology

Term	Definition
Skin	A named set of properties and templates that can be applied to one or more controls on a page. A skin is always associated with a specific control type.
Style sheet	A CSS or server-side style sheet file that can be used by pages on a site.
StyleSheet Theme	A theme used to abstract control properties from controls. The application of this theme means that the control can still override the theme.
Customization Theme	A theme used to abstract control properties from controls, but the theme overrides the control and any style sheet theme.

Imagine you are creating a new Web site and would like it to be visually appealing from the start. Instead of having to learn all the available style properties of each employed control, you just use ASP.NET themes. Using a built-in theme in a page is as easy as setting a property, as we'll see in a moment. With this change, pages automatically inherit a new and, one hopes, attractive appearance. For example, if you add a *Calendar* control to a page, it automatically renders with the default appearance defined in the theme.

Selecting a theme for one or more pages doesn't necessarily bind you to the settings of that theme. Through the Visual Studio .NET designer, you can review the pages and manually adjust some styles in a control if you want to.

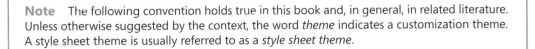

> **Note**   The following convention holds true in this book and, in general, in related literature. Unless otherwise suggested by the context, the word *theme* indicates a customization theme. A style sheet theme is usually referred to as a *style sheet theme*.

Structure of a Theme

Themes are expressed as the union of various files and folders living under a common root directory. Themes can be global or local. Global themes are visible to all Web applications installed on a server machine. Local themes are visible only to the application that defines them. Global themes are contained in child directories located under the following path. The name of the directory is the name of the theme:

```
%WINDOWS%\Microsoft.NET\Framework\[version]\ASP.NETclientFiles\Themes
```

Local themes are specialized folders that live under the *App_Themes* folder at the root of the application. Figure 6-10 shows a sample theme (named ProAspNet20) in a Web application.

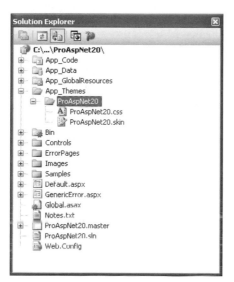

Figure 6-10   A view of this book's companion code's official theme in Visual Studio .NET 2005.

As you can see, the theme in the figure consists of a *.css* file and a *.skin* file. Generally, themes can contain a mix of the following resources:

- **CSS files.**   Also known as *style sheets*, CSS files contain style definitions to be applied to elements in an HTML document. Written according to a tailor-made syntax, CSS styles define how elements are displayed and where they are positioned on your page. Web browsers that support only HTML 3.2 and earlier will not apply CSS styles. The World Wide Web Consortium (W3C) maintains and constantly evolves CSS standards. Visit *http://www.w3.org* for details on current CSS specifications. CSS files are located in the root of the theme folder.

- **Skin files.**   A skin file contains the theme-specific markup for a given set of controls. A skin file is made by a sequence of control definitions that include predefined values for most visual properties and supported templates. Each skin is control-specific and has a unique name. You can define multiple skins for a given control. A skinned control has the original markup written in the *.aspx* source file modified by the content of the skin. The way the modification occurs depends on whether a customization or a style sheet theme is used. Skin files are located in the root of the theme folder.

- **Image files.**   Feature-rich ASP.NET controls might require images. For example, a page-able *DataGrid* control might want to use bitmaps for first or last pages that are graphically compliant to the skin. Images that are part of a skin are typically located in an *Images* directory under the theme folder. (You can change the name of the folder as long as the name is correctly reflected by the skin's attributes.)

- **Templates.**   A control skin is not limited to graphical properties but extends to define the layout of the control—for templated controls that support this capability. By stuffing template definitions in a theme, you can alter the internal structure of a control while leaving the programming interface and behavior intact. Templates are defined as part of the control skin and persisted to skin files.

The content types just listed are not exhaustive, but they do cover the most commonly used data you might want to store in a theme. You can have additional subdirectories filled with any sort of data that makes sense to skinned controls. For example, imagine you have a custom control that displays its own user interface through the services of an external ASP.NET user control (*.ascx*). Skinning this control entails, among other things, indicating the URL to the user control. The user control becomes an effective part of the theme and must be stored under the theme folder. Where exactly? That depends on you, but opting for a *Controls* subdirectory doesn't seem to be a bad idea. We'll return to this point later when building a sample theme.

Customization Themes vs. Style Sheet Themes

There are two forms of themes—customization themes and style sheet themes. Customization themes are used for post-customization of a site. The theme overrides any property definition on the control found in the *.aspx* source. By changing the page's theme, you entirely modify the appearance of the page without touching the source files. If you opt for customization theming, you just need minimal markup for each control in the ASP.NET page.

Style sheet themes are similar to CSS style sheets, except that they operate on control properties rather than on HTML element styles. Style sheet themes are applied immediately after the control is initialized and before the attributes in the *.aspx* file are applied. In other words, with a style sheet theme developers define default values for each control that are in fact overridden by settings in the *.aspx* source.

> **Important** Customization themes and style sheet themes use the same source files. They differ only in how the ASP.NET runtime applies them to a page. The same theme can be applied as a customization theme or a style sheet theme at different times.

The difference between customization and style sheet themes is purely a matter of which takes priority over which. Let's review the resultant form of a control when a customization theme and style sheet theme are applied. Imagine you have the following markup:

```
<asp:Calendar ID="Calendar1" runat="server" backcolor="yellow" />
```

If the page that contains this markup is bound to a customization theme, the calendar shows up as defined in the theme. In particular, the background of the calendar will be of the color defined by the theme.

If the page is bound to a style sheet theme, instead, the background color of the calendar is yellow. The other properties are set in accordance with the theme.

Theming Pages and Controls

You can apply themes at various levels—application, folder, and individual pages. In addition, within the same theme you can select different skins for the same type of control.

Setting a theme at the application level affects all the pages and controls in the application. It's a feature you configure in the application's *web.config* file:

```
<system.web>
    <pages theme="ProAspNet20" />
</system.web>
```

The *theme* attribute sets a customization theme, while the *styleSheetTheme* attribute sets a style sheet theme. Note that the case is important in the *web.config*'s schema. Likewise, a theme can be applied to all the pages found in a given folder and below that folder. To do so, you create a new *web.config* file in an application's directory and add the section just shown to it. All the pages in that directory and below it will be themed accordingly. Finally, you can select the theme at the page level and have styles and skins applied only to that page and all its controls.

Enabling Themes on a Page

To associate a theme with a page, you set the *Theme* or *StyleSheetTheme* attribute on the *@Page* directive, and you're all set:

```
<% @Page Language="C#" Theme="ProAspNet20" %>
<% @Page Language="C#" StyleSheetTheme="ProAspNet20" %>
```

Also in this case, *Theme* sets a customization theme, whereas *StyleSheetTheme* indicates a style sheet theme.

Bear in mind that the name of the selected theme must match the name of a subdirectory under the *App_Themes* path or the name of a global theme. If a theme with a given name exists both locally to the application and globally to the site, the local theme takes precedence. Figure 6-11 shows IntelliSense support for themes in Visual Studio .NET 2005.

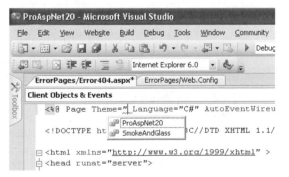

Figure 6-11   IntelliSense support for themes in Visual Studio .NET 2005.

While we're speaking of precedence, it is important to note that themes have a hierarchical nature: directory-level themes takes precedence over application-level themes, and page-level themes override any other themes defined around the application. This hierarchy is independent of which attributes are used—*Theme* or *StyleSheetTheme*—to enable theming.

> **Note**   Setting both *Theme* and *StyleSheetTheme* attributes is not prohibited, though it is not a recommended practice. There's a behavioral gap between the two forms of themes that should make clear which one you need in any situation. However, if you set both attributes, consider that both themes will be applied—first the style sheet theme and then the customization theme. The final results depend on the CSS cascading mechanism and ultimately are determined by the CSS settings of each theme.

Applying Skins

A skin file looks like a regular ASP.NET page as it is populated by control declaration and import directives. Each control declaration defines the default appearance of a particular control. Consider the following excerpt from a skin file:

```
<!-- This is a possible skin for a Button control -->
<asp:Button runat="server"
    BorderColor="darkgray"
    Font-Bold="true"
    BorderWidth="1px"
    BorderStyle="outset"
    ForeColor="DarkSlateGray"
    BackColor="gainsboro" />
```

The net effect of the skin is that every *Button* control in a themed page will be rendered as defined by the preceding markup. If the theme is applied as a style sheet, the settings just shown will be overridable by the developer; if the theme is a customization theme, those settings determine the final look and feel of the control. Properties that the theme leave blank are set according to the control's defaults or the *.aspx* source.

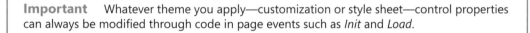

> **Important**   Whatever theme you apply—customization or style sheet—control properties can always be modified through code in page events such as *Init* and *Load*.

A theme can contain multiple skins for a given control, each identified with a unique name—the *SkinID* attribute. When the *SkinID* attribute is set, the skin is said to be a named *skin*. A theme can contain any number of named skins per control, but just one unnamed (default) skin. You select the skin for a control in an ASP.NET themed page by setting the control's *SkinID* property. The value of the control's *SkinID* property should match an existing skin in the current theme. If the page theme doesn't include a skin that matches the *SkinID* property, the default skin for that control type is used. The following code shows two named skins for a button within the same theme:

```
<!-- Place these two definitions in the same .skin file -->
<asp:button skinid="skinClassic" BackColor="gray" />
<asp:button skinid="skinTrendy" BackColor="lightcyan" />
```

When you enable theming on a page, by default all controls in that page will be themed except controls, and individual control properties, that explicitly disable theming.

> **Note**   The automatic application of themes to all controls in a page makes it easy to customize a page that has no knowledge of skins, including existing pages written for ASP.NET 1.x.

Taking Control of Theming

The ASP.NET 2.0 theming infrastructure provides the *EnableTheming* Boolean property to disable skins for a control and all its children. You can configure a page or control to ignore themes by setting the *EnableTheming* property to *false*. The default value of the property is *true*. *EnableTheming* is defined on the *Control* class and inherited by all server controls and pages. If you want to disable theme support for all controls in a page, you can set the *EnableTheming* attribute on the *@Page* directive.

> **Important**   Note that the *EnableTheming* property can be set only in the *Page_PreInit* event for static controls—that is, controls defined in the *.aspx* source. For dynamic controls—controls created programmatically—you must have set the property before adding the control to the page's control tree. A control is added to the page's control tree when you add to the *Controls* collection of the parent control—typically, the form or another control in the form.

When is disabling themes useful? Themes are great at ensuring that all page controls have a consistent look and feel, but at the same time themes override the visual attributes of any control for which a skin is defined. You can control the overriding mechanism a bit by switching style sheet and customization themes. However, when you want a control or page to maintain its predefined look, you just disable themes for that page or control.

Note that disabling themes affects *only* skins, not CSS styles. When a theme includes one or more CSS style-sheet files, they are linked to the *<head>* tag of the resulting HTML document and, after that, are handled entirely by the browser. As you can easily guess, there's not much a Web browser can know about ASP.NET themes!

Theming Controls

Themes style server controls to the degree that each control allows. By default, all control properties are themeable. Theming can be disabled on a particular property by applying the *Themeable* attribute on the property declaration, as follows:

```
[Themeable(false)]
public virtual bool CausesValidation
{
    get { … }
    set { … }
}
```

You can't change the *Themeable* attribute for built-in server controls. You have that option for custom controls instead. Moreover, for custom controls you should use the *Themeable* attribute to prevent theming of behavioral properties such as the *CausesValidation* property just shown. Themes should be used only on visual properties that uniquely affect the appearance of the control:

```
[Themeable(false)]
public MyControl : Control
{
    ...
}
```

Finally, the *Themeable* attribute can be applied to the class declaration of a custom control to stop it from ever bothering about themes.

Putting Themes to Work

Finding a bunch of themes that suit your needs, free or for a small fee, shouldn't be a problem. However, this is a bad reason for not learning how to build your own themes. As mentioned, themes consist of several supporting files, including CSS style sheets and control skins to decorate HTML elements and server controls, respectively, and any other supporting images or files that make up the final expected result.

I firmly believe that building nice-looking, consistent, usable themes is not a programmer's job. It is a task that designers and graphics people can easily accomplish ten times better and faster. However, themes are more than CSS files, and what's more, they are in the area of control properties—exactly the realm of the developer. In short, developers should provide guidance to theme designers much more than we did in the past with CSS authors.

As a first step, let's review the key differences between CSS files and themes.

CSS vs. Themes

Themes are similar to CSS style sheets in that both apply a set of common attributes to any page where they are declared. Themes differ from CSS style sheets in a few key ways, however.

First and foremost, themes work on control properties, whereas CSS style sheets operate on styles of HTML elements. Because of this, with themes you can include auxiliary files and specify standard images for a *TreeView* or *Menu* control, the paging template of a *DataGrid*, or the layout of a *Login* control. In addition, themes can optionally force overriding of local property values (customization themes) and not cascade as CSS style sheets do.

Because themes incorporate CSS style-sheet definitions and apply them along with other property settings, there's no reason for preferring CSS style sheets over themes in ASP.NET 2.0 applications.

Creating a Theme

To create a new theme in a Visual Studio .NET 2005 solution, you start by creating a new folder under *App_Themes*. The simplest way to do this is by right-clicking the *App_Themes* node and selecting a theme folder. Next, you add theme files to the folder, and, when you're done, you can even move the entire directory to the root path of global themes on the Web server.

Typical auxiliary files that form a theme are listed in Figure 6-12. They are CSS style-sheet files, skin files, XML or text files, and extensible style-sheet files (XSLT). Empty files of the specified type are created in the theme folder and edited through more or less specialized text editors in Visual Studio .NET 2005.

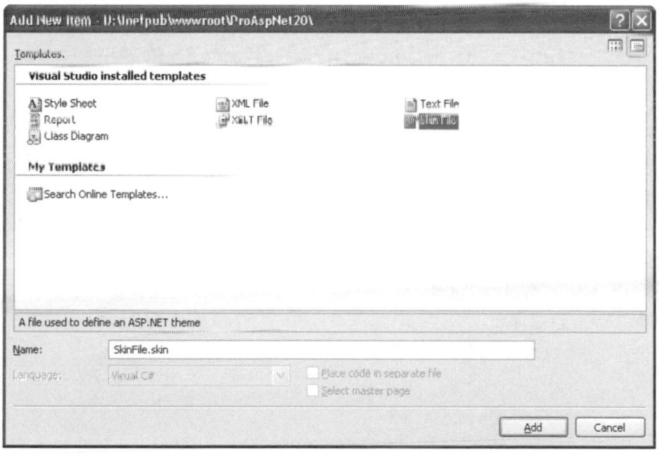

Figure 6-12 Adding auxiliary files to an ASP.NET theme.

A skin file is a collection of a control's markup chunks, optionally named through the *SkinID* attribute. You can create a skin file by cutting and pasting the markup of controls you visually configured in a sample page. If some properties of the skinned controls require resources, you can point them to a path inside the theme folder. Here's an example:

```
<asp:BulletedList runat="server"
    Font-Names="Verdana"
```

```
BulletImageURL="Images/smokeandglass_bullet2.gif"
BulletStyle="CustomImage"
BackColor="transparent"
ForeColor="#585880" />
```

This skin of the *BulletedList* control points to a theme-specific URL for the bullet image. The directory *Images* is intended to be relative to the theme folder. Needless to say, the name *Images* is totally arbitrary. Should the skin require other external files, you could group them in other theme subdirectories.

A skin file can define the appearance of built-in server controls as well as custom controls. To skin a custom control, though, you must first reference it in the file, as follows:

```
<%@ Register TagPrefix="expo"
            Namespace="Expoware.ProAspNet20.Controls"
            Assembly="ProAspNet20.Controls" %>
```

Next, you add the desired default markup for any control defined in the specified assembly and namespace.

Loading Themes Dynamically

You can apply themes dynamically, but this requires a bit of care. The ASP.NET runtime loads theme information immediately after the *PreInit* event fires. When the *PreInit* event fires, the name of any theme referenced in the *@Page* directive is already known and will be used unless it is overridden during the event. If you want to enable your users to change themes on the fly, you create a *Page_PreInit* event handler. The following code shows the code file of a sample page that changes themes dynamically:

```
public partial class TestThemes : System.Web.UI.Page
{
    protected void Page_Load(object sender, EventArgs e)
    {
        if (!IsPostBack) {
            ThemeList.DataSource = GetAvailableThemes();
            ThemeList.DataBind();
        }
    }

    void Page_PreInit(object sender, EventArgs e)
    {
        string theme = "";
        if (Page.Request.Form.Count > 0)
            theme = Page.Request["ThemeList"].ToString();
        if (theme == "None")
            theme = "";
        this.Theme = theme;
    }

    protected StringCollection GetAvailableThemes()
```

```
    {
        string path = Request.PhysicalApplicationPath + @"App_Themes";
        DirectoryInfo dir = new DirectoryInfo(path);
        StringCollection themes = new StringCollection();
        foreach (DirectoryInfo di in dir.GetDirectories())
            themes.Add(di.Name);

        return themes;
    }
}
```

Figure 6-13 shows the page in action. The drop-down list control enumerates the installed application themes and lets you choose the one to apply. The selected theme is then applied in the *PreInit* event and immediately reflected. In the *PreInit* event, no view state has been restored yet; *Request.Form* is the only safe way to access a posted value like the selected theme.

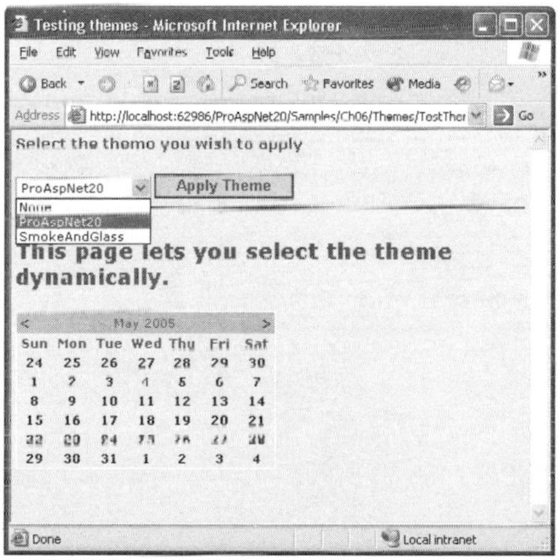

Figure 6-13   Changing themes dynamically in a sample page.

Working with Wizards

Master pages and themes give you the power of building similar-looking, rich pages that share graphics, control layout, and even some functionality. A special type of rich page is the page that implements a wizard. More common in Windows desktop applications than in Web scenarios, wizards are typically used to break up large forms to collect user input. A wizard is a sequence of related steps, each associated with an input form and a user interface. Users move through the wizard sequentially, but they are normally given a chance to skip a step or jump back to modify some of the entered values. A wizard is conceptually pretty simple, but implementing it over HTTP connections can be tricky. Everybody involved with serious Web development can only heartily welcome the introduction of the *Wizard* control in ASP.NET 2.0.

An Overview of the *Wizard* Control

The *Wizard* control supports both linear and nonlinear navigation. It allows you to move backward to change values and to skip steps that are unnecessary due to previous settings or because users don't want to fill those fields. Like many other ASP.NET 2.0 controls, the *Wizard* supports themes, styles, and templates.

The *Wizard* is a composite control and automatically generates some constituent controls such as navigation buttons and panels. As you'll see in a moment, the programming interface of the control has multiple templates that provide for in-depth customization of the overall user interface. The control also guarantees that state is maintained no matter where you move—backward, forward, or to a particular page. All the steps of a wizard must be declared within the boundaries of the same *Wizard* control. In other words, the wizard must be self-contained and not provide page-to-page navigation.

Structure of a Wizard

As shown in Figure 6-14, a wizard has four parts: header, view, navigation bar, and sidebar.

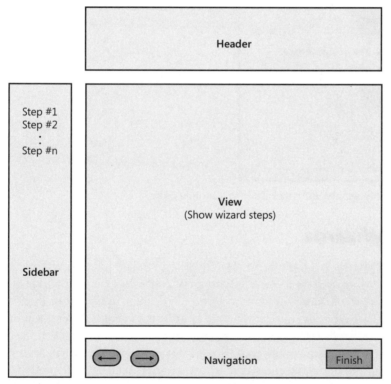

Figure 6-14   The four parts of a *Wizard* control.

The header consists of text you can set through the *HeaderText* property. You can change the default appearance of the header text by using its style property; you can also change the structure of the header by using the corresponding header template property. If *HeaderText* is empty and no custom template is specified, no header is shown for the wizard.

The view displays the contents of the currently active step. The wizard requires you to define each step in an *<asp:wizardstep>* element. An *<asp:wizardstep>* element corresponds to a *WizardStep* control. Different types of wizard steps are supported; all wizard step classes inherit from a common base class named *WizardStepBase*.

All wizard steps must be grouped in a single *<wizardsteps>* tag, as shown in the following code:

```
<asp:wizard runat="server" DisplaySideBar="true">
  <wizardsteps>
    <asp:wizardstep runat="server" steptype="auto" id="step1">
      First step
    </asp:wizardstep>
    <asp:wizardstep runat="server" steptype="auto" id="step2">
      Second step
    </asp:wizardstep>
    <asp:wizardstep runat="server" steptype="auto" id="finish">
      Final step
    </asp:wizardstep>
  </wizardsteps>
</asp:wizard>
```

The navigation bar consists of auto-generated buttons that provide any needed functionality—typically, going to the next or previous step or finishing. You can modify the look and feel of the navigation bar by using styles and templates.

The optional sidebar is used to display content in the left side of the control. It provides an overall view of the steps needed to accomplish the wizard's task. By default, it displays a description of each step, with the current step displayed in boldface type. You can customize styles and templates. Figure 6-15 shows the default user interface. Each step is labeled using the ID of the corresponding *<asp:wizardstep>* tag.

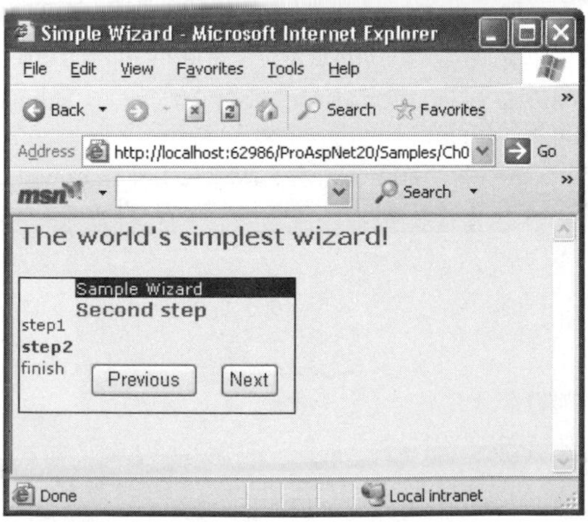

Figure 6-15   A wizard with the default sidebar on the left side.

Wizard Styles and Templates

You can style all the various parts and buttons of a *Wizard* control by using the properties listed in Table 6-4.

Table 6-4 The *Wizard* Control's Style Properties

Style	Description
CancelButtonStyle	Sets the style properties for the wizard's Cancel button
FinishCompleteButtonStyle	Sets the style properties for the wizard's Finish button
FinishPreviousButtonStyle	Sets the style properties for the wizard's Previous button when at the *Finish* step
HeaderStyle	Sets the style properties for the wizard's header
NavigationButtonStyle	Sets the style properties for navigation buttons
NavigationStyle	Sets the style properties for the navigation area
SideBarButtonStyle	Sets the style properties for the buttons on the sidebar
SideBarStyle	Sets the style properties for the wizard's sidebar
StartStepNextButtonStyle	Sets the style properties for the wizard's Next button when at the *Start* step
StepNextButtonStyle	Sets the style properties for the wizard's Next button
StepPreviousButtonStyle	Sets the style properties for the wizard's Previous button
StepStyle	Sets the style properties for the area where steps are displayed

The contents of the header, sidebar, and navigation bar can be further customized with templates. Table 6-5 lists the available templates.

Table 6-5 The *Wizard* Control's Template Properties

Style	Description
FinishNavigationTemplate	Specifies the navigation bar shown before the last page of the wizard. By default, the navigation bar contains the Previous and Finish buttons.
HeaderTemplate	Specifies the title bar of the wizard.
SideBarTemplate	Used to display content in the left side of the wizard control.
StartNavigationTemplate	Specifies the navigation bar for the first view in the wizard. By default, it contains only the Next button.
StepNavigationTemplate	Specifies the navigation bar for steps other than first, finish, or complete. By default, it contains Previous and Next buttons.

In addition to using styles and templates, you can control the programming interface of the *Wizard* control through a few properties.

The Wizard's Programming Interface

Table 6-6 lists the properties of the *Wizard* control, excluding style and template properties and properties defined on base classes.

Table 6-6   Main Properties of the *Wizard* Control

Property	Description
ActiveStep	Returns the current wizard step object. The object is an instance of the *WizardStep* class.
ActiveStepIndex	Gets and sets the 0-based index of the current wizard step.
DisplayCancelButton	Toggles the visibility of the *Cancel* button. The default value is *false*.
DisplaySideBar	Toggles the visibility of the sidebar. The default value is *false*.
HeaderText	Gets and sets the title of the wizard.
SkipLinkText	The ToolTip string that the control associates with an invisible image, as a hint to screen readers. The default value is *Skip Navigation Links* and is localized based on the server's current locale.
WizardSteps	Returns a collection containing all the *WizardStep* objects defined in the control.

A wizard in action is fully represented by its collection of step views and buttons. In particular, you'll recognize the following buttons: *StartNext*, *StepNext*, *StepPrevious*, *FinishComplete*, *FinishPrevious*, and *Cancel*. Each button is characterized by properties to get and set the button's image URL, caption, type, and destination URL after click. The name of a property is the name of the button followed by a suffix. The available suffixes are listed in Table 6-7.

Table 6-7   Suffixes of Button Properties

Suffix	Description
ButtonImageUrl	Gets and sets the URL of the image used to render the button
ButtonText	Gets and sets the text for the button
ButtonType	Gets and sets the type of the button: push button, image, or link button
DestinationPageUrl	Gets and sets the URL to jump to once the button is clicked

Note that names in Table 6-7 do not correspond to real property names. You have the four properties in this table for each distinct type of wizard button. The real name is composed by the name of the button followed by any of the suffixes—for example, *CancelButtonText*, *Finish-CompleteDestinationPageUrl*, and so on.

The *Wizard* control also supplies a few interesting methods—for example, *GetHistory*, which is defined as follows:

```
public ICollection GetHistory()
```

GetHistory returns a collection of *WizardStepBase* objects. The order of the items is determined by the order in which the wizard's pages were accessed by the user. The first object returned—the one with an index of 0—is the currently selected wizard step. The second object represents the view before the current one, and so on.

The second method, *MoveTo*, is used to move to a particular wizard step. The method's prototype is described here:

```
public void MoveTo(WizardStepBase step)
```

The method requires you to pass a *WizardStepBase* object, which can be problematic. However, the method is a simple wrapper around the setter of the *ActiveStepIndex* property. If you want to jump to a particular step and not hold an instance of the corresponding *WizardStep* object, setting *ActiveStepIndex* is just as effective.

Table 6-8 lists the key events in the life of a *Wizard* control in an ASP.NET 2.0 page.

Table 6-8 Events of the *Wizard* Control

Event	Description
ActiveViewChanged	Raised when the active step changes
CancelButtonClick	Raised when the Cancel button is clicked
FinishButtonClick	Raised when the Finish Complete button is clicked
NextButtonClick	Raised when any Next button is clicked
PreviousButtonClick	Raised when any Previous button is clicked
SideBarButtonClick	Raised when a button on the sidebar is clicked

As you can see, there's a common click event for all Next and Previous buttons you can find on your way. A Next button can be found on the Start page as well as on all step pages. Likewise, a Previous button can be located on the Finish page. Whenever a Next button is clicked, the page receives a *NextButtonClick* event; whenever a Previous button is clicked, the control raises a *PreviousButtonClick* event.

Adding Steps to a Wizard

A *WizardStep* object represents one of the child views that the wizard can display. The *WizardStep* class ultimately derives from *View* and adds just a few public properties to it. A *View* object represents a control that acts as a container for a group of controls. A view is hosted within a *MultiView* control. (See Chapter 4.) To create its output, the wizard makes internal use of a *MultiView* control. However, the wizard is not derived from the *MultiView* class.

You define the views of a wizard through distinct instances of the *WizardStep* class, all grouped under the <*WizardSteps*> tag. The <*WizardSteps*> tag corresponds to the *WizardSteps* collection property exposed by the *Wizard* control:

```
<WizardSteps>
    <asp:WizardStep>
        ...
    </asp:WizardStep>
    <asp:WizardStep>
        ...
    </asp:WizardStep>
</WizardSteps>
```

Each wizard step is characterized by a title and a type. The *Title* property provides a brief description of the view. This information is not used unless the sidebar is enabled. If the sidebar is enabled, the title of each step is used to create a list of steps. If the sidebar is enabled but no title is provided for the various steps, the ID of the *WizardStep* objects is used to populate the sidebar, as shown earlier in Figure 6-15.

While defining a step, you can also set the *AllowReturn* property, which indicates whether the user is allowed to return to the current step from a subsequent step. The default value of the property is *true*.

Types of Wizard Steps

The *StepType* property indicates how a particular step should be handled and rendered within a wizard. Acceptable values for the step type come from the *WizardStepType* enumeration, as listed in Table 6-9.

Table 6-9   Wizard Step Types

Property	Description
Auto	The default setting, which forces the wizard to determine how each contained step should be treated.
Complete	The last page that the wizard displays, usually after the wizard has been completed. The navigation bar and the sidebar aren't displayed.
Finish	The last page used for collecting user data. It lacks the Next button, and it shows the Previous and Finish buttons.
Start	The first screen displayed, with no Previous button.
Step	All other intermediate pages, in which the Previous and Next buttons are displayed.

When the wizard is in automatic mode—the default type *Auto*—it determines the type of each step based on the order in which the steps appear in the source code. For example, the first step is considered of type *Start* and the last step is marked as *Finish*. No *Complete* step is assumed. If you correctly assign types to steps, the order in which you declare them in the *.aspx* source is not relevant.

Creating an Input Step

The following code shows a sample wizard step used to collect the provider name and the connection string to connect to a database and search for some data. For better graphical results, the content of the step is encapsulated in a fixed-height *<div>* tag. If all the steps are configured in this way, users navigating through the wizard won't experience sudden changes in the overall page size and layout.

```
<asp:wizardstep ID="Wizardstep1" runat="server" title="Connect">
    <div style="height:200px;width:400px;margin:10;">
        <table>
            <tr><td>Provider</td><td>
                <asp:textbox runat="server" id="ProviderName" width="250px"
                            text="System.Data.SqlClient" />
            </td></tr>
            <tr><td>Connection String</td><td>
```

```
                        <asp:textbox runat="server" id="ConnString" width="250px"
                            text="SERVER=(local);DATABASE=northwind;UID=...;" />
                    </td></tr>
                    <tr><td height="100px"></td></tr>
                </table>
            </div>
        </asp:wizardstep>
```

Figure 6-16 shows a preview of the step. As you can guess, the step is recognized as a *Start* step. As a result, the wizard is added only to the Next button.

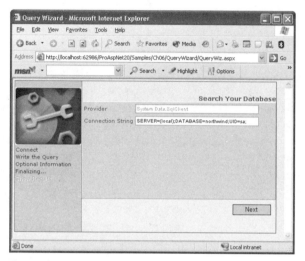

Figure 6-16   A sample *Start* wizard step.

A wizard is usually created for collecting input data, so validation becomes a critical issue. You can validate the input data in two nonexclusive ways—using validators and using transition event handlers.

The first option involves placing validator controls in the wizard step. This guarantees that invalid input—empty fields or incompatible data types—is caught quickly and, optionally, already on the client:

```
<asp:requiredfieldvalidator ID="RequiredField1" runat="server"
    text="*"
    errormessage="Must indicate a connection string"
    setfocusonerror="true"
    controltovalidate="ConnString" />
```

If you need to access server-side resources to validate the input data, you're better off using transition event handlers. A transition event is an event the wizard raises when it is about to switch to another view. For example, the *NextButtonClick* event is raised when the user clicks the Next button to jump to the subsequent step. You can intercept this event, do any required validation, and cancel the transition if necessary. We'll return to this topic in a moment.

Defining the Sidebar

The sidebar is a left-side panel that lists buttons to quickly and randomly reach any step of the wizard. It's a sort of quick-launch menu for the various steps that form the wizard. You control the sidebar's visibility through the Boolean *DisplaySideBar* attribute and define its contents through the *SideBarTemplate* property.

Regardless of the template, the internal layout of the sidebar is not left entirely to your imagination. In particular, the *<SideBarTemplate>* tag must contain a *DataList* control with a well-known ID—*SideBarList*. In addition, the *<ItemTemplate>* block must contain a button object with the name of *SideBarButton*. The button object must be any object that implements the *IButtonControl* interface.

> **Note**   For better graphical results, you might want to use explicit heights and widths for all steps and the sidebar as well. Likewise, the push buttons in the navigation bar might look better if they are made the same size. You do this by setting the *Width* and *Height* properties on the *NavigationButtonStyle* object.

Navigating Through the Wizard

When a button is clicked to move to another step, an event is fired to the hosting page. It's up to you to decide when and how to perform any critical validation, such as deciding whether conditions exist to move to the next step.

In most cases, you'll want to perform server-side validation only when the user clicks the Finish button to complete the wizard. You can be sure that whatever route the user has taken within the wizard, clicking the Finish button will complete it. Any code you bind to the *FinishButtonClick* event is executed only once, and only when strictly necessary.

By contrast, any code bound to the Previous or Next button executes when the user moves back or forward. The page posts back on both events.

Filtering Page Navigation with Events

You should perform server-side validation if what the user can do next depends on the data he or she entered in the previous step. This means that in most cases you just need to write a *NextButtonClick* event handler:

```
<asp:wizard runat="server" id="QueryWizard"
    OnNextButtonClick="OnNext">
    ...
</asp:wizard>
```

If the user moves back to a previously visited page, you can usually ignore any data entered in the current step and avoid validation. Because the user is moving back, you can safely assume he or she is not going to use any fresh data. When a back movement is requested, you can assume that any preconditions needed to visit that previous page are verified. This happens by design if your users take a sequential route.

If the wizard's sidebar is enabled, users can jump from page to page in any order. If the logic you're implementing through the wizard requires that preconditions be met before a certain step is reached, you should write a *SideBarButtonClick* event handler and ensure that the requirements have been met.

A wizard click event requires a *WizardNavigationEventHandler* delegate:

```
public delegate void WizardNavigationEventHandler(
    object sender,
    WizardNavigationEventArgs e);
```

The *WizardNavigationEventArgs* structure contains two useful properties that inform you about the 0-based indexes of the page being left and the page being displayed. The *CurrentStepIndex* property returns the index of the last page visited; the *NextStepIndex* returns the index of the next page. Note that both properties are read-only.

The following code shows a sample handler for the Next button. The handler prepares a summary message to show when the user is going to the Finish page.

```
void OnNext(object sender, WizardNavigationEventArgs e)
{
    // Collect the input data if going to the last page
    // -1 because of 0-based indexing, add -1 if you have a Complete page
    if (e.NextStepIndex == QueryWizard.WizardSteps.Count - 2)
        PrepareFinalStep();
}
void PrepareFinalStep()
{
    string cmdText = DetermineCommandText();

    // Show a Ready-to-go message
    StringBuilder sb = new StringBuilder("");
    sb.AppendFormat("You're about to run: <br><br>{0}<hr>", cmdText);
    sb.Append("<b><br>Ready to go?</b>");
    ReadyMsg.Text = sb.ToString();
}

string DetermineCommandText()
{
    // Generate and return command text here
}
```

Each page displayed by the wizard is a kind of panel (actually, a view) defined within a parent control—the wizard. This means that all child controls used in all steps must have a unique ID. It also means that you can access any of these controls just by name. For example, if one of the pages contains a text box named, say, ProviderName, you can access it from any event handler by using the *ProviderName* identifier.

The preceding code snippet is an excerpt from a sample wizard that collects input and runs a database query. The first step picks up connection information, whereas the second step lets users define table, fields, and optionally a *WHERE* clause. The composed command is shown in the Finish page, where the wizard asks for final approval. (See Figure 6-17.)

The full source code of the wizard is in the companion code for this book.

Figure 6-17   Two successive pages of the sample wizard: query details and the *Finish* step.

Canceling Events

The *WizardNavigationEventArgs* structure also contains a read/write Boolean property named *Cancel*. If you set this property to *true*, you just cancel the ongoing transition to the destination page. The following code shows how to prevent the display of the next step if the user is on the Start page and types in **sa** as the user ID:

```
void OnNext(object sender, WizardNavigationEventArgs e)
{
    if (e.CurrentStepIndex == 0 &&
        ConnString.Text.IndexOf("UID=sa") > -1)
    {
        e.Cancel = true;
        return;
    }
}
```

You can cancel events from within any transition event handler and not just from the *NextButtonClick* event handler. This trick is useful to block navigation if the server-side validation of the input data has failed. In this case, though, you're responsible for showing some feedback to the user.

> **Note**   You can't cancel navigation from within the *ActiveViewChanged* event. This event follows any transition events, such as the *NextButtonClick* or *PreviousButtonClick* event, and occurs when the transition has completed. Unlike transition events, the *ActiveViewChanged* event requires a simpler, parameterless handler—*EventHandler*.

Finalizing the Wizard

All wizards have some code to execute to finalize the task. If you use the ASP.NET 2.0 *Wizard* control, you place this code in the *FinishButtonClick* event handler. Figure 6-18 shows the final step of a wizard that completed successfully.

```
void OnFinish(object sender, WizardNavigationEventArgs e)
{
    string finalMsg = "The operation completed successfully.";
    try {
        // Complete the wizard (compose and run the query)
        string cmd = DetermineCommandText();
        DataTable table = ExecuteCommand(ConnString.Text, cmd);
        grid.DataSource = table;
        grid.DataBind();

        // OK color
        FinalMsg.ForeColor = Color.Blue;
    }
    catch (Exception ex) {
        FinalMsg.ForeColor = Color.Red;
        finalMsg = String.Format("The operation cannot be completed
                                 due to:<br>{0}", ex.Message);
    }
    finally {
        FinalMsg.Text = finalMsg;
    }
}

string DetermineCommandText()
{
    // Generate and return command text here
}

DataTable ExecuteCommand()
{
    // Execute database query here
}
```

If the wizard contains a *Complete* step, that page should be displayed after the Finish button is clicked and the final task has completed. If something goes wrong with the update, you should either cancel the transition to prevent the Complete page from even appearing or adapt the user interface of the completion page to display an appropriate error message. Which option you choose depends on the expected behavior of the implemented operation. If the wizard's operation can fail or succeed, you let the wizard complete and display an error message in case something went wrong. If the wizard's operation must complete successfully unless the user quits, you should not make the transition to the Complete page; instead, provide users with feedback on what went wrong and give them a chance to try again.

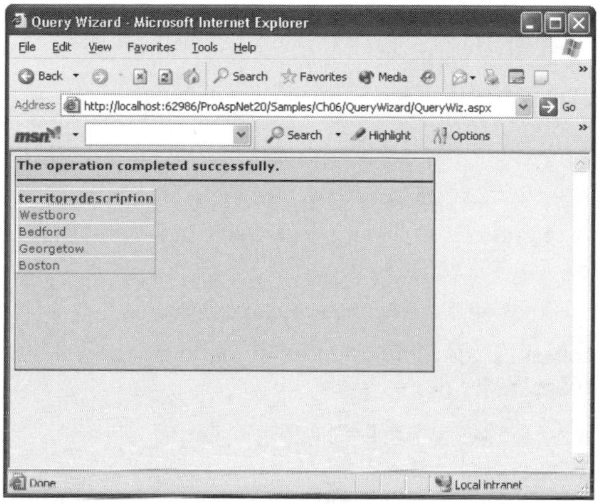

Figure 6-18   The final step of a wizard that completed successfully.

Conclusion

Since version 1.0, ASP.NET has been characterized by a well-balanced mix of low-level and fea-ture-rich tools. Using low-level tools such as events, HTTP modules, and HTTP handlers, you can plug into the ASP.NET pipeline to influence the processing of requests at every stage. At the same time, ASP.NET offers a wealth of feature-rich components for those who don't need control over every little step.

The quantity and quality of application services has grown significantly in ASP.NET 2.0, which was designed with the goal of making things happen with the least amount of code. The intro-duction of rich composition tools for building pages like the ones we examined in this chapter is just a confirmation of the trend. In this chapter, we explored master pages to create content pages based on a predefined template made of graphics and, optionally, code. Master pages are not pure object-oriented visual inheritance a là Windows Forms; instead, they benefit from aggregation and let derived pages personalize well-known regions of the master. With full support from the Visual Studio .NET 2005 environment, master pages are a time-saving feature that brings concrete added value to ASP.NET 2.0 solutions.

Likewise, themes let developers code pages and controls that allow users to apply skins at will. ASP.NET themes work like Windows XP themes, and overall they're a superset of CSS that covers control properties in addition to HTML element styles. Themes work well in con-junction with the user profile API we discussed in Chapter 5. Using both, developers can let end users choose the theme and persist its name back to the personalization storage layer.

Finally, wizards are made-to-measure controls to quickly and efficiently write multistep input forms that divide complex operations into simple steps.

With this chapter, we completed the first part of the book, dedicated to building ASP.NET pages. With the next chapter, we approach the world of data access and explore ways to add data to a Web site.

Just the Facts

- A master page is a distinct file referenced at the application or page level that contains the static layout of the page.
- A master page contains regions that each *derived* page can customize.
- A *derived* page, known as a content page, is a collection of markup blocks that the runtime will use to fill the regions in the master page.
- Content pages can't contain information other than contents for the master's placeholders.
- Regions in the master page can have default content that can be used if the content page doesn't provide any.
- You can define various masters for a page and have the system automatically pick up a particular one based on the browser's user agent string.
- Master pages can be nested and expose a strong-typed object model.
- Themes are a collection of settings spread over various files that the ASP.NET runtime uses to give the whole site (or page) a consistent user interface.
- Themes become a kind of attribute, and they can be exported from one application to the next and applied to pages on the fly.
- Themes differ from CSS files because they let you style ASP.NET control properties and not just HTML elements.
- A theme contains skin files, CSS files, and images, plus any other auxiliary file you might find useful.
- A skin file is a collection of ASP.NET control declarations. The system ensures that after instantiation each control of that type in the page will have exactly the same set of attributes.
- The wizard control manages multiple views inside a single control and provides an auto-generated user interface for you to move back and forth between views as you do in a desktop wizard.

Part II
Adding Data in an ASP.NET Site

Chapter 7

ADO.NET Data Providers

In this chapter:

.NET Data Access Infrastructure. 264

Connecting to Data Sources. 274

Executing Commands 293

Conclusion 317

ADO.NET is a data-access subsystem in the Microsoft .NET Framework. It was heavily inspired by ActiveX Data Objects (ADO), which has emerged over the past few years as a very successful object model for writing data-aware applications. The key design criteria for ADO.NET are simplicity and performance. Those criteria typically work against each other, but with ADO.NET you get the power and performance of a low-level interface combined with the simplicity of a modern object model. Unlike ADO, though, ADO.NET has been purposely designed to observe general, rather than database-oriented, guidelines.

Several syntactical differences exist between the object models of ADO and ADO.NET. In spite of this, the functionalities of ADO and ADO.NET look much the same. This is because Microsoft put a lot of effort in aligning some programming aspects of the ADO.NET object model with ADO. In this way, seasoned data developers new to .NET don't need to become familiar with too many new concepts and can work with a relatively short learning curve. With ADO.NET, you probably won't be able to reuse much of your existing code. You'll certainly be able, though, to reuse all your skills. At the same time, novice developers face a relatively simple and easy-to-understand model, with a consistent design and a powerful set of features.

The ADO.NET framework is made of two distinct but closely related sets of classes—data providers and data containers. We tackle providers in this chapter and save containers for the next chapter.

.NET Data Access Infrastructure

ADO.NET is the latest in a long line of database-access technologies that began with the Open Database Connectivity (ODBC) API several years ago. Written as a C-style library, ODBC was designed to provide a uniform API to issue SQL calls to various database servers. In the ODBC model, database-specific drivers hide any difference and discrepancy between the SQL language used at the application level and the internal query engine. Next, COM landed in the database territory and started a colonization process that culminated with OLE DB.

OLE DB has evolved from ODBC and, in fact, the open database connectivity principle emerges somewhat intact in it. OLE DB is a COM-based API aimed at building a common layer of code for applications to access any data source that can be exposed as a tabular rowset of data. The OLE DB architecture is composed of two elements—a consumer and a provider. The consumer is incorporated in the client and is responsible for setting up COM-based communication with the data provider. The OLE DB data provider, in turn, receives calls from the consumer and executes commands on the data source. Whatever the data format and storage medium are, an OLE DB provider returns data formatted in a tabular layout—that is, with rows and columns. OLE DB uses COM to make client applications and data sources to communicate.

Because it isn't especially easy to use and is primarily designed for coding from within C++ applications, OLE DB never captured the hearts of programmers, even though it could guarantee a remarkable mix of performance and flexibility. Next came ADO—roughly, a COM automation version of OLE DB—just to make the OLE DB technology accessible from Microsoft Visual Basic and classic Active Server Pages (ASP) applications. When used, ADO acts as the real OLE DB consumer embedded in the host applications. ADO was invented in the age of connected, two-tier applications, and the object model design reflects that. ADO makes a point of programming redundancy: it usually provides more than just one way of accomplishing key tasks, and it contains a lot of housekeeping code. For all these reasons, although it's incredibly easy to use, an ADO-based application doesn't perform as efficiently as a pure OLE DB application.

> **Note** Using ADO in .NET applications is still possible, but for performance and consistency reasons its use should be limited to a few very special cases. For example, ADO is the only way you have to work with server cursors. In addition, ADO provides a schema management API to .NET Framework 1.x applications. On the other hand, ADO recordsets can't be directly bound to ASP.NET or Microsoft Windows Forms data-bound controls. We'll cover ASP.NET data binding in Chapter 9 and Chapter 10. The key improvements in ADO.NET are the rather powerful disconnected model exposed through the *DataSet* object, the strong integration with XML, and the seamless integration with the rest of the .NET Framework. Additionally, the performance of ADO.NET is very good, and the integration with Microsoft Visual Studio .NET is unprecedented. If you're writing a new application in the .NET Framework, deciding whether to use ADO.NET is a no-brainer.

.NET Managed Data Providers

A key architectural element in the ADO.NET infrastructure is the *managed provider*, which can be considered the .NET counterpart of the OLE DB provider. A managed data provider enables you to connect to a data source and retrieve and modify data. Compared to the OLE DB provider, a .NET managed provider has a simplified data-access architecture made of a smaller set of interfaces and based on .NET Framework data types.

Building Blocks of a .NET Data Provider

The classes in the managed provider interact with the specific data source and return data to the application using the data types defined in the .NET Framework. The logical components implemented in a managed provider are those graphically featured in Figure 7-1.

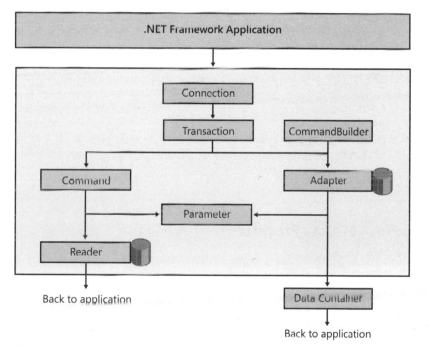

Figure 7-1   The .NET Framework classes that form a typical managed provider and their interconnections.

The functionalities supplied by a .NET data provider fall into a couple of categories:

- Support for disconnected data—that is, the capability of populating ADO.NET container classes with fresh data

- Support for connected data access, which includes the capability of setting up a connection and executing a command

Table 7-1 details the principal components of a .NET data provider.

Table 7-1   Principal Components of a .NET Data Provider

Component	Description
Connection	Creates a connection with the specified data source, including Microsoft SQL Server, Oracle, and any data source for which you can indicate either an OLE DB provider or an ODBC driver
Transaction	Represents a transaction to be made in the source database server
Command	Represents a command that hits the underlying database server
Parameter	Represents a parameter you can pass to the command object
DataAdapter	Represents a database command that executes on the specified database server and returns a disconnected set of records
CommandBuilder	Represents a helper object that automatically generates commands and parameters for a DataAdapter
DataReader	Represents a read-only, forward-only cursor created on the underlying database server

Each managed provider that wraps a real-world database server implements all the objects in Table 7-1 in a way that is specific to the data source.

> **Caution**   You won't find any class named *Connection* in the .NET Framework. You'll find instead several connection-like classes, one for each supported .NET managed provider—for example, *SqlConnection* and *OracleConnection*. The same holds true for the other objects listed in Table 7-1.

Interfaces of a .NET Data Provider

The components listed in Table 7-1 are implemented based on methods and properties defined by the interfaces you see in Table 7-2.

Table 7-2   Interfaces of .NET Data Providers

Interface	Description
IDbConnection	Represents a unique session with a data source
IDbTransaction	Represents a local, nondistributed transaction
IDbCommand	Represents a command that executes when connected to a data source
IDataParameter	Allows implementation of a parameter to a command
IDataReader	Reads a forward-only, read-only stream of data created after the execution of a command
IDataAdapter	Populates a DataSet object, and resolves changes in the DataSet object back to the data source
IDbDataAdapter	Supplies methods to execute typical operations on relational databases (such as insert, update, select, and delete)

Note that all these interfaces except *IDataAdapter* are officially considered to be optional. However, any realistic data provider that manages a database server would implement them all.

> **Note**   Individual managed providers are in no way limited to implementing all and only the interfaces listed in Table 7-2. Based on the capabilities of the underlying data source and its own level of abstraction, each managed provider can expose more components. A good example of this is the data provider for Microsoft SQL Server that you get in the .NET Framework 2.0. It adds several additional classes to handle special operations such as bulk copy, data dependency, and connection string building.

Managed Providers vs. OLE DB Providers

OLE DB providers and managed data providers are radically different types of components that share a common goal—to provide a unique and uniform programming interface for data access. The differences between OLE DB providers and .NET data providers can be summarized in the following points:

- **Component technology.**   OLE DB providers are in-process COM servers that expose a suite of COM interfaces to consumer modules. The dialog between consumers and providers takes place through COM and involves a number of interfaces. A .NET data provider is a suite of managed classes whose overall design looks into one *particular* data source rather than blinking at an abstract and universal data source, as is the case with OLE DB.

- **Internal implementation.**   Both types of providers end up making calls into the data-source programming API. In doing so, though, they provide a dense layer of code that separates the data source from the calling application. Learning from the OLE DB experience, Microsoft designed .NET data providers to be more agile and simple. Fewer interfaces are involved, and the conversation between the caller and the callee is more direct and as informal as possible.

- **Application integration.**   Another aspect of .NET that makes the conversation between caller and callee more informal is the fact that managed providers return data using the same data structures that the application would use to store it. In OLE DB, the data-retrieval process is more flexible, but it's also more complex because the provider packs data in flat memory buffers and leaves the consumer responsible for mapping that data into usable data structures.

Calling into an OLE DB provider from within a .NET application is more expensive because of the data conversion necessary to make the transition from the managed environment of the common language runtime (CLR) to the COM world. Calling a COM object from within a .NET application is possible through the COM interop layer, but doing so comes at a cost. In general, to access a data source from within a .NET application, you should always use a managed provider instead of OLE DB providers or ODBC drivers. You should be doing this primarily because of the transition costs, but also because managed providers are normally more modern tools based on an optimized architecture.

Some data sources, though, might not have a .NET data provider available. In these cases, resorting to old-fashioned OLE DB providers or ODBC drivers is a pure necessity. For this reason, the .NET Framework encapsulates in managed wrapper classes the logic needed to call into a COM-style OLE DB provider or a C-style ODBC driver.

Data Sources You Access Through ADO.NET

The .NET data provider is the managed component of choice for database vendors to expose their data in the most effective way. Ideally, each database vendor should provide a .NET-compatible API that is seamlessly callable from within managed applications. Unfortunately, this is not always the case. However, at least for the major database management systems (DBMS), a managed data provider can be obtained from either Microsoft or third-party vendors.

As of version 2.0, the .NET Framework supports the data providers listed in Table 7-3.

Table 7-3   Managed Data Providers in the .NET Framework

Data Source	Namespace	Description
SQL Server	*System.Data.SqlClient*	Targets various versions of SQL Server, including SQL Server 7.0, SQL Server 2000, and the newest SQL Server 2005
OLE DB providers	*System.Data.OleDb*	Targets OLE DB providers, including SQLOLEDB, MSDAORA, and the Jet engine
ODBC drivers	*System.Data.Odbc*	Targets several ODBC drivers, including those for SQL Server, Oracle, and the Jet engine
Oracle	*System.Data.OracleClient*	Targets Oracle 9i, and supports all of its data types

The OLE DB and ODBC managed providers listed in Table 7-3 are not specific to a physical database server, but rather they serve as a bridge that gives instant access to a large number of existing OLE DB providers and ODBC drivers. When you call into OLE DB providers, your .NET applications jumps out of the managed environment and issues COM calls through the COM interop layer.

Accessing SQL Server

As mentioned, Microsoft supplies a managed provider for SQL Server 7.0 and newer versions. Using the classes contained in this provider is by far the most effective way of accessing SQL Server. Figure 7-2 shows how SQL Server is accessed by .NET and COM clients.

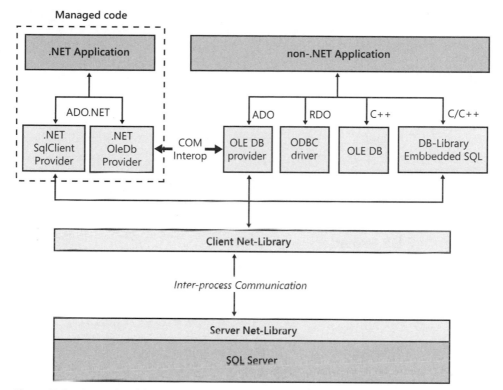

Figure 7-2   Accessing SQL Server by using the managed provider for OLE DB adds overhead because the objects called must pass through the COM interop layer.

A .NET application should always access a SQL Server database using the native data provider. Although it's possible to do so, you should have a good reason to opt for an alternative approach such as using the OLE DB provider for SQL Server (named SQLOLEDB). A possible good reason is the need to use ADO rather than ADO.NET as the data-access library. The SQL Server native provider not only avoids paying the performance tax of going down to COM, but it also implements some small optimizations when preparing the command for SQL Server.

Accessing Oracle Databases

The .NET Framework 1.1 and 2.0 include a managed provider for Oracle databases. The classes are located in the *System.Data.OracleClient* namespace in the *System.Data.OracleClient* assembly. Instead of using the managed provider, you can resort to the COM-based OLE DB provider (named MSDAORA) or the ODBC driver. Note, though, that the Microsoft OLE DB provider for Oracle does not support Oracle 9i and its specific data types. In contrast, Oracle 9i data types are fully supported by the .NET managed provider. So by using the .NET component to connect to Oracle, you not only get a performance boost but also increased programming power.

> **Note** The .NET data provider for Oracle requires Oracle client software (version 8.1.7 or later) to be installed on the system before you can use it to connect to an Oracle data source.

Microsoft is not the only company to develop a .NET data provider for Oracle databases. Data Direct, Core Lab, and Oracle itself also shipped one. Each provider has its own set of features; for example, the Oracle provider (named ODP.NET) has many optimizations for retrieving and manipulating Oracle native types, such as any flavor of large objects (LOBs) and REF cursors. ODP.NET can participate in transactional applications, with the Oracle database acting as the resource manager and the Microsoft Distributed Transaction Coordinator (DTC) coordinating transactions.

Using OLE DB Providers

The .NET data provider for OLE DB providers is a data-access bridge that allows .NET applications to call into data sources for which a COM OLE DB provider exists. While this approach is architecturally less effective than using native providers, it is the only way to access those data sources when no managed providers are available.

The classes in the *System.Data.OleDb* namespace, though, don't support all types of OLE DB providers and have been optimized to work with only a few of them, as listed in Table 7-4.

Table 7-4   OLE DB Providers Tested

Name	Description
Microsoft.Jet.OLEDB.4.0	The OLE DB provider for the Jet engine implemented in Microsoft Office Access
MSDAORA	The Microsoft OLE DB provider for Oracle 7 that partially supports some features in Oracle 8
SQLOLEDB	The OLE DB provider for SQL Server 6.5 and newer

Table 7-4 does not include all the OLE DB providers that really work through the OLE DB .NET data provider. However, only the components in Table 7-4 are guaranteed to work well in .NET. In particular, the classes in the *System.Data.OleDb* namespace don't support OLE DB providers that implement any of the OLE DB 2.5 interfaces for semistructured and hierarchical rowsets. This includes the OLE DB providers for Exchange (EXOLEDB) and for Internet Publishing (MSDAIPP).

In general, what really prevents existing OLE DB providers from working properly within the .NET data provider for OLE DB is the set of interfaces they actually implement. Some OLE DB providers—for example, those written using the Active Template Library (ATL) or with Visual Basic and the OLE DB Simple Provider Toolkit—are likely to miss one or more COM interfaces that the .NET wrapper requires.

Using ODBC Drivers

The .NET data provider for ODBC lets you access ODBC drivers from managed, ADO.NET-driven applications. Although the ODBC .NET data provider is intended to work with all compliant ODBC drivers, it is guaranteed to work well only with the drivers for SQL Server, Oracle, and Jet. Although ODBC might appear to now be an obsolete technology, it is still used in several production environments, and for some vendors it is still the only way to connect to their products.

You can't access an ODBC driver through an OLE DB provider. There's no technical reason behind this limitation—it's just a matter of common sense. In fact, calling the MSDASQL OLE DB provider from within a .NET application would drive your client through a double data-access bridge—one going from .NET to the OLE DB provider, and one going one level down to the actual ODBC driver.

The Provider Factory Model

Unlike ADO and OLE DB, ADO.NET takes into careful account the particularity of each DBMS and provides a programming model tailor-made for each one. All .NET data providers share a limited set of common features, but each has unique capabilities. The communication between the user code and the DBMS takes place more directly using ADO.NET. This model works better and faster and is probably clearer to most programmers.

But until version 2.0 of the .NET Framework, ADO.NET has one key snag. Developers must know in advance the data source they're going to access. Generic programming—that is, programming in which the same code targets different data sources at different times—is hard (but not impossible) to do. You can create a generic command object and a generic data reader, but not a generic data adapter and certainly not a generic connection. However, through the *IDbConnection* interface, you can work with a connection object without knowing the underlying data source. But you can never create a connection object in a weakly typed manner—that is, without the help of the *new* operator.

Instantiating Providers Programmatically

ADO.NET 2.0 enhances the provider architecture and introduces the factory class. Each .NET data provider encompasses a factory class derived from the base class *DbProviderFactory*. A factory class represents a common entry point for a variety of services specific to the provider. Table 7-5 lists the main methods of a factory class.

Table 7-5   Principal Methods of a Factory Class

Method	Description
CreateCommand	Returns a provider-specific command object
CreateCommandBuilder	Returns a provider-specific command builder object
CreateConnection	Returns a provider-specific connection object
CreateDataAdapter	Returns a provider-specific data adapter object
CreateParameter	Returns a provider-specific parameter object

How do you get the factory of a particular provider? By using a new class, *DbProviderFactories*, that has a few static methods. The following code demonstrates how to obtain a factory object for the SQL Server provider:

```
DbProviderFactory fact;
fact = DbProviderFactories.GetFactory("System.Data.SqlClient");
```

The *GetFactory* method takes a string that represents the invariant name of the provider. This name is hard-coded for each provider in the configuration file where it is registered. By convention, the provider name equals its unique namespace.

GetFactory enumerates all the registered providers and gets assembly and class name information for the matching invariant name. The factory class is not instantiated directly. Instead, the method uses reflection to retrieve the value of the static *Instance* property of the factory class. The property returns the instance of the factory class to use. Once you hold a factory object, you can call any of the methods listed earlier in Table 7-5.

The following pseudocode gives an idea of the internal implementation of the *CreateConnection* method for the *SqlClientFactory* class—the factory class for the SQL Server .NET data provider:

```
public DbConnection CreateConnection()
{
    return new SqlConnection();
}
```

Enumerating Installed Data Providers

In the .NET Framework 2.0, you can use all .NET data providers registered in the configuration file. The following excerpt is from the *machine.config* file:

```
<system.data>
  <DbProviderFactories>
    <add name="SqlClient Data Provider"
         invariant="System.Data.SqlClient"
         description=".Net Framework Data Provider for SqlServer"
         type="System.Data.SqlClient.SqlClientFactory, System.Data "/>
    <add name="OracleClient Data Provider"
         invariant="System.Data.OracleClient"
         description=".Net Framework Data Provider for Oracle"
         type="System.Data.OracleClient.OracleFactory,
               System.Data.OracleClient" />
    ...
  </DbProviderFactories>
</system.data>
```

Each provider is characterized by an invariant name, a description, and a type that contains assembly and class information. The *GetFactoryClasses* method on the *DbProviderFactories* class returns this information packed in an easy-to-use *DataTable* object. The following sample page demonstrates how to get a quick list of the installed providers:

```
<%@ page language="C#" %>
<%@ import namespace="System.Data" %>
<%@ import namespace="System.Data.Common" %>

<script runat="server">
    void Page_Load (object sender, EventArgs e) {
        DataTable providers = DbProviderFactories.GetFactoryClasses();
        provList.DataSource = providers;
        provList.DataBind();
    }
</script>

<html>
<head runat="server"><title>List Factory Objects</title></head>
<body>
    <form runat="server">
        <asp:datagrid runat="server" id="provList" />
    </form>
</body>
</html>
```

The final page is shown in Figure 7-3.

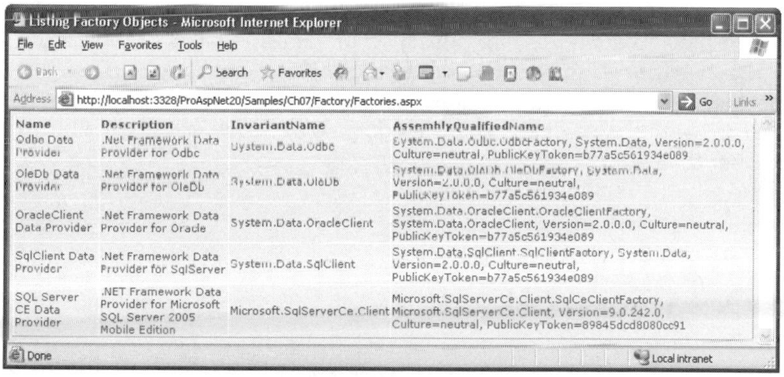

Figure 7-3   The list of the installed .NET data providers.

Database-Agnostic Pages

Let's write out some sample code to demonstrate how to craft database-agnostic pages. The sample page will contain three text boxes to collect the name of the provider, connection string, and command text:

```
protected void RunButton_Click(object sender, EventArgs e)
{
    string provider = ProviderNameBox.Text;
    string connString = ConnectionStringBox.Text;
    string commandText = CommandTextBox.Text;
```

```
    // Get the provider
    DbProviderFactory fact = DbProviderFactories.GetFactory(provider);

    // Create the connection
    DbConnection conn = fact.CreateConnection();
    conn.ConnectionString = connString;

    // Create the data adapter
    DbDataAdapter adapter = fact.CreateDataAdapter();
    adapter.SelectCommand = conn.CreateCommand();
    adapter.SelectCommand.CommandText = commandText;

    // Run the query
    DataTable table = new DataTable();
    adapter.Fill(table);

    // Shows the results
    Results.DataSource = table;
    Results.DataBind();
}
```

By changing the provider name and properly adapting the connection string and command, the same core code can now be used to work on other database servers.

> **Caution**   Nothing presented here is invented; no magic and no tricks apply. This said, though, don't be fooled by the apparent simplicity of this approach. Be aware that in real-world applications data access is normally insulated in the boundaries of the Data Access Layer (DAL) and that practice suggests you have one DAL per supported data source. This is because the complexity of real problems needs to be addressed by getting the most out of each data server. In the end, you need optimized data access code to exploit all the features of the DBMS rather than generic code that you write once and which queries everywhere and everything.

Connecting to Data Sources

The ADO.NET programming model is based on a relatively standard and database-independent sequence of steps. You first create a connection, then prepare and execute a command, and finally process the data retrieved. As far as basic operations and data types are involved, this model works for most providers. Some exceptions are binary large object (BLOB) fields management for Oracle databases and perhaps bulk copy and XML data management for SQL Server databases.

In the rest of the chapter, we'll mostly discuss how ADO.NET data classes work with SQL Server 7.0 and newer versions. However, we'll promptly point out any aspect that is significantly different from other .NET data providers. To start out, let's see how connections take place.

More Info   For in-depth coverage of ADO.NET 2.0, see *Programming Microsoft ADO.NET 2.0 Applications: Advanced Topics* by Glenn Johnson (Microsoft Press, 2005) and *Programming ADO.NET 2.0 Core Reference* by David Sceppa (Microsoft Press, 2005).

The *SqlConnection* Class

The first step in working with an ADO.NET-based application is setting up the connection with the data source. The class that represents a physical connection to SQL Server is *SqlConnection*, and it is located in the *System.Data.SqlClient* namespace. The class is sealed (that is, not inheritable) and cloneable, and it implements the *IDbConnection* interface. In ADO.NET 2.0, the interface is implemented through the intermediate base class *DbConnection*, which also provides additional features shared by all providers. (In fact, adding new members to the interface would have broken existing code.)

The *SqlConnection* class features two constructors, one of which is the default parameterless constructor. The second class constructor, on the other hand, takes a string containing the connection string:

```
public SqlConnection();
public SqlConnection(string);
```

The following code snippet shows the typical way to set up and open a SQL Server connection:

```
string connString = "SERVER=…;DATABASE=…;UID=...;PWD=...";
SqlConnection conn = new SqlConnection(connString);
conn.Open();
...
conn.Close();
```

Properties of the *SqlConnection* Class

Table 7-6 details the public properties defined on the *SqlConnection* class.

Table 7-6   Properties of the *SqlConnection* Class

Property	*IDbConnection* Interface	Description
ConnectionString	Yes	Gets or sets the string used to open the database.
ConnectionTimeout	Yes	Gets the number of seconds to wait while trying to establish a connection.
Database	Yes	Gets the name of the database to be used.
DataSource		Gets the name of the instance of SQL Server to connect to. It corresponds to the *Server* connection string attribute.

Table 7-6 Properties of the *SqlConnection* Class

Property	*IDbConnection* Interface	Description
PacketSize		Gets the size in bytes of network packets used to communicate with SQL Server. Set to 8192, it can be any value in the range from 512 through 32767.
ServerVersion		Gets a string containing the version of the current instance of SQL Server. The version string is in the form of *major.minor.release*.
State	Yes	Gets the current state of the connection: open or closed. Closed is the default.
StatisticsEnabled		Enables the retrieval of statistical information over the current connection. *Not available in ADO.NET 1.x.*
WorkStationId		Gets the network name of the client, which normally corresponds to the *WorkStation ID* connection string attribute.

An important characteristic to note about the properties of the connection classes is that they are all read-only except *ConnectionString*. In other words, you can configure the connection only through the tokens of the connection string, but you can read attributes back through handy properties. This characteristic of connection class properties in ADO.NET is significantly different than what you find in ADO, where many of the connection properties—for example, *ConnectionTimeout* and *Database*—were read/write.

Methods of the *SqlConnection* Class

Table 7-7 shows the methods available in the *SqlConnection* class.

Table 7-7 Methods of the *SqlConnection* Class

Method	*IDbConnection* Interface	Description
BeginTransaction	Yes	Begins a database transaction. Allows you to specify a name and an isolation level.
ChangeDatabase	Yes	Changes the current database on the connection. Requires a valid database name.
Close	Yes	Closes the connection to the database. Use this method to close an open connection.
CreateCommand	Yes	Creates and returns a *SqlCommand* object associated with the connection.

Table 7-7   Methods of the *SqlConnection* Class

Method	*IDbConnection* Interface	Description
Dispose		Calls *Close*.
EnlistDistributedTransaction		If auto-enlistment is disabled, enlists the connection in the specified distributed Enterprise Services DTC transaction. *Not supported in version 1.0 of the .NET Framework.*
EnlistTransaction	No, but defined on *DbConnection* in ADO.NET 2.0	Enlists the connection on the specified local or distributed transaction. *Not available in ADO.NET 1.x.*
GetSchema	No, but defined on *DbConnection* in ADO.NET 2.0	Retrieve schema information for the specified scope (that is, tables, databases). *Not available in ADO.NET 1.x.*
ResetStatistics		Resets the statistics service. *Not available in ADO.NET 1.x.*
RetrieveStatistics		Gets a hash table filled with the information about the connection, such as data transferred, user details, transactions. *Not available in ADO.NET 1.x.*
Open	Yes	Opens a database connection.

Note that if the connection goes out of scope, it is not automatically closed. Later on, but not especially soon, the garbage collector picks up the object instance, but the connection won't be closed because the garbage collector can't recognize the peculiarity of the object and handle it properly. Therefore, you must explicitly close the connection by calling *Close* or *Dispose* before the object goes out of scope.

> **Note**   Like many other disposable objects, connection classes implement the *IDisposable* interface, thus providing a programming interface for developers to dispose of the object. The dispose pattern entails the sole *Dispose* method; *Close* is not officially part of the pattern, but most classes implement it as well.

Changing Passwords

In ADO.NET 2.0, the *SqlConnection* class provides a static method named *ChangePassword* to let developers change the SQL Server password for the user indicated in the supplied connection string:

```
public static void ChangePassword(
    string connectionString, string newPassword)
```

An exception will be thrown if the connection string requires integrated security (that is, *Integrated Security=True* or an equivalent setting). The method opens a new connection to the server, requests the password change, and closes the connection once it has completed. The connection used to change the password is not taken out of the connection pool. The new password must comply with any password security policy set on the server, including minimum length and requirements for specific characters.

Note that *ChangePassword* works only on SQL Server 2005.

Accessing Schema Information

In ADO.NET 2.0, all managed providers are expected to implement a *GetSchema* method for retrieving schema information. The standard providers offer the following overloads of the method:

```
public override DataTable GetSchema();
public override DataTable GetSchema(string collection);
public override DataTable GetSchema(string collection, string[] filterVal)
```

The schema information you can retrieve is specific to the back-end system. For the full list of valid values, call *GetSchema* with no parameters. The following code shows how to retrieve all available collections and bind the results to a drop-down list:

```
// Get schema collections
SqlConnection conn = new SqlConnection(connString);
conn.Open();
DataTable table = conn.GetSchema();
conn.Close();

// Display their names
CollectionNames.DataSource = table;
CollectionNames.DataTextField = "collectionname";
CollectionNames.DataBind();
```

Figure 7-4 shows the available schema collections for a SQL Server 2000 machine. (For SQL Server 2005, it adds only a *UserDefinedTypes* collection.) Call *GetSchema* on, say, the *Databases* collection and you will get the list of all databases for the instance of SQL Server you are connected to. Likewise, if you call it on *Tables*, you will see the tables in the connected database.

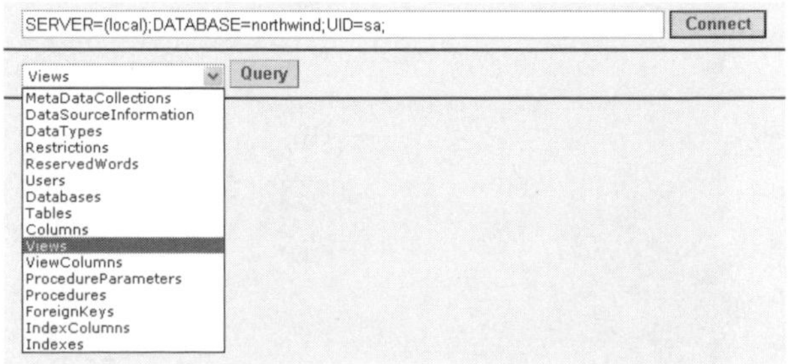

Figure 7-4   The list of available schema collections for SQL Server 2000.

> **Note** The preceding code snippet introduces the *DataTable* class as well as data binding. We will cover the *DataTable* class—one of the most important ADO.NET container classes—in the next chapter. Data binding, on the other hand, will be the subject of Chapter 9.

The list of schema collections is expressed as a *DataTable* object with three columns—*CollectionName* is the column with names. The following code shows how to retrieve schema information regarding the collection name currently selected in the drop-down list—the *Views*:

```
string coll = CollectionNames.SelectedValue;
string connString = ConnStringBox.Text;
SqlConnection conn = new SqlConnection(connString);
conn.Open();
DataTable table = conn.GetSchema(coll);
conn.Close();
GridView1.DataSource = table;
GridView1.DataBind();
```

As Figure 7-5 demonstrates, the data is then bound to a grid for display.

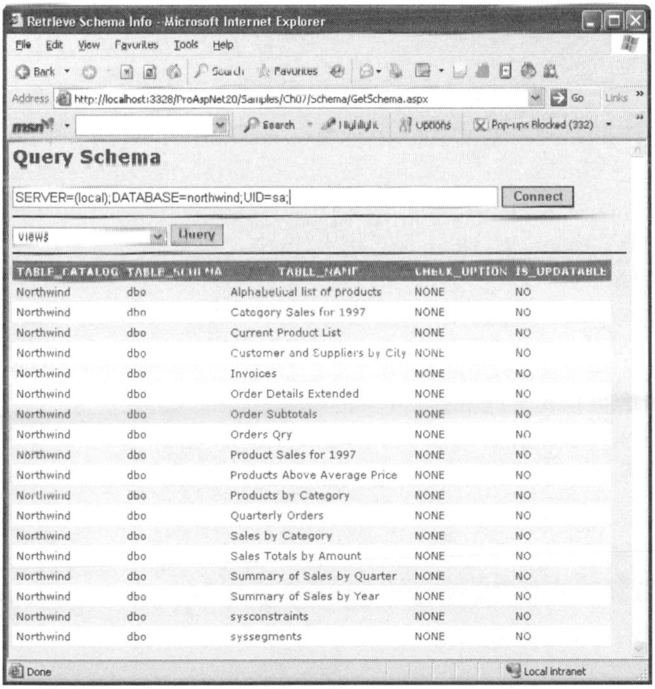

Figure 7-5 The list of views found in the Northwind database.

In ADO.NET 2.0, all connection objects support *GetSchema* methods, as they are part of the new intermediate *DbConnection* class. In ADO.NET 1.x, you have different approaches depending on the target source. If you work with OLE DB, you get schema information through the OLE DB native provider calling the *GetOleDbSchemaTable* method. The following code shows how to get table information:

```
OleDbConnection conn = new OleDbConnection(connString);
conn.Open();
DataTable schema = cConn.GetOleDbSchemaTable(
    OleDbSchemaGuid.Tables,
    new object[] {null, null, null, "TABLE"});
conn.Close();
```

GetOleDbSchemaTable takes an *OleDbSchemaGuid* argument that identifies the schema information to return. In addition, it takes an array of values to restrict the returned columns. *GetOleDbSchemaTable* returns a *DataTable* populated with the schema information. Alternately, you can get information on available databases, tables, views, constraints, and so on through any functionality provided by the specific data source, such as stored procedures and views.

```
SqlConnection conn = new SqlConnection(connString);
SqlDataAdapter adapter = new SqlDataAdapter(
    "SELECT * FROM INFORMATION_SCHEMA.TABLES " +
        "WHERE TABLE_TYPE = 'BASE TABLE' " +
        "ORDER BY TABLE_TYPE", conn);
DataTable schema = new DataTable();
adapter.Fill(schema);
```

In ADO.NET 2.0, the *GetSchema* method unifies the approach for retrieving schema information. The *SqlDataAdapter* class that appears in the preceding code snippet is a special type of command that we'll explore in depth in the next chapter. One of its key characteristics is that it returns disconnected data packed in a *DataTable* or *DataSet*.

Connection Strings

To connect to a data source, you need a connection string. Typically made of semicolon-separated pairs of names and values, a connection string specifies settings for the database runtime. Typical information contained in a connection string includes the name of the database, location of the server, and user credentials. Other, more operational information, such as connection timeout and connection pooling settings, can be specified, too.

In many enterprise applications, the usage of connection strings is related to a couple of issues: how to store and protect them, and how to build and manage them. The .NET Framework 2.0 provides excellent solutions to both issues, as we'll see in a moment.

Needless to say, connection strings are database-specific, although huge differences don't exist between, say, a connection string for SQL Server and Oracle databases. In this chapter, we mainly focus on SQL Server but point out significant differences.

Configuring Connection Properties

The *ConnectionString* property of the connection class can be set only when the connection is closed. Many connection string values have corresponding read-only properties in the connection class. These properties are updated when the connection string is set. The contents of the connection string are checked and parsed immediately after the *ConnectionString* property is set. Attribute names in a connection string are not case-sensitive, and if a given name appears multiple times, the value of the last occurrence is used. Table 7-8 lists the keywords that are supported.

Table 7-8   Connection String Keywords for SQL Server

Keyword	Description
Application Name	Name of the client application as it appears in the SQL Profiler. Defaults to *.Net SqlClient Data Provider*.
Async	When *true*, enables asynchronous operation support. *Not supported in ADO.NET 1.x.*
AttachDBFileName or *Initial File Name*	The full path name of the file (.mdf) to use as an attachable database file.
Connection Timeout	The number of seconds to wait for the connection to take place. Default is 15 seconds.
Current Language	The SQL Server language name.
Database or *Initial Catalog*	The name of the database to connect to.
Encrypt	Indicates whether Secure Sockets Layer (SSL) encryption should be used for all data sent between the client and server. Needs a certificate installed on the server. Default is *false*.
Failover Partner	The name of the partner server to access in case of errors. Connection failover allows an application to connect to an alternate, or backup, database server if the primary database server is unavailable. *Not supported in ADO.NET 1.x.*
Integrated Security or *Trusted_Connection*	Indicates whether current Windows account credentials are used for authentication. When set to *false*, explicit user ID and password need to be provided. The special value *sspi* equals *true*. Default is *false*.
MultipleActiveResultSets	When *true*, an application can maintain multiple active result sets. Set to *true* by default, this feature requires SQL Server 2005. *Not supported in ADO.NET 1.x.*
Network Library or *Net*	Indicates the network library used to establish a connection to SQL Server. Default is *dbmssocn*, which is based on TCP/IP.
Packet Size	Bytes that indicate the size of the packet being exchanged. Default is 8192.
Password or *pwd*	Password for the account logging on.

Table 7-8 Connection String Keywords for SQL Server

Keyword	Description
Persist Security Info	Indicates whether the managed provider should include password information in the string returned as the connection string. Default is *false*.
Server or *Data Source*	Name or network address of the instance of SQL Server to connect to.
User ID or *uid*	User name for the account logging on.
Workstation ID	Name of the machine connecting to SQL Server.

The network DLL specified by the *Network Library* keyword must be installed on the system to which you connect. If you use a local server, the default library is *dbmslpcn*, which uses shared memory. For a list of options, consult the MSDN documentation.

Any attempt to connect to an instance of SQL Server should not exceed a given time. The *Connection Timeout* keyword controls just this. Note that a connection timeout of 0 causes the connection attempt to wait indefinitely; it does not indicate no wait time.

You normally shouldn't change the default packet size, which has been determined based on average operations and workload. However, if you're going to perform bulk operations in which large objects are involved, increasing the packet size can be of help because it decreases the number of reads and writes.

Some of the attributes you see listed in Table 7-8 are specific to ADO.NET 2.0 and address features that have been introduced lately. They are asynchronous commands and multiple active result sets (MARS). MARS, in particular, removes a long-time constraint of the SQL Server programming model—that is, the constraint of having at most one pending request on a given session at a time. Before ADO.NET 2.0 and SQL Server 2005, several approaches have been tried to work around this limitation, the most common of which is using server-side cursors through ADO. We'll return to MARS later, in the section dedicated to SQL Server 2005.

Connection String Builders

How do you build the connection string to be used in an application? In many cases, you just consider it constant and read it out of a secured source. In other cases, though, you might need to construct it based on user input—for example, when retrieving user ID and password information from a dialog box. In ADO.NET 1.x, you can build the string only by blindly concatenating any name/value pairs. There are two major drawbacks with this technique. One is that the use of wrong keywords is caught only when the application undergoes testing. More serious than the lack of compile-time check, though, is that a blind-pair concatenation leaves room for undesired data injections to attach users to a different database or to change in some way the final goal of the connection. Any measures to fend off injections and check the syntax should be manually coded, resulting in a specialized builder class—just like the brand new connection string builder classes you find in ADO.NET 2.0.

All default data providers support connection string builders in a guise that perfectly applies to the underlying provider. The following code snippet (and its result, shown in Figure 7-6) builds and displays a connection string for SQL Server:

```
SqlConnectionStringBuilder builder = new SqlConnectionStringBuilder();
builder.DataSource = serverName;
builder.UserID = userid;
builder.Password = pswd;
NewConnString.Text = builder.ConnectionString;
```

Figure 7-6   Building connection strings programmatically and securely.

By using connection string builders, you gain a lot in terms of security because you dramatically reduce injection. Imagine that a malicious user types in the password **Foo;Trusted_Connection=true**. If you blindly concatenate strings, you might get the following:

```
Password=Foo;Trusted_Connection=true
```

Because the last pair wins, the connection will be opened based on the credentials of the logged-on user. If you use the builder class, you get the following appropriately quoted string:

```
Password="Foo;Trusted_Connection=true"
```

In addition, the builder class exposes the 20-plus supported keywords through easier-to-remember properties recognized by Microsoft IntelliSense.

Storing and Retrieving Connection Strings

Savvy developers avoid hard-coding connection strings in the compiled code. Configuration files (such as the *web.config* file) purposely support the *<appSettings>* named section, which is used to store custom data through name/value pairs. All these values populate the *AppSettings* collection and can be easily retrieved programmatically, as shown here:

```
string connString = ConfigurationSettings.AppSettings["NorthwindConn"];
```

This approach is far from perfect for two reasons. First, connection strings are not just data—they're a special kind of data not to be mixed up with general-purpose application settings. Second, connection strings are a critical parameter for the application and typically contain sensitive data. Therefore, at a minimum they need transparent encryption. Let's tackle storage first.

In the .NET Framework 2.0, configuration files define a new section specifically designed to contain connection strings. The section is named *<connectionStrings>* and is laid out as follows:

```
<connectionStrings>
    <add name="NWind"
        connectionString="SERVER=...;DATABASE=...;UID=...;PWD=...;"
        providerName="System.Data.SqlClient"  />
</connectionStrings>
```

You can manipulate the contents of the section by using *<add>*, *<remove>*, and *<clear>* nodes. You use an *<add>* node to add a new connection string to the current list, *<remove>* to remove a previously defined connection, and *<clear>* to reset all connections and create a new collection. By placing a *web.config* file in each of the application's directories, you can customize the collection of connection strings that are visible to the pages in the directory. Configuration files located in child directories can remove, clear, and extend the list of connection strings defined at the upper level. Note that each stored connection is identified with a name. This name references the actual connection parameters throughout the application. Connection names are also used within the configuration file to link a connection string to other sections, such as the *<providers>* section of *<membership>* and *<profile>* nodes.

All the connection strings defined in the *web.config* file are loaded into the new *ConfigurationManager.ConnectionStrings* collection. To physically open a connection based on a string stored in the *web.config* file, use following code:

```
string connStr;
connStr = ConfigurationManager.ConnectionStrings["NWind"].ConnectionString;
SqlConnection conn = new SqlConnection(connStr);
```

The full support from the configuration API opens up an interesting possibility for consuming connection strings—declarative binding. As we'll see in Chapter 9, ASP.NET 2.0 supports quite a few data source objects. A data source object is a server control that manages all aspects of data source interaction, including connection setup and command execution. You bind data source objects to data-bound controls and instruct the data source to retrieve data from a specific source. The great news is that you can now indicate the connection string declaratively, as follows:

```
<asp:SqlDataSource id="MySource" runat="server"
  ProviderName="System.Data.SqlClient"
  ConnectionString='<%#
    ConfigurationSettings.ConnectionStrings["NWind"].ConnectionString %>'
  SelectCommand="SELECT * FROM employees">
```

There's a lot more to be known about this feature, though, and we'll delve deeply into that later in the book. For now, it suffices to say that connection strings are much more than strings in the .NET Framework 2.0.

Protecting Connection Strings

ASP.NET 2.0 introduces a system for protecting sensitive data stored in the configuration system. It uses industry-standard XML encryption to encrypt specific sections of configuration files that might contain sensitive data. XML encryption (which you can learn more about at *http://www.w3.org/TR/xmlenc-core*) is a way to encrypt data and represent the result in XML. Prior to version 2.0, only a few specific ASP.NET sections that contain sensitive data support protection of this data using a machine-specific encryption in a registry key. This approach requires developers to come up with a utility to protect their own secrets—typically connection strings, credentials, and encryption keys.

In the .NET Framework 2.0, encryption of configuration sections is optional, and you can enable it for any configuration sections you want by referencing the name of the section in the *<protectedData>* section of the *web.config* file, as shown here:

```
<protectedData>
    <protectedDataSections>
        <add name="connectionStrings"
            provider="RSAProtectedConfigurationProvider" />
    </protectedDataSections>
</protectedData>
```

You can specify the type of encryption you want by selecting the appropriate provider from the list of available encryption providers. The .NET Framework 2.0 comes with two predefined providers:

- **DPAPIProtectedConfigurationProvider.**   Uses the Windows Data Protection API (DPAPI) to encrypt and decrypt data

- **RSAProtectedConfigurationProvider.**   Default provider; uses the RSA encryption algorithm to encrypt and decrypt data

Being able to protect data stored in the *web.config* file is not a feature specific to connection strings. It applies, instead, to all sections, with very few exceptions. This said, let's see how to encrypt connection strings stored in the *web.config* file.

You can use the newest version of a popular system tool—*aspnet_regiis.exe*—or write your own tool by using the ASP.NET 2.0 configuration API. If you use *aspnet_regiis*, examine the following code, which is a sample used to encrypt connection strings for the ProAspNet20 application:

```
aspnet_regiis.exe -pe connectionStrings -app /ProAspNet20
```

Note that the section names are case-sensitive. Note also that connection strings are stored in a protected area that is completely transparent to applications, which continue working as before. If you open the *web.config* file after encryption, you see something like the following:

```
<configuration>
  <protectedData>
    <protectedDataSections>
      <add name="connectionStrings"
           provider="RSAProtectedConfigurationProvider" />
    </protectedDataSections>
  </protectedData>
  <connectionStrings>
    <EncryptedData …>

      ...

      <CipherData>
        <CipherValue>cQyofWFQ… =</CipherValue>
      </CipherData>
    </EncryptedData>
  </connectionStrings>
</configuration>
```

To restore the *web.config* file to its original clear state, you use the –*pd* switch in lieu of the –*pe* in the aforementioned command line.

> **Caution**   Any page that uses protected sections works like a champ as long as you run it inside the local Web server embedded in Visual Studio .NET 2005. You might get an RSA provider configuration error if you access the same page from within a canonical (and much more realistic) IIS virtual folder. What's up with that?
>
> The RSA-based provider—the default protection provider—needs a key container to work. A default key container is created upon installation and is named *NetFrameWorkConfiguration-Key*. The *aspnet_regiis.exe* utility provides a lot of command-line switches for you to add, remove, and edit key containers. The essential point is that you have a key container created before you dump the RSA-protected configuration provider. The container must not only exist, it also needs to be associated with the user account attempting to call it. The system account (running the local Web server) is listed with the container; the ASP.NET account on your Web server might not be. Assuming you run ASP.NET under the NETWORK SERVICE account (the default on Windows Server 2003 machines), you need the following code to add access to the container for the user:
>
> ```
> aspnet_regiis.exe –pa "NetFrameworkConfigurationKey"
>                      "NT AUTHORITY\NETWORK SERVICE"
> ```
>
> It is important that you specify a complete account name, as in the preceding code. Note that granting access to the key container is necessary only if you use the RSA provider.

Both the RSA and DPAPI providers are great options for encrypting sensitive data. The DPAPI provider dramatically simplifies the process of key management—keys are generated based on machine credentials and can be accessed by all processes running on the machine. For the same reason, the DPAPI provider is not ideal to protect sections in a Web farm scenario where the same encrypted *web.config* file will be deployed to several servers. In this case, either you manually encrypt all *web.config* files on each machine or you copy the same container key to all servers. To accomplish this, you create a key container for the application, export it to an XML file, and import it on each server that will need to decrypt the encrypted *web.config* file. To create a key container, you do as follows:

```
aspnet_regiis.exe -pc YourContainerName -exp
```

Next, you export the key container to an XML file:

```
aspnet_regiis.exe -px YourContainerName YourXmlFile.xml
```

Next, you move the XML file to each server and import it as follows:

```
aspnet_regiis.exe -pi YourContainerName YourXmlFile.xml
```

As a final step, grant the ASP.NET account permission to access the container.

> **Note**   We won't cover the .NET Framework configuration API in this book. You can find deep coverage of the structure of configuration files and related APIs in my other recent book, *Programming Microsoft ASP.NET 2.0 Applications: Advanced Topics* (Microsoft Press, 2005).

Connection Pooling

Connection pooling is a fundamental aspect of high-performance, scalable applications. For local or intranet desktop applications that are not multithreaded, connection pooling is no big deal—you'll get nearly the same performance with and without pooling. Furthermore, using a nonpooled connection gives you more control over the lifetime. For multithreaded applications, the use of connection pooling is a necessity for performance reasons and to avoid nasty, hardware-dependent bugs. Finally, if ASP.NET applications are involved, every millisecond that the connection is idle steals valuable resources from other requests. Not only should you rely on connection pooling, but you should also open the connection as late as possible and close it as soon as you can.

Using connection pooling makes it far less expensive for the application to open and close the connection to the database, even if that is done frequently. (We'll cover this topic in more detail later.) All standard .NET data providers have pooling support turned on by default. The .NET data providers for SQL Server and Oracle manage connection pooling internally using ad hoc classes. For the OLE DB data provider, connection pooling is implemented through the OLE DB service infrastructure for session pooling. Connection-string arguments (for example, *OLE DB Service*) can be used to enable or disable various OLE DB services, including pooling. A similar situation occurs with ODBC, in which pooling is controlled by the ODBC driver manager.

Configuring Pooling

Some settings in the connection string directly affect the pooling mechanism. The parameters you can control to configure the SQL Server environment are listed in Table 7-9.

Table 7-9   SQL Server Connection Pooling Keywords

Keyword	Description
Connection Lifetime	Sets the maximum duration in seconds of the connection object in the pool. This keyword is checked only when the connection is returned to the pool. If the time the connection has been open is greater than the specified lifetime, the connection object is destroyed. (We'll cover this topic in more detail later.)
Connection Reset	Determines whether the database connection is reset when being drawn from the pool. Default is *true*.
Enlist	Indicates that the pooler automatically enlists the connection in the creation thread's current transaction context. Default is *true*.
Max Pool Size	Maximum number of connections allowed in the pool. Default is 100.
Min Pool Size	Minimum number of connections allowed in the pool. Default is 0.
Pooling	Indicates that the connection object is drawn from the appropriate pool or, if necessary, is created and added to the appropriate pool. Default is *true*.

With the exception of *Connection Reset*, all the keywords listed in Table 7-9 are acceptable to the Oracle managed provider, too.

As far as SQL Server and Oracle providers are concerned, connection pooling is automatically enabled; to disable it, you need to set *Pooling* to *false* in the connection string. To control pooling for an ODBC data source, you use the ODBC Data Source Administrator in the Control Panel. The Connection Pooling tab allows you to specify connection pooling parameters for each ODBC driver installed. Note that any changes to a specific driver affect all applications that make use of it. The .NET data provider for OLE DB automatically pools connections using OLE DB session pooling. You can disable pooling by setting the *OLE DB Services* keyword to −4.

In ADO.NET 2.0, auto enlistment (the *Enlist* keyword) works in the connection strings of all standard data providers, including providers for OLE DB and ODBC. In ADO.NET 1.x, only managed providers for SQL Server and Oracle support auto-enlistment because they are made of native managed code instead of being wrappers around existing code. The new *EnlistTransaction* method on connection classes allows you to enlist a connection object programmatically, be it pooled or not.

Getting and Releasing Objects

Each connection pool is associated with a distinct connection string and the transaction context. When a new connection is opened, if the connection string does not exactly match an existing pool, a new pool is created. Once created, connection pools are not destroyed until the process ends. This behavior does not affect the system performance because maintenance of inactive or empty pools requires only minimal overhead.

When a pool is created, multiple connection objects are created and added so that the minimum size is reached. Next, connections are added to the pool on demand, up to the maximum pool size. Adding a brand-new connection object to the pool is the really expensive operation here, as it requires a roundtrip to the database. Next, when a connection object is requested, it is drawn from the pool as long as a usable connection is available. A usable connection must currently be unused, have a matching or null transaction context, and have a valid link to the server. If no usable connection is available, the pooler attempts to create a new connection object. When the maximum pool size is reached, the request is queued and served as soon as an existing connection object is released to the pool.

Connections are released when you call methods such as *Close* or *Dispose*. Connections that are not explicitly closed might not be returned to the pool unless the maximum pool size has been reached and the connection is still valid.

A connection object is removed from the pool if the lifetime has expired (which will be explained further in a moment) or if a severe error has occurred. In these cases, the connection is marked as invalid. The pooler periodically scavenges the various pools and permanently removes invalid connection objects.

> **Important**   Unlike in ADO, connection pools in ADO.NET are created based on the connection string applying an exact match algorithm. In other words, to avoid the creation of an additional connection pool you must ensure that two connection strings carrying the same set of parameters are expressed by two byte-per-byte identical strings. A different order of keywords, or blanks interspersed in the text, is not ignored and ends up creating additional pools and therefore additional overhead.

To make connection pooling work effectively, it is extremely important that connection objects are returned to the pool as soon as possible. It is even more important, though, that connections are returned. Note that a connection object that goes out of scope is not closed and, therefore, not immediately returned. For this reason, it is highly recommended that you work with connection objects according to the following pattern:

```
SqlConnection conn = new SqlConnection(connString);
try {
    conn.Open();
    // Do something here
}
catch {
    // Trap errors here
}
finally {
    conn.Close();
}
```

Alternately, you can resort to the C# *using* statement, as follows:

```
using (SqlConnection conn = new SqlConnection(connString))
{
    // Do something here
    // Trap errors here
}
```

The *using* statement is equivalent to the preceding *try/catch/finally* block in which *Close* or *Dispose* is invoked in the *finally* block. You can call either *Close* or *Dispose* or even both—they do the same thing. *Dispose* cleans the connection string information and then calls *Close*. In addition, note that calling each multiple times doesn't result in run-time troubles, as closing or disposing an already closed or disposed connection is actually a no-operation.

> **Note** Before the .NET Framework 2.0, there was no sort of *using* statement in Visual Basic .NET. Starting with Visual Studio .NET 2005, you can rely on a shortcut keyword for *try/catch/finally* blocks also in Visual Basic .NET. The keyword is *Using ... End Using*:
>
> ```
> Using conn As New SqlConnection()
>     ...
> End Using
> ```

Detecting Connections Leaks

In ADO.NET 2.0, you can more easily figure out whether you're leaking connections, thanks to some new performance counters. In particular, you can monitor the *Number-OfReclaimedConnections* counter; if you see it going up, you have the evidence that your application is making poor use of connection objects. A good symptom of connection leaking is when you get an invalid operation exception that claims the timeout period elapsed prior to obtaining a connection from the pool. You can make this exception disappear or, more exactly, become less frequent by tweaking some parameters in the connection string. Needless to say, this solution doesn't remove the leak; it simply changes run-time conditions to make it happen less frequently. Here's a quick list of things you should not do that relate to connection management:

- **Do not turn connection pooling off.** With pooling disabled, a new connection object is created every time. No timeout can ever occur, but you lose a lot in performance and, more important, you are still leaking connections.

- **Do not shrink the connection lifetime.** Reducing the lifetime of the connection will force the pooler to renew connection objects more frequently. A short lifetime (a few seconds) will make the timeout exception extremely unlikely, but it adds significant overhead and doesn't solve the real problem. Let's say that it is only a little better than turning pooling off.

- **Do not increase the connection timeout.**   You tell the pooler to wait a longer time before throwing the timeout exception. Whatever value you set here, ASP.NET aborts the thread after three minutes. In general, this option worsens performance without alleviating the problem.

- **Do not increase the pool size.**   If you set the maximum pool size high enough (how high depends on the context), you stop getting timeout exceptions while keeping pooling enabled. The drawback is that you greatly reduce your application's scalability because you force your application to use a much larger number of connections than is actually needed.

To avoid leaking connections, you need to guarantee *only* that the connection is closed or disposed of when you're done, and preferably soon after.

In the previous section, I emphasized the importance of writing code that guarantees the connection is always closed. However, there might be nasty cases in which your code places a call to *Close*, but it doesn't get called. Let's see why. Consider the following code:

```
SqlConnection conn = new SqlConnection(connString);
conn.Open();
SqlCommand cmd = new SqlCommand(cmdText, conn);
cmd.ExecuteNonQuery();
conn.Close();
```

What if the command throws an exception? The *Close* method is not called, and the connection is not returned to the pool. Wrapping the code in a *using* statement would do the trick because it ensures that *Dispose* is always invoked on the object being used. Here's the correct version of the code:

```
using (SqlConnection conn = new SqlConnection(connString))
{
    conn.Open();
    SqlCommand cmd = new SqlCommand(cmdText, conn);
    cmd.ExecuteNonQuery();
    conn.Close();  // Not called in case of exception
} // Dispose always called
```

That's the only way to avoid connection leaking.

Managing Connection Lifetime

The *Connection Lifetime* keyword indicates in seconds the time a connection object is considered valid. When the time has elapsed, the connection object should be disposed of. But why on earth should you get rid of a perfectly good connection object? This keyword is useful only in a well-known situation, and it should never be used otherwise. Imagine that you have a cluster of servers sharing the workload. At some point, you realize the load is too high and you turn on an additional server. With good reason, you expect the workload to be distributed among all servers. However, this might not happen—the newly added server is idle.

A plausible and common reason for this is that middle-tier components cache the connections and never open new ones. By disposing of working connections, you force the middle-tier applications to create new connections. Needless to say, new connections will be assigned to the least loaded server. In the end, you should set *Connection Lifetime* only if you're in a cluster scenario. Finally, note that in ADO.NET 2.0 the connection builder classes use a different (and more intuitive) name to address the keyword—*LoadBalanceTimeout*.

> **Note**   The *LoadBalanceTimeout* is not a newly supported attribute for a connection string. If you use the *SqlConnectionStringBuilder* class to programmatically build the connection string, you'll find a *LoadBalanceTimeout* property to set the *Connection Lifetime* attribute.

Clearing the Connection Pool

Until ADO.NET 2.0, there was no way to programmatically clear the pool of open connections. Admittedly, this is not an operation you need to perform often, but it becomes essential in case the database server goes down for whatever reason. Consider the following scenario: your ASP.NET pages open and then successfully close some connections out of the same pool. Next, the server suddenly goes down and is restarted. As a result, all connection objects in the pool are now invalid because each of them holds a reference to a server connection that no longer exists. What happens when a new page request is issued?

The answer is that the pooler returns an apparently valid connection object to the page, and the page runs the command. Unfortunately, the connection object is not recognized by the database server, resulting in an exception. The connection object is removed from the pool and replaced. The exception will be raised for each command as long as there are connection objects in the pool. In summary, shutting down the server without shutting down the application brings the connection pool into an inconsistent, corrupted state.

This situation is common for applications that deal with server reboots, like a failover cluster. Only one solution is possible—flushing the connection pool. It is not as easy to implement as it might seem at first, though. An easier workaround is catching the exception and changing the connection string slightly to force the use of a new connection pool.

In ADO.NET 2.0, the solution to this issue comes with the framework. ADO.NET 2.0 is smart enough to recognize when an exception means that the pool is corrupted. When an exception is thrown during the execution of a command, ADO.NET 2.0 determines if the exception means that the pool is corrupted. In this case, it walks down the pool and marks each connection as obsolete. When does an exception indicate pool corruption? It has to be a fatal exception raised from the network layer on a previously opened connection. All other exceptions are ignored and bubble up as usual.

Two new static methods—*ClearPool* and *ClearAllPools,* defined for both *SqlConnection* and *OracleConnection*—can be used to programmatically clear the pool, if you know that the server has been stopped and restarted. These methods are used internally by ADO.NET 2.0 to clear the pool as described earlier.

Executing Commands

Once you have a physical channel set up between your client and the database, you can start preparing and executing commands. The ADO.NET object model provides two types of command objects—the traditional one-off command and the data adapter. The one-off command executes a SQL command or a stored procedure and returns a sort of cursor. Using that, you then scroll through the rows and read data. While the cursor is in use, the connection is busy and open. The data adapter, on the other hand, is a more powerful object that internally uses a command and a cursor. It retrieves and loads the data into a data container class—*DataSet* or *DataTable*. The client application can then process the data while disconnected from the source.

We'll cover container classes and data adapters in the next chapter. Let's focus on one-off commands, paying particular attention to SQL Server commands.

The *SqlCommand* Class

The *SqlCommand* class represents a SQL Server statement or stored procedure. It is a cloneable and sealed class that implements the *IDbCommand* interface. In ADO.NET 2.0, it derives from *DbCommand* which, in turn, implements the interface. A command executes in the context of a connection and, optionally, a transaction. This situation is reflected by the constructors available in the *SqlCommand* class:

```
public SqlCommand();
public SqlCommand(string);
public SqlCommand(string, SqlConnection);
public SqlCommand(string, SqlConnection, SqlTransaction);
```

The string argument denotes the text of the command to execute (and it can be a stored procedure name), whereas the *SqlConnection* parameter is the connection object to use. Finally, if specified, the *SqlTransaction* parameter represents the transactional context in which the command has to run. ADO.NET command objects never implicitly open a connection. The connection must be explicitly assigned to the command by the programmer and opened and closed with direct operations. The same holds true for the transaction.

Properties of the *SqlCommand* Class

Table 7-10 shows the attributes that make up a command in the .NET data provider for SQL Server.

Table 7-10   Properties of the *SqlCommand* Class

Property	*IDbCommand* Interface	Description
CommandText	Yes	Gets or sets the statement or the stored procedure name to execute.
CommandTimeout	Yes	Gets or sets the seconds to wait while trying to execute the command. The default is 30.
CommandType	Yes	Gets or sets how the *CommandText* property is to be interpreted. Set to *Text* by default, which means the *CommandText* property contains the text of the command.
Connection	Yes	Gets or sets the connection object used by the command. It is null by default.
Notification		Gets or sets the *SqlNotificationRequest* object bound to the command. *This property requires SQL Server 2005.*
NotificationAutoEnlist		Indicates whether the command will automatically enlist the SQL Server 2005 notification service. *This property requires SQL Server 2005.*
Parameters	Yes	Gets the collection of parameters associated with the command.
Transaction	Yes	Gets or sets the transaction within which the command executes. The transaction must be connected to the same connection as the command.
UpdatedRowSource	Yes	Gets or sets how query command results are applied to the row being updated. The value of this property is used only when the command runs within the *Update* method of the data adapter. Acceptable values are in the *UpdateRowSource* enumeration.

Commands can be associated with parameters, and each parameter is rendered using a provider-specific object. For the SQL Server managed provider, the parameter class is *SqlParameter*. The command type determines the role of the *CommandText* property. The possible values for *CommandType* are:

- **Text.** The default setting, which indicates the property contains Transact-SQL text to execute directly.

- **StoredProcedure.** Indicates that the content of the property is intended to be the name of a stored procedure contained in the current database.

- **TableDirect.** Indicates the property contains a comma-separated list containing the names of the tables to access. All rows and columns of the tables will be returned. It is supported only by the data provider for OLE DB.

To execute a stored procedure, you need the following:

```
using (SqlConnection conn = new SqlConnection(ConnString))
{
    SqlCommand cmd = new SqlCommand(sprocName, conn);
    cmd.CommandType = CommandType.StoredProcedure;
    cmd.Connection.Open();
    cmd.ExecuteNonQuery();
}
```

In ADO.NET 2.0, commands have two main new features—asynchronous executors and support for notification services. We'll cover both later.

Methods of the *SqlCommand* Class

Table 7-11 details the methods available for the *CommandText* class.

Table 7-11   Methods of the *CommandText* Class

Property	IDbCommand Interface	Description
BeginExecuteNonQuery		Executes a nonquery command in a nonblocking manner. *Not supported in ADO.NET 1.x.*
BeginExecuteReader		Executes a query command in a nonblocking manner. *Not supported in ADO.NET 1.x.*
BeginExecuteXmlReader		Executes an XML query command in a nonblocking manner. *Not supported in ADO.NET 1.x.*
Cancel	Yes	Attempts to cancel the execution of the command. No exception is generated if the attempt fails.
CreateParameter	Yes	Creates a new instance of a *SqlParameter* object.
EndExecuteNonQuery		Completes a nonquery command executed asynchronously. *Not supported in ADO.NET 1.x.*
EndExecuteReader		Completes a query command executed asynchronously. *Not supported in ADO.NET 1.x.*
EndExecuteXmlReader		Completes an XML query command executed asynchronously. *Not supported in ADO.NET 1.x.*
ExecuteNonQuery	Yes	Executes a nonquery command, and returns the number of rows affected.
ExecuteReader	Yes	Executes a query, and returns a read-only cursor—the data reader—to the data.
ExecuteScalar	Yes	Executes a query, and returns the value in the 0,0 position (first column of first row) in the result set. Extra data is ignored.
ExecuteXmlReader		Executes a query that returns XML data and builds an *XmlReader* object.
Prepare	Yes	Creates a prepared version of the command in an instance of SQL Server.
ResetCommandTimeout		Resets the command timeout to the default.

Parameterized commands define their own arguments using instances of the *SqlParameter* class. Parameters have a name, value, type, direction, and size. In some cases, parameters can also be associated with a source column. A parameter is associated with a command by using the *Parameters* collection:

```
SqlParameter parm = new SqlParameter();
parm.ParameterName = "@employeeid";
parm.DbType = DbType.Int32;
parm.Direction = ParameterDirection.Input;
cmd.Parameters.Add(parm);
```

The following SQL statement uses a parameter:

```
SELECT * FROM employees WHERE employeeid=@employeeid
```

The .NET data provider for SQL Server identifies parameters by name, using the @ symbol to prefix them. In this way, the order in which parameters are associated with the command is not critical.

> **Note**   Named parameters are supported by the managed provider for Oracle but not by the providers for OLE DB and ODBC data sources. The OLE DB and ODBC data sources use positional parameters identified with the question mark (?) placeholder. The order of parameters is important.

Ways to Execute

As Table 7-11 shows, a *SqlCommand* object can be executed either synchronously or asynchronously. Let's focus on synchronous execution, which is supported on all .NET platforms. Execution can happen in four different ways: *ExecuteNonQuery*, *ExecuteReader*, *ExecuteScalar*, and *ExecuteXmlReader*. The various executors work in much the same way, but they differ in the return values. Typically, you use the *ExecuteNonQuery* method to perform update operations such as those associated with UPDATE, INSERT, and DELETE statements. In these cases, the return value is the number of rows affected by the command. For other types of statements, such as SET or CREATE, the return value is −1.

The *ExecuteReader* method is expected to work with query commands, and returns a data reader object—an instance of the *SqlDataReader* class. The data reader is a sort of read-only, forward-only cursor that client code scrolls and reads from. If you execute an update statement through *ExecuteReader*, the command is successfully executed but no affected rows are returned. We'll return to data readers in a moment.

The *ExecuteScalar* method helps considerably when you have to retrieve a single value. It works great with SELECT COUNT statements or for commands that retrieve aggregate values. If you call the method on a regular query statement, only the value in the first column of the first row is read and all the rest is discarded. Using *ExecuteScalar* results in more compact code than you'd get by executing the command and manually retrieving the value in the top-left corner of the rowset.

These three executor methods are common to all command objects. The *SqlCommand* class also features the *ExecuteXmlReader* method. It executes a command that returns XML data and builds an XML reader so that the client application can easily navigate through the XML tree. The *ExecuteXmlReader* method is ideal to use with query commands that end with the FOR XML clause or with commands that query for text fields filled with XML data. Note that while the *XmlReader* object is in use, the underlying connection is busy.

ADO.NET Data Readers

The data reader class is specific to a DBMS and works like a firehose-style cursor. It allows you to scroll through and read one or more result sets generated by a command. The data reader operates in a connected way and moves in a forward-only direction. A data reader is instantiated during the execution of the *ExecuteReader* method. The results are stored in a buffer located on the client and are made available to the reader.

By using the data reader object, you access data one record at a time as soon as it becomes available. An approach based on the data reader is effective both in terms of system overhead and performance. Only one record is cached at any time, and there's no wait time to have the entire result set loaded in memory.

Table 7-12 shows the properties of the *SqlDataReader* class—that is, the data reader class for SQL Server.

Table 7-12   Properties of the *SqlDataReader* Class

Property	Description
Depth	Indicates the depth of nesting for the current row. For the *SqlDataReader* class, it always returns 0.
FieldCount	Gets the number of columns in the current row.
HasRows	Gets a value that indicates whether the data reader contains one or more rows. *Not supported in ADO.NET 1.0.*
IsClosed	Gets a value that indicates whether the data reader is closed.
Item	Indexer property, gets the value of a column in the original format.
RecordsAffected	Gets the number of rows modified by the execution of a batch command.

The *Depth* property is meant to indicate the level of nesting for the current row. The depth of the outermost table is always 0; the depth of inner tables grows by one. Most data readers, including the *SqlDataReader* and *OracleDataReader* classes, do not support multiple levels of nesting so that the *Depth* property always returns 0.

The *RecordsAffected* property is not set until all rows are read and the data reader is closed. The default value of *RecordsAffected* is −1. Note that *IsClosed* and *RecordsAffected* are the only properties you can invoke on a closed data reader.

Table 7-13 lists the methods of the SQL Server data reader class.

Table 7-13   Methods of the *SqlDataReader* Class

Methods	Description
Close	Closes the reader object. Note that closing the reader does not automatically close the underlying connection.
GetBoolean	Gets the value of the specified column as a Boolean.
GetByte	Gets the value of the specified column as a byte.
GetBytes	Reads a stream of bytes from the specified column into a buffer. You can specify an offset both for reading and writing.
GetChar	Gets the value of the specified column as a single character.
GetChars	Reads a stream of characters from the specified column into a buffer. You can specify an offset both for reading and writing.
GetDataTypeName	Gets the name of the back-end data type in the specified column.
GetDateTime	Gets the value of the specified column as a *DateTime* object.
GetDecimal	Gets the value of the specified column as a decimal.
GetDouble	Gets the value of the specified column as a double-precision floating-point number.
GetFieldType	Gets the *Type* object for the data in the specified column.
GetFloat	Gets the value of the specified column as a single-precision floating-point number.
GetGuid	Gets the value of the specified column as a globally unique identifier (GUID).
GetInt16	Gets the value of the specified column as a 16-bit integer.
GetInt32	Gets the value of the specified column as a 32-bit integer.
GetInt64	Gets the value of the specified column as a 64-bit integer.
GetName	Gets the name of the specified column.
GetOrdinal	Given the name of the column, returns its ordinal number.
GetSchemaTable	Returns a *DataTable* object that describes the metadata for the columns managed by the reader.
GetString	Gets the value of the specified column as a string.
GetValue	Gets the value of the specified column in its original format.
GetValues	Copies the values of all columns in the supplied array of objects.
IsDbNull	Indicates whether the column contains null values. The type for a null column is *System.DBNull*.
NextResult	Moves the data reader pointer to the beginning of the next result set, if any.
Read	Moves the data reader pointer to the next record, if any.

The SQL Server data reader also features a variety of other DBMS-specific get methods. They include methods such as *GetSqlDouble*, *GetSqlMoney*, *GetSqlDecimal*, and so on. The difference between the *GetXXX* and *GetSqlXXX* methods is in the return type. With the *GetXXX* methods, a base .NET Framework type is returned; with the *GetSqlXXX* methods, a .NET Framework wrapper for a SQL Server type is returned—such as *SqlDouble*, *SqlMoney*, or *SqlDecimal*. The SQL Server types belong to the *SqlDbType* enumeration.

All the *GetXXX* methods that return a value from a column identify the column through a 0-based index. Note that the methods don't even attempt a conversion; they simply return data as is and just make a cast to the specified type. If the actual value and the type are not compatible, an exception is thrown.

> **Note**   The *GetBytes* method is useful to read large fields one step at a time. However, the method can also be used to obtain the length in bytes of the data in the column. To get this information, pass a buffer that is a null reference and the return value of the method will contain the length.

Reading Data with the Data Reader

The key thing to remember when using a data reader is that you're working while connected. The data reader represents the fastest way to read data out of a source, but you should read your data as soon as possible and then release the connection. One row is available at a time, and you must move through the result set by using the *Read* method. The following code snippet illustrates the typical loop you implement to read all the records of a query:

```
using (SqlConnection conn = new SqlConnection(connstring))
{
    string cmdText = "SELECT * FROM customers";
    SqlCommand cmd = new SqlCommand(cmdText, conn);
    cmd.Connection.Open();
    SqlDataReader reader = cmd.ExecuteReader();
    while (reader.Read())
        CustomerList.Items.Add(reader["companyname"].ToString());
    reader.Close();
}
```

You have no need to explicitly move the pointer ahead and no need to check for the end of the file. The *Read* method returns *false* if there are no more records to read. A data reader is great if you need to consume data by processing the records in some way. If you need to cache values for later use, the data reader is not appropriate. You need a container object in this case, as we'll see in Chapter 8.

> **Note**   Although accessing row fields by name is easy to read and understand, it is not the fastest approach. Internally, in fact, the data reader needs to resolve the name to a 0-based index. If you provide the index directly, you get slightly faster code:
>
> ```
> const int Customers_CustomerID = 0;
> ...
> Response.Write(reader[Customers_CustomerID].ToString());
> ```
>
> The preceding code shows that using constants turns out to be a good compromise between speed and readability.

Command Behaviors

When calling the *ExecuteReader* method on a command object—on any command object, regardless of the underlying DBMS—you can require a particular working mode known as a command behavior. *ExecuteReader* has a second overload that takes an argument of type *CommandBehavior*:

```
cmd.ExecuteReader(CommandBehavior.CloseConnection);
```

CommandBehavior is an enumeration. Its values are listed in Table 7-14.

Table 7-14   Command Behaviors for the Data Reader

Behavior	Description
CloseConnection	Automatically closes the connection when the data reader is closed.
Default	No special behavior is required. Setting this option is functionally equivalent to calling *ExecuteReader* without parameters.
KeyInfo	The query returns only column metadata and primary key information. The query is executed without any locking on the selected rows.
SchemaOnly	The query returns only column metadata and does not put any lock on the database rows.
SequentialAccess	Enables the reader to load data as a sequential stream. This behavior works in conjunction with methods such as *GetBytes* and *GetChars*, which can be used to read bytes or characters having a limited buffer size for the data being returned.
SingleResult	The query is expected to return only the first result set.
SingleRow	The query is expected to return a single row.

The sequential access mode applies to all columns in the returned result set. This means you can access columns only in the order in which they appear in the result set. For example, you cannot read column 2 before column 1. More exactly, if you read or move past a given location, you can no longer read or move back. Combined with the *GetBytes* method, sequential access can be helpful in cases in which you must read BLOBs with a limited buffer.

> **Note**   You can also specify *SingleRow* when executing queries that are expected to return multiple result sets. In this case, all the generated result sets are correctly returned, but each result set has a single row. *SingleRow* and *SingleResult* serve the purpose of letting the underlying provider machinery know about the expected results so that some internal optimization can optionally be made.

Closing the Reader

The data reader is not a publicly creatable object. It does have a constructor, but not one that is callable from within user applications. The data reader constructor is marked as internal and can be invoked only from classes defined in the same assembly—*System.Data*. The data reader is implicitly instantiated when the *ExecuteReader* method is called. Opening and closing the reader are operations distinct from instantiation and must be explicitly invoked by the application. The *Read* method advances the internal pointer to the next readable record in the current result set. The *Read* method returns a Boolean value indicating whether more records can be read. While records are being read, the connection is busy and no operation—other than closing—can be performed on the connection object.

The data reader and the connection are distinct objects and should be managed and closed independently. Both objects provide a *Close* method that should be called twice—once on the data reader (first) and once on the connection. When the *CloseConnection* behavior is required, closing the data reader also closes the underlying connection. In addition, the data reader's *Close* method fills in the values for any command output parameters and sets the *RecordsAffected* property.

> **Tip**   Because of the extra work *Close* always performs on a data reader class, closing a reader with success can sometimes be expensive, especially in cases of long-running and complicated queries. In situations in which you need to squeeze out every bit of performance, and where the return values and number of records affected are not significant, you can invoke the *Cancel* method of the associated *SqlCommand* object instead of closing the reader. *Cancel* aborts the operation and closes the reader faster. Aside from this, you're still responsible for properly closing the underlying connection.

Accessing Multiple Result Sets

Depending on the syntax of the query, multiple result sets can be returned. By default, the data reader is positioned on the first of them. You use the *Read* method to scroll through the various records in the current result set. When the last record is found, the *Read* method returns *false* and does not advance further. To move to the next result set, you should use the *NextResult* method. The method returns *false* if there are no more result sets to read. The following code shows how to access all records in all returned result sets:

```
using (SqlConnection conn = new SqlConnection(connString))
{
    string cmdText = Query.Text;
```

```
SqlCommand cmd = new SqlCommand(cmdText, conn);
cmd.Connection.Open();
SqlDataReader reader = cmd.ExecuteReader();

do {
    // Move through the first result set
    while (reader.Read())
        sb.AppendFormat("{0}, {1}<br/>", reader[0], reader[1]);

    // Separate result sets
    sb.Append("<hr />");
} while (reader.NextResult());

reader.Close();
}

// Display results in the page
Results.Text = sb.ToString();
```

Figure 7-7 shows the output generated by the sample page based on this code.

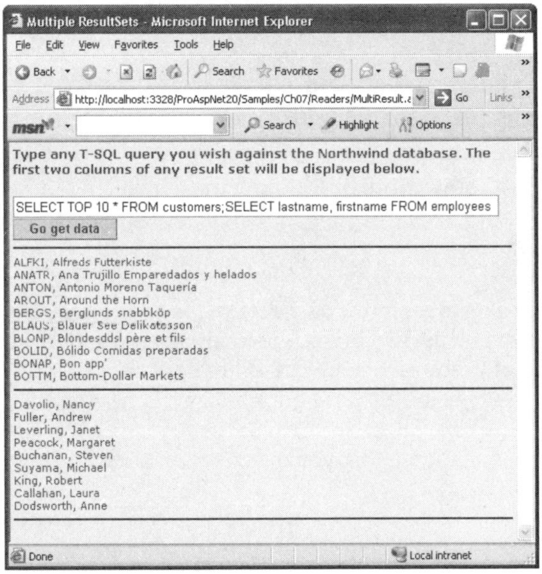

Figure 7-7 Processing multiple result sets.

> **Note** The .NET Framework version 1.1 extends the programming interface of data readers by adding the *HasRows* method, which returns a Boolean value indicating whether there are more rows to read. However, the method does not tell anything about the number of rows available. Similarly, there is no method or trick for knowing in advance how many result sets have been returned.

Asynchronous Commands

A database operation is normally a synchronous operation—the caller regains control of the application only after the interaction with the database is completed. This approach can lead to performance and scalability issues in lengthy operations—a common scenario when you interact with a DBMS. The .NET Framework 1.x supports asynchronous operations, but the model is implemented around user-level code. In other words, you can implement your own procedures asynchronously and connect to databases and run commands as part of the code, but connection management and command execution remain atomic operations that execute synchronously.

The .NET data provider for SQL Server in ADO.NET 2.0 provides true asynchronous support for executing commands. This offers a performance advantage because you can perform other actions until the command completes. However, this is not the only benefit. The support for asynchronous operations is built into the *SqlCommand* class and is limited to executing non-query commands and getting a reader or an XML reader. You can use three different approaches to build commands that work asynchronously: nonblocking, polling, and callback.

Setting Up Asynchronous Commands

To enable asynchronous commands, you must set the new *Async* attribute to *true* in the connection string. You'll receive an exception if any of the asynchronous methods are called over a connection that doesn't have asynchronous capabilities explicitly turned on. Enabling asynchronous commands does have a cost in terms of overall performance; for this reason, you're better off using the *Async* keyword only with connection objects that execute asynchronous operations only.

If you need both synchronous and asynchronous commands, employ different connections wherever possible. Note, though, that you can still call synchronous methods over connections enabled to support asynchronous operations. However, you'll only end up using more resources than needed and experience a performance degradation.

> **Note** Asynchronous commands are not implemented by creating a new thread and blocking execution on it. Among other things, ADO.NET is not thread-safe and blocking threads would be a serious performance hit. When asynchronous commands are enabled, ADO.NET opens the TCP socket to the database in overlapped mode and binds it to the I/O completion port. In light of this, synchronous operations execute as the emulation of asynchronous operations, and this explains why they're more expensive than asynchronous-enabled connections.

Nonblocking Commands

Nonblocking commands are the simplest case of asynchronous commands. The code starts the operation and continues executing other unrelated methods; then it comes back to get the results. Whatever the model of choice happens to be, the first step of an asynchronous command is calling one of the *BeginExecuteXXX* methods. For example, if you want to execute a reading command, you call *BeginExecuteReader*:

```
// Start a non-blocking execution
IAsyncResult iar = cmd.BeginExecuteReader();

// Do something else meanwhile
...

// Block the execution until done
SqlDataReader reader = cmd.EndExecuteReader(iar);

// Process data here ...
ProcessData(reader);
```

The *BeginExecuteReader* function returns an *IAsyncResult* object you will use later to complete the call. Note that *EndExecuteReader* is called to finish the operation and will block execution until the ongoing command terminates. The *EndExecuteReader* function will automatically sync up the command with the rest of the application, blocking the code whenever the results of the command are not ready.

As an alternative to the aforementioned approach, the client code might want to check the status of a running asynchronous operation and poll for completion. The following code illustrates the polling option with a query statement:

```
// Executes a query statement
IAsyncResult iar = cmd.BeginExecuteReader();
do {
    // Do something here
} while (!iar.IsCompleted);

// Sync up
SqlDataReader reader = cmd.EndExecuteReader(iar);
ProcessData(reader);
```

It is important to note that if *iar.IsCompleted* returns *true*, the *EndExecuteReader* method will not block the application.

The third option for nonblocking commands has the client code start the database operation and continue without waiting. Later on, when the operation is done, it receives a call. In this case, you pass a delegate to a *BeginExecuteXXX* method and any information that constitutes the state of the particular call. The state is any information you want to pass to the callback function. In this case, you pass the command object:

```
// Begin executing the command
IAsyncResult ar = cmd.BeginExecuteReader(
    new AsyncCallback(ProcessData), cmd);
```

After initiating the asynchronous operation, you can forget about it and do any other work. The specified callback function is invoked at the end of the operation. The callback must have the following layout:

```
public void ProcessData(IAsyncResult ar)
{
    // Retrieve the context of the call
    SqlCommand cmd = (SqlCommand) iar.AsyncState;

    // Complete the async operation
    SqlDataReader reader = cmd.EndExecuteReader(iar);
    ...
}
```

The context of the call you specified as the second argument to *BeingExecuteReader* is packed in the *AsyncState* property of the *IAsyncResult* object.

> **Note** The callback will be called in a thread-pool thread, which is likely to be different from the thread that initiated the operation. Proper thread synchronization might be needed, depending on the application. This also poses a problem with the user interface of applications, especially Windows Forms applications. Ensuring that the UI is refreshed in the right thread is up to you. Windows Forms controls and forms provide mechanisms for deciding if the correct thread is currently executing and for accessing the correct thread if it isn't. You should consult the MSDN documentation or a good Windows Forms programming book for more information regarding multithreaded Windows Forms programming. Note that if you fail to use the threading model correctly, your application will almost certainly lock up and quite possibly even crash.

Executing Parallel Commands in an ASP.NET Page

Having asynchronous commands available is not necessarily a good reason for using them without due forethought. Let's examine a couple of scenarios where asynchronous commands are useful for building better Web pages. The first scenario we'll consider is the execution of multiple SQL statements in parallel, either against the same or different database servers.

Imagine that your page displays information about a particular customer—both personal and accounting data. The former block of data comes from the client's database; the latter is excerpted from the accounting database. You can fire both queries at the same time and have them execute in parallel on distinct machines—thus benefiting from true parallelism. Here's an example:

```
protected void QueryButton_Click(object sender, EventArgs e)
{
    string custID = CustomerList.SelectedValue;
```

```
using (SqlConnection conn1 = new SqlConnection(ConnString1))
using (SqlConnection conn2 = new SqlConnection(ConnString2))
{
  // Fire the first command: get customer info
  SqlCommand cmd1 = new SqlCommand(CustomerInfoCmd, conn1);
  cmd1.Parameters.Add("@customerid", SqlDbType.Char, 5).Value = custID;
  conn1.Open();
  IAsyncResult arCustomerInfo = cmd1.BeginExecuteReader();

  // Fire the second command: get order info
  SqlCommand cmd2 = new SqlCommand(CustomerOrderHistory, conn2);
  cmd2.CommandType = CommandType.StoredProcedure;
  cmd2.Parameters.Add("@customerid", SqlDbType.Char, 5).Value = custID;
  conn2.Open();
  IAsyncResult arOrdersInfo = cmd2.BeginExecuteReader();

  // Prepare wait objects to sync up
  WaitHandle[] handles = new WaitHandle[2];
  handles[0] = arCustomerInfo.AsyncWaitHandle;
  handles[1] = arOrdersInfo.AsyncWaitHandle;
  SqlDataReader reader;

  // Wait for all commands to terminate (no longer than 5 secs)
  for (int i=0; i<2; i++)
  {
    StringBuilder builder = new StringBuilder();
    int index = WaitHandle.WaitAny(handles, 5000, false);
        if (index == WaitHandle.WaitTimeout)
                throw new Exception("Timeout expired");

    if (index == 0) {    // Customer info
      reader = cmd1.EndExecuteReader(arCustomerInfo);
      if (!reader.Read())
        continue;

      builder.AppendFormat("{0}<br>", reader["companyname"]);
      builder.AppendFormat("{0}<br>", reader["address"]);
      builder.AppendFormat("{0}<br>", reader["country"]);
      Info.Text = builder.ToString();
      reader.Close();
    }
    if (index == 1) {    // Orders info
      reader = cmd2.EndExecuteReader(arOrdersInfo);
      gridOrders.DataSource = reader;
      gridOrders.DataBind();
      reader.Close();
    }
  }
}
```

The page fires the two commands and then sits waiting for the first command to terminate. The *AsyncWaitHandle* object of each *IAsyncResult* is stored in an array and passed to the *WaitAny* method of the *WaitHandle* class. *WaitAny* signals out when any of the commands terminates, but the surrounding *for* statement reiterates the wait until all pending commands terminate. You could have more easily opted for the *WaitAll* method. In this case, though, you can process results as they become available. This fact ensures a performance gain, especially for long-running stored procedures.

> **Note**   You can implement the same behavior in ADO.NET 1.x without asynchronous commands by simply assigning each command to a different thread—either a user-defined one or one from the thread pool. In this case, though, each command would have blocked a thread. Blocking threads is fine for client-side applications, but it might compromise scalability in server-side applications such as ASP.NET applications.

Nonblocking Data-Driven ASP.NET Pages

Imagine a data-driven ASP.NET page that employs long-running, synchronous commands. The more the page is requested, the more likely it is that a large share of system threads are blocked while waiting for the database to return results. The paradoxical effect of this is that the Web server is virtually idle (with almost no CPU and network usage) but can't accept new requests because it has very few threads available.

To address this problem, since version 1.0 ASP.NET supports asynchronous HTTP handlers—that is, a special breed of page classes that implement the *IHttpAsyncHandler* interface instead of *IHttpHandler*. Asynchronous HTTP handlers take care of a request and produce a response in an asynchronous manner. In the .NET Framework 2.0, asynchronous handlers can combine with asynchronous commands to boost data-driven pages.

The *IHttpAsyncHandler* interface counts *BeginProcessRequest* and *EndProcessRequest* methods. In the former method, you connect to the database and kick off the query. *BeginProcessRequest* receives a callback function directly from ASP.NET; the same callback is used to detect the completion of the asynchronous command.

When *BeginProcessRequest* returns, the page gives the control back to ASP.NET as if it was served. ASP.NET is now free to reuse the thread to process another request while the database server proceeds. When the query is complete, the signaling mechanism ends up invoking the *EndProcessRequest* method, although not necessarily on the same thread as the rest of the page, so to speak. The *EndProcessRequest* method is where you simply collect the data and render the page out.

We'll cover asynchronous handlers in my other book on this subject, *Programming Microsoft ASP.NET 2.0 Applications: Advanced Topics*.

> **Note**   A fair number of methods work synchronously even in the context of asynchronous commands. The list includes *BeginXXX* methods and most methods of the data reader class, such as *GetXXX* methods *Read*, *Close*, and *Dispose*.

Working with Transactions

In ADO.NET, you can choose between two types of transactions: local and distributed. A local transaction involves a single resource—typically, the database you're connected to. You begin the transaction, you attach one or more commands to its context, and decide whether the whole operation was successful or whether it failed. The transaction is then committed or rolled back accordingly. This approach is functionally similar to simply running a SQL stored procedure that groups a few commands under the same transaction. Using ADO.NET code makes it more flexible but doesn't change the final effect.

A distributed transaction spans multiple heterogeneous resources and ensures that if the entire transaction is committed or rolled back, all modifications made at the various steps are committed or rolled back as well. A distributed transaction requires a Transaction Processing (TP) monitor. The Distributed Transaction Coordinator (DTC) is the TP monitor for Microsoft Windows 2000 and later.

In ADO.NET 1.x, you manage a local transaction through a bunch of database-specific transaction objects—for example, *SqlTransaction* for SQL Server transactions. You begin the transaction, associate commands to it, and decide the outcome. For distributed transactions, you need Enterprise Services and serviced components. You can enlist database connections to Enterprise Services DTC managed transactions by using the aforementioned *EnlistDistributedTransaction* method on the connection class.

In ADO.NET 2.0, local and distributed transactions can also be managed (more easily, actually) through the new classes defined in the *System.Transactions* namespace—specifically, with the *TransactionScope* class.

Managing Local Transactions as in ADO.NET 1.x

You start a new local transaction through the *BeginTransaction* method of the connection class. You can give the transaction a name and an isolation level. The method maps to the SQL Server implementation of *BEGIN TRANSACTION*. The following code snippet shows the typical flow of a transactional piece of code:

```
SqlTransaction tran;
tran = conn.BeginTransaction();
SqlCommand cmd1 = new SqlCommand(cmdText1);
cmd1.Connection = conn;
cmd1.Transaction = tran;
...
SqlCommand cmd2 = new SqlCommand(cmdText2);
cmd2.Connection = conn;
cmd2.Transaction = tran;
...
try {
  cmd1.ExecuteNonQuery();
  cmd2.ExecuteNonQuery();
```

```
  tran.Commit();
}
catch {
  tran.Rollback();
}
finally {
  conn.Close();
}
```

The newly created transaction object operates on the same connection represented by the connection object you used to create it. To add commands to the transaction, you set the *Transaction* property of command objects. Note that if you set the *Transaction* property of a command to a transaction object that is not connected to the same connection, an exception will be thrown as you attempt to execute a statement. Once all the commands have terminated, you call the *Commit* method of the transaction object to complete the transaction, or you call the *Rollback* method to cancel the transaction and undo all changes.

The isolation level of a transaction indicates the locking behavior for the connection. Common values are: *ReadCommitted* (default), *ReadUncommitted, RepeatableRead*, and *Serializable*. Imagine a situation in which one transaction changes a value that a second transaction might need to read. *ReadCommitted* locks the row and prevents the second transaction from reading until the change is committed. *ReadUncommitted* doesn't hold locks, thus improving the overall performance. In doing so, though, it allows the second transaction to read a modified row before the original change is committed or rolled back. This is a "dirty read" because if the first transaction rolls the change back, the read value is invalid and there's nothing you can do about it. (Of course, you set *ReadUncommitted* only if dirty reads are not a problem in your scenario.) Note also that disallowing dirty reads also decreases overall system concurrency.

Imagine one transaction reads a committed row; next, another transaction modifies or deletes the row and commits the change. At this point, if the first transaction attempts to read the row again, it will obtain different results. To prevent this, you set the isolation level to *Repeatable-Read*, which prevents further updates and dirty reads but not other operations that can generate phantom rows. Imagine that a transaction runs a query; next, another transaction does something that modifies the results of the previous query. When the first transaction ends, it returns an inconsistent result to the client. The *Serializable* level prevents concurrent transactions from updating or inserting rows until a given transaction is complete. Table 7-15 summarizes the isolation levels.

Table 7-15   Isolation Levels

Level	Dirty Reads	Nonrepeatable	Phantom Rows
ReadUncommitted	Yes	Yes	Yes
ReadCommitted	No	Yes	Yes
RepeatableRead	No	No	Yes
Serializable	No	No	No

The highest isolation level, *Serializable*, provides a high degree of protection against concurrent transactions, but it requires that each transaction complete before any other transaction is allowed to work on the database.

The isolation level can be changed at any time and remains in effect until explicitly changed. If changed during a transaction, the server is expected to apply the new locking level to all statements remaining.

You terminate a transaction explicitly by using the *Commit* or *Rollback* method. The *SqlTransaction* class supports named savepoints in the transaction that can be used to roll back a portion of the transaction. Named savepoints exploit a specific SQL Server feature—the SAVE TRANSACTION statement.

This approach to local transactions is only possible in ADO.NET 1.x and is, of course, fully supported in ADO.NET 2.0. Let's explore alternative approaches.

Introducing the *TransactionScope* Object

The preceding code based on *BeginTransaction* ties you to a specific database and requires you to start a new transaction to wrap a few database commands. What if you need to work with distinct databases and then, say, send a message to a message queue? In ADO.NET 1.x, you typically create a distributed transaction in Enterprise Services. In ADO.NET 2.0, you can perform both local and distributed transactions through a new object—*TransactionScope*. Here's the code:

```
using (TransactionScope ts = new TransactionScope())
{
  using (SqlConnection conn = new SqlConnection(ConnString))
  {
    SqlCommand cmd = new SqlCommand(cmdText, conn);
    cmd.Connection.Open();
    try {
      cmd.ExecuteNonQuery();
    }
    catch (SqlException ex) {
      // Error handling code goes here
      lblMessage.Text = ex.Message;
    }
  }

  // Must call to complete; otherwise abort
  ts.Complete();
}
```

The connection object is defined within the scope of the transaction, so it automatically participates in the transaction. The only thing left to do is commit the transaction, which you do by placing a call to the method *Complete*. If you omit that call, the transaction fails and rolls back no matter what really happened with the command or commands. Needless to say, any exceptions will abort the transaction.

> **Important**   You must guarantee that the *TransactionScope* object will be disposed of. By design, the transaction scope commits or rolls back on disposal. Waiting for the garbage collector to kick in and dispose of the transaction scope can be expensive because distributed transactions have a one-minute timeout by default. Keeping multiple databases locked for up to a minute is an excellent scalability killer. Calling *TransactionScope.Dispose* manually in the code might not be enough, as it won't be called in case of exceptions. You should either opt for a *using* statement or a *try/catch/finally* block.

Distributed Transactions with *TransactionScope*

Let's consider a transaction that includes operations on different databases—the Northwind database of SQL Server 2000 and a custom *MyData.mdf* file managed through SQL Server 2005 Express. The file is available in the *app_Data* directory of the sample project. The sample table we're interested in here can be created with the following command:

```
CREATE TABLE Numbers (ID int, Text varchar(50))
```

You create a unique and all-encompassing *TransactionScope* instance and run the various commands, even on different connections. You track the outcome of the various operations and call *Complete* if all went fine. Here's an example:

```
bool canCommit = true;

using (TransactionScope ts = new TransactionScope())
{
    // ************************************************************
    // Update Northwind on SQL Server 2000
    using (SqlConnection conn = new SqlConnection(ConnString))
    {
        SqlCommand cmd = new SqlCommand(UpdateCmd, conn);
        cmd.Connection.Open();
        try {
            cmd.ExecuteNonQuery();
        }
        catch (SqlException ex) {
            canCommit &= false;
        }
    }

    // ************************************************************
    // Update Numbers on SQL Server 2005
    using (SqlConnection conn = new SqlConnection(ConnString05))
    {
        SqlCommand cmd = new SqlCommand(InsertCmd, conn);
        cmd.Connection.Open();
        try {
            cmd.ExecuteNonQuery();
        }
        catch (SqlException ex) {
            canCommit &= false;
```

```
        }
    }

    // Must call to complete; otherwise abort
    if (canCommit)
        ts.Complete();
}
```

If an error occurs, say, on the SQL Server 2005 database, any changes successfully entered on the SQL Server 2000 database are automatically rolled back.

TransactionScope is a convenience class that supports the dispose pattern, and internally it simply sets the current transaction, plus it has some state to track scoping. By wrapping everything in a *TransactionScope* object, you're pretty much done, as the object takes care of everything else for you. For example, it determines whether you need a local or distributed transaction, enlists any necessary distributed resources, and proceeds with local processing otherwise. As the code reaches a point where it won't be running locally, *TransactionScope* escalates to DTC as appropriate.

Which objects can be enlisted with a transaction? Anything that implements the required interface—*ITransaction*—can be enlisted. ADO.NET 2.0 ships all standard data providers with support for *System.Transactions*. MSMQ works in compatibility mode.

When some code invokes the *Complete* method, it indicates that all operations in the scope are completed successfully. Note that the method does not physically terminate the distributed transaction, as the commit operation will still happen on *TransactionScope* disposal. However, after calling the method, you can no longer use the distributed transaction.

> **Note**   There are a number of differences between *System.Transactions* and Enterprise Services as far as distributed transactions are concerned. First, *System.Transactions* is a transaction framework designed specifically for the managed environment, so it fits more naturally into .NET applications. Of course, internally the classes of the *System.Transactions* namespace might end up delegating some work to DTC and COM+, but that is nothing more than an implementation detail. Another important difference between the two is the existence of a lightweight transaction manager implemented on the managed side that allows for a number of optimizations, including presenting several enlistments as only one for DTC and support for promotable transactions.

Enlisting in a Distributed Transaction in ADO.NET 1.x

If your code uses *TransactionScope*, there's no need for a connection object to explicitly enlist in a transaction. However, if needed, the *EnlistTransaction* method provides you with exactly that capability.

Manually enlisting connections into distributed transactions is a feature already available in ADO.NET 1.1 through the *EnlistDistributedTransaction* method of the connection class. The method manually enlists the connection into a transaction being managed by the Enterprise Services DTC. In this case, you work with a distributed transaction that is defined elsewhere and takes direct advantage of the DTC.

> **Note**   *EnlistDistributedTransaction* is useful when you have pooled business objects with an open connection. In this case, enlistment occurs only when the connection is opened. If the object participates in multiple transactions, the connection for that object is not reopened and therefore has no way to automatically enlist in new transactions. In this case, you can disable automatic transaction enlistment and enlist the connection explicitly by using *EnlistDistributedTransaction*.

SQL Server 2005–Specific Enhancements

The .NET data provider for SQL Server also has new features that are tied to the enhancements in SQL Server 2005. SQL Server 2005 introduces significant enhancements in various areas, including data-type support, query dependency and notification, and multiple active result sets (MARS).

Support for CLR Types

SQL Server 2005 supports any CLR types. In addition to default types, you can store into and retrieve from SQL Server tables any object that is a valid .NET type. This includes both system types—such as a *Point*—and user-defined classes. This extended set of capabilities is reflected in the ADO.NET 2.0 provider for SQL Server.

CLR types appear as objects to the data reader, and parameters to commands can be instances of CLR types. The following code snippet demonstrates how to retrieve a value from the MyCustomers table that corresponds to an instance of user-defined *Customer* class:

```
string cmdText = "SELECT CustomerData FROM MyCustomers";
SqlConnection conn = new SqlConnection(connStr);
SqlCommand cmd = new SqlCommand(cmdText, conn);
cmd.Connection.Open();
SqlDataReader reader = cmd.ExecuteReader();
while(reader.Read())
{
  Customer cust = (Customer) reader[0];
  // Do some work
}
cmd.Connection.Close();
```

A SQL Server 2005 user-defined type is stored as a binary stream of bytes. The *get* accessor of the data reader gets the bytes and deserializes them to a valid instance of the original class. The reverse process (serialization) takes place when a user-defined object is placed in a SQL Server column.

Support for XML as a Native Type

SQL Server 2005 natively supports the XML data type, which means you can store XML data in columns. At first glance, this feature seems to be nothing new because XML data is plain text and to store XML data in a column you only need the column to accept text. Native XML support in SQL Server 2005, however, means something different—you can declare the type of a given column as native XML, not plain text adapted to indicate markup text.

In ADO.NET 1.x, the *ExecuteXmlReader* method allows you to process the results of a query as an XML stream. The method builds an *XmlTextReader* object on top of the data coming from SQL Server. Therefore, for the method to work, the entire result set must be XML. Scenarios in which this method is useful include when the FOR XML clause is appended or when you query for a scalar value that happens to be XML text.

In ADO.NET 2.0, when SQL Server 2005 is up and running, you can obtain an *XmlTextReader* object for each table cell (row, column) whose type is XML. You obtain a *SqlDataReader* object and have it return XML to you using the new *GetSqlXml* method. The following code snippet provides a useful example:

```
string cmdText = " SELECT * FROM MyCustomers";
SqlCommand cmd = new SqlCommand(cmdText, conn);
SqlDataReader reader = cmd.ExecuteReader();
while(reader.Read())
{
  // Assume that field #3 contains XML data

  // Get data and do some work
  SqlXml xml = reader.GetSqlXml(3);
  ProcessData(xml.Value);
}
```

The *SqlXml* class represents the XML data type. The *Value* property of the class returns the XML text as a string.

SQL Notifications and Dependencies

Applications that display volatile data or maintain a cache would benefit from friendly server notification whenever their data changes. SQL Server 2005 offers this feature—it notifies client applications about dynamic changes in the result set generated by a given query. Suppose your application manages the results of a query. If you register for a notification, your application is informed if something happens at the SQL Server level that modifies the result set generated by that query. This means that if a record originally selected by your query is updated or deleted, or if a new record is added that meets the criteria of the query, you're notified. Note, though, the notification reaches your application only if it is still up and running—which poses a clear issue with ASP.NET pages. But let's move forward one step at a time.

The SQL Server provider in ADO.NET 2.0 provides two ways to use this notification feature and two related classes—*SqlDependency* and *SqlNotificationRequest*. *SqlNotificationRequest* is a lower-level class that exposes server-side functionality, allowing you to execute a command with a notification request. When a T-SQL statement is executed in SQL Server 2005, the notification mechanism keeps track of the query, and if it detects a change that might cause the result set to change, it sends a message to a queue. A queue is a new SQL Server 2005 database object that you create and manage with a new set of T-SQL statements. How the queue is polled and how the message is interpreted is strictly application-specific.

The *SqlDependency* class provides a high-level abstraction of the notification mechanism and allows you to set an application-level dependency on the query so that changes in the server can be immediately communicated to the client application through an event. The following code binds a command to a SQL dependency:

```
SqlCommand cmd = new SqlCommand("SELECT * FROM Employees", conn);
SqlDependency dep = new SqlDependency(cmd);
dep.OnChange += new OnChangeEventHandler(OnDependencyChanged);
SqlDataReader reader = cmd.ExecuteReader();
```

The *OnChange* event on the *SqlDependency* class fires whenever the class detects a change that affects the result set of the command. Here's a typical handler:

```
void OnDependencyChanged(object sender, SqlNotificationsEventArgs e)
{
    ...
}
```

When the underlying machinery detects a change, it fires the event to the application.

As mentioned, using notifications in this way is not particularly interesting from an ASP.NET perspective because the page returns immediately after running the query. However, the caching API of ASP.NET 2.0 provides a similar feature that automatically tracks the results of a query via the ASP.NET cache. What you have in ASP.NET 2.0 is a custom type of cache dependency that monitors the results of a query for both SQL Server 2000 and SQL Server 2005, although in radically different ways. You create a dependency on a command or a table, and place it in the ASP.NET *Cache* object. The cache item will be invalidated as soon as a change in the monitored command or table is detected. If a SQL Server 2000 instance is involved, you can detect changes to only one of the tables touched by the query; if SQL Server 2005 is involved, you get finer control and can track changes to the result set of the query. We'll cover ASP.NET caching in great detail in Chapter 14.

Multiple Active Result Sets

Version 1.x of the SQL Server managed provider, along with the SQL Server ODBC driver, supports only one active result set per connection. The (unmanaged) OLE DB provider and the outermost ADO library appear to support multiple active result sets, but this is an illusion. In OLE DB, the effect is obtained by opening additional and nonpooled connections.

In SQL Server 2005, the multiple active result set (MARS) feature is natively implemented and allows an application to have more than one *SqlDataReader* open on a connection, each started from a separate command. Having more than one data reader open on a single connection offers a potential performance improvement because multiple readers are much less expensive than multiple connections. At the same time, MARS adds some hidden per-operation costs that are a result of its implementation. Considering the tradeoffs and making a thoughtful decision is up to you.

The canonical use of MARS is when you get a data reader to walk through a result set while using another command on the same connection to issue update statements to the database. The following code demonstrates a sample page that walks through a data reader and updates the current record using a second command. If you try this approach in ADO.NET 1.x, or in ADO.NET 2.0 with MARS disabled, you get an exception complaining that the data reader associated with this connection is open and should be closed first.

```
using (SqlConnection conn = new SqlConnection(connString))
{
    SqlCommand cmd1 = new SqlCommand("SELECT * FROM employees", conn);
    cmd1.Connection.Open();
    SqlDataReader reader = cmd1.ExecuteReader();

    // Walks the data reader
    while (reader.Read())
    {
        // Reverses the first name
        string firstNameReversed = reader["firstname"].ToString();
        char[] buf = firstNameReversed.ToCharArray();
        Array.Reverse(buf);
        firstNameReversed = new string(buf);

        // Set the new first name on the same connection
        int id = (int)reader["employeeid"];
        SqlCommand cmd2 = new SqlCommand(
                "UPDATE employees SET firstname=@newFirstName WHERE
                 employeeid=@empID", conn);
        cmd2.Parameters.AddWithValue("@newFirstName", firstNameReversed);
        cmd2.Parameters.AddWithValue("empID", id);
        cmd2.ExecuteNonQuery();
    }
    reader.Close();

    // Get a new reader to refresh the UI
    grid.DataSource = cmd1.ExecuteReader();
    grid.DataBind();
    cmd1.Connection.Close();
}
```

Note that for MARS to work, you must use a distinct *SqlCommand* object, as shown in the following code. If you use a third command object to re-execute the query to get up-to-date records, there's no need to close the reader explicitly.

Another big benefit of MARS is that, if you're engaged in a transaction, it lets you execute code in the same isolation-level scope of the original connection. You won't get this benefit if you open a second connection under the covers.

In ADO.NET 2.0, the MARS feature is enabled by default when SQL Server 2005 is the database server. To disable MARS, you set the *MultipleActiveResultSets* attribute to *false* in the connection string. There are some hidden costs associated with MARS. First, MARS requires the continuous creation of *SqlCommand* objects. To deal with this issue, a pool of command objects is constituted and maintained. Second, there is a cost in the network layer as a result of multiplexing the I/O stream of data. Most of these costs are structural, and you should not expect a great performance improvement by disabling the MARS feature. So what's the purpose of the *MultipleActiveResultSets* attribute? The attribute appears mostly for backward compatibility. In this way, applications that expect an exception when more than one result set is used can continue working.

> **Note**   MARS-like behavior is available in the .NET Framework 2.0 versions of the OLE DB and Oracle managed providers. The Oracle provider doesn't support the MARS attribute on the connection string, but it enables the feature automatically. The OLE DB provider doesn't support the connection string attribute either—it simulates multiple result sets when you connect to earlier versions of SQL Server or when the MDAC 9.0 library is not available. When you operate through OLE DB on a version of SQL Server 2005 equipped with MDAC 9.0, multiple result sets are active and natively implemented.

Conclusion

The .NET data access subsystem is made of two main subtrees—the managed providers and the database-agnostic container classes. ADO.NET managed providers are a new type of data source connectors and replace the COM-based OLE DB providers of ADO and ASP. As of this writing, the .NET Framework includes two native providers—one for SQL Server and one for Oracle—and support for all OLE DB providers and ODBC drivers. Third-party vendors also support MySQL, DB2, and Sybase, and they have alternate providers for Oracle.

A managed provider is faster and more appropriate than any other database technology for data-access tasks in .NET. Especially effective with SQL Server, a managed provider hooks up at the wire level and removes any sort of abstraction layer. In this way, a managed provider makes it possible for the ADO.NET to return to callers the same data types they would use to refresh the user interface. A managed provider supplies objects to connect to a data source, execute a command, start a transaction, and then grab or set some data.

In this chapter, we focused on establishing a connection to the data source and setting up commands and transactions. In the next chapter, we'll complete our look at ADO.NET by exploring data container classes such as *DataSet* and *DataTable*.

Just the Facts

- ADO.NET is a data-access subsystem in the Microsoft .NET Framework and is made of two distinct but closely related sets of classes—data providers and data containers.

- The functionalities supplied by a .NET data provider fall into a couple of categories: the capability of populating container classes, and the capability of setting up a connection and executing commands.

- The .NET Framework comes with data providers for SQL Server, Oracle, and all OLE DB and ODBC data sources.

- A data provider is faster and more appropriate than any other database technology for data-access tasks in .NET. Especially effective with SQL Server, a managed data provider hooks up at the wire level and removes any sort of abstraction layer.

- The data provider supplies an object to establish and manage the connection to a data source. This object implements connection pooling.

- In .NET applications, connection strings can be stored in a special section of the configuration file and encrypted if required.

- The data provider supplies an object to execute commands on an open connection and optionally within a transaction. The command object lists various execute methods to account for query and nonquery commands. Commands can execute either synchronously or asynchronously.

- Data returned by a query command are cached in a data reader object, which is a kind of optimized read-only, forward-only cursor.

- Local and distributed transactions can be managed through the *TransactionScope* class introduced with ADO.NET 2.0.

Chapter 8
ADO.NET Data Containers

In this chapter:
Data Adapters. 319
In-Memory Data Container Objects 332
Conclusion 351

To enhance aggregation and delivery of data across the tiers of distributed enterprise systems, ADO.NET introduces a new breed of object that looks and acts like the in-memory version of a modern powerful database—the *DataSet*. At its core, the *DataSet* is merely a data container—a sort of super dictionary—specifically designed to manage tabular data expressed in terms of tables, columns, and rows. Nothing in the *DataSet* is tied to a physical database—be it Microsoft SQL Server, Microsoft Office Access, or even Oracle databases. The *DataSet* has no notion of the provider that served its data, it is a mere data container that is serializable, feature-rich, and tightly integrated with ADO.NET providers. *DataSet* and related objects such as *DataTable*, *DataView*, and *DataRelation*—form the second leg of the ADO.NET framework that is, smart containers of data filled by enabled managed providers.

ADO.NET containers expose an API to let application developers populate them with any sort of data. In many cases, though, you want a *DataSet* to contain the results of a database query. This entails various steps: running the query, processing the results, filling the container, closing the connection. To get the results, you need a command and a data reader; next, you need some code to walk through the reader and copy the records in a proper table layout. All this behavior (and much more, actually) is incorporated in a made-to-measure ADO.NET object—the data adapter. Without further adieu, let's start the second part of our ADO.NET exploration with a look at adapters. Next, we'll take the plunge and dive into the *DataSet*, *DataTable*, and *DataView* classes. As their names suggest, these classes mimic the behavior of well-known database objects but remain database-agnostic—that is, they remain as purely in-memory objects.

Data Adapters

In ADO.NET, the data adapter object acts as a two-way bridge between a data source and the *DataSet* object. The *DataSet* is a disconnected container of data, and the adapter takes care of filling it and submitting its data back to a particular data source. Viewed from an abstract point of view, a data adapter is similar to a command and represents another way of executing a command against the data source.

> **Note**   In a certain way, the concepts of *command*, *data reader*, and *data adapter* are the results of the ADO *Recordset* split. Born to be a simple COM wrapper around an SQL result set, the ADO *Recordset* soon became a rather bloated object incorporating three types of cursors—read-only, disconnected, and server. Compared to ADO, the ADO.NET object model is simpler overall and, more important, made of simpler objects. Instead of providing a big monolithic object such as the *Recordset*, ADO.NET supplies three smaller and highly specialized objects—the command, data reader, and *DataSet*. The data reader is generated only by a direct query command; *DataSet* is generated only by a data adapter. To complete the comparison, note that ADO.NET has no native support for database server cursors.

The big difference between commands and data adapters is just in the way each one returns the retrieved data. A query command returns a read-only cursor—the data reader. The data adapter performs its data access, grabs all the data, and packs it into an in-memory container—the *DataSet* or *DataTable*. Under the hood, the data adapter is just an extra layer of abstraction built on top of the command/data reader pair. Internally, in fact, the data adapter just uses a command to query and a data reader to walk its way through the records and fill a user-provided *DataSet*.

Like commands and data readers, data adapters are specific to each data provider. So expect to find a data adapter class for SQL Server, one for Oracle, and so on. To come to grips with data adapters, let's examine the SQL Server adapter.

The *SqlDataAdapter* Class

By definition, a data adapter is a class that implements the *IDataAdapter* interface. However, looking at the actual implementation of the adapters in the supported providers, you can see that multiple layers of code are used. In particular, all data adapter classes inherit from a base class named *DbDataAdapter* and implement the *IDbDataAdapter* interface. The relationship is shown in Figure 8-1.

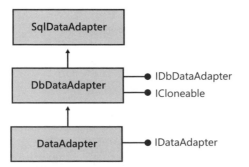

Figure 8-1   The hierarchy of data adapters and implemented interfaces.

Programming the SQL Server Data Adapter

Table 8-1 shows the properties of the *SqlDataAdapter* class—that is, the data adapter class for SQL Server.

Table 8-1   Properties of the *SqlDataAdapter* Class

Property	Description
AcceptChangesDuringFill	Indicates whether insertions of a row during a fill operation should be committed. *True* by default.
AcceptChangesDuring-Update	Indicates whether changed rows processed during a batch update operation should be committed. *True* by default. *Not supported in ADO.NET 1.x.*
ContinueUpdateOnError	Indicates whether in case of row conflicts the batch update continues or an exception is generated.
DeleteCommand	Gets or sets a statement or stored procedure to delete records from the database during batch update. Is a member of the *IDbDataAdapter* interface.
FillLoadOption	Indicates how retrieved values will be applied to existing rows. *Not supported in ADO.NET 1.x.*
InsertCommand	Gets or sets a statement or stored procedure to insert new records in the database during batch update. Is a member of the *IDbDataAdapter* interface.
MissingMappingAction	Determines the action to take when a table or column in the source data is not mapped to a corresponding element in the in-memory structure. Is a member of the *IDataAdapter* interface.
MissingSchemaAction	Determines the action to take when source data does not have a matching table or column in the corresponding in-memory structure. Is a member of the *IDataAdapter* interface.
ReturnProviderSpecific-Types	Indicates whether provider-specific types should be used to create table layouts to contain result sets during a fill operation. *Not supported in ADO.NET 1.x.*
SelectCommand	Gets or sets a statement or stored procedure to select records from the database. During batch update, the method is used to download metadata; it is used to select records in a query statement. Is a member of the *IDbDataAdapter* interface.
TableMappings	Gets a collection that provides the mappings between a source table and an in-memory table. Is a member of the *IDataAdapter* interface.
UpdateBatchSize	Indicates the size of the blocks of records submitted at a time during the batch update. Set to 1 by default. *Not supported in ADO.NET 1.x.*
UpdateCommand	Gets or sets a statement or stored procedure to update records in the database during batch update. Is a member of the *IDbDataAdapter* interface.

One thing is essential to know about a data adapter: It is a two-way channel used to read data from a data source into a memory table and to write in-memory data back to a data source. The data source used in both cases is likely to be the same, but it's not necessarily the same.

These two operations, known as *fill* and *update*, can be clearly identified in the preceding list of properties.

The four *xxxCommand* members of the *IDbDataAdapter* interface are used to control how in-memory data is written to the database during an *update* operation. This is not entirely true of *SelectCommand*. Although *SelectCommand* plays a role in the batch update process, it is the key member in performing the *fill* operation. The *MissingXXX* properties, *TableMappings* collection, and, in ADO.NET 2.0, *FillLoadOption* and *ReturnProviderSpecificTypes* indicate how data read out of the data source is mapped onto client memory.

Once loaded in memory, the (disconnected) data is available for client-side updates performed by a Windows Forms application or an ASP.NET page. Client updates consist of adding new rows and deleting or updating existing ones. A batch update is the data provider procedure that, triggered by the client application, posts all the pending in-memory changes back to a data source. In carrying out this procedure, a bunch of database management system (DBMS)–specific commands are required to carry out the three basic operations—insert, update, and delete. The *InsertCommand*, *UpdateCommand*, and *DeleteCommand* properties are *SqlCommand* objects that do just this.

> **Important**   ADO.NET batch updates consist of a series of commands sequentially submitted to the database, by means of the data adapter. As a developer, you fire the batch update process with a single command. Bear in mind that conceptually ADO.NET batch updates don't equate to a series of queries submitted in a single command. "Batch update" doesn't really mean that a batch of commands and data is moved on the DBMS and executes there.
>
> Using a batch update is a powerful approach, but it's not particularly suited to ASP.NET applications. The difficulty lies in the fact that Web applications work over a stateless protocol such as HTTP. So to make the whole scheme work well, you should cache the in-memory table in the session, which is not something all applications can afford. In addition, note that using a batch update saves you from a lot of coding and can be easily configured to serve complex update scenarios. Using a batch update, though, doesn't necessarily give you significant performance advantages because each update requires its own command in ADO.NET 1.x. In ADO.NET 2.0, you can group more updates in a unique command instead, through the new *UpdateBatchSize* property.

Table 8-2 lists the methods of the data adapter objects.

Table 8-2   Methods of the *SqlDataAdapter* Class

Method	Description
Fill	Populates an in-memory table with rows read from the source.
FillSchema	Configures an in-memory table so that the schema matches the schema in the data source.
GetFillParameters	Returns the parameters the user set on the query statement.
Update	Updates the data source based on the current content of the specified in-memory table. It works by calling the respective INSERT, UPDATE, or DELETE statements for each inserted, updated, or deleted row, respectively, in the table.

The data adapter uses the *SelectCommand* property to retrieve schema and data from the data source. The connection object associated with the *SelectCommand* does not need to be open. If the connection is closed before the reading occurs, it is opened to retrieve data and then closed. If the connection is open when the adapter works, it remains open.

Filling a *DataSet* Using a Data Adapter

A data adapter object uses the *Fill* method to populate an in-memory object with data retrieved through a query. The in-memory structure is a *DataSet* or *DataTable* object. As we'll see more clearly in a moment, the *DataSet* is the in-memory counterpart of a DBMS database. It might contain multiple tables (that is, multiple *DataTable* objects) and set up relationships and constraints between tables. Each table, in turn, is made of a number of columns and rows.

Filling a *DataSet* object ultimately means filling one of its tables. The data adapter can create a new table for each result set generated by the query. The table mapping code decides how. (If the table exists already, it is updated.) Mapping a result set to a *DataSet* is a process articulated in two phases: table mapping and column mapping. During the first step, the data adapter determines the name of the *DataTable* that will contain the rows in the current result set. Each *DataTable* is given a default name that you can change at will.

> **Note**   Although you can fill a *DataTable* with any kind of data from any existing source, the name of the table doesn't have to reflect necessarily the name of a database table, even when the data comes out of a database query. The *DataTable*'s table name serves only to identify the object. Changing the name of a *DataTable* doesn't have any impact on the name of the database table that might have been used to fill it.

The default name of the *DataTable* depends on the signature of the *Fill* method that was used for the call. For example, let's consider the following two *Fill* calls:

```
DataSet ds = new DataSet();
adapter.Fill(ds);
adapter.Fill(ds, "MyTable");
```

In the first call, the name of the first result set generated by the query defaults to "Table". If the query produces multiple result sets, additional tables will be named Table1, Table2, and so on, appending a progressive index to the default name. In the second call, the first result set is named MyTable and the others are named after it: MyTable1, MyTable2, and so forth. The procedure is identical; what really changes in the two cases is the base name.

The names of the tables can be changed at two different moments. You can change them after the *DataSet* has been populated or, when using table mapping, you can define settings that will be used to name the tables upon creation. You define a table mapping on a data adapter object by using the *TableMappings* property.

> **Note** You can also use the *Fill* method to populate a single *DataTable*. In this case, only the first result set is taken into account and only one mapping phase occurs—column mapping:
>
> ```
> DataTable dt = new DataTable();
> adapter.Fill(dt);
> ```
>
> The preceding code shows how to use the *Fill* method to populate a *DataTable*.

Loading Options

In ADO.NET 2.0, you can better control the way data is loaded into the various data tables during a fill operation. By setting the *FillLoadOption* property, you indicate how rows already in a *DataTable* combine with rows being loaded. The *FillLoadOption* property accepts a value from the *LoadOption* enumeration. Table 8-3 describes the feasible values.

Table 8-3   Values from the *LoadOption* Enumeration

Value	Description
OverwriteChanges	Updates the current and original versions of the row with the value of the incoming row.
PreserveChanges	Default option. Updates the original version of the row with the value of the incoming row.
Upsert	Updates the current version of the row with the value of the incoming row.

In each case, the description indicates the behavior when the primary key of a row in the incoming data matches the primary key of an existing row.

OverwriteChanges addresses the need to initialize tables with fresh data. *PreserveChanges*, on the other hand, is useful when you are in the process of synchronizing existing in-memory data with the current state of the database. In this case, you want to preserve any changes you entered on the client—that is, the current values you're working with and that you plan to submit back to the database later. At the same time, you might want to update the values in the *DataSet* that represent the original values read from the database. Finally, *Upsert* simply overwrites the current value, leaving the original value intact.

It is important to note that in-memory rows maintain two distinct values—current and original. The current value is the value that you receive when you read the content of a cell. The original value is the last value stored in the cell that was committed. When you assign a value to a newly created row, you set the current value. The original value is null. The assigned value must be committed to become an effective part of the row. You commit a row by invoking the *AcceptChanges* method (which will be discussed in more detail later). When this happens, the current value is duplicated as the original value and the overall state of the row is modified to *unchanged*. The row has no pending changes.

A *DataSet* populated with a fill operation presents all committed rows where current and original values coincide. Or at least this is the default behavior that you can alter by setting the

AcceptChangesDuringFill property. Once the data is downloaded on the client, the client application can work with it and enter changes, as shown here:

```
DataTable table = _data.Tables[0];
DataRow row = table.Rows[0];
row["firstname"] = "Lucy";
```

The assignment simply alters the current value of the row; the original value remains set to null or what it was before the assignment. To make "Lucy" become the effective original value of the row, you have to explicitly accept or commit the change:

```
// Accept all pending (uncommitted) changes on the row
row.AcceptChanges();
```

Uncommitted changes are important because only pending uncommitted changes are taken into account during a batch update operation. To read the current value of a row value, you do as follows:

```
Response.Write(row["firstname"].ToString());
```

To read the original value, you resort to the following:

```
Response.Write(row["firstname", DataRowVersion.Original].ToString());
```

Figure 8-2 shows the output of the sample page that illustrates the *FillLoadOption* property and the adapter's *Fill* method.

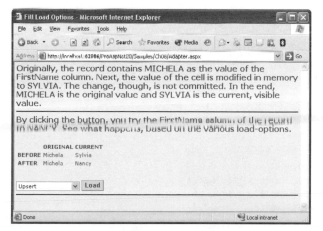

Figure 8-2 Examining the effect of the various load options.

As you can see, the *Upsert* option replaces the current value, leaving the original intact.

> **Note** In ADO.NET 1.x, the default behavior is *OverwriteChanges*; if *AcceptChangesDuringFill* is *false*, the actual behavior you get is *Upsert*. You never preserve client changes in ADO.NET 1.x. In ADO.NET 2.0, the value of *AcceptChangesDuringFill* is taken into account only for rows added, not for existing rows that get updated by the fill operation.

The *DataSet* is an empty container that a data adapter fills with the results of a query. But what about the number and structure of the child tables? The number of tables depends on the number of result sets. The structure of the tables depends on the table-mapping mechanism.

The Table-Mapping Mechanism

The .NET data provider assigns a default name to each result set generated by the query. The default name is *Table* or any name specified by the programmer in the call to *Fill*. The adapter looks up its *TableMappings* collection for an entry that matches the default name of the result set being read. If a match is found, the data adapter reads the mapped name. Next, it attempts to locate in the *DataSet* a *DataTable* object with the name specified in the mapping, as shown in Figure 8-3.

If the result set named *Table* has been mapped to Employees, a table named Employees is searched in the *DataSet*. If no such *DataTable* object exists, it gets created and filled. If such a *DataTable* exists in the *DataSet*, its content is merged with the contents of the result set.

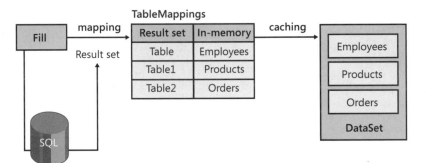

Figure 8-3   Mapping a result set onto a *DataSet* object.

The *TableMappings* property represents a collection object of type *DataTableMapping-Collection*. Each contained *DataTableMapping* object defines a pair of names: a source table name and an in-memory table name. Here's how to configure a few table mappings:

```
DataSet ds = new DataSet();
DataTableMapping dtm1, dtm2, dtm3;
dtm1 = adapter.TableMappings.Add("Table", "Employees");
dtm2 = adapter.TableMappings.Add("Table1", "Products");
dtm3 = adapter.TableMappings.Add("Table2", "Orders");
adapter.Fill(ds);
```

It goes without saying that the default names you map onto your own names must coincide with the default names originated by the call to the *Fill* method. In other words, suppose you change the last line of the previous code snippet with the following one:

```
adapter.Fill(ds, "MyTable");
```

In this case, the code won't work any longer because the default names will now be MyTable, MyTable1, and MyTable2. For these names, the *TableMappings* collection would have no entries defined. Finally, bear in mind you can have any number of table mappings. The overall number of mappings doesn't necessarily have to be related to the expected number of result sets.

The Column-Mapping Mechanism

If table mapping ended here, it wouldn't be such a big deal for us. In fact, if your goal is simply to give a mnemonic name to your *DataSet* tables, use the following code. The final effect is exactly the same.

```
DataSet ds = new DataSet();
adapter.Fill(ds);
ds.Tables["Table"].TableName = "Employees";
ds.Tables["Table1"].TableName = "Products";
```

The mapping mechanism, though, has another, rather interesting, facet: column mapping. Column mapping establishes a link between a column in the result set and a column in the mapped *DataTable* object. Column mappings are stored in the *ColumnMappings* collection property defined in the *DataTableMapping* class. The following code shows how to create a column mapping:

```
DataSet ds = new DataSet();
DataTableMapping dtm1;
dtm1 = adapter.TableMappings.Add("Table", "Employees");
dtm1.ColumnMappings.Add("employeeid", "ID");
dtm1.ColumnMappings.Add("firstname", "Name");
dtm1.ColumnMappings.Add("lastname", "FamilyName");
adapter.Fill(ds);
```

Figure 8-4 extends the previous diagram (Figure 8-3) and includes details of the column-mapping mechanism.

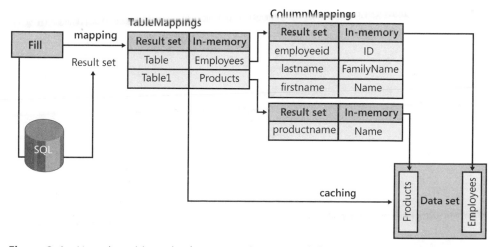

Figure 8-4   How the table and column mappings control the population of the *DataSet*.

In the preceding code, the source column *employeeid* is renamed *ID* and placed in a *DataTable* named *Employees*. The name of the column is the only argument you can change at this level. Bear in mind that all this mapping takes place automatically within the body of the *Fill* method. When *Fill* terminates, each column in the source result set has been transformed into a *DataTable* column object—an instance of the *DataColumn* class.

Missing Mapping Action

The *Fill* method accomplishes two main operations. First, it maps the source result sets onto in-memory tables. Second, it fills the tables with the data fetched from the physical data source. While accomplishing either of these tasks, the *Fill* method could raise some special exceptions. An exception is an anomalous situation that needs to be specifically addressed codewise. When the adapter can't find a table or column mapping, or when a required *Data-Table* or *DataColumn* can't be found, the data adapter throws a kind of lightweight exception.

Unlike real exceptions that must be resolved in code, this special breed of data adapter exceptions has to be resolved declaratively by choosing an action from a small set of allowable options. Data adapters raise two types of lightweight exceptions: missing mapping actions and missing schema actions.

A missing mapping action is required in two circumstances that can occur when the data adapter is collecting data to fill the *DataSet*. You need it if a default name is not found in the *TableMappings* collection, or if a column name is not available in the table's *ColumnMappings* collection. The data adapter's *MissingMappingAction* property is the tool you have to customize the behavior of the data adapter in the face of such exceptions. Allowable values for the property come from the *MissingMappingAction* enumeration and are listed in Table 8-4.

Table 8-4   The *MissingMappingAction* Enumeration

Value	Description
Error	An exception is generated if a missing column or table is detected.
Ignore	The unmapped column or table is ignored.
Passthrough	Default option. It adds the missing table or column to the structure.

Unless you explicitly set the *MissingMappingAction* property prior to filling the data adapter, the property assumes a default value of *Passthrough*. As a result, missing tables and columns are added using the default name. If you set the *MissingMapping-Action* property to *Ignore*, any unmapped table or column is simply ignored. No error is detected, but there will be no content for the incriminating result set (or one of its columns) in the target *DataSet*. If the *MissingMappingAction* property is set to *Error*, the adapter is limited to throwing an exception whenever a missing mapping is detected.

Once the data adapter is done with the mapping phase, it takes care of actually populating the target *DataSet* with the content of the selected result sets. Any required *DataTable* or *DataColumn* object that is not available in the target *DataSet* triggers another lightweight exception and requires another declarative action: the missing schema action.

Missing Schema Action

A missing schema action is required if the *DataSet* does not contain a table with the name that has been determined during the table-mapping step. Similarly, the same action is required if the *DataSet* table does not contain a column with the expected mapping name. *MissingSchemaAction* is the property you set to indicate the action you want to be taken in case of an insufficient table schema. Allowable values for the property come from the *MissingSchemaAction* enumeration and are listed in Table 8-5.

Table 8-5   The *MissingSchemaAction* Enumeration

Value	Description
Error	Generates an exception if a missing column or table is detected.
Ignore	Ignores the unmapped column or table.
Add	The default option. Completes the schema by adding any missing item.
AddWithKey	Also adds primary key and constraints.

By default, the *MissingSchemaAction* property is set to *Add*. As a result, the *DataSet* is completed by adding any constituent item that is missing—*DataTable* or *DataColumn*. Bear in mind, though, that the schema information added in this way for each column is very limited. It simply includes name and type. If you want extra information—such as the primary key, autoincrement, read-only, and allow-null settings—use the *AddWithKey* option instead.

Note that even if you use the *AddWithKey* option, not all available information about the column is really loaded into the *DataColumn*. For example, *AddWithKey* marks a column as autoincrement but does not set the related seed and step properties. Also the default value for the source column, if any, is not automatically copied. Only the primary key is imported; any additional indexes you might have set in the database are not. As for the other two options, *Ignore* and *Error*, they work exactly as they do with the *MissingMappingAction* property.

Prefilling the Schema

MissingMappingAction and *MissingSchemaAction* are not as expensive as real exceptions, but they still affect your code. Put another way, filling a *DataSet* that already contains all the needed schema information results in faster code. The advantage of this approach is more evident if your code happens to repeatedly fill an empty *DataSet* with a fixed schema. In this case, using a global *DataSet* object pre-filled with schema information helps to prevent all those requests for recovery actions. The *FillSchema* method just ensures that all the required objects are created beforehand:

```
DataTable[] FillSchema(DataSet ds, SchemaType mappingMode);
```

FillSchema takes a *DataSet* and adds as many tables to it as needed by the query command associated with the data adapter. The method returns an array with all the *DataTable* objects created (only schema, no data). The mapping-mode parameter can be one of the values defined in the *SchemaType* enumeration. The *SchemaType* enumeration values are listed in Table 8-6.

Table 8-6 The *SchemaType* Enumeration

Value	Description
Mapped	Apply any existing table mappings to the incoming schema. Configure the *DataSet* with the transformed schema. Recommended option.
Source	Ignore any table mappings on the data adapter. Configure the *DataSet* using the incoming schema without applying any transformations.

The *Mapped* option describes what happens when mappings are defined. *Source*, on the other hand, deliberately ignores any mappings you might have set. In this case, the tables in the *DataSet* retain their default name and all the columns maintain the original name they were given in the source tables.

How Batch Update Works

Batch update consists of the submission of an entire set of changes to the database. The batch update basically repeats the user actions that produced the changes that have the database—rather than the *DataSet*—as the target. Batch update assumes that the application enters its changes to the dataset in an offline manner. In a multiuser environment, this might pose design problems if users concurrently access on the server the same data you're editing offline. When you post your changes on a record that another person has modified in the meantime, whose changes win out?

Data Conflicts and Optimistic Lock

The possibility of data conflicts represents a design issue, but it isn't necessarily a problem for the application. Batch update in a multiuser environment creates conflict only if the changes you enter are somewhat implied by the original values you have read. In such a case, if someone else has changed the rows in the time elapsed between your fetch and the batch update, you might want to reconsider or reject your most recent updates. Conflicts detected at update time might introduce significant overhead that could make the batch update solution much less exciting. In environments with a low degree of data contention, batch updates can be effective because they allow for disconnected architectures, higher scalability, and considerably simpler coding.

To submit client changes to the server, use the data adapter's *Update* method. Data can be submitted only on a per-table basis. If you call *Update* without specifying any table name, a default name of Table is assumed. If no table exists with that name, an exception is raised:

```
adapter.Update(ds, "MyTable");
```

The *Update* method prepares and executes a tailor-made INSERT, UPDATE, or DELETE statement for each inserted, updated, or deleted row in the specified table. Rows are processed according to their natural order, and the row state determines the operation to accomplish. The *Update* method has several overloads and returns an integer, which represents the number of rows successfully updated.

When a row being updated returns an error, an exception is raised and the batch update process is stopped. You can prevent this from happening by setting the *ContinueUpdateOnError* property to *true*. In this case, the batch update terminates only when all the rows have been processed. Rows for which the update completed successfully are committed and marked as unchanged in the *DataSet*. For other rows, the application must decide what to do and restart the update if needed.

Command Builders

The data adapter provides a bunch of command properties—*InsertCommand*, *DeleteCommand*, and *UpdateCommand*—to let the programmer control and customize the way in which in-memory updates are submitted to the database server. These properties represent a quantum leap from ADO, in which update commands were SQL commands silently generated by the library. If you don't quite see the importance of this change, consider that with ADO.NET you can use stored procedures to perform batch updates and even work with non-SQL data providers.

The commands can also be generated automatically and exposed directly to the data-adapter engine. Command builder objects do that for you. A command builder object—for example, the *SqlCommandBuilder* class—cannot be used in all cases. The automatic generation of commands can take place only under certain circumstances. In particular, command builders do not generate anything if the table is obtained by joining columns from more than one table and if calculated—or aggregate—columns are detected. Command builders are extremely helpful and code-saving only when they are called to deal with single-table updates. How can a command builder generate update statements for a generic table? This is where a fourth command property—the *SelectCommand* property—fits in.

A command builder employs *SelectCommand* to obtain all the metadata necessary to build the update commands. To use command builders, you must set *SelectCommand* with a query string that contains a primary key and a few column names. Only those fields will be used for the update, and the insertion and key fields will be used to uniquely identify rows to update or delete. Note that the command text of *SelectCommand* runs in the provider-specific way that makes it return only metadata and no rows.

The association between the data adapter and the command builder is established through the builder's constructor, as shown in the following code:

```
SqlCommand cmd = new SqlCommand();
cmd.CommandText = "SELECT employeeid, lastname FROM Employees";
cmd.Connection = conn;
```

```
adapter.SelectCommand = cmd;
SqlCommandBuilder builder = new SqlCommandBuilder(adapter);
```

The builder requests metadata and generates the commands the first time they are required and then caches them. Each command is exposed through a particular method—*GetInsertCommand*, *GetUpdateCommand*, and *GetDeleteCommand*. Note that using the command builder *does not* automatically set the corresponding command properties on the data adapter.

> **Note**   The behavior of data adapters and command builders for other managed providers does not differ in a relevant way from what we described here for the SQL Server .NET data provider.

In-Memory Data Container Objects

The *System.Data* namespace contains several collection-like objects that, combined, provide an in-memory representation of the DBMS relational programming model. The *DataSet* class looks like a catalog, whereas the *DataTable* maps to an individual table. The *DataRelation* class represents a relationship between tables, and the *DataView* creates a filtered view of a table's data. In addition, the *System.Data* namespace also supports constraints and a relatively simple model of indexing.

The facilities of the memory-resident database model feature a programming model in which disconnection is a key feature rather than a precise requirement. Using the *DataSet* model, for example, you can filter and sort the data on the client before it gets to the middle tier. Having such facilities available within the *DataSet* means that once the data is there, you don't need to go back to the database to get a different view on the data. The data stored in the *DataSet* is self-sufficient, which makes the whole model inherently disconnected.

> **Note**   An interesting use of the *DataSet* that makes sense both for Web and desktop scenarios is in moving data around between components and tiers. The *DataSet* is great at encapsulating tables of data and relationships. It can also be passed around between tiers as a monolithic object. Finally, it can be serialized, meaning that data and related schema can be moved between tiers in a loosely coupled manner.

The *DataSet* class is the principal component in the ADO.NET object model, but several others are satellite classes that play a fundamental role. ADO.NET container classes are listed Table 8-7.

Table 8-7   ADO.NET Container Classes

Class	Description
DataSet	An in-memory cache of data made of tables, relations, and constraints. Serializable and remotable, it can be filled from a variety of data sources and works regardless of which one is used.
DataTable	Represents a relational table of data with a collection of columns and rows.
DataColumn	Represents a column in a DataTable object.
DataRow	Represents a row in a DataTable object.
DataView	Defined on top of a particular table, it creates a filtered view of data. Can be configured to support editing and sorting. The data view is not a copy of the data—just a mask.
DataRelation	Represents a relationship between two tables in the same DataSet. The relationship is set on a common column.

A key point to remember about ADO.NET container classes is that they work regardless of the data source used. You can populate the tables in a *DataSet* using the results of a SQL Server query as well as file system information or data read out of a real-time device. Even more important, none of the ADO.NET container classes retains information about the source. Like array or collection objects, they just contain data. Unlike array or collection objects, though, they provide facilities to relate and manage data in a database-like fashion.

The *DataSet* Object

The *DataSet* class implements three important interfaces—*IListSource* makes it possible to return a data-bound list of elements, *ISerializable* makes the class capable of controlling how its data is serialized to a .NET formatter, and *IXmlSerializable* guarantees the class can serialize itself to XML. Table 8-8 lists the properties of the *DataSet* class.

Table 8-8   Properties of the *DataSet* Class

Property	Description
CaseSensitive	Gets or sets a value that indicates whether string comparisons within DataTable objects are case-sensitive.
DataSetName	Gets or sets the name of the DataSet.
DefaultViewManager	Gets the default view manager object—an instance of the DefaultViewManager class—that contains settings for each table in the DataSet.
EnforceConstraints	Gets or sets a value that indicates whether constraint rules are enforced when attempting any update operation.
ExtendedProperties	Gets the collection of customized user information associated with the DataSet.
HasErrors	Gets whether there are errors in any of the child DataTable objects.
Locale	Gets or sets the locale information used to compare strings within the tables.

Table 8-8   Properties of the *DataSet* Class

Property	Description
Namespace	Gets or sets the namespace of the *DataSet*.
Prefix	Gets or sets the prefix that aliases the namespace of the *DataSet*.
Relations	Gets the collection of the relations set between pairs of child tables.
RemotingFormat	Indicates the desired serialization format—binary or XML. *Not supported in ADO.NET 1.x.*
SchemaSerialization-Mode	Indicates whether schema should be included in the serialized data. *Not supported in ADO.NET 1.x.*
Tables	Gets the collection of contained tables.

The *Namespace* and *Prefix* properties affect the way in which the *DataSet* serializes itself to XML. The name of the *DataSet* is also used to set the root node of the XML representation. If the *DataSetName* is empty, the *NewDataSet* string is used. The methods of the class are listed in Table 8-9.

Table 8-9   Methods of the *DataSet* Class

Method	Description
AcceptChanges	Commits all the changes made to all the tables in the *DataSet* since it was loaded or since the last time the method was called.
Clear	Removes all rows in all tables.
Clone	Copies the structure of the *DataSet*, including all table schemas, relations, and constraints. No data is copied.
Copy	Makes a deep copy of the object, including schema and data.
CreateDataReader	Returns a *DataTable*-specific data reader object with one result set per table, in the same sequence as they appear in the *Tables* collection. *Not supported in ADO.NET 1.x.*
GetChanges	Returns a copy of the *DataSet* containing only the changes made to it since it was last loaded or since *AcceptChanges* was called.
GetXml	Returns the XML representation of the data stored.
GetXmlSchema	Returns the XSD schema for the XML string representing the data stored in the *DataSet*.
HasChanges	Indicates whether there are new, deleted, or modified rows in any of the contained tables.
InferXmlSchema	Replicates into the *DataSet* the table structure inferred from the specified XML document.
Merge	Merges the specified ADO.NET object (*DataSet*, *DataTable*, or an array of *DataRow* objects) into the current *DataSet*.
ReadXml	Populates the *DataSet* by reading schema and data from the specified XML document.
ReadXmlSchema	Replicates into the *DataSet* the table structure read from the specified XML schema.

Table 8-9   **Methods of the *DataSet* Class**

Method	Description
RejectChanges	Rolls back all the changes made to all the tables since it was created or since the last time *AcceptChanges* was called.
Reset	Empties tables, relations, and constraints, resetting the *DataSet* to its default state.
WriteXml	Serializes the *DataSet* contents to XML.
WriteXmlSchema	Writes the *DataSet* structure as an XML schema.

To make a full, deep copy of the *DataSet*, you must resort to the *Copy* method—except that in this case you duplicate the object. The following code does not duplicate the object:

```
DataSet tmp = ds;
```

If you simply assign the current *DataSet* reference to another variable, you duplicate the reference but not the object. Use the following code to duplicate the object:

```
DataSet tmp = ds.Copy();
```

The *Copy* method creates and returns a new instance of the *DataSet* object and ensures that all the tables, relations, and constraints are duplicated. The *Clone* method is limited to returning a new *DataSet* object in which all the properties have been replicated but no data in the tables is copied.

Reading Stored Data

DataSets and data readers are often presented as mutually exclusive and alternative ways to read data in ADO.NET applications. At its core, there's just one physical way of reading data in ADO.NET—using data readers. *DataSets* are disconnected containers automatically filled using a reader, and they are ideal for caching data. Data readers are ideal tools for consuming data as you walk your way through the result set.

Imagine now that you have access to some previously cached data—say, a *DataSet* stored in the session state. How do you find and read a particular record? You typically indicate the coordinates of the record (row and column) and perform a random access to it. If you need to read two or more records, you just repeat the operation. In ADO.NET 2.0, there's a better way—using in-memory, disconnected readers that you create through the *CreateDataReader* method. A reader obtained in this way is different from the connected, cursor-like data reader you get out of the *ExecuteReader* method on the command class. What you get here is a *DataTableReader* object, good at scrolling the contents of an in-memory data table using the same cursor-like programming interface of data readers. Here's an example:

```
DataSet data = new DataSet();
SqlDataAdapter adapter = new SqlDataAdapter(
    "SELECT * FROM employees;SELECT * FROM customers",
    ConfigurationManager.ConnectionStrings["LocalNWind"].ConnectionString);
adapter.Fill(data);
```

```
// Access the whole data set record by record
DataTableReader reader = data.CreateDataReader();
do
{
    while (reader.Read()) {
        // reader[1] indicates the second column
        Response.Write(String.Format("{0} <br>", reader[1]));
    }
    Response.Write("<hr>");
} while (reader.NextResult());

reader.Close();
```

The *do* statement loops through all the result sets and lists the content of the second field for the record. This code is not really different from the code we examined in Chapter 7 for multiple result sets except that all this code runs in-memory without any connection to the database.

What's the purpose of table readers? Your code runs faster when repeated reads of many consecutive records should be performed.

Merging *DataSet* Objects

A merge operation is typically accomplished by a client application to update an existing *DataSet* object with the latest changes read from the data source. The *Merge* method should be used to fuse together two *DataSet* objects that have nearly identical schemas. The two schemas, though, are not strictly required to be identical.

The first step in the merge operation compares the schemas of the involved *DataSet* objects to see whether they match. If the *DataSet* to be imported contains new columns or a new table source, what happens depends on the missing schema action specified. By default, any missing schema element is added to the target *DataSet*, but you can change the behavior by choosing the *Merge* overload that allows for a *MissingSchemaAction* parameter.

At the second step, the *Merge* method attempts to merge the data by looking at the changed rows in the *DataSet* to be imported. Any modified or deleted row is matched to the corresponding row in the existing *DataSet* by using the primary key value. Added rows are simply added to the existing *DataSet* and retain their primary key value.

The merge operation is an atomic operation that must guarantee integrity and consistency only at its end. For this reason, constraints are disabled during a merge operation. However, if at the end of the merge the original constraints can't be restored—for example, a unique constraint is violated—an exception is thrown, but no uploaded data gets lost. In this case, the *Merge* method completely disables constraints in the *DataSet*. It sets the *EnforceConstraints* property to *false* and marks all invalid rows in error. To restore constraints, you must first resolve errors.

The *DataSet* Commit Model

When the *DataSet* is first loaded, all the rows in all tables are marked as unchanged. (All rows are marked *Added* if the *AcceptChangesDuringFill* property is *false* on the adapter used to fill the *DataSet*.) The state of a table row is stored in a property named *RowState*. Allowable values for the row state are in the *DataRowState* enumeration listed in Table 8-10.

Table 8-10   States of a Table Row

Value	Description
Added	The row has been added to the table.
Deleted	The row is marked for deletion from the parent table.
Detached	Either the row has been created but not yet added to the table or the row has been removed from the rows collection.
Modified	Some columns within the row have been changed.
Unchanged	No changes have been made since the last call to *AcceptChanges*. This is also the state of all rows when the table is first created.

Each programmatic operation accomplished on a *DataSet* member changes the state of the involved rows. All changes remain pending in an uncommitted state until a specific call is made to make the changes persistent. The *AcceptChanges* method has the power to commit all the changes and accept the current values as the new original values of the table. After *AcceptChanges* is called, all changes are cleared and rows incorporate the changed values and appear as unchanged. The *RejectChanges* method, on the other hand, rolls back all the pending changes and restores the original values. Note that the *DataSet* retains original values until changes are committed or rejected.

The commit model is applicable at various levels. In particular, by calling *AcceptChanges* or *RejectChanges* on the *DataSet* object, you commit or roll back changes for all the rows in all the contained tables. If you call the same methods on a *DataTable* object, the effect applies to all the rows in the specified table. Finally, you can also accept or reject changes for an individual row in a particular table.

Serializing Contents to XML

The contents of a *DataSet* object can be serialized as XML in two ways, which I'll call *stateless* and *stateful*. Although these expressions are not common throughout the ADO.NET documentation, I feel that they perfectly describe the gist of the two possible approaches. A stateless representation takes a snapshot of the current instance of the data and renders it according to a particular XML schema—the ADO.NET normal form—which is shown in the following code:

```
<MyDataSet>
   <Employees>
      <ID>...</ID>
```

```
            <Name>...</Name>
        </Employees>
        ...
        <Orders>
            <OrderID>...</OrderID>
            <OrderDate>...</OrderDate>
            <Amount>...</Amount>
        </Orders>
    </MyDataSet>
```

The root node appears after the *DataSetName* property. Nodes one level deeper represent rows of all tables and are named as the table. Each row node contains as many children as there are columns in the row. This code snippet refers to a *DataSet* with two tables—Employees and Orders—with two and three columns, respectively. That kind of string is what the *GetXml* method returns and what the *WriteXml* method writes out when the default write mode is chosen:

```
dataSet.WriteXml(fileName);
dataSet.WriteXml(fileName, mode);
```

A stateful representation, on the other hand, contains the history of the data in the object and includes information about changes as well as pending errors. Table 8-11 summarizes the writing options available for use with *WriteXml* through the *WriteXmlMode* enumeration.

Table 8-11   The *WriteXmlMode* Enumeration

Write Mode	Description
IgnoreSchema	Writes the contents of the *DataSet* as XML data without schema.
WriteSchema	Writes the contents of the *DataSet*, including an inline XSD schema. The schema cannot be inserted as XDR, nor can it be added as a reference.
DiffGram	Writes the contents of the *DataSet* as a DiffGram, including original and current values

IgnoreSchema is the default option. The following code demonstrates the typical way to serialize a *DataSet* to an XML file:

```
StreamWriter sw = new StreamWriter(fileName);
dataset.WriteXml(sw);    // defaults to XmlWriteMode.IgnoreSchema
sw.Close();
```

A DiffGram is an XML serialization format that includes both the original values and current values of each row in each table. In particular, a DiffGram contains the current instance of rows with the up-to-date values plus a section where all the original values for changed rows are grouped. Each row is given a unique identifier that is used to track changes between the two sections of the DiffGram. This relationship looks a lot like a foreign-key relationship. The following listing outlines the structure of a DiffGram:

```
<diffgr:diffgram
    xmlns:msdata="urn:schemas-microsoft-com:xml-msdata"
```

```
      xmlns:diffgr="urn:schemas-microsoft-com:xml-diffgram-v1">
      <DataSet>
      ...
      </DataSet>

      <diffgr:before>
      ...
      </diffgr:before>

      <diffgr:errors>
      ...
      </diffgr:errors>
</diffgr:diffgram>
```

The *<diffgr:diffgram>* root node can have up to three children. The first is the *DataSet* object with its current contents, including newly added rows and modified rows (but not deleted rows). The actual name of this subtree depends on the *DataSetName* property of the source *DataSet* object. If the *DataSet* has no name, the subtree's root is *NewDataSet*. The subtree rooted in the *<diffgr:before>* node contains enough information to restore the original state of all modified rows. For example, it still contains any row that has been deleted as well as the original content of any modified row. All columns affected by any change are tracked in the *<diffgr:before>* subtree. The last subtree is *<diffgr:errors>*, and it contains information about any errors that might have occurred on a particular row.

Serialization and Remoting Format

In addition to XML serialization, the *DataSet* class fully supports .NET binary serialization. Marked with the *[Serializable]* attribute, the *DataSet* object implements the *ISerializable* interface and gains full control over the serialization process. Put another way, the *DataSet* itself embeds the code that generates the stream of bytes saved as the serialized version of the object.

In ADO.NET 1.x, the *DataSet* serializes as XML even when binary serialization is requested through a .NET formatter. Worse yet, the *DataSet* uses the fairly verbose DiffGram format, topped with any related schema information. All .NET distributed systems that make intensive use of disconnected data (as Microsoft's architecture patterns and practices suggests) are sensitive to the size of serialized data. The larger the *DataSet*, the more these systems suffer from consumption of CPU, memory, and bandwidth. Nicely enough, ADO.NET 2.0 provides a great fix for this limitation through the *RemotingFormat* property.

The property accepts values from the *SerializationFormat* enum type: *Xml* (the default) or *Binary*. When a *DataSet* instance is being serialized through a .NET formatter (say, in a .NET Remoting scenario), it looks at the value of the *RemotingFormat* property and decides about the persistence format. Needless to say, if you set *RemotingFormat* to *Binary* you get a much more compact output:

```
DataSet ds = GetData();
ds.RemotingFormat = SerializationFormat.Binary;
```

```
StreamWriter writer = new StreamWriter(BinFile);
BinaryFormatter bin = new BinaryFormatter();
bin.Serialize(writer.BaseStream, ds);
writer.Close();
```

The preceding code shows how to serialize to disk a *DataSet* in a truly binary format. If you omit the statement that sets the remoting format, you obtain the same behavior as in ADO.NET 1.x. If you're passing a *DataSet* through a .NET Remoting channel, the only thing you have to do is set the *RemotingFormat* property.

The *DataTable* Object

The *DataTable* object represents one table of in-memory data. Mostly used as a container of data within a *DataSet*, the *DataTable* object is also valid as a standalone object that contains tabular data. The *DataTable* and *DataSet* are the only ADO.NET objects that can be remoted and serialized. Just as with a *DataSet*, a *DataTable* can be created programmatically. In this case, you first define its schema and then add new rows. The following code snippet shows how to create a new table within a *DataSet*:

```
DataSet ds = new DataSet();
DataTable tableEmp = new DataTable("Employees");
tableEmp.Columns.Add("ID", typeof(int));
tableEmp.Columns.Add("Name", typeof(string));
ds.Tables.Add(tableEmp);
```

The table is named Employees and features two columns—ID and Name. The table is empty because no rows have been added yet. To add rows, you first create a new row object by using the *NewRow* method:

```
DataRow row = tableEmp.NewRow();
row["ID"] = 1;
row["Name"] = "Joe Users";
tableEmp.Rows.Add(row);
```

The *DataTable* contains a collection of constraint objects that can be used to ensure the integrity of the data and signals changes to its data-firing events. Let's have a closer look at the programming interface of the *DataTable*, beginning with properties. Table 8-12 lists the properties of the *DataTable* class.

Table 8-12   Properties of the *DataTable* Class

Property	Description
CaseSensitive	Gets or sets whether string comparisons are case-sensitive.
ChildRelations	Gets the collection of child relations for this table.
Columns	Gets the collection of columns that belong to this table.
Constraints	Gets the collection of constraints maintained by this table.
DataSet	Gets the *DataSet* this table belongs to.

Table 8-12   Properties of the *DataTable* Class

Property	Description
DefaultView	Gets the default *DataView* object for this table.
DisplayExpression	Gets or sets a display string for the table. Used in the *ToString* method together with *TableName*.
ExtendedProperties	Gets the collection of customized user information.
HasErrors	Gets a value that indicates whether there are errors in any of the rows.
Locale	Gets or sets locale information used to compare strings.
MinimumCapacity	Gets or sets the initial starting size for the table.
Namespace	Gets or sets the namespace for the XML representation of the table.
ParentRelations	Gets the collection of parent relations for this table.
Prefix	Gets or sets the prefix that aliases the table namespace.
PrimaryKey	Gets or sets an array of columns that function as the primary key for the table.
RemotingFormat	Indicates the desired serialization format— binary or XML. *Not supported in ADO.NET 1.x.*
Rows	Gets the collection of rows that belong to this table.
TableName	Gets or sets the name of the *DataTable* object.

Shared by several ADO.NET objects, the *ExtendedProperties* collection manages name/value pairs and accepts values of type *object*. You can use this collection as a generic cargo variable in which to store any user information. The methods of the *DataTable* class are listed in Table 8-13.

Table 8-13   Methods of the *DataTable* Class

Method	Description
AcceptChanges	Commits all the pending changes made to the table.
BeginInit	Begins the initialization of the table. Used when the table is used on a form or by another component.
BeginLoadData	Turns off notifications, index maintenance, and constraints while loading data.
Clear	Removes all the data from the table.
Clone	Clones the structure of the table. Copies constraints and schema, but doesn't copy data.
Compute	Computes the given expression on the rows that meet the specified filter criteria. Returns the result of the computation as an object.
Copy	Copies both the structure and data for the table.
CreateDataReader	Returns a *DataTableReader* object for the current table. *Not supported in ADO.NET 1.x.*
EndInit	Ends the initialization of the table. Closes the operation started with *BeginInit*.
EndLoadData	Turns on notifications, index maintenance, and constraints after loading data.

Table 8-13   Methods of the *DataTable* Class

Method	Description
GetChanges	Gets a copy of the table containing all changes made to it since it was last loaded or since *AcceptChanges* was called.
GetErrors	Gets an array of all the *DataRow* objects that contain errors.
ImportRow	Performs a deep copy of a *DataRow*, and loads it into the table. Settings, including original and current values, are preserved.
LoadDataRow	Finds and updates a specific row. If no matching row is found, a new row is created using the given values. Uses the primary keys to locate the row.
NewRow	Creates a new *DataRow* object with the schema as the table.
ReadXml	Populates the *DataTable* reading schema and data from the specified XML document. *Not supported in ADO.NET 1.x.*
ReadXmlSchema	Replicates into the *DataTable* the table structure read from the specified XML schema. *Not supported in ADO.NET 1.x.*
RejectChanges	Rolls back all changes that have been made to the table since it was loaded or since the last time *AcceptChanges* was called.
Reset	Resets the *DataTable* object to its default state.
Select	Gets the array of *DataRow* objects that match the criteria.
WriteXml	Serializes the *DataTable* contents to XML. *Not supported in ADO.NET 1.x.*
WriteXmlSchema	Writes the *DataTable* structure as an XML schema. *Not supported in ADO.NET 1.x.*

In ADO.NET 2.0, the *DataTable* implements the *IXmlSerializable* interface and provides public methods to load and save its contents from and to XML streams. The implementation of the interface is also the key that now allows *DataTable* to be used as parameters and return values from .NET Web service methods.

Any row in the *DataTable* is represented by a *DataRow* object, whereas the *DataColumn* object represents a column. The *Select* method implements a simple but effective query engine for the rows of the table. The result set is an array of *DataRow* objects. The filter string is expressed in an internal language that looks like that used to build WHERE clauses in a SQL SELECT statement. The following line of code is a valid expression that selects all records in which the ID is greater than 5 and the name begins with A:

```
tableEmp.Select("ID >5 AND Name LIKE 'A%'");
```

Refer to the .NET Framework documentation for the full syntax supported by the *Select* method. Note that it is the same language you can use to define expression-based *DataTable* columns.

Performing Computations

The *Compute* method of the *DataTable* class calculates a value by applying a given expression to the table rows that match a specified filter. Expressions can include any sort of Boolean and arithmetic operators, but they can also include more interesting aggregate functions such as *Min*, *Max*, *Count*, and *Sum*, plus a few more statistical operators such as average, standard deviation, and variance. The following code counts the rows in which the Name column begins with A:

```
int numRecs = (int) tableEmp.Compute("Count(ID)", " Name LIKE 'A%'");
```

The *Compute* method has two possible overloads—one that takes only the expression to compute and one that also adds a filter string, as shown in the preceding code. Note that all aggregate functions can operate on a single column. This means you can directly compute the sum on two columns, as in the following pseudocode:

```
Sum(quantity * price)
```

To compute functions on multiple columns, you can leverage the capabilities of the *Data-Column* object and, in particular, its support for dynamic expressions. For example, you can define an in-memory column named *order_item_price* as follows:

```
tableEmp.Columns.Add("order_item_price", typeof(double), "quantity*price");
```

At this point, you can compute the sum of that column using the following expression:

```
Sum(order_item_price)
```

Columns of a Table

A *DataColumn* object represents the schema of a column in a *DataTable* object. It provides properties that describe the characteristics and capabilities of the column. The *DataColumn* properties include *AllowDBNull*, *Unique*, *ReadOnly*, *DefaultValue*, and *Expression*. As discussed earlier, some of these properties are automatically set with the corresponding information read from the data source—at least when the data source is a database.

A *DataColumn* object has a name and type; sometimes it can also have an associated expression. The content of an expression-based column is a function of one or more columns combined with operators and aggregates to form a full expression. When an expression-based column is created, ADO.NET precalculates and caches all the values for the column as if they were native data. At the same time, ADO.NET tracks the columns involved and monitors them for changes. It does so by registering an internal handler for the *DataTable*'s *RowChanged* event. When a row changes in one of the columns involved in the expression, the computed column is automatically refreshed.

Expression-based columns are extremely powerful for setting up more effective and practical forms of data binding, as we'll see in the next chapter. In addition, expression-based columns work side by side with table relations and, using both, you can implement really powerful features. We'll demonstrate this later in the "Data Relations" section.

Rows of a Table

The data in a table is represented with a collection of *DataRow* objects. A row has a state, an array of values, and possibly error information. The *DataTable* maintains various versions of the row. You can query for a particular version at any time using the *Item* accessor property. The following code snippet shows how to read the original value of a column in a particular *DataRow* object. By default, you are returned the current value.

```
Response.Write(row["Name", DataRowVersion.Original].ToString());
```

All the values in a row can be accessed either individually or as a whole. When accessing all the values in a row, you use the *ItemArray* property, which passes you an array of objects, one per each column. The *ItemArray* property is a quick way to read values from a row and to set all the columns on a row in a single shot.

The *DataRow* class doesn't have a public constructor. As a result, a data row can be created only implicitly using the *NewRow* method on a base table. The *NewRow* method populates the *DataRow* object with as many entries as there are columns in the *DataTable*. In this case, the table provides the schema for the row, but the row is in no way a child of the table. To add a row to a *DataTable*, you must explicitly add it to the *Rows* collection:

```
tableEmp.Rows.Add(row);
```

Note that a *DataRow* object cannot be associated with more than one table at a time. To load a row into another table, you can use the *ImportRow* method, which basically duplicates the *DataRow* object and loads it into the specified table. A row can be detached from its parent table by using the *Remove* method. If you use the *Delete* method, on the other hand, the row will be marked for deletion but still remain part of the table.

> **Note**   Objects removed from a parent collection are not automatically destroyed or, at least, not until they go out of scope and become fodder for the garbage collector. This consideration holds true for several ADO.NET objects including, but not limited to, the *DataRow*. A *Data-Table*, for example, can be detached from the *DataSet* by simply removing it from the *Tables* collection. However, this doesn't mean that the *DataTable* is automatically deleted as an object.

Table Constraints

A constraint is a logical rule set on a table to preserve the integrity of the data. For example, a constraint determines what happens when you delete a record in a table that is related to another one. The .NET Framework supports two types of constraints—*ForeignKeyConstraint* and *UniqueConstraint*.

In particular, the *ForeignKeyConstraint* class sets the rules that govern how the table propagates, updates, and deletes child tables. For example, suppose you have two related tables, one with employees and one with orders. What happens when an employee is deleted?

Should you delete all the related records, too? The *ForeignKeyConstraint* object associated with the Employees table will determine what is related to it in the Orders table. You create a *ForeignKeyConstraint* object as shown here:

```
DataColumn c1 = tableEmp.Columns("empID");
DataColumn c2 = tableOrd.Columns("empID");
ForeignKeyConstraint fk = new ForeignKeyConstraint("EmpOrders", c1, c2);

// Run some code to configure the constraint object
...

tableOrd.Constraints.Add(fk);
```

The *ForeignKeyConstraint* constructor takes the name of the object plus two *DataColumn* objects. The first *DataColumn* object represents the column (or columns) on the parent table; the second *DataColumn* object represents the column (or columns) in the child table. The constraint is added to the child table and is configured using the *UpdateRule*, *DeleteRule*, and *AcceptRejectRule* properties. While setting the *UpdateRule* and *DeleteRule* properties, you use values taken from the *Rule* enumeration. The *AcceptRejectRule* is the enumeration used to look for the property with the same name. For updates and deletions, the child table can cascade the change or set the involved rows to null or default values. Alternately, the child table can simply ignore the changes. The *AcceptRejectRule* property is processed when the *AcceptChanges* method is called on the parent row to commit changes. The choices for the constraint are limited to either cascading or ignoring changes.

The *UniqueConstraint* class ensures that a single column (or an array of columns) have unique, nonduplicated values. There are several ways to set a unique constraint. You can create one explicitly using the class constructor and adding the resulting object to the *Constraints* collection of the *DataTable*:

```
UniqueConstraint uc;
uc = new UniqueConstraint(tableEmp.Columns("empID"));
tableEmp.Constraints.Add(uc);
```

A unique constraint can also be created implicitly by setting the *Unique* property of the column to *true*. In contrast, setting the *Unique* property to *false* resets the constraint. In addition, adding a column to the in-memory primary key for a table would automatically create a unique constraint for the column. Note that a primary key on a *DataTable* object is an array of *DataColumn* objects that is used to index and sort the rows. The *Select* method on the *DataTable* benefits from the index as much as other methods on the *DataView* class do.

> **Note**   When you define a *DataColumn* as the primary key for a *DataTable* object, the table automatically sets the *AllowDBNull* property of the column to *false* and the *Unique* property to *true*. If the primary key is made of multiple columns, only the *AllowDBNull* property is automatically set to *false*.

Data Relations

A data relation represents a parent/child relationship between two *DataTable* objects in the same *DataSet*. In the .NET Framework, a data relation is represented by a *DataRelation* object. You set a relation between two tables based on matching columns in the parent and child tables. The matching columns in the two related tables can have different names, but they must have the same type. All the relations for the tables in a *DataSet* are stored in the *Relations* collection. Table 8-14 lists the properties of the *DataRelation* class.

Table 8-14   Properties of the *DataRelation* Class

Property	Description
ChildColumns	Gets the child *DataColumn* objects for the relation.
ChildKeyConstraint	Gets the *ForeignKeyConstraint* object for the relation.
ChildTable	Gets the child *DataTable* object for the relation.
DataSet	Gets the *DataSet* to which the relation belongs.
ExtendedProperties	Gets the collection that stores user information.
Nested	Gets or sets a value that indicates whether the relation should render its data as nested subtrees when the *DataSet* is rendered to XML (more on this later in the "Serializing a Data Relation" section).
ParentColumns	Gets the parent *DataColumn* objects for the relation.
ParentKeyConstraint	Gets the *UniqueConstraint* object that ensures unique values on the parent column of the relation.
ParentTable	Gets the parent *DataTable* object for the relation.
RelationName	Gets or sets the name of the *DataRelation* object. The name is used to identify the relation in the *Relations* collection of the parent *DataSet* object.

When a *DataRelation* is created, two constraints are silently created. A foreign-key constraint is set on the child table using the two columns that form the relation as arguments. In addition, the parent table is given a unique constraint that prevents it from containing duplicates. The constraints are created by default, but by using a different constructor you can instruct the *DataRelation* to skip that step. The *DataRelation* class has no significant methods.

Creating a Data Relation

The *DataRelation* class can be seen as the memory counterpart of a database table relationship. However, when a *DataSet* is loaded from a database, DBMS-specific relationships are not processed and loaded. As a result, data relations are exclusively in-memory objects that must be created explicitly with code. The following snippet shows how:

```
DataColumn c1 = tableEmp.Columns("empID");
DataColumn c2 = tableOrd.Columns("empID");
DataRelation rel = new DataRelation("Emp2Orders", c1, c2);
DataSet.Relations.Add(rel);
```

Given two tables, Employees and Orders, the preceding code sets up a relationship between the two based on the values of the common column empID. What are the practical advantages of such a relation? After the relation is set, the parent *DataTable* knows that each row might be bound to a bunch of child related rows. In particular, each employee in the Employees table has an array of related rows in the Orders table. The child rows are exactly those where the value of the Orders.empID column matches the empID column on the current Employees row.

ADO.NET provides an automatic mechanism to facilitate the retrieval of these related rows. The method is *GetChildRows* and is exposed by the *DataRow* class. *GetChildRows* takes a relation and returns an array filled with all the *DataRow* objects that match:

```
foreach(DataRow childRow in parentRow.GetChildRows("Emp2Orders"))
{
    // Process the child row[s]
}
```

Another important facility ADO.NET provides for data relations has to do with table calculations and expression-based columns.

Performing Calculations on Relations

A common task in many real-world applications entails that you manage two related tables and, given a parent row, process the subset of child records. In many situations, processing the child rows just means performing some aggregate computations on them. This is just one of the facilities that ADO.NET and relations provide for free. Let's suppose that, given the previous employees-to-orders relation, you need to compute the total of orders issued by a given employee. You could simply add a dynamically computed column to the parent table and bind it to the data in the relation:

```
tableEmp.Columns.Add("Total", typeof(int),
    "Sum(child(Emp2Orders).Amount)");
```

The new column Total contains, per each employee, a value that represents the sum of all the values in the Amount column for the child rows of the relation. In other words, now you have a column that automatically computes the total of orders issued by each employee. The keyword *child* is a special syntax element of the language that ADO.NET expressions support. Basically, the *child* keyword takes a relation name and returns an array of *DataRow* objects that is the child of that relation.

Serializing a Data Relation

The *Nested* property on the *DataRelation* object affects the way in which the parent *DataSet* is rendered to XML. By default, the presence of a relation doesn't change the XML schema used to serialize a *DataSet*. All the tables are therefore rendered sequentially under the root node. A nested relation changes this default schema. In particular, a nested relation is rendered hierarchically with child rows nested under the parent row.

A *DataSet* with Employees and Orders tables is rendered according to the following pattern:

```
<MyDataSet>
    <Employees empid="1" name="Joe Users" />
    ...
    <Orders empid="1" amount="6897" … />
    <Orders empid="1" amount="19713" … />
    ...
</MyDataSet>
```

If a relation exists between the tables and is set as nested, the XML schema changes as follows:

```
<MyDataSet>
    <Employees empid="1" name="Joe Users">
        <Orders empid="1" amount="6897" … />
        <Orders empid="1" amount="19713" … />
    </Employees>
    ...
</MyDataSet>
```

The child rows are taken out of their natural place and placed within the subtree that represents the parent row.

The *DataView* Object

The *DataView* class represents a customized view of a *DataTable*. The relationship between *DataTable* and *DataView* objects is governed by the rules of a well-known design pattern: the document/view model. The *DataTable* object acts as the document, whereas the *DataView* behaves as the view. At any moment, you can have multiple, different views of the same underlying data. More important, you can manage each view as an independent object with its own set of properties, methods, and events.

The view is implemented by maintaining a separate array with the indexes of the original rows that match the criteria set on the view. By default, the table view is unfiltered and contains all the records included in the table. By using the *RowFilter* and *RowStateFilter* properties, you can narrow the set of rows that fit into a particular view. Using the *Sort* property, you can apply a sort expression to the rows in the view. Table 8-15 lists the properties of the *DataView* class.

Table 8-15 Properties of the *DataView* Class

Property	Description
AllowDelete	Gets or sets a value that indicates whether deletes are allowed in the view.
AllowEdit	Gets or sets a value that indicates whether edits are allowed in the view.
AllowNew	Gets or sets a value that indicates whether new rows can be added through the view.
ApplyDefaultSort	Gets or sets a value that indicates whether to use the default sort.
Count	Gets the number of rows in the view after the filter has been applied.
DataViewManager	Gets the *DataViewManager* object associated with this view.

Table 8-15   Properties of the *DataView* Class

Property	Description
Item	An indexer property. Gets a row of data from the underlying table.
RowFilter	Gets or sets the expression used to filter out rows in the view.
RowStateFilter	Gets or sets the row state filter used in the view.
Sort	Gets or sets the sorting of the view in terms of columns and order.
Table	Gets or sets the source *DataTable* for the view.

The filter can be an expression, the state of the rows, or both. The *RowStateFilter* property, in particular, takes its acceptable values from the *DataViewRowState* enumeration and allows you to filter based on the original or current values of the row, or on modified, added, or deleted rows. The *RowFilter* property supports the same syntax as the *DataTable's Select* method.

A *DataView* does not contain copies of the table's rows. It is limited to storing an array of indexes that is updated whenever any of the filter properties is set. The *DataView* object is already connected to the underlying *DataTable*, of which it represents a possibly filtered and/ or sorted view. The *AllowXXX* properties only let you control whether the view is editable. By default, the view is fully editable. Table 8-16 lists the methods of the *DataView* class.

Table 8-16   Methods of the *DataView* Class

Method	Description
AddNew	Adds a new row to the view and the underlying table.
BeginInit	Begins the initialization of the view.
CopyTo	Copies items from the view into an array.
Delete	Deletes the row at the specified index in the view. The row is deleted from the table, too.
EndInit	Ends the initialization of the view.
Find	Finds a row in the view by the specified key value.
FindRows	Returns an array of row objects that match the specified key value.
GetEnumerator	Returns an enumerator object for the *DataView*.

Both the *AddNew* and *Delete* methods affect the underlying *DataTable* object. Multiple changes can be grouped using the pair *BeginInit*/*EndInit*.

Navigating the View

The contents of a *DataView* object can be scrolled through a variety of programming interfaces, including collections, lists, and enumerators. The *GetEnumerator* method, in particular, ensures that you can walk your way through the records in the view by using the familiar *for...each* statement. The following code shows how to access all the rows that fit into the view:

```
DataView myView = new DataView(table);
foreach(DataRowView rowview in myView)
{
```

```
    // dereferences the DataRow object
    DataRow row = rowview.Row;
    ...
}
```

When client applications access a particular row in the view, the *DataView* class expects to find it in an internal cache of rows. If the cache is not empty, the specified row is returned to the caller via an intermediate *DataRowView* object. The *DataRowView* object is a kind of wrapper for the *DataRow* object that contains the actual data. You access row data through the *Row* property. If the row cache is empty, the *DataView* class fills it up with an array of *DataRowView* objects, each of which references an original *DataRow* object. The row cache is refreshed whenever the sort expression or the filter string is updated. The row cache can be empty either because it's never been used or because the sort expression or the filter string has been changed in the meantime. Figure 8-5 illustrates the internal architecture of a *DataView* object.

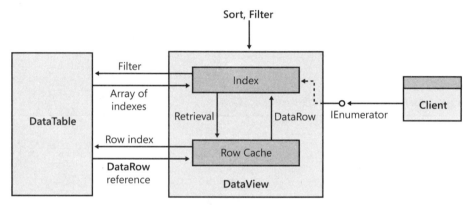

Figure 8-5   The internal structure of a *DataView* object.

Finding Rows

The link between the *DataTable* and the *DataView* is typically established at creation time through the constructor:

```
public DataView(DataTable table);
```

However, you could also create a new view and associate it with a table at a later time using the *DataView*'s *Table* property, as shown here:

```
DataView dv = new DataView();
dv.Table = dataSet.Tables["Employees"];
```

You can also obtain a *DataView* object from any table. In fact, the *DefaultView* property of a *DataTable* object just returns a *DataView* object initialized to work on that table:

```
DataView dv = dt.DefaultView;
```

Originally, the view is unfiltered and the index array contains as many elements as the rows in the table. To quickly find a row, you can use either the *Find* or *FindRows* method. The *Find* method takes one or more values and returns an array with the indexes of the rows that match. The *FindRows* method works in much the same way, but it returns an array of *DataRowView* objects rather than indexes. Both methods accept a sort key value to identify the rows to return.

Note   The contents of a *DataView* can be sorted by multiple fields by using the *Sort* property. You can assign to *Sort* a comma-separated list of column names, and even append them with *DESC* or *ASC* to indicate the direction.

Conclusion

Centered around the disconnected model, ADO.NET incorporates a made-to-measure API to let developers store and consume data through special in-memory containers with two key capabilities. First, they behave like real databases and provide interface and functions similar to those of a server DBMS. Second, they're serializable and implement a commit model for you to handle changes in an extremely flexible way.

Classes such as *DataSet* and *DataTable* are ideal to package data to be moved across the tiers of a distributed system. They offer advanced, database-like features such as referential integrity, optimistic locking, constraints, indexing, and filtering. They lend themselves to operate well in batch update scenarios, where client code connects to a back-end database and submits changes. *DataSet* objects don't know anything about databases and, in general, data providers. They're sort of super-arrays enriched with advanced and database-like features. *DataSet* objects can be filled programmatically with any data that can be represented in a tabular manner. Adapters are special command objects that fill *DataSet* and *DataTable* objects with the results of a query. Likewise, adapters take care of moving the contents of ADO.NET containers back to a connected database table with a compatible layout.

DataSet and *DataTable* are frequently used for binding data to data-bound controls. In the next chapter, we'll address this.

Just the Facts

■ ADO.NET data container classes such as *DataSet* and *DataTable* have no notion of the provider that served them any data. They are serializable, feature-rich classes and offer a bunch of database-like functions, such as referential integrity, optimistic locking, constraints, indexing, and filtering.

■ The data adapter is a command-like object that performs data access, grabs all the data, and packs it into a data container. Like commands and data readers, data adapters are specific to each data provider.

■ The *Fill* method of the data adapter maps the source result sets onto in-memory tables and fills the tables with the data fetched from the physical data source.

■ In ADO.NET 2.0, you can better control the way data is loaded into the various data tables during a fill operation. You can choose, for example, to override current or underlying values.

■ *DataSet* is great at encapsulating tables of data and relationships and moving it between the tiers of an application in a loosely coupled manner.

■ ADO.NET batch update consists of a series of commands that the data adapter submits sequentially to the database. Batch update is triggered by a single instruction but doesn't necessarily equate to a series of queries submitted in a single command.

■ Batch update is particularly effective in environments with a low degree of data contention because it allows for disconnected architectures, higher scalability, and considerably simpler code.

■ In ADO.NET 2.0, *DataSet* can be serialized in a true binary format, which gets you a much more compact output.

■ In ADO.NET 2.0, *DataTable* implements the *IXmlSerializable* interface and provides public methods to load and save its contents from and to XML streams. The implementation of the interface also enables *DataTable* to be used as a parameter and return value from .NET Web service methods.

Chapter 9
The Data-Binding Model

In this chapter:

Data Source–Based Data Binding 354

Data-Binding Expressions. 373

Data Source Components. 382

Conclusion 411

To write effective ASP.NET 1.x data-driven applications, you need a deep understanding of ADO.NET objects. You have to be familiar with connections, commands, transactions, parameters, and all the objects we dealt with in the previous two chapters. In ASP.NET 2.0, the role of ADO.NET object is more blurred because of the introduction of a new family of data-related and more programmer friendly components—the data source objects. In ASP.NET 2.0, you use ADO.NET objects directly much less frequently. You also use them in relatively standard data-driven pages belonging to relatively simple or prototype Web sites. Does this mean that ADO.NET objects have suddenly become unnecessary? Will ASP.NET 2.0 magically let you write data applications without having to really know about databases? Of course not.

Complex and sophisticated enterprise systems typically isolate ADO.NET code in the data tier, and they often have it wrapped up by an additional layer of helper libraries such as the Microsoft Data Access Application Block. Realistic pages belonging to similar systems never call ADO.NET objects directly, like we did in the demonstration pages of the past two chapters. In ASP.NET 2.0, ADO.NET objects are still essential pieces of the .NET Framework, but they have been pushed into the back-end infrastructure of most common data-binding operations. ASP.NET 2.0 offers the possibility of writing data access code that hides many essential steps from view and buries them in the framework's code. Basically, what many ASP.NET 1.x developers called "that boring ADO.NET boilerplate code" is now packed into a bunch of new data source controls.

Overall, the data-binding model of ASP.NET is founded on three pillars: data-binding expressions, classic data source–based binding, and data source controls, which are limited to ASP.NET 2.0. Let's start with data source–based binding, which is probably the most common form.

Data Source–Based Data Binding

Web applications are, for the most part, just data-driven applications. For this reason, the ability to bind HTML elements such as drop-down lists or tables to structured data is a key feature for any development platform. Data binding is the process that retrieves data from a fixed source and dynamically associates this data to properties on server controls. Valid target controls are those that have been specifically designed to support data binding—that is, data-bound controls. Data-bound controls are not another family of controls; they're simply server controls that feature a few well-known data-related properties and feed them using a well-known set of collection objects.

Feasible Data Sources

Many .NET classes can be used as data sources—and not just those that have to do with database content. In ASP.NET, any object that exposes the *IEnumerable* interface is a valid bindable data source. The *IEnumerable* interface defines the minimal API to enumerate the contents of the data source:

```
public interface IEnumerable
{
    IEnumerator GetEnumerator();
}
```

Many bindable objects, though, actually implement more advanced versions of *IEnumerable*, such as *ICollection* and *IList*. In particular, you can bind a Web control to the following classes:

- ADO.NET container classes such as *DataSet*, *DataTable*, and *DataView*
- Data readers
- Custom collections, dictionaries, and arrays

To be honest, I should note that the *DataSet* and *DataTable* classes don't actually implement *IEnumerable* or any other interfaces that inherit from it. However, both classes do store collections of data internally. These collections are accessed using the methods of an intermediate interface—*IListSource*—which performs the trick of making *DataSet* and *DataTable* classes look like they implement a collection.

ADO.NET Classes

As we saw in Chapter 8, ADO.NET provides a bunch of data container classes that can be filled with any sort of data, including results of a database query. These classes represent excellent resources for filling data-bound controls such as lists and grids. If having memory-based classes such as the *DataSet* in the list is no surprise, it's good to find data readers there, too. An open data reader can be passed to the data-binding engine of a control. The control will then walk its way through the reader and populate the user interface while keeping the connection to the database busy.

> **Note**   Data binding works differently for Web pages and Microsoft Windows desktop appli-
> cations. Aside from the internal implementations, both Web and Windows Forms can share the
> same data source objects with the exception of the data reader. You can bind a data reader
> only to ASP.NET controls. Likewise, only Windows Forms controls can be bound to instances of
> the *DataViewManager* class that we briefly mentioned in Chapter 8.

The *DataSet* class can contain more than one table; however, only one table at a time can be
associated with standard ASP.NET data-bound controls. If you bind the control to a *DataSet*,
you need to set an additional property to select a particular table within the *DataSet*. Be aware
that this limitation is not attributable to ASP.NET as a platform; it is a result of the implementation of the various data-bound controls. In fact, you could write a custom control that
accepts a *DataSet* as its sole data-binding parameter.

DataSet and *DataTable* act as data sources through the *IListSource* interface; *DataView* and data
readers, on the other hand, implement *IEnumerable* directly.

Collection-Based Classes

At the highest level of abstraction, a collection serves as a container for instances of other
classes. All collection classes implement the *ICollection* interface, which in turn implements
the *IEnumerable* interface. As a result, all collection classes provide a basic set of functionalities. All collection classes have a *Count* property to return the number of cached items; they
have a *CopyTo* method to copy their items, in their entirety or in part, to an external array; they
have a *GetEnumerator* method that instantiates an enumerator object to loop through the
child items. *GetEnumerator* is the method behind the curtain whenever you call the *foreach*
statement in C# and the *For...Each* statement in Microsoft Visual Basic .NET.

IList and *IDictionary* are two interfaces that extend *ICollection*, giving a more precise character-
ization to the resultant collection class. *ICollection* provides only basic and minimal functionality for a collection. For example, *ICollection* does not have any methods to add or remove
items. Add and remove functions are exactly what the *IList* interface provides. In the *IList*
interface, the *Add* and *Insert* methods place new items at the bottom of the collection or at the
specified index. The *Remove* and *RemoveAt* methods remove items, while *Clear* empties the
collection. Finally, *Contains* verifies whether an item with a given value belongs to the collection, and *IndexOf* returns the index of the specified item. Commonly used container classes
that implement both *ICollection* and *IList* are *Array*, *ArrayList*, and *StringCollection*.

The *IDictionary* interface defines the API that represents a collection of key/value pairs. The
interface exposes methods similar to *IList*, but with different signatures. Dictionary classes
also feature two extra properties: *Keys* and *Values*. They return collections of keys and values,
respectively, found in the dictionary. Typical dictionary classes are *ListDictionary*, *Hashtable*,
and *SortedList*.

You'll likely use custom collection classes in ASP.NET data-binding scenarios more often than you'll use predefined collection classes. The simplest way to code a custom collection in .NET 1.x is to derive a new class from *CollectionBase* and override at least the *Add* method and the *Item* property, as shown in the following code snippet:

```
public class OrderCollection : CollectionBase
{
    public OrderCollection()
    {
    }

    // Add method
    public void Add(OrderInfo o)
    {
        InnerList.Add(o);
    }

    // Indexer ("Item") property
    public OrderInfo this[int index]
    {
        get { return (OrderInfo) InnerList[index]; }
        set { InnerList[index] = value; }
    }
}
public class OrderInfo
{
    private int _id;
    public int ID
    {
        get { return _id; }
        set { _id = value; }
    }
    private DateTime _date;
    public DateTime Date
    {
        get { return _date; }
        set { _date = value; }
    }
    ...
}
```

It is important that the element class—*OrderInfo*, in the preceding code—implements data members as properties, instead of fields, as shown below:

```
public class OrderInfo
{
    public int ID;
    public DateTime Date;
}
```

Data members coded as fields are certainly faster to write, but they are not discovered at run time unless the class provides a custom type descriptor (in other words, it implements the *ICustomTypeDescriptor* interface) that exposes fields as properties.

In ASP.NET 2.0, the advent of generics greatly simplifies the development of custom collections. In some cases, the code to write reduces to the following:

```
public class OrderCollection : List<OrderInfo>
{
}
```

Data-Binding Properties

In ASP.NET, there are two main categories of data-bound controls—list controls and iterative controls. As we'll see in more detail later on, list controls repeat a fixed template for each item found in the data source. Iterative controls are more flexible and let you define the template to repeat explicitly, as well as other templates that directly influence the final layout of the control.

All data-bound controls implement the *DataSource* and *DataSourceID* properties, plus a few more, as detailed in Figure 9-1.

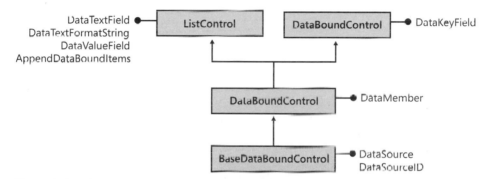

Figure 9-1   Class diagram for data binding in ASP.NET 2.0.

Note that the figure refers to the ASP.NET 2.0 object model. In ASP.NET 1.x, there's no *DataSourceID* property. Likewise, no intermediate classes exist such as *BaseDataBoundControl* and *DataBoundControl*. *ListControl* and *BaseDataList* form the common base for list and iterative controls.

> **Note**   Both in ASP.NET 1.x and ASP.NET 2.0 the *Repeater* control—a low-level iterative control—doesn't inherit from either of the classes in the diagram. It inherits directly from the *Control* class.

The *DataSource* Property

The *DataSource* property lets you specify the data source object the control is linked to. Note that this link is logical and does not result in any overhead or underlying operation until you explicitly order to bind the data to the control. As mentioned, you activate data binding on a control by calling the *DataBind* method. When the method executes, the control actually loads data from the associated data source, evaluates the data-bound properties (if any), and generates the markup to reflect changes:

```
public virtual object DataSource {get; set;}
```

The *DataSource* property is declared of type *object* and can ultimately accept objects that implement either *IEnumerable* (including data readers) or *IListSource*. By the way, only *DataSet* and *DataTable* implement the *IListSource* interface.

The *DataSource* property of a data-bound control is generally set programmatically. However, nothing prevents you from adopting a kind of declarative approach, as follows:

```
<asp:DropDownList runat="server" id="theList"
    DataSource="<%# GetData() %>"
    ...
/>
```

GetData is a public or protected member of the host page class that returns a bindable object.

> **Note**   How can a data-bound control figure out which actual object it is bound to? Will it be a collection, a data reader, or perhaps a *DataTable*? All standard data-bound controls are designed to work only through the *IEnumerable* interface. For this reason, any object bound to *DataSource* is normalized to an object that implements *IEnumerable*. In some cases, the normalization is as easy (and fast) as casting the object to the *IEnumerable* interface. In other cases—specifically, when *DataTable* and *DataSet* are involved—an extra step is performed to locate a particular named collection of data that corresponds to the value assigned to the *DataMember* property. We'll return to this point and discuss some code in my other recent book, *Programming Microsoft ASP.NET 2.0 Applications: Advanced Topics* (Microsoft Press, 2005), while developing custom data-bound controls.

The *DataSourceID* Property

Introduced with ASP.NET 2.0, the *DataSourceID* property gets or sets the ID of the data source component from which the data-bound control retrieves its data. This property is the point of contact between ASP.NET 2.0 data-bound controls and the new family of data source controls that includes *SqlDataSource* and *ObjectDataSource*. (I'll cover these controls in more detail later in the chapter.)

```
public virtual string DataSourceID {get; set;}
```

By setting *DataSourceID*, you tell the control to turn to the associated data source control for any needs regarding data—retrieval, paging, sorting, counting, or updating.

Like *DataSource*, *DataSourceID* is available on all data-bound controls. The two properties are mutually exclusive. If both are set, you get an invalid operation exception at run time. Note, though, that you also get an exception if *DataSourceID* is set to a string that doesn't correspond to an existing data source control.

The *DataMember* Property

The *DataMember* property gets or sets the name of the data collection to extract when data binding to a data source:

```
public virtual string DataMember {get; set;}
```

You use the property to specify the name of the *DataTable* to use when the *DataSource* property is bound to a *DataSet* object:

```
DataSet data = new DataSet();
SqlDataAdapter adapter = new SqlDataAdapter(cmdText, connString);
adapter.Fill(data);

// Table is the default name of the first table in a
// DataSet filled by an adapter
grid.DataMember = "Table";
grid.DataSource = data;
grid.DataBind();
```

DataMember and *DataSource* can be set in any order, provided that both are set before *DataBind* is invoked. *DataMember* has no relevance if you bind to data using *DataSourceID* with standard data source components.

> **Note**   This is not a limitation of the binding technology, but rather a limitation of standard data source components, which don't support multiple views. We'll return to this point later when discussing data source components.

The *DataTextField* Property

Typically used by list controls, the *DataTextField* property specifies which property of a data-bound item should be used to define the display text of the nth element in a list control:

```
public virtual string DataTextField {get; set;}
```

For example, for a drop-down list control the property feeds the displayed text of each item in the list. The following code creates the control shown in Figure 9-2:

```
CountryList.DataSource = data;
CountryList.DataTextField = "country";
CountryList.DataBind();
```

The same happens for *ListBox*, *CheckBoxList*, and other list controls. Unlike *DataMember*, the *DataTextField* property is necessary also in case the binding is operated by data source components.

Figure 9-2   A drop-down list control filled with the country column of a database table.

> **Note**   List controls can automatically format the content of the field bound through the *DataTextField* property. The format expression is indicated via the *DataTextFormatString* property.

The *DataValueField* Property

Similar to *DataTextField*, the *DataValueField* property specifies which property of a data-bound item should be used to identify the nth element in a list control:

```
public virtual string DataValueField {get; set;}
```

To understand the role of this property, consider the markup generated for a drop-down list, set as in the code snippet shown previously:

```
<select name="CountryList" id="CountryList">
    <option selected="selected" value="[All]">[All]</option>
    <option value="Argentina">Argentina</option>
    <option value="Austria">Austria</option>

    ...
</select>
```

The text of each *<option>* tag is determined by the field specified through *DataTextField*; the value of the value attribute is determined by *DataValueField*. Consider the following code filling a *ListBox* with customer names:

```
CustomerList.DataMember = "Table";
CustomerList.DataTextField = "companyname";
CustomerList.DataValueField = "customerid";
CustomerList.DataSource = data;
CustomerList.DataBind();
```

If *DataValueField* is left blank, the value of the *DataTextField* property is used instead. Here's the corresponding markup:

```
<select size="4" name="CustomerList" id="CustomerList">
    <option value="BOTTM">Bottom-Dollar Markets</option>
    <option value="LAUGB">Laughing Bacchus Wine Cellars</option>
    ...
</select>
```

As you can see, the *value* attribute now is set to the customer ID—the unique, invisible value determined by the *customerid* field. The content of the *value* attribute for the currently selected item is returned by the *SelectedValue* property of the list control. If you want to access programmatically the displayed text of the current selection, use the *SelectedItem.Text* expression.

The *AppendDataBoundItems* Property

Introduced in ASP.NET 2.0, *AppendDataBoundItems* is a Boolean property that indicates whether the data-bound items should be appended to or whether they should overwrite the existing contents of the control. By default, *AppendDataBoundItems* is set to *false*, meaning that data-bound contents replace any existing contents. This behavior is the same as you have in ASP.NET 1.x, where this property doesn't exist:

```
public virtual bool AppendDataBoundItems {get; set;}
```

AppendDataBoundItems is useful when you need to combine constant items with data-bound items. For example, imagine you need to fill a drop-down list with all the distinct countries in which you have a customer. The user will select a country and see the list of customers who live there. To let users see all the customers in any country, you add an unbound element, such as [All]:

```
<asp:DropDownList runat="server" ID="CountryList"
    AppendDataBoundItems="true">
    <asp:ListItem Text="[All]" />
</asp:DropDownList>
```

With *AppendDataBoundItems* set to *false* (which is the default behavior in ASP.NET 1.x), the [All] item will be cleared before data-bound items are added. In ASP.NET 1.x, you need to add it programmatically after the binding operation completes.

The *DataKeyField* Property

The *DataKeyField* property gets or sets the key field in the specified data source. The property serves the needs of ASP.NET 1.x grid-like controls (*DataList* and *DataGrid*) and lets them (uniquely) identify a particular record. Note that the identification of the record is univocal only if the original data source has a unique-constrained field:

```
public virtual string DataKeyField {get; set;}
```

The *DataKeyField* property is coupled with the *DataKeys* array property. When *DataKeyField* is set, *DataKeys* contains the value of the specified key field for all the control's data items currently displayed in the page. We'll cover this in more detail in the next chapter when we talk about *DataGrid* controls.

The new grid control of ASP.NET (the *GridView* control) extends the *DataKeyField* to an array of strings and renames it *DataKeyNames*. The *DataKeys* property is maintained, though defined differently, as we'll see in the next chapter.

List Controls

List controls display (or at least need to have in memory) many items at the same time—specifically, the contents of the data source. Depending on its expected behavior, the control will pick the needed items from memory and properly format and display them. List controls include *DropDownList*, *CheckBoxList*, *RadioButtonList*, *ListBox*, and, in ASP.NET 2.0, also the *BulletedList* control. All list controls inherit from the base *ListControl* class both in ASP.NET 1.x and 2.0.

The *DropDownList* Control

The *DropDownList* control enables users to select one item from a single-selection drop-down list. You can specify the size of the control by setting its height and width in pixels, but you can't control the number of items displayed when the list drops down. Table 9-1 lists the most commonly used properties of the control.

Table 9-1 Properties of the *DropDownList* Control

Property	Description
AppendDataBoundItems	Indicates whether statically defined items should be maintained or cleared when adding data-bound items. *Not supported in ASP.NET 1.x.*
AutoPostBack	Indicates whether the control should automatically post back to the server when the user changes the selection.
DataMember	The name of the table in the *DataSource* to bind.
DataSource	The data source that populates the items of the list.
DataSourceID	ID of the data source component to provide data. *Not supported in ASP.NET 1.x.*
DataTextField	Name of the data source field to supply the text of list items.
DataTextFormatString	Formatting string used to control list items are displayed.
DataValueField	Name of the data source field to supply the value of a list item.
Items	Gets the collection of items in the list control.
SelectedIndex	Gets or sets the index of the selected item in the list.
SelectedItem	Gets the selected item in the list.
SelectedValue	Gets the value of the selected item in the list.

The programming interface of the *DropDownList* control also features three properties to configure the border of the drop-down list: *BorderColor*, *BorderStyle*, and *BorderWidth*. Although the properties are correctly transformed by style properties, most browsers won't use them to change the appearance of the drop-down list.

The *DataTextField* and *DataValueField* properties don't accept expressions, only plain column names. To combine two or more fields of the data source, you can use a calculated column. You can either use a column computed by the database or exploit the power of the ADO.NET object model and add an in-memory column. The following SQL query returns a column obtained by concatenating *lastname* and *firstname*:

```
SELECT lastname + ', ' + firstname AS 'EmployeeName'
FROM Employees
```

The same result can also be obtained without the involvement of the database. Once you've filled a *DataTable* object with the result of the query, you add a new column to its *Columns* collection. The content of the column is based on an expression. The following code adds an EmployeeName column to the data source that concatenates the last name and first name:

```
dataTable.Columns.Add("EmployeeName",
    typeof(string),
    "lastname + ', ' + firstname");
```

An expression-based column does not need to be filled explicitly. The values for all the cells in the column are calculated and cached when the column is added to the table. The table tracks any dependencies and updates the calculated column whenever any of the constituent columns are updated.

The *CheckBoxList* Control

The *CheckBoxList* control is a single monolithic control that groups a collection of checkable list items, each of which is rendered through an individual *CheckBox* control. The properties of the child check boxes are set by reading the associated data source. You insert a check box list in a page as follows:

```
<asp:CheckBoxList runat="server" id="employeesList">
```

Table 9-2 lists the specific properties of the *CheckBoxList* control.

Table 9-2   Properties of the *CheckBoxList* Control

Property	Description
AppendDataBoundItems	Indicates whether statically defined items should be maintained or cleared when adding data-bound items. *Not supported in ASP.NET 1.x.*
AutoPostBack	Indicates whether the control should automatically post back to the server when the user changes the selection.
CellPadding	Indicates pixels between the border and contents of the cell.

Table 9-2 Properties of the *CheckBoxList* Control

Property	Description
CellSpacing	Indicates pixels between cells.
DataMember	The name of the table in the *DataSource* to bind.
DataSource	The data source that populates the items of the list.
DataSourceID	ID of the data source component to provide data. *Not supported in ASP.NET 1.x.*
DataTextField	Name of the data source field to supply the text of list items.
DataTextFormatString	Formatting string used to control list items are displayed.
DataValueField	Name of the data source field to supply value of a list item.
Items	Gets the collection of items in the list control.
RepeatColumns	Gets or sets the number of columns to display in the control.
RepeatDirection	Gets or sets a value that indicates whether the control displays vertically or horizontally.
RepeatLayout	Gets or sets the layout of the check boxes (table or flow).
SelectedIndex	Gets or sets the index of the first selected item in the list—the one with the lowest index.
SelectedItem	Gets the first selected item.
SelectedValue	Gets the value of the first selected item.
TextAlign	Gets or sets the text alignment for the check boxes.

The *CheckBoxList* control does not supply any properties that know which items have been selected. But this aspect is vital for any Web application that uses checkable elements. The *CheckBoxList* control can have any number of items selected, but how can you retrieve them?

Any list control has an *Items* property that contains the collection of the child items. The *Items* property is implemented through the *ListItemCollection* class and makes each contained item accessible via a *ListItem* object. The following code loops through the items stored in a *CheckBoxList* control and checks the *Selected* property of each of them:

```
foreach(ListItem item in chkList.Items)
{
    if (item.Selected) {
        // this item is selected
    }
}
```

Figure 9-3 shows a sample page that lets you select some country names and composes an ad hoc query to list all the customers from those countries.

Note that the *SelectedXXX* properties work in a slightly different manner for a *CheckBoxList* control. The *SelectedIndex* property indicates the lowest index of a selected item. By setting *SelectedIndex* to a given value, you state that no items with a lower index should be selected any longer. As a result, the control automatically deselects all items with an index lower than the new value of *SelectedIndex*. Likewise, *SelectedItem* returns the first selected item, and *SelectedValue* returns the value of the first selected item.

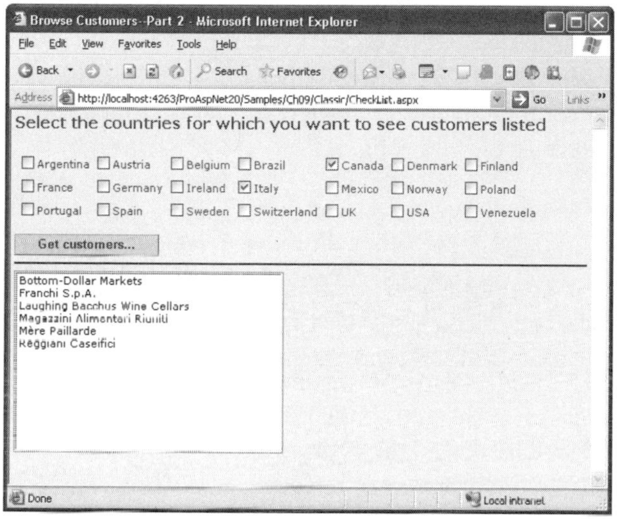

Figure 9-3   A horizontally laid out *CheckBoxList* control in action.

The *RadioButtonList* Control

The *RadioButtonList* control acts as the parent control for a collection of radio buttons. Each of the child items is rendered through a *RadioButton* control. By design, a *RadioButtonList* control can have zero or one item selected. The *SelectedItem* property returns the selected element as a *ListItem* object. Note, though, that there is nothing to guarantee that only one item is selected at any time. For this reason, be extremely careful when you access the *SelectedItem* of a *RadioButtonList* control—it could be null:

```
if (radioButtons.SelectedValue != null)
{
    // Process the selection here
    ...
}
```

The *RadioButtonList* control supports the same set of properties as the *CheckBoxList* control and, just like it, accepts some layout directives. In particular, you can control the rendering process of the list with the *RepeatLayout* and *RepeatDirection* properties. By default, the list items are rendered within a table, which ensures the vertical alignment of the companion text. The property that governs the layout is *RepeatLayout*. The alternative is displaying the items as free HTML text, using blanks and breaks to guarantee some sort of minimal structure. *RepeatDirection* is the property that controls the direction in which—with or without a tabular structure—the items flow. Feasible values are *Vertical* (the default) and *Horizontal*. *RepeatColumns* is the property that determines how many columns the list should have. By default, the value is 0, which means all the items will be displayed in a single row, vertical or horizontal, according to the value of *RepeatDirection*.

The *ListBox* Control

The *ListBox* control represents a vertical sequence of items displayed in a scrollable window. The *ListBox* control allows single-item or multiple-item selection and exposes its contents through the usual *Items* collection, as shown in the following code:

```
<asp:listbox runat="server" id="theListBox"
    rows="5" selectionmode="Multiple" />
```

You can decide the height of the control through the *Rows* property. The height is measured in number of rows rather than pixels or percentages. When it comes to data binding, the *ListBox* control behaves like the controls discussed earlier in the chapter.

Two properties make this control slightly different from other list controls—the *Rows* property, which represents the number of visible rows in the control, and the *SelectionMode* property, which determines whether one or multiple items can be selected. The programming interface of the list box also contains the set of *SelectedXXX* properties we considered earlier. In this case, they work as they do for the *CheckBoxList* control—that is, they returns the selected item with the lowest index.

> **Note**   All the list controls examined so far support the *SelectedIndexChanged* event, which is raised when the selection from the list changes and the page posts back to the server. You can use this event to execute server-side code whenever a control is selected or deselected.

The *BulletedList* Control

The *BulletedList* control is a programming interface built around the *<ul>* and *<ol>* HTML tags, with some extra features such as the bullet style, data binding, and support for custom images. The *BulletedList* control is not supported in ASP.NET 1.x. The following example uses a custom bullet object:

```
<asp:bulletedlist runat="server" bulletstyle="Square">
    <asp:listitem>One</asp:listitem>
    <asp:listitem>Two</asp:listitem>
    <asp:listitem>Three</asp:listitem>
</asp:bulletedlist>
```

The bullet style lets you choose the style of the element that precedes the item. You can use numbers, squares, circles, and uppercase and lowercase letters. The child items can be rendered as plain text, hyperlinks, or buttons. Table 9-3 details the main properties of a *BulletedList* control.

Table 9-3   Properties of the *BulletedList* Control

Property	Description
AppendDataBoundItems	Indicates whether statically defined items should be maintained or cleared when adding data-bound items
BulletImageUrl	Gets or sets the path to the image to use as the bullet
BulletStyle	Determines the style of the bullet
DataMember	The name of the table in the *DataSource* to bind
DataSource	The data source that populates the items of the list
DataSourceID	ID of the data source component to provide data
DataTextField	Name of the data source field to supply text of list items
DataTextFormatString	Formatting string used to control list items are displayed
DataValueField	Name of the data source field to supply value of a list item
DisplayMode	Determines how to display the items: plain text, link buttons, or hyperlinks
FirstBulletNumber	Gets or sets the value that starts the numbering
Items	Gets the collection of items in the list control
Target	Indicates the target frame in case of hyperlink mode

The items of a *BulletedList* control supports a variety of graphical styles—disc, circle, and custom image, plus a few numberings including roman numbering. The initial number can be programmatically set through the *FirstBulletNumber* property. The *DisplayMode* property determines how to display the content of each bullet—plain text (the default), link button, or hyperlink. In the case of link buttons, the *Click* event is fired on the server to let you handle the event when the page posts back. In the case of hyperlinks, the browser will display the target page in the specified frame—the *Target* property. The target URL coincides with the contents of the field specified by *DataValueField*.

Figure 9-4 shows a sample page that includes a *RadioButtonList* and a *BulletedList* control. The radio-button list is bound to the contents of a system enumerated type—*BulletStyle*—and displays as selectable radio buttons the various bullet styles. To bind the contents of an enumerated type to a data-bound control, you do as follows:

```
BulletOptions.DataSource = Enum.GetValues(typeof(BulletStyle));
BulletOptions.SelectedIndex = 0;
BulletOptions.DataBind();
```

To retrieve and set the selected value, use the following code:

```
BulletStyle style = (BulletStyle) Enum.Parse(typeof(BulletStyle), BulletOptions.SelectedValue);
BulletedList1.BulletStyle = style;
```

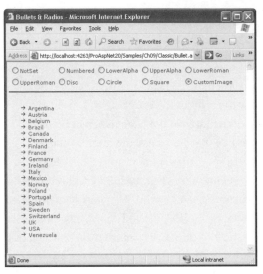

Figure 9-4   A sample page to preview the style of a *BulletedList* control.

Iterative Controls

Iterative controls are a special type of data-bound controls that supply a template-based mechanism to create free-form user interfaces. Iterative controls take a data source, loop through the items, and iteratively apply user-defined HTML templates to each row. This basic behavior is common to all three ASP.NET iterators—*Repeater*, *DataList*, and *DataGrid*. Beyond that, iterative controls differ from each other in terms of layout capabilities and functionality.

Iterative controls differ from list controls because of their greater rendering flexibility. An iterative control lets you apply an ASP.NET template to each row in the bound data source. A list control, on the other hand, provides a fixed and built-in template for each data item. List controls are customizable to some extent, but you can't change anything other than the text displayed. No changes to layout are supported. On the other hand, using a list control is considerably easier than setting up an iterative control, as we'll see in a moment. Defining templates requires quite a bit of declarative code, and if accomplished programmatically, it requires that you write a class that implements the *ITemplate* interface. A list control only requires you to go through a few data-binding properties.

We'll take a look at *DataGrid* controls in Chapter 10 and reserve more space for lower-level iterators such as *Repeater* and *DataList* in my other recent book, *Programming Microsoft ASP.NET 2.0 Applications: Advanced Topics*. When they are properly customized and configured, there's no graphical structure—be it flat or hierarchical—that the *Repeater* and *DataList* controls can't generate. Let's briefly meet each control.

The *Repeater* Control

The *Repeater* control displays data using user-provided layouts. It works by repeating a specified ASP.NET template for each item displayed in the list. The *Repeater* is a rather basic templated data-bound control. It has no built-in layout or styling capabilities. All formatting and layout information must be explicitly declared and coded using HTML tags and ASP.NET classes.

The *Repeater* class acts as a naming container by implementing the marker interface *INamingContainer*. (See Chapter 3.) Table 9-4 lists the main properties exposed by the control, not including those inherited from the base class.

Table 9-4 Properties of the *Repeater* Control

Property	Description
AlternatingItemTemplate	Template to define how every other item is rendered.
DataMember	The name of the table in the *DataSource* to bind.
DataSource	The data source that populates the items of the list.
DataSourceID	ID of the data source component to provide data. *Not supported in ASP.NET 1.x.*
FooterTemplate	Template to define how the footer is rendered.
HeaderTemplate	Template to define how the header is rendered.
Items	Gets a *RepeaterItemCollection* object—that is, a collection of *RepeaterItem* objects. Each element of the collection represents a displayed data row in the *Repeater*.
ItemTemplate	Template to define how items are rendered.
SeparatorTemplate	Template to define how the separator between items is to be rendered.

For the most part, properties are the template elements that form the control's user interface. The *Repeater* populates the *Items* collection by enumerating all the data items in the bound data source. For each data-bound item (for example, a table record), it creates a *RepeaterItem* object and adds it to the *Items* collection. The *RepeaterItemCollection* class is a plain collection class with no special or peculiar behavior. The *RepeaterItem* class represents a displayed element within the overall structure created by the *Repeater*. The *RepeaterItem* contains properties to point to the bound data item (such as a table record), the index, and the type of the item (regular item, alternating item, header, footer, and so on). Here's a quick example of a *Repeater*:

```
<asp:Repeater ID="Repeater1" runat="server">
    <HeaderTemplate>
        <h2>We have customers in the following cities</h2>
        <hr />
    </HeaderTemplate>
    <SeparatorTemplate>
        <hr noshade style="border:dashed 1px blue" />
    </SeparatorTemplate>
    <ItemTemplate>
        <%# Eval("City")%>   <b><%# Eval("Country")%></b>
    </ItemTemplate>
    <FooterTemplate>
        <hr />
```

```
            <%# CalcTotal() %> cities
      </FooterTemplate>
</asp:Repeater>
```

Bound to the output of the following query, the structure produces what is shown in Figure 9-5:

```
SELECT DISTINCT country, city FROM customers WHERE country=@TheCountry
```

The *@TheCountry* parameter is the name of the country picked from the drop-down list:

```
data = new DataTable();
SqlDataAdapter adapter = new SqlDataAdapter(cmdText, connString);
adapter.SelectCommand.Parameters.AddWithValue("@TheCountry",
Countries.SelectedValue);
adapter.Fill(data);
Repeater1.DataSource = data;
Repeater1.DataBind();
```

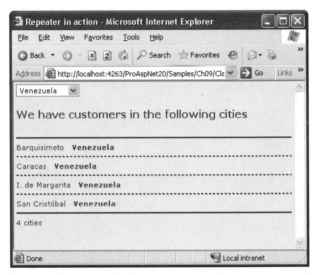

Figure 9-5   A sample *Repeater* control in action. No predefined list control can generate such free-form output.

Of all templates, only *ItemTemplate* and *AlternatingItemTemplate* are data-bound, meaning that they are repeated for each item in the data source. You need a mechanism to access public properties on the data item (such as a table record) from within the template. The *Eval* method takes the name of the property (for example, the name of the table column) and returns the content. We'll learn more about *Eval* and <%# ... %> code blocks in a moment when discussing data-binding expressions.

The *DataList* Control

The *DataList* is a data-bound control that begins where the *Repeater* ends and terminates a little before the starting point of the *DataGrid* control. In some unrealistically simple cases, you could even take some code that uses a *Repeater*, replace the control, and not even notice any difference. The *DataList* overtakes the *Repeater* in several respects, mostly in the area of graphical layout. The *DataList* supports directional rendering, meaning that items can flow horizontally or vertically to match a specified number of columns. Furthermore, it provides facilities to retrieve a key value associated with the current data row and has built-in support for selection and in-place editing. (I discuss these features in *Programming Microsoft ASP.NET 2.0 Applications: Advanced Topics.*)

In addition, the *DataList* control supports more templates and can fire some extra events beyond those of the *Repeater* control. Data binding and the overall behavior are nearly identical for the *Repeater* and *DataList* controls.

The *DataList* works by making some assumptions about the expected results. This is both good and bad news for you as a programmer. It means that in some cases much less code is needed to accomplish the same effect; on the other hand, it also indicates that you should know the behavior of the control very well to govern it. For example, the *DataList* assumes that no HTML tag is split across templates. This fact isn't a problem per se, but it can result in badly formed or totally unexpected HTML output. In addition, by default the *DataList* renders its entire output as an HTML table, meaning that if this is exactly what you want, there's no need for you to comply with *<table>* or *<td>* elements.

In addition to being a naming container, the *DataList* class implements the *IRepeatInfoUser* interface. The *IRepeatInfoUser* interface defines the properties and methods that must be implemented by any list control that repeats a list of items. This interface is also supported by the *CheckBoxList* and *RadioButtonList* controls and is the brains behind the *RepeatXXX* properties we met earlier. Here's how to rewrite the previous example to get stricter control over the output:

```
<asp:DataList ID="DataList1" runat="server" RepeatColumns="5"
    GridLines="Both">
  <FooterStyle Font-Bold="true" ForeColor="blue" />
  <HeaderTemplate>
    <h2>We have customers in the following cities</h2>
  </HeaderTemplate>
  <ItemTemplate>
    <%# Eval("City") %>   <b><%# Eval("Country")%></b>
  </ItemTemplate>
  <FooterTemplate>
    <%# CalcTotal() %> cities
  </FooterTemplate>
</asp:DataList>
```

The output is shown in Figure 9-6. Note the *FooterStyle* tag; the *DataList* also lets you explicitly style the content of each supported template. In this case, we're going to get boldface and blue text in the footer panel.

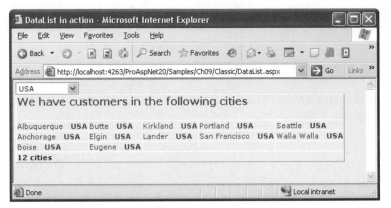

Figure 9-6 A sample *DataList* control in action. Note the extended layout capabilities that let you divide by columns by simply setting a property.

The *DataGrid* Control

The *DataGrid* is an extremely versatile data-bound control that is a fixed presence in any real-world ASP.NET 1.x application. While fully supported, in ASP.NET 2.0, the *DataGrid* is pushed into the background by the introduction of a new and much more powerful grid control—the *GridView*. We'll cover both in the next chapter.

The *DataGrid* control renders a multicolumn, fully templated grid and provides a highly customizable, Microsoft Office Excel–like user interface. In spite of the rather advanced programming interface and the extremely rich set of attributes, the *DataGrid* simply generates an HTML table with interspersed hyperlinks to provide interactive functionalities such as sorting, paging, selection, and in-place editing.

The *DataGrid* is a column-based control and supports various types of data-bound columns, including text columns, templated columns, and command columns. You associate the control with a data source using the *DataSource* property. Just as for other data-bound controls, no data will be physically loaded and bound until the *DataBind* method is called. The simplest way of displaying a table of data using the ASP.NET grid is as follows:

```
<asp:DataGrid runat="server" id="grid" />
```

The control will then automatically generate an HTML table column for each property available in the bound data source. This is only the simplest scenario, however. If needed, you can specify which columns should be displayed and style them at will:

```
grid.DataSource = data;
grid.DataBind();
```

Figure 9-7 demonstrates the grid's output for a sample that returns three fields. As mentioned, we'll cover the *DataGrid* control in much greater detail in the next chapter.

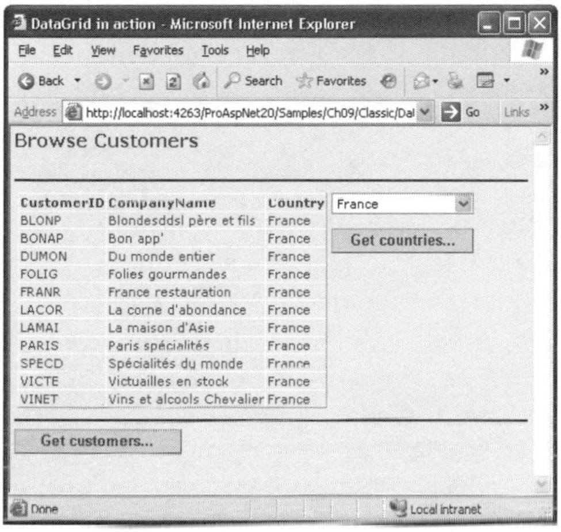

Figure 9-7   A sample *DataGrid* control in action.

Data-Binding Expressions

What we have examined so far is the most common form of data binding that involves list and iterative controls and collections of data. Note that any ASP.NET controls support some minimal form of data binding, including text boxes and labels, through the *DataBind* method. In its simplest form, a binding is a connection between one piece of data and a server control property. This simple form of binding is established through a special expression that gets evaluated when the code in the page calls the *DataBind* method on the control.

Simple Data Binding

A data-binding expression is any executable code wrapped by <% ... %> and prefixed by the symbol #. Typically, you use data-binding expressions to set the value of an attribute in the opening tag of a server control. A data-binding expression is programmatically managed via an instance of the *DataBoundLiteralControl* class.

> **Note**   The binding expression is really any executable code that can be evaluated at run time. Its purpose is to generate data that the control can use to bind for display or editing. Typically, the code retrieves data from the data source, but there is no requirement that this be the case. Any executable code is acceptable as long as it returns data for binding.

The following code snippet shows how to set the text of a label with the current time:

```
<asp:label runat="server" Text='<%# DateTime.Now %>' />
```

Within the delimiters, you can invoke user-defined page methods, static methods, and properties and methods of any other page components. The following code demonstrates a label bound to the name of the currently selected element in a drop-down list control:

```
<asp:label runat="server" Text='<%# dropdown.SelectedItem.Text %>' />
```

Note that if you're going to use quotes within the expression, you should wrap the expression itself with single quotes. The data-binding expression can accept a minimal set of operators, mostly for concatenating subexpressions. If you need more advanced processing and use external arguments, resort to a user-defined method. The only requirement is that the method is declared public or protected.

> **Important**   Any data-bound expression you define in the page is evaluated only after *DataBind* is called. You can either call *DataBind* on the page object or on the specific control. If you call *DataBind* on the page object, it will recursively call *DataBind* on all controls defined in the page. If *DataBind* is not called, no <%# ...%> expressions will ever be evaluated.

Binding in Action

Data-binding expressions are particularly useful to update, in a pure declarative manner, properties of controls that depend on other controls in the same page. For example, suppose you have a drop-down list of colors and a label, and you want the text of the label to reflect the selected color:

```
<asp:DropDownList ID="SelColors" runat="server" AutoPostBack="True">
    <asp:ListItem>Orange</asp:ListItem>
    <asp:ListItem>Green</asp:ListItem>
    <asp:ListItem>Red</asp:ListItem>
    <asp:ListItem>Blue</asp:ListItem>
</asp:DropDownList>
<asp:Label runat="server" ID="lblColor"
    Text='<%# "<b>You selected: </b>" + SelColors.SelectedValue %>' />
```

Note that in the <%# ... %> expression you can use any combination of methods, constants, and properties as long as the final result matches the type of the bound property. Also note that the evaluation of the expression requires a postback and a call to *DataBind*. We set the *AutoPostBack* property to *true* just to force a postback when the selection changes in the drop-down list. At the same time, a call to the page's or label's *DataBind* method is required for the refresh to occur:

```
protected void Page_Load(object sender, EventArgs e) {
    DataBind();
}
```

You can bind to expressions virtually any control properties regardless of the type. Let's see how to bind the *ForeColor* property of the *Label* control to the color string picked from the drop-down list:

```
ForeColor='<%# Color.FromName(SelColors.SelectedValue) %>'
```

Note that you can't just set *ForeColor* to an expression that evaluates to a color string, such as "orange":

```
ForeColor='<%# SelColors.SelectedValue %>'
```

The preceding code won't compile because of the impossible automatic conversion between a string (your expression) and a color (the type of the *ForeColor* property). Interestingly enough, of the two following statements only the second will work fine:

```
ForeColor='<%# "orange" %>'
ForeColor="orange"
```

The upshot is that a data-binding expression requires that the return type match the type of the property represented via an attribute. Using a plain constant string is fine, on the other hand, because the page parser recognizes the expression and seamlessly inserts proper conversion code, if such a conversion is possible. Figure 9-8 shows the sample page in action.

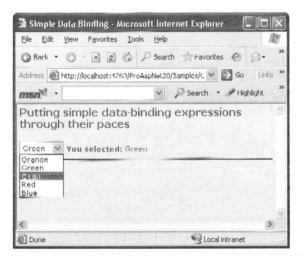

Figure 9-8   A drop-down list and a label tied up together using a data-binding expression.

Implementation of Data-Binding Expressions

What really happens when a data-binding expression is found in a Web page? How does the ASP.NET runtime process it? Let's consider the following code:

```
<asp:label runat="server" id="today" text='<%# DateTime.Now %>' />
```

When the page parser takes care of the *.aspx* source code, it generates a class where each server control has a factory method. The factory method simply maps the tag name to a server-side control class and transforms attributes on the tag into property assignments. In addition, if a data-binding expression is found, the parser adds a handler for the *DataBinding* event of the control—a *Label* in this case. Here's some pseudocode to illustrate the point:

```
private Control __BuildControlToday() {
    Label __ctrl = new Label();
```

```
    this.today = __ctrl;
    __ctrl.ID = "today";

    __ctrl.DataBinding += new EventHandler(this.__DataBindToday);
    return __ctrl;
}
```

The handler assigns the data-binding expression verbatim to the property:

```
public void __DataBindToday(object sender, EventArgs e) {
    Label target;
    target = (Label) sender;
    target.Text = Convert.ToString(DateTime.Now);
}
```

If the value returned by the data-binding expression doesn't match the expected type, you generally get a compile error. However, if the expected type is *string*, the parser attempts a standard conversion through the *Convert.ToString* method. (All .NET Framework types are convertible to a string because they inherit the *ToString* method from the root *object* type.)

The *DataBinder* Class

Earlier in this chapter, we met <%# ... %> expressions in the context of templates along with the *Eval* method. The *Eval* method is a kind of tailor-made operator you use in data-binding expressions to access a public property on the bound data item. The *Eval* method as used earlier is an ASP.NET 2.0–only feature and will generate a compile error if used in ASP.NET 1.x applications. For all versions of ASP.NET, you can use a functionally equivalent method, also named *Eval*, but from another class–*DataBinder*.

> **Important**   Through the *Eval* method—even if it comes from *DataBinder* or *Page*—you can access public properties on the bound data item. Let me clarify what public properties are in this context and why I insist on calling them properties. Any class that implements *IEnumerable* can be bound to a control. The list of actual classes certainly includes *DataTable* (where a data item logically corresponds to table record), but it also includes custom collections (where a data item corresponds to an instance of a given class). The *Eval* method ends up querying the data item object for its set of properties. The object that represents a table record will return descriptors for its columns; other objects will return their set of public properties.

The *DataBinder* class supports generating and parsing data-binding expressions. Of particular importance is its overloaded static method *Eval*. The method uses reflection to parse and evaluate an expression against a run-time object. Clients of the *Eval* method include RAD tools such as Microsoft Visual Studio .NET designers and Web controls that declaratively place calls to the method to feed properties dynamically changing values.

The *Eval* Method

The syntax of *DataBinder.Eval* typically looks like this:

```
<%# DataBinder.Eval(Container.DataItem, expression) %>
```

A third, optional parameter is omitted in the preceding snippet. This parameter is a string that contains formatting options for the bound value. The *Container.DataItem* expression references the object on which the expression is evaluated. The expression is typically a string with the name of the field to access on the data item object. It can be an expression that includes indexes and property names. The *DataItem* property represents the object within the current container context. Typically, a container is the current instance of the item object—for example, a *DataGridItem* object—that is about to be rendered.

The code shown earlier is commonly repeated, always in the same form. Only the expression and the format string change from page to page.

A More Compact *Eval*

The original syntax of *DataBinder.Eval* can be simplified in ASP.NET 2.0, as we already saw earlier in the *Repeater* example. In ASP.NET 2.0, you can use

```
<%# Eval(expression) %>
```

wherever the following expression is accepted in ASP.NET 1.x:

```
<%# DataBinder.Eval(Container.DataItem, expression) %>
```

It goes without saying that the *DataBinder* object is also fully supported in ASP.NET 2.0.

Any piece of code that appears within the <%# ... %> delimiters enjoys special treatment from the ASP.NET runtime. Let's briefly look at what happens with this code. When the page is compiled for use, the *Eval* call is inserted in the source code of the page as a standalone call. The following code gives an idea of what happens:

```
object o = Eval("lastname");
string result = Convert.ToString(o);
```

The result of the call is converted to a string and is assigned to a data-bound literal control—an instance of the *DataBoundLiteralControl* class. Then the data-bound literal is inserted in the page's control tree.

In ASP.NET 2.0, the *TemplateControl* class—the parent of *Page*—is actually enriched with a new, protected (but not virtual) method named *Eval*. The following pseudocode illustrates how the method works:

```
protected object Eval(string expression)
{
    if (Page == null)
```

```
        throw new InvalidOperationException(…);
    return DataBinder.Eval(Page.GetDataItem(), expression);
}
```

As you can see, *Eval* is a simple wrapper built around the *DataBinder.Eval* method. The *DataBinder.Eval* method is invoked using the current container's data item. Quite obviously, the current container's data is null outside a data-binding operation—that is, in the stack of calls following a call to *DataBind*. This fact brings up a key difference between *Eval* and *DataBinder.Eval*.

Important   The *TemplateControl*'s *Eval* is a data-binding method and can be used only in the context of a data-bound control during a data-binding operation. On the other hand, *DataBinder.Eval* is a fully fledged method that can be used anywhere in the code. Typically, you use it in the implementation of custom data-bound controls. I'll show this in the companion volume, *Programming Microsoft ASP.NET 2.0 Applications: Advanced Topics*.

Getting the Default Data Item

The pseudocode that illustrates the behavior of the page's *Eval* method shows a *GetDataItem* method off the *Page* class. What is it? As mentioned, the simplified syntax assumes a default *Container.DataItem* context object. *GetDataItem* is simply the function that returns that object.

More precisely, *GetDataItem* is the endpoint of a stack-based mechanism that traces the current binding context for the page. Each control in the control tree is pushed onto this stack at the time the respective *DataBind* method is called. When the *DataBind* method returns, the control is popped from the stack. If the stack is empty, and you attempt to call *Eval* programmatically, *GetDataItem* throws an invalid operation exception. In summary, you can use the Eval shortcut only in templates; if you need to access properties of a data item anywhere else in the code, resort to *DataBinder.Eval* and indicate the data item object explicitly.

Tip   As mentioned, you generally need to call *DataBinder.Eval* directly only in the code of custom data-bound controls. (I cover custom controls in *Programming Microsoft ASP.NET 2.0 Applications: Advanced Topics*.) When this happens, though, you might want to save a few internal calls and CPU cycles by calling *DataBinder.GetPropertyValue* instead. This is exactly what *DataBinder.Eval* does in the end.

Other Data-Binding Methods

In ASP.NET 2.0, data-binding expressions go far beyond read-only evaluation of enumerable and tabular data. In addition to *DataBinder*, ASP.NET 2.0 provides a class that can bind to the result of XPath expressions that are executed against an object that implements the *IXPathNavigable* interface. This class is named *XPathBinder*; it plays the same role as *DataBinder*, except it works on XML data. The *XPathBinder* class backs up a new data-binding method named *XPath*.

ASP.NET 2.0 also supports declarative two-way data binding, meaning that you can read and write data item properties through a new data-binding method named *Bind*.

Finally, ASP.NET 2.0 supports user-defined expressions that operate outside the boundaries of data-binding operations. It might seem weird that I discuss non-data-binding expressions in a section explicitly dedicated to data-binding expressions. The reason I mention this option here is to avoid confusion, as the syntax for custom expressions is nearly identical.

The *XPath* Method

In ASP.NET 2.0, data-bound controls can be associated with raw XML data. You can bind XML data in version 1.x, but you have to first fit XML data into a relational structure such as a *DataSet*. When a templated control such as *DataList* or *Repeater* is bound to an XML data source (such as the new *XmlDataSource* control, which we'll cover in the next section), individual XML fragments can be bound inside the template using the *XPathBinder* object.

The *XPathBinder.Eval* method accepts an *XmlNode* object along with an XPath expression, and it evaluates and returns the result. The output string can be formatted if a proper format string is specified. *XPathBinder.Eval* casts the container object to *IXPathNavigable*. This is a prerequisite to applying the XPath expression. If the object doesn't implement the interface, an exception is thrown. The *IXPathNavigable* interface is necessary because in the .NET Framework the whole XPath API is built for, and works only with, objects that provide a navigator class. The goal of the interface is creating an XPath navigator object for the query to run.

Like *DataBinder*, the *XPathBinder* class supports a simplified syntax for its evaluator method. The syntax assumes a default container context that is the same object that is tracked for the data binder. The following example demonstrates using the simplified XPath data-binding syntax:

```
<%# XPath("Orders/Order/Customer/LastName") %>
```

The output value is the object returned by *XPathBinder.Eval* converted to a string. Internally, *XPathBinder.Eval* gets a navigator object from the data source and evaluates the expression. The managed XPath API is used.

> **Note** In this book, we don't cover XML classes in the .NET Framework. A good reference is my book *Applied XML with the .NET Framework* (Microsoft Press, 2003). The book covers .NET Framework 1.x, but as far as XPath is concerned, what you can learn from that source is exactly what you need to know.

The *XPathSelect* Method

The *XPathBinder* class also features a *Select* method. The method executes an XPath query and retrieves a nodeset—an enumerable collection of XML nodes. This collection can be assigned as a late-bound value to data-bound controls (such as the *Repeater* control). An equivalent simplified syntax exists for this scenario, too:

```
<asp:Repeater runat="server"
    DataSource='<%# XPathSelect("orders/order/summary") %>'>
...
</asp:Repeater>
```

XPathSelect is the keyword you use in data-binding expressions to indicate the results of an XPath query run on the container object. If the container object does not implement *IXPathNavigable*, an exception is thrown. Like *Eval* and *XPath*, *XPathSelect* assumes a default data item context object.

The *Bind* Method

As we'll see in Chapter 11, ASP.NET 2.0 supports two-way data binding—that is, the capability to bind data to controls and submit changes back to the database. The *Eval* method is representative of a one-way data binding that automates data reading but not data writing. The new *Bind* method can be used whenever *Eval* is accepted and through a similar syntax:

```
<asp:TextBox Runat="server" ID="TheNotes" Text='<%# Bind("notes") %>' />
```

The big difference is that *Bind* works in both directions—reading and writing. For example, when the *Text* property is being set, *Bind* behaves exactly like *Eval*. In addition, when the *Text* property is being read, *Bind* stores the value into a collection. Enabled ASP.NET 2.0 data-bound controls (for example, the new *FormView* control and other templated controls) automatically retrieve these values and use them to compose the parameter list of the insert or edit command to run against the data source. The argument passed to *Bind* must match the name of a parameter in the command. For example, the text box shown earlier provides the value for the *@notes* parameter.

User-Defined Dynamic Expressions

Data-binding expressions are not really dynamic expressions because they are evaluated only within the context of a data-binding call. ASP.NET 2.0 provides a made-to-measure infrastructure for dynamic expressions based on a new breed of components—the expression builders. (I cover expression builders in *Programming Microsoft ASP.NET 2.0 Applications: Advanced Topics*.)

Dynamic expressions have a syntax that is similar to data binding, except that they use the $ prefix instead of #. Dynamic expressions are evaluated when the page compiles. The content of the expression is extracted, transformed into code, and injected into the code created for the page. A few predefined expression builders exist, as listed in Table 9-5.

Table 9-5 Custom Expressions

Syntax	Description
AppSettings:XXX	Returns the value of the specified setting from the *<appSettings>* section of the configuration file.
ConnectionStrings:XXX[.YYY]	Returns the value of the specified XXX string from the *<connectionStrings>* section of the configuration file. The optional YYY parameter indicates which attribute is read from the section. It can be either *connectionString* (default) or *providerName*.
Resources:XXX, YYY	Returns the value of the YYY global resource read from the XXX resource file (*.resx*).

To declaratively bind a control property to the value of the expression, you follow the schema shown here:

```
<%$ expression %>
```

The exact syntax is defined by the builder associated with each expression. Note, though, that literal expressions are not permitted in the body of the page. In other words, you can use expression only to set a control property. You can't have the following:

```
<h1><%$ AppSettings:AppVersionNumber %></h1>
```

Instead, you should wrap the expression in a server control, the simplest of which would be the *Literal* control. The following code generates the page in Figure 9-9:

```
<h1><asp:Literal runat="server"
        Text="<%$ Resources.Resource, AppWelcome %>" /></h1>
<hr />
<b>Code version <asp:Literal runat="server"
    Text="<%$ AppSettings:AppVersionNumber %>" /></b>
```

Needless to say, you need to have an *AppVersionNumber* string resource in the *App_GlobalResource* and an *AppWelcome* setting in the *web.config* file:

```
<appSettings>
    <add key="AppVersionNumber" value="8.2.2001" />
</appSettings>
```

Figure 9-9 The heading text and the version number are obtained through declarative expressions.

The remaining expression—*ConnectionStrings*—is extremely helpful with data source controls to avoid hard-coding the connection string in the *.aspx* file.

> **Note**   Microsoft provides the few built-in expression builders listed in Table 9-5. Developers can define others by simply writing new classes that inherit from *ExpressionBuilder*. To be recognized and properly handled, custom expression builders must be registered in the *web.config* file. I'll touch on this topic in *Programming Microsoft ASP.NET 2.0 Applications: Advanced Topics*.

Data Source Components

ASP.NET 1.x has an extremely flexible and generic data-binding architecture that gives developers full control of the page life cycle. Developers can link data-bound controls such as the *DataGrid* to any enumerable collection of data. While this approach represents a quantum leap from classic ASP, it still requires page developers to learn a lot of architectural details to create even relatively simple read-only pages. This is a problem for Web developers with limited skills because they soon get into trouble if left alone to decide how (or whether) to implement paging, sorting, updates, or perhaps a master/detail view. But this is a (different) problem for experienced developers, as they have to continually reimplement the same pattern to access data sources, get data, and make the data consistent with the programming interface of data controls.

The key issue with ASP.NET 1.x data binding is a lack of a higher-level and possibly declarative model for data fetching and data manipulation. As a result, an ASP.NET 1.x data access layer is boring to write and requires hundreds of lines of code even for relatively simple scenarios. Enter ASP.NET 2.0 data source components.

Overview of Data Source Components

A data source component is a server control designed to interact with data-bound controls and hide the complexity of the manual data-binding pattern. Data source components not only provide data to controls, but they also support data-bound controls in the execution of other common operations such as insertions, deletions, sorting, and updates. Each data source component wraps a particular data provider—relational databases, XML documents, or custom classes. The support for custom classes means that you can now directly bind your controls to existing classes—for example, classes in your business or data access layer. (I'll say more about this later.)

Existing ASP.NET 1.x controls have been extended in ASP.NET 2.0 to support binding to data source controls as far as data retrieval is concerned. The *DataSourceID* property represents the point of contact between old-style data-bound controls and the new data source components. In ASP.NET 2.0, you can successfully bind a *DataGrid* to a data source control without writing a single line of code—not even the ritual call to *DataBind*. However, achieving codeless programming is not the primary goal of data source controls. Think of data source controls as the natural tool to achieve a less complex and semi-automatic interaction between a variety of data sources and controls.

Existing controls such as *DataGrid* and *Repeater* don't take full advantage of data source components. Only ASP.NET 2.0–specific controls such as *GridView*, *FormView*, and *DetailsView* benefit from the true power of data source controls. This is because new controls have a different internal structure specifically designed to deal with data source controls and share with them the complexity of the data-binding pattern.

A Click in the Life of *DataGrid*

To understand the primary goal of data source components, consider what happens when the user performs an action on some data displayed through a *DataGrid*. Imagine that you display an editable grid—that is, a grid that contains an edit column. Users click a cell to edit the corresponding row; the *DataGrid* posts back and fires an event. Page authors handle the event by writing some code to turn on the control in edit mode. A pair of OK/Cancel buttons replaces the edit button. The user edits the contents of the row and then clicks to save or cancel changes. What happens at this point?

The *DataGrid* control captures the event, validates, and then fires the *UpdateCommand* event. The page author is in charge of handling the event, collecting new data, and building and running any required command against the data source. All these steps require code. The same happens if you need to sort data, view a new page, or drill down into the currently selected record.

A Click in the Life of *GridView*

Let's see what happens if you use the successor to the *DataGrid* control—the *GridView* control—which is specifically designed to adhere to the data source model. Let's assume the same scenario: the user clicks, and the control enters edit mode. The first difference is that you don't need to write any code to turn on edit mode. If you click on a cell within an edit column, the control "knows" what you want to do and intelligently takes the next step and executes the requested action—turning on the edit mode.

When the user clicks to save changes, again the *GridView* control anticipates the user's next action and talks to the data source control to have it perform the requested operation (update) on the data source. All this requires no code from the page author; only a few settings, such as the command text and the connection string, are required and can be set declaratively.

The combination of data source controls and new, smarter data-bound controls demonstrates its true power when your code addresses relatively common scenarios, which is probably 70 to 80 percent of the time. If you need to have things done in a particular way, just work the old way and take full control of the page life cycle. This said, in data source controls you find much more than just a deep understanding of the page life cycle. Data source controls support declarative parameters, transparent data caching, server-side paging ability, hierarchical data support, and the ability to work asynchronously. Implementing all these features manually would require quite a bit of code.

Internals of Data Source Controls

A data source control represents one or more named views of data. Each view manages a collection of data. The data associated with a data source control is managed through SQL-like operations such as SELECT, INSERT, DELETE, and COUNT and through capabilities such as sorting and paging. Data source controls come in two flavors—tabular and hierarchical. Tabular controls are described in Table 9-6.

Table 9-6 Tabular Data Source Controls

Class	Description
AccessDataSource	Represents a connection to a Microsoft Office Access database. Inherits from the SqlDataSource control but points to an MDB file and uses the Jet 4.0 OLE DB provider to connect to the database.
ObjectDataSource	Allows binding to a custom .NET business object that returns data. The class is expected to follow a specific design pattern and include, for example, a parameterless constructor and methods that behave in a certain way.
SqlDataSource	Represents a connection to an ADO.NET data provider that returns SQL data, including data sources accessible through OLE DB and ODBC. The name of the provider and the connection string are specified through properties.

Note that the SqlDataSource class is not specific to SQL Server. It can connect to any ADO.NET provider that manages relational data. Hierarchical data source controls are listed in Table 9-7.

Table 9-7 Hierarchical Data Source Controls

Class	Description
SiteMapDataSource	Allows binding to any provider that supplies site map information. The default provider supplies site map data through an XML file in the root folder of the application.
XmlDataSource	Allows binding to XML files and strings with or without schema information.

Note that data source controls have no visual rendering. They are implemented as controls to allow for "declarative persistence" (automatic instantiation during the request processing) as a native part of the .aspx source code and to gain access to the page view state.

Data Source Views

A named view is represented by a data source view object—an instance of the DataSourceView class. These classes represent a customized view of data in which special settings for sorting, filtering, and other data operations have been defined. The DataSourceView class is the base class for all views associated with a data source control. The number of views in a data source control depends on the connection string, characteristics, and actual contents of the underlying data source. In ASP.NET 2.0, built-in controls support only one view, the default view. Table 9-8 lists the properties of the *DataSourceView* class.

Table 9-8   Properties of the *DataSourceView* Class

Property	Description
CanDelete	Indicates whether deletions are allowed on the underlying data source. The deletion is performed by invoking the *Delete* method.
CanInsert	Indicates whether insertions are allowed on the underlying data source. The insertion is performed by invoking the *Insert* method.
CanPage	Indicates whether the data in the view can be paged.
CanRetrieveTotalRowCount	Indicates whether information about the total row count is available.
CanSort	Indicates whether the data in the view can be sorted.
CanUpdate	Indicates whether updates are allowed on the underlying data source. The update is performed by invoking the *Update* method.
Name	Returns the name of the current view.

The *CanXXX* properties indicate not only whether the data source control is capable of performing the specified operation but also whether that operation is appropriate given the current status of the data. Table 9-9 lists all the methods supported by the class.

Table 9-9   Methods of the *DataSourceView* Class

Method	Description
Delete	Performs a delete operation on the data associated with the view
Insert	Performs an insert operation on the data associated with the view
Select	Returns an enumerable object filled with the data contained in the underlying data storage
Update	Performs an update operation on the data associated with the view

All data source view objects support data retrieval through the *Select* method. The method returns an object that implements the *IEnumerable* interface. The real type of the object depends on the data source control and the attributes set on it.

Interaction with Data-Bound Controls

Figure 9-10 shows the interaction between a data source control and data-bound control in ASP.NET 2.0.

ASP.NET 2.0 controls are aware of the full potential of the data source control and, through the data source control, they use the methods of *IDataSource* to connect to the underlying data repository. Implementing the interface is the only official requirement for a control that intends to behave like a data source control. Once it gets hold of a data source view object, the control can call the properties and methods shown in Table 9-8 and Table 9-9 to perform required tasks.

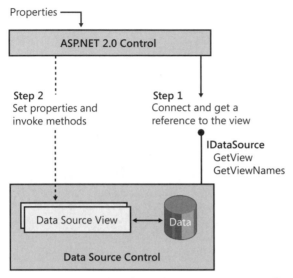

Figure 9-10   The data-bound control gets a view object and talks about capabilities and operations.

Hierarchical Data Source Views

Unlike tabular data source controls, which typically have only one named view, hierarchical data source controls support a view for each level of data that the data source control represents. Hierarchical and tabular data source controls share the same conceptual specification of a consistent and common programming interface for data-bound controls. The only difference is the nature of the data they work with—hierarchical versus flat and tabular.

The view class is different and is named *HierarchicalDataSourceView*. The class features only one method—*Select*—which returns an enumerable hierarchical object. Hierarchical data source controls are, therefore, read-only.

The *SqlDataSource* Control

The *SqlDataSource* control is a data source control that represents a connection to a relational data store such as SQL Server or Oracle or any data source accessible through OLE DB and ODBC bridges.

You set up the connection to the data store using two main properties, *ConnectionString* and *ProviderName*. The former represents the connection string and contains enough information to open a session with the underlying engine. The latter specifies the namespace of the ADO.NET managed provider to use for the operation. The *ProviderName* property defaults to *System.Data.SqlClient*, which means that the default data store is SQL Server. For example, to target an OLE DB provider, use the *System.Data.OleDb* string instead.

The control can retrieve data using either a data adapter or a command object. Depending on your choice, fetched data will be packed in a *DataSet* object or a data reader. The following code snippet shows the minimal code necessary to activate a SQL data source control bound to a SQL Server database:

```
<asp:SqlDataSource runat="server" ID="MySqlSource"
    ProviderName='<%$ ConnectionStrings:LocalNWind.ProviderName %>'
    ConnectionString='<%$ ConnectionStrings:LocalNWind %>'
    SelectCommand="SELECT * FROM employees" />
<asp:DataGrid runat="server" ID="grid" DataSourceID="MySqlSource" />
```

Programming Interface of *SqlDataSource*

The data operations supported by the associated view class are provided by the property groups listed in Table 9-10.

Table 9-10   Properties for Configuring Data Operations

Property Group	Description
DeleteCommand, DeleteParameters, DeleteCommandType	Gets or sets the SQL statement, related parameters, and type (text or stored procedure) used to delete rows in the underlying data store.
FilterExpression, FilterParameters	Gets or sets the string (and related parameters) to create a filter on top of the data retrieved using the *Select* command. Only works if the control manages data through a *DataSet*.
InsertCommand, InsertParameters, InsertCommandType	Gets or sets the SQL statement, related parameters, and type (text or stored procedure) used to insert new rows in the underlying data store.
SelectCommand, SelectParameters, SelectCommandType	Gets or sets the SQL statement, related parameters, and type (text or stored procedure) used to retrieve data from the underlying data store.
SortParameterName	Gets or sets the name of an input parameter that a command's stored procedure will use to sort data. (The command in this case must be a stored procedure.) It raises an exception if the parameter is missing.
UpdateCommand, UpdateParameters, UpdateCommandType	Gets or sets the SQL statement, related parameters, and type (text or stored procedure) used to update rows in the underlying data store.

Each command property is a string that contains the SQL text to be used. The command can optionally contain the parameters listed in the associated parameter collection. The managed provider and its underlying relational engine determine the exact syntax of the SQL to use and the syntax of the embedded parameters. For example, if the data source control points to SQL Server, command parameter names must be prefixed with the @ symbol. If the target data source is an OLE DB provider, parameters are unnamed, identified with a ? placeholder symbol, and located by position. The following code snippet shows a more complex data source control in which parametric delete and update commands have been enabled:

```
<asp:SqlDataSource runat="server" ID="MySqlSource"
    ConnectionString='<%$ ConnectionStrings:LocalNWind %>'
    SelectCommand="SELECT * FROM employees"
    UpdateCommand="UPDATE employees SET lastname=@lname"
    DeleteCommand="DELETE FROM employees WHERE employeeid=@TheEmp"
    FilterExpression="employeeid > 3">
    <!-- parameters go here -->
</asp:SqlDataSource>
```

The syntax used for the *FilterExpression* property is the same as the syntax used for the *RowFilter* property of the *DataView* class, which in turn is similar to that used with the SQL WHERE clause. If the *FilterExpression* property needs to be parametric, you can indicate parameters through the *FilterParameters* collection. Filtering is enabled only when *DataSourceMode* is set to *DataSet*.

> **Note**   Note the difference between filter expressions and parameters on the *Select* command. Parameters on the command influence the result set returned by the data store; a filter expression restricts for display the result set returned through the *Select* command.

Table 9-11 details other operational properties defined on the *SqlDataSource* class. The list doesn't include cache-related properties, which we'll cover in a moment.

Table 9-11   Other Properties on *SqlDataSource*

Property	Description
CancelSelectOnNullParameter	Indicates whether a data-retrieval operation is cancelled if a parameter evaluates to *null*. The default value is *true*.
ConflictDetection	Determines how the control should handle data conflicts during a delete or update operation. By default, changes that occurred in the meantime are overwritten.
ConnectionString	The connection string to connect to the database.
DataSourceMode	Indicates how data should be returned—via a *DataSet* or data reader.
OldValuesParameterFormatString	Gets or sets a format string to apply to the names of any parameters passed to the *Delete* or *Update* method.
ProviderName	Indicates the namespace of the ADO.NET managed provider to use.

It is interesting to note that many of these properties mirror identical properties defined on the actual view class, as illustrated earlier in Figure 9-10.

The *SqlDataSource* object features a few methods and events, which in most cases are common to all data source components. The methods are *Delete*, *Insert*, *Select*, and *Update*, and they're implemented as mere wrappers around the corresponding methods of the underlying data source view class. Events exist in pairs—*Deleting/Deleted*, *Inserting/Inserted*, *Selecting/Selected*, and *Updating/Updated*—and fire before and after any of the methods just mentioned. The beginning of a filtering operation is signaled through the *Filtering* event.

As mentioned, ASP.NET 2.0–specific controls are the only ones to really take advantage of the capabilities of data source controls. For this reason, in the next two chapters devoted to *GridView*, *DetailsView*, and *FormView* controls, we'll see a lot of sample code showing how to use the *SqlDataSource* control for selecting, updating, paging, and sorting. In this chapter, we'll need to spend more time discussing other features of the control that can be particularly useful in real-world applications.

Declarative Parameters

Each command property has its own collection of parameters—an instance of a collection class named *ParameterCollection*. ASP.NET 2.0 supports quite a few parameter types, which are listed in Table 9-12.

Table 9-12   Parameter Types in ASP.NET 2.0

Parameter	Description
ControlParameter	Gets the parameter value from any public property of a server control
CookieParameter	Sets the parameter value based on the content of the specified HTTP cookie
FormParameter	Gets the parameter value from the specified input field in the HTTP request form
Parameter	Gets the parameter value assigned by the code
ProfileParameter	Gets the parameter value from the specified property name in the profile object created from the application's personalization scheme
QueryStringParameter	Gets the parameter value from the specified variable in the request query string
SessionParameter	Sets the parameter value based on the content of the specified session state slot

Each parameter class has a *Name* property and a set of properties specific to its role and implementation. To understand declarative parameters in data source controls, take a look at the following code:

```
<asp:SqlDataSource runat="server" ID="MySource"
    ConnectionString='<%$ ConnectionStrings:LocalNWind %>'
    SelectCommand="SELECT * FROM employees WHERE employeeid > @MinID">
    <SelectParameters>
        <asp:ControlParameter Name="MinID" ControlId="EmpID"
            PropertyName="Text" />
    </SelectParameters>
</asp:SqlDataSource>
```

The query contains a placeholder named *@MinID*. The data source control automatically populates the placeholder with the information returned by the *ControlParameter* object. The value of the parameter is determined by the value of a given property on a given control. The name of the property is specified by the *PropertyName* attribute. The ID of the control is in the *ControlId* attribute. For the previous code to work, page developers must guarantee that the page contains a control with a given ID and property; otherwise, an exception is thrown. In the example, the value of the property *Text* on the *EmpID* control is used as the value for the matching parameter.

The binding between formal parameters (the placeholders in the command text) and actual values depends on how the underlying managed provider handles and recognizes parameters. If the provider type supports named parameters—as is the case with SQL Server and Oracle—the binding involves matching the names of placeholders with the names of the parameters. Otherwise, the matching is based on the position. Hence, the first placeholder is bound to the first parameter, and so on. This is what happens if OLE DB is used to access the data.

Conflicts Detection

The *SqlDataSource* control can optionally perform database-intrusive operations (deletions and updates) in either of two ways. The data source control is associated with a data-bound control, so it is not a far-fetched idea that data is read at the same time, perhaps modified on the client, and then updated. In a situation in which multiple users have read/write access to the database, what should be the behavior of the update/delete methods if the record they attempt to work on has been modified in the meantime?

The *SqlDataSource* control uses the *ConflictDetection* property to determine what to do when performing update and delete operations. The property is declared as type *ConflictOptions*—an enum type. The default value is *OverwriteChanges*, which means that any intrusive operation happens regardless of whether values in the row have changed since they were last read. The alternative is the *CompareAllValues* value, which simply ensures that the *SqlDataSource* control passes the original data read from the database to the *Delete* or *Update* method of the underlying view class.

It is important to note that changing the value of *ConflictDetection* doesn't produce any significant effect unless you write your delete or update statements in such a way that the command fails if the data in the row doesn't match the data that was initially read. To get this, you should define the command as follows:

```
UPDATE employees SET firstname=@firstname
WHERE employeeid=@employeeid AND firstname=@original_firstname
```

In other words, you must explicitly add to the command an extra clause to check whether the current value of the field being modified still matches the value initially read. In this way, intermediate changes entered by concurrent users make the WHERE clause fail and make the command fail. You are in charge of tweaking the command text yourself; setting *ConflictDetection* to *CompareAllValues* is not enough.

How would you format the name of the parameters that represent old values? The *SqlDataSource* control uses the *OldValuesParameterFormatString* property to format these parameter names. The default value is *original_{0}*.

When you use the *CompareAllValues* option, you can handle the *Deleted* or *Updated* event on the data source control to check how many rows are affected. If no rows are affected by the operation, a concurrency violation might have occurred:

```
void OnUpdated(object sender, SqlDataSourceStatusEventArgs e)
{
    if (e.AffectedRows == 0) {
        ...
    }
}
```

Caching Behavior

The data binding between a data-bound control and its data source component is automatic and takes place on each postback caused by the data-bound control. Imagine a page with grid, a data source control, and a button. If you turn on the grid in edit mode, the *Select* command is run; if you click the button (outside the boundaries of the data-bound control) the UI of the grid is rebuilt from the view state and no *Select* statement is run.

To save a query on each postback, you can ask the data source control to cache the result set for a given duration. While data is cached, the *Select* method retrieves data from the cache rather than from the underlying database. When the cache expires, the *Select* method retrieves data from the underlying database, and stores the fresh data back to the cache. The caching behavior of the *SqlDataSource* control is governed by the properties in Table 9-13.

Table 9-13 Caching Properties on *SqlDataSource*

Property	Description
CacheDuration	Indicates in seconds how long the data should be maintained in the cache.
CacheExpirationPolicy	Indicates if the cache duration is absolute or sliding. If absolute, data is invalidated after the specified number of seconds. If sliding, data is invalidated if not used for the specified duration.
CacheKeyDependency	Indicates the name of a user-defined cache key that is linked to all cache entries created by the data source control. By expiring the key, you can clear the control's cache.
EnableCaching	Enables or disables caching support.
SqlCacheDependency	Gets or sets a semicolon-delimited string that indicates which databases and tables to use for the SQL Server cache dependency.

A single cache entry is created for each distinct combination of *SelectCommand*, *ConnectionString*, and *SelectParameters*. Multiple *SqlDataSource* controls can share the same cache entries if they happen to load the same data from the same database. You can take control of cache entries managed by the data source control through the *CacheKeyDependency* property. If set to a non-null string, the property forces the *SqlDataSource* control to create a dependency between that key and all cache entries created by the control. At this point, to clear the control's cache, you only have to assign a new value to the dependency key:

```
Cache["ClearAll"] = anyInitializationValue;
SqlDataSource1.CacheKeyDependency = "ClearAll";
...
Cache["ClearAll"] = anyOtherValue;
```

The *SqlDataSource* control can cache data only when working in *DataSet* mode. You get an exception if *DataSourceMode* is set to *DataReader* and caching is enabled.

Finally, the *SqlCacheDependency* property links the *SqlDataSource* cached data with the contents of the specified database table (typically, the same table where the cached data comes from):

```
<asp:SqlDataSource ID="SqlDataSource1" runat="server"
  CacheDuration="1200"
  ConnectionString="<%$ ConnectionStrings:LocalNWind %>"
  EnableCaching="true"
  SelectCommand="SELECT * FROM employees"
  SqlCacheDependency="Northwind:Employees">
</asp:SqlDataSource>
```

Whenever the underlying table changes, the cached data is automatically flushed. We'll cover SQL cache dependencies in detail in Chapter 14.

The *AccessDataSource* Class

The *AccessDataSource* control is a data source control that represents a connection to an Access database. It is based on the *SqlDataSource* control and provides a simpler, made-to-measure programming interface. As a derived class, *AccessDataSource* inherits all members defined on its parent and overrides a few of them. In particular, the control replaces the *ConnectionString* and *ProviderName* properties with a more direct *DataFile* property. You set this property to the *.mdb* database file of choice. The data source control resolves the file path at run time and uses the Microsoft Jet 4 OLE DB provider to connect to the database.

> **Note**   *AccessDataSource* actually inherits from *SqlDataSource* and for this reason can't make base members disappear, as hinted at earlier. *AccessDataSource* doesn't really replace the *ConnectionString* and *ProviderName* properties; it overrides them so that an exception is thrown whenever someone attempts to set their value. Another property overridden only to throw exceptions is *SqlCacheDependency*. This feature, of course, is not supported.

Working with an Access Database

The following code shows how to use the *AccessDataSource* control to open an *.mdb* file and bind its content to a drop-down list control. Note that the control opens Access database files in read-only mode by default:

```
<asp:AccessDataSource runat="server" ID="MyAccessSource"
    DataFile="nwind.mdb"
    SelectCommand="SELECT * FROM Customers" />
Select a Customer:
<asp:DropDownList runat="server" DataSourceId="MyAccessSource" />
```

Several features of the *AccessDataSource* control are inherited from the base class, *SqlDataSource*. In fact, the Access data source control is basically a SQL data source control optimized to work with Access databases. Like its parent control, the *AccessDataSource* control supports two distinct data source modes—*DataSet* and *DataReader*, depending on the ADO.NET classes used to retrieve data. Filtering can be applied to the selected data only if the fetch operation returns a *DataSet*. Caching works as on the parent class except for the *SqlCacheDependency* feature.

Updating an Access Database

The *AccessDataSource* can also be used to perform insert, update, or delete operations against the associated database. This is done using ADO.NET commands and parameter collections. Updates are problematic for Access databases when performed from within an ASP.NET application because an Access database is a plain file and the default account of the ASP.NET process (ASPNET or NetworkService, depending on the host operating system) might not have sufficient permission to write to the database file. For the data source updates to work, you should grant write permission to the ASP.NET account on the database file. Alternatively, you can use a different account with adequate permission.

> **Note** Most Internet service providers (ISPs) normally give you one directory in which ASPNET and NetworkService accounts have been granted write permission. In this case, you just place your Access file in this directory and you can read and write seamlessly. In general, though, Access databases are plain files and, as such, are subject to the security rules of ASP.NET.

The *ObjectDataSource* Control

The *ObjectDataSource* class enables user-defined classes to associate the output of their methods to data-bound controls. Like other data source controls, *ObjectDataSource* supports declarative parameters to allow developers to pass page-level variables to the object's methods. The *ObjectDataSource* class makes some assumptions about the objects it wraps. As a consequence, an arbitrary class can't be used with this data source control. In particular, bindable classes are expected to have a default constructor, to be stateless, and to have methods that easily map to select, update, insert, and delete semantics. Also, the object must perform updates one item at a time; objects that update their states using batch operations are not supported. The bottom line is that managed objects that work well with *ObjectDataSource* are designed with this data source class in mind.

Programming Interface of *ObjectDataSource*

The *ObjectDataSource* component provides nearly the same programmatic interface (events, methods, and properties, and associated behaviors) as the *SqlDataSource*, with the addition of three new events and a few properties. The events are related to the lifetime of the underlying business object—*ObjectCreating*, *ObjectCreated*, and *ObjectDisposing*. Table 9-14 lists other key properties of *ObjectDataSource*.

Table 9-14 Main Properties of *ObjectDataSource*

Property	Description
ConvertNullToDBNull	Indicates whether null parameters passed to insert, delete, or update operations are converted to *System.DBNull*. False by default.
DataObjectTypeName	Gets or sets the name of a class that is to be used as a parameter for a *Select*, *Insert*, *Update*, or *Delete* operation.
DeleteMethod, DeleteParameters	Gets or sets the name of the method and related parameters used to perform a delete operation.
EnablePaging	Indicates whether the control supports paging.
FilterExpression, FilterParameters	Indicates the filter expression (and parameters) to filter the output of a select operation.
InsertMethod, InsertParameters	Gets or sets the name of the method and related parameters used to perform an insert operation.
MaximumRowsParameterName	If the *EnablePaging* property is set to *true*, indicates the parameter name of the *Select* method that accepts the value for the number of records to retrieve.
OldValuesParameterFormatString	Gets or sets a format string to apply to the names of any parameters passed to the *Delete* or *Update* methods.
SelectCountMethod	Gets or sets the name of the method used to perform a select count operation.
SelectMethod, SelectParameters	Gets or sets the name of the method and related parameters used to perform a select operation.
SortParameterName	Gets or sets the name of an input parameter used to sort retrieved data. It raises an exception if the parameter is missing.
StartRowIndexParameterName	If the *EnablePaging* property is set to *true*, indicates the parameter name of the *Select* method that accepts the value for the starting record to retrieve.
UpdateMethod, UpdateParameters	Gets or sets the name of the method and related parameters used to perform an update operation.

The *ObjectDataSource* control uses reflection to locate and invoke the method to handle the specified operation. The *TypeName* property returns the fully qualified name of the assembly that defines the class to call. If the class is defined in the *App_Code* directory, you don't need to indicate the assembly name. Otherwise, you use a comma-separated string in the form of *[classname, assembly]*. Let's see an example.

> **Warning**   Having too many classes in the *App_Code* directory can become a nightmare at development time because any changes to any files will cause Visual Studio .NET to recompile the whole set of files in the project.

Implementing Data Retrieval

The following code snippet illustrates a class that can be used with an object data source. Architected according to the Table Data Gateway (TDG) pattern, the class represents employees and takes advantage of two other helper classes (at the very minimum): *Employee* and *Employee-Collection*. The class *Employee* contains information about the entity being represented; the class *EmployeeCollection* represents a collection of employees. The behavior of the entity "employee" is codified in a bunch of methods exposed out of the gateway class—*Employees*:

```
public class Employees
{
    public static string ConnectionString {
        ...
    }
    public static void Load(int employeeID) {
        ...
    }
    public static EmployeeCollection LoadAll() {
        ...
    }
    public static EmployeeCollection LoadByCountry(string country) {
        ...
    }
    public static void Save(Employee emp) {
        ...
    }
    public static void Insert(Employee emp) {
        ...
    }
    public static void Delete(int employeeID) {
        ...
    }
    ...
}
```

The TDG pattern requires the gateway to be shared among instances of the entity class—in the following example, I implemented the class with static methods. If you don't use static methods, the worker class you use with *ObjectDataSource* must have a default parameterless constructor. Furthermore, the class should not maintain any state.

> **Warning** Using static methods in the context of a TDG pattern is fine from an architectural viewpoint, but it might pose practical problems with unit testing. What if you test a business class that calls the Data Access Layer (DAL) internally and the DAL fails? Can you figure out what really happened? Does the business class work or not? To effectively test a business layer that calls into a DAL, you need to focus on the object under test. Mock objects come to the rescue. Mock objects are programmable polymorphic objects that present themselves as others and can wrap DAL anomalies and signal them out clearly, making the test succeed if nothing else happens. The point is that mocking toolkits typically don't like static methods. That's why instance methods might be preferable in real-world implementations of the TDG pattern.

The worker class must be accessible from within the *.aspx* page and can be bound to the *ObjectDataSource* control, as shown here:

```
<asp:ObjectDataSource runat="server" ID="MyObjectSource"
    TypeName="ProAspNet20.DAL.Employees"
    SelectMethod="LoadAll" />
```

When the HTTP runtime encounters a similar block in a Web page, it generates code that calls the *LoadAll* method on the specified class. The returned data—an instance of the *EmployeeCollection*—is bound to any control that links to *MyObjectSource* via the *DataSourceID* property. Let's take a brief look at the implementation of the *LoadAll* method:

```
public static EmployeeCollection LoadAll()
{
    EmployeeCollection coll = new EmployeeCollection();

    using (SqlConnection conn = new SqlConnection(ConnectionString))
    {
        SqlCommand cmd = new SqlCommand("SELECT * FROM employees", conn);
        conn.Open();
        SqlDataReader reader = cmd.ExecuteReader();
        HelperMethods.FillEmployeeList(coll, reader);
        reader.Close();
        conn.Close();
    }
    return coll;
}
```

A bit oversimplified to fit in the section, the preceding code remains quite clear: you execute a command, fill in a custom collection class, and return it to the data-bound control. The only piece of code you need to write is the worker class—you don't need to put any code in the code-behind class of the page:

```
<asp:DataGrid ID="grid" runat="server" DataSourceID="MyObjectSource" />
```

The *DataGrid* receives a collection of *Employee* objects defined as follows:

```
public class EmployeeCollection : List<Employee>
{
}
```

Binding is totally seamless, even without ADO.NET container objects. (See the companion code for full details.)

The method associated with the *SelectMethod* property must return any of the following: an *IEnumerable* object such as a collection, *DataSet*, *DataTable*, or *Object*. Preferably, the *Select* method is not overloaded, although *ObjectDataSource* doesn't prevent you from using overloading in your business classes.

Using Parameters

In most cases, methods require parameters. *SelectParameters* is the collection you use to add input parameters to the select method. Imagine you have a method to load employees by country. Here's the code you need to come up with:

```
<asp:ObjectDataSource ID="ObjectDataSource1" runat="server"
    TypeName="ProAspNet20.DAL.Employees"
    SelectMethod="LoadByCountry">
    <SelectParameters>
        <asp:ControlParameter Name="country" ControlID="Countries"
            PropertyName="SelectedValue" />
    </SelectParameters>
</asp:ObjectDataSource>
```

The preceding code snippet is the declarative version of the following pseudocode, where *Countries* is expected to be a drop-down list filled with country names:

```
string country = Countries.SelectedValue;
EmployeeCollection coll = Employees.LoadByCountry(country);
```

The *ControlParameter* class automates the retrieval of the actual parameter value and the binding to the parameter list of the method. What if you add an *[All Countries]* entry to the drop-down list? In this case, if the *All Countries* option is selected, you need to call *LoadAll* without parameters; otherwise, if a particular country is selected, you need to call *LoadByCountry* with a parameter. Declarative programming works great in the simple scenarios; otherwise, you just write code:

```
void Page_Load(object sender, EventArgs e)
{
    // Must be cleared every time (or disable the viewstate)
    ObjectDataSource1.SelectParameters.Clear();

    if (Countries.SelectedIndex == 0)
        ObjectDataSource1.SelectMethod = "LoadAll";
    else
    {
        ObjectDataSource1.SelectMethod = "LoadByCountry";
        ControlParameter cp = new ControlParameter("country",
            "Countries", "SelectedValue");
        ObjectDataSource1.SelectParameters.Add(cp);
    }
}
```

Note that data source controls are like ordinary server controls and can be programmatically configured and invoked. In the code just shown, you first check the selection the user made and if it matches the first option (*All Countries*), configure the data source control to make a parameterless call to the *LoadAll* method.

You must clean up the content of the *SelectParameters* collection upon page loading. The data source control (more precisely, the underlying view control) caches most of its properties to the view state. As a result, *SelectParameters* is not empty when you refresh the page after changing the drop-down list selection. The preceding code clears only the *SelectParameters* collection; performance-wise, it could be preferable to disable the view state altogether on the data source control. However, if you disable the view state, all collections will be empty on the data source control upon loading.

> **Important** *ObjectDataSource* allows data retrieval and update while keeping data access and business logic separate from user interface. The use of the *ObjectDataSource* class doesn't automatically transform your system into a well-designed, effective n-tiered system. Data source controls are mostly a counterpart to data-bound controls so that the latter can work more intelligently. To take full advantage of *ObjectDataSource*, you need to have your DAL already in place. It doesn't work the other way around. *ObjectDataSource* doesn't necessarily have to be bound to the root of the DAL, which could be on a remote location and perhaps behind a firewall. In this case, you write a local intermediate object and connect it to *ObjectDataSource* on one end and to the DAL on the other end. The intermediate object acts as an application-specific proxy and works according to the application's specific rules. *ObjectDataSource* doesn't break n-tiered systems, nor does it transform existing systems into truly n-tier systems. It greatly benefits, instead, from existing business and data layers.

Caching Data and Object Instances

The *ObjectDataSource* component supports caching only when the specified select method returns a *DataSet* or *DataTable* object. If the wrapped object returns a custom collection (as in the example we're considering), an exception is thrown.

ObjectDataSource is designed to work with classes in the business layer of the application. An instance of the business class is created for each operation performed and destroyed shortly after the operation is complete. This model is the natural offspring of the stateless programming model that ASP.NET promotes. In case of business objects that are particularly expensive to initialize, you can resort to static classes or static methods in instance classes. (If you do so, bear in mind what we said earlier regarding unit testing classes with static methods.)

Instances of the business object are not automatically cached or pooled. Both options, though, can be manually implemented by properly handling the *ObjectCreating* and *Object-Disposing* events on an *ObjectDataSource* control. The *ObjectCreating* event fires when the data source control needs to get an instance of the business class. You can write the handler to retrieve an existing instance of the class and return that to the data source control:

```
// Handle the ObjectCreating event on the data source control
public void BusinessObjectBeingCreated(object sender,
        ObjectDataSourceEventArgs e)
{
    BusinessObject bo = RetrieveBusinessObjectFromPool();
    if (bo == null)
        bo = new BusinessObject();
    e.ObjectInstance = bo;
}
```

Likewise, in *ObjectDisposing* you store the instance again and cancel the disposing operation being executed:

```
// Handle the ObjectDisposing event on the data source control
public void BusinessObjectBeingDisposed(object sender,
        ObjectDataSourceDisposingEventArgs e)
{
    ReturnBusinessObjectToPool(e.ObjectInstance);
    e.Cancel = true;
}
```

It is not only object instances that aren't cached. In some cases, even retrieved data is not persisted in memory for the specified duration. More precisely, the *ObjectDataSource* control does support caching just as *SqlDataSource* does, except that caching is enabled only if the select method returns a *DataTable* or *DataSet* object. A *DataView*, and in general a simple enumerable collection of data, isn't cached; if you enable caching in this scenario, an exception will be thrown.

> **Note**   Just as with caching, filtering is also not permitted when the return value is not an ADO.NET container class

Setting Up for Paging

Unlike *SqlDataSource*, *ObjectDataSource* also supports paging. Three properties in Table 9-14 participate in paging—*EnablePaging*, *StartRowIndexParameterName*, and *MaximumRowsParameterName*.

As the name clearly suggests, *EnablePaging* toggles support for paging on and off. The default value is *false*, meaning that paging is not turned on automatically. *ObjectDataSource* provides an infrastructure for paging, but actual paging must be implemented in the class bound to *ObjectDataSource*. In the following code snippet, the *Customers* class has a method, *LoadByCountry*, that takes two additional parameters to indicate the page size and the index of the first record in the page. The names of these two parameters must be assigned to *MaximumRowsParameterName* and *StartRowIndexParameterName*, respectively:

```
<asp:ObjectDataSource ID="ObjectDataSource1" runat="server"
    TypeName="ProAspNet20.DAL.Customers"
    StartRowIndexParameterName="firstRow"
    MaximumRowsParameterName="totalRows"
    SelectMethod="LoadByCountry">
  <SelectParameters>
    <asp:ControlParameter Name="country" ControlID="Countries"
        PropertyName="SelectedValue" />
    <asp:ControlParameter Name="totalRows" ControlID="PageSize"
        PropertyName="Text" />
    <asp:ControlParameter Name="firstRow" ControlID="FirstRow"
        PropertyName="Text" />
  </SelectParameters>
</asp:ObjectDataSource>
```

The implementation of paging is up to the method and must be coded manually. *LoadByCountry* provides two overloads, one of which supports paging. Internally, paging is actually delegated to *FillCustomerList*:

```
public static CustomerCollection LoadByCountry(string country)
{
    return LoadByCountry(country, -1, 0);
}
public static CustomerCollection LoadByCountry(string country,
        int totalRows, int firstRow)
{
    CustomerCollection coll = new CustomerCollection();

    using (SqlConnection conn = new SqlConnection(ConnectionString))
    {
        SqlCommand cmd;
        cmd = new SqlCommand(CustomerCommands.cmdLoadByCountry, conn);
        cmd.Parameters.AddWithValue("@country", country);

        conn.Open();
        SqlDataReader reader = cmd.ExecuteReader();
        HelperMethods.FillCustomerList(coll, reader, totalRows, firstRow);
        reader.Close();
        conn.Close();
    }

    return coll;
}
```

As you can see in the companion source code, *FillCustomerList* doesn't use a particularly smart approach. It simply scrolls the whole result set using a reader and discards all the records that don't belong in the requested range. You could improve upon this approach to make paging smarter. What's important here is that paging is built into your business object and exposed by data source controls to the pageable controls through a well-known interface.

Updating and Deleting Data

To update underlying data using *ObjectDataSource*, you need to define an update/insert/ delete method. All the actual methods you use must have semantics that are well-suited to implement such operations. Again, this requirement is easily met if you employ the TDG pattern in the design of your DAL. Here are some good prototypes for the update operations:

```
public static void Save(Employee emp)
public static void Insert(Employee emp)
public static void Delete(int id)
```

More than select operations, update operations require parameters. To update a record, you need to pass new values and one or more old values to make sure the right record to update is located and to take into account the possibility of data conflicts. To delete a record, you need to identify it by matching a supplied primary key parameter. To specify input parameters, you can use command collections such as *UpdateParameters*, *InsertParameters*, or *DeleteParameters*. Let's examine update/insert scenarios first.

To update an existing record or insert a new one, you need to pass new values. This can be done in either of two ways—listing parameters explicitly or aggregating all parameters in an all-encompassing data structure. The prototypes shown previously for *Save* and *Insert* follow the latter approach. An alternative might be the following:

```
public static void Save(int id, string firstName, string lastName, ...)

public static void Insert(string firstName, string lastName, ...)
```

You can use command parameter collections only if the types involved are simple types—numbers, strings, dates. If your DAL implements the TDG pattern (or a similar one, such as Data Mapper), your update/insert methods are likely to accept a custom aggregate data object as a parameter—the *Employee* class seen earlier. To make a custom class such as *Employee* acceptable to the *ObjectDataSource* control, you need to set the *DataObjectTypeName* property:

```
<asp:ObjectDataSource ID="RowDataSource" runat="server"
    TypeName="ProAspNet20.DAL.Employees"
    SelectMethod="Load"
    UpdateMethod="Save"
    DataObjectTypeName="ProAspNet20.DAL.Employee">
  <SelectParameters>
      <asp:ControlParameter Name="id" ControlID="GridView1"
          PropertyName="SelectedValue" />
  </SelectParameters>
</asp:ObjectDataSource>
```

The preceding *ObjectDataSource* control saves rows through the *Save* method, which takes an *Employee* object. Note that when you set the *DataObjectTypeName* property, the *UpdateParameters* collection is ignored. The *ObjectDataSource* instantiates a default instance of the object before the operation is performed and then attempts to fill its public members with the values of any matching input fields found around the bound control. Because this work is performed using reflection, the names of the input fields in the bound control must match the names of public properties exposed by the object in the *DataObjectTypeName* property. A practical limitation you must be aware of is that you can't define the *Employee* class using complex data types, as follows:

```
public class Employee {
    public string LastName {…}
    public string FirstName {…}
    ...
    public Address HomeAddress {…}
}
```

Representing individual values (*strings* in the sample), the *LastName* and *FirstName* members have good chances to match an input field in the bound control. The same can't be said for the *HomeAddress* member, which is declared of a custom aggregate type like *Address*. If you go with this schema, all the members in *Address* will be ignored; any related information won't be carried into the *Save* method, with resulting null parameters. All the members in the *Address* data structure should become members of the *Employee* class.

> **Note**   Recall that data source controls work at their fullest only with a few ASP.NET 2.0 controls, such as *GridView* (Chapter 10) and *DetailsView* (Chapter 11). We'll return to the topic of the internal mechanism of parameter binding later in the book. For now, it suffices to say that as a page author you're responsible for making input fields and member names match in the following way: columns in *GridView* and rows in *DetailsView* have a *DataField* attribute pointing to the data source field to use (that is, *lastname*, where *lastname* is typically a database column retrieved by the select operation). The data field name must match (case-insensitive) a public property in the class used as a parameter in the update/insert operation—in this case, the *Employee* class.

Unlike the insert operation, the update operation also requires a primary key value to identify uniquely the record being updated. If you use an explicit parameter listing, you just append an additional parameter to the list to represent the ID, as follows:

```
<asp:ObjectDataSource runat="server" ID="MyObjectSource"
    TypeName="ProAspNet20.SimpleBusinessObject"
    SelectMethod="GetEmployees"
    UpdateMethod="SetEmployee">
  <UpdateParameters>
      <asp:Parameter Name="employeeid" Type="Int32" />
      <asp:Parameter Name="firstname" Type="string" />
      <asp:Parameter Name="lastname" Type="string" />
      <asp:Parameter Name="country" Type="string" DefaultValue="null" />
  </UpdateParameters>
</asp:ObjectDataSource>
```

Note that by setting the *DefaultValue* attribute to *null*, you can make a parameter optional. A null value for a parameter must then be gracefully handled by the method to implement the update.

There's an alternative method to set the primary key—through the *DataKeyNames* property of *GridView* and *DetailsView* controls. I'll briefly mention it here and cover it in much greater detail in the next two chapters:

```
<asp:GridView runat="server" ID="grid1"
    DataKeyNames="employeeid"
    DataSourceId="MyObjectSource"
    AutoGenerateEditButton="true">
  ...
</asp:GridView>
```

When *DataKeyNames* is set on the bound control, data source controls automatically add a parameter to the list of parameters for update and delete commands. The default name of the parameter is *original_XXX*, where *XXX* stands for the value of *DataKeyNames*. For the operation to succeed, the method (or the SQL command if you're using *SqlDataSource*) must handle a parameter with the same name. Here's an example:

```
UPDATE employees SET lastname=@lastname
    WHERE employeeid=@original_employeeid
```

The name format of the key parameter can be changed at will through the *OldValuesParameterFormatString* property. For example, a value of "{0}" assigned to the property would make the following command acceptable:

```
UPDATE employees SET lastname=@lastname
    WHERE employeeid=@employeeid
```

Setting the *DataKeyNames* property on the bound control (hold on, it's *not* a property on the data source control) is also the simplest way to configure a delete operation. For a delete operation, in fact, you don't need to specify a whole record with all its fields; the key is sufficient.

> **Note**   In ASP.NET 2.0 data-bound controls such as *GridView* and *DetailsView*, the *DataKeyNames* property replaces *DataKeyField*, which we found on *DataGrid* and *DataList* controls in ASP.NET 1.x. The difference between the two lies in the fact that *DataKeyNames* support keys based on multiple fields. If *DataKeyNames* is set to multiple fields (for example, *id,name*), two parameters are added: *original_id* and *original_name*.

Configuring Parameters at Run Time

When using *ObjectDataSource* with an ASP.NET 2.0 made-to-measure control (for example, *GridView*), most of the time the binding is totally automatic and you don't have to deal with it. If you need it, though, there's a back door you can use to take control of the update process— the *Updating* event:

```
protected void Updating(object sender, ObjectDataSourceMethodEventArgs e)
{
    Employee emp = (Employee) e.InputParameters[0];
    emp.LastName = "Whosthisguy";
}
```

The event fires before the update operation climaxes. The *InputParameters* collection lists the parameters being passed to the update method. The collection is read-only, meaning that you can't add or delete elements. However, you can modify objects being transported, as the preceding code snippet demonstrates.

This technique is useful when, for whatever reasons, the *ObjectDataSource* control doesn't load all the data its method needs to perform the update. A similar approach can be taken for deletions and insertions as well.

The *SiteMapDataSource* Class

Site maps are a common feature of cutting-edge Web sites. A site map is the graph that represents all the pages and directories found in a Web site. Site map information is used to show users the logical coordinates of the page they are visiting, allow users to access site locations dynamically, and render all the navigation information in a graphical fashion (as shown in Figure 9-11).

Figure 9-11   The graphical layout that the *MSDN Magazine* Web site uses to represent the location of a page in the site hierarchy.

ASP.NET 2.0 contains a rich navigation infrastructure that allows developers to specify the site structure. I cover site navigation in detail in *Programming Microsoft ASP.NET 2.0 Applications: Advanced Topics*. For now, it suffices to say that the site map is a hierarchical piece of information that can be used as input for a hierarchical data source control such as *SiteMapDataSource*. The output of *SiteMapDataSource* can bound to hierarchical data-bound controls such as *Menu*.

Displaying Site Map Information

The site map information can appear in many ways, the simplest of which is an XML file named *web.sitemap* located in the root of the application. To give you the essence of site maps and site map data sources, let's briefly review a few usage scenarios. Suppose you're writing a Web site and your client asks for a sequence of hyperlinks that indicate the location of the page in the site map. In ASP.NET 1.x, you have to create your own infrastructure to hold site map information and render the page location. (Typically, you would use a configuration file and a user control.) ASP.NET 2.0 provides richer support for site maps. You start by creating a configuration file named *web.sitemap* in the root of the Web application. The file describes the relationship between pages on the site. Your next step will depend on the expected output.

If the common representation shown in Figure 9-11 (a sequence of hyperlinks with a separator) is what you need, add a *SiteMapPath* control to the page. This control retrieves the site map and produces the necessary HTML markup. In this simple case, there is no need to resort to a site map data source control. If you need to build a more complex hierarchical layout—for example, a tree-based representation—you need the *SiteMapDataSource* control.

The *SiteMapDataSource* control pumps site map information to a hierarchical data-bound control (for example, the new *TreeView* control) so that it can display the site's structure. Here's a quick example:

```
<%@ Page Language="C#" %>
<html>
<body>
    <form runat="server">
        <asp:SiteMapDataSource runat="server" ID="MySiteMapSource" />
        <asp:TreeView runat="server" DataSourceId="MySiteMapSource" />
    </form>
</body>
</html>
```

Figure 9-12 shows the final output as it appears to the end user.

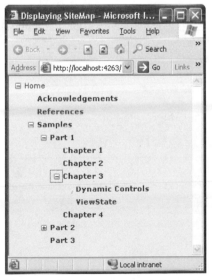

Figure 9-12   The site map information rendered through a *TreeView* control.

The site map information might look like the following:

```
<siteMap>
    <siteMapNode title="Home" url="default.aspx" >
        <siteMapNode title="Acknowledgements" url="ack.aspx"/>
        <siteMapNode title="References" url="ref.aspx" />
        <siteMapNode title="Samples">
            <siteMapNode title="Part 1">
                <siteMapNode title="Chapter 1" />
                <siteMapNode title="Chapter 2" />
                <siteMapNode title="Chapter 3">
                    <siteMapNode title="Dynamic Controls" url=".../dynctls.aspx" />
                    <siteMapNode title="ViewState" url=".../viewstate.aspx" />
                </siteMapNode>
                <siteMapNode title="Chapter 4" />
            </siteMapNode>
            <siteMapNode title="Part 2">
                <siteMapNode title="Chapter 9">
                    <siteMapNode title="Site map" url=".../sitemapinfo.aspx" />
                </siteMapNode>
            </siteMapNode>
            <siteMapNode title="Part 3" url="samples.aspx?partid=3" />
        </siteMapNode>
    </siteMapNode>
</siteMap>
```

Note that the *url* attribute is optional. If not defined, the node is intended to be an inert container and won't be made clickable.

> **Note**   As mentioned, ASP.NET 2.0 introduces a new type of data-bound control that was completely unsupported in previous versions—the hierarchical data-bound control. A new base class is defined to provide a minimum set of capabilities: *HierarchicalDataBoundControl*. The *TreeView* and *Menu* controls fall into this category.

Programming Interface of *SiteMapDataSource*

Table 9-15 details the properties available in the *SiteMapDataSource* class.

Table 9-15   Properties of *SiteMapDataSource*

Property	Description
Provider	Indicates the site map provider object associated with the data source control.
ShowStartingNode	True by default, indicates whether the starting node is retrieved and displayed.
SiteMapProvider	Gets and sets the name of the site map provider associated with the instance of the control.
StartFromCurrent-Node	False by default, indicates whether the node tree is retrieved relative to the current page.
StartingNodeOffset	Gets and sets a positive or negative offset from the starting node that determines the root hierarchy exposed by the control. Set to 0 by default.
StartingNodeUrl	Indicates the URL in the site map in which the node tree is rooted.

By default, the starting node is the root node of the hierarchy, but you can change the starting node through a pair of mutually exclusive properties—*StartFromCurrentNode* and *Starting-NodeUrl*. If you explicitly indicate the URL of the page that should appear as the root of the displayed hierarchy, make sure the *StartFromCurrentNode* property is *false*. Likewise, if you set *StartFromCurrentNode* to *true*, ensure the *StartingNodeUrl* property evaluates to the empty string.

Properly used, the *StartingNodeOffset* property lets you restrict the nodes of the site map that are actually displayed. The default value of 0 indicates that the root hierarchy exposed by the *SiteMapDataSource* control is the same as the starting node. A value greater than 0 goes as many levels down in the hierarchy proceeding from the root to the requested node and uses the node found as the root. Look at the sample site map we considered earlier. If you request *sitemapinfo.aspx* with an offset of 1, the displayed hierarchy will be rooted in the *Samples* node—that is, one level down the real root. If you set it to 2, the effective root will be the *Part 2* node. A negative offset, on the other hand, ensures that the specified number of child levels will be displayed if possible.

The *SiteMapDataSource* class features a couple of properties that relate to the site map provider: *SiteMapProvider* and *Provider*. The former specifies the name of the site map provider to use; the latter returns a reference to the object.

The *XmlDataSource* Class

The *XmlDataSource* control is a special type of data source control that supports both tabular and hierarchical views of data. The tabular view of XML data is just a list of nodes at a given level of hierarchy, whereas the hierarchical view shows the complete hierarchy. An XML node is an instance of the *XmlNode* class; the complete hierarchy is an instance of the *XmlDocument* class. The XML data source supports only read-only scenarios.

> **Important** The *XmlDataSource* control is unique in that it is the only built-in data source control to implement both *IDataSource* and *IHierarchicalDataSource* interfaces. For both interfaces, though, the control doesn't go further than implementing the *Select* method. Hence, the *XmlDataSource* control is not suitable for Web applications using read/write XML data stores, as it doesn't support methods such as *Delete*, *Insert*, and *Update*.

Programming Interface of *XmlDataSource*

Table 9-16 details the properties of the *XmlDataSource* control.

Table 9-16   Properties of *XmlDataSource*

Property	Description
CacheDuration	Indicates in seconds how long the data should be maintained in the cache.
CacheExpirationPolicy	Indicates whether the cache duration is absolute or sliding. If absolute, data is invalidated after the specified number of seconds. If sliding, data is invalidated if not used for the specified duration.

Table 9-16   Properties of *XmlDataSource*

Property	Description
CacheKeyDependency	Indicates the name of a user-defined cache key that is linked to all cache entries created by the data source control. By expiring the key, you can clear the control's cache.
Data	Contains a block of XML text for the data source control to bind.
DataFile	Indicates the path to the file that contains data to display.
EnableCaching	Enables or disables caching support.
Transform	Contains a block of XSLT text that will be used to transform the XML data bound to the control.
TransformArgumentList	A list of input parameters for the XSLT transformation to apply to the source XML.
TransformFile	Indicates the path to the *.xsl* file that defines an XSLT transformation to be performed on the source XML data.
XPath	Indicates an XPath query to be applied to the XML data.

The *XmlDataSource* control can accept XML input data as a relative or absolute filename assigned to the *DataFile* property or as a string containing the XML content assigned to the *Data* property. If both properties are set, *DataFile* takes precedence. Note that the *Data* property can also be set declaratively through the *<Data>* tag. Furthermore, the contents assigned to *Data*—a potentially large chunk of text—are stored in the view state regardless of the caching settings you might have. If you bind the control to static text, the risk is that you move the XML data back and forth with the page view state while keeping it also stored in the cache for faster access. If you use *Data* and enable caching, consider disabling the view state for the control. (It should be noted, though, that disabling the view state on a control usually affects more than one property.)

If caching is enabled and you change the value of the *DataFile* or *Data* property, the cache is discarded. The *DataSourceChanged* event notifies pages of the event.

Displaying XML Data

The *XmlDataSource* control is commonly bound to a hierarchical control, such as the *TreeView* or *Menu*. (These are the only two built-in hierarchical controls we have in ASP.NET 2.0, but others can be created by developers and third-party vendors.)

To understand how the XML data source works, consider a file that is a kind of XML representation of a *DataSet*—the Employees table of Northwind:

```
<MyDataSet>
    <NorthwindEmployees>
        <Employee>
            <employeeid>1</employeeid>
            <lastname>Davolio</lastname>
            <firstname>Nancy</firstname>
```

```
            <title>Sales Representative</title>
        </Employee>
        ...
    <NorthwindEmployees>
<MyDataSet>
```

Next you bind this file to an instance of the *XmlDataSource* control and the data source to a tree view:

```
<asp:XmlDataSource runat="server" ID="XmlSource"
    DataFile="employees.xml" />
<asp:TreeView runat="server" DataSourceId="XmlSource">
</asp:TreeView>
```

The result (which is not as useful as it could be) is shown in Figure 9-13.

Figure 9-13   The layout (rather than contents) of the bound XML file displayed using a *TreeView* control.

To display data in a way that is really helpful to users, you need to configure node bindings in the tree view:

```
<asp:TreeView runat="server" DataSourceId="XmlSource">
    <DataBindings>
        <asp:TreeNodeBinding Depth="3" DataMember="employeeid"
            TextField="#innertext" />
        <asp:TreeNodeBinding Depth="3" DataMember="lastname"
            TextField="#innertext" />
        <asp:TreeNodeBinding Depth="3" DataMember="firstname"
            TextField="#innertext" />
        <asp:TreeNodeBinding Depth="3" DataMember="title"
            TextField="#innertext" />
    </DataBindings>
</asp:TreeView>
```

The *<DataBindings>* section of the *TreeView* control lets you control the layout and the contents of the tree nodes. The *<TreeNodeBinding>* node indicates the 0-based depth (attribute *Depth*) of the specified XML node (attribute *DataMember*), as well as which attributes determine the text displayed for the node in the tree view and value associated with the node. The *TextField* attribute can be set to the name of the attribute to bind or *#innertext* if you want to display the body of the node. Figure 9-14 provides a preview.

There's a lot more to know about the *TreeView* configuration. I delve into that in *Programming Microsoft ASP.NET 2.0 Applications: Advanced Topics.*

Figure 9-14 XML data bound to a *TreeView* control.

The contents returned by the *XmlDataSource* control can be filtered using XPath expressions:

```
<asp:xmldatasource runat="server" ID="XmlSource"
    DataFile="employees.xml"
    XPath="MyDataSet/NorthwindEmployees/Employee" />
```

The preceding expression displays only the *<Employee>* nodes, with no unique root node in the tree view. XPath expressions are case-sensitive.

> **Note** The *XmlDataSource* control automatically caches data as the *EnableCaching* property is set to *true* by default. Note also that by default the cache duration is set to 0, which means an infinite stay for data. In other words, the data source will cache data until the XML file that it depends on is changed.

Transforming XML Data

The *XmlDataSource* class can also transform its data using Extensible Stylesheet Language Transformations (XSLT). You set the transform file by using the *TransformFile* property or by assigning the XSLT content to the string property named *Transform*. Using the *TransformArgumentList* property, you can also pass arguments to the style sheet to be used during the XSL transformation. An XSL transformation is often used when the structure of an XML document does not match the structure needed to process the XML data. Note that once the data is transformed, the *XmlDataSource* becomes read-only and the data cannot be modified or saved back to the original source document.

Conclusion

ASP.NET data binding has three faces—classic source-based binding as in ASP.NET 1.x, data source controls, and data-binding expressions. Data-binding expressions serve a different purpose from the other two binding techniques. Expressions are used declaratively and within templated controls. They represent calculated values bindable to any property. In ASP.NET 2.0, support for expressions has been empowered to go beyond the boundaries of classic data binding. ASP.NET 2.0 supports custom expressions that are evaluated when the page loads, not when the data-binding process is triggered.

The data-binding model of ASP.NET 1.x is maintained intact with enumerable collections of data bound to controls through the *DataSource* property and a few related others. In addition, a new family of controls makes its debut—data source controls. By virtue of being implemented as a control, a data source component can be declaratively persisted into a Web page without any further effort in code. In addition, data source controls can benefit from other parts of the page infrastructure, such as the view state and ASP.NET cache. Data source controls accept parameters, prepare and execute a command, and return results (if any). Commands include the typical data operations—select, insert, update, delete, and total count.

The most interesting consequence of data source controls is the tight integration with some new data-bound controls. These smarter data-bound controls (*GridView*, *DetailsView*) contain logic to automatically bind at appropriate times on behalf of the page developer, and they interact with the underlying data source intelligently, requiring you to write much less code. Existing data-bound controls have been extended to support data source controls, but only for select operations.

Data source controls make declarative, codeless programming easier and likely to happen in reality. Data source controls, though, are just tools and not necessarily the right tool for the job you need to do.

In the next chapter, we continue our examination of data binding from another perspective—data-bound controls.

Just the Facts

- In ASP.NET 2.0, all data-bound controls support two binding mechanisms: the classic binding available in ASP.NET 1.x done through enumerable data source objects, and data source controls.

- Data source controls are regular server controls with no user interface that intelligently cooperate with the control they're bound to in an effort to anticipate the user's next request.

- Data source controls simplify programming in a quite a few scenarios by reducing the code you need to write.

- ASP.NET 1.x data-bound controls have been modified to support data source controls; they have not been redesigned to take full advantage of data source controls. For this reason, new controls have been added, such as *GridView* and *DetailsView*.

- A new type of expression ($-expression) partners data-binding expressions to provide for declarative expressions that can be used primarily in the design-time configuration of data source controls.

- $-expressions differ from #-expressions because they are evaluated at parse time and their output becomes part of the page source.

- *ObjectDataSource* is the most interesting of the data source controls because it can bridge your presentation layer to the DAL, even remotely. The *ObjectDataSource* control takes advantage of existing tiers and overall promotes a domain-based design over a purely tiered design.

- *XmlDataSource* is both a hierarchical and tabular data source, but only supports read-only scenarios.

Chapter 10
Creating Bindable Grids of Data

In this chapter:

The *DataGrid* Control 414
The *GridView* Control 427
Conclusion 464

Data-bound controls play a key role in the development of ASP.NET applications. Data-driven controls allow you to associate the whole interface, or individual properties, with one or more columns read out of a .NET-compliant data source. We already mentioned data-bound controls in Chapter 9 and reviewed their basics. In this chapter, we'll delve into the details of a couple of extremely versatile data-bound controls that are a fixed presence in any real-world ASP.NET application—the *DataGrid* control in ASP.NET 1.x and the *GridView* control in ASP.NET 2.0.

Both controls render a multicolumn, templated grid and provide a largely customizable user interface with read/write options. In spite of the rather advanced programming interface and the extremely rich set of attributes, the *DataGrid* and *GridView* controls simply generate an HTML table with interspersed hyperlinks to provide interactive functionalities such as sorting, paging, selection, and in place editing.

Although they are customizable at will, grid controls feature a relatively rigid and inflexible graphical model. The data bound to a *DataGrid* or *GridView* is always rendered like a table, therefore, in terms of rows and columns. As we'll see later in the chapter, though, the contents of the cells in a column can be customizable to some extent using system-provided as well as user-defined templates.

The *DataGrid* is the principal control of most data-driven ASP.NET 1.x applications. Like all ASP.NET 1.x controls, the *DataGrid* is fully supported in ASP.NET 2.0 but is partnered with a newer control that is meant to replace it in the long run. The new grid control, *GridView*, is complemented by other view controls, such as *DetailsView* and *FormView*. (We'll cover *DetailsView* and *FormView* in the next chapter.) The *GridView* is a major upgrade of the ASP.NET 1.x *DataGrid* control. It provides the same basic set of capabilities, plus a long list of extensions and improvements.

In this chapter, we'll first take a look at the *DataGrid* capabilities and try to identify and discuss its major shortcomings and limitations. Then we'll consider the *GridView* control and its modified programming interface. For brand-new ASP.NET 2.0 applications, choosing the *GridView* over the *DataGrid* is a no-brainer. For ASP.NET 1.x applications that are being maintained, a move to the *GridView* doesn't present any significant difficulties and such a move positions you well for future enhancements.

The *DataGrid* Control

The *DataGrid* is a column-based control that supports various types of data-bound columns, including text, templated, and command columns. You associate the control with a data source using either the *DataSource* property or, in ASP.NET 2.0, the *DataSourceID* property. The simplest way of displaying a table of data using the ASP.NET grid is as follows:

```
<asp:DataGrid runat="server" id="grid" />
```

Once the control has been placed into the page, you bind it to the data source and have it display the resulting markup.

The *DataGrid* Object Model

The *DataGrid* control provides a grid-like view of the contents of a data source. Each column represents a data source field, and each row represents a record. The *DataGrid* control supports several style and visual properties; in a more realistic scenario, the markup required to embed the control in a page is significantly larger and complex enough to include all those attributes. In ASP.NET 2.0, themes can wrap control-specific visual settings and apply them seamlessly while leaving the markup as slim as possible.

Properties of the *DataGrid* Control

Table 10-1 lists the properties of the control, except those that the control inherits from *Control* and *WebControl*.

Table 10-1   Properties of the *DataGrid* Control

Property	Description
AllowCustomPaging	Gets or sets whether custom paging is enabled. *AllowPaging* must be set to *true* for this setting to work.
AllowPaging	Gets or sets whether paging is enabled.
AllowSorting	Gets or sets whether sorting is enabled.
AlternatingItemStyle	Gets the style properties for alternating rows.
AutoGenerateColumns	Gets or sets whether columns are automatically created and displayed for each field in the data source. *True* by default.
BackImageUrl	Gets or sets the URL of the image to display as the background of the control.

Table 10-1   Properties of the *DataGrid* Control

Property	Description
Caption	The text to render in the control's caption. *Not available in ASP.NET 1.x.*
CaptionAlign	Alignment of the caption. *Not available in ASP.NET 1.x.*
CellPadding	Gets or sets the space (in pixels) remaining between the cell's border and the embedded text.
CellSpacing	Gets or sets the space (in pixels) remaining, both horizontally and vertically, between two consecutive cells.
Columns	Gets a collection of *DataGridColumn* objects.
CurrentPageIndex	Gets or sets the index of the currently displayed page.
DataKeyField	Gets or sets the key field in the bound data source.
DataKeys	Gets a collection that stores the key values of all records displayed as a row in the grid. The column used as the key is defined by the *DataKeyField* property.
DataMember	Indicates the specific table in a multimember data source to bind to the grid. The property works in conjunction with *DataSource*. If *DataSource* is a *DataSet* object, it contains the name of the particular table to bind.
DataSource	Gets or sets the data source object that contains the values to populate the control.
DataSourceID	Indicates the data source object to populate the control. *Not available in ASP.NET 1.x.*
EditItemIndex	Gets or sets the index of the grid's item to edit.
EditItemStyle	Gets the style properties for the item being edited.
FooterStyle	Gets the style properties for the footer section of the grid.
GridLines	Gets or sets whether all cells must have the border drawn.
HeaderStyle	Gets the style properties for the heading section of the grid.
HorizontalAlign	Gets or sets the horizontal alignment of the text in the grid.
Items	Gets the collection of the currently displayed items.
ItemStyle	Gets the style properties for the items in the grid.
PageCount	Gets the number of pages required to display all bound items.
PagerStyle	Gets the style properties for the paging section of the grid.
PageSize	Gets or sets the number of items to display on a single page.
SelectedIndex	Gets or sets the index of the currently selected item.
SelectedItem	Gets a *DataGridItem* object representing the selected item.
SelectedItemStyle	Gets the style properties for the currently selected item.
ShowFooter	Indicates whether the footer is displayed. *False* by default.
ShowHeader	Indicates the header is displayed. *True* by default.
UseAccessibleHeader	Indicates whether the control's header is rendered in an accessible format—that is, using <th> tags instead of <td>. *Not available in ASP.NET 1.x.*
VirtualItemCount	Gets or sets the virtual number of items in the *DataGrid* control when custom paging is used.

The characteristic traits of the *DataGrid* control are the *Columns* and *Items* collections, the style and data-binding properties. All columns in the grid are represented by an object with its own set of properties and methods. Several types of columns are available to implement the most common tasks. In general, not all rows in the bound data source are included in the HTML code for the client. The *Items* collection returns a collection of *DataGridItem* objects, one per each displayed row. The *DataGridItem* class is a specialized version of the *TableRow* class.

> **Note**   In ASP.NET 2.0, a bunch of new properties make their debut to improve the usability of the control especially for users with accessibility problems. *Caption*, *CaptionAlign*, and *UseAccessibleHeader* let you tweak the markup that the control generates to make it easier to users of Assistive Technology devices.

Constituent Elements of a *DataGrid*

The output of a *DataGrid* control is made of several constituent elements grouped in the *List-ItemType* enumeration. Each element plays a clear role and has a precise location in the user interface of the control, as Figure 10-1 shows.

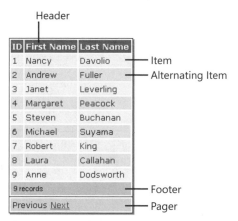

Figure 10-1   The layout of a *DataGrid* control.

The *DataGrid* user interface comprises the logical elements listed in Table 10-2. Each element has its own style property—that is, the set of graphical settings that are automatically applied by the control.

Table 10-2   Graphical Elements That Form a Data Grid

Item Type	Description
AlternatingItem	Represents a data-bound row placed in an odd position. Useful if you want to use different styles for alternating rows. *AlternatingItemStyle* is the property that lets you control the look and feel of the element.
EditItem	Represents the item currently displayed in edit mode. *EditItemStyle* lets you control the look and feel of the element.

Table 10-2   Graphical Elements That Form a Data Grid

Item Type	Description
Footer	Represents the grid's footer. The element can't be bound to a data source and is styled using the settings in the *FooterStyle* property.
Header	Represents the grid's header. The element can't be bound to a data source and is styled using the settings in the *HeaderStyle* property.
Item	Represents a data-bound row placed in an even position. Styled through the *ItemStyle* property.
Pager	Represents the pager element you use to scroll between pages. The element can't be bound to a data source and is styled using the settings in the *PagerStyle* property. The pager can be placed at the top or bottom of the grid's table and even in both places.
SelectedItem	Represents the item, or alternating item, currently selected. The property that defines its look and feel is *SelectedItemStyle*.

Each time one of the constituent elements is about to be created, the grid fires an *ItemCreated* event for you to perform some application-specific tasks. We'll return to grid events in a moment.

Data Source Rows and Displayed Rows

By design, the *DataGrid* control displays the data stored in a data source object—be it an enumerable data object or, in ASP.NET 2.0, a data source control. Each row in the bound data source is potentially a row in the grid. However, this one-to-one mapping doesn't always correspond to reality. Each displayed grid row finds a place in the *Items* collection. Each element in the *Items* collection is an instance of the *DataGridItem* class—a slightly richer table row object—and supplies a *DataItem* property set to the object that corresponds to the row in the bound data source. Note that only bindable items are contained in the *Items* collection. The header, footer, and pager are not included in the collection.

The index properties of the *DataGrid* refer to the rows displayed rather than to the underlying data source. When the item with an index of 1 is selected, the second displayed item is selected, but this piece of information says nothing about the position of the corresponding source record. The data source index for the item object is stored in the *DataSetIndex* property on the *DataGridItem* class. *DataSetIndex* returns the absolute position in the overall data source of the record represented by the current item. Although functional, this method isn't especially handy in some common scenarios, such as when you want to select a row and retrieve a bunch of associated records. In such a case, you need to know the value of the key field in the underlying data source row.

The *DataKeys* collection and the *DataKeyField* property provide an effective shortcut designed specifically to work in similar situations. When you configure a *DataGrid*, you can store the name of a key field in the *DataKeyField* property. During the data-binding phase, the control extracts from the data source the values for the specified key field that correspond to the rows being displayed. As a result, the index of the selected row in the *Items* collection can be used with *DataKeys* to get the key value for the underlying data source row. Let's consider the following declaration, which refers to a grid that displays information about the employees of a company:

```
<asp:DataGrid runat="server" id="grid" DataKeyField="employeeid" ... >
```

To get the ID of the selected employee–to be used to implement, say, a drill-down view–you simply use the following code:

```
// empID is the key of the currently selected item
int empID = grid.DataKeys[grid.SelectedIndex];
```

The *DataKeys* collection is automatically filled by the control based on the value of the *DataKeyField* property and the bound data source.

Events of the *DataGrid* Control

The *DataGrid* control has no specific methods worth mentioning. Table 10-3 lists the events that the control fires during its life cycle.

Table 10-3   Events of the *DataGrid* Control

Event	Description
CancelCommand	The user clicked to cancel any updates made on the current item being edited.
DeleteCommand	The user clicked to start a delete operation on the current item.
EditCommand	The user clicked to put the current item in edit mode.
ItemCommand	The user clicked any command button within the grid control.
ItemCreated	This event occurs after a new grid item is created.
ItemDataBound	This event occurs after a grid item is bound to data.
PageIndexChanged	The user clicked to see a new page of data.
SelectedIndexChanged	The user clicked to select a different item.
SortCommand	The user clicked to start a sort operation on a column.
UpdateCommand	The user clicked to save any updates made on the current item being edited.

The *CancelCommand* and *UpdateCommand* events are fired under special circumstances–that is, when an item is being edited. (We'll cover the *DataGrid* in-place editing feature later in the chapter.) The *CancelCommand* event signals that the user clicked the Cancel button to cancel all pending changes. The *UpdateCommand* event denotes the user's intention to persist all the changes. The other command events–*EditCommand*, *DeleteCommand*, and *SortCommand*– indicate that the user required a particular action by clicking on command buttons within the user interface of the grid.

In addition to the events just listed, the *DataGrid* control fires all the standard events of Web controls, including *Load*, *Init*, *PreRender*, and *DataBinding*. In particular, you might want to write a handler for *PreRender* if you need to modify the HTML code generated for the grid. The *DataBinding* event, on the other hand, is the entry point in the grid's binding process. The event is fired as the first step before the whole binding process begins, regardless of the type of object bound—be it an enumerable object or a data source control.

> **Note**   These command events mark a key difference between the *DataGrid* and the newer *GridView* control. While the *DataGrid* is limited to firing an event to let the page know the user's intention, the *GridView* proactively handles the event by executing the configured command through the bound data source control. The *DataGrid* supports data source controls too, but the support is limited to showing read-only data.

Binding Data to the Grid

A *DataGrid* control is formed by data-bindable columns. By default, the control includes all the data source columns in the view. You can change this behavior by setting the *AutoGenerate-Columns* property to *false*. In this case, only the columns explicitly listed in the *Columns* collection are displayed. The *DataGrid* control supports a variety of column types, which mostly differ from one another in how each represents the data. You are required to indicate the type of the column if you add it to the *Columns* collection; otherwise, if automatic generation is used, all columns are of the simplest type—the *BoundColumn* column type. Table 10-4 details the various types of columns supported.

Table 10-4   Types of Columns

Column Type	Description
BoundColumn	The contents of the column are bound to a field in a data source. Each cell displays as plain text.
ButtonColumn	Displays a button for each item in the column. The text of the button can be data-bound and buttons have a common command name.
EditCommandColumn	Particular type of button column associated with a command named *Edit*. When in edit mode, the whole row is drawn using text boxes rather than literals.
HyperLinkColumn	Displays the contents of each item in the column as a hyperlink. The text of the hyperlink can be bound to a column in the data source or it can be static text. The target URL can be data-bound, too. Clicking a hyperlink column causes the browser to jump to the specified URL.
TemplateColumn	This type displays each cell of the column following a specified ASP.NET template. It also allows you to provide custom behaviors.

Note that the *AutoGenerateColumns* property and the *Columns* collection are not mutually exclusive. If both properties are set to *true* and the collection is not empty, the grid will show the user-defined columns followed by all the ones that auto-generation would produce.

You normally bind columns using the *<columns>* tag in the body of the *<asp:datagrid>* server control, as the following code demonstrates:

```
<asp:datagrid runat="server" id="grid" ... >
  ...
  <columns>
    <asp:BoundColumn runat="server" DataField="employeeid"
        HeaderText="ID" />
    <asp:BoundColumn runat="server" DataField="firstname"
        HeaderText="First Name" />
    <asp:BoundColumn runat="server" DataField="lastname"
        HeaderText="Last Name" />
  </columns>
</asp:datagrid>
```

Alternately, you can create a new column of the desired class, fill its member properly, and then add the class instance to the *Columns* collection. Here is some code to add a *Bound-Column* object to a grid:

```
BoundColumn bc = new BoundColumn();
bc.DataField = "firstname";
bc.HeaderText = "First Name";
grid.Columns.Add(bc);
```

The order of the columns in the collection determines the order in which the columns are displayed in the *DataGrid* control.

> **Note**   The *Columns* collection doesn't persist its contents to the view state, and it is empty whenever the page posts back. To preserve any dynamically added column, you need to re-add it on each and every postback.

Data-Bound Columns

All grid column types inherit from the *DataGridColumn* class and have a few common properties such as the header text, footer and item style, and visibility flag. Table 10-5 details the properties shared by all types of columns.

Table 10-5   Common Properties for All Column Types

Property	Description
FooterStyle	Gets the style properties for the footer of the column
FooterText	Gets or sets the static text displayed in the footer of the column
HeaderImageUrl	Gets or sets the URL of an image to display in the header

Table 10-5   Common Properties for All Column Types

Property	Description
HeaderStyle	Gets the style properties for the header of the column
HeaderText	Gets or sets the static text displayed in the header of the column
ItemStyle	Gets the style properties for the item cells of the column
SortExpression	Gets or sets the expression to sort the data in the column
Visible	Gets or sets whether the column is visible

The *BoundColumn* class represents a column type that is bound to a data field. The key properties to set up a grid column are *DataField*, which represents the name of the column to bind, and *DataFormatString*, which allows you to format the displayed text to some extent. The *ReadOnly* property has an effect only if an edit command column is added to the grid. In this case, the cells in the column are switched to edit mode according to the value of the property.

The following code snippet adds two columns and specifies the header text and the source column for each. In addition, the second column is given a format string to make it look like a currency value with right alignment.

```
<asp:boundcolumn runat="server" datafield="quantityperunit"
    headertext="Packaging" />
<asp:boundcolumn runat="server" datafield="unitprice"
    headertext="Price" DataFormatString="{0:c}">
    <itemstyle width="80px" horizontalalign="right" />
</asp:boundcolumn>
```

Graphical settings for a column must be specified using a child style element.

HyperLink Columns

The *HyperLinkColumn* class is a column type that contains a hyperlink for each cell. The programmer can control the text of the hyperlink and the URL to navigate. Both fields can be bound to a column in the data source. The *DataTextField* takes the name of the field to use for the text of the hyperlink. *DataNavigateUrlField*, on the other hand, accepts the field that contains the URL. Another property, named *DataNavigateUrlFormatString*, defines the format of the final URL to use. By combining the two properties, you can redirect users to the same page, passing row-specific information on the query string, as shown in the following code:

```
<asp:hyperlinkcolumn runat="server" datatextfield="productname"
    headertext="Product"
    datanavigateurlfield="productid"
    datanavigateurlformatstring="productinfo.aspx?id={0}"
    target="ProductView">
    <itemstyle width="200px" />
</asp:hyperlinkcolumn>
```

The hyperlinks will point to the same page—*productinfo.aspx*—each with the product ID associated with the corresponding row of the bound data. The column class is responsible for building the real URL correctly.

> **Note** By using the *DataNavigateUrlField* and *DataNavigateUrlFormatString* properties together, you can make the URL of the hyperlink parametric. However, by default you are limited to just one parameter—the value of the field bound through the *DataNavigateUrlField* property. To use a hyperlink bound to any number of arguments, you should resort to templated columns or use a *GridView*.

Button Columns

The *ButtonColumn* class represents a command column and contains a user-defined button for each cell in the column. Functionally similar to hyperlink columns, button columns are different because they generate a postback event on the same URL. Although the caption of each button can be bound to a data-source column, more often than not a button column has static text displayed through all the cells.

The key idea behind the button column is that you execute a particular action after the user clicks on a row. All buttons in the column are associated with some script code that posts the page back and executes the *ItemCommand* server-side procedure. Within that procedure, you use the command name (the *CommandName* property) to distinguish between multiple button columns, and you use the *ItemIndex* property of the *DataGridItem* class to know the particular row that was clicked. A reference to a *DataGridItem* object is passed through the *ItemCommand* event.

The *select* column is a special type of button column. It is a normal button column with the command name of *select*. When you click on such a column, the *DataGrid* automatically redraws the selected row using a different class of settings—those determined by the *SelectedItemStyle* property. There is no need for you to write an *ItemCommand* handler; the described behavior is built in:

```
<asp:ButtonColumn runat="server" text="Select" CommandName="Select" />
```

The style of the selected row—at most one at a time—is set using the *SelectedItemStyle* property. It can be as easy as the following code:

```
<selecteditemstyle backcolor="cyan" />
```

The change of the selected item is signaled with the *SelectedIndexChanged* event. However, before this event is fired, the application can handle the related *ItemCommand* event. When *SelectedIndexChanged* reaches the application, the *SelectedIndex* property indicates the new selected index.

Templated Columns

Templated columns allow you to create combinations of HTML text and server controls to design a custom layout for any cells in the column. The controls within a templated column can be bound to any combination of fields in the data source. In particular, you can group more fields in a single expression and even embellish it with HTML attributes such as bold-face or italic style. Templates are column-specific and cannot be applied to auto-generated columns. If you want more columns to share the same template, you can duplicate the code only in the ASP.NET page for each column.

A templated column is recognized by the *<TemplateColumn>* tag and rendered by the *Template-Column* class. The body of the tag can contain up to four different templates: *ItemTemplate*, *EditItemTemplate*, *HeaderTemplate*, and *FooterTemplate*. Just as with any other column type, a templated column can have header text and a sort expression. Templated columns, though, do not have an explicit data source field to bind. To bind a templated column to one or more data fields, you use a data-binding expression. (See Chapter 9.) In particular, you use the *Eval* method to evaluate data-bound expressions at run time and return the value properly cast. For example, the following code snippet shows a templated column that mimics the behavior of a *BoundColumn* object associated with the lastname column:

```
<asp:templatecolumn runat="server" headertext="Last Name">
    <itemtemplate>
        <asp:label runat="server" Text='<%#
            DataBinder.Eval(Container.DataItem, "lastname") %>' />
    </itemtemplate>
</asp:templatecolumn>
```

By using *DataBinder.Eval* (or simply *Eval* in ASP.NET 2.0), you can access any number of fields in the currently bound data source. In addition, you can combine them in any order to obtain any sort of expression, which is otherwise impossible using a simpler bound or button column.

Working with the *DataGrid*

The *DataGrid* control is not simply a tool to display static data; it also provides advanced functionalities to page, sort, and edit bound data. The interaction that is established between a *DataGrid* and the host page is limited to exchanging notifications in the form of postback events. The *DataGrid* lets the page know that something happened and leaves the page free to react as appropriate. This pattern is common to most supported operations, with the notable exception of item selection. As mentioned, in fact, if you add a Select button column to the grid and define a proper style for selected items, clicking on a Select button makes the page post back and forces the *DataGrid* to change the appearance of the corresponding row. Other operations for which the *DataGrid* simply fires an event to the page are paging, sorting, and in-place editing.

As you can see, these are relatively common operations that plenty of pages need to accomplish. If you choose to use a *DataGrid* control, be ready to write much more boilerplate code than you would with the newer *GridView* control.

Paging Through the Data Source

In real-world scenarios, the size of a data source easily exceeds the real estate of the page. Data paging is the contrivance that many applications adopt to both gain in scalability and present a more helpful page to the user. Especially on the Web, displaying only a few rows at a time is a more effective approach than downloading hundreds of records that stay hidden most of the time. The *DataGrid* control provides some built-in facilities to let the programmer easily switch to a new page according to the user's clicking.

The control needs to know how many items should be displayed per page, what type of functionality is required for the pager, and the data source to page through. In return for this, the control tracks the current page index, extracts the rows that fit into the particular page, and refreshes the user interface. Whenever the page index changes, an event is fired to the application—the *PageIndexChanged* event.

Note, however, that the host page is still responsible for ensuring that all the rows that fit into the new page are bound to the control. This holds true even if the *DataGrid* is bound to a data source control or a classic enumerable object. With a *DataGrid*, a handler for the *PageIndexChanged* event is always required. What you do in the handler might be different, though, depending on the actual data source. Here's the code you need to use if the *DataGrid* is bound to a data source control:

```
protected void grid_PageIndexChanged(object sender,
        DataGridPageChangedEventArgs e)
{
    grid.CurrentPageIndex = e.NewPageIndex;

    // Must be repeated to force a refresh
    grid.DataSourceID = "SqlDataSource1";
}
```

Note that you still need to reassign *DataSourceID* to trigger an internal data source changed event and cause the control to load its new dataset. If the grid is bound to an enumerable object, you simply assign a new bunch of rows to the *DataSource* property.

Overall, paging is a tough feature and a potential scalability killer. If you leave grid controls in charge of handling paging more or less automatically, caching data is a must. A data source control makes it as easy as turning on the *EnableCaching* property, as you saw in Chapter 9. Caching a lot of data, though, might pose a serious problem, especially if you have to do that for each user.

DataGrid controls also support custom paging, an alternative and cost-effective approach to paging that binds to the control only the records that fit in the current page:

```
protected void grid_PageIndexChanged(object sender,
        DataGridPageChangedEventArgs e)
{
    grid.CurrentPageIndex = e.NewPageIndex;
    grid.DataSource = GetRecordsInPage(grid.CurrentPageIndex);
}

protected object GetRecordsInPage(int pageIndex)
{
    // Retrieve and return data that fit in the given page
}
```

As we'll see later, the *GridView* doesn't explicitly support custom paging. On the other hand, the *GridView* doesn't prevent server paging from working if it is supported by the underlying data source control or the (data access layer) DAL.

Sorting Columns of Data

The *AllowSorting* property enables sorting on all or some of the *DataGrid*'s displayed columns. Just as for paging, clicking to sort data by a column doesn't really produce any visible effect unless you add a handler for the *SortCommand* event. Here's a simple handler you can use if the *DataGrid* is bound to a data source control:

```
protected void grid_SortCommand(object sender,
        DataGridSortCommandEventArgs e)
{
    SqlDataSource1.SelectCommand += " ORDER BY " + e.SortExpression;
    grid.DataSourceID = "SqlDataSource1";
}
```

Sorting is a potentially slow operation to accomplish and can have significant repercussions on scalability. For this reason, it is important to understand how it really works in the context of grids. In ASP.NET 1.x, you can employ in the *SortCommand* event handler only your own logic to sort. You can sort in memory using the *Sort* method of the *DataView* object (which is a very slow process, indeed); you can rely on the database sort capabilities (which is typically the fastest approach to sort data, but note that communication latency and network bandwidth may serve to slow things down from the user's perspective); sometimes, you can also maintain presorted caches of data. Whatever you choose, you need to know what you're doing.

In ASP.NET 2.0, data source controls tend to hide some details. If the data source control is configured to retrieve data via a *DataSet* (the default setting), sorting happens in memory via the *Sort* method. This approach is not really efficient, and it should be avoided unless you have only a few records to sort. If the data source control works via data readers and stored procedures, sorting can take place on the server and data will be returned in the correct order. In the end, sorting is a delicate operation no matter which controls you use. Only careful benchmarks and an application-specific combination of tools and options can deliver the perfect result. To get this, you need to understand how controls work internally.

Editing Existing Rows

A *DataGrid* control displays mostly read-only data. If editing is needed, you select the row to update and post a request for editing. The new page contains an edit form with input fields and links to persist or reject the changes. This pattern is probably the most effective one for editing data over the Web, and it's certainly the pattern that provides the highest level of flexibility. With *DataGrid* controls, though, a simpler model of data editing is possible. The new model is known as in-place editing and mimics the behavior of a Microsoft Office Excel worksheet. When you trigger the event that begins the editing phase, the visible part of the grid is redrawn and—like cells in Excel—the row selected for editing is rendered in a different way, using text-box controls instead of literals and labels. At the same time, the *DataGrid* control completes its own user interface with a couple of button links to allow you to commit or roll back changes.

In-place editing does not require much work to be completely set up, but at the same time it is not appropriate for all types of applications, and it is not functional in all operating contexts. All in all, if you have to edit the content of single and relatively small tables that have no special validation or business logic to apply, in-place editing is extremely handy and powerful.

The key object for in-place editing is the *EditCommandColumn* class. The column adds a link button to all rows of the grid. When the link is clicked, the page posts back and the cells of the row are drawn in edit mode. How a column behaves in edit mode depends on the column type. For example, button and hyperlink columns are completely ignored in edit mode. Bound and templated columns, on the other hand, change their rendering when the row is being edited. In particular, bound columns are rendered using text boxes in place of literals, whereas templated columns display the contents of the *<EditItemTemplate>* section, if any.

As with paging and sorting, code is required to have the *DataGrid* complete an in-place editing operation, too. You typically need to write three event handlers—*EditCommand*, to put the grid in edit mode; *CancelCommand*, to put the grid back in read-only mode; and *UpdateCommand*, to persist changes and refresh the grid. Handlers for *EditCommand* and *CancelCommand* are relatively simple and standard. Writing a handler for *UpdateCommand* might not be that easy, though.

Basically, the *UpdateCommand* handler must accomplish two key operations—retrieving input data and persisting changes. Both operations are hard-coded in the *GridView*, performed in collaboration with the underlying data source control, and mostly configured at design time by the page author.

> **Important**   Admittedly, this section about *DataGrid* controls didn't get into the nitty-gritty details of how the control works and deliberately avoided describing how to implement paging, sorting, and editing properly in real-world scenarios. The reason for this approach lies in the structural difference that exists between *DataGrid* and *GridView* controls. To a large extent, the two controls provide the same set of abstract features—grid-like display, paging, sorting, editing, and templates. How each control implements individual features and binds to data is radically different. In one word, the *philosophy* behind each control is different. Now, the *GridView* control is newer, richer, and smarter, and it would probably have been the only grid control in ASP.NET 2.0 if it weren't for compatibility issues.
>
> If you have an existing ASP.NET application to maintain, and you don't feel like leaping to *GridView*, you already know all the details and techniques omitted here. If you're building a new application and want to take advantage of grids, you don't need to know about *DataGrid* controls and are better off focusing entirely on *GridView* controls. The purpose of this section is to help people in the middle make a decision about which control to use while explaining why Microsoft decided to go with a new control that is designed to complement the changes in the data-binding model we explored in Chapter 9. The *GridView* control is also complemented by other view controls—specifically, *FormView* and *DetailsView*—that we'll cover in the next chapter.

The *GridView* Control

The *GridView* is the successor to the ASP.NET 1.x *DataGrid* control. It provides the same base set of capabilities, plus a long list of extensions and improvements. As mentioned, the *DataGrid*—which is still fully supported in ASP.NET 2.0—is an extremely powerful and versatile control. However, it has one big drawback: it requires you to write a lot of custom code, even to handle relatively simple and common operations such as paging, sorting, editing, or deleting data. The *GridView* control was designed to work around this limitation and make two-way data binding happen with as little code as possible. The control is tightly coupled to the family of new data source controls, and it can handle direct data source updates as long as the underlying data source object supports these capabilities.

This virtually codeless two-way data binding is by far the most notable feature of the new *GridView* control, but other enhancements are numerous. The control is an improvement over the *DataGrid* control because it has the ability to define multiple primary key fields, new column types, and style and templating options. The *GridView* also has an extended eventing model that allows you to handle or cancel events.

The *GridView* Object Model

The *GridView* control provides a tabular grid-like view of the contents of a data source. Each column represents a data source field, and each row represents a record. The class is declared as follows:

```
public class GridView : CompositeDataBoundControl,
                        ICallbackContainer,
                        ICallbackEventHandler
```

The base class ensures data-binding and naming-container support. The *ICallbackContainer* and *ICallbackEventHandler* interfaces provide more effective paging and sorting than is now supported. It does this through client-side, out-of-band calls that use the new script callback technology. (I'll talk more about this later.) Let's begin our tour of the *GridView* control by looking at the control's programming interface.

Properties of the *GridView* Control

The *GridView* supports a large set of properties that fall into the following broad categories: behavior, visual settings, style, state, and templates. Table 10-6 details the properties that affect the behavior of the *GridView*.

Table 10-6   Behavior Properties of the *GridView* Control

Property	Description
AllowPaging	Indicates whether the control supports paging.
AllowSorting	Indicates whether the control supports sorting.
AutoGenerateColumns	Indicates whether columns are automatically created for each field in the data source. The default is *true*.
AutoGenerateDeleteButton	Indicates whether the control includes a button column to let users delete the record that is mapped to the clicked row.
AutoGenerateEditButton	Indicates whether the control includes a button column to let users edit the record that is mapped to the clicked row.
AutoGenerateSelectButton	Indicates whether the control includes a button column to let users select the record that is mapped to the clicked row.
DataMember	Indicates the specific table in a multimember data source to bind to the grid. The property works in conjunction with *DataSource*. If *DataSource* is a *DataSet* object, it contains the name of the particular table to bind.
DataSource	Gets or sets the data source object that contains the values to populate the control.
DataSourceID	Indicates the bound data source control.
EnableSortingAndPagingCallbacks	Indicates whether sorting and paging are accomplished using script callback functions. Disabled by default.
RowHeaderColumn	Name of the column to use as the column header. This property is designed for improving accessibility.

Table 10-6   Behavior Properties of the *GridView* Control

Property	Description
SortDirection	Gets the direction of the column current sort.
SortExpression	Gets the current sort expression.
UseAccessibleHeader	Specifies whether to render *<th>* tags for the column headers instead of default *<td>* tags.

The *SortDirection* and *SortExpression* properties specify the direction and the sort expression on the column that currently determines the order of the rows. Both properties are set by the control's built-in sorting mechanism when users click a column's header. The whole sorting engine is enabled and disabled through the *AllowSorting* property. The *EnableSortingAnd-PagingCallbacks* property toggles on and off the control's capability of using script callbacks to page and sort without doing roundtrips to the server and changing the entire page.

Each row displayed within a *GridView* control corresponds to a special type of grid item. The list of predefined types of items is nearly identical to that of the *DataGrid* and includes items such as the header, rows and alternating rows, footer, and pager. These items are static in the sense that they remain in place for the lifetime of the control in the application. Other types of items are active for a short period of time—the time needed to accomplish a certain operation. Dynamic items are the edit row, the selected row, and the *EmptyData* item. *EmptyData* identifies the body of the grid when the grid is bound to an empty data source.

> **Note**   The *GridView* control provides a few properties specifically designed for accessibility. They are *UseAccessibleHeader*, *Caption*, *CaptionAlign*, and *RowHeaderColumn*. When you set *RowHeaderColumn*, all the column cells will be rendered with the default header style (bold face type). However, *ShowHeader*, *HeaderStyle*, and other header-related properties don't affect the column indicated by *RowHeaderColumn*.

Table 10-7 details the style properties available on the *GridView* control.

Table 10-7   Style Properties of the *GridView* Control

Style	Description
AlternatingRowStyle	Defines the style properties for every other row in the table
EditRowStyle	Defines the style properties for the row being edited
FooterStyle	Defines the style properties for the grid's footer
HeaderStyle	Defines the style properties for the grid's header
EmptyDataRowStyle	Defines the style properties for the empty row, which is rendered when the *GridView* is bound to empty data sources
PagerStyle	Defines the style properties for the grid's pager
RowStyle	Defines the style properties for the rows in the table
SelectedRowStyle	Defines the style properties for the currently selected row

Table 10-8 lists most of the properties that affect the appearance of the control, and Table 10-9 details the templating properties.

Table 10-8   Appearance Properties of the *GridView* Control

Property	Description
BackImageUrl	Indicates the URL to an image to display in the background
Caption	The text to render in the control's caption
CaptionAlign	Alignment of the caption text
CellPadding	Indicates the amount of space (in pixels) between the contents of a cell and the border
CellSpacing	Indicates the amount of space (in pixels) between cells
GridLines	Indicates the gridline style for the control
HorizontalAlign	Indicates the horizontal alignment of the control on the page
EmptyDataText	Indicates the text to render in the control when it is bound to an empty data source
PagerSettings	References an object that lets you set the properties of the pager buttons
ShowFooter	Indicates whether the footer row is displayed
ShowHeader	Indicates whether the header row is displayed

The *PagerSettings* object groups together all the visual properties you can set on the pager. Many of these properties should sound familiar to *DataGrid* programmers. The *PagerSettings* class also adds some new properties to accommodate new predefined buttons (first and last pages), and it uses images instead of text in the links. (You need to figure out a trick to do the same with a *DataGrid*.)

Table 10-9   Templating Properties of the *GridView* Control

Template	Description
EmptyDataTemplate	Indicates the template content to be rendered when the control is bound to an empty source. This property takes precedence over *EmptyDataText* if both are set. If neither is set, the grid isn't rendered if bound to an empty data source.
PagerTemplate	Indicates the template content to be rendered for the pager. This property overrides any settings you might have made through the *PagerSettings* property.

The final block of properties—the state properties—is shown in Table 10-10. State properties return information about the internal state of the control.

Table 10-10   State Properties

Property	Description
BottomPagerRow	Returns a *GridViewRow* object that represents the bottom pager of the grid.
Columns	Gets a collection of objects that represent the columns in the grid. The collection is always empty if columns are auto-generated.

Table 10-10   **State Properties**

Property	Description
DataKeyNames	Gets an array that contains the names of the primary key fields for the currently displayed items.
DataKeys	Gets a collection of DataKey objects that represent the values of the primary key fields set in DataKeyNames for the currently displayed records.
EditIndex	Gets and sets the 0-based index that identifies the row currently rendered in edit mode.
FooterRow	Returns a GridViewRow object that represents the footer.
HeaderRow	Returns a GridViewRow object that represents the header.
PageCount	Gets the number of pages required to display the records of the data source.
PageIndex	Gets and sets the 0-based index that identifies the currently displayed page of data.
PageSize	Indicates the number of records to display on a page.
Rows	Gets a collection of GridViewRow objects that represent the data rows currently displayed in the control.
SelectedDataKey	Returns the DataKey object for the currently selected record.
SelectedIndex	Gets and sets the 0-based index that identifies the row currently selected.
SelectedRow	Returns a GridViewRow object that represents the currently selected row.
SelectedValue	Returns the explicit value of the key as stored in the DataKey object. Similar to SelectedDataKey.
TopPagerRow	Returns a GridViewRow object that represents the top pager of the grid.

The *GridView* is designed to leverage the new data source object model, and it works best when bound to a data source control via the *DataSourceID* property. The *GridView* also supports the classic *DataSource* property, but if you bind data in that way, some of the features (such as built-in updates and paging) become unavailable.

Events of the *GridView* Control

The *GridView* control doesn't have methods other than *DataBind*. As mentioned, though, in many situations you don't need to call methods on the *GridView* control. The data-binding process is started implicitly when you bind the *GridView* to a data source control.

In ASP.NET 2.0, many controls, and the *Page* class itself, feature pairs of events of the type doing/done. Key operations in the control life cycle are wrapped by a pair of events—one firing before the operation takes place, and one firing immediately after the operation is completed. The *GridView* class is no exception. The list of events is shown in Table 10-11.

Table 10-11   Events Fired by the *GridView* Control

Event	Description
PageIndexChanging, *PageIndexChanged*	Both events occur when one of the pager buttons is clicked. They fire before and after the grid control handles the paging operation, respectively.
RowCancelingEdit	Occurs when the Cancel button of a row in edit mode is clicked, but before the row exits edit mode.
RowCommand	Occurs when a button is clicked.
RowCreated	Occurs when a row is created.
RowDataBound	Occurs when a data row is bound to data.
RowDeleting, RowDeleted	Both events occur when a row's Delete button is clicked. They fire before and after the grid control deletes the row, respectively.
RowEditing	Occurs when a row's Edit button is clicked but before the control enters edit mode.
RowUpdating, *RowUpdated*	Both events occur when a row's Update button is clicked. They fire before and after the grid control updates the row, respectively.
SelectedIndexChanging, *SelectedIndexChanged*	Both events occur when a row's Select button is clicked. The two events occur before and after the grid control handles the select operation, respectively.
Sorting, Sorted	Both events occur when the hyperlink to sort a column is clicked. They fire before and after the grid control handles the sort operation, respectively.

RowCreated and *RowDataBound* events are the same as the *DataGrid*'s *ItemCreated* and *ItemDataBound* events, with new names. They behave exactly as they do in ASP.NET 1.x. The same is true of the *RowCommand* event, which is the same as the *DataGrid*'s *ItemCommand* event.

The availability of events that announce a certain operation significantly enhances your programming power. By hooking the *RowUpdating* event, you can cross-check what is being updated and validate the new values. Likewise, you might want to handle the *RowUpdating* event to HTML-encode the values supplied by the client before they are persisted to the underlying data store. This simple trick helps you to fend off script injections.

Simple Data Binding

The following code demonstrates the simplest way to bind data to a *GridView* control. The data source object keeps the page virtually code-free.

```
<asp:ObjectDataSource ID="MySource" runat="server"
    TypeName="ProAspNet20.DAL.Customers"
    SelectMethod="LoadAll">
</asp:ObjectDataSource>
<asp:GridView runat="server" id="grid" DataSourceID="MySource"  />
```

Setting the *DataSourceID* property triggers the binding process, which runs the data source query and populates the user interface of the grid. You need not write any binding code. (Note that you still have to write the *LoadAll* method and the DAL.)

By default, the *GridView* control auto-generates enough columns to contain all the data coming through the data source. In other cases, you might want to control and style each column individually. For this to happen, the binding process should be refined a little bit.

Binding Data to a *GridView* Control

If no data source property is set, the *GridView* control doesn't render anything. If an empty data source object is bound and an *EmptyDataTemplate* template is specified, the results shown to the user have a more friendly look:

```
<asp:gridview runat="server" datasourceid="MySource">
   <emptydatatemplate>
      <asp:label runat="server">
         There's no data to show in this view.
      </asp:label>
   </emptydatatemplate>
</asp:gridview>
```

The *EmptyDataTemplate* property is ignored if the bound data source is not empty. Figure 10-2 shows the output generated by the empty template.

Figure 10-2   The *GridView* control in action on an empty data source.

When you use a declared set of columns, the *AutoGenerateColumns* property of the grid is typically set to *false*. However, this is not a strict requirement—a grid can have declared and auto-generated columns. In this case, declared columns appear first. Note also that auto-generated columns are not added to the *Columns* collection. As a result, when column auto-generation is used, the *Columns* collection is typically empty.

Configuring Columns

The *Columns* property is a collection of *DataControlField* objects. The *DataControlField* object is akin to the *DataGrid*'s *DataGridColumn* object, but it has a more general name because these field objects can be reused in other data-bound controls that do not necessarily render columns. (For example, in the *DetailsView* control, the same class is used to render a row.)

You can define your columns either declaratively or programmatically. In the latter case, you just instantiate any needed data field objects and add them to the *Columns* collection. The following code adds a data-bound column to the grid:

```
BoundField field = new BoundField();
field.DataField = "companyname";
field.HeaderText = "Company Name";
grid.ColumnFields.Add(field);
```

Columns of data are displayed in the order that the column fields appear in the collection. To statically declare your columns in the *.aspx* source file, you use the *<Columns>* tag, as shown here:

```
<columns>
    <asp:boundfield datafield="customerid" headertext="ID" />
    <asp:boundfield datafield="companyname" headertext="Company Name" />
</columns>
```

Table 10-12 lists the column field classes that can be used in a *GridView* control. All the classes inherit *DataControlField*.

Table 10-12   Supported Column Types in *GridView* Controls

Type	Description
BoundField	Default column type. Displays the value of a field as plain text.
ButtonField	Displays the value of a field as a command button. You can choose the link button or the push button style.
CheckBoxField	Displays the value of a field as a check box. It is commonly used to render Boolean values.
CommandField	Enhanced version of *ButtonField*, represents a special command such as *Select*, *Delete*, *Insert*, or *Update*. It's rarely useful with *GridView* controls; the field is tailor-made for *DetailsView* controls. (*GridView* and *DetailsView* share the set of classes derived from *DataControlField*.)
HyperLinkField	Displays the value of a field as a hyperlink. When the hyperlink is clicked, the browser navigates to the specified URL.
ImageField	Displays the value of a field as the *Src* property of an *<img>* HTML tag. The content of the bound field should be the URL to the physical image.
TemplateField	Displays user-defined content for each item in the column. You use this column type when you want to create a custom column field. The template can contain any number of data fields combined with literals, images, and other controls.

Table 10-13 lists the main properties shared by all column types.

Table 10-13   Common Properties of *GridView* Columns

Property	Description
AccessibleHeaderText	The text that represents abbreviated text read by screen readers of Assistive Technology devices.
FooterStyle	Gets the style object for the column's footer.
FooterText	Gets and sets the text for the column's footer.
HeaderImageUrl	Gets and sets the URL of the image to place in the column's header.
HeaderStyle	Gets the style object for the column's header.
HeaderText	Gets and sets the text for the column's header.
InsertVisible	Indicates whether the field is visible when its parent data-bound control is in insert mode. This property does not apply to *GridView* controls.
ItemStyle	Gets the style object for the various columns' cells.
ShowHeader	Indicates whether the column's header is rendered.
SortExpression	Gets and sets the expression used to sort the grid contents when the column's header is clicked. Typically, this string property is set to the name of the bound data field.

The properties listed in Table 10-13 represent a subset of the properties that each column type actually provides. In particular, each type of column defines a tailor-made set of properties to define and configure the bound field. Refer to the MSDN documentation for details on the programming interface of *GridView*'s column types.

Bound Fields

The *BoundField* class represents a field that is displayed as plain text in a data-bound control such as *GridView* or *DetailsView*. To specify the field to display, you set the *DataField* property to the field's name. You can apply a custom formatting string to the displayed value by setting the *DataFormatString* property. The *NullDisplayText* property lets you specify alternative text to display should the value be *null*. Finally, by setting the *ConvertEmptyStringToNull* property to *true*, you force the class to consider empty strings as null values.

A *BoundField* can be programmatically hidden from view through the *Visible* property while the *ReadOnly* property prevents the displayed value from being modified in edit mode. To display a caption in the header or footer sections, set the *HeaderText* and *FooterText* properties, respectively. You can also choose to display an image in the header instead of text. In this case, you set the *HeaderImageUrl* property.

Button Fields

A button field is useful to put a clickable element in a grid's column. You typically use a button field to trigger an action against the current row. A button field represents any action that you want to handle through a server-side event. When the button is clicked, the page posts back and fires a *RowCommand* event. Figure 10-3 shows a sample.

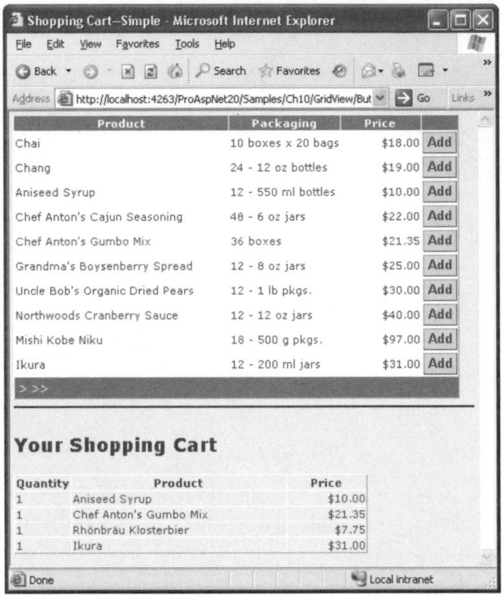

Figure 10-3 Button fields in a *GridView* control.

The following listing shows the markup code behind the grid in the figure:

```
<asp:GridView ID="GridView1" runat="server" DataSourceID="SqlDataSource1"
    AutoGenerateColumns="false" AllowPaging="true"
    OnRowCommand="GridView1_RowCommand">
    <HeaderStyle backcolor="gray" font-bold="true" height="200%" />
    <PagerStyle backcolor="gray" font-bold="true" height="200%" />
    <PagerSettings Mode="NextPreviousFirstLast" />
    <Columns>
        <asp:BoundField datafield="productname"
            headertext="Product" />
        <asp:BoundField datafield="quantityperunit"
            headertext="Packaging" />
        <asp:BoundField datafield="unitprice"
            headertext="Price" DataFormatString="{0:c}">
          <itemstyle width="80px" horizontalalign="right" />
        </asp:BoundField>
        <asp:ButtonField buttontype="Button" text="Add" CommandName="Add" />
    </Columns>
</asp:GridView>
```

Product information is displayed using a few *BoundField* objects. The sample button column allows you to add the product to the shopping cart. When users click the button, the *RowCommand* server event is fired. In case multiple button columns are available, the *CommandName* attribute lets you figure out which button was clicked. The value you assign to *CommandName* is any unique string that the code-behind class can understand. Here's an example:

```
void GridView1_RowCommand(object sender, GridViewCommandEventArgs e)
{
    if (e.CommandName.Equals("Add"))
```

```
    {
        // Get the index of the clicked row
        int index = Convert.ToInt32(e.CommandArgument);

        // Create a new shopping item and add it to the cart
        AddToShoppingCart(index);
    }
}
```

In the sample, the button column shows a fixed text for all data items. You get this by setting the *Text* property on the *ButtonField* class. If you want to bind the button text to a particular field on the current data item, you set the *DataTextField* property to the name of that field.

You can choose different styles for the button—push, link, or image. To render the button as an image, do as follows:

```
<asp:buttonfield buttontype="Image" CommandName="Add"
    ImageUrl="/proaspnet20/images/cart.gif"  />
```

To add a ToolTip to the button (or the image), you need to handle the *RowCreated* event. (I'll discuss this in more detail later in the chapter.)

Hyperlink Fields

Hyperlink columns point the user to a different URL, optionally displayed in an inner frame. Both the text and URL of the link can be obtained from the bound source. In particular, the URL can be set in either of two ways: through a direct binding to a data source field or by using a hard-coded URL with a customized query string. You choose the direct binding if the URL is stored in one of the data source fields. In this case, you set the *DataNavigateUrlFields* property to the name of the column. In some situations, though, the URL to access is application-specific and not stored in the data source. In this case, you can set the *DataNavigateUrl-FormatString* property with a hard-coded URL and with an array of parameters in the query string, as follows:

```
<asp:HyperLinkField DataTextField="productname"
    HeaderText="Product"
    DataNavigateUrlFields="productid"
    DataNavigateUrlFormatString="productinfo.aspx?id={0}"
    Target="ProductView" />
```

When the user clicks, the browser fills the specified frame window with the contents of the *productinfo.aspx?id=xxx* URL, where *xxx* comes from the *productid* field. The URL can include multiple parameters. To include more data-bound values, just set the *DataNavigateUrlFields* property to a comma-separated list of field names. This behavior extends that of the *Data-Grid*'s hyperlink column in that it supports multiple parameters.

The text of the hyperlink can be formatted too. The *DataTextFormatString* property can contain any valid markup and uses the {0} placeholder to reserve space for the data-bound value. (See Figure 10-4.)

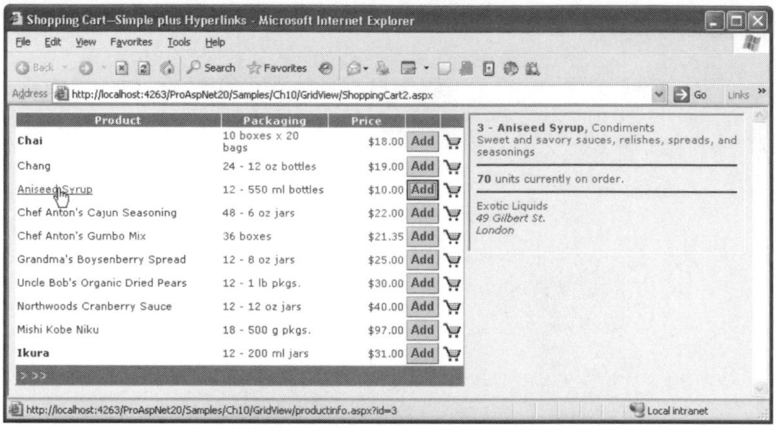

Figure 10-4 Hyperlink fields in a *GridView* control.

> **Tip** When choosing a target for the hyperlinked pages, you can also use any of the following standard targets: *_self*, *_parent*, *_new*. Both Microsoft Internet Explorer and Firefox support *_search*, which uses a companion Web panel docked at the left edge of the browser's real estate. (See Figure 10-5.)

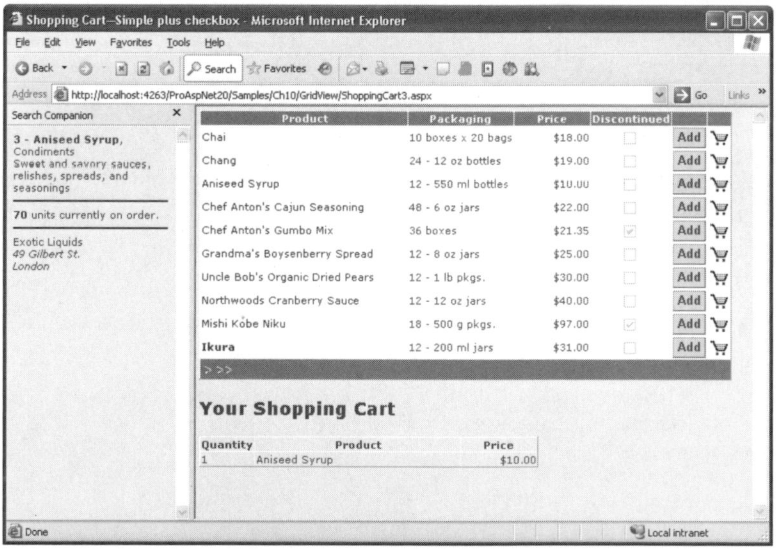

Figure 10-5 Checkbox fields in a *GridView* control.

CheckBox Fields

The column types we hitherto considered are nothing new for seasoned ASP.NET 1.x developers. Although renamed, their overall behavior remains very similar to that of analogous column types for *DataGrids*. The *CheckBoxField* type, on the other hand, is a new entry in

ASP.NET 2.0 and is limited to *GridView* and other view controls. The simplest way in which you can get a checkbox column in ASP.NET 1.x (or in general for *DataGrids*) is through templates.

The *CheckBoxField* column is a relatively simple bound column that displays a check box. You can bind it only to a data field that contains Boolean values. A valid Boolean value is a value taken from a column of type *Bit* in a SQL Server table (and analogous types in other databases) or a property of type *bool* if the control is bound to a custom collection. Any other form of binding will result in a parsing exception. In particular, you get an exception if you bind a *CheckBoxField* column to an integer property, thus implicitly assuming that 0 is false and non-zero values are true.

Image Fields

The *ImageField* column type represents a field that is displayed as an image in a data-bound control. The cell contains an *<img>* element, so the underlying field must reference a valid URL. You can compose the URL at will, though. For example, you can use the *DataImageUrlField* to perform a direct binding where the content of the field fills the *Src* attribute of the *<img>* tag. Alternately, you can make the column cells point to an external page (or HTTP handler) that retrieves the bytes of the image from any source and passes them down to the browser. The following code illustrates this approach:

```
<columns>
  <asp:ImageField DataImageUrlField="employeeid"
    DataImageUrlFormatString="showemployeepicture.aspx?id={0}"
    DataAlternateTextField="lastname">
    <ControlStyle width="120px" />
  </asp:ImageField>
  <asp:TemplateField headertext="Employee">
    <ItemStyle width="220px" />
    <ItemTemplate>
        <b><%# Eval("titleofcourtesy") + " " +
            Eval("lastname") + ", " +
            Eval("firstname") %></b> <br />
        <%# Eval("title")%>
        <hr />
        <i><%# Eval("notes")%></i>
    </ItemTemplate>
  </asp:templatefield>
</Columns>
```

Cells in the *ImageField* column are filled with the output of the next URL:

```
ShowEmployeePicture.aspx?id=xxx
```

Needless to say, *xxx* is the value in the *employeeid* field associated with *DataImageUrlField*. Interestingly enough, the alternate text can also be data bound. You use the *DataAlternateText-Field* property. Figure 10-6 gives a sneak preview of the feature. The page in Figure 10-6 employs a template column to render the employee's information. I'll return to the subject of template columns in a moment.

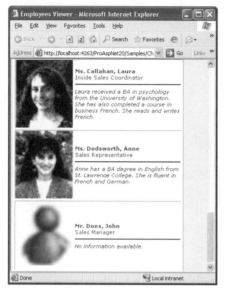

Figure 10-6 Image fields in a *GridView* control.

The following code demonstrates the world's simplest page to retrieve and serve an image out of a database table:

```
void Page_Load(object sender, EventArgs e)
{
    int id = Convert.ToInt32(Request.QueryString["id"]);
    string connString = "...";
    string cmdText = "SELECT photo FROM employees WHERE employeeid=@empID";

    using (SqlConnection conn = new SqlConnection(connString))
    {
        SqlCommand cmd = new SqlCommand(cmdText, conn);
        cmd.Parameters.AddWithValue("@empID", id);
        byte[] img = null;
        conn.Open();

        try
        {
            img = (byte[])cmd.ExecuteScalar();
            if (img != null)
            {
                Response.ContentType = "image/png";
                Response.OutputStream.Write(img, EMP_IMG_OFFSET, img.Length);
            }
        }
        catch
        {
```

```
         Response.WriteFile("/proaspnet20/images/noimage.gif");
     }
     conn.Close();
}
```

The preceding code serves a standard image if the value of the field specified is *null*. You can obtain the same result by setting the *NullImageUrl* property if you're using direct binding—that is, not passing through an external page or handler.

> **Note** The EMP_IMG_OFFSET constant in the code snippet should normally be just 0. However, given the particular structure of the photo column of the Northwind's *Employees* database, it has to be 78. But, again, this is required only with that table.

Templated Fields

Figure 10-6 shows a customized column where the values of several fields are combined. This is exactly what you can get by using templates. A *TemplateField* column gives each row in the grid a personalized user interface that is completely defined by the page developer. You can define templates for various rendering stages, including the default view, in-place editing, the header, and the footer. The supported templates are listed in Table 10-14.

Table 10-14 Supported Templates

Template	Description
AlternatingItemTemplate	Defines the contents and appearance of alternating rows. If not specified, the *ItemTemplate* is used.
EditItemTemplate	Defines the contents and appearance of the row currently being edited. This template should contain input fields and possibly validators.
FooterTemplate	Defines the contents and appearance of the row's footer.
HeaderTemplate	Defines the contents and appearance of the row's header.
ItemTemplate	Defines the default contents and appearance of the rows.

A templated view can contain anything that makes sense to the application you're building—server controls, literals, and data-bound expressions. Data-bound expressions allow you to insert values contained in the current data row. You can use as many fields as needed in a template. Notice, though, that not all templates support data-bound expressions. The header and footer templates are not data-bound, and any attempt to use expressions will result in an exception.

The following code shows how to define the item template for a product column. The column displays on two lines and includes the name of the product and some information about the packaging. You use data-bound expressions (which are discussed in Chapter 9) to refer to data fields.

```
<asp:templatefield headertext="Product">
    <itemtemplate>
```

```
        <b><%# Eval("productname")%></b> <br />
        available in <%# Eval("quantityperunit")%>
    </itemtemplate>
</asp:templatefield>
```

Figure 10-7 demonstrates template fields in action.

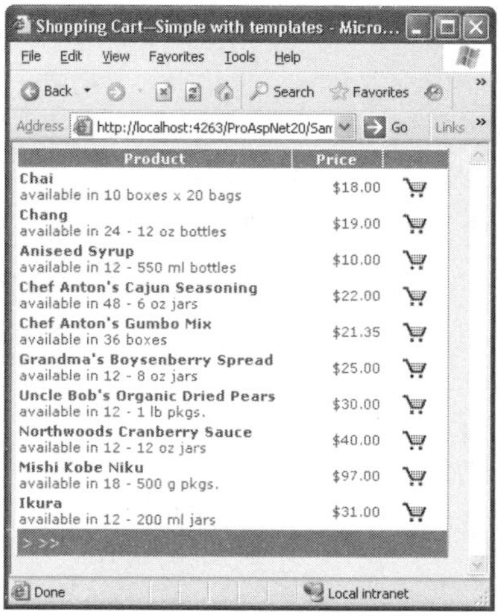

Figure 10-7   Template fields in a *GridView* control.

> **Note**   The *TemplateField* class also features an *InsertTemplate* property. However, this type of template is never used by the *GridView* control. The *InsertTemplate* is used by the *FormView* control instead. As mentioned earlier, in ASP.NET 2.0 view controls share some field classes, such as *TemplateField*. As a result, *TemplateField* (and a few more classes) provide a superset of properties that serves the needs of multiple view controls. We'll cover the *FormView* control in the next chapter.

Paging Data

The *GridView* is designed to take advantage of specific capabilities of the underlying data source control. In this way, the grid control can handle common operations on data such as sorting, paging, updating, and deleting. In general, not all data source components support all possible and feasible data operations. Data source components expose Boolean properties (such as the *CanSort* property) to signal whether they can perform a given operation.

> **Important**   If a *GridView* control is bound to its data source through the *DataSource* property—that is, it doesn't leverage data source controls—its overall behavior as far as paging and other operations are concerned (for example, sorting and editing) is nearly identical to that of the *DataGrid* control. In this case, the *GridView* fires events and expects the binding code in the page to provide instructions and fresh data. In the remainder of this chapter, unless explicitly mentioned, we refer to a *GridView* bound to a data source control.

To some extent, the *GridView* makes transparent for the page developer the implementation of commonly required features such as sorting and paging. In most cases, you need only a fraction of the code you need with the *DataGrid*; in some cases, no code at all is required. This said, don't forget what one old and wise proverb says—not all that glitters is gold. Put another way, be aware that the less code you write, the more you rely on the existing infrastructure to get things done. In doing so, you let the system make important decisions on your behalf. Paging and sorting are key operations in Web applications. You can still accept what the *GridView* does by default, but if you get to know exactly what happens under the hood, you have a better chance of diagnosing and fixing in a timely manner any performance problems that show up in the lifetime of the application.

Codeless Data Paging

The ability to scroll a potentially large set of data is an important but challenging feature for modern, distributed applications. An effective paging mechanism allows customers to interact with a database without holding resources. To enable paging on a *GridView* control, all you do is set the *AllowPaging* property to *true*. When the *AllowPaging* property is set to *true*, the grid displays a pager bar and prepares to detect a user's pager button clicks.

When a user clicks to see a new page, the page posts back, but the *GridView* traps the event and handles it internally. This marks a major difference between *GridView* and the *DataGrid* and programming model you might know from ASP.NET 1.x. With the *GridView*, there's no need to write a handler for the *PageIndexChanged* event. The event is still exposed (and partnered with *PageIndexChanging*), but you should handle it only to perform extra actions. The *GridView* knows how to retrieve and display the requested new page. Let's take a look at the following control declaration:

```
<asp:GridView ID="GridView1" runat="server"
    DataSourceID="SqlDataSource1" AllowPaging="true" />
```

Any data *SqlDataSource1* binds to the grid is immediately pageable. As in Figure 10-8, the control displays a pager with a few predefined links (first, previous, next, and last) and automatically selects the correct subset of rows that fit in the selected page.

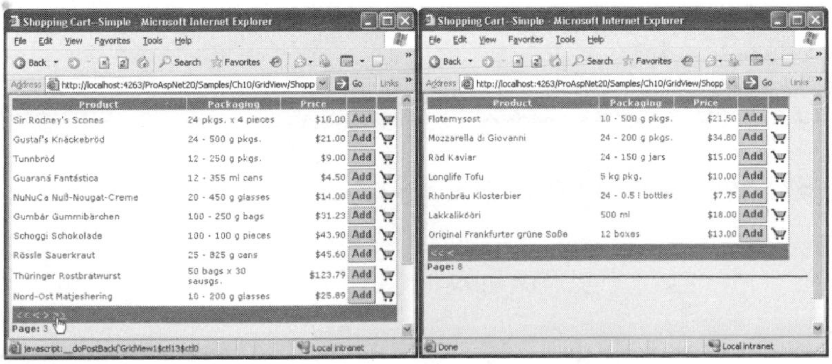

Figure 10-8 Moving through pages in a *GridView* control.

The default user interface you get with the *GridView* doesn't include the page number. Adding a page number label is as easy as writing a handler for the *PageIndexChanged* event:

```
protected void GridView1_PageIndexChanged(object sender, EventArgs e)
{
    ShowPageIndex();
}
private void ShowPageIndex()
{
    CurrentPage.Text = (GridView1.PageIndex + 1).ToString();
}
```

Once again, note that the *PageIndexChanged* handler is not involved with data binding or page selection as it is with *DataGrids*. If you don't need any post-paging operation, you can blissfully omit it altogether.

What's the cost of this apparently free (and magical) paging mechanism?

The *GridView* control doesn't really know how to get a new page. It simply asks the bound data source control to return the rows that fit in the specified page. Paging is ultimately up to the data source control. When a grid is bound to a *SqlDataSource* control, paging requires that the whole data source be bound to the control. When a grid is bound to an *ObjectDataSource* control, paging depends on the capabilities of the business object you're connecting to.

Let's tackle *SqlDataSource* first. It is mandatory that you set *DataSourceMode* to *DataSet* (the default setting). This means that the whole dataset is retrieved and only the few records that fit in the current page size are displayed. In an extreme scenario, you might end up downloading 1,000 records for each postback to show only 10. Things go much better if you enable caching on *SqlDataSource* by setting *EnableCaching* to *true*. In this case, the whole data set is downloaded only once and stored in the ASP.NET cache for the specified duration. As long as the data stays cached, any page is displayed almost for free. However, a potentially large chunk of data is stored in memory. This option is therefore recommended only for relatively small sets of records shared by all users.

> **Tip**   If you want to page records at the database level, the best that you can do is code the desired behavior in a stored procedure and bind the stored procedure to the *SelectCommand* property of the *SqlDataSource* control. In this case, turn caching off.

Moving the Burden of Paging to the DAL

As we discussed in Chapter 9, the *ObjectDataSource* control supplies a rather generic interface for paging that heavily relies on the capabilities of the underlying business and data access layers (DALs).

The key point is that you should have a paging-enabled business object. You configure the *ObjectDataSource* control based on the characteristics of your business object method. Once you have identified the select method, you overload it with a version that takes two extra parameters—the page size and start index for the page. In the end, the select method must be able to retrieve pages of records. In the declaration of the *ObjectDataSource* control, you set the *StartRowIndexParameterName* and *MaximumRowsParameterName* properties to the name of the method parameter that denotes the start index and page size, respectively.

One more step is needed to enable the *GridView* to page the data source provided by the *ObjectDataSource* control. You also need to set the *EnablePaging* property of *ObjectDataSource* to *true*:

```
<asp:ObjectDataSource ID="ObjectDataSource1" runat="server"
    EnablePaging="true"
    TypeName="ProAspNet20.DAL.Customers"
    StartRowIndexParameterName="firstRow"
    MaximumRowsParameterName="totalRows"
    SelectMethod="LoadByCountry">
    <SelectParameters>
        <asp:ControlParameter Name="country" ControlID="Countries"
            PropertyName="SelectedValue" />
    </SelectParameters>
</asp:ObjectDataSource>

<asp:GridView ID="GridView1" runat="server" AutoGenerateColumns="false"
    DataSourceID="ObjectDataSource1" AllowPaging="true"
    OnPageIndexChanged="GridView1_PageIndexChanged">
    <PagerSettings Mode="NextPreviousFirstLast" />
    <Columns>
        <asp:BoundField DataField="id" HeaderText="ID" />
        <asp:BoundField DataField="companyname" HeaderText="Company" />
        <asp:BoundField DataField="contactname" HeaderText="Contact" />
    </Columns>
</asp:GridView>
<b>Page: </b><asp:Label runat="server" ID="CurrentPage" />
```

In the preceding code, you explicitly specify only the parameters whose contents are important for the method to work. The two paging-related parameters are left to the *GridView* to set. The page size parameter is automatically bound to the *PageSize* property of the *GridView*; the first index to retrieve is determined by multiplying page size by page index. Here are the prototypes of the *LoadByCountry* method:

```
public static CustomerCollection LoadByCountry(string country) {
    LoadByCountry(country, -1, 0);
}
public static CustomerCollection LoadByCountry(string country,
        int totalRows, int firstRow) {
    // Retrieve the specified subset of records
}
```

The mechanics of *ObjectDataSource* doesn't say much about the effectiveness of the paging algorithm. How the business object actually retrieves the records in the requested page is an implementation- and application-specific detail. In the sample code, *LoadByCountry* runs the original query and retrieves a data reader to the whole data set. Next, it discards all the records that don't fit in the specified range. This implementation is a good compromise between simplicity and effectiveness. It is not the best solution possible, but it's easy to implement and demonstrate. The memory consumption is limited to one record at a time, but the database returns the whole data set.

Paging Algorithms

The *GridView* doesn't support the *AllowCustomPaging* property you find on *DataGrid*s. However, customizing the paging algorithm is definitely possible. At its core, a custom paging algorithm provides a way to extract pages of records that minimizes caching of records. Ideally, you would ask the database to page the results of a particular query. Very few databases, though, support this feature. Several alternative approaches exist, with pros and cons.

A possible strategy entails creating temporary tables to select only the subset of records you really need. You build a stored procedure and pass it parameters to indicate the page size and index. Alternately, you can use nested SELECT commands and the TOP statement to retrieve all the records up to the last record in the requested page, reverse the order, and discard unneeded records. Again, the TOP clause is not common to all databases. Another possible approach based on dynamically built SQL code is discussed in the following blog post: *http://weblogs.sqlteam.com/jeffs/archive/2004/03/22/1085.aspx*.

If you can collaborate with the database administrator (DBA), you can require that an ad hoc column be added to index the queries. In this case, the DAL must guarantee that the values in the column form a regular succession of values and can be computable. The simplest way of accomplishing this is by giving the column progressive numbers.

Configuring the Pager

When the *AllowPaging* property is set to *true*, the grid displays a pager bar. You can control the characteristics of the pager to a large extent, through the *<PagerSettings>* and *<PagerStyle>* tags or their equivalent properties. The pager of the *GridView* control also supports first and last page buttons and lets you assign an image to each button. (This is also possible for *DataGrid*s, but it requires a lot of code.) The pager can work in either of two modes—displaying explicit page numbers, or providing a relative navigation system. In the former case, the pager contains numeric links, one representing a page index. In the latter case, buttons are present to navigate to the next or previous page and even to the first or last page. The *Mode* property rules the user interface of the pager. Available modes are listed in the Table 10-15.

Table 10-15   Modes of a Grid Pager

Mode	Description
NextPrevious	Displays next and previous buttons to access the next and previous pages of the grid
NextPreviousFirstLast	Displays next and previous buttons plus first and last buttons to directly access first and last pages of the grid
Numeric	Displays numeric link buttons corresponding to the pages of the grid
NumericFirstLast	Displays numeric link buttons corresponding to the pages of the grid plus first and last buttons to directly access first and last pages of the grid

Ad hoc pairs of properties—*xxxPageText* and *xxxPageImageUrl*—let you set the labels for these buttons as desired. The *xxx* stands for any of the following: *First*, *Last*, *Next*, or *Previous*. Figure 10-9 shows a sample page in action.

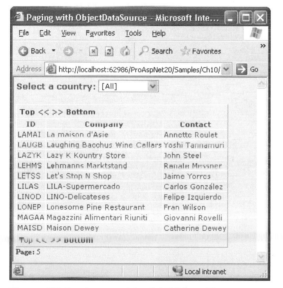

Figure 10-9   A pageable *GridView* with two pagers.

Depending on the size of the grid, the first and last rows in a grid might not necessarily fit in the screen real estate. To make it easier for users to page regardless of the scrollbar position, you can enable top and bottom pagers for a grid. You do this by setting the *Position* attribute on the *<PagerSettings>* element:

```
<PagerSettings Position="TopAndBottom" />
```

Other options are to display the pager only at the top or only at the bottom of the grid.

The pager of the *GridView* control can be entirely replaced with a new one, in case of need. (See Figure 10-10.) You do this by adding the *<PagerTemplate>* element to the control's declaration. Here's an example:

```
<PagerTemplate>
    <asp:Button ID="BtnFirst" runat="server" commandname="First"
        Text="First" />
    <asp:Button ID="BtnPrev" runat="server" commandname="Prev"
        Text="<<" />
    <asp:Button ID="BtnNext" runat="server" commandname="Next"
        Text=">>" />
    <asp:Button ID="BtnLast" runat="server" commandname="Last"
        Text="Last" />
</PagerTemplate>
```

To handle clickings on the buttons, you write a *RowCommand* event handler and set the page index explicitly:

```
void GridView1_RowCommand(object sender, GridViewCommandEventArgs e)
{
    if (e.CommandName == "Last")
        GridView1.PageIndex = GridView1.PageCount - 1;
    if (e.CommandName == "First")
        GridView1.PageIndex = 0;
    if (e.CommandName == "Next")
        GridView1.PageIndex ++;
    if (e.CommandName == "Prev")
        GridView1.PageIndex --;
}
```

Admittedly, this code is quite simple and should be fleshed out a little bit, at least to make it capable of disabling buttons when the first or last index is reached.

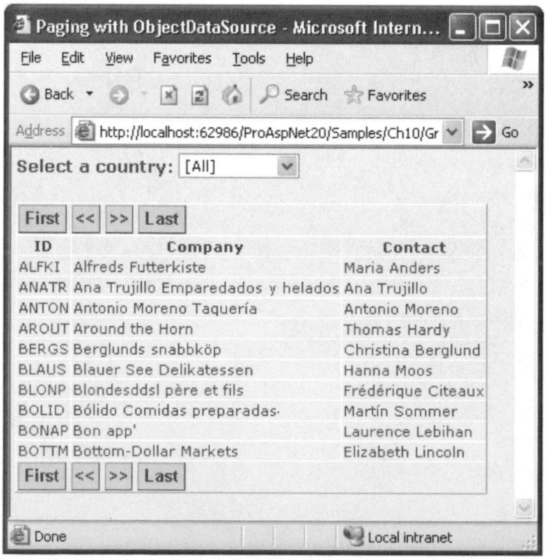

Figure 10-10   A pageable *GridView* with a custom pager.

Sorting Data

Sorting is a delicate, nonlinear operation that normally is quite expensive if performed on the client. Generally speaking, in fact, the best place to sort records is in the database environment because of the super-optimized code you end up running most of the time. Be aware of this as we examine the sorting infrastructure of the *GridView* control and data source controls. The *GridView* doesn't implement a sorting algorithm; instead, it relies on the data source control (or the page, if bound to an enumerable object) to provide sorted data.

Codeless Data Sorting

To enable the *GridView*'s sorting capabilities, you set the *AllowSorting* property to *true*. When sorting is enabled, the *GridView* gains the ability to render the header text of columns as links. You can associate each column with a sorting expression by using the *SortExpression* property. A sorting expression is any comma-separated sequence of column names. Each column name can be enriched with an order qualifier such as DESC or ASC. DESC indicates a descending order, while ASC denotes the ascending order. The ASC qualifier is the default; if omitted, the column is sorted ascendingly. The following code sets up the GridView column for sorting on the *productname* data source column:

```
<asp:GridView runat="server" id="MyGridView" DataSourceID="MySource"
   AllowSorting="true" AutoGenerateColumns="false">
   <Columns>
      <asp:BoundField datafield="productname" headertext="Product"
         sortexpression="productname" />
      <asp:BoundField datafield="quantityperunit"
         headertext="Packaging" />
   </Columns>
</asp:Gridview>
```

Just as for paging, with a *GridView* no manually written code is required to make sorting work. Properly configured, the *GridView*'s sorting infrastructure works without further intervention and in a bidirectional way—that is, if you click on a column sorted descendingly, it is sorted ascendingly and vice versa. You need to add some custom code only if you want to implement more advanced capabilities such as showing a glyph in the header to indicate the direction. (I'll say more about that in a moment.)

Just as for paging, the main snag with sorting is how the underlying data source control implements it. Let's see what happens when the grid is bound to a *SqlDataSource* object. Other than setting *AllowSorting* to *true* and adding the sort expression to the sortable columns, no other action is required. (See Figure 10-11.)

When the user clicks to sort, the grid asks the *SqlDataSource* control to return sorted data. As mentioned, the *SqlDataSource* control returns a *DataSet* by default. If this is the case, the control retrieves the data, builds a *DataView* out of it, and calls the *DataView*'s *Sort* method. This approach works fine, but it's not exactly the fastest way you have to sort. You might still find it to be a good fit for your application, but be aware that sorting is performed using the Web server's memory. Combined with caching, both paging and sorting in memory are a feasible solution for shared and relatively small sets of records.

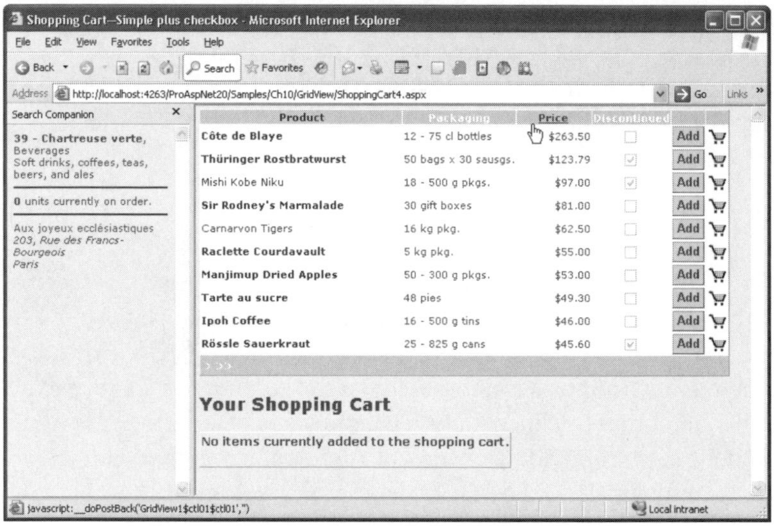

Figure 10-11   A sortable *GridView* bound to a *SqlDataSource* control.

Is there any chance to get pre-sorted data from the database server? The first step is to set the *DataSourceMode* property of the *SqlDataSource* control to *DataReader*. If you leave it set to *DataSet*, sorting will occur in memory. The second step requires you to write a stored procedure to retrieve data. To get data sorted, you also set the *SortParameterName* property of the data source control to the name of the stored procedure parameter that indicates the sort expression. Obviously, you need the stored procedure to build its command text dynamically to incorporate the proper *ORDER BY* clause. Here's how to modify the *CustOrderHist*, Northwind's stored procedure, to make its results sortable at will:

```
CREATE PROCEDURE CustOrderHistSorted
     @CustomerID nchar(5), @SortedBy varchar(20)='total'  AS
SET QUOTED_IDENTIFIER OFF
IF @SortedBy = ''
BEGIN
   SET @SortedBy = 'total'
END

EXEC (
   'SELECT ProductName, Total=SUM(Quantity)  ' +
   'FROM Products P, [Order Details] OD, Orders O, Customers C ' +
   'WHERE C.CustomerID = "' + @CustomerID + '" ' +
   'AND C.CustomerID = O.CustomerID AND O.OrderID = OD.OrderID ' +
   'AND OD.ProductID = P.ProductID GROUP BY ProductName ' +
   'ORDER BY ' + @SortedBy)
GO
```

At this point, the grid is ready to show sorted columns of data and the burden of sorting has moved to the database management system (DBMS):

```
<asp:SqlDataSource ID="SqlDataSource1" runat="server"
    DataSourceMode="DataReader"
    ConnectionString='<%$ ConnectionStrings:LocalNWind %>'
    SortParameterName="SortedBy"
    SelectCommand="CustOrderHistSorted"
    SelectCommandType="StoredProcedure">
  <SelectParameters>
    <asp:ControlParameter ControlID="CustList"
        Name="CustomerID" PropertyName="SelectedValue" />
  </SelectParameters>
</asp:SqlDataSource>
```

It is essential to know that sorting data on the database, as shown here, is incompatible with caching. You need to set *EnableCaching* to *false*; otherwise, an exception is thrown. As a result, you go back to the database every time the user clicks to sort.

If you use the *DataSet* mode and enable caching, you initially get data from the database, sorted as expected, but successive sorting operations are resolved in memory. Finally, if you use the *DataSet* mode and disable caching, you still go down to the database for sorting each time. Note that this option is mentioned only for completeness: the effect is the same as using *DataReader*, but a data reader is a more efficient approach when caching is not required.

In general, the availability of the *SortParameterName* property opens up a world of possibility for sorting the contents of other data-bound controls (for example, *Repeater* and custom controls) that mostly consume data and don't require paging or caching.

Moving the Burden of Sorting to the DAL

What if you use an *ObjectDataSource* control instead? In this case, the burden of sorting should be moved to the DAL or business layer and exposed to the data source control by the programming interface of the bound business object. Let's modify the *LoadByCountry* method we considered earlier for paging and add to it a new parameter to indicate the sort expression:

```
public static CustomerCollection LoadByCountry(
    string country, int totalRows, int firstRow, string sortExpression)
{
    CustomerCollection coll = new CustomerCollection();
    using (SqlConnection conn = new SqlConnection(ConnectionString))
    {
        SqlCommand cmd;
        cmd = new SqlCommand(cmdLoadByCountry, conn);
        cmd.Parameters.AddWithValue("@country", country);
        if (!String.IsNullOrEmpty(sortExpression))
            cmd.CommandText += " ORDER BY " + sortExpression;
        conn.Open();
        SqlDataReader reader = cmd.ExecuteReader();
        HelperMethods.FillCustomerList(coll, reader, totalRows, firstRow);
```

```
            reader.Close();
            conn.Close();
        }
        return coll;
    }
```

The *cmdLoadByCountry* constant represents the SQL command or stored procedure we use to retrieve data. As you can see, this implementation of the method simply adds an optional *ORDER BY* clause to the existing command. This might not be the best approach ever devised, but it certainly fits the bill of having the burden of sorting moved down to the DAL and from there to the database. At this point, you set the *SortParameterName* on the *ObjectDataSource* control to the method's parameter that determines the sorting—in this case, *sortExpression*:

```
<asp:ObjectDataSource ID="ObjectDataSource1" runat="server"
    EnablePaging="true"
    TypeName="ProAspNet20.DAL.Customers"
    SortParameterName="sortExpression"
    StartRowIndexParameterName="firstRow"
    MaximumRowsParameterName="totalRows"
    SelectMethod="LoadByCountry">
    <SelectParameters>
        ...
    </SelectParameters>
</asp:ObjectDataSource>
```

The advantage of this approach is that you take full control of the sorting machinery, and you can decide how, where, and when to implement it. You might have to write some code in your DAL for sorting, but consider that you only write highly focused code. In fact, no infrastructural code is required, as the machinery is set up for you by ASP.NET.

> **Note** One more item worth mentioning about sorting on a *GridView* control is that you can cancel the sorting operation if need be. To do this, you write a handler for the *Sorting* event, get the event argument data (of type *GridViewSortEventArgs*), and set its *Cancel* property to *true*.

Give Users Feedback

The *GridView* control doesn't automatically add any visual element to the output that indicates the direction of the sorting. This is one of the few cases in which some coding is needed to complete sorting:

```
<script runat="server">
void GridView1_RowCreated (object sender, GridViewRowEventArgs e) {
    if (e.Row.RowType == DataControlRowType.Header)
        AddGlyph(MyGridView, e.Row);
}

void AddGlyph(GridView grid, GridViewRow item) {
    Label glyph = new Label();
    glyph.EnableTheming = false;
    glyph.Font.Name = "webdings";
```

```
    glyph.Font.Size = FontUnit.Small;
    glyph.Text = (grid.SortDirection==SortDirection.Ascending ?"5" :"6");


    // Find the column you sorted by
    for(int i=0; i<grid.Columns.Count; i++) {
        string colExpr = grid.Columns[i].SortExpression;
        if (colExpr != "" && colExpr == grid.SortExpression)
            item.Cells[i].Controls.Add (glyph);
    }
}
}
</script>
```

The idea is that you write a handler for the *RowCreated* event and look for the moment when the header is created. Next you create a new *Label* control that represents the glyph you want to add. Where should the *Label* control be added?

The newly created *Label* control has font and text adequately set to generate a glyph (typically ▲ and ▼) that indicates the direction of the sorting. (The glyphs correspond to 5 and 6 in the Microsoft Webdings font.) You must add it alongside the header text of the clicked column. The index of the column can be stored to the view state during the *Sorting* event. Alternately, it can simply be retrieved, comparing the current sort expression—the grid's *SortExpression* property—to the column's sort expression. Once you know the index of the column, you retrieve the corresponding table cells and add the *Label*:

```
item.Cells[i].Controls.Add (glyph);
```

The results are shown in Figure 10-12. If your page is based on a theme, the font of the *Label* control—essential for rendering the glyph correctly—might be overridden. To avoid that, you should disable theming support for the label control. The *EnableTheming* property does just that.

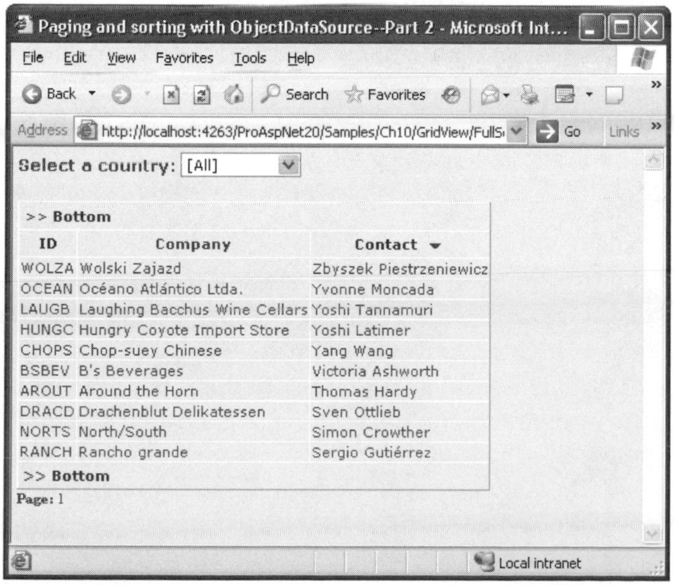

Figure 10-12   Enhancing the sorting capabilities of the *GridView* control.

Using Callbacks for Paging and Sorting

Both sorting and paging operations require a postback with subsequent full refresh of the page. In most cases, this is a heavy operation, as the page usually contains lots of graphics. To provide the user with a better experience, wouldn't it be nice if the grid could go down to the Web server, grab the new set of records, and update only a portion of the interface? Thanks to ASP.NET script callbacks (which I cover in greater detail in my other recent book, *Programming Microsoft ASP.NET 2.0 Applications: Advanced Topics* [Microsoft Press, 2005]), the *GridView* control is capable of offering this feature. All that you have to do is turn on the Boolean property *EnableSortingAndPagingCallbacks*.

As mentioned, the feature relies on the services of the ASP.NET script callback engine, which is designed to work also with non–Internet Explorer browsers, including Firefox, Netscape 6.x and newer, Safari 1.2, and the latest Opera browser.

SqlDataSource vs. *ObjectDataSource*

A few considerations will help clarify when to use *SqlDataSource* and *ObjectDataSource* controls. First, remember that these data source controls are not the only two choices for developers who want to do sane data binding. By far, though, they are the most popular and commonly used. It is also essential to bear in mind that data binding in ASP.NET 2.0 is in no way limited to using data source controls. This said, *SqlDataSource* and *ObjectDataSource* are just tools in the ASP.NET toolbox and should be used if they're right for the job.

As I see things, *SqlDataSource* is optimized for a disconnected approach to data binding. It works at its best if you retrieve data through a *DataSet*. Only in this case are paging, sorting, and caching capabilities enabled. Of these three functionalities, only sorting is somehow replicable in data reader mode. If using *DataSet*s is fine for your application, using *SqlDataSource* is an excellent choice. It gives you ready-made solutions with mostly declarative code that is simple to write, but it's not necessarily effective in a real-world application. Put another way, using *SqlDataSource* in an application might be good for certain features, but it's hardly sufficient to power the whole DAL.

Should you instead realize that you need more control over paging and sorting operations (such as custom paging or server-side sorting), switching to *ObjectDataSource* appears to me a sounder idea. In this case, you start by designing and implementing a fully fledged DAL and, optionally, a business layer, too. In this layer, you craft any capabilities you need to be supported from the grid—paging, sorting, or even data caching. Note that caching is not supported if you use custom collections instead of ADO.NET container classes, but implementing a personal caching layer is not a hard challenge.

With *ObjectDataSource*, you make yourself responsible for the implementation of such key features more or less like with *DataGrids* in ASP.NET 1.x. What's the deal? You don't simply inject sparse code in some code-behind class; you inject logic in the application's DAL. You're still writing code, but the quality of the code you get to write is quite different!

In addition, the *ObjectDataSource* control fully supports custom entity classes and custom collections. The support for generics in the .NET Framework 2.0 makes writing custom collections a snap, and it significantly reduces the cost of writing a fully custom DAL built on made-to-measure and domain-specific objects.

Editing Data

A major strength of the *GridView* control—which makes up for a major shortcoming of the *DataGrid*—is the ability to handle updates to the data source. The *DataGrid* control provides only an infrastructure for data editing. It provides the necessary user interface elements and fires appropriate events when the user modifies the value of a certain data field, but it does not submit those changes back to the data source. Developers are left with the disappointing realization that they have to write a huge amount of boilerplate code to really persist changes.

With the *GridView* control, when the bound data source supports updates, the control can automatically perform this operation, thus providing a truly out-of-the-box solution. The data source control signals its capability to update through the *CanUpdate* Boolean property.

Much like the *DataGrid*, the *GridView* can render a column of command buttons for each row in the grid. These special command columns contain buttons to edit or delete the current record. With the *DataGrid*, you must explicitly create an edit command column using a special column type—the *EditCommandColumn* class. The *GridView* simplifies things quite a bit for update and delete operations.

In-Place Editing and Updates

In-place editing refers to the grid's ability to support changes to the currently displayed records. You enable in-place editing on a grid view by turning on the *AutoGenerateEditButton* Boolean property:

```
<asp:gridview runat="server" id="Gridview1" datasourceid="MySource"
    autogeneratecolumns="false" autogenerateeditbutton="true">
...
</asp:gridview>
```

When the *AutoGenerateEditButton* property is set to *true*, the *GridView* displays an additional column, like that shown in Figure 10-13. By clicking the Edit button, you put the selected row in edit mode and can enter new data at will.

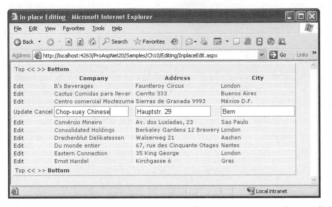

Figure 10-13   A *GridView* control that supports in-place editing.

To stop editing and lose any changes, users simply click the Cancel button. *GridView* can handle this click without any external support; the row returns to its original read-only state; and the *EditIndex* property takes back its −1 default value–meaning no row is currently being edited. But what if users click the update link? *GridView* first fires the *RowUpdating* event and then internally checks the *CanUpdate* property on the data source control. If *CanUpdate* returns false, an exception is thrown. *CanUpdate* returns false if the data source control has no update command defined.

Suppose your grid is bound to a *SqlDataSource* object. To persist changes when the user updates, you have to design your code as follows:

```
<asp:sqldatasource runat="server" ID="EmployeesSource"
    ConnectionString="<%$ ConnectionStrings:LocalNWind %>"
    SelectCommand="SELECT employeeid, firstname, lastname FROM employees"
    UpdateCommand="UPDATE employees SET
            firstname=@firstname, lastname=@lastname
            WHERE employeeid=@original_employeeid">
</asp:sqldatasource>
<asp:gridview runat="server" id="GridView1" datasourceid="EmployeesSource"
        AutoGenerateColumns="false"
        DataKeyNames="employeeid" AutoGenerateEditButton="true">
        <columns>
            <asp:boundfield datafield="firstname" headertext="First" />
            <asp:boundfield datafield="lastname" headertext="Last" />
        </columns>
</asp:gridview>
```

The *UpdateCommand* attribute is set to the SQL command to use to perform updates. When you write the command, you declare as many parameters as needed. However, if you stick with a particular naming convention, parameter values are automatically resolved. Parameters that represent fields to update (such as *firstname*) must match the name of *DataField* property of a grid column. The parameter used in the WHERE clause to identify the working record must match the *DataKeyNames* property–the key for the displayed records. The *original_XXX* format string is required for identity parameters. You can change this scheme through the *OldValuesParameterFormatString* property on the data source control.

The successful completion of an update command is signaled throughout the grid via the
RowUpdated event.

> **Note** The *GridView* collects values from the input fields and populates a dictionary of name/
> value pairs that indicate the new values for each field of the row. The *GridView* also exposes a
> *RowUpdating* event that allows the programmer to validate the values being passed to the
> data source object. In addition, the *GridView* automatically calls *Page.IsValid* before starting
> the update operation on the associated data source. If *Page.IsValid* returns false, the operation
> is canceled. This is especially useful if you're using a custom template with validators.

If the grid is bound to an *ObjectDataSource* control, things go a bit differently. The bound
business object must have an update method. This method will receive as many arguments
as it needs to work. You can decide to pass parameters individually or grouped in a unique
data structure. This second option is preferable if you have a well-done DAL. Here's an
example:

```
<asp:ObjectDataSource ID="CustomersSource" runat="server"
    TypeName="ProAspNet20.DAL.Customers"
    SelectMethod="LoadAll"
    UpdateMethod="Save"
    DataObjectTypeName="ProAspNet20.DAL.Customer">
</asp:ObjectDataSource>
<asp:GridView ID="GridView1" runat="server" DataSourceID="CustomersSource"
    DataKeyNames="id" AutoGenerateColumns="false">
    AutoGenerateEditButton="true"
    <Columns>
        <asp:BoundField DataField="companyname" HeaderText="Company" />
        <asp:BoundField DataField="street" HeaderText="Address" />
        <asp:BoundField DataField="city" HeaderText="City" />
    </Columns>
</asp:GridView>
```

The *Save* method can have the following prototype and implementation:

```
public static void Save(Customer cust)
{
    using (SqlConnection conn = new SqlConnection(ConnectionString))
    {
        SqlCommand cmd = new SqlCommand(cmdSave, conn);
        cmd.Parameters.AddWithValue("@id", cust.ID);
        cmd.Parameters.AddWithValue("@companyname", cust.CompanyName);
        cmd.Parameters.AddWithValue("@city", cust.City);
        cmd.Parameters.AddWithValue("@address", cust.Street);
        ...

        conn.Open();
        cmd.ExecuteNonQuery();
        conn.Close();
        return;
    }
}
```

The physical SQL command (or stored procedure) to run is nothing more than a classic UPDATE statement with a list of SET clauses. The *DataObjectTypeName* attribute indicates the name of a class that the *ObjectDataSource* uses for a parameter in a data operation.

> **Note** If you set the *DataObjectTypeName* property, all data methods can either be parameterless or accept an object of the specified type. This happens regardless of whether you declarative fill the parameters collection for the method. The *DataObjectTypeName* property takes precedence over parameter collections.

Deleting Displayed Records

From the *GridView*'s standpoint, deleting records is not much different from updating. In both cases, the *GridView* takes advantage of a data source ability to perform data operations. You enable record deletion by specifying a value of *true* for the *AutoGenerateDeleteButton* property. The *GridView* renders a column of buttons that, if clicked, invokes the delete command for the row on the bound data source control. The data source method is passed a dictionary of key field name/value pairs that are used to uniquely identify the row to delete:

```
<asp:sqldatasource runat="server" ID="EmployeesSource"
    ConnectionString="<%$ ConnectionStrings:LocalNWind %>"
    SelectCommand="SELECT employeeid, firstname, lastname FROM employees"
    UpdateCommand="UPDATE employees SET
            firstname=@firstname, lastname=@lastname
            WHERE employeeid=@original_employeeid"
    DeleteCommand="DELETE employees WHERE
                    employeeid=@original_employeeid" />
```

The *GridView* doesn't provide any feedback about the operation that will take place. Before proceeding, it calls *Page.IsValid*, which is useful if you have a custom template with validators to check. In addition, the *RowDeleting* event gives you another chance to programmatically control the legitimacy of the operation.

The delete operation fails if the record can't be deleted because of database-specific constraints. For example, the record can't be deleted if child records refer to it through a relationship. In this case, an exception is thrown.

To delete a record through an *ObjectDataSource* control, you give your business object a couple of methods, as follows:

```
public static void Delete(Customer cust)
{
    Delete(cust.ID);
}
public static void Delete(string id)
{
    using (SqlConnection conn = new SqlConnection(ConnectionString))
    {
        SqlCommand cmd = new SqlCommand(cmdDelete, conn);
```

```
        cmd.Parameters.AddWithValue("@id", id);
        conn.Open();
        cmd.ExecuteNonQuery();
        conn.Close();
        return;
    }
}
```

Overloading the delete method is not mandatory, but it can be useful and certainly make your DAL more flexible and easier to use.

Inserting New Records

In its current form, the *GridView* control doesn't support inserting data against a data source object. This omission is a result of the *GridView* implementation and not the capabilities and characteristics of the underlying data source. In fact, all data source controls support an insert command property. As you'll see in the next chapter, the insertion of new records is a scenario fully supported by the *DetailsView* and *FormView* control.

In ASP.NET 1.x, a common practice to make *DataGrid* controls support record insertions entails that you modify the footer or the pager to make room for empty text boxes and buttons. The *GridView* supports the same model and makes it slightly simpler through the *Pager-Template* property as far as the pager is concerned. Modifying the contents of the footer is possible through the *RowCreated* event (which I'll say more about in a moment). Note, though, that if the grid is bound to an empty data, the footer bar is hidden. What if you want your users to be able to add a new record to an empty grid? Resort to the *EmptyDataTemplate*, as follows:

```
<emptydatatemplate>
    <asp:label ID="Label1" runat="server">
      There's no data to show in this view.
      <asp:Button runat="server" ID="btnAddNew" CommandName="AddNew"
          Text="Add New Record" />
    </asp:label>
</emptydatatemplate>
```

To trap the user's clicking on the button, you write a handler for the *RowCommand* event:

```
void Gridview1_RowCommand(object sender, GridViewCommandEventArgs e)
{
    if (e.CommandName == "AddNew")
    { ... }
}
```

Advanced Capabilities

To complete the overview of the *GridView* control, we just need to take a look at a couple of common programming scenarios—drill-down and row customization. A grid presents a list of items to the user; in many cases, the user needs to select one of those items and start an operation on it. As discussed earlier, button columns exist to facilitate this task. We'll delve deeper into this topic in a moment. Row customization is another common feature, which gives you a chance to modify the standard rendering of the grid. You can edit the row layout, add or remove cells, or modify visual attributes on a per-row basis so that certain rows show up distinct from others (for example, rows representing negative values).

Executing an Operation on a Given Row

Let's return to a problem that we briefly mentioned earlier in the chapter while discussing button columns. Imagine you're building an e-commerce application; one of your pages shows a grid of products with buttons for users to add products to their shopping cart. You add a button column and write a handler for the *RowCommand* event:

```
void GridView1_RowCommand(object sender, GridViewCommandEventArgs e)
{
    if (e.CommandName.Equals("Add"))
    {
        // Get the index of the clicked row
        int index = Convert.ToInt32(e.CommandArgument);

        // Create a new shopping item and add it to the cart
        AddToShoppingCart(index);
    }
}
```

This is where we left off earlier. Let's go one step ahead now and expand the code of *AddTo-ShoppingCart*. What's the purpose of this method? Typically, it retrieves some information regarding the clicked product and stores that in the data structure that represents the shopping cart. In the sample code, the shopping cart is a custom collection named *ShoppingCart*:

```
public class ShoppingCart : List<ShoppingItem>
{
    public ShoppingCart()
    {
    }
}
```

ShoppingItem is a custom class that describes a bought product. It contains a few properties—product ID, product name, price per unit, and quantity bought. The shopping cart is stored in the session state and exposed through a page-wide property named *MyShoppingCart*:

```
protected ShoppingCart MyShoppingCart
{
    get
    {
        object o = Session["ShoppingCart"];
        if (o == null) {
            InitShoppingCart();
            return (ShoppingCart) Session["ShoppingCart"];
        }
        return (ShoppingCart) o;
    }
}
```

```
private void InitShoppingCart()
{
    ShoppingCart cart = new ShoppingCart();
    Session["ShoppingCart"] = cart;
}
```

At its core, the goal of *AddToShoppingCart* is merely that of creating a *ShoppingItem* object filled with the information of the clicked product. How would you retrieve that information?

As you can see, the *GridView* stores the index of the clicked row in the *CommandArgument* property of the *GridViewCommandEventArgs* structure. This information is necessary but not sufficient for our purposes. We need to translate that index into the key of the product behind the grid's row. Better yet, we need to translate the grid row index into a data set index to retrieve the data item object rendered in the clicked grid's row.

The *DataKeyNames* property of the *GridView* indicates the names of the data fields to persist in the view state to be retrieved later during postback events such as *RowCommand*. Implemented as a string array, *DataKeyNames* is the *GridView*'s counterpart of the *DataKeyField* of *DataGrid* controls. It carries the value of the primary key for a displayed row in a *DataGrid* and a slew of properties for a *GridView*:

```
<asp:GridView ID="GridView1" runat="server"
     DataSourceID="SqlDataSource1"
     DataKeyNames="productid,productname,unitprice" ... />
```

How many fields should you list in *DataKeyNames*? Consider that every field you list there takes up some view-state space. On the other hand, if you limit yourself to storing only the primary key field, you need to run a query to retrieve all the data you need. Which approach is better depends on what you really need to do. In our sample scenario, we need to make a copy of a product that is already cached in the Web server's memory. There's no need to run a query to retrieve data we already know. To fill a *ShoppingItem* object, you need the product ID, name, and unit price:

```
private void AddToShoppingCart(int rowIndex)
{
    DataKey data = GridView1.DataKeys[rowIndex];
    ShoppingItem item = new ShoppingItem();
    item.NumberOfItems = 1;
    item.ProductID = (int) data.Values["productid"];
    item.ProductName = data.Values["productname"].ToString();
    item.UnitPrice = (decimal) data.Values["unitprice"];
    MyShoppingCart.Add(item);

    ShoppingCartGrid.DataSource = MyShoppingCart;
    ShoppingCartGrid.DataBind();
}
```

The values of the fields listed in *DataKeyNames* are packed in the *DataKeys* array—an old acquaintance for *DataGrid* developers. *DataKeys* is an array of *DataKey* objects. *DataKey*, in turn, is a sort of ordered dictionary. You access the values of the persisted fields through the *Values* collection, as shown in the preceding code.

For user-interface purposes, the contents of the shopping cart are bound to a second *GridView* control so that users can see what's in their basket at any time. The binding takes place through the classic *DataSource* object. Look back to Figure 10-3 for a view of this feature.

> **Caution**   Each grid row gets bound to a data item—a row from the data source—only when the control is rendered out. A postback event such as *RowCommand* fires before this stage is reached. As a result, the *DataItem* property of the clicked *GridViewRow* object—where the data we need is expected to be—is inevitably null if accessed from within the *RowCommand* handler. That's why you need *DataKeyNames* and the related *DataKeys* properties.

Selecting a Given Row

A more general mechanism to select clicked rows can be implemented through a special command button—the select button. As with delete and edit buttons, you bring it on by setting the *AutoGenerateSelectButton* Boolean property. To fully take advantage of the selection feature, it is recommended that you also add a style for selected rows:

```
<asp:GridView ID="GridView1" runat="server" ... >
   <SelectedRowStyle BackColor="cyan" />
   ...
</asp:GridView>
```

When users click a select-enabled button, the page receives a more specific *SelectedIndex-Changed* event. Some properties such as *SelectedIndex*, *SelectedRow*, and *SelectedDataKey* are updated too. For completeness, note that when a row is selected the page first receives a *Row-Command* event, and later it is reached by the *SelectedIndexChanged* event. When *RowCommand* fires, though, none of the select properties is updated yet.

The following code shows how to rewrite the previous example to add the product being selected to the cart:

```
protected void GridView1_SelectedIndexChanged(object sender, EventArgs e)
{
    AddToShoppingCart();
}
private void AddToShoppingCart()
{
    DataKey data = GridView1.SelectedDataKey;
    ShoppingItem item = new ShoppingItem();
    item.NumberOfItems = 1;
    item.ProductID = (int) data.Values["productid"];
    item.ProductName = data.Values["productname"].ToString();
    item.UnitPrice = (decimal) data.Values["unitprice"];
    MyShoppingCart.Add(item);

    ShoppingCartGrid.DataSource = MyShoppingCart;
    ShoppingCartGrid.DataBind();
}
```

As you can see, there's no need to pass the row index, as the corresponding *DataKey* object is served by the *SelectedDataKey* property. (See Figure 10-14.)

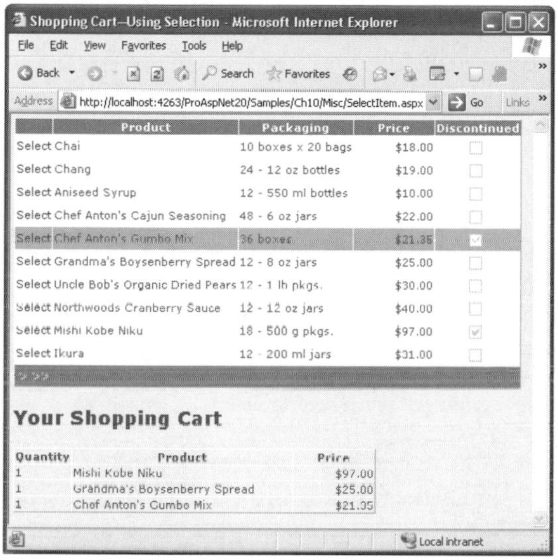

Figure 10-14   Adding the selected item to the shopping cart.

Row Customization

Want a quick example of why it's often important to render grid rows in a customized way? Take a look at Figure 10-14. The user just added to the cart a product that has been discontinued. Wouldn't it be nice if you could disable any rows matching certain criteria or, more simply, customize the row layout according to runtime conditions? Let's see how to do it.

There are two *GridView* events that are essential for the task—*RowCreated* and *RowDataBound*. The former is fired when any grid row is being created—whether it's a header, footer, item, alternating item, pager, and so on. The latter fires when the newly created row is bound to its data item—that is, the corresponding record in the bound data source. The *RowDataBound* event is not fired for all rows in the grid, but only for those which represent bound items. No event fires for the header, footer, and pager.

As a first example, let's see how to disable the Select link for rows where the *Discontinued* field returns true. In this case, you need a handler to *RowDataBound* because the required customization depends on the values on the bound data row. As mentioned, this information is not available yet when *RowCreated* fires:

```
void GridView1_RowDataBound(object sender, GridViewRowEventArgs e)
{
    if (e.Row.RowType == DataControlRowType.DataRow)
    {
        object dataItem = e.Row.DataItem;
```

```
        bool discontinued = (bool) DataBinder.Eval(dataItem, "discontinued");
        e.Row.Enabled = !discontinued;
    }
}
```

In general, you start by checking the type of the row. To be precise, this test is not strictly necessary for a *RowDataBound* event, which fires only for data rows. The data item—that is, the corresponding record—is retrieved through the *DataItem* property of the *GridViewRow* object. Next, you retrieve the field of interest and apply your logic. You might not know in advance the type of the data object bound to the row. The *DataBinder.Eval* method is a generic accessor that works through reflection and regardless of the underlying object. If you want to disable the whole row (and contained controls), you can turn off the *Enabled* property of the grid row object. To access a particular control, you need to find your way in the grid's object model. Here's how to access (and disable) the Select link alone:

```
((WebControl)e.Row.Cells[0].Controls[0]).Enabled = !discontinued;
```

This code works because in the sample grid the Select link is always the first control in the first cell of each data row. Figure 10-15 shows the previous product list with discontinued products disabled.

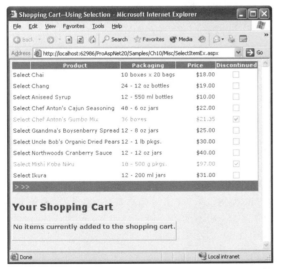

Figure 10-15   The rows corresponding to discontinued products are now disabled.

Once you gain access to the grid row object model, you can do virtually whatever you want.

Conclusion

In this chapter, we examined the grid controls available in ASP.NET—*DataGrid* and the newer *GridView*. Grids are a type of component that all Web applications need to employ in one shape or another. All Web applications, in fact, at a certain point of their life cycles are called to display data. More often than not, this data is in tabular format.

As long as the data to be displayed can be articulated in rows and columns, a grid is ideal for displaying it. Such controls provides facilities to select and edit single rows, page through a bound data source, and sort views. In addition, you can customize all the cells in a column by using any data-bound template made of any combination of HTML and ASP.NET text. To top it off, a fair number of events signal to user applications the key events in the control's life cycle.

The in-place editing feature is a piece of cake to use, as it is powerful and easy to configure. Even though this type of editing—designed to resemble Excel worksheets—is not appropriate for all applications and pages, as long as you can functionally afford the feature, in-place editing can save you a lot of coding and increase productivity by at least one order of magnitude.

Why are there two grid controls in ASP.NET 2.0? Let's state the answer clearly—the *DataGrid* control is supported mostly for backward compatibility. If you're writing a new ASP.NET 2.0 application, choosing to use the *GridView* is a no-brainer. The *GridView* has a newer and more effective design and totally embraces the data-binding model of ASP.NET 2.0. The key shortcoming of ASP.NET 1.x data binding is that it requires too much code for common, relatively boilerplate operations. This has been addressed with the introduction of data source controls. But data source controls require richer data-bound controls that are capable of working with the new model. This explains why ASP.NET 2.0 offers a brand-new control—the *GridView*—rather than just enhancing the existing *DataGrid*.

In the next chapter, we'll cover a pair of controls named *DetailsView* and *FormView*—the perfect complements to the *GridView*. These two controls fill another hole in the ASP.NET 1.x data toolbox, as they offer a smart interface for displaying individual records.

Just the Facts

- ASP.NET comes with two grid controls—*DataGrid* and *GridView*. The *DataGrid* works as it did in ASP.NET 1.x, whereas the *GridView* has a newer and more effective design and totally embraces the new data-binding model of ASP.NET 2.0.

- The *GridView* supports more column types, including checkbox and image columns.

- The *GridView* provides paging, sorting, and editing capabilities, and it relies on the bound data source control for effective implementation. If bound to an enumerable data source object (ASP.NET 1.x-style binding), it behaves like a *DataGrid* control.

- If bound to a *SqlDataSource* control, the *GridView* heavily relies on the *DataSet* capabilities for paging and sorting data in memory.

- If bound to an *ObjectDataSource* control, the *GridView* requires a fully fledged DAL that contains any custom logic for paging, sorting, and sometimes caching.

- Compared to the *DataGrid* control, the *GridView* provides an extended eventing model: pre/post pairs of events, possibility of canceling ongoing operations, and more events.

- To retrieve information about a clicked row, you use the *CommandArgument* property of the event data structure to get the index and you use the newest version of the *DataKeys* collection to access selected fields on the data item. With *DataGrid*, you can select only the primary key field and you need to run a query to access row data in drill-down scenarios.

Chapter 11

Managing Views of a Record

In this chapter:

The *DetailsView* Control 467

The *FormView* Control 489

Conclusion 497

Many applications need to work on a single record at a time. ASP.NET 1.x has no built in support for this scenario. Creating a single record view is possible, but it requires some coding and, possibly, a custom control. You have to fetch the record, bind its fields to a data-bound form, and optionally provide paging buttons to navigate between records. Displaying the contents of a single record is a common and necessary practice when you build master/detail views. Typically, the user selects a master record from a list or a grid, and the application drills down to show all the available fields. In ASP.NET 2.0, the *DetailsView* control fulfills this role and is the ideal complement to the *DataGrid* and *GridView* controls that we examined in the previous chapter.

The *DetailsView* control deliberately doesn't support templates. The *FormView* control, which we'll also cover in this chapter, is a fully templated details-view control.

The *DetailsView* Control

The *DetailsView* control is a data-bound control that renders a single record at a time from its associated data source, optionally providing paging buttons to navigate between records. It is similar to the Form View of a Microsoft Office Access database and is typically used for updating and inserting records in a master/details scenario.

The *DetailsView* control binds to any data source control and executes its set of data operations. It can page, update, insert, and delete data items in the underlying data source as long as the data source supports these operations. In most cases, no code is required to set up any of these operations. You can customize the user interface of the *DetailsView* control by choosing the most appropriate combination of data fields and styles in much the same way that you do with the *GridView*.

Finally, note that although the *DetailsView* is commonly used as an update and insert interface, it does not perform any input validation against the data source schema, nor does it provide any schematized user interface such as foreign key field drop-down lists or made-to-measure edit templates for particular types of data.

The *DetailsView* Object Model

The *DetailsView* is to a single record what a *GridView* is to a page of records. Just as the grid lets you choose which columns to display, the *DetailsView* allows you to select a subset of fields to display in read-only or read/write fashion. The rendering of the *DetailsView* is largely customizable using templates and styles. The default rendering consists of a vertical list of rows, one for each field in the bound data item. *DetailsView* is a composite data-bound control and acts as a naming and binding container. Much like the *GridView*, the *DetailsView* control also supports out-of-band calls for paging through the *ICallbackContainer* and *ICallbackEventHandler* interfaces. Here's the declaration of the control class:

```
public class DetailsView : CompositeDataBoundControl,
                           IDataItemContainer,
                           ICallbackContainer,
                           ICallbackEventHandler,
                           INamingContainer
```

The typical look and feel of the control is shown in Figure 11-1.

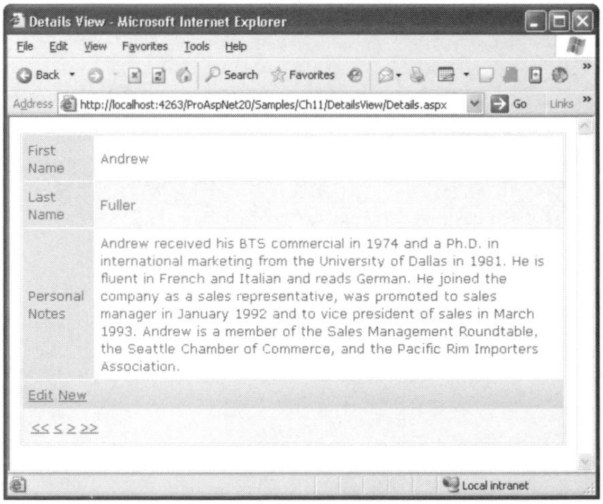

Figure 11-1   A *DetailsView* control in action.

The control is formed by a few main areas—header, field rows, pager bar, command bar, and footer.

Properties of the *DetailsView*

The *DetailsView* layout supports several properties that fall into the following categories: behavior, appearance, style, state, and templates. Table 11-1 lists the behavioral properties.

Table 11-1 *DetailsView* Behavior Properties

Property	Description
AllowPaging	Indicates whether the control supports navigation.
AutoGenerateDeleteButton	Indicates whether the command bar includes a Delete button. The default is *false*.
AutoGenerateEditButton	Indicates whether the command bar includes an Edit button. The default is *false*.
AutoGenerateInsertButton	Indicates whether the command bar includes an Insert button. The default is *false*.
AutoGenerateRows	Indicates whether the control auto-generates the rows. The default is *true*—all the fields of the record are displayed.
DataMember	Indicates the specific table in a multimember data source to bind to the control. The property works in conjunction with *DataSource*. If *DataSource* is a *DataSet* object, it contains the name of the particular table to bind.
DataSource	Gets or sets the data source object that contains the values to populate the control.
DataSourceID	Indicates the bound data source control.
DefaultMode	Indicates the default display mode of the control. It can be any value from the *DetailsViewMode* enumeration (read-only, insert, or edit).
EnablePagingCallbacks	Indicates whether client-side callback functions are used for paging operations.
PagerSettings	Gets a reference to the *PagerSettings* object that allows you to set the properties of the pager buttons.
UseAccessibleHeader	Determines whether to render <*th*> tags for the column headers instead of default <*td*> tags.

The *DefaultMode* property determines the initial working mode of the control and also the mode that the control reverts to after an edit or insert operation is performed.

The output generated by the *DetailsView* control is a table in which each row corresponds to a record field. Additional rows represent special items such as the header, footer, pager, and new command bar. The command bar is a sort of toolbar where all the commands available on the record are collected. Auto-generated buttons go to the command bar.

The user interface of the control is governed by a handful of visual properties, which are listed in Table 11-2.

Table 11-2 *DetailsView* Appearance Properties

Property	Description
BackImageUrl	Indicates the URL to an image to display in the background
Caption	The text to render in the control's caption
CaptionAlign	Alignment of the caption
CellPadding	Gets or sets the space (in pixels) remaining between the cell's border and the embedded text

Table 11-2 *DetailsView* **Appearance Properties**

Property	Description
CellSpacing	Gets or sets the space (in pixels) remaining, both horizontally and vertically, between two consecutive cells
EmptyDataText	Indicates the text to render in the control when bound to an empty data source
FooterText	Indicates the text to render in the control's footer
Gridlines	Indicates the gridline style for the control
HeaderText	Indicates the text to render in the control's header
HorizontalAlign	Indicates the horizontal alignment of the control on the page

The properties listed in the table apply to the control as a whole. You can program specific elements of the control's user interface by using styles. The supported styles are listed in Table 11-3.

Table 11-3 *DetailsView* **Style Properties**

Property	Description
AlternatingRowStyle	Defines the style properties for the fields that are displayed for each even-numbered row
CommandRowStyle	Defines the style properties for the command bar
EditRowStyle	Defines the style properties of individual rows when the control renders in edit mode
EmptyDataRowStyle	Defines the style properties for the displayed row when no data source is available
FieldHeaderStyle	Defines the style properties for the label of each field value
FooterStyle	Defines the style properties for the control's footer
HeaderStyle	Defines the style properties for the control's header
InsertRowStyle	Defines the style properties of individual rows when the control renders in insert mode
PagerStyle	Defines the style properties for the control's pager
RowStyle	Defines the style properties of the individual rows

The *DetailsView* control can be displayed in three modes, depending on the value—*ReadOnly*, *Insert*, or *Edit*—of the *DetailsViewMode* enumeration. The read-only mode is the default display mode in which users see only the contents of the record. To edit or add a new record, users must click the corresponding button (if any) on the command bar. Such buttons must be explicitly enabled on the command bar through the *AutoGenerateXxxButton* properties. Each mode has an associated style. The current mode is tracked by the *CurrentMode* read-only property.

Other state properties are listed in Table 11-4.

Table 11-4 *DetailsView* State Properties

Property	Description
BottomPagerRow	Returns a *DetailsViewRow* object that represents the bottom pager of the control.
CurrentMode	Gets the current mode for the control—any of the values in the *DetailsView-Mode* enumeration. The property determines how bound fields and templates are rendered.
DataItem	Returns the data object that represents the currently displayed record.
DataKey	Returns the *DataKey* object for the currently displayed record. The *DataKey* object contains the key values corresponding to the key fields specified by *DataKeyNames*.
DataItemCount	Gets the number of items in the underlying data source.
DataItemIndex	Gets or sets the index of the item being displayed from the underlying data source.
DataKeyNames	An array specifying the primary key fields for the records being displayed. These keys are used to uniquely identify an item for update and delete operations.
Fields	Returns the collection of *DataControlField* objects for the control that was used to generate the *Rows* collection.
FooterRow	Returns a *DetailsViewRow* object that represents the footer of the control.
HeaderRow	Returns a *DetailsViewRow* object that represents the header of the control.
PageCount	Returns the total number of items in the underlying data source bound to the control.
PageIndex	Returns the 0-based index for the currently displayed record in the control. The index is relative to the total number of records in the underlying data source.
Rows	Returns a collection of *DetailsViewRow* objects representing the individual rows within the control. Only data rows are taken into account.
SelectedValue	Returns the value of the key for the current record as stored in the *DataKey* object.
TopPagerRow	Returns a *DetailsViewRow* object that represents the top pager of the control.

If you're not satisfied with the default control rendering, you can use certain templates to better adapt the user interface to your preferences. Table 11-5 details the supported templates.

Table 11-5 *DetailsView* Template Properties

Property	Description
EmptyDataTemplate	The template for rendering the control when it is bound to an empty data source. If set, this property overrides the *EmptyDataText* property.
FooterTemplate	The template for rendering the footer row of the control.
HeaderTemplate	The template for rendering the header of the control. If set, this property overrides the *HeaderText* property.
PagerTemplate	The template for rendering the pager of the control. If set, this property overrides any existing pager settings.

As you can see, the list of templates is related to the layout of the control and doesn't include any template that influences the rendering of the current record. This is by design. For more ambitious template properties, such as *InsertTemplate* or perhaps *ItemTemplate*, you should resort to the *FormView* control, which is the fully templated sibling of the *DetailsView* control.

The *DetailsView* control has only one method, *ChangeMode*. As the name suggests, the *Change-Mode* method is used to switch from one display mode to the next:

```
public void ChangeMode(DetailsViewMode newMode)
```

This method is used internally to change views when a command button is clicked.

Events of the *DetailsView*

The *DetailsView* control exposes several events that enable the developer to execute custom code at various times in the life cycle. The event model is similar to that of the *GridView* control in terms of supported events and because of the pre/post pair of events that characterize each significant operation. Table 11-6 details the supported events.

Table 11-6   Events of the *DetailsView* Control

Event	Description
ItemCommand	Occurs when any clickable element in the user interface is clicked. This doesn't include standard buttons (such as Edit, Delete, and Insert), which are handled internally, but it does include custom buttons defined in the templates.
ItemCreated	Occurs after all the rows are created.
ItemDeleting, ItemDeleted	Both events occur when the current record is deleted. They fire before and after the record is deleted.
ItemInserting, ItemInserted	Both events occur when a new record is inserted. They fire before and after the insertion.
ItemUpdating, ItemUpdated	Both events occur when the current record is updated. They fire before and after the row is updated.
ModeChanging, ModeChanged	Both events occur when the control switches to a different display mode. They fire before and after the mode changes.
PageIndexChanging, PageIndexChanged	Both events occur when the control moves to another record. They fire before and after the display change occurs.

The *ItemCommand* event fires only if the original click event is not handled by a predefined method. This typically occurs if you define custom buttons in one of the templates. You do not need to handle this event to intercept any clicking on the Edit or Insert buttons.

Simple Data Binding

Building a record viewer with the *DetailsView* control is easy and quick. You just drop an instance of the control onto the Web form, bind it to a data source control, and add a few decorative settings. The following listing shows the very minimum that's needed:

```
<asp:DetailsView runat="server" id="RecordView"
    DataSourceID="MySource"
    HeaderText="Employees">
</asp:DetailsView>
```

When the *AllowPaging* property is set to *true*, a pager bar is displayed for users to navigate between bound records. As you'll see in more detail later, this works only if multiple records are bound to the control. Here's a more realistic code snippet—the code behind the control in Figure 11-2:

```
<asp:ObjectDataSource ID="RowDataSource" runat="server"
    TypeName="ProAspNet20.DAL.Employees"
    SelectMethod="LoadAll">
</asp:ObjectDataSource>

<asp:DetailsView ID="RecordView" runat="server"
    DataSourceID="RowDataSource" AllowPaging="true"
    HeaderText="Northwind Employees"
    AutoGenerateRows="false">
    <PagerSettings Mode="NextPreviousFirstLast" />
    <Fields>
        <asp:BoundField DataField="firstname" HeaderText="First Name" />
        <asp:BoundField DataField="lastname" HeaderText="Last Name" />
        <asp:BoundField DataField="title" HeaderText="Title" />
        <asp:BoundField DataField="birthdate" HeaderText="Birth"
            DataFormatString="{0:d}" />
    </Fields>
</asp:DetailsView>
```

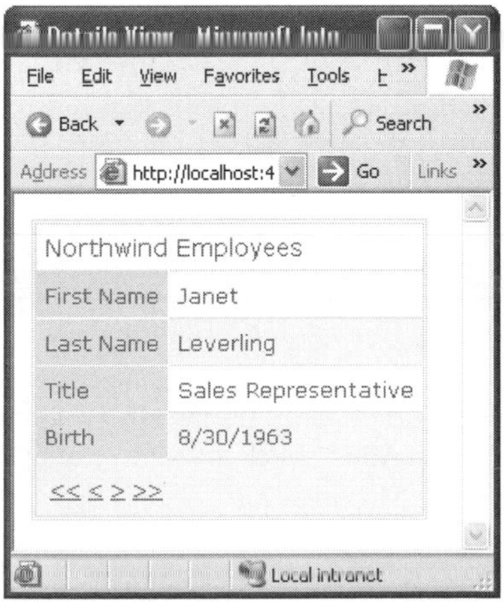

Figure 11-2 A *DetailsView* control to explore the results of a query.

Binding Data to a *DetailsView* Control

A *DetailsView* control is formed by data-bindable rows—one for each field in the displayed data item. By default, the control includes all the available fields in the view. You can change this behavior by setting the *AutoGenerateRows* property to *false*. In this case, only the fields explicitly listed in the *Fields* collection are displayed. Just as grids do, the *DetailsView* control can have both declared and auto-generated fields. In this case, declared fields appear first and auto-generated fields are not added to the *Fields* collection. The *DetailsView* supports the same variety of field types as the *GridView*. (See Chapter 10.)

If no data source property is set, the *DetailsView* control doesn't render anything. If an empty data source object is bound and an *EmptyDataTemplate* template is specified, the results shown to the user have a more friendly look:

```
<asp:DetailsView runat="server" datasourceid="MySource">
   <EmptyDataTemplate>
      <asp:label runat="server">
         There's no data to show in this view.
      </asp:label>
   </EmptyDataTemplate>
</asp:DetailsView>
```

The *EmptyDataTemplate* property is ignored if the bound data source is not empty. If you simply plan to display a message to the user, you can more effectively resort to the *EmptyDataText* property. Plain text properties, in fact, are faster than templates.

Fields can be defined either declaratively or programmatically. If you opt for the latter, instantiate any needed data field objects and add them to the *Fields* collection, as shown in the following code snippet:

```
BoundField field = new BoundField();
field.DataField = "companyname";
field.HeaderText = "Company Name";
detailsView1.Fields.Add(field);
```

Rows in the control's user interface reflect the order of fields in the *Fields* collection. To statically declare your columns in the *.aspx* source file, you use the *<Fields>* tag.

> **Note**   If you programmatically add fields to the control, be aware of the view state. The field is not automatically added to the view state and won't be there the next time the page posts back. (This is the same snag we encountered in the previous chapter for the columns of a *Grid-View* or *DataGrid* control.) If some fields have to be added programmatically all the time, you put the code in the *Page_Load* event handler. If field insertion is conditional, after adding fields you write a custom flag to the view state. In *Page_Load*, you then check the view-state flag and, if it is set, you add fields as expected.

Controlling the Displayed Fields

Just as grid controls can display only a selected range of columns, the *DetailsView* control can display only a subset of the available fields for the current record. As mentioned, you disable the automatic generation of all fields by setting the *AutoGenerateRows* property to *false*. Then you declare as many fields as needed under the *<Fields>* element, as shown here:

```
<asp:detailsview>
    ...
    <fields>
        <asp:boundfield datafield="firstname" headertext="First Name" />
        <asp:boundfield datafield="lastname" headertext="Last Name" />
        <asp:boundfield datafield="title" headertext="Position" />
    </fields>
</asp:detailsview>
```

The *HeaderText* attribute refers to the label displayed alongside the field value. You can style this text using the *FieldHeaderStyle* property. The following code makes field labels appear in boldface type:

```
<FieldHeaderStyle Font-Bold="true" />
```

To improve the readability of displayed data, you select the field type that best suits the data to display. For example, Boolean data is better displayed through *CheckBoxField* rows, whereas URLs render the best via *HyperLinkField*. Admittedly, the list is not exhaustive, but the main issues won't show up until you turn on the record in edit mode. By default, in fact, in edit or insert mode the content of the field is displayed using a text box, which is great for many data types but not for all. For example, what if your users need to edit a date? In this case, the *Calendar* control would be far more appropriate. However, you can't use templates to modify the default rendering because the *DetailsView* control doesn't support data-bound templates on rows. You should resort to the *FormView* control if template support is an unavoidable necessity.

Paging Through Bound Data

The *DetailsView* control is designed to display one record at a time, but it allows you to bind multiple records. In a master/detail scenario, you really need to bind a single record. In a record-viewer scenario, you might find it useful to bind the whole cached data source and have the control to page through. The following paragraph details the rules for paging in the *DetailsView* control.

No paging is allowed if *AllowPaging* is set to *false* (the default setting). If *AllowPaging* is turned on, paging is allowed only if more than one record is bound to the control. When paging is possible, the pager is displayed to let users select the next record to view. Just as for grids, the pager can provide numeric links to the various records (the first, the third, the last, and so forth) as well as relative hyperlinks to the first, previous, next, or last record. The *PagerSettings* type determines the attributes and behavior of the pager bar. *PagerStyle*, on the other hand, governs the appearance of the pager.

The *DetailsView* paging mechanism is based on the *PageIndex* property, which indicates the index of the current record in the bound data source. Clicking any pager button updates the property; the control does the data binding and refreshes the view. *PageCount* returns the total number of records available for paging. Changing the record is signaled by a pair of events—*PageIndexChanging* and *PageIndexChanged*.

The *PageIndexChanging* event allows you to execute custom code before the *PageIndex* actually changes—that is, before the control moves to a different record. You can cancel the event by setting the *Cancel* property of the event argument class to *true*:

```
void PageIndexChanging(object sender, DetailsViewPageEventArgs e)
{
    e.Cancel = true;
}
```

Note that when the event fires you don't have much information about the new record being displayed. You can read everything about the currently displayed record, but you know only the index of the next one. To retrieve details of the current record, you proceed as you would with *GridView*s and use the *DataKey* property:

```
DataKey data = DetailsView1.DataKey;
string country = (string) data.Values["country"];
if (country == "Mexico" || country == "USA" || country == "Brazil")
{
    ...
}
```

To be able to use the *DataKey* property within data-bound events, you must set the *DataKeyNames* property to the comma-separated list of fields you want to be persisted in the view state and exposed by the *DataKey* structure later:

```
<asp:DetailsView ID="DetailsView1" runat="server"
   DataKeyNames="id, country"
   ...
/>
```

It is essential that *DataKeyNames* contains public properties of the bound data type. In other words, *id* and *country* must be record fields if the *DetailsView* control is bound to a *DataSet* or *DataTable*. They must be property names if the *DetailsView* control is bound to a custom collection via *ObjectDataSource*.

There's no easy way to look up the next record from within the *PageIndexChanging* event. The simplest thing you can do is cache the dataset bound to the *DetailsView*, get a reference to the cached data, and select in that list the record that corresponds to the index of the next page.

> **Note** Paging with the *DetailsView* control is subject to the same paging issues for *GridView* and *DataGrid* that we examined in the previous chapter. If you bind the control to *SqlDataSource*, you're better off caching the data source; if you bind to *ObjectDataSource*, it is preferable that you use business objects that page themselves through the data source.

Paging via Callbacks

Paging is normally implemented through a server-side event and requires a full page refresh. The *DetailsView* control provides the *EnablePagingCallbacks* property to specify whether paging operations are performed using client-side callback functions.

Based on ASP.NET script callbacks, when enabled, paging callbacks prevent the need to post the page back to the server. At the same time, new data for the requested page is retrieved through an out-of-band call. The control is responsible for grabbing the server data and refreshing its own user interface on browsers that support a Dynamic HTML–compliant document object model.

For a developer, turning on the client paging feature couldn't be easier. You just set the *EnablePagingCallbacks* property to *true* and you're done.

Creating Master/Detail Views

In ASP.NET 1.x, implementing master/detail views is not particularly hard to do, but it's certainly not automatic and codeless. In ASP.NET 2.0, combining the *DetailsView* control with another data-bound control such as the *GridView* or *DropDownList* greatly simplifies the creation of master/detail views of data. The master control (such as the *GridView*) selects one particular record in its own data source, and that record becomes the data source for a *DetailsView* control in the same form. Let's see how.

Drill Down into the Selected Record

A typical master/detail page contains a master control (such as a *GridView*) and a detail control (such as a *DetailsView*), each bound to its own data source. The trick is in binding the detail control to a data source represented by the currently selected record. The following code snippet shows the configuration of the "master" block. It consists of a *GridView* bound to a pageable *ObjectDataSource*:

```
<asp:ObjectDataSource ID="CustomersDataSource" runat="server"
    EnablePaging="true"
    StartRowIndexParameterName="firstRow"
    MaximumRowsParameterName="totalRows"
    TypeName="ProAspNet20.DAL.Customers"
    SelectMethod="LoadAll">
</asp:ObjectDataSource>
```

```
<asp:GridView ID="GridView1" runat="server"
    DataSourceID="CustomersDataSource"
    DataKeyNames="id" AllowPaging="True"
    AutoGenerateSelectButton="True"
    AutoGenerateColumns="False">
    <PagerSettings Mode="NextPreviousFirstLast" />
    <Columns>
        <asp:BoundField DataField="CompanyName" HeaderText="Company" />
        <asp:BoundField DataField="Country" HeaderText="Country" />
    </Columns>
</asp:GridView>
```

The grid shows a Select column for users to select the record to drill down into. However, you don't need to handle the corresponding *SelectedIndexChanged* event for the details view to kick in. The following code shows the "detail" block of the master/detail scheme:

```
<asp:ObjectDataSource ID="RowDataSource" runat="server"
    TypeName="ProAspNet20.DAL.Customers"
    SelectMethod="Load">
    <SelectParameters>
        <asp:ControlParameter Name="id" ControlID="GridView1"
            PropertyName="SelectedValue" />
    </SelectParameters>
</asp:ObjectDataSource>
<asp:DetailsView ID="DetailsView1" runat="server"
    HeaderText="Customer Details"
    EmptyDataText="No customer currently selected"
    DataSourceID="RowDataSource"
    AutoGenerateRows="False"
    AutoGenerateInsertButton="True"
    AutoGenerateDeleteButton="True"
    AutoGenerateEditButton="True">
    <Fields>
        <asp:BoundField DataField="ID" HeaderText="ID" />
        <asp:BoundField DataField="CompanyName" HeaderText="Company" />
        <asp:BoundField DataField="ContactName" HeaderText="Contact" />
        <asp:BoundField DataField="Street" HeaderText="Address" />
        <asp:BoundField DataField="City" HeaderText="City" />
        <asp:BoundField DataField="Country" HeaderText="Country" />
    </Fields>
</asp:DetailsView>
```

The *DetailsView* control is bound to the return value of the *Load* method on the *Customer* Data Access Layer (DAL) class. The *Load* method requires an argument to be the ID of the customer. This parameter is provided by the grid through its *SelectedValue* property. Whenever the user selects a new row in the grid, the *SelectedValue* property changes (as discussed in Chapter 10), the page posts back, and the *DetailsView* refreshes its user interface accordingly. No code should be written in the code-behind class for this to happen.

Figure 11-3 shows the page in action when no row is selected in the grid. This is a great example for understanding the importance of the empty data row template.

Figure 11-4 shows the two controls in action when a record is selected.

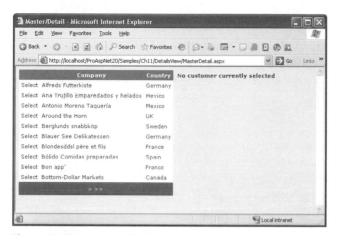

Figure 11-3 A no-code implementation of a master/detail scheme based on a combination of *GridView* and *DetailsView* controls.

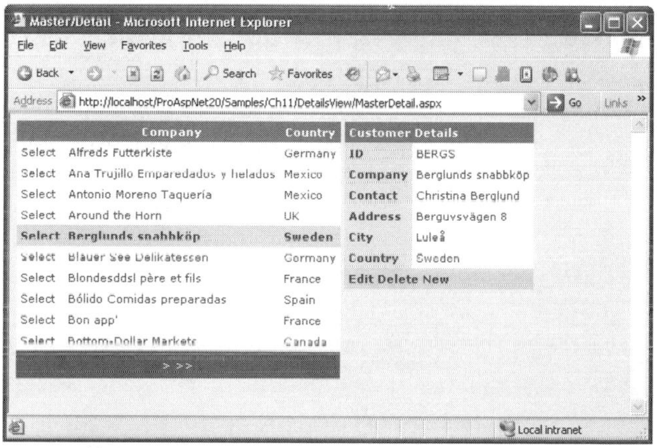

Figure 11-4 The *DetailsView* control shows the details of the selected customer.

Note that the internal page mechanics places a call to the *Load* method at all times, even when the page first loads and there's no record selected in the grid. Even when there's no record selected, the *Load* method is passed the value of the *SelectedValue* property on the grid, which is null. What happens in this case? It depends on the implementation of the *Load* method. If *Load* can handle null input values and degrades gracefully, nothing bad happens and the page displays the empty data template. Otherwise, you typically get a run-time exception from the ADO.NET infrastructure in charge of retrieving data because of the invalid parameter you provided to the method. Here's a good code sequence to use for methods with data source controls:

```
public static Customer Load(string id)
{
    if (String.IsNullOrEmpty(id))
        return null;
    ...
}
```

Caching Issues

The preceding scheme for master/detail pages is easy to understand and arrange. Furthermore, you can design it through a full point-and-click metaphor directly in the Microsoft Visual Studio .NET 2005 IDE without writing a single line of code. Can you ask for more? Actually, what you should do is ensure that it works the way you want it to. Let's delve a bit deeper into this type of automatic master/detail binding.

The grid is bound to a list of customers as returned by the data source control. As you would expect, this list is cached somewhere. If you use *SqlDataSource*, you can control caching to some extent through a bunch of properties. If you use *ObjectDataSource* as in the previous example, you have no caching at all unless you instruct the *Load* method or, more generally, you instruct your DAL and business layer to cache data. All the data bound to the grid is retrieved from the database whenever the grid is paged or sorted. But there's more.

When the user selects a given record, the *DetailsView* gets bound to a particular record whose details are retrieved through another query. This repeated query might or might not be necessary. It might not be necessary if you're building a master/detail scheme on a single table (Customers, in this case) and if the "master" control already contains all the data. In the previous example, the *LoadAll* method that populates the grid returns a collection based on the results of *SELECT [fields] FROM customers*. In light of this, there would be no need for the *DetailsView* to run a second query to get details that could already be available, if only they were cached.

In summary, *ObjectDataSource* doesn't support caching unless you use ADO.NET data containers. Generally speaking, caching is a performance booster if the overall size of cached data is limited to hundreds of records. If you can't get caching support from the data source control, build it in the business objects you use. If you use *SqlDataSource*, or *ObjectDataSource* with ADO.NET objects, enable caching, but keep an eye on the size of the cached data. And in all cases, use the SQL Server profiler (or similar tools if you use other database management systems) to see exactly when data is being retrieved from the database.

Working with Data

A detailed view like that of the *DetailsView* control is particularly useful if users can perform basic updates on the displayed data. Basic updates include editing and deleting the record, as well as inserting new records. The *DetailsView* command bar gathers all the buttons needed to start data operations. You tell the control to create those buttons by setting to *true* the following properties: *AutoGenerateEditButton* (for updates), *AutoGenerateDeleteButton* (for deletions), and *AutoGenerateInsertButton* (for adding new records).

Editing the Current Record

As with the *GridView*, data operations for the *DetailsView* control are handled by the bound data source control, as long as the proper commands are defined and a key to identify the correct record to work on is indicated through the *DataKeyNames* property. Let's test *SqlData-Source* first:

```
<asp:SqlDataSource runat="server" id="SqlDataSource1"
    ConnectionString="<%$ ConnectionStrings:LocalNWind %>"
    SelectCommand="SELECT * FROM customers"
    UpdateCommand="UPDATE customers SET
                    companyname=@companyname, contactname=@contactname,
                    city=@city, country=@country
                 WHERE customerid=@original_customerid"
    DeleteCommand="DELETE customers WHERE customerid=@original_customerid"
/>
<asp:DetailsView ID="DetailsView1" runat="server"
    DataKeyNames="customerid"
    DataSourceID="SqlDataSource1"
    AllowPaging="True"
    AutoGenerateRows="False"
    HeaderText="Customers"
    AutoGenerateEditButton="True"
    AutoGenerateDeleteButton="True">
    <PagerSettings Mode="NextPreviousFirstLast" />
    <Fields>
        <asp:BoundField DataField="CompanyName" HeaderText="Company" />
        <asp:BoundField DataField="ContactName" HeaderText="Contact" />
        <asp:BoundField DataField="City" HeaderText="City" />
        <asp:BoundField DataField="Country" HeaderText="Country" />
    </Fields>
</asp:DetailsView>
```

The *SqlDataSource* must expose SQL commands (or stored procedures) for deleting and updating records. (See Chapter 9 for details.) Once this has been done, the *DetailsView* control does all the rest. Users click to edit or delete the current record and the control ultimately calls upon the underlying data source to accomplish the action.

Figure 11-5 shows the changed user interface of the *DetailsView* control when it works in edit mode. Note that in edit mode, the default set of buttons in the command is replaced by a pair of update/cancel buttons.

If you attach the *DetailsView* control to an *ObjectDataSource* control, make sure you properly bind the update and delete methods of the business object:

```
<asp:ObjectDataSource runat="server" id="ObjectDataSource1"
    TypeName="ProAspNet20.DAL.Customers"
    SelectMethod="LoadAll"
    DeleteMethod="Delete"
    UpdateMethod="Save"
    DataObjectTypeName="ProAspNet20.DAL.Customer"
/>
```

The *DataKeyNames* property must be set to the name of the public property that represents the key for identifying the record to delete or update.

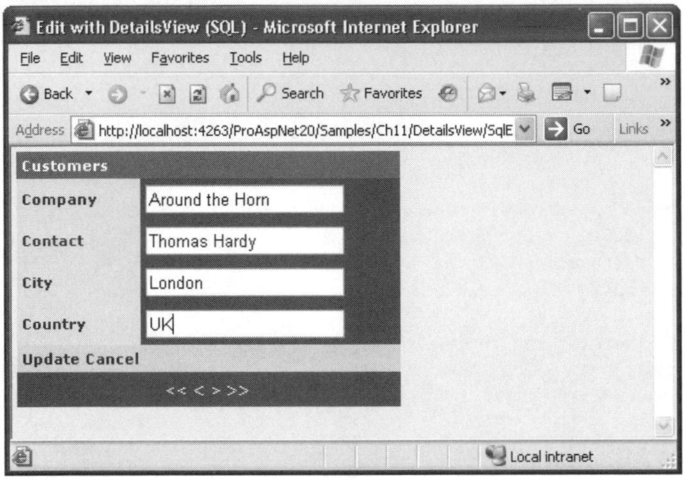

Figure 11-5   A *DetailsView* control working in edit mode.

Deleting the Current Record

Although the delete operation can be pre- and post-processed by a pair of events such as *Item-Deleting/ItemDeleted*, there's not much a page author can do to give users a chance to recall an inadvertently started delete operation. The bad news is that unlike other data-bound controls, the *DetailsView* doesn't offer easy-to-use events and properties for you to override default behaviors. You might think that the *ItemCreated* event is the right place to handle the interception of the command bar creation and add some script code to the delete button. *ItemCreated* is still the right (the only, actually) entry point in the control's machinery, but adding a client-side message box to the delete button is a difficult challenge.

ItemCreated fires whenever a *DetailsView* row is being created, but it doesn't supply additional information about the newly created row. Furthermore, the command row is not exposed through a direct property as is the case with a pager, header, and footer. A trick is needed to access the row representing the command bar. If you turn tracing on and snoop into the contents of the *Rows* collection while debugging, you can easily figure out that the *Rows* collection contains as many elements as there are data rows in the control, plus one. The extra row is just the command bar. You get it with the following code:

```
protected void DetailsView1_ItemCreated(object sender, EventArgs e)
{
    if (DetailsView1.FooterRow != null)
    {
        int commandRowIndex = DetailsView1.Rows.Count-1;
        DetailsViewRow commandRow = DetailsView1.Rows[commandRowIndex];
        ...
    }
}
```

To be sure that your code kicks in when the command bar exists, you check the *FooterRow* property for nullness. The footer row is always created regardless of whether it is displayed; in addition, it is always created after all the data rows have been created. The command bar is the last row in the *Rows* collection and is an object of type *DetailsViewRow*—a special type of table row. The row contains a cell—an internal object of type *DataControlFieldCell*—which in turn contains edit, delete, and insert buttons. The tracing tool reveals that buttons are not plain buttons, but instances of the internal *DataControlLinkButton* class, a class derived from *LinkButton*. You get the cell with the following code:

```
DataControlFieldCell cell;
cell = (DataControlFieldCell) commandRow.Controls[0];
```

At this point, you're pretty much done. What remains for you to do is loop through all the child controls of the cell and get a reference to all link buttons. How can you distinguish the delete button from the edit button? What if one of these controls is not enabled? Link buttons have the *CommandName* property, which assigns them a characteristic and unique name—Delete, Edit, or New for the data operations we're interested in here. Have a look at the following code:

```
protected void DetailsView1_ItemCreated(object sender, EventArgs e)
{
    if (DetailsView1.FooterRow != null)
    {
        int commandRowIndex = DetailsView1.Rows.Count-1;
        DetailsViewRow commandRow = DetailsView1.Rows[commandRowIndex];

        DataControlFieldCell cell;
        cell = (DataControlFieldCell) commandRow.Controls[0];
        foreach(Control ctl in cell.Controls)
        {
            LinkButton link = ctl as LinkButton;
            if (link != null)
            {
                if (link.CommandName == "Delete")
                {
                    link.ToolTip = "Click here to delete";
                    link.OnClientClick = "return confirm('Do you really want
                                        to delete this record?');";
                }
                else if (link.CommandName == "New")
                {
                    link.ToolTip = "Click here to add a new record";
                }
                else if (link.CommandName == "Edit")
                {
                    link.ToolTip = "Click here to edit the current record";
                }
            }
        }
    }
}
```

Once you have received a valid reference to the link button that represents, say, the delete button, you can do whatever you want—for example, add a ToolTip and a JavaScript confirmation popup. (See Figure 11-6.)

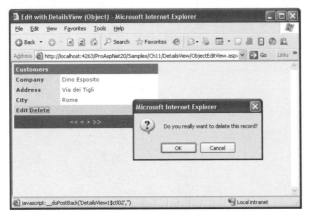

Figure 11-6   Ask for confirmation before you delete the current record.

Inserting a New Record

The process of adding a new record is much like the process for editing or deleting. You add an insert command in the bound data source control and enable the insert button on the *DetailsView* control. Here is a valid insert command:

```
<asp:SqlDataSource ID="SqlDataSource1" runat="server"
    EnableCaching="true"
    ConnectionString='<%$ ConnectionStrings:LocalNWind %>'
    SelectCommand="SELECT employeeid, firstname, lastname, title, hiredate
                FROM employees"
    InsertCommand="INSERT INTO employees
                    (firstname, lastname, title, hiredate) VALUES
                    (@firstname, @lastname, @title, @hiredate)"
/>
<asp:DetailsView ID="DetailsView1" runat="server"
    AllowPaging="true"
    DataSourceID="SqlDataSource1"
    AutoGenerateInsertButton="true"
    HeaderText="Employee Details" >
    <PagerSettings Mode="NextPreviousFirstLast" />
</asp:DetailsView>
```

Figure 11-7 shows how it works.

When you implement the insert command, you should pay attention to primary keys. In particular, the preceding command doesn't specify the primary key (*employeeid*) because, in this example, the underlying database auto-generates values for the field. Generally, for a database that accepts user-defined keys, you should provide a validation mechanism in the page before you push the new record. Once again, all this code is best placed in the DAL and bound to *DetailsView* through an *ObjectDataSource* control. I'll say more about input data validation in a moment.

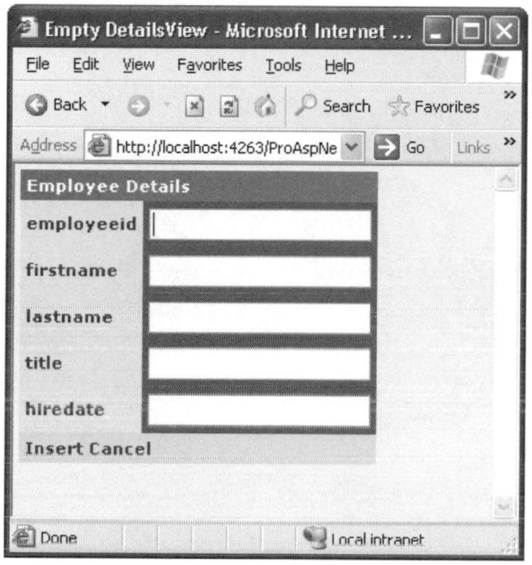

Figure 11-7   A *DetailsView* control working in insert mode.

Templated Fields

The *DetailsView* control doesn't support edit and insert templates to change the layout of the control entirely. When editing the contents of a data source, you either go through the standard layout of the user interface—a vertical list of header/value pairs—or resort to another control, such as the *FormView* or a custom control. Designed to be simple and effective, the *DetailsView* turns out to be not very flexible and hard to hook up. As seen earlier, walking your way through the internal object model of the *DetailsView* control is not impossible. The real problem, though, is forcing the control to play by rules that it hasn't set.

You can change, instead, the way in which a particular field is displayed within the standard layout. For example, you can use a *Calendar* control to render a date field. To do this, you employ the *TemplateField* class, as we did for grid controls. By using a *TemplateField* class to render a data field, you are free to use any layout you like for view, edit, and insert operations, as shown in the following code:

```
<asp:TemplateField HeaderText="Country">
    <ItemTemplate>
        <asp:literal runat="server" Text='<%# Eval("country") %>' />
    </ItemTemplate>
    <EditItemTemplate>
        <asp:dropdownlist ID="DropDownList1" runat="server"
            datasourceid="CountriesDataSource"
            selectedvalue='<%# Bind("country") %>' />
    </EditItemTemplate>
</asp:TemplateField>
```

The field *Country* is rendered through a literal in view mode, and it turns to a data-bound drop-down list control in edit mode. The bound data source control is responsible for providing all the displayable countries. The *Bind* operator is like *Eval* except that it writes data back to the data source—this is the power of ASP.NET two-way data binding. (See Chapter 9.) Figure 11-8 shows a sample page.

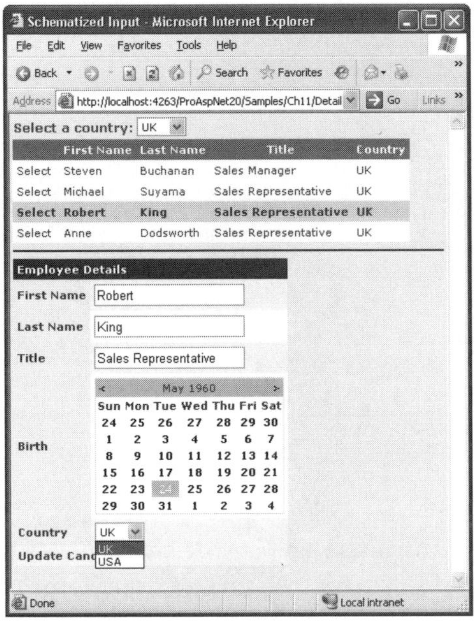

Figure 11-8   Template fields in a *DetailsView* control.

Adding Validation Support

By using templated fields, you can also add any validator control you need where you need it. What if you don't want templated fields? Limited to validator controls, you have an alternate approach. With this approach, you still use *BoundField* controls to render fields, but you attach validators to them programmatically.

You start by adding an *ItemCreated* event handler to the *DetailsView* control in the page, as follows:

```
protected void DetailsView1_ItemCreated(object sender, EventArgs e)
{
    if (DetailsView1.CurrentMode == DetailsViewMode.ReadOnly)
        return;
    if (DetailsView1.FooterRow == null)
        return;

    AddRequiredFieldValidator(0, "First name required");
    AddRequiredFieldValidator(1, "Last name required");
}
```

First you ensure that the control is in edit mode and all the data rows have been created. Next, you assume that you know the ordinal position of the fields you want to modify. (This is a reasonable assumption, as we're not designing a general-purpose solution, but simply adjusting a particular ASP.NET page that we created.)

The *AddRequiredFieldValidator* method takes the index of the field you want to validate and the message to display in case the field is left blank. It instantiates and initializes a validator, and then adds it to the corresponding cell, as in the following code:

```
void AddRequiredFieldValidator(int rowIndex, string msg)
{
    // Retrieve the data row to extend
    const int DataCellIndex = 1;
    DetailsViewRow row = DetailsView1.Rows[rowIndex];

    // Get the second cell-the first contains the label
    DataControlFieldCell cell;
    cell = (DataControlFieldCell) row.Cells[DataCellIndex];

    // Initialize the validator
    RequiredFieldValidator req = new RequiredFieldValidator();
    req.Text = String.Format("<span title='{0}'>*</span>", msg);

    // Get the ID of the TextBox control to validate
    string ctlID = cell.Controls[0].UniqueID;
    int pos = ctlID.LastIndexOf("$");
    if (pos < 0)
        return;
    string temp = ctlID.Substring(pos + 1);
    req.ControlToValidate = temp;

    // Insert the validator
    cell.Controls.Add(req);
}
```

You retrieve the data row to extend with a validator control and get a reference to its second cell. A *DetailsView* row has two cells—one for the field header and one for the field value. In edit/insert mode, the second cell contains a *TextBox* control.

The validator control—a *RequiredFieldValidator* in this example—requires some behavior settings (say, the message to display). More important, it requires the ID of the control to validate. Nobody knows the ID of the dynamically generated *TextBox* control. However, you can get a reference to the control and read the *UniqueID* property.

The *DetailsView* is a naming container, which means that it prefixes the names of contained controls. For example, an internal *TextBox* named, say, *clt01* is publicly known as *DetailsView1$clt01*, where *DetailsView1* is the ID of the *DetailsView* control. You need to pass the real control's ID to the validator. That's why the preceding code locates the last occurrence of the $ symbol and discards all that precedes it. The equivalent of *clt01* is finally assigned to the *ControlToValidate* property of the validator and the validator is added to the cell.

You have added a new control with its own behavior, and you have no need to interact with the remainder of the host control. In this case, it works just fine, as shown in Figure 11-9.

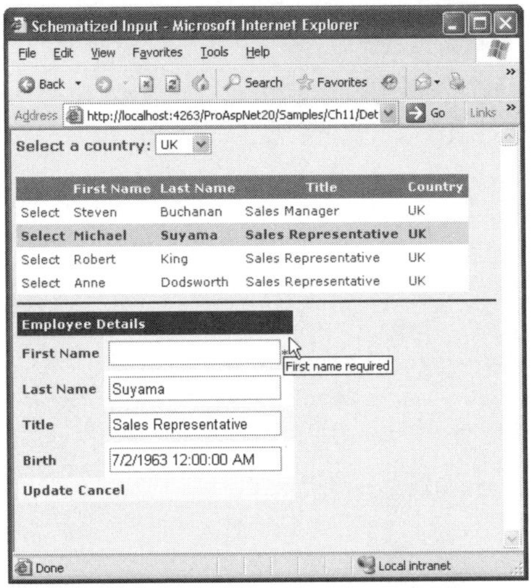

Figure 11-9   Validation support added to a *DetailsView* control.

The preceding code always displays an asterisk to signal an incomplete field. The actual text is wrapped by a *<span>* tag to include a ToolTip. This is arbitrary; you can configure the validator control at your leisure.

Validating Without Validators

So far, we considered two different scenarios for validating data manipulated with the *DetailsView* control. In the first scenario, you employ templates and explicitly add validator controls. In the second, you stick to nontemplated bound fields but use a slick piece of code to add validators programmatically. It is important to mention that there's also a simpler, and perhaps more natural, way of approaching the problem of validating data—using events.

You write a handler for the *ItemUpdating* event (*ItemInserting* or *ItemDeleting* for insert and delete operations, respectively), check the new values, and cancel the operation if there's something wrong. The following code ensures that the *title* field contains one of two hard-coded strings:

```
void DetailsView1_ItemUpdating(object sender, DetailsViewUpdateEventArgs e)
{
    string title = (string) e.NewValues["title"];
    if (!title.Equals("Sales Representative") &&
        !title.Equals("Sales Manager"))
    {
        e.Cancel = true;
    }
}
```

The *NewValues* dictionary you get through the event data contains new values as edited by the user; the *OldValues* dictionary contains the original data. What's the difference between this approach and validators? *ItemUpdating* (and similar events) are run on the server during the postback event. Validators can catch patently invalid input data already on the client. However, a golden rule of validation states that you should never, ever rely on client-side validation only. You should always do some validation on the server, so performance is not the issue here. The event-based approach is easier to set up and is ideal for quick pages where you don't bother using a more advanced and templated user interface. Validators are a more complete toolkit for validation and, of course, include a control for server-side validation, as we saw in Chapter 4. The validation-without-validators scheme can be applied for any view control—*DetailsView*, *FormView*, and *GridView*.

The *FormView* Control

FormView is a new data-bound control that can be considered the templated version of the *DetailsView*. It renders one record at a time, picked from the associated data source and, optionally, provides paging buttons to navigate between records. Unlike the *DetailsView* control, *FormView* doesn't use data control fields and requires the user to define the rendering of each item by using templates. The *FormView* can support any basic operation its data source provides.

Note that the *FormView* requires you to define everything through templates, and not just the things you want to change. The *FormView* has no built-in rendering engine and is limited to printing out the user-defined templates.

The *FormView* Object Model

Two functional aspects mark the difference between *FormView* and *DetailsView*. First, the *FormView* control has properties such as *ItemTemplate*, *EditItemTemplate*, and *InsertItemTemplate* that—as we've seen thus far—the *DetailsView* lacks entirely. Second, the *FormView* lacks the command row—that is, a sort of toolbar where available functions are grouped. The graphical layout of a *FormView* control is completely customizable using templates. Therefore, each template will include all command buttons needed by the particular record.

The control's definition is shown in the following code:

```
public class FormView : CompositeDataBoundControl,
                        IDataItemContainer,
                        INamingContainer
```

As you can see, *FormView* has the same root and implements the same interfaces as *DetailsView* except for the interfaces related to ASP.NET script callbacks.

Members of the *FormView* Control

The *FormView* control exposes many of the properties that we've seen already for the *DetailsView* control. This aspect is no surprise, as the two controls serve as two sides of the same coin—a record viewer control—one with and one without templates. Only the templates and related styles mark the difference between *FormView* and *DetailsView*. You can refer to Table 11-1 through Table 11-6 for the complete list of properties and events supported by the *FormView* control.

Supported Templates

The output of the *FormView* control is exclusively based on templates. This means that you always need to specify the item template at a very minimum. Table 11-7 shows the list of data-bound supported templates.

Table 11-7   Templates of the *FormView* Control

Template	Description
EditItemTemplate	The template to use when an existing record is being updated
InsertItemTemplate	The template to use when a new record is being created
ItemTemplate	The template to use when an existing record is rendered for viewing only

It's not a coincidence that the *FormView* templates match the three feasible states of the control—ReadOnly, Edit, and Insert. You use the *ItemTemplate* to define the control's layout when in view mode. You use *EditItemTemplate* to edit the contents of the current record, and you use *InsertItem-Template* to add a new record.

In addition to these templates, the control features the same set of templates offered by the *DetailsView*—that is, *HeaderTemplate*, *FooterTemplate*, and the other templates listed in Table 11-5.

Supported Operations

Because the user interface of the control is largely defined by the page author, you cannot expect a *FormView* control to understand the click on a particular button and act accordingly. For this reason, the *FormView* control exposes a few publicly callable methods to trigger common actions, such as those listed in Table 11-8.

Table 11-8   Methods of the *FormView* Control

Method	Description
ChangeMode	Changes the working mode of the control from the current to any of the modes defined in the *FormViewMode* type—ReadOnly, Edit, or Insert.
DeleteItem	Deletes the current record in the *FormView* control from the data source.
InsertItem	Inserts the current record in the data source. The *FormView* control must be in insert mode when this method is called; otherwise, an exception is thrown.
UpdateItem	Updates the current record in the data source. The *FormView* control must be in edit mode when this method is called; otherwise, an exception is thrown.

Both *InsertItem* and *UpdateItem* require a Boolean indicating whether input validation should be performed. In this context, performing validation simply means that any validator controls you might have in the template will be called. If no validators are found, no other form of validation ever occurs. The *InsertItem* and *UpdateItem* methods are designed to start a basic operation from within controls in any of the supported templates. You don't have to pass the record to insert, the values to update, or the key of the record to delete. The *FormView* control knows how to retrieve that information internally in much the same way the *DetailsView* does.

The *DeleteItem*, *InsertItem*, and *UpdateItem* methods let you define your own delete, insert, and edit user interface and attach it to the standard data-binding model of ASP.NET controls. In the *DetailsView* control, this association is implicit because the user interface is relatively static and fixed; in the *FormView*, the same association must be explicitly defined in light of the totally customizable user interface.

Binding Data to a *FormView* Control

Let's see how to use templates to configure and run a *FormView* control in a sample ASP.NET Web page. All templates must contain everything needed to accomplish tasks—user interface elements and command buttons. The control itself provides the pager bar and the surrounding table.

Header, Footer, and Pager

The final output of the *FormView* control takes the form of an HTML table with a header and footer row, plus an optional row for the pager. Just like the *DetailView*, the *FormView* control provides templates for the header and footer; unlike the *DetailsView*, though, it doesn't provide simpler and handy text properties such as *HeaderText* and *FooterText*:

```
<asp:FormView ID="FormView1" runat="server"
    AllowPaging="true"
    DataSourceID="CustomersDataSource">
    <PagerSettings Mode="NextPreviousFirstLast" />

    <HeaderTemplate>
        <h1>Customer Viewer</h1>
    </HeaderTemplate>

    <FooterTemplate>
        <h3>Courtesy of "Programming ASP.NET"</h3>
    </FooterTemplate>
</asp:FormView>
```

The pager is dual in the sense that you can have the control to render it as the settings established through *PagerSettings* and *PagerStyle* properties dictate, or create it from scratch via the *PagerTemplate* property.

Displaying Data

The following code snippet shows the typical layout of the code you write to embed a *Form-View* in your pages:

```
<asp:FormView ID="FormView1" runat="server"
    DataSourceId="CustomersDataSource" AllowPaging="true">
    <ItemTemplate>
      ...
    </ItemTemplate>
    <EditItemTemplate>
      ...
    </EditItemTemplate>
    < InsertItemTemplate >
      ...
    </InsertItemTemplate>
</asp:FormView>
```

The following code generates the page in Figure 11-10:

```
<asp:FormView runat="server" id="FormView1"
    DataKeyNames="employeeid"
    DataSourceID="MySource" AllowPaging="true">
    <ItemTemplate>
        <table style="border:solid 1px black;" width="100%">
        <tr>
            <td bgcolor="yellow" width="50px" align="center">
                <b><%# Eval("id") %></b></td>
            <td bgcolor="lightyellow" >
                <b><%# Eval("companyname") %></b></td>
        </tr>
        </table>
        <table style="font-family:Verdana;font-size:8pt;">
          <tr>
            <td><b>Contact</b></td>
            <td><%# Eval("contactname") %></td>
          </tr>
          <tr>
            <td><b>City</b></td>
            <td><%# Eval("city") %></td>
          </tr>
          <tr>
            <td valign="top"><b>Country</b></td>
            <td><%# Eval("country") %></td>
          </tr>
          </table>
          <br />
          <asp:Button ID="EditButton" runat="server" CommandName="Edit"
                    Text="Edit" />
      </ItemTemplate>
</asp:FormView>
```

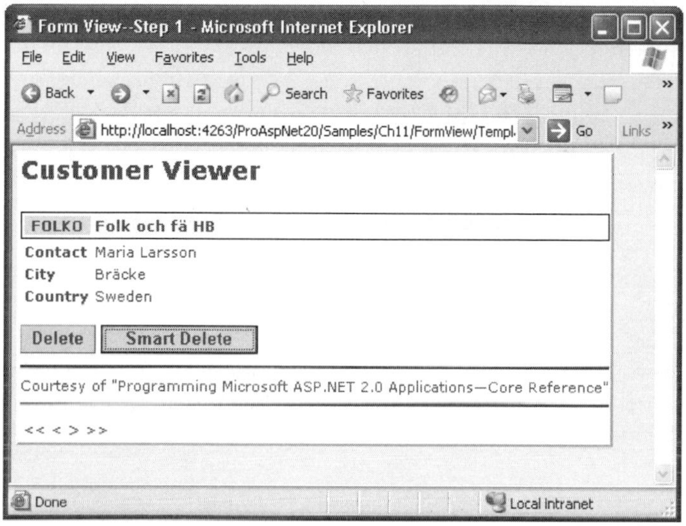

Figure 11-10   A *FormView* control in action.

All the markup you place in the *ItemTemplate* is rendered in a table cell that spans over two columns. As mentioned, the overall layout of the *FormView* is a table.

```
<td colspan="2">
  ...
</td>
```

If you want to obtain a tabular output, feel free to define an inner table, as in the preceding code.

The Edit button is added using a classic *<asp:Button>* button with the *Edit* command name. The command name will cause the *FormView* to automatically switch from the read-only mode to edit mode and display using the edit item template, if any is defined. You can use any button control with whatever command name and caption you like. If it doesn't change mode automatically, you call *ChangeMode* and the other methods supported by the *FormView* control.

The *Eval* Function

How can you insert data fields in a template? You resort to data-binding expressions and, in particular, use the *Eval* function:

```
<td><%# Eval("city") %></td>
```

As mentioned in Chapter 9, *Eval* exists in two forms, one of which is also supported in ASP.NET 1.x. The two forms are functionally equivalent, as one of them is implemented in terms of the other. The first form you can use is the following:

```
<%# DataBinder.Eval(Container.DataItem, "city")%>
```

The static function *Eval* on the *DataBinder* class uses reflection to parse and evaluate a data-binding expression against an object at run time. The object it works with is the data item object from the bound data source that corresponds to the record being rendered. Most of the time, the data-binding expression will be the name of a property on the data item bound to a row. The *Eval* function counts a third overload to specify a format string.

In ASP.NET 2.0, a similar function is available that has a more compact syntax—the *Eval* function defined on the *TemplateControl* class and inherited by all ASP.NET pages. *Eval* is an instance function and accepts only the data-binding expression, and optionally a format string. The *Eval* function ends up calling into the *DataBinder.Eval* function.

The *Eval* is useful only in read-only, one-way data-binding scenarios. For implementing real two-way data binding, an extension to *Eval* is required—the *Bind* function, which we'll discuss in a moment.

Editing Data

To edit bound records, you define an ad hoc edit template through the *EditItemTemplate* property. You can place on the form any combination of input controls, including validators. You are not limited to using text boxes and can unleash your imagination to build the user interface.

How do you retrieve values to update the bound record? You enable two-way binding by using the newest *Bind* function in lieu of *Eval*.

The Edit Template

The following code snippet shows a sample *TextBox* control bound to the *companyname* property of the data source. This is the key difference between item and edit item templates.

```
<asp:TextBox runat="server" Text='<%# Bind("companyname") %>' />
```

The following code snippet shows a sample edit template. It contains quite a few standard text boxes but also a data-bound drop-down list.

```
<EditItemTemplate>
  <table style="border:solid 1px black;" width="100%">
  <tr>
  <td bgcolor="yellow" align="center">
      <b><%# Eval("id") %></b></td>
      <td bgcolor="lightyellow">
      <asp:textbox runat="server" text='<%# Bind("companyname") %>' /></td>
  </tr>
  </table>
  <table style="font-family:Verdana;font-size:8pt;">
  <tr>
      <td><b>Contact</b></td>
```

```
        <td><%# Eval("contactname") %></td>
    </tr>
    <tr>
        <td><b>Address</b></td><td>
        <asp:textbox runat="server" text='<%# Bind("street") %>' /></td>
    </tr>
    <tr>
        <td><b>City</b></td>
        <td><asp:textbox runat="server" text='<%# Bind("city") %>' /></td>
    </tr>
    <tr>
        <td valign="top"><b>Country</b></td>
        <td><asp:dropdownlist runat="server"
                datasourceid="CountriesDataSource"
                selectedvalue='<%# Bind("country") %>' /></td>   </tr>
    </table>
    <br />
    <asp:Button runat="server" CommandName="Update" Text="Update" />
    <asp:Button runat="server" CommandName="Cancel" Text="Cancel" />
</EditItemTemplate>
```

You use *Eval* to populate control properties not involved in the update process. Wherever you need two-way data binding—that is, read/write capabilities—you use the *Bind* function instead of *Eval*, with the same syntax. For text boxes, you bind the *Text* property; for drop-down lists, you typically bind the *SelectedValue* property. Finally, for a *Calendar* control you would bind the *SelectedDate* property.

How would you populate a data-bound drop-down list? You would do it by using another data source control, properly configured and parameterized to retrieve its data based on any input that proves necessary. In the sample code, you bind the drop-down list with all possible countries. Similarly, you might bind an employee ID field to the list of all employees from an external, foreign data source.

Finally, bear in mind that the edit template must contain buttons to save changes. These are ordinary buttons with specific command names—*Update* to save and *Cancel* to abort. Buttons trigger update commands whose details are stored in the associated data source object. You can choose any text for the captions as long as you don't change the command names. If you want to modify the command names, be prepared to handle the *ItemCommand* event on the *FormView* and call the *UpdateItem* method in response.

Figure 11-11 demonstrates the output of the preceding code.

For the update command to work, the *DataKeyNames* property must be set on the *FormView* to identify the key field. For deleting a record, just add a button with the *Delete* command name and configure the underlying data source control.

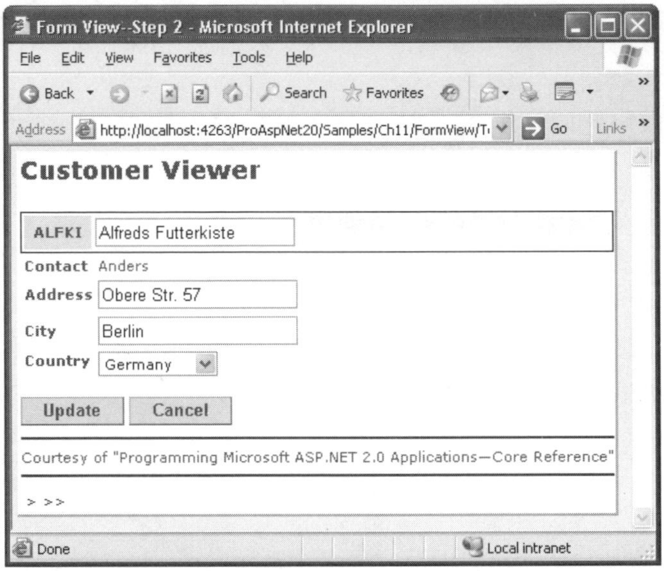

Figure 11-11   A *FormView* control running in edit mode.

The *Bind* Function

How does the *Bind* function work? The function stores the value of the bound control property into a collection of values that the *FormView* control automatically retrieves and uses to compose the parameter list of the edit command.

The argument passed to *Bind* must match the name of a parameter in the update command or method or one of the properties on the type used as an argument to the update method. This is the case in the example shown earlier, where the update method takes an instance of the *ProAspNet20.DAL.Customer* class. An exception is raised if no parameter match is found.

The Insert Template

The *InsertItemTemplate* property allows you to define the input layout when a new record is being added. To avoid confusion, an insert template should not be much different from an edit template. At the same time, you should be aware that edit and insert are distinct operations with different requirements. For example, an insert template should provide default values to controls wherever that is acceptable, and it should display neutral or null values elsewhere.

To start an insert operation, you also need a button with a command name of *New*. Clicking on this button will force the *FormView* control to change mode to Insert and render the contents defined for the insert template. The insert template should also provide a couple of Update/Cancel buttons with the same command names discussed for edit operations.

When the Function Is Not Supported

Both *DetailsView* and *FormView* controls expose some predefined operations such as Insert, Edit, and Delete. As we've seen thus far, these operations are implemented inside the data source control bound to the view control. What if, say, the *Edit* function is enabled on the *FormView* control but not supported by the underlying data source control? When this happens, a *NotSupportedException* exception is thrown and the application fails.

It's hard to imagine a team of developers who release some production code that has an Edit button associated with a non-updateable data source. However, checking whether a requested function is available is a good measure to make any application more robust and stable. The following code demonstrates this feature:

```
if (e.CommandName == "Edit")
{
    IDataSource obj = (IDataSource) FindControl(FormView1.DataSourceID);
    DataSourceView view = obj.GetView("DefaultView");
    if (!view.CanUpdate)
    {
        Response.Write("Sorry, you can't update");
        return;
    }
    else
        FormView1.UpdateItem();
}
```

The code retrieves the data source control and obtains a reference to its default data source view object. (See Chapter 9.) At this point, it checks whether the requested functionality is available. You can place this code in the *ItemCommand* event handler of any view controls—*DetailsView*, *FormView*, or *GridView*. Note that all ASP.NET built-in data source controls have only one view, named *DefaultView*.

Conclusion

In ASP.NET 2.0, the developer's toolbox for data-binding operations is definitely richer and more complete than in ASP.NET 1.x. You not only have a new and radically revised grid control, but you also have two other controls to manage views of a single record. There's nothing like this in ASP.NET 1.x.

The *DetailsView* and *FormView* control are two sides of the same coin. Both offer a user interface for viewing the contents of a single record. In both cases, the user interface is largely customizable and associated with predefined data operations such as delete, update, and insert. Bound to a data source control, both *DetailsView* and *FormView* can manage an underlying data source effectively without forcing developers to write ad hoc code. (Well, this is not entirely true. If you expose your data source through a DAL—as recommended for large systems—you have to write that code at least.)

The key difference between *DetailsView* and *FormView* lies in the support for templates. The former is perhaps a richer control with good basic support for templates limited to individual fields, and it has a relatively rich set of styles and visual properties. If you want to create your own form to edit and insert records, you should use the *FormView* control. If you do so, though, forget about standard rendering—a form view, in fact, is 100-percent templated and requires you to specify every single byte of markup.

With this chapter, we conclude the second part of the book—the part devoted to data access and related tools. Starting with the next chapter, we'll begin a new trip in the ASP.NET infrastructure, one that shows you how to make pages and applications run.

Just the Facts

- Both the *DetailsView* and *FormView* controls render a single record at a time from the associated data source, optionally providing paging buttons to navigate between records.

- Both the *DetailsView* and *FormView* controls lend themselves very well to implementing master/detail views.

- The *DetailsView* control has a fixed tabular layout and is formed by a few main areas—a header, field rows, a pager bar, a command bar, and a footer.

- The *FormView* control has areas such as a header, footer, and pager, plus a completely templated item area. You can define a custom form to render the contents of a single record.

- The *DetailsView* control typically uses text boxes to render fields. If a particular field defines a template, any markup can be displayed. This feature is useful for representing dates and foreign keys through ad hoc controls such as calendars and drop-down lists.

- Both the *DetailsView* and *FormView* controls support basic I/O operations such as insert, delete, and update. If bound to data source controls such as *ObjectDataSource* or *SqlDataSource*, *DetailsView* and *FormView* leverage the capabilities of the bound data source control to execute data-binding operations.

- Both the *DetailsView* and *FormView* controls support two-way data binding through which data can be read automatically from a bound data source and also written back.

- During updates and insertions, validation is possible in either of two ways. If templates are used, you can insert validator controls to sanitize the input both on the client and the server. If templates are not used, you can intercept events fired by *DetailsView* and *Form-View*, control values being passed, and modify them at will or just cancel the operation.

Part III
ASP.NET Infrastructure

Chapter 12
The HTTP Request Context

In this chapter:
Initialization of the Application. 502
The *global.asax* File 507
The *HttpContext* Class 514
The *Server* Object. 518
The *HttpResponse* Object 524
The *HttpRequest* Object 530
Conclusion 535

Various steps are involved in having the ASP.NET worker process serve an incoming HTTP request. The request is assigned to the *aspnet_isapi.dll* ISAPI extension which, in turn, hands it over to the HTTP runtime pipeline. The entry point in the ASP.NET pipeline is the *HttpRuntime* class. A new instance of this class is created for each request, governs its overall execution, and generates the response text for the browser. Upon instantiation, the *HttpRuntime* class performs a number of initialization tasks, the first of which is the creation of a wrapper object to encapsulate all the HTTP-specific information available about the request. The newly created object—an instance of the *HttpContext* class—is then passed along to the pipeline and is used by the various modules to access intrinsic worker objects such as *Request*, *Response*, and *Server*.

In this chapter, we'll first review the startup process of the ASP.NET application and then move on to examine the various objects that form the context of the HTTP request. If you're a former classic ASP developer, some material in this chapter might sound familiar, especially as we discuss old acquaintances such as *Request* and *Response*. Although these objects are much more feature-rich and powerful than in ASP, they should be considered lower-level tools; their use is necessary and unavoidable only in a relatively small number of situations. In general, too-frequent use of these objects in your code should be considered an alarm bell, warning you of possible non-optimal use of the ASP.NET programming toolkit.

Initialization of the Application

Once the context for the request is created, the *HttpRuntime* class sets up an ASP.NET application object to carry out the request. An ASP.NET application consists of an instance of the *HttpApplication* class that we briefly met in Chapter 3. *HttpApplication* is a *global.asax*-derived object that handles all HTTP requests directed to a particular virtual folder.

An ASP.NET running application is wholly represented by its virtual folder and, optionally, by the *global.asax* file. The virtual folder name is a sort of key that the HTTP runtime uses to selectively identify which of the running applications should take care of the incoming request. The *global.asax* file, if present, contains settings and code for responding to application-level events raised by ASP.NET or by registered HTTP modules that affect the application.

The particular *HttpApplication* class selected is responsible for managing the entire lifetime of the request it is assigned to. That instance of *HttpApplication* can be reused only after the request has been completed. If no *HttpApplication* object is available, either because the application has not been started yet or all valid objects are busy, a new *HttpApplication* is created and pooled.

Properties of the *HttpApplication* Class

Although the *HttpApplication* provides a public constructor, user applications never need to create instances of the *HttpApplication* class directly. The ASP.NET runtime infrastructure always does the job for you. As mentioned, instances of the class are pooled and, as such, can process many requests in their lifetime, but always one at a time. Should concurrent requests arrive for the same application, additional instances are created. Table 12-1 lists the properties defined for the *HttpApplication* class.

Table 12-1   *HttpApplication* Properties

Property	Description
Application	Instance of the *HttpApplicationState* class. It represents the global and shared state of the application. It is functionally equivalent to the ASP intrinsic *Application* object.
Context	Instance of the *HttpContext* class. It encapsulates in a single object all HTTP-specific information about the current request. Intrinsic objects (for example, *Application* and *Request*) are also exposed as properties.
Modules	Gets the collection of modules that affect the current application.
Request	Instance of the *HttpRequest* class. It represents the current HTTP request. It is functionally equivalent to the ASP intrinsic *Request* object.
Response	Instance of the *HttpResponse* class. It sends HTTP response data to the client. It is functionally equivalent to the ASP intrinsic *Response* object.
Server	Instance of the *HttpServerUtility* class. It provides helper methods for processing Web requests. It is functionally equivalent to the ASP intrinsic *Server* object.
Session	Instance of the *HttpSessionState* class. It manages user-specific data. It is functionally equivalent to the ASP intrinsic *Session* object.
User	An *IPrincipal* object that represents the user making the request.

The *HttpApplication* is managed by the ASP.NET infrastructure, so how can you take advantage of the fairly rich, public programming interface of the class? The answer is that properties and, even more, overridable methods and class events can be accessed and programmatically manipulated in the *global.asax* file. (We'll return to *global.asax* in a moment.)

Application Modules

The property *Modules* returns a collection of application-wide components providing ad hoc services. An HTTP module component is a class that implements the *IHttpModule* interface. Modules can be considered the managed counterpart of ISAPI filters; they are a kind of request interceptor with the built-in capability of modifying the overall context of the request being processed. The Microsoft .NET Framework defines a number of standard modules, as listed in Table 12-2. Custom modules can be defined, too. I cover this particular aspect of HTTP programming in my other recent book, *Programming Microsoft ASP.NET 2.0 Applications: Advanced Topics* (Microsoft Press, 2005).

Table 12-2   ASP.NET Modules

Module	Description
AnonymousIdentification	Assigns anonymous users a fake identity. *Not installed in ASP.NET 1.x.*
FileAuthorization	Verifies that the remote user has Microsoft Windows NT permissions to access the requested resource.
FormsAuthentication	Enables applications to use forms authentication.
OutputCache	Provides page output caching services.
PassportAuthentication	Provides a wrapper around Passport authentication services.
Profile	Provides user profile services. *Not installed in ASP.NET 1.x.*
RoleManager	Provides session-state services for the application. *Not installed in ASP.NET 1.x.*
SessionState	Provides session-state services for the application.
UrlAuthorization	Provides URL-based authorization services to access specified resources.
WindowsAuthentication	Enables ASP.NET applications to use Windows and IIS-based authentication.

The list of default modules is defined in the *machine.config* file. The modules listed in *machine.config* are available to all applications. By creating a proper *web.config* file, you can also create an application-specific list of modules. (Configuration is also covered in *Programming Microsoft ASP.NET 2.0 Applications: Advanced Topics.*)

Methods of the *HttpApplication* Class

The methods of the *HttpApplication* class can be divided in two groups—operational methods and event handler managers. The *HttpApplication* operational methods are described in Table 12-3.

Table 12-3   *HttpApplication* Operational Methods

Method	Description
CompleteRequest	Sets an internal flag that causes ASP.NET to skip all successive steps in the pipeline and directly execute *EndRequest*. Mostly useful to HTTP modules.
Dispose	Overridable method, cleans up the instance variables of all registered modules once the request has been served. At this time, *Request, Response, Session,* and *Application* are no longer available.
GetVaryByCustomString	Overridable method, provides a way to set output caching based on a custom string for all pages in the application. (We'll say more about output page caching in Chapter 14.)
Init	Overridable method that executes custom initialization code after all modules have been linked to the application to serve the request. You can use it to create and configure any object that you want to use throughout the request processing. At this time, *Request, Response, Session,* and *Application* are not yet available.

Note that *Init* and *Dispose* methods are quite different from well-known event handlers such as *Application_Start* and *Application_End*.

Init executes for every request directed at the Web application, whereas *Application_Start* fires only once in the Web application's lifetime. *Init* indicates that a new instance of the *HttpApplication* class has been created to serve an incoming request; *Application_Start* denotes that the first instance of the *HttpApplication* class has been created to start up the Web application and serve its very first request. Likewise, *Dispose* signals the next termination of the request processing but not necessarily the end of the application. *Application_End* is raised only once, when the application is being shut down.

> **Note**   The lifetime of any resources created in the *Init* method is limited to the execution of the current request. Any resource you allocate in *Init* should be disposed of in *Dispose*, at the latest. If you need persistent data, resort to other objects that form the application or session state. You can find more information on these objects in Chapter 13 and Chapter 14.

In addition to the operational methods in Table 12-3, a few other *HttpApplication* methods are available to register asynchronous handlers for application-level events. These methods are of little interest to user applications and are used only by HTTP modules to hook up the events generated during the request's chain of execution.

Events of the *HttpApplication* Class

Table 12-4 describes the event model of the *HttpApplication* class—that is, the set of events that HTTP modules, as well as user applications, can listen to and handle.

Table 12-4   *HttpApplication* Events

Event	Description
AcquireRequestState, PostAcquireRequestState	Occurs when the handler that will actually serve the request acquires the state information associated with the request. *The post event is not available in ASP.NET 1.x.*
AuthenticateRequest, PostAuthenticateRequest	Occurs when a security module has established the identity of the user. *The post event is not available in ASP.NET 1.x.*
AuthorizeRequest, PostAuthorizeRequest	Occurs when a security module has verified user authorization. *The post event is not available in ASP.NET 1.x.*
BeginRequest	Occurs as soon as the HTTP pipeline begins to process the request.
Disposed	Occurs when the *HttpApplication* object is disposed of as a result of a call to *Dispose.*
EndRequest	Occurs as the last event in the HTTP pipeline chain of execution.
Error	Occurs when an unhandled exception is thrown.
PostMapRequestHandler	Occurs when the HTTP handler to serve the request has been found. *The event is not available in ASP.NET 1.x.*
PostRequestHandlerExecute	Occurs when the HTTP handler of choice finishes execution. The response text has been generated at this point.
PreRequestHandlerExecute	Occurs just before the HTTP handler of choice begins to work.
PreSendRequestContent	Occurs just before the ASP.NET runtime sends the response text to the client.
PreSendRequestHeaders	Occurs just before the ASP.NET runtime sends HTTP headers to the client.
ReleaseRequestState, PostReleaseRequestState	Occurs when the handler releases the state information associated with the current request. *The post event is not available in ASP.NET 1.x.*
ResolveRequestCache, PostResolveRequestCache	Occurs when the ASP.NET runtime resolves the request through the output cache. *The post event is not available in ASP.NET 1.x.*
UpdateRequestCache, PostUpdateRequestCache	Occurs when the ASP.NET runtime stores the response of the current request in the output cache to be used to serve subsequent requests. *The post event is not available in ASP.NET 1.x.*

To handle any of these events asynchronously, an application will use the corresponding method whose name follows a common pattern: *AddOnXXXAsync*, where *XXX* stands for the event name. To hook up some of these events in a synchronous manner, an application will define in *global.asax* event handler procedures with the following signature:

```
public void Application_XXX(object sender, EventArgs e)
{
    // Do something here
}
```

Of course, the *XXX* placeholder must be replaced with the name of the event. All the events in the preceding table provide no event-specific data. You could also use the following simpler syntax without losing additional information and programming power:

```
public void Application_XXX()
{
    // Do something here
}
```

In addition to the events listed in Table 12-4, in *global.asax* an application can also handle *Application_Start* and *Application_End*. When ASP.NET is about to fire *BeginRequest* for the very first time in the application lifetime, it makes *Application_Start* precede it. *EndRequest* will happen at the end of every request to an application. *Application_End* occurs outside the context of a request, when the application is ending.

Application events are fired in the following sequence:

1. ***BeginRequest.*** The ASP.NET HTTP pipeline begins to work on the request. This event reaches the application after *Application_Start*.

2. ***AuthenticateRequest.*** The request is being authenticated. All the internal ASP.NET authentication modules subscribe to this event and attempt to produce an identity. If no authentication module produced an authenticated user, an internal default authentication module is invoked to produce an identity for the unauthenticated user. This is done for the sake of consistency so that code doesn't need to worry about null identities.

3. ***PostAuthenticateRequest.*** The request has been authenticated. All the information available is stored in the *HttpContext*'s *User* property.

4. ***AuthorizeRequest.*** The request authorization is about to occur. This event is commonly handled by application code to do custom authorization based on business logic or other application requirements.

5. ***PostAuthorizeRequest.*** The request has been authorized.

6. ***ResolveRequestCache.*** The ASP.NET runtime verifies whether returning a previously cached page can resolve the request. If a valid cached representation is found, the request is served from the cache and the request is short-circuited, calling only any registered *EndRequest* handlers.

7. ***PostResolveRequestCache.*** The request can't be served from the cache, and the procedure continues. An HTTP handler corresponding to the requested URL is created at this point. If the requested resource is an *.aspx* page, an instance of a page class is created.

8. ***PostMapRequestHandler.*** The event fires when the HTTP handler corresponding to the requested URL has been successfully created.

9. ***AcquireRequestState.*** The module that hooks up this event is willing to retrieve any state information for the request. A number of factors are relevant here: the handler must support session state in some form, and there must be a valid session ID.

10. *PostAcquireRequestState.* The state information (such as *Application* or *Session*) has been acquired.

11. *PreRequestHandlerExecute.* This event is fired immediately prior to executing the handler for a given request. The handler does its job and generates the output for the client.

12. *PostRequestHandlerExecute.* This event is raised when the handler has generated the response text.

13. *ReleaseRequestState.* This event is raised when the handler releases its state information and prepares to shut down. This event is used by the session state module to update the dirty session state if necessary.

14. *PostReleaseRequestState.* The state, as modified by the page execution, has been persisted. Any relevant response filtering is done at this point. (I'll say more about this topic later.)

15. *UpdateRequestCache.* The ASP.NET runtime determines whether the generated output, now also properly filtered by registered modules, should be cached to be reused with upcoming identical requests.

16. *PostUpdateRequestCache.* The page has been saved to the output cache if it was configured to do so.

17. *EndRequest.* This event fires as the final step of the HTTP pipeline. The control passes back to the *HttpRuntime* object, which is responsible for the actual forwarding of the response to the client. At this point, the text has not been sent yet.

Another pair of events can occur during the request, but in a nondeterministic order: *PreSendRequestHeaders* and *PreSendRequestContent.* The *PreSendRequestHeaders* event informs the *HttpApplication* object in charge of the request that HTTP headers are about to be sent. The event normally fires after *EndRequest* but not always. For example, if buffering is turned off, the event gets fired as soon as some content is going to be sent to the client. Finally, with the *PreSendRequestContent* event, the *HttpApplication* object in charge of the request learns that the response body is about to be sent. Speaking of nondeterministic application events, it must be said that a third nondeterministic event is, of course, *Error.*

The *global.asax* File

The *global.asax* file is used by Web applications to handle some application-level events raised by the ASP.NET runtime or by registered HTTP modules. The *global.asax* file is optional. If the *global.asax* file is missing, the ASP.NET runtime environment simply assumes you have no application or module event handlers defined. To be functional, the *global.asax* file must be located in the root directory of the application. Only one *global.asax* file per application is accepted. Any *global.asax* files placed in subdirectories are simply ignored. Note that Microsoft Visual Studio .NET 2005 doesn't list *global.asax* in the items that you can add to the project if there already is one.

Compiling *global.asax*

When the application is started, *global.asax*, if present, is parsed into a source class and compiled. The resultant assembly is created in the temporary directory just as any other dynamically generated assembly would be. The following listing shows the skeleton of the C# code that ASP.NET generates for any *global.asax* file:

```
namespace ASP
{
    public class global_asax : System.Web.HttpApplication
    {
        //
        // The source code of "global.asax" file is flushed
        // here verbatim. For this reason, the following code
        // in global.asax would generate a compile error.
        //     int i;
        //     i = 2;  // can't have statements outside methods
        //
    }
}
```

The class is named *ASP.global_asax* and is derived from the *HttpApplication* base class. In most cases, you deploy *global.asax* as a separate text file; however, you can also write it as a class and compile it either in a separate assembly or within your project's assembly. The class source code must follow the outline shown earlier and, above all, must derive from *HttpApplication*. The assembly with the compiled version of *global.asax* must be deployed in the application's *Bin* subdirectory.

Note, though, that even if you isolate the logic of the *global.asax* file in a precompiled assembly, you still need to have a (codeless) *global.asax* file that refers to the assembly, as shown in the following code:

```
<%@ Application Inherits="ProAspNet.Global" %>
```

We'll learn more about the syntax of *global.asax* in the next section. With a precompiled global application file, you certainly don't risk exposing your source code over the Web to malicious attacks. However, even if you leave it as source code, you're somewhat safe.

The *global.asax* file, in fact, is configured so that any direct URL request for it is automatically rejected by Internet Information Server (IIS). In this way, external users cannot download or view the code it contains. The trick that enables this behavior is the following line of code, excerpted from *machine.config*:

```
<add verb="*" path="*.asax" type="System.Web.HttpForbiddenHandler" />
```

ASP.NET registers with IIS to handle *.asax* resources, but then it processes those direct requests through the *HttpForbiddenHandler* HTTP handler. As a result, when a browser requests an *.asax* resource, an error message is displayed on the page, as shown in Figure 12-1.

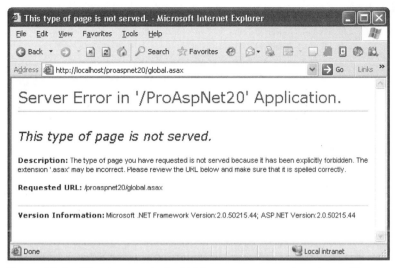

Figure 12-1 Direct access to forbidden resources, such as *.asax* files, results in a server error.

> **Tip** You can duplicate the line of code listed above in your application's *web.config* file and block direct access to other types of resources specific to your application. For this trick to work, though, make sure that the resource type is redirected to ASP.NET at the IIS level. In other words, you must first register *aspnet_isapi.dll* to handle those files in the IIS metabase and then ask ASP.NET to block any requests. You accomplish this through the IIS manager applet, which is accessible from Control Panel.

When the *global.asax* file of a running application is modified, the ASP.NET runtime detects the change and prepares to shut down and restart the application. It waits until all pending requests are completed and then fires the *Application_End* event. When the next request from a browser arrives, ASP.NET reparses and recompiles the *global.asax* file, and again raises the *Application_Start* event.

Syntax of *global.asax*

Four elements determine the syntax of the *global.asax* file: application directives, code declaration blocks, server-side *<object>* tags, and server-side includes. These elements can be used in any order and number to compose a *global.asax* file.

Application Directives

The *global.asax* file supports three directives: *@Application*, *@Import*, and *@Assembly*. The *@Import* and *@Assembly* directives work as we have seen in Chapter 3. The *@Import* directive imports a namespace into an application; the *@Assembly* directive links an assembly to the application at compile time.

The *@Application* directive supports a few attributes—*Description*, *Language*, and *Inherits*. *Description* can contain any text you want to use to describe the behavior of the application. This text only serves a documentation purpose and is blissfully ignored by the ASP.NET parser. *Language* indicates the language being used in the file. The *Inherits* attribute indicates a code-behind class for the application to inherit. It can be the name of any class derived from the *HttpApplication* class. The assembly that contains the class must be located in the *Bin* subdirectory of the application.

Code Declaration Blocks

A *global.asax* file can contain code wrapped by a *<script>* tag. Just as for pages, the *<script>* tag must have the *runat* attribute set to *server*. The *language* attribute indicates the language used throughout:

```
<script language="C#" runat="server">
   ...
</script>
```

If the *language* attribute is not specified, ASP.NET defaults to the language set in the configuration, which is Microsoft Visual Basic .NET. The source code can also be loaded from an external file, whose virtual path is set in the *Src* attribute. The location of the file is resolved using *Server.MapPath*—that is, starting under the physical root directory of the Web application:

```
<script language="C#" runat="server" src="global.aspx.cs" />
```

In this case, any other code in the declaration *<script>* block is ignored. Notice that ASP.NET enforces syntax rules on the *<script>* tag. The *runat* attribute is mandatory, and if the block has no content, the *Src* must be specified.

Server-Side *<object>* Tags

The server-side *<object>* tag lets you create new objects using a declarative syntax. As shown in the following lines of code, the *<object>* tag can take three forms, depending on the specified reference type:

```
<object id="..." runat="server" scope="..." class="..." />
<object id="..." runat="server" scope="..." progid="..." />
<object id="..." runat="server" scope="..." classid="..." />
```

In the first case, the object is identified by the name of the class and assembly that contains it. In the last two cases, the object to create is a COM object identified by the program identifier (*progid*) and the 128-bit CLSID, respectively. As one can easily guess, the *classid*, *progid*, and *class* attributes are mutually exclusive. If you use more than one within a single server-side *<object>* tag, a compile error is generated. Objects declared in this way are loaded when the application is started.

The *scope* attribute indicates the scope at which the object is declared. The allowable values are defined in Table 12-5. Unless otherwise specified, the server-side object is valid only within the boundaries of the HTTP pipeline that processes the current request. Other settings that increase the object's lifetime are *application* and *session*.

Table 12-5   Feasible Scopes for Server-Side *<object>* Tags

Scope	Description
Pipeline	Default setting, indicates the object is available only within the context of the current HTTP request
Application	Indicates the object is added to the *StaticObjects* collection of the *Application* object and is shared among all pages in the application
Session	Indicates the object is added to the *StaticObjects* collection of the *Session* object and is shared among all pages in the current session

Server-Side Includes

An *#include* directive inserts the contents of the specified file as-is into the ASP.NET file that uses it. The directive for file inclusion can be used in *global.asax* pages as well as in *.aspx* pages. The directive must be enclosed in an HTML comment so that it isn't mistaken for plain text to be output verbatim:

```
<!-- #include file="filename" -->
<!-- #include virtual="filename"  >
```

The directive supports two mutually exclusive attributes—*file* and *virtual*. If the *file* attribute is used, the file name must be a relative path to a file located in the same directory or in a sub-directory; the included file cannot be in a directory above the file with the *#include* directive. With the *virtual* attribute, the file name can be indicated by using a full virtual path from a virtual directory on the same Web site.

Static Properties

If you define static properties in the *global.asax* file, they will be accessible for reading and writing by all pages in the application:

```
<script language="C#" runat="server">
    public static int Counter = 0;
</script>
```

The *Counter* property defined in the preceding code works like an item stored in *Application*—namely, it is globally visible across pages and sessions. Consider that concurrent access to *Counter* is not serialized; on the other hand, you have a strong-typed, direct global item whose access speed is much faster than retrieving the same piece of information from a generic collection such as *Application*.

To access the property from a page, you must use the *ASP.global_asax* qualifier, shown here:

```
Response.Write(ASP.global_asax.Counter.ToString());
```

If you don't particularly like the *ASP.global_asax* prefix, you can alias it as long as you use C#. Add the following code to a C#-based page (or code-behind class) for which you need to access the globals:

```
using Globals = ASP.global_asax;
```

The preceding statement creates an alias for the *ASP.global_asax* class (or whatever name your *global.asax* class has). The alias—*Globals* in this sample code—can be used throughout your code wherever *ASP.global_asax* is accepted:

```
Response.Write(Globals.Counter.ToString());
```

> **Important**   You can use the *global.asax* file to handle any event exposed by the modules called to operate on the request. Handlers for events exposed by an HTTP module must have a name that conforms to the following scheme: *ModuleName_EventName*. The module name to use is defined in the *<httpModules>* section of the configuration file.

Tracking Errors and Anomalies

When an error occurs, displaying a friendly page to the user is only half the job a good programmer should do. The second half of the work consists of sending appropriate notifications to the system administrator—if possible, in real time. A great help is the *Error* event of the *HttpApplication* object, as we have already seen in Chapter 5. Write an *Application_Error* event handler in your *global.asax* file, and the system will call it back whenever an unhandled error occurs in the application—either in the user code, a component's code, or ASP.NET code.

In the *Application_Error* event handler, you first obtain specific information about the error and then implement the tracking policy that best suits your needs—for example, e-mailing the administrator, writing to the Windows Event Log, or dumping errors to a text file. The *Server.GetLastError* method returns an *Exception* object that represents the unhandled exception you want to track down. URL information is contained in the *Request* object, and even session or application state is available.

The following code demonstrates how to write an *Application_Error* event handler in *global.asax* to report run-time anomalies to the Event Log. An example of this code in action is shown in Figure 12-2. The code retrieves the last exception and writes out available information to the event log. Note that the *ToString* method on an exception object returns more information than the *Message* property. Additional information includes the stack trace.

```
<%@ Import Namespace="System.Diagnostics" %>
<%@ Import Namespace="System.Text" %>
```

```
<script language="C#" runat="server">
void Application_Error(object sender, EventArgs e)
{
    // Obtain the URL of the request
    string url = Request.Path;

    // Obtain the Exception object describing the error
    Exception error = Server.GetLastError();

    // Build the message --> [Error occurred. XXX at url]
    StringBuilder text = new StringBuilder("Error occurred. ");
    text.Append(error.ToString());
    text.Append(" at ");
    text.Append(url);

    // Write to the Event Log
    EventLog log = new EventLog();
    log.Source = "ProAspNet20 Log";
    log.WriteEntry(text.ToString(), EventLogEntryType.Error);
}
</script>
```

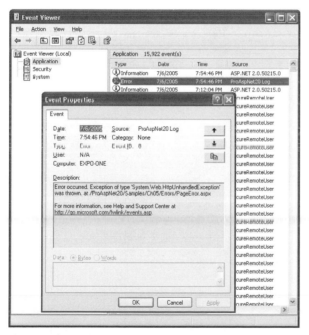

Figure 12-2   The Event Viewer tracks an error on an ASP.NET application.

Your code doesn't necessarily have to create the event source. If the source specified in the *Source* property does not exist, it will be created before writing to the event log. The *WriteEntry* method takes care of that. Windows provides three log files: Application, Security, and System. System is reserved for device drivers. The *Log* property of the *EventLog* class gets and sets the log file to use, which is Application by default.

> **Caution** To create new event logs, applications should use the static method *CreateEventSource* on the *EventLog* class. Note, though, that ASP.NET applications can't create new event logs because the running account (ASPNET or NETWORK SERVICE) doesn't have enough permissions. If you want your ASP.NET application to use a custom log, create that at setup time.

The *HttpContext* Class

During the various steps of the request's chain of execution, an object gets passed along from class to class—this object is the *HttpContext* object. *HttpContext* encapsulates all the information available about an individual HTTP request that ASP.NET is going to handle. The *HttpContext* class is instantiated by the *HttpRuntime* object while the request processing mechanism is being set up. Next, the object is flowed throughout the various stages of the request's lifetime, as Figure 12-3 demonstrates.

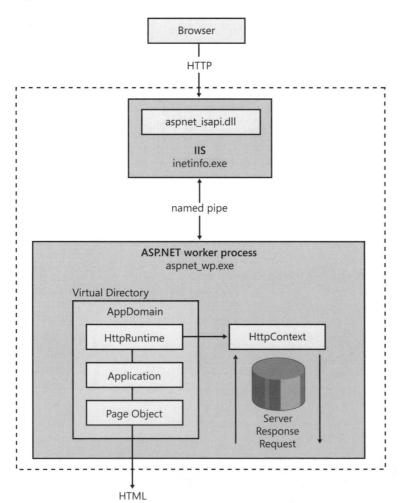

Figure 12-3 The *HttpContext* object encapsulates all the request information and gets flowed through the HTTP pipeline until the client response is generated.

Properties of the *HttpContext* Class

Table 12-6 enumerates all the properties exposed by the *HttpContext* class. The class represent a single entry point for a number of intrinsic objects such as classic ASP's intrinsics and ASP.NET-specific *Cache* and *User* objects.

Table 12-6   *HttpContext* Properties

Property	Description
AllErrors	Gets an array of *Exception* objects, each of which represents an error that occurred while processing the request.
Application	Gets an instance of the *HttpApplicationState* class, which contains the global and shared states of the application.
ApplicationInstance	Gets or sets the *HttpApplication* object for the current request. The actual type is the *global.asax* code-behind class. Make a cast to access public properties and methods you might have defined in *global.asax*.
Cache	Gets the ASP.NET *Cache* object for the current request.
Current	Gets the *HttpContext* object for the current request.
CurrentHandler	Gets the handler for the request that is currently being executed by the application. *Not supported in ASP.NET 1.x.*
Error	Gets the first exception (if any) that has been raised while processing the current request.
Handler	Gets or sets the HTTP handler for the current request.
IsCustomErrorEnabled	Indicates whether custom error handling is enabled for the current request.
IsDebuggingEnabled	Indicates whether the current request is in debug mode.
Items	Gets a name/value collection (hash table) that can be used to share custom data and objects between HTTP modules and HTTP handlers during the request lifetime.
PreviousHandler	Gets the last handler before the current request was executed. *Not supported in ASP.NET 1.x.*
Profile	Gets the object that represents the profile of the current user. *Not supported in ASP.NET 1.x.*
Request	Gets an instance of the *HttpRequest* class, which represents the current HTTP request.
Response	Gets an instance of the *HttpResponse* class, which sends HTTP response data to the client.
Server	Get an instance of the *HttpServerUtility* class, which provides helper methods for processing Web requests.
Session	Gets an instance of the *HttpSessionState* class, which manages session-specific data.
SkipAuthorization	Gets or sets a Boolean value that specifies whether the URL-based authorization module will skip the authorization check for the current request. This is *false* by default. It is mostly used by authentication modules that need to redirect to a page that allows anonymous access.

Table 12-6   *HttpContext* **Properties**

Property	Description
Timestamp	Gets a *DateTime* object that represents the initial timestamp of the current request.
Trace	Gets the *TraceContext* object for the current response.
User	Gets or sets the *IPrincipal* object that represents the identity of the user making the request.

The *Current* property is a frequently used static member that returns the *HttpContext* object for the request being processed.

The *Items* property is a dictionary object—a hash table, to be exact—that can be used to share information between the modules and handlers involved with the particular request. By using this property, each custom HTTP module or handler can add its own information to the *HttpContext* object serving the request. The information stored in *Items* is ultimately made available to the page. The lifetime of this information is limited to the request.

Methods of the *HttpContext* Class

Table 12-7 lists the methods specific to the *HttpContext* class.

Table 12-7   *HttpContext* **Methods**

Method	Description
AddError	Adds an exception object to the *AllErrors* collection.
ClearError	Clears all errors for the current request.
GetAppConfig	Returns requested configuration information for the current application. The information is collected from *machine.config* and the application's main *web.config* files. *Marked as obsolete in ASP.NET 2.0.*
GetConfig	Returns requested configuration information for the current request. The information is collected at the level of the requested URL, taking into account any child *web.config* files defined in subdirectories. *Marked as obsolete in ASP.NET 2.0.*
GetGlobalResourceObject	Loads a global resource. *Not available in ASP.NET 1.x.*
GetLocalResourceObject	Loads a local, page-specific resource. *Not available in ASP.NET 1.x.*
GetSection	Returns requested configuration information for the current request. *Not available in ASP.NET 1.x.*
RewritePath	Mostly for internal use; overwrites URL and query string of the current *Request* object.

In ASP.NET 2.0, the *GetSection* replaces *GetConfig*, which has been marked as obsolete and should not be used. If you have old code using *GetConfig*, just change the name of the method. The prototype is the same. *GetAppConfig* is also marked as obsolete in ASP.NET 2.0. It has been replaced by *GetWebApplicationSection*, a static member of the new *WebConfigurationManager* class. Also in this case, no changes to the prototype are required. Let's take some time to dig out some interesting characteristics of other methods of the *HttpContext* class.

URL Rewriting

The *RewritePath* method lets you change the URL of the current request on the fly, thus performing a sort of internal redirect. As a result, the displayed page is the one you set through *RewritePath*; the page shown in the address bar remains the originally requested one. The change of the final URL takes place on the server and, more important, within the context of the same call. *RewritePath* should be used carefully and mainly from within the *global.asax* file. If you use *RewritePath* in the context of a postback event, you can experience some view-state troubles.

```
protected void Application_BeginRequest(object sender, EventArgs e)
{
    HttpContext context = HttpContext.Current;
    object o = context.Request["id"];
    if (o != null) {
        int id = (int) o;
        string url = GetPageUrlFromId(id);
        context.RewritePath(url);
    }
}
```

The preceding code rewrites a URL such as *page.aspx?id=1234* to a specific page whose real URL is read out of a database or a configuration file.

Loading Resources Programmatically

In Chapter 2, we discussed expressions allowed in ASP.NET 2.0 pages to bind control properties to embedded global or local resources. The *$Resources* and *meta:resourcekey* expressions for global and local resources, respectively, work only at design time. What if you instead need to generate text programmatically that embeds resource expressions? Both the *Page* and *HttpContext* classes support a pair of programmatic methods to retrieve the content of resources embedded in the application.

GetGlobalResourceObject retrieves a global resource—that is, a resource defined in an *.resx* file located in the *App_GlobalResources* special folder. *GetLocalResourceObject* does the same for an *.resx* file located in the *App_LocalResources* special folder of a given page:

```
msg1.Text = (string) HttpContext.GetGlobalResourceObject(
    "Test", "MyString");
msg2.Text = (string) HttpContext.GetLocalResourceObject(
    "/ProAspNet20/Samples/Ch02/ResPage.aspx", "PageResource1.Title");
```

The first parameter you pass to *GetGlobalResourceObject* indicates the name of the *.resx* resource file without extension; the second parameter is the name of the resource to retrieve. As for *GetLocalResourceObject*, the first argument indicates the virtual path of the page; the second is the name of the resource.

The *Server* Object

In the all-encompassing container represented by the *HttpContext* object, a few popular objects also find their place. Among them are *Server*, *Request*, and *Response*. They are old acquaintances for ASP developers and, indeed, they are feature-rich elements of the ASP.NET programming toolkit. The set of properties and methods still makes these objects a fundamental resource for developers. Let's learn more about them, starting with the *Server* object.

The functionality of the ASP intrinsic *Server* object in ASP.NET is implemented by the *HttpServerUtility* class. An instance of the type is created when ASP.NET begins to process the request and is then stored as part of the request context. The bunch of helper methods that *HttpServerUtility* provides are publicly exposed to modules and handlers—including *global.asax*, pages, and Web services—through the *Server* property of the *HttpContext* object. In addition, to maintain ASP.NET coding as close as possible to the ASP programming style, several other commonly used ASP.NET objects also expose their own *Server* property. In this way, developers can use, say, *Server.MapPath* in the code without incurring compile errors.

Properties of the *HttpServerUtility* Class

This class provides two properties, named *MachineName* and *ScriptTimeout*. The *MachineName* property returns the machine name, whereas *ScriptTimeout* gets and sets the time in seconds that a request is allowed to be processed. This property accepts integers and defaults to 90 seconds; however, it is set to a virtually infinite value if the page runs with the attribute *debug=true*, as shown here:

```
this.Server.ScriptTimeout = 30000000;
```

The *ScriptTimeout* property is explicitly and automatically set in the constructor of the dynamically created class that represents the page.

Methods of the *HttpServerUtility* Class

Table 12-8 lists all methods exposed by the *HttpServerUtility* class. As you can see, they constitute a group of helper methods that come in handy at various stages of page execution. The class provides a couple of methods to create instances of COM components and a few others to deal with errors. Another group of methods relates to the decoding and encoding of content and URL.

Table 12-8   Methods of the *HttpServerUtility* Class

Method	Description
ClearError	Clears the last exception that was thrown for the request.
CreateObject	Creates an instance of the specified COM object.
CreateObjectFromClsid	Creates an instance of the COM object identified by the specified CLSID. The class identifier is expressed as a string.

Table 12-8   **Methods of the *HttpServerUtility* Class**

Method	Description
Execute	Passes control to the specified page for execution. The child page executes like a subroutine. The output can be retained in a writer object or automatically flushed in the parent response buffer.
GetLastError	Returns the last exception that was thrown.
HtmlDecode	Decodes a string that has been encoded to eliminate invalid HTML characters. For example, it translates *<* into <.
HtmlEncode	Encodes a string to be displayed in a browser. For example, it encodes < into *<*.
MapPath	Returns the physical path that corresponds to the specified virtual path on the Web server.
Transfer	Works as a kind of server-side redirect. It terminates the execution of the current page and passes control to the specified page. Unlike *Execute*, control is not passed back to the caller page.
UrlDecode	Decodes a string encoded for HTTP transmission to the server in a URL. The decoded string can be returned as a string or output to a writer.
UrlEncode	Encodes a string for HTTP transmission to a client in a URL. The encoded string can be returned as a string or output to a writer.
UrlPathEncode	Encodes only the path portion of a URL string and returns the encoded string. This method leaves the query string content intact.

HTML and URL encoding are ways of encoding characters to ensure that the transmitted text is not misunderstood by the receiving browser. HTML encoding, in particular, replaces <, >, &, and quotes with equivalent HTML entities such as *<*, *>*, *&*, and *"*. It also encodes blanks, punctuation characters, and in general, all characters not allowed in an HTML stream. On the other hand, URL encoding is aimed at fixing the text transmitted in URL strings. In URL encoding, the same critical characters are replaced with different character entities than in HTML encoding.

In ASP.NET 2.0, two new static methods have been added to encode and decode a token. The *UrlTokenEncode* method accepts a byte array containing Base64 data and converts it into a URL-encoded token. *UrlTokenDecode* does the reverse.

Embedding Another Page's Results

The *Execute* method allows you to consider an external page as a subroutine. When the execution flow reaches the *Server.Execute* call, control is passed to the specified page. The execution of the current page is suspended, and the external page is spawned. The response text generated by the child execution is captured and processed according to the particular overload of *Execute* that has been used. Table 12-9 lists the overloads of the *Execute* method.

Table 12-9 Overloads of the *Execute* Method

Overload	Description
Execute(string);	You pass the URL of the page, and the response text is automatically embedded in the main page.
Execute(string, TextWriter);	The response text is accumulated in the specified text writer.
Execute(string, bool);	The same description as for previous item, except that you can choose whether to preserve the *QueryString* and *Form* collections. *True* is the default setting.
Execute(IHttpHandler, TextWriter, bool);	You indicate the HTTP handler to transfer the current request to. The response is captured by the text writer.
Execute(string, TextWriter, bool);	The response text is captured by the specified text writer, and the *QueryString* and *Form* collections are either preserved or not preserved, as specified.

Only the first two overloads listed in Table 12-9 are supported in ASP.NET 1.x.

It is important to note that if a *TextWriter* object is specified, the response text of the child execution is accumulated into the writer object so that the main page can be used later at will. Figure 12-4 shows this approach in action—the main page generates the boldfaced text, while the child page's output is shown in normal font sandwiched between the main page output.

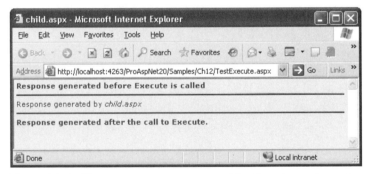

Figure 12-4 The response text generated by *Execute* can be automatically embedded in the main response or cached in a writer object.

The source code for the main page in Figure 12-4 is as follows:

```
void Page_Load(object sender, EventArgs e)
{
    Response.Write("Response generated before Execute is called<hr>");
    Server.Execute("child.aspx");
    Response.Write("<hr>Response generated after the call to Execute.");
}
```

It's interesting to look at the internal implementation of the *Execute* method. Both the main and child pages are run by the same *HttpApplication* object as if they were the same request. What happens within the folds of *Execute* is a sort of context switch. First, the method obtains an HTTP handler from the application factory to serve the new request. The original handler of the main request is cached and replaced with the new handler. The spawned page inherits the context of the parent; when finished, any modification made to *Session* or *Application* is immediately visible to the main page.

The handler switching makes the whole operation extremely fast, as there's no need to create a new object to serve the request. When the child page returns, the original handler is restored. The execution of the main page continues from the point in which it was stopped, but it uses the context inherited from the child page.

> **Caution**   ASP.NET directly calls the handler indicated by the *Execute* method without reapplying any authentication and authorization logic. If your security policy requires clients to have proper authorization to access the resource, the application should force reauthorization. You can force reauthorization by using the *Response.Redirect* method instead of *Execute*. When *Redirect* is called, the browser places a new request in the system, which will be authenticated and authorized as usual by IIS and ASP.NET. As an alternative, you can verify whether the user has permission to call the page by defining roles and checking the user's role before the application calls the *Execute* method.

Server-Side Redirection

The *Transfer* method differs from the *Execute* method in that it terminates the current page after executing the specified page. The new page runs as if it was the originally requested one. The *Transfer* method has the following overloads:

```
public void Transfer(string);
public void Transfer(string, bool);
public void Transfer(IHttpHandler, bool);
```

The string parameter indicates the destination URL. The Boolean parameter indicates what to do with regard to the *QueryString* and *Form* collections. If true, the collections are preserved; otherwise, they are cleared and made unavailable to the destination page (which is the recommended approach). In ASP.NET 2.0 only, you can also directly indicate the HTTP handler to invoke with the same security issues that were mentioned for *Execute*.

Any code that might be following the call to *Transfer* in the main page is never executed. In the end, *Transfer* is just a page redirect method. However, it is particularly efficient for two reasons. First, no roundtrip to the client is requested, as is the case, for example, with *Response.Redirect*. Second, the same *HttpApplication* that was serving the caller request is reused, thus limiting the impact on the ASP.NET infrastructure.

Late-Bound COM Objects

The *HttpServerUtility* class provides you with the ability to create late-bound COM objects in much the same way you do in ASP. The methods are *CreateObject* and *CreateObjectFromClsid*.

Objects can be created either from the string representation of the class CLSID or from the progID. The following code creates an instance of a COM component using the CLSID:

```
// Only in VB (and in non-strict mode) can you call methods
// on an Object variable beyond the members of the Object class.
// The code here will work written in C# but it will be hardly usable
Dim strClsid As String = "42754580-16b7-11ce-80eb-00aa003d7352"
Dim comObj As Object = Server.CreateObject(strClsid)
```

When assigned to a variable declared of type *Object*, an object is said to be late bound—as opposed to early-bound, strongly typed objects. Late-bound objects can hold references to any object, but they lack many advantages of early-bound objects. Early-bound objects should be used whenever possible because they are significantly faster than late-bound objects and provide strong type checking, thus making your code easier to develop, read, and maintain.

Primarily for backward-compatibility reasons, you might sometimes create late-bound instances of COM objects. Using COM objects in ASP.NET applications is a common necessity in real-world projects. The best way to import COM functionality in .NET applications entails the use of managed wrappers—special classes that expose the type library of the COM class as a .NET class. Managed wrappers are usually created by Visual Studio .NET when you reference a COM object in your project.

> **Note** A command-line utility is also available should you need to generate the class assembly using a particular namespace, language, or file name different from those automatically set by Visual Studio .NET. The utility is the Type Library Importer (*tlbimp.exe*) and is located in the installation path of Visual Studio .NET.

Although it's not an especially effective approach, the *Server.CreateObject* method can be used to create a late-bound instance of a COM component. The ideal language for late binding is Visual Basic .NET; however, bear in mind that late binding is supported only if the *Strict* option is *Off* (the default).

The following code shows how to fill an ADO *Recordset* object using the ASP programming style:

```
<%@ Page Language="VB" AspCompat="true" %>

<script runat="server">
Sub Page_Load(sender as object, e as EventArgs)
    Dim rs As Object = Server.CreateObject("ADODB.Recordset")
    rs.Open("SELECT firstname, lastname FROM employees", _
        "PROVIDER=sqloledb;DATABASE=northwind;SERVER=localhost;UID=sa;")

    Dim sb As StringBuilder = New StringBuilder("")
    While Not rs.EOF
        sb.Append(rs.Fields("lastname").Value.ToString())
        sb.Append(", ")
```

```
        sb.Append(rs.Fields("firstname").Value.ToString())
        sb.Append("<br>")
        rs.MoveNext
    End While

    Response.Write(sb.ToString())
End Sub
</script>
```

Note the use of the *AspCompat* attribute in the *@Page* directive. Apartment-threaded COM components can be created only in ASP.NET pages that have the *AspCompat* attribute set to *true*. Before an attempt to create the object is made, the *CreateObject* method checks the threading model of the component. If the page is already working in ASP compatibility mode— that is, the *AspCompat* attribute is *true*—the object is created, regardless of the threading model of the component. If the *AspCompat* attribute is set to *false* (the default), *CreateObject* reads the threading model of the COM component from the registry. If the threading model is *apartment* or no threading model is specified, an exception is thrown; otherwise, the object is successfully created.

Note also that the use of the *AspCompat* attribute is not strictly necessary with the ADO library because the ADO library supports both the apartment and free-threading models.

> **Note**   COM components developed using Visual Basic 6.0 need the *AspCompat* attribute to be used in ASP.NET pages because they typically use the single-threaded apartment model (STA). This situation is detected and throws an exception.
>
> Note, though, that if your code instantiates the COM object through a managed wrapper (instead of creating the instance using *CreateObject*), the runtime will no longer be able to detect the apartment nature of the component and does not throw an exception. A managed wrapper saves you from a run-time exception but not from the need of setting *AspCompat* to *true*.

The Importance of *AspCompat*

Running STA components in a multithreaded apartment environment (MTA) such as ASP.NET is strongly discouraged for performance reasons. The *AspCompat* attribute is designed specifically to avoid this critical situation. Let's see how and why.

To process HTTP requests, normally ASP.NET uses a pool of threads from an MTA. Objects in an MTA execute on any thread and allow any number of methods to occur simultaneously. Single-threaded apartment COM components (that is, all Visual Basic 6 COM components) execute on the particular thread in which they were created and allow only one method to execute at a time. Until special countermeasures are taken, when you run an STA component in an MTA environment continued thread switching is likely to happen. More important, a thread switch can happen only when the particular thread in the pool that can serve the STA component is available. As you see, this situation is heralding poor performance issues, and possibly even deadlock.

By setting the *AspCompat* attribute to *true*, you force ASP.NET to use an STA thread pool to accommodate the COM object on a per-page basis. In this case, both the caller thread and the callee component live in the same apartment, and extra overhead is involved. As a matter of fact, ASP.NET pages that contain STA COM components run better in STA mode than in an otherwise generally faster MTA mode.

Because the *AspCompat* attribute is processed after the instance of the page class is created, you should also avoid creating instances of STA COM objects in the page constructor. If you don't avoid this, the page will be served by an MTA thread regardless of the value of *AspCompat*, and you'll probably experience poor performance.

Setting *AspCompat* to *true* has another advantage—it makes ASP's intrinsic objects (*ObjectContext*, *Request*, *Response*, and so on) available to the COM component. ASP.NET creates unmanaged ASP intrinsic objects and passes them to the COM components used in the page.

The *HttpResponse* Object

In ASP.NET, the HTTP response information is encapsulated in the *HttpResponse* class. An instance of the class is created when the HTTP pipeline is set up to serve the request. The instance is then linked to the *HttpContext* object associated with the request and exposed via the *Response* property. The *HttpResponse* class defines methods and properties to manipulate the text that will be sent to the browser. Although user-defined ASP.NET code never needs to use the *HttpResponse* constructor, looking at it is still useful to get the gist of the class:

```
public HttpResponse(TextWriter writer);
```

As you can see, the constructor takes a writer object, which will then be used to accumulate the response text. All calls made to *Response.Write* (and similar output methods) are resolved in terms of internal calls to the specified writer object.

Properties of the *HttpResponse* Class

All properties of the class are grouped and described in Table 12-10. You set a few of these properties to configure key fields on the HTTP response packet, such as content type, character set, page expiration, and status code.

Table 12-10   *HttpResponse* Properties

Property	Description
Buffer	Indicates whether the response text should be buffered and sent only at the end of the request. This property is deprecated and provided only for backward compatibility with classic ASP. ASP.NET applications should instead use *BufferOutput*.
BufferOutput	Gets or sets a Boolean value that indicates whether response buffering is enabled. The default is *true*.

Table 12-10   *HttpResponse* Properties

Property	Description
Cache	Gets the caching policy set for the page. The caching policy is an *HttpCachePolicy* object that can be used to set the cache-specific HTTP headers for the current response.
CacheControl	Sets the *Cache-Control* HTTP header. Acceptable values are *Public*, *Private*, or *No-Cache*. The property is deprecated in favor of *Cache*.
Charset	Gets or sets a string for the HTTP character set of the output stream. If set to *null*, it suppresses the *Content-Type* header.
ContentEncoding	Gets or sets an object of type *Encoding* for the character encoding of the output stream.
ContentType	Gets or sets the string that represents the MIME type of the output stream. The default value is *text/html*.
Cookies	Gets a collection (*HttpCookieCollection*) object that contains instances of the *HttpCookie* class generated on the server. All the cookies in the collection will be transmitted to the client through the *set-cookie* HTTP header.
Expires	Gets or sets the number of minutes before a page cached on a browser expires. Provided for compatibility with ASP, the property is deprecated in favor of *Cache*.
ExpiresAbsolute	Gets or sets the absolute date and time at which the page expires in the browser cache. Provided for compatibility with ASP, the property is deprecated in favor of *Cache*.
Filter	Gets or sets a filter *Stream* object through which all HTTP output is directed.
IsClientConnected	Indicates whether the client is still connected.
IsRequestBeing-Redirected	Indicates whether the request is being redirected. *Not available in ASP.NET 1.x.*
Output	Gets the writer object used to send text out.
OutputStream	Gets the *Stream* object used to output binary data to the response stream.
RedirectLocation	Gets or a sets a string for the value of the *Location* header.
Status	Sets the string returned to the client describing the status of the response. Provided for compatibility with ASP, the property is deprecated in favor of *StatusDescription*.
StatusCode	Gets or sets an integer value for the HTTP status code of the output returned to the client. The default value is *200*.
StatusDescription	Gets or sets the HTTP status string, which is a description of the overall status of the response returned to the client. The default value is *OK*.
SuppressContent	Gets or sets a Boolean value that indicates whether HTTP content should be sent to the client. This is set to *false* by default; if it is set to *true*, only headers are sent.

As you can see, a few of the *HttpResponse* properties are provided only for backward compatibility with classic ASP. In some cases (for example, *BufferOutput*), the property has just been renamed; in other cases, the deprecated properties have been replaced by a more general and powerful API. This is certainly the case for cache and expiration properties.

Setting the Response Cache Policy

The response object has three properties dedicated to controlling the ability of the page being sent to the browser to be cached. The *Expires* and *ExpiresAbsolute* properties define relative and absolute times at which the page cached on the client expires and is no longer used by the browser to serve a user request. In fact, if the user navigates to a currently cached page, the cached version is displayed and no roundtrip occurs to the server. *CacheControl* is a third property somehow related to page caching. The property sets a particular HTTP header—the *Cache-Control* header. The *Cache-Control* header controls how a document is to be cached across the network. These properties represent the old-fashioned programming style and exist mostly for compatibility with classic ASP applications.

In ASP.NET, all caching capabilities are grouped in the *HttpCachePolicy* class. With regard to page caching, the class has a double role. It provides methods for both setting cache-specific HTTP headers and controlling the ASP.NET page output cache. (In this chapter, we're mostly interested in the HTTP headers, and we'll keep page output caching warm for Chapter 14.)

To set the visibility of a page in a client cache, use the *SetCacheability* method of the *HttpCachePolicy* class. To set an expiration time, use the *SetExpires* method, which takes for input an absolute *DateTime* object. Finally, to set a lifetime for the cached page, pass to *SetExpires* the current time plus the desired interval.

> **Note** In the case of conflicting cache policies, ASP.NET maintains the most restrictive settings. For example, if a page contains two controls that set the *Cache-Control* header to *public* and *private*, the most restrictive policy will be used. In this case, *Cache-Control: Private* is what will be sent to the client.

Setting an Output Filter

In ASP.NET, a new component makes its debut—the *response filter*. A response filter is a *Stream*-derived object associated with the *HttpResponse* object. It monitors and filters any output being generated by the page. If you set the *Filter* property with the instance of a class derived from *Stream*, all output being written to the underlying HTTP writer first passes through your output filter.

The custom filter, if any, is invoked during the *HttpResponse*'s *Flush* method before the actual text is flushed to the client. An output filter is useful for applying the final touches to the markup, and it is sometimes used to compact or fix the markup generated by controls.

Building a response filter is a matter of creating a new stream class and overriding some of the methods. The class should have a constructor that accepts a *Stream* object. In light of this, a response filter class is more a wrapper stream class than a purely inherited stream class. If you simply try to set *Response.Filter* with a new instance of, say, *MemoryStream* or *FileStream*, an exception is thrown.

The following listing shows how to create a stream class that works as a response filter. For simplicity, the class inherits from *MemoryStream*. You might want to make it inherit from *Stream*, but in this case you need to override a number of methods, such as *CanRead*, *CanWrite*, *CanSeek*, and *Read* (because they are abstract). The class converts lowercase characters to uppercase ones:

```
public class MyFilterStream : MemoryStream
{
    private Stream m_Stream;

    public MyFilterStream(Stream filterStream)
    {
        m_Stream = filterStream;
    }

    // The Write method actually does the filtering
    public override void Write(byte[] buffer, int offset, int count)
    {
        // Grab the output as a string
        string buf = UTF8Encoding.UTF8.GetString(buffer, offset, count);

        // Apply some changes
        // Change lowercase chars to uppercase
        buf = buf.ToUpper();

        // Write the resulting string back to the response stream
        byte[] data = UTF8Encoding.UTF8.GetBytes(buf.ToString());
        m_Stream.Write(data, 0, data.Length);
    }
}
```

Use the following code to associate this output filter with the *Response.Filter* property. Here's a sample page:

```
void Page_Load(object sender, EventArgs e)
{
    Response.Filter = new MyFilterStream(Response.Filter);
}
```

Figure 12-5 shows a page that uses the sample filter.

Response filters are an interesting opportunity for developers to build more powerful applications, but I caution you to be careful when considering this option. As the sample demonstrates, changing the case of the entire output is not a smart move. If done without care, the change ends up affecting the view state and the internal script code, seriously compromising the functionality of the page. In addition, filters must be activated on a per-page basis. If you need to filter all the pages in a Web site, you're better off writing an HTTP module.

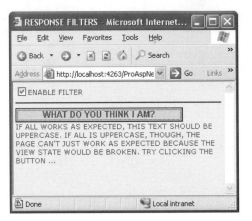

Figure 12-5   This page uses a response filter to turn on uppercase characters.

Methods of the *HttpResponse* Class

Table 12-11 lists all the methods defined on the *HttpResponse* class.

Table 12-11   *HttpResponse* Methods

Method	Description
AddCacheDependency	Adds an array of cache dependencies to make the cached page output invalid if any dependency gets broken. In the array, you can have any class that inherits from *Cache-Dependency*. *Not available in ASP.NET 1.x.*
AddCacheItemDependencies	Adds an array of strings representing names of items in the ASP.NET *Cache*. When any of the specified items vary, the cached page output becomes invalid.
AddCacheItemDependency	Description is the same as for the previous item, except that *AddCacheItemDependency* adds a single cache item name.
AddFileDependencies	Adds a group of file names to the collection of file names on which the current page is dependent. When any of the files is modified, the cached output of the current page is deemed invalid.
AddFileDependency	Adds a single file name to the collection of file names on which the current page is dependent. If the file is modified, the cached output of the current page becomes invalid.
AddHeader	Adds an HTTP header to the output stream. It is provided for compatibility with previous versions of ASP. In ASP.NET, you should use *AppendHeader*.
AppendCookie	Adds an HTTP cookie to the cookie collection.
AppendHeader	Adds an HTTP header to the output stream.
AppendToLog	Adds custom log information to the IIS log file.
ApplyAppPathModifier	Adds a session ID to the specified virtual path, and returns the result. It is mostly used with cookieless sessions to construct absolute *HREF*s for hyperlinks.

Table 12-11 *HttpResponse* Methods

Method	Description
BinaryWrite	Writes binary characters to the HTTP output stream. It is subject to failures with very large files. (See the references to this method later in the chapter.)
Clear	Clears all content output from the buffer stream.
ClearContent	Calls into *Clear*.
ClearHeaders	Clears all headers from the buffer stream.
Close	Closes the socket connection with the client.
End	Sends all buffered text to the client, stops execution, and raises the end event for the request.
Flush	Sends all currently buffered output to the client.
Pics	Appends a PICS-Label HTTP header to the output. PICS stands for Platform for Internet Content Selection and is a World Wide Web Consortium (W3C) standard for rating pages. Any string is acceptable as long as it doesn't exceed 255 characters.
Redirect	Redirects a client to a new URL. Needs a roundtrip.
RemoveOutputCacheItem	A static method that takes a file system path and removes from the cache all cached items associated with the specified path.
SetCookie	Updates an existing cookie in the cookie collection.
TransmitFile	Just as *BinaryWrite* and *WriteFile*, it writes the specified file directly to the output stream. You can safely use *TransmitFile* regardless of the size of the file that you want to transmit. *Available in ASP.NET 1.x through the Service Pack 1.*
Write	Writes content to the underlying output stream. The method can write a string, a single character, or an array of characters, as well as an object. In this case, though, what gets written is the output of the object's *ToString* method.
WriteFile	Writes the specified file (or a portion of it) directly to the output stream. The file can be identified with its path or a Win32 handle (an *IntPtr* object). It is subject to failures with very large files. (See the references to this method later in the chapter.)
WriteSubstitution	Allows fragments of a page to be substituted and sent to the output cache. (We'll cover this method in more detail in Chapter 14.) *Not available in ASP.NET 1.x.*

Output Caching Features

The *HttpResponse* class has several methods to make the page response it represents dependent on files or cache item changes. The methods *AddFileDependency* and *AddCacheItemDependency* (and their version-handling multiple dependencies) make the page response invalid when the specified file(s) or cached item(s) is modified.

This is a simple form of programmatic page output caching, and although it's not as powerful as the API that we'll examine in Chapter 14, it's still worth a look. The API discussed in Chapter 14 is superior because it allows you to control how the page response is cached by also assigning the cached output a duration and perhaps a location.

In ASP.NET 2.0, the new method *AddCacheDependency* completes the offering, as it gives you the possibility of making the page response dependent on any dependency object available to your application, including custom dependency objects. See Chapter 14 for more details on custom-dependency objects.

Large Files Transmission

As you can see, there are three methods for writing potentially large chunks of data down to the output stream—*BinaryWrite*, *WriteFile*, and *TransmitFile*. You might think that *TransmitFile* is new to ASP.NET 2.0. In reality, it was introduced with ASP.NET 1.x through a hotfix package documented in Microsoft Knowledge Base article KB823409 and later incorporated in the .NET Framework 1.x SP1. In summary, *TransmitFile* is the most stable and reliable of the three methods, although you won't notice any significant difference for most files.

Both *WriteFile* and *BinaryWrite* methods seem perfect for streaming binary data down to the client. However, both can put the Web server memory under pressure if called to work on very large files. Why? Because both methods load the entire data block (the contents of the file or the byte array) into the Web server's memory. For large files, this can cause severe problems that can culminate in the recycling of the ASP.NET process. The *TransmitFile* method is designed to elegantly work around the problem. It sends output directly from a file to the ASP.NET ISAPI extension and then down to the client, without passing a humongous string to the ISAPI extension.

> **Note**   Although *TransmitFile* makes large file downloads more stable than ever and defeats the problem of recycling, it is far from being a full solution to the problem of tracking and resuming large file downloads. For example, if a download fails, for whatever reason, *Transmit-File* can start it again only from the beginning. The article located at the Web site *http:// www.devx.com/dotnet/Article/22533* discusses a better approach to the problem.

The *HttpRequest* Object

The *HttpRequest* object groups all the information contained in the HTTP packet that represents the incoming Web request. The contents of the various HTTP headers, the query string, or the form's input fields, path, and URL information are organized in a series of collections and other ad hoc objects for easy and effective programmatic access. The *HttpRequest* object is populated as soon as ASP.NET begins working on a Web request, and it's made available through the *Request* property of *HttpContext*.

HttpRequest exposes a fair number of properties and is one of the objects that has been more significantly enriched in the transition from ASP to ASP.NET.

Properties of the *HttpRequest* Class

The class properties can be categorized into three groups based on the type of information they contain: the type of the request, client data, and connection.

Information about the Request

Table 12-12 lists the properties that define the type of request being issued.

Table 12-12   Properties Describing the Request Type

Property	Description
AcceptTypes	Gets an array of strings denoting the list of MIME types supported by the client for the specified request.
AnonymousID	Indicates the ID of the anonymous user, if any. The identity refers to the string generated by the *AnonymousIdentification* module and has nothing to do with the identify of the IIS anonymous user. *Not available in ASP.NET 1.x.*
Browser	Gets an *HttpBrowserCapabilities* object that contains information about the capabilities of the client's browser.
ContentEncoding	Gets or sets an *Encoding* object that represents the client's character set. If specified, this property overrides the ASP.NET default encoding.
ContentLength	Gets the length in bytes of the content sent by the client.
ContentType	Gets or sets the MIME content type of the incoming request.
CurrentExecutionFilePath	Gets the current virtual path of the request even when the client is redirected to another page via *Execute* or *Transfer*. The *FilePath* property, on the other hand, always returns the path to the originally requested page.
FilePath	Gets the virtual path of the current request. The path doesn't change in cases of server-side page redirection.
HttpMethod	Gets a string that denotes the HTTP method used for the request. Values are *GET*, *POST*, or *HEAD*.
RequestType	Gets or sets a string that denotes the HTTP command used to issue the request. It can be *GET* or *POST*.
TotalBytes	Gets the total number of bytes in the input stream. This property differs from *ContentLength* in that it also includes headers.
UserAgent	Gets a string that identifies the browser. This property gets the raw content of the user agent header.

In ASP.NET 2.0, the anonymous ID is usually transmitted through a cookie (default name is *.ASPXANONYMOUS*) and serves the purpose of giving an identity to nonauthenticated users, mainly for user profile functions. The anonymous ID is a Guid and is transmitted as clear text.

It doesn't play any relevant role with authentication and security but is merely a way to track nonregistered users as they move around the site. (See Chapter 5 for profiles and Chapter 15 for user authentication.)

Initially, *CurrentExecutionFilePath* and *FilePath* share the same content—the requested URL. However, in cases of server-side redirects, the value of *CurrentExecutionFilePath* is automatically updated. You should check *CurrentExecutionFilePath* for up-to-date information about the target URL.

The *HttpBrowserCapabilities* object groups in a single place values that identify a fair number of browser capabilities, including support for ActiveX controls, scripting languages, frames, cookies, and more. When the request arrives, the user agent information is used to identify the requesting browser and an instance of the *HttpBrowserCapabilities* class is created and populated with browser-specific information. The information is in no way dynamically set by the browser, but is retrieved from an offline server-side repository.

> **Note**   The *Browser* property also supports mobile scenarios in version 1.1 of the .NET Framework and newer versions. In this case, the actual object returned is of class *MobileCapabilities*—an *HttpBrowserCapabilities*-derived class. When you obtain the *Browser* property reference, you should cast it as a *MobileCapabilities* class if you are interested in the mobile browser capabilities.

Information from the Client

Table 12-13 lists the *HttpRequest* properties that expose the client data that ASP.NET pages might want to use for server-side processing. The following table includes, for example, cookies, forms, and query string collections.

Table 12-13   Properties Describing the Client Data

Property	Description
ClientCertificate	Gets an *HttpClientCertificate* object with information on the client's security certificate settings, if any. The certificate object wraps up information such as number, validity, and issuer of the certificate.
Cookies	Gets a collection representing all cookies sent by the client. A cookie is identified by the *HttpCookie* object.
Files	Gets a collection of client-uploaded files. The property requires the HTTP *Content-Type* header to be set to *multipart/form-data*.
Filter	Gets or sets a *Stream*-based object through which all HTTP input passes when received. The filtered input is anything read via *InputStream*.
Form	Gets a name-value collection filled with the values of the input fields in the form posted. The collection is populated when the *Content-Type* header is either *application/x-www-form-urlencoded* or *multipart/form-data*.
Headers	Gets a name-value collection filled with all the header values in the request.

Table 12-13   Properties Describing the Client Data

Property	Description
InputStream	Gets a *Stream* object representing the contents of the incoming HTTP content body.
Params	Gets a name-value collection that is a union of four other similar collections: *QueryString*, *Form*, *ServerVariables*, and *Cookies*.
QueryString	Gets a name-value collection containing all the query string variables sent by the client.
ServerVariables	Gets a name-value collection filled with a collection of Web server–defined variables.
UserHostAddress	Gets the Internet Protocol (IP) address of the remote client.
UserHostName	Gets the Domain Name System (DNS) name of the remote client.
UserLanguages	Gets an array of strings denoting the list of the languages accepted by the client for the specified request. The languages are read from the *Accept-Language* header.

The *Params* collection combines four different but homogeneous collections—*QueryString*, *Form*, *ServerVariables*, and *Cookies*—and replicates the information contained in each of them. The collections are added in the following order: *QueryString*, *Form*, *Cookies*, and finally *ServerVariables*.

Information about the Connection

Table 12-14 lists the properties that relate to the open connection.

Table 12-14   Properties Describing the Connection

Property	Description
ApplicationPath	Gets the virtual path of the current application.
IsAuthenticated	Indicates whether the user has been authenticated.
IsLocal	Indicates if it is a local request. *Not available in ASP.NET 1.x.*
IsSecureConnection	Indicates whether the connection is taking place over a Secure Sockets Layer (SSL) using HTTPS.
LogonUserIdentity	Gets an object representing the Windows identity of the current user as logged at the IIS gate. *Not available in ASP.NET 1.x.*
Path	Gets the virtual path of the current request.
PathInfo	Gets additional path information for the requested resource, if any. The property returns any text that follows the URL.
PhysicalApplicationPath	Gets the file system path of the current application's root directory.
PhysicalPath	Gets the physical file system path corresponding to the requested URL.
RawUrl	Gets the raw URL of the current request.
Url	Gets the *Uri* object that represents the URL of the current request.
UrlReferrer	Gets the *Uri* object that represents the URL from which the current request originated.

The *Uri* class provides an object representation of a Uniform Resource Identifier (URI)—a unique name for a resource available on the Internet. The *Uri* class provides easy access to the parts of the URI as well as properties and methods for checking host, loopback, ports, and DNS.

The server variables set in the *ServerVariables* collection are decided by the run-time environment that processes the request. The information packed in the collection is for the most part excerpted from the HTTP worker request object; another part contains Web server–specific information. The *ServerVariables* collection is just a friendly name/value model to expose that information.

Methods of the *HttpRequest* Class

Table 12-15 lists all methods exposed by the *HttpRequest* class.

Table 12-15 *HttpRequest* Methods

Method	Description
BinaryRead	Performs a binary read from the current input stream. The method lets you specify the number of bytes to read and returns an array of bytes. The method is provided for compatibility with ASP. ASP.NET applications should read from the stream associated with the *InputStream* property.
MapImageCoordinates	Maps an incoming image-field form parameter to x/y coordinate values.
MapPath	Maps the specified virtual path to a physical path on the Web server.
SaveAs	Saves the current request to a file disk with or without headers. This method is especially useful for debugging.
ValidateInput	Performs a quick, non-exhaustive check to find potentially dangerous input data in the request.

Saving the Request to Disk

The *SaveAs* method lets you create a file to store the entire content of the HTTP request. Note that the storage medium can only be a disk file; no stream or writer can be used. Because ASP.NET by default isn't granted write permissions, this method causes an access denied exception unless you take ad hoc measures. Granting the ASP.NET account full control over the file to be created (or over the whole folder) is one of the possible ways to successfully use the *SaveAs* method. The following listing shows possible content that *SaveAs* writes to disk:

```
GET /ProAspNet20/Samples/Ch12/TestFilter.aspx HTTP/1.1
Connection: Keep-Alive
Accept: */*
```

```
Accept-Encoding: gzip, deflate
Accept-Language: en-us,it;q=0.5
Authorization: NTLM TlRMTVNTUAADAAAAIAAAA … BcKIogUCzg4AAAAP
Cookie: .ASPXANONYMOUS=AcW35sC18TwwNDcyYTMxY … w2
Host: localhost
User-Agent: Mozilla/4.0 (compatible; MSIE 6.0; Windows NT 5.2; SV1;
snprtz|S04739424200867; .NET CLR 1.1.4322; .NET CLR 2.0.50215)
UA-CPU: x86
```

If, instead, the intercepted request is a *POST*, you'll find posted values at the bottom of the string.

Validating Client Input

A golden rule of Web security claims that all user input is evil and should always be filtered and sanitized before use. Starting with ASP.NET 1.x, Microsoft added an attribute to the *@Page* directive that automatically blocks postbacks that contain potentially dangerous data. This feature is not the silver bullet of Web input security, but it helps detect possible problems. From a general security perspective, you're better off replacing the automatic input validation with a strong, application-specific validation layer.

The automatic input validation feature—*ValidateRequest*—is enabled by default and implemented via a call to the *HttpRequest*'s *ValidationInput* method. *ValidateInput* can be called by your code if the validation feature is not enabled. Request validation works by checking all input data against a hard-coded list of potentially dangerous data. The contents of the collections *QueryString*, *Form*, and *Cookies* are checked during request validation.

Conclusion

In this chapter, we covered some basic objects that are the foundation of ASP.NET programming—*Server*, *Response*, *Request*, and others. An ASP.NET application is represented by an instance of the *IHttpApplication* class properly configured by the contents of the *global.asax* file. And both the *HttpApplication* class and the *global.asax* file found their space in this chapter, too.

While discussing the interface of the objects that generate the context of an HTTP request, we reviewed in detail some specific programming issues such as the instantiation of late-bound COM objects, server-side page redirection, and the setup of response filters. In the next chapter, we'll discuss an important topic related to Web applications and ASP.NET—state management. Fundamentally, Web applications are stateless, but ASP.NET provides various mechanisms for maintaining application state and caching pages.

Just the Facts

- Any ASP.NET request is served by making it flow through a pipeline of internal components. The entry point in the ASP.NET pipeline is the *HttpRuntime* class.

- The *HttpRuntime* creates an object that represents the context of the request—the *HttpContext* class. An instance of this class accompanies the request for the entire request lifetime.

- The HTTP context of a request is enriched with references to the intrinsic worker objects such as *Request*, *Response*, and *Server*. In addition, it references the session state, ASP.NET cache, tracer, and identity object.

- The execution of the request is governed by a pooled *HttpApplication* object. An instance of this class is created based on the contents of the *global.asax* file, if any.

- *HttpApplication* makes the request flow through the pipeline along with its associated HTTP context so that registered HTTP modules can intercept the request, consume any contained information, and add new information if needed.

- Modules can fire their own events, and the *global.asax* file is the place where page authors can put code to catch application-level events.

- Standard intrinsic objects—such as *Request*, *Response*, and *Server*—look like their classic ASP counterparts but provide some specific functionalities. For example, *Response* manages file downloads and filters page output; *Request* allows you to manage the incoming request and its values.

Chapter 13
State Management

In this chapter:

The Application's State 538
The Session's State 542
Working with Session's State 549
Customizing Session State Management 567
The View State of a Page 573
Conclusion 589

All real-world applications of any shape and form need to maintain their own state to serve users' requests. ASP.NET applications are no exception, but unlike other types of applications, they need special system-level tools to achieve the result. The reason for this peculiarity lies in the stateless nature of the underlying protocol that Web applications still rely upon. As long as HTTP remains the transportation protocol for the Web, all applications will run into the same trouble figuring out the most effective way to persist state information.

Application state is a sort of blank container that each application and programmer can fill with whatever piece of information makes sense to persist: from user preferences to global settings, from worker data to hit counters, from lookup tables to shopping carts. This extremely variegated mess of data can be organized and accessed according to a number of different usage patterns. Typically, all the information contributing to the application state is distributed in various layers, each with its own settings for visibility, programmability, and lifetime.

ASP.NET provides state-management facilities at four levels: application, session, page, and request. Each level has its own special container object, which is a topic we'll cover in this chapter, along with the *HttpApplicationState*, *HttpSessionState*, and *ViewState* objects, which provide for application, session, and page state maintenance, respectively. In the next chapter, we'll dive into the *Cache* object. In Chapter 12, you will recall, we covered the *HttpContext* object, which is the primary tool used to manage state and information across the entire request lifetime. The context of the request is different from all other state objects in that the request has a limited lifetime but passes through the entire pipeline of objects processing an HTTP request.

The Application's State

Table 13-1 summarizes the main features of the various state objects.

Table 13-1   State Management Objects at a Glance

Object	Lifetime	Data Visibility	Location
Cache	Implements an automatic scavenging mechanism, and periodically clears less frequently used contents	Global to all sessions	Does not support Web farm or Web garden scenarios
HttpApplicationState	Created when the first request hits the Web server, and released when the application shuts down	Same as for *Cache*	Same as for *Cache*
HttpContext	Spans the entire lifetime of the individual request	Global to the objects involved with the request	Same as for *Cache*
HttpSessionState	Created when the user makes the first request, and lasts until the user closes the session	Global to all requests issued by the user who started the session	Configurable to work on Web farms and gardens
ViewState	Represents the calling context of each page being generated	Limited to all requests queued for the same page	Configurable to work on Web farms and gardens

In spite of their quite unfamiliar names, the *HttpApplicationState* and *HttpSessionState* objects are state facilities totally compatible with classic Active Server Pages (ASP) intrinsic objects such as *Application* and *Session*. Ad hoc properties known as *Application* and *Session* let you use these objects in much the same way you did in ASP.

> **Note**   In this chapter, we'll review several objects involved, at various levels, with the state management. We won't discuss cookies in detail, but cookies are definitely useful for storing small amounts of information on the client. The information is sent with the request to the server and can be manipulated and re-sent through the response. The cookie is a text-based structure with simple key/value pairs, and it consumes no resources on the server. In e-commerce applications, for example, cookies are the preferred way of storing user preferences. In addition, cookies have a configurable expiration policy. The downside of cookies is their limited size (browser-dependent, but seldom greater than 8 KB) and the fact that the user can disable them.

The *HttpApplicationState* object makes a dictionary available for storage to all request handlers invoked within an application. In classic ASP, only pages have access to the application state; this is no longer true in ASP.NET, in which all HTTP handlers and modules can store and retrieve values within the application's dictionary. The application state is accessible only within the context of the originating application. Other applications running on the system cannot access or modify the values.

An instance of the *HttpApplicationState* class is created the first time a client requests any resource from within a particular virtual directory. Each running application holds its own global state object. The most common way to access application state is by means of the *Application* property of the *Page* object. Application state is not shared across either a Web farm or Web garden.

Properties of the *HttpApplicationState* Class

The *HttpApplicationState* class is sealed and inherits from a class named *NameObjectCollection-Base*. In practice, the *HttpApplicationState* class is a collection of pairs, each made of a string key and an object value. Such pairs can be accessed either using the key string or the index. Internally, the base class employs a hashtable with an initial capacity of zero that is automatically increased as required. Table 13-2 lists the properties of the *HttpApplicationState* class.

Table 13-2   *HttpApplicationState* **Properties**

Property	Description
AllKeys	Gets an array of strings containing all the keys of the items currently stored in the object.
Contents	Gets the current instance of the object. But wait! What this property returns is simply a reference to the application state object, not a clone. Provided for ASP compatibility.
Count	Gets the number of objects currently stored in the collection.
Item	Indexer property, provides read/write access to an element in the collection. The element can be specified either by name or index. Accessors of this property are implemented using *Get* and *Set* methods.
StaticObjects	Gets a collection including all instances of all objects declared in *global.asax* using an <*object*> tag with the *scope* attribute set to *Application*.

Notice that static objects and actual state values are stored in separate collections. The exact type of the static collection is *HttpStaticObjectsCollection*.

Methods of the *HttpApplicationState* Class

The set of methods that the *HttpApplicationState* class features are mostly specialized versions of the typical methods of a name/value collection. As Table 13-3 shows, the most significant extension entails the locking mechanism necessary to serialize access to the state values.

Table 13-3   *HttpApplicationState* **Methods**

Method	Description
Add	Adds a new value to the collection. The value is boxed as an *object*.
Clear	Removes all objects from the collection.
Get	Returns the value of an item in the collection. The item can be specified either by key or index.

Table 13-3   *HttpApplicationState* Methods

Method	Description
GetEnumerator	Returns an enumerator object to iterate through the collection.
GetKey	Gets the string key of the item stored at the specified position.
Lock	Locks writing access to the whole collection. No concurrent caller can write to the collection object until *UnLock* is called.
Remove	Removes the item whose key matches the specified string.
RemoveAll	Calls *Clear*.
RemoveAt	Removes the item at the specified position.
Set	Assigns the specified value to the item with the specified key. The method is thread-safe, and the access to the item is blocked until the writing is completed.
UnLock	Unlocks writing access to the collection.

Note that the *GetEnumerator* method is inherited from the base collection class and, as such, is oblivious to the locking mechanism of the class. If you enumerate the collection using this method, each returned value is obtained through a simple call to one of the *get* methods on the base *NameObjectCollectionBase* class. Unfortunately, that method is not aware of the locking mechanism needed on the derived *HttpApplicationState* class because of the concurrent access to the application state. As a result, your enumeration would not be thread-safe. A better way to enumerate the content of the collection is by using a *while* statement and the *Get* method to access an item. Alternatively, you could lock the collection before you enumerate.

State Synchronization

Notice that all operations on *HttpApplicationState* require some sort of synchronization to ensure that multiple threads running within an application safely access values without incurring deadlocks and access violations. The writing methods, such as *Set* and *Remove*, as well as the *set* accessor of the *Item* property implicitly apply a writing lock before proceeding. The *Lock* method ensures that only the current thread can modify the application state. The *Lock* method is provided to apply the same writing lock around portions of code that need to be protected from other threads' access.

You don't need to wrap a single call to *Set*, *Clear*, or *Remove* with a lock/unlock pair of statements—those methods, in fact, are already thread-safe. Using *Lock* in these cases will only have the effect of producing additional overhead, increasing the internal level of recursion:

```
// This operation is thread-safe
Application["MyValue"] = 1;
```

Use *Lock* instead if you want to shield a group of instructions from concurrent writings:

```
// These operations execute atomically
Application.Lock();
int val = (int) Application["MyValue"];
```

```
if (val < 10)
    Application["MyValue"] = val + 1;
Application.UnLock();
```

Reading methods such as *Get*, the *get* accessor of *Item*, and even *Count* have an internal synchronization mechanism that, when used along with *Lock*, will protect them against concurrent and cross-thread readings and writings:

```
// The reading is protected from concurrent read/writes
Application.Lock();
int val = (int) Application["MyValue"];
Application.UnLock();
```

You should always use *Lock* and *UnLock* together. However, if you omit the call to *UnLock*, the likelihood of incurring a deadlock is not high because the Microsoft .NET Framework automatically removes the lock when the request completes or times out, or when an unhandled error occurs. For this reason, if you handle the exception, consider using a *finally* block to clear the lock or expect to face some delay while ASP.NET clears the lock for you when the request ends.

Tradeoffs of Application State

Instead of writing global data to the *HttpApplicationState* object, you could use public members within the *global.asax* file. Compared to entries in the *HttpApplicationState* collection, a global member is preferable because it is strongly typed and does not require a hashtable access to locate the value. On the other hand, a global variable is not synchronized per se and must be manually protected. You have to use language constructs to protect access to these members—for example, the C# *lock* operator or, in Microsoft Visual Basic .NET, the *SyncLock* operator. We demonstrated global members in Chapter 12.

Memory Occupation

Whatever form you choose to store the global state of an application, some general considerations apply about the opportunity of storing data globally. For one thing, global data storage results in permanent memory occupation. Unless explicitly removed by the code, any data stored in the application global state is removed only when the application shuts down. On one hand, putting a few megabytes of data in the application's memory speeds up access; on the other hand, doing this occupies valuable memory for the entire duration of the application.

For this reason, it is extremely important that you consider using the *Cache* object (which is discussed further in the next chapter) whenever you need globally shared data. Unlike *Application* and global members, data stored in the ASP.NET *Cache* is subject to an automatic scavenging mechanism that ensures that data is removed when a too-high percentage of virtual memory is being consumed. In addition, the *Cache* object has a lot of other features that we'll explore in the next chapter. The bottom line is that the *Cache* object was introduced just to mitigate the problem of memory occupation and to replace the *Application* object.

Concurrent Access to Data

Storing data globally is also problematic because of locking. Synchronization is necessary to ensure that concurrent thread access doesn't cause inconsistencies in the data. But locking the application state can easily become a performance hit that leads to nonoptimal use of threads. The application global state is held in memory and never trespasses the machine's boundaries. In multimachine and multiprocessor environments, the application global state is limited to the single worker process running on the individual machine or CPU. As such, it is not something really global. Finally, the duration of the data in memory is at risk because of possible failures in the process or, more simply, because of the ASP.NET process recycling. If you're going to use the application state feature and plan to deploy the application in a Web farm or Web garden scenario, you're probably better off dropping global state in favor of database tables. At the very least, you should wrap your global data in smart proxy objects that check for the existence of data and refill if it's not there, for whatever reason. Here's a quick snapshot:

```
// Retrieve data
public object GetGlobalData(string entry)
{
    object o = Application[entry];
    if (o == null)
    {
        // TODO:: Reload the data from its source
        return Application[entry];
    }
    return o;
}
```

The Session's State

The *HttpSessionState* class provides a dictionary-based model of storing and retrieving session-state values. Unlike *HttpApplicationState*, this class doesn't expose its contents to all users operating on the virtual directory at a given time. Only the requests that originate in the context of the same session—that is, generated across multiple page requests made by the same user—can access the session state. The session state can be stored and published in a variety of ways, including in a Web farm or Web garden scenario. By default, though, the session state is held within the ASP.NET worker process.

Compared to *Session*, the intrinsic object of ASP, the ASP.NET session state is nearly identical in use, but it's significantly richer in functionality and radically different in architecture. In addition, it provides some extremely handy facilities—such as support for cookieless browsers, Web farms, and Web gardens—and the capability of being hosted by external processes, including Microsoft SQL Server. In this way, ASP.NET session management can provide an unprecedented level of robustness and reliability.

In ASP.NET 2.0, developers can create custom data stores for session state. For example, if you need the robustness that a database-oriented solution can guarantee, but you work with Oracle databases, you need not install SQL Server as well. By writing a piece of additional code, you can support an Oracle session data store while using the same *Session* semantics and classes.

The extensibility model for session state offers two options: customizing bits and pieces of the existing ASP.NET session-state mechanism (for example, creating an Oracle session provider or a module controlling the generation of the ID) and replacing the standard session-state HTTP module with a new one. The former option is easier to implement but provides a limited set of features you can customize. The latter option is more complicated to code but provides the greatest flexibility.

The Session-State HTTP Module

Regardless of the internal implementation, the programmer's API for session-state management is just one—the old acquaintance known as the *Session* object. It was a COM object in classic ASP that was instantiated in the *asp.dll* ISAPI extension and injected in the memory space of the ActiveX Scripting engine called to parse and process the *.asp* script. It is a collection object in ASP.NET, living behind the *Session* property of the *Page* class. The exact type is *HttpSessionState*; it's a class that's not further inheritable and which implements *ICollection* and *IEnumerable*. An instance of this class is created during the startup of each request that requires session support. The collection is filled with name/value pairs read from the specified medium and attached to the context of the request—the *HttpContext* class. The *Page*'s *Session* property just mirrors the *Session* property of the *HttpContext* class.

If developers can simply work with one object—the *Session* object—regardless of other details, most of the credit goes to an HTTP module that governs the process of retrieving and storing session state with some help from special provider objects. The ASP.NET module in charge of setting up the session state for each user connecting to an application is an HTTP module named *SessionStateModule*. Structured after the *IHttpModule* interface, the *SessionStateModule* object provides session-state services for ASP.NET applications.

Although as an HTTP module it is required to supply a relatively simple programming interface— the *IHttpModule* interface contracts only for *Init* and *Dispose* methods—*SessionStateModule* does perform a number of quite sophisticated tasks, most of which are fundamental for the health and functionality of the Web application. The session-state module is invoked during the setup of the *HttpApplication* object that will process a given request and is responsible for either generating or obtaining a unique session ID string and for storing and retrieving state data from a state provider—for example, SQL Server or the Web server's memory.

State Client Managers

When invoked, the session-state HTTP module reads the settings in the *<sessionState>* section of the *web.config* file and determines what the expected state client manager is for the application. A state client manager is a component that takes care of storing and retrieving data of all currently active sessions. The *SessionStateModule* component queries the state client manager to get the name/value pairs of a given session.

In ASP.NET 2.0, there are four possibilities for working with the session state. The session state can be stored locally in the ASP.NET worker process; the session state can be maintained in an external, even remote, process named *aspnet_state.exe*; the session state can be managed by SQL Server and stored in an ad hoc database table. Finally, a fourth option is added in ASP.NET 2.0 and entails storing the sessions in a custom component. Table 13-4 briefly discusses the various options.

Table 13-4 State Client Providers

Mode	Description
Custom	The values for all the sessions are stored in a custom data store. *Not available in ASP.NET 1.x.*
InProc	The values for all the sessions are maintained as live objects in the memory of the ASP.NET worker process (*aspnet_wp.exe* or *w3wp.exe* in Microsoft Windows Server 2003). This is the default option.
Off	Session state is disabled, and no state client provider is active.
SQLServer	The values for all the sessions are serialized and stored in a SQL Server table. The instance of SQL Server can run either locally or remotely.
StateServer	The values for all the sessions are serialized and stored in the memory of a separate system process (*aspnet_state.exe*). The process can also run on another machine. Session values are deserialized into the session dictionary at the beginning of the request. If the request completes successfully, state values are serialized into the process memory and made available to other pages.

The *SessionStateMode* enum type lists the available options for the state client provider. The *InProc* option is by far the fastest possible in terms of access. However, bear in mind that the more data you store in a session, the more memory is consumed on the Web server, thereby increasing the risk of performance hits. If you plan to use any of the out-of-process solutions, the possible impact of serialization and deserialization should be carefully considered. We'll discuss this aspect in detail later in the chapter, starting with the "Persist Session Data to Remote Servers" section.

The session-state module determines the state provider to use based on what it reads out of the *<sessionState>* section of the *web.config* file. Next, it instantiates and initializes the state provider for the application. Each provider continues its own initialization, which is quite different depending on the type. For example, the SQL Server state manager opens a connection to the given database, whereas the out-of-process manager checks the specified TCP port. The *InProc* state manager, on the other hand, stores a reference to the callback function that will be used to fire the *Session_End* event. (I'll discuss this further in the section "Lifetime of a Session.")

All state providers expose a common set of methods to communicate with the caller. The schema is outlined in Figure 13-1.

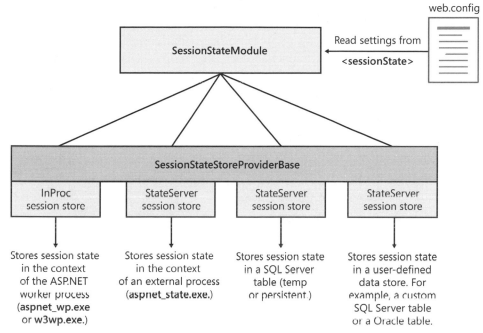

Figure 13-1   *SessionStateModule* and its child-state client managers.

> **Note**   In ASP.NET 2.0, all the actual state provider objects derive from a base class—
> *SessionStateStoreProviderBase*. In ASP.NET 1.x, on the other hand, all state providers implement
> a common interface, named *IStateClientManager*. This interface has been lost in the transition
> to version 2.0, a victim of the refactoring process and the advent of the provider model. (See
> Chapter 1.) However, the switch to base classes from interfaces is a pervasive design choice that
> affects all of ASP.NET Framework 2.0.

Creating the *HttpSessionState* Object

The state module is responsible for retrieving and attaching the session state to the context
of each request that runs within the session. The session state is available only after
the *HttpApplication.AcquireRequestState* event fires, and it gets irreversibly lost after the
HttpApplication.ReleaseRequestState event. Subsequently, this means that no state is still
available when *Session_End* fires.

The session module creates the *HttpSessionState* object for a request while processing the
HttpApplication.AcquireRequestState event. At this time, the *HttpSessionState* object—a sort
of collection—is given its session ID and the session dictionary. The session dictionary is
the actual collection of state values that pages will familiarly access through the *Session*
property.

If a new session is being started, such a data dictionary is simply a newly created empty object. If the module is serving a request for an existing session, the data dictionary will be filled by deserializing the contents supplied by the currently active session-state provider. At the end of the request, the current content of the dictionary, as modified by the page request, is flushed back to the state provider through a serialization step. The whole process is depicted in Figure 13-2.

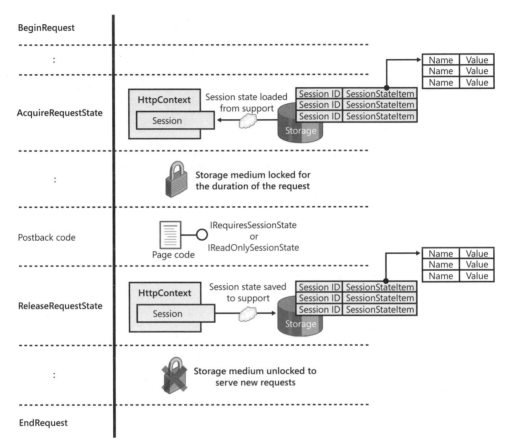

Figure 13-2 The session-state management timeline.

Synchronizing Access to the Session State

So when your Web page makes a call into the *Session* property, it's actually accessing a local, in-memory copy of the data. What if other pages (in the same session) attempt to concurrently access the session state? In that case, the current request might end up working on inconsistent data or data that isn't up to date.

To avoid that, the session-state module implements a reader/writer locking mechanism and queues the access to state values. A page that has session-state write access will hold a writer lock on the session until the request finishes. A page gains write access to the session state by setting the *EnableSessionState* attribute on the *@Page* directive to *true*. A page that has session-state read access—for example, when the *EnableSessionState* attribute is set to *ReadOnly*—will hold a reader lock on the session until the request finishes.

If a page request sets a reader lock, other concurrently running requests cannot update the session state but are allowed to read. If a page request sets a writer lock on the session state, all other pages are blocked regardless of whether they have to read or write. For example, if two frames attempt to write to *Session*, one of them has to wait until the other finishes. Figure 13-3 shows the big picture.

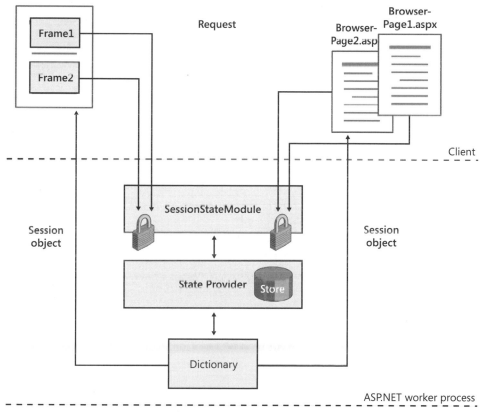

Figure 13-3   Page access to the session state is synchronized, and a serialization/deserialization layer ensures that each request is served an up-to-date dictionary of values, stored at the application's convenience.

Tip   Concurrent access to the session state is not very common in reality. It might happen if you have a multiframe page or if your users work with two copies of the same page or multiple pages of the same application at the same time. It also happens when you use session-enabled HTTP handlers to serve embedded resources such as images or CSS files. By default, you are protected against concurrent accesses. However, declaring the exact use of the session state that a page is going to make (read/write, read-only, or no use) is an excellent form of optimization. You do this through the *EnableSessionState* attribute on the *@Page* directive.

Properties of the *HttpSessionState* Class

The *HttpSessionState* class is defined in the *System.Web.SessionState* namespace. It is a generic collection class and implements the *ICollection* interface. The properties of the *HttpSession-State* class are listed in Table 13-5.

Table 13-5   *HttpSessionState* **Properties**

Property	Description
CodePage	Gets or sets the code page identifier for the current session.
Contents	Returns a reference to *this* object. Provided for ASP compatibility.
CookieMode	Details the application's configuration for cookieless sessions. Declared to be of type *HttpCookieMode*. (I'll discuss this in more detail later.) *Not available in ASP.NET 1.x.*
Count	Gets the number of items currently stored in the session state.
IsCookieless	Indicates whether the session ID is embedded in the URL or stored in an HTTP cookie. *IsCookieless* is more specific than *CookieMode*.
IsNewSession	Indicates whether the session was created with the current request.
IsReadOnly	Indicates whether the session is read-only. The session is read-only if the *EnableSessionState* attribute on the *@Page* directive is set to the keyword *ReadOnly*.
IsSynchronized	Returns *false*. (See references to this later in the chapter.)
Item	Indexer property, provides read/write access to a session-state value. The value can be specified either by name or index.
Keys	Gets a collection of the keys of all values stored in the session.
LCID	Gets or sets the locale identifier (LCID) of the current session.
Mode	Gets a value denoting the state client manager being used. Acceptable values are listed in Table 13-4.
SessionID	Gets a string with the ID used to identify the session.
StaticObjects	Gets a collection including all instances of all objects declared in *global.asax* using an *<object>* tag with the *scope* attribute set to *Session*. Note that you cannot add objects to this collection from within an ASP.NET application—that is, programmatically.
SyncRoot	Returns a reference to *this* object. (See references to this later in the chapter.)
Timeout	Gets or sets the minutes that the session module should wait between two successive requests before terminating the session.

The *HttpSessionState* class is a normal collection class because it implements the *ICollection* interface, but synchronization-wise it is a very special collection class. As mentioned, the synchronization mechanism is implemented in the *SessionStateModule* component, which guarantees that at most one thread will ever access the session state. However, because *HttpSessionState* implements the *ICollection* interface, it must provide an implementation for both *IsSynchronized* and *SyncRoot*. Notice that *IsSynchronized* and *SyncRoot* are collection-specific properties for synchronization and have nothing to do with the session synchronization discussed previously. They refer to the ability of the collection class (*HttpSessionState* in this case) to work synchronistically. Technically speaking, the *HttpSessionState* is not synchronized, but access to session state is.

Methods of the *HttpSessionState* Class

Table 13-6 shows all the methods available in the *HttpSessionState* class. They mostly have to do with the typical operations on a collection. In this sense, the only exceptional method is *Abandon*, which causes the session to be canceled.

Table 13-6   *HttpSessionState* Methods

Method	Description
Abandon	Sets an internal flag that instructs the session module to cancel the current session.
Add	Adds a new item to the session state. The value is boxed in an *object* type.
Clear	Clears all values from the session state.
CopyTo	Copies the collection of session-state values to a one-dimensional array, starting at the specified index in the array.
GetEnumerator	Gets an enumerator to loop through all the values in the session.
Remove	Deletes an item from the session-state collection. The item is identified by the key
RemoveAll	Calls *Clear*.
RemoveAt	Deletes an item from the session-state collection. The item is identified by position.

When running the procedure to terminate the current request, the session state module checks an internal flag to verify whether the user ordered that the session be abandoned. If the flag is set—that is, the *Abandon* method was called—any response cookie is removed and the procedure to terminate the session is begun. Notice, though, that this does not necessarily mean that a *Session_End* event will fire.

First, the *Session_End* event fires only if the session mode is *InProc*; second, the event does not fire if the session dictionary is empty and no real session state exists for the application. In other words, at least one request must have been completed for the *Session_End* to fire when the session is closed either naturally or after a call to *Abandon*.

Working with Session's State

Now that you have grabbed hold of the session-state basics, we can sharpen our skills by looking into more technically relevant aspects of session-state management. Handling session state is a task that can be outlined in three steps: assigning a session ID, obtaining session data from a provider, and stuffing it into the context of the page. As mentioned, the session-state module governs the execution of all these tasks. In doing so, it takes advantage of a couple of additional components: the session ID generator and session-state provider. In ASP.NET 2.0, both can be replaced with custom components, as we'll discuss later. For now, let's tackle some of the practical issues you face when working with session state.

Identifying a Session

Each active ASP.NET session is identified using a 120-bit string made only of URL-allowed characters. Session IDs are guaranteed to be unique and randomly generated to avoid data conflicts and prevent malicious attacks. Obtaining a valid session ID algorithmically from an existing ID is virtually impossible. In ASP.NET 1.x, the generator of the session ID is a system component buried in the framework and invisible from outside. In ASP.NET 2.0, it has become a customizable component that developers can optionally replace.

> **Note**   An old proverb reminds us that nothing should be done only because it is doable. This motto is particularly apt here as we talk about parts of the session-state management that are customizable in ASP.NET 2.0. These subsystems, such as the session ID generator, should be customized only with good reason and with certainty that it won't make things worse or lower the level of security. I'll return to this point in a moment with more details.

Generating the Session ID

A session ID is 15 bytes long by design ($15 \times 8 = 120$ bits). The session ID is generated using the Random Number Generator (RNG) cryptographic provider. The service provider returns a sequence of 15 randomly generated numbers. The array of numbers is then mapped to valid URL characters and returned as a string.

If the session contains nothing, a new session ID is generated for each request and the session state is not persisted to the state provider. However, if a *Session_Start* handler is used, the session state is always saved, even if empty. For this reason, and especially if you're not using the in-process session provider, define *Session_Start* handlers with extreme care and only if strictly necessary.

In contrast, the session ID remains the same after a nonempty session dictionary times out or is abandoned. By design, even though the session state expires, the session ID lasts until the browser session is ended. This means that the same session ID is used to represent multiple sessions over time as long as the browser instance remains the same.

Session Cookies

The *SessionID* string is communicated to the browser and then returned to the server application in either of two ways: using a cookie or a modified URL. By default, the session-state module creates an HTTP cookie on the client, but a modified URL can be used—especially for cookieless browsers—with the *SessionID* string embedded. Which approach is taken depends on the configuration settings stored in the application's *web.config* file. By default, session state uses cookies.

A cookie is really nothing more than a text file placed on the client's hard disk by a Web page. In ASP.NET, a cookie is represented by an instance of the *HttpCookie* class. Typically, a cookie has a name, a collection of values, and an expiration time. In addition, you can configure the cookie to operate on a particular virtual path and over secure connections (for example, HTTPS).

> **Important**   ASP.NET 2.0 takes advantage of the HTTP-only feature for session cookies on the browsers that supports it. For example, it is supported on Microsoft Internet Explorer 6.0 SP1 or with Windows XP SP2 installed. The HTTP-only feature prevents cookies from being available to client-side script, thus raising a barrier against potential cross-site scripting attacks aimed at stealing session IDs.

When cookies are enabled, the session-state module actually creates a cookie with a particular name and stores the session ID in it. The cookie is created as shown in the following pseudocode:

```
HttpCookie sessionCookie;
sessionCookie = new HttpCookie("ASP.NET_SessionId", sessionID);
sessionCookie.Path = "/";
```

ASP.NET_SessionId is the name of the cookie, and the *sessionID* string is its value. The cookie is also associated with the root of the current domain. The *Path* property describes the relative URL that the cookie applies to. A session cookie is given a very short expiration term and is renewed at the end of each successful request. The cookie's *Expires* property indicates the time of day on the client at which the cookie expires. If not explicitly set, as is the case with session cookies, the *Expires* property defaults to *DateTime.MinValue*—that is, the smallest possible unit of time in the .NET Framework.

> **Note**   A server-side module that needs to write a cookie adds an *HttpCookie* object to the *Response.Cookies* collection. All cookies found on the client and associated with the requested domain are uploaded and made available for reading through the *Request.Cookies* collection.

Cookieless Sessions

For the session state to work, the client must be able to pass the session ID to the server application. How this happens depends on the configuration of the application. ASP.NET applications define their session-specific settings through the *<sessionState>* section of the configuration file. To decide about the cookie support, you set the *cookieless* attribute to one of the values in Table 13-7. The listed values belong to the *HttpCookieMode* enumerated type.

Table 13-7 *HttpCookieMode* Enumerated Type

Mode	Description
AutoDetect	Use cookies only if the requesting browser supports cookies.
UseCookies	Use cookies to persist the session ID regardless of whether the browser supports cookies. This is the default option.
UseDeviceProfile	Base the decision on the browser's capabilities as listed in the device profile section of the configuration file.
UseUri	Store the session ID in the URL regardless of whether the browser supports cookies. Use this option if you want to go cookieless no matter what.

When *AutoDetect* is used, ASP.NET will query the browser to determine whether it supports cookies. If the browser supports cookies, the session ID will be stored in a cookie; otherwise, the session ID will be stored in the URL. When *UseDeviceProfile* is set, on the other hand, the effective capabilities of the browser are not checked. For the session HTTP module to make the decision about cookies or URL, the declared capabilities of the browser are used as they result from the *SupportsRedirectWithCookie* property of the *HttpBrowserCapabilities* object. Note that even though a browser can support cookies, a user might have disabled cookies. In this case, session state won't work properly.

> **Note** In ASP.NET 1.x, you have fewer options to choose from. The *cookieless* attribute of the *<sessionState>* section can accept only a Boolean value. To disable cookies in sessions, you set the attribute to *true*.

With cookie support disabled, suppose that you request a page at the following URL:

```
http://www.contoso.com/test/sessions.aspx
```

What is displayed in the browser's address bar is slightly different and now includes the session ID, as shown here:

```
http://www.contoso.com/test/(S(5ylg0455mrvws1uz5mmaau45))/sessions.aspx
```

When instantiated, the session-state module checks the value of the *cookieless* attribute. If the value is *true*, the request is redirected (HTTP 302 status code) to a modified virtual URL that includes the session ID just before the page name. When processed again, the request embeds the session ID. A special ISAPI filter—the *aspnet_filter.exe* component—preprocesses the request, parses the URL, and rewrites the correct URL if it incorporates a session ID. The detected session ID is also stored in an extra HTTP header named *AspFilterSessionId* and retrieved later.

Issues with Cookieless Sessions

Designed to make stateful applications also possible on a browser that does not support cookies or on one that does not have cookies enabled, cookieless sessions are not free of issues. First, they cause a redirect when the session starts and whenever the user follows an absolute URL from within an application's page.

When cookies are used, you can clear the address bar, go to another application, and then return to the previous one and retrieve the same session values. If you do this when session cookies are disabled, the session data is lost. This feature is not problematic for postbacks, which are automatically implemented using relative URLs, but it poses a serious problem if you use links to absolute URLs. In this case, a new session will always be created. For example, the following code breaks the session:

```
<a runat="server" href="/test/sessions.aspx">Click</a>
```

Is there a way to automatically mangle absolute URLs in links and hyperlinks so that they incorporate session information? You can use the following trick, which uses the *ApplyAppPathModifier* method of the *HttpResponse* class:

```
<a href='<% =Response.ApplyAppPathModifier("test/page.aspx")%>' >Click</a>
```

The *ApplyAppPathModifier* method takes a string representing a relative URL and returns an absolute URL, which embeds session information. This trick is especially useful when you need to redirect from an HTTP page to an HTTPS page, where the full, absolute address is mandatory. Note that *ApplyAppPathModifier* returns the original URL if session cookies are enabled and if the path is an absolute path.

> **Caution**   You can't use < %...% > code blocks in server-side expressions—that is, expressions flagged with the *runat=server* attribute. It works in the preceding code because the *<a>* tag is emitted verbatim, being devoid of the *runat* attribute.

Cookieless Sessions and Security

Another issue regarding the use of cookieless sessions is connected with security. Session hijacking is one of the most popular types of attacks and consists of accessing an external system through the session ID generated for another, legitimate user. Try this: set your application for work without cookies and visit a page. Grab the URL with the session ID as it appears in the browser's address bar, and send it immediately in an e-mail to a friend. Have your friend paste the URL in his or her own machine and click Go. Your friend will gain access to your session state as long as the session is active. The session ID is certainly not well-protected information (and probably couldn't work otherwise). For the safety of a system, an unpredictable generator of IDs is key because it makes it difficult to guess a valid session ID. With cookieless sessions, the session ID is exposed in the address bar and visible to all. For this reason, if you are storing private or sensitive information in the session state, it is recommended that you use Secure Sockets Layer (SSL) or Transport Layer Security (TLS) to encrypt any communication between the browser and server that includes the session ID.

In addition, you should always provide users the ability to log out and call the *Abandon* method when they think security has been breached in this way. This contrivance reduces the amount of time available for anybody getting to use your session ID to exploit data stored in the session state. And, speaking of security, it is important that you configure the system to avoid the reuse of expired session IDs when cookieless sessions are used. This behavior is configurable in ASP.NET 2.0 through the *<sessionState>* section, as you can read in the following section.

Configuring the Session State

The *<sessionState>* section has grown significantly in the transition from ASP.NET 1.x to ASP.NET 2.0. Here's how it looks now:

```
<sessionState
    mode="Off|InProc|StateServer|SQLServer|Custom"
    timeout="number of minutes"
    cookieName="session cookie name"
    cookieless="http cookie mode"
    regenerateExpiredSessionId="true|false"
    sqlConnectionString="sql connection string"
    sqlCommandTimeout="number of seconds"
    allowCustomSqlDatabase="true|false"
    useHostingIdentity="true|false"
    partitionResolverType=""
    sessionIDManagerType="custom session ID generator"
    stateConnectionString="tcpip=server:port"
    stateNetworkTimeout="number of seconds"
    customProvider="custom provider name">
    <providers>
        ...
    </providers>
</sessionState>
```

Table 13-8 details goals and characteristics of the various attributes. Note that only *mode*, *timeout*, *stateConnectionString*, and *sqlConnectionString* are identical to ASP.NET 1.x. The attribute *cookieless* also exists in ASP.NET 1.x but accepts Boolean values. All the others are new in ASP.NET 2.0.

Table 13-8   *<sessionState>* Attributes

Mode	Description
allowCustomSqlDatabase	If *true*, enables specifying a custom database table to store session data instead of using the standard *ASPState*.
Cookieless	Specifies how to communicate the session ID to clients.
cookieName	Name of the cookie, if cookies are used for session IDs.
customProvider	The name of the custom session-state store provider to use for storing and retrieving session-state data.
mode	Specifies where to store session state.
partitionResolverType	Indicates type and assembly of the partition resolver component to be loaded to provide connection information when session state is working in *SQLServer* or *StateServer* mode. If a partition resolver can be correctly loaded, *sqlConnectionString* and *stateConnectionString* attributes are ignored.

Table 13-8 *<sessionState>* **Attributes**

Mode	Description
regenerateExpiredSessionId	When a request is made with a session ID that has expired, if this attribute is *true*, a new session ID is generated; otherwise, the expired one is revived. The default is *false*.
sessionIDManagerType	Null by default. If set, it indicates the component to use as the generator of session IDs.
sqlCommandTimeout	Specifies the number of seconds a SQL command can be idle before it is canceled. The default is 30.
sqlConnectionString	Specifies the connection string to SQL Server.
stateConnectionString	Specifies the server name or address and port where session state is stored remotely.
stateNetworkTimeout	Specifies the number of seconds the TCP/IP network connection between the Web server and the state server can be idle before the request is canceled. The default is 10.
timeout	Specifies the number of minutes a session can be idle before it is abandoned. The default is 20.
useHostingIdentity	*True* by default. It indicates that the ASP.NET process identity is impersonated when accessing a custom state provider or the *SQLServer* provider configured for integrated security.

In addition, the child *<providers>* section lists custom session-state store providers. ASP.NET session state is designed to enable you to easily store user session data in different sources, such as a Web server's memory or SQL Server. A store provider is a component that manages the storage of session-state information and stores it in alternative media (for example, Oracle) and layout. We'll return to this topic later in the chapter.

Lifetime of a Session

The life of a session state begins only when the first item is added to the in-memory dictionary. The following code demonstrates how to modify an item in the session dictionary. "*MyData*" is the key that uniquely identifies the value. If a key named "*MyData*" already exists in the dictionary, the existing value is overwritten:

```
Session["MyData"] = "I love ASP.NET";
```

The *Session* dictionary generically contains *object* types; to read data back, you need to cast the returned values to a more specific type:

```
string tmp = (string) Session["MyData"];
```

When a page saves data to *Session*, the value is loaded into an in-memory dictionary—an instance of an internal class named *SessionDictionary*. (See Figure 13-2.) Other concurrently running pages cannot access the session until the ongoing request completes.

The *Session_Start* Event

The session startup event is unrelated to the session state. The *Session_Start* event fires when the session-state module is servicing the first request for a given user that requires a new session ID. The ASP.NET runtime can serve multiple requests within the context of a single session, but only for the first of them does *Session_Start* fire.

A new session ID is created and a new *Session_Start* event fires whenever a page is requested that doesn't write data to the dictionary. The architecture of the session state is quite sophisticated because it has to support a variety of state providers. The overall schema entails that the content of the session dictionary is serialized to the state provider when the request completes. However, to optimize performance, this procedure really executes only if the content of the dictionary is not empty. As mentioned earlier, though, if the application defines a *Session_Start* event handler, the serialization takes place anyway.

The *Session_End* Event

The *Session_End* event signals the end of the session and is used to perform any cleanup code needed to terminate the session. Notice, though, that the event is supported only in *InProc* mode—that is, only when the session data is stored in the ASP.NET worker process.

For *Session_End* to fire, the session state has to exist first. That means you have to store some data in the session state and you must have completed at least one request. When the first value is added to the session dictionary, an item is inserted into the ASP.NET cache—the afore-mentioned *Cache* object that we'll cover in detail in the next chapter. The behavior is specific to the in-process state provider; neither the out-of-process state server nor the SQL Server state server work with the *Cache* object.

However, much more interesting is that the item added to the cache—only one item per active session—is given a special expiration policy. You'll also learn more about the ASP.NET cache and related expiration policies in the next chapter. For now, suffice it to say that the session-state item added to the cache is given a sliding expiration, with the time interval set to the session timeout. As long as there are requests processed within the session, the sliding period is automatically renewed. The session-state module resets the timeout while processing the *EndRequest* event. It obtains the desired effect by simply performing a read on the cache! Given the internal structure of the ASP.NET *Cache* object, this evaluates to renewing the sliding period. As a result, when the cache item expires, the session has timed out.

An expired item is automatically removed from the cache. As part of the expiration policy for this item, the state-session module also indicates a remove callback function. The cache automatically invokes the remove function which, in turn, fires the *Session_End* event.

> **Note**   The items in *Cache* that represent the state of a session are not accessible from outside the *system.web* assembly and can't even be enumerated, as they are placed in a system-reserved area of the cache. In other words, you can't programmatically access the data resident in another session or even remove it.

Why Does My Session State Sometimes Get Lost?

Values parked in a *Session* object are removed from memory either programmatically by the code or by the system when the session times out or is abandoned. In some cases, though, even when nothing of the kind seemingly happens, the session state gets lost. Is there a reason for this apparently weird behavior?

When the working mode is *InProc*, the session state is mapped in the memory space of the AppDomain in which the page request is being served. In light of this, the session state is subject to process recycling and AppDomain restarts. The ASP.NET worker process is periodically restarted to maintain an average good performance; when this happens, the session state is lost. Process recycling depends on the percentage of memory consumption and maybe the number of requests served. Although cyclic, no general estimate can be made regarding the interval of the cycle. Be aware of this when designing your session-based, in-process application. As a general rule, bear in mind that the session state might not be there when you try to access it. Use exception handling or recovery techniques as appropriate for your application.

Consider that some antivirus software might be marking the *web.config* or *global.asax* file as modified, thus causing a new application to be started and subsequently causing the loss of the session state. This holds true also if you or your code modify the timestamp of those files or alter the contents of one of the special folders such as *Bin* or *App_Code*.

> **Note**   What happens to the session state when a running page hits an error? Will the current dictionary be saved or is it just lost? The state of the session is not saved if, at the end of the request, the page results in an error—that is, the *GetLastError* method of the *Server* object returns an exception. However, if in your exception handler you reset the error state by calling *Server.ClearError*, the values of the session are saved regularly as if no error ever occurred.

Persist Session Data to Remote Servers

The session-state loss problem that we mentioned earlier for *InProc* mode can be neatly solved by employing either of the two predefined out-of-process state providers—*StateServer* and *SQLServer*. In this case, though, the session state is held outside the ASP.NET worker process and an extra layer of code is needed to serialize and deserialize it to and from the actual storage medium. This operation takes place whenever a request is processed.

The need of copying session data from an external repository into the local session dictionary might tax the state management process to the point of causing a 15 percent to 25 percent decrease in performance. Notice, though, that this is only a rough estimate, and it's closer to the minimum impact rather than to the maximum impact. The estimate, in fact, does not fully consider the complexity of the types actually saved into the session state.

Caution   When you get to choose an out-of-process state provider (for example, *StateServer* and *SQLServer*), be aware that you need to set up the run-time environment before putting the application in production. This means either starting a Windows service for *StateServer* or configuring a database for *SQLServer*. No preliminary work is needed if you stay with the default, in-process option.

State Serialization and Deserialization

When you use the *InProc* mode, objects are stored in the session state as live instances of classes. No real serialization and deserialization ever takes place, meaning that you can actually store in *Session* whatever objects (including COM objects) you have created and access them with no significant overhead. The situation is less favorable if you opt for an out-of-process state provider.

In an out-of-process architecture, session values are to be copied from the native storage medium into the memory of the AppDomain that processes the request. A serialization/ deserialization layer is needed to accomplish the task and represents one of the major costs for out-of-process state providers. How does this affect your code? First, you should make sure that only serializable objects are ever stored in the session dictionary; otherwise, as you can easily imagine, the session state can't be saved.

To perform the serialization and deserialization of types, ASP.NET uses two methods, each providing different results in terms of performance. For basic types, ASP.NET resorts to an optimized internal serializer; for other types, including objects and user-defined classes, ASP.NET makes use of the .NET binary formatter, which is slower. Basic types are *string*, *DateTime*, *Guid*, *IntPtr*, *TimeSpan*, *Boolean*, *byte*, *char*, and all numeric types.

The optimized serializer—an internal class named *AltSerialization*—employs an instance of the *BinaryWriter* object to write out one byte to denote the type and then the value. While reading, the *AltSerialization* class first extracts one byte, detects the type of the data to read, and then resorts to a type-specific method of the *BinaryReader* class to take data. The type is associated to an index according to an internal table, as shown in Figure 13-4.

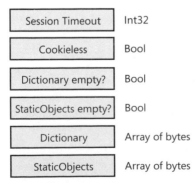

Session Timeout	Int32
Cookieless	Bool
Dictionary empty?	Bool
StaticObjects empty?	Bool
Dictionary	Array of bytes
StaticObjects	Array of bytes

Figure 13-4   The serialization schema for basic types that the internal *AltSerialization* class uses.

> **Note** While Booleans and numeric types have a well-known size, the length of a string can vary quite a bit. How can the reader determine the correct size of a string? The *BinaryReader* *.ReadString* method exploits the fact that on the underlying stream the string is always prefixed with the length, encoded as an integer seven bits at a time. Values of the *DateTime* type, on the other hand, are saved by writing only the total number of ticks that form the date and are read as an *Int64* type.

As mentioned, more complex objects are serialized using the relatively slower *BinaryFormatter* class as long as the involved types are marked as serializable. Both simple and complex types use the same stream, but all nonbasic types are identified with the same type ID. The performance-hit range of 15 percent to 25 percent is a rough estimate based on the assumption that basic types are used. The more you use complex types, the more the overhead grows and reliable numbers can be calculated only by testing a particular application scenario.

In light of this, if you plan to use out-of-process sessions, make sure you store data effectively. For example, if you need to persist an instance of a class with three string properties, performancewise you are *probably* better off using three different slots filled with a basic type rather than one session slot for which the binary formatter is needed. Better yet, you can use a type converter class to transform the object to and from a string format. However, understand that this is merely a guideline to be applied case by case and with a grain of salt.

> **Caution** In classic ASP, storing an ADO *Recordset* object in the session state was a potentially dangerous action because of threading issues. Fortunately, in ASP.NET no thread-related issues exist to cause you to lose sleep. However, you can't just store any object to *Session* and be happy. If you use an out-of-process scheme, you ought to pay a lot of attention to storing *DataSet* objects. The reason has to do with the serialization process of the *DataSet* class. Because the *DataSet* is a complex type, it gets serialized through the binary formatter. The serialization engine of the *DataSet*, though, generates a lot of XML data and turns out to be a serious flaw, especially for large applications that store a large quantity of data. In fact, you can easily find yourself moving megabytes of data for each request. Just avoid *DataSet* objects in ASP.NET 1.x out-of-process sessions and opt for plain arrays of column and row data. In ASP.NET 2.0, set the new *RemotingFormat* property before you store it.

Storing Session Data

When working in *StateServer* mode, the entire content of the *HttpSessionState* object is serialized to an external application—a Microsoft Windows NT service named *aspnet_state.exe*. The service is called to serialize the session state when the request completes. The service internally stores each session state as an array of bytes. When a new request begins processing, the array corresponding to the given session ID is copied into a memory stream and then deserialized into an internal session-state item object. This object really represents the contents of the whole session. The *HttpSessionState* object that pages actually work with is only its application interface.

As mentioned, nonbasic types are serialized and deserialized using the system's binary formatter class, which can handle only classes explicitly marked to be serializable. This means that COM objects, either programmatically created or declared as static objects with a session scope in *global.asax*, can't be used with an out-of-process state provider. The same limitation applies to any nonserializable object.

Configuring the *StateServer* Provider

Using out-of-process storage scenarios, you give the session state a longer life and your application greater robustness. Out-of-process session-state storage basically protects the session against Internet Information Services (IIS) and ASP.NET process failures. By separating the session state from the page itself, you can also much more easily scale an existing application to Web farm and Web garden architectures. In addition, the session state living in an external process eliminates at the root the risk of periodically losing data because of process recycling.

As mentioned, the ASP.NET session-state provider is a Windows NT service named *aspnet_state.exe*. It normally resides in the installation folder of ASP.NET:

```
%WINDOWS%\Microsoft.NET\Framework\[version]
```

As usual, notice that the final directory depends on the .NET Framework version you're actually running. Before using the state server, you should make sure that the service is up and running on the local or remote machine used as the session store. The state service is a constituent part of ASP.NET and gets installed along with it, so you have no additional setup application to run.

By default, the state service is stopped and requires a manual start. You can change its configuration through the property dialog box of the service, as shown in Figure 13-5.

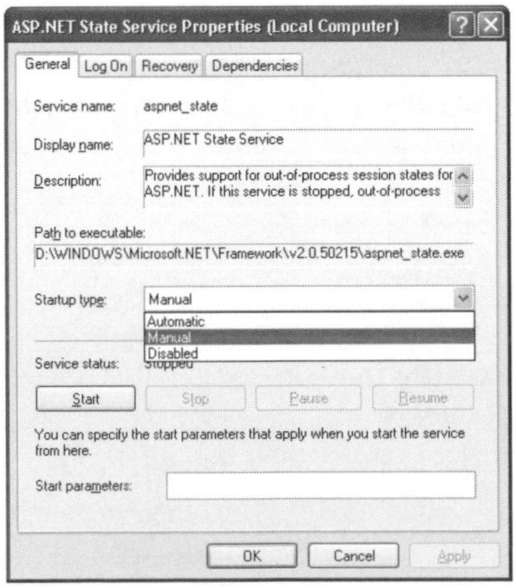

Figure 13-5 The property dialog box of the ASP.NET state server.

An ASP.NET application needs to specify the TCP/IP address of the machine hosting the session-state service. The following listing shows the changes that need to be made to the *web.config* file to enable the remote session state:

```
<configuration>
    <system.web>
        <sessionState
            mode="StateServer"
            stateConnectionString="tcpip=MyMachine:42424" />
    </system.web>
</configuration>
```

Note that the value assigned to the *mode* attribute is case sensitive. The format of the *stateConnectionString* attribute is shown in the following line of code. The default machine address is 127.0.0.1, while the port is 42424.

```
stateConnectionString="tcpip=server:port"
```

The server name can be either an IP address or a machine name. In this case, though, non-ASCII characters in the name are not supported. Finally, the port number is mandatory and cannot be omitted.

> **Important** The state server doesn't oppose any authentication barrier to requestors, meaning that anyone who can get access to the network is potentially free to access sessions data. To protect session state and make sure that it is only accessed by the Web server machine, you can use a firewall or IPSec policies. Another security-related countermeasure consists of changing the default port number. To change the port, you edit the *Port* entry under the registry key: *HKEY_LOCAL_MACHINE\SYSTEM\CurrentControlSet\Services\aspnet_state\Parameters*. Writing the port in the *web.config* file isn't enough.

The ASP.NET application attempts to connect to the session-state server immediately after loading. The *aspnet_state* service must be up and running; otherwise, an HTTP exception is thrown. By default, the service is not configured to start automatically. The state service uses .NET Remoting to move data back and forth.

> **Note** The ASP.NET state provider runs under the ASP.NET account. The account, though, can be configured and changed at will using the Service Control Manager interface. The state service is slim and simple and does not implement any special features. It is limited to holding data and listens to the specified port for requests to serve. In particular, the service isn't cluster-aware (that is, it doesn't provide a failover monitor to be error tolerant) and can't be used in a clustered world when another server takes on the one that fails. Finally, note that by default the state server only listens to local connections. If the state server and Web server live on different machines, you need to enable remote connections. You do this through another entry in the same registry key as listed above. The entry is *AllowRemoteConnection* and must be set to a nonzero value.

Persist Session Data to SQL Server

Maintaining the session state in an external process certainly makes the whole ASP.NET application more stable. Whatever happens to the worker process, the session state is still there, ready for further use. If the service is paused, the data is preserved and automatically retrieved when the service resumes. Unfortunately, if the state provider service is stopped or if a failure occurs, the data is lost. If robustness is key for your application, drop the *StateServer* mode in favor of *SQLServer*.

Performance and Robustness

When ASP.NET works in *SQLServer* mode, the session data is stored in a made-to-measure database table. As a result, the session data survives even if SQL Server crashes, but you have to add higher overhead to the bill. *SQLServer* mode allows you to store data on any connected machine, as long as the machine runs SQL Server 7.0 or newer. Besides the different medium, the storage mechanism is nearly identical to that described for remote servers. In particular, the serialization and deserialization algorithm is the same, only it's a bit slower because of the characteristics of storage. When storing data of basic types, the time required to set up the page's *Session* object is normally at least 25 percent longer than in an *InProc* scenario. Also in regard to this issue, the more complex the types you use, the more time will probably be required to manage the session data.

> **Note**   When you have to make a decision between state server or SQL server storage, consider the fact that SQL Server is cluster-aware, which makes a solution based on it more robust and reliable than one based on a state server.

Configuring Session State for SQL Server Support

To use SQL Server as the state provider, enter the following changes in the *<sessionState>* section of the *web.config* file:

```
<configuration>
  <system.web>
    <sessionState
        mode="SQLServer"
        sqlConnectionString="server=127.0.0.1;integrated security=SSPI;" />
  </system.web>
</configuration>
```

In particular, you need to set the *mode* attribute (which is case sensitive) to *SQLServer* and specify the connection string through the *sqlConnectionString* attribute. Notice that the *sqlConnectionString* attribute string must include a user ID, password, and server name. It cannot, however, contain tokens such as *Database* and *Initial Catalog*, unless (and only in ASP.NET 2.0) a custom database is enabled, as mentioned in Table 13-8. You can specify a SQL Server *Initial Catalog* database name or use the SQL Server Express *attachDBFileName* to point to an MDB file in the connection string only if the *allowCustomSqlDatabase* configuration setting is enabled. If that setting is disabled, any attempts to specify these settings in the connection string will result in an exception.

Note In ASP.NET 2.0, the connection string for an out-of-process session-state implementation (both *SQLServer* and *StateServer*) can also be specified referring to a connection string defined in the *<connectionStrings>* section. The session-state module will first attempt to look up a connection string from the *<connectionStrings>* section with the name specified in the appropriate *<sessionState>* attribute; if it is not found, the session state will attempt to use the specified string directly.

As for credentials to access the database, you can either use User ID and passwords or resort to integrated security.

Note Whatever account you use to access session state in SQL Server, make sure that it is granted the *db_datareader* and *db_datawriter* permissions at the very least. Note also that to configure the SQL Server environment for storing session state, administrative privileges are required, as a new database and stored procedures need to be created.

In ASP.NET 2.0, session state in SQL Server mode now supports the specification of a custom command timeout value (in seconds) to accommodate slow-responding-server scenarios. You control this value through the *sqlCommandTimeout* attribute, as mentioned in Table 13-8.

Creating the SQL Server Data Store

ASP.NET provides two pairs of scripts to configure the database environment by creating any needed tables, stored procedures, triggers, and jobs. The scripts in the first pair are named *InstallSqlState.sql* and *UninstallSqlState.sql*. They create a database called *ASPState* and several stored procedures. The data, though, is stored in a couple tables belonging to the *TempDB* database. In SQL Server, the *TempDB* database provides a storage area for temporary tables, temporary stored procedures, and other temporary working storage needs. This means that the session data is lost if the SQL Server machine is restarted.

The second pair consists of the scripts *InstallPersistSqlState.sql* and *UninstallPersistSqlState.sql*. Also in this case, an *ASPState* database is created but the tables are persistent because they are created within the same database. All scripts are located in the following path:

```
%SystemRoot%\Microsoft.NET\Framework\[version]
```

Important In ASP.NET 2.0, these script files are included for backward compatibility only. You should use *aspnet_regsql.exe* to install and uninstall a SQL session state. Among other things, the newest *aspnet_regsql.exe* supports more options, such as using a custom database table. In ASP.NET 1.x, you still have a version of *aspnet_regsql* but with some limitations—there are no persistent tables and no custom tables.

The tables that get created are named ASPStateTempApplications and ASPStateTempSessions. Figure 13-6 shows a view of the session database in SQL Server.

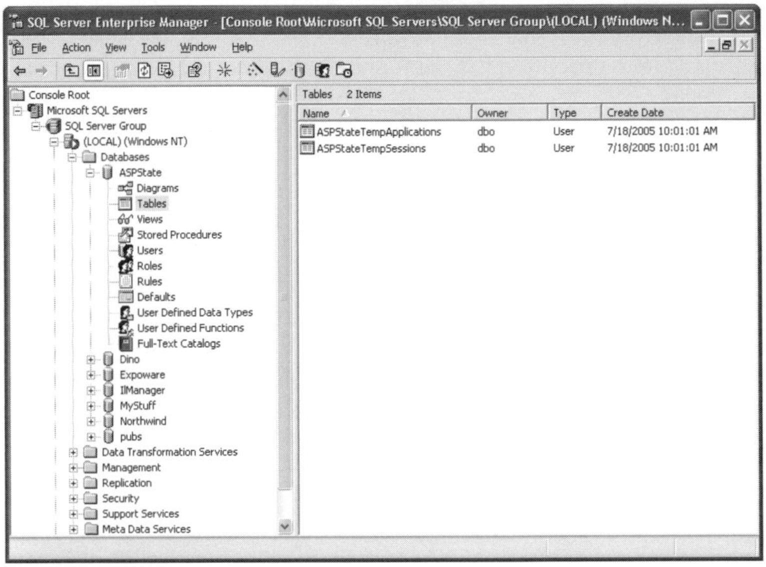

Figure 13-6 The *ASPState* database in SQL Server 2000.

The ASPStateTempApplications table defines a record for each currently running ASP.NET application. The table columns are listed in Table 13-9.

Table 13-9 The ASPStateTempApplications Table

Column	Type	Description
AppId	*Int*	Indexed field. It represents a sort of auto-generated ID that identifies a running application using the *SQLServer* session mode.
AppName	*char(280)*	Indicates the application ID of the AppDomain running the application. It matches the contents of the *AppDomainAppId* property on the *HttpRuntime* object.

The ASPStateTempSessions table stores the actual session data. The table contains one row for each active session. The structure of the table is outlined in Table 13-10.

Table 13-10 The ASPStateTempSessions Table

Column	Type	Description
SessionId	*char(88)*	Indexed field. It represents the session ID.
Created	*DateTime*	Indicates the time at which the session was created. It defaults to the current date.
Expires	*DateTime*	Indicates the time at which the session will expire. This value is normally the time at which the session state was created plus the number of minutes specified in *Timeout*. Notice that *Created* refers to the time at which the session started, whereas *Expires* adds minutes to the time in which the first item is added to the session state.

Table 13-10   The ASPStateTempSessions Table

Column	Type	Description
LockDate	*DateTime*	Indicates the time in which the session was locked to add the last item. The value is expressed as the current Universal Time Coordinate (UTC).
LockDateLocal	*DateTime*	Like the previous item (LockDate), except that this one expresses the system's local time. *Not available in ASP.NET 1.x.*
LockCookie	*int*	Indicates the number of times the session was locked— that is, the number of accesses.
Timeout	*int*	Indicates the timeout of the session in minutes.
Locked	*bit*	Indicates whether the session is currently locked.
SessionItemShort	*VarBinary(7000)*	Nullable field. It represents the values in the specified session. The layout of the bytes is identical to the layout discussed for *StateServer* providers. If more than 7000 bytes are needed to serialize the dictionary, the *SessionItemLong* field is used instead.
SessionItemLong	*Image*	Nullable field, represents the serialized version of a session longer than 7000 bytes.
Flags	*Int*	Indicates action flags—initialize item or none—from the *SessionStateActions* enum. *Not available in ASP.NET 1.x.*

The column *SessionItemLong* contains a long binary block of data. Although the user always works with image data as if it were a single, long sequence of bytes, the data is not stored in that format. The data is stored in a collection of 8-KB pages that aren't necessarily located next to each other.

When installing the SQL Server support for sessions, a job is also created to delete expired sessions from the session-state database. The job, which is shown in Figure 13-7, is named *ASPState_Job_DeleteExpiredSessions*, and the default configuration makes it run every minute. You should note that the SQLServerAgent service needs to be running for this to work.

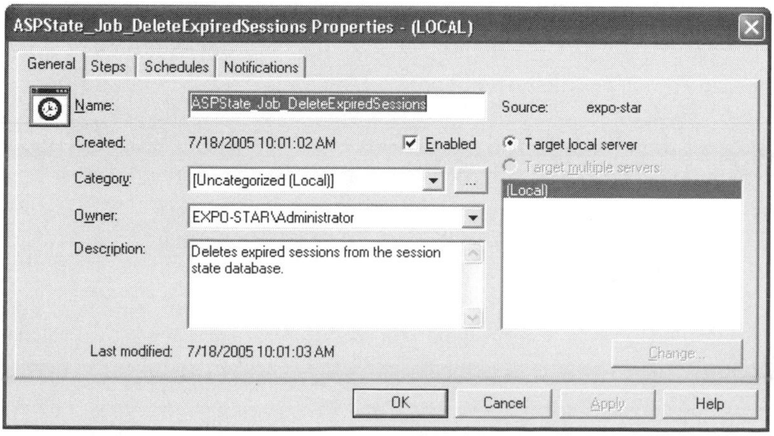

Figure 13-7   The SQL Server job to delete expired sessions.

Reverting to the Hosting Identity

In ASP.NET 1.x, credentials used to access the SQL Server stored session state depend on the connection string. If explicitly provided, the user name and password will be used to access the database. Otherwise, if integrated security is requested, the account of the currently logged-in client is used. This approach clashes with the *StateServer* state provider, which uses the ASP.NET identity to do its job. More important, though, it poses some administrative issues for intranet sites using client impersonation. In these cases, in fact, you have to grant access to the database to every client account that might be making calls.

In ASP.NET 2.0, the *useHostingIdentity* attribute (shown in Table 13-8) lets you decide the identity to be effectively used. Breaking the ASP.NET 1.x behavior, in ASP.NET 2.0—when the *SQLServer* state provider is used with integrated security—the identity is that impersonated by ASP.NET. It will typically be ASPNET or NETWORK SERVICE or any other account impersonated by the ASP.NET worker process through the *<identity>* section of the configuration file. This simplifies the administrative experience for intranet sites, requiring that only the ASP.NET account is granted access to protected and critical resources. The *useHostingIdentity* attribute defaults to *true*, which enables you to revert to the ASP.NET identity before making calls to the *SQLServer* session-state provider. This will also happen if a custom provider is used.

> **Note** If you're using Windows integrated authentication to access SQL Server, reverting to the host identity is the most highly recommended option for security reasons. Otherwise, it is advisable that you create a specific account and grant it only rights to execute session-state stored procedures and access related resources.

Session State in a Web Farm Scenario

ASP.NET applications designed to run in a Web farm or Web garden hardware configuration cannot implement an in-process session state. The *InProc* mode won't work on a Web farm because a distinct worker process will be running on each connected machine, with each process maintaining its own session state. It doesn't even work on a Web garden because multiple worker processes will be running on the same machine.

Keeping all states separate from worker processes allows you to partition an application across multiple worker processes even when they're running on multiple computers. In both Web farm and Web garden scenarios, there can be only one *StateServer* or *SQLServer* process to provide session-state management.

If you're running a Web farm, make sure you have the same *<machineKey>* in all of your Web servers. (More details can be found in Knowledge Base article Q313091.) In addition, for the session state to be maintained across different servers in the Web farm, all applications should have the same application path stored in the IIS metabase. This

> value is set as the AppDomain application ID and identifies a running application in the ASP.NET state database. (See Knowledge Base article Q325056 for more details.)
>
> In ASP.NET 2.0, partition resolvers are also introduced to let a session-state provider partition its data onto multiple back-end nodes. This allows you to scale session state on large Web farms, according to a custom, user-defined load-balancing scheme. A partition provider is a component that supplies the connection string (the actual string, not the pointer to a string in the *web.config* file) to the session state that is used to access data, overriding any other settings in the *<sessionState>* section.

Customizing Session State Management

Since its beginning, the ASP.NET session state was devised to be an easy-to-customize and extensible feature. For various reasons, in ASP.NET 1.x it came out with a high degree of customization but a total lack of extensibility. In ASP.NET 2.0, the session-state subsystem was refactored to allow developers to replace most of the functionalities—a characteristic that is often referred to as *session-state pluggability*.

All things considered, you have the following three options to customize session-state management.

- You can stay with the default session-state module but write a custom state provider to change the storage medium (for example, a non–SQL Server database or a different table layout). In doing so, you also have the chance to override some of the helper classes (mostly collections) that are used to bring data from the store to the *Session* object and back.

- You can stay with the default session state module but replace the session ID generator. But hold on! The algorithm that generates session IDs is a critical element of the application, as making session IDs too easy for attackers to guess can lead straight to session hijacking attacks. Nonetheless, this remains a customizable aspect of session state that, properly used, can make your application even more secure.

- You can unplug the default session-state module and roll your own. Technically possible also in ASP.NET 1.x, this option should be used as a last resort. Obviously, it provides the maximum flexibility, but it is also extremely complicated and is recommended only if strictly necessary and if you know exactly what you're doing. We won't cover this topic in the book.

The first option—the easiest and least complicated of all—addresses most of the scenarios for which some custom session management is desirable. So let's tackle it first.

Building a Custom Session-State Provider

A session-state provider is the component in charge of serving any data related to the current session. Invoked when the request needs to acquire state information, it retrieves data from a given storage medium and returns that to the module. Invoked by the module when the request ends, it writes the supplied data to the storage layer. As mentioned, ASP.NET supports three state providers, as listed in Table 13-11.

Table 13-11 Default State Providers

Name	Class	Storage Medium
InProc	*InProcSessionStateStore*	Stores data as live objects in the ASP.NET *Cache*.
StateServer	*OutOfProcSessionStateStore*	Stores data as serialized objects to the memory of a Windows service named *aspnet_state.exe*.
SQLServer	*SqlSessionStateStore*	Stores data as serialized objects into a SQL Server database.

In ASP.NET 2.0, you can write your own state-provider class that uses the storage medium of your choice. Note that the default state providers also make use of various helper classes to move data around. In your custom provider, you can replace these classes, too, or just stick to the standard ones.

Defining the Session-State Store

A state provider (also often referred to as a *session-state store*) is a class that inherits from *SessionStateStoreProviderBase*. The main methods of the interface are listed in Table 13-12.

Table 13-12 Methods of the *SessionStateStoreProviderBase* Class

Method	Description
CreateNewStoreData	Creates an object to contain the data of a new session. It should return an object of type *SessionStateStoreData*.
CreateUninitializedItem	Creates a new and uninitialized session in the data source. The method is called when an expired session is requested in a cookieless session state. In this case, the module has to generate a new session ID. The session item created by the method prevents the next request with the newly generated session ID from being mistaken for a request directed at an expired session.
Dispose	Releases all resources (other than memory) used by the state provider.
EndRequest	Called by the default session-state module when it begins to handle the *EndRequest* event.
GetItem	Returns the session item matching the specified ID from the data store. The session item selected is locked for reading. The method serves requests from applications that use read-only session state.

Table 13-12   Methods of the *SessionStateStoreProviderBase* Class

Method	Description
GetItemExclusive	Returns the session item matching the specified ID from the data store and locks it for writing. Used for requests originated by applications that use read/write session state.
Initialize	Inherited from base provider class, performs one-off initialization.
InitializeRequest	Called by the default session-state module when it begins to handle the *AcquireRequestState* event.
ReleaseItemExclusive	Unlocks a session item that was previously locked by a call to the *GetItemExclusive* method.
RemoveItem	Removes a session item from the data store. Called when a session ends or is abandoned.
ResetItemTimeout	Resets the expiration time of a session item. Invoked when the application has session support disabled.
SetAndReleaseItemExclusive	Writes a session item to the data store.
SetItemExpireCallback	The default module calls this method to notify the data store class that the caller has registered a *Session_End* handler.

Classes that inherit the *SessionStateStoreProviderBase* class work with the default ASP.NET session-state module and replace only the part of it that handles session-state data storage and retrieval. Nothing else in the session functionality changes.

Locking and Expiration

Can two requests for the same session occur concurrently? You bet. Take a look at Figure 13-3. Requests can arrive in parallel—for example, from two frames or when a user works with two instances of the same browser, the second of which is opened as a new window. To avoid problems, a state provider must implement a locking mechanism to serialize access to a session. The session-state module determines whether the request requires read-only or read/write access to the session state and calls *GetItem* or *GetItemExclusive* accordingly. In the implementation of these methods, the provider's author should create a reader/writer lock mechanism to allow multiple concurrent reads but prevent writing on locked sessions.

Another issue relates to letting the session-state module know when a given session has expired. The session-state module calls the method *SetItemExpireCallback* when there's a *Session_End* handler defined in *global.asax*. Through the method, the state provider receives a callback function with the following prototype:

```
public delegate void SessionStateItemExpireCallback(
    string sessionID, SessionStateStoreData item);
```

It has to store that delegate internally and invoke it whenever the given session times out. Supporting expiration callbacks is optional and, in fact, only the *InProc* provider actually supports it. If your custom provider is not willing to support expiration callbacks, you should instruct the *SetItemExpireCallback* method to return *false*.

> **Note**   A provider that intends to support cookieless sessions must also implement the *CreateUninitialized* method to write a blank session item to the data store. More precisely, a blank session item means an item that is complete in every way except that it contains no session data. In other words, the session item should contain the session ID, creation date, and perhaps lock IDs, but no data. ASP.NET 2.0 generates a new ID (in cookieless mode only) whenever a request is made for an expired session. The session-state module generates the new session ID and redirects the browser. Without an uninitialized session item marked with a newly generated ID, the new request will again be recognized as a request for an expired session.

Replacing the Session Data Dictionary

SessionStateStoreData is the class that represents the session item—that is, a data structure that contains all the data that is relevant to the session. *GetItem* and *GetItemExclusive*, in fact, are defined to return an instance of this class. The class has three properties: *Items*, *StaticObjects*, and *Timeout*.

Items indicates the collection of name/values that will ultimately be passed to the page through the *Session* property. *StaticObjects* lists the static objects belonging to the session, such as objects declared in the *global.asax* file and scoped to the session. As the name suggests, *Timeout* indicates how long, in minutes, the session-state item is valid. The default value is 20 minutes.

Once the session-state module has acquired the session state for the request, it flushes the contents of the *Items* collection to a new instance of the *HttpSessionStateContainer* class. This object is then passed to the constructor of the *HttpSessionState* class and becomes the data container behind the familiar *Session* property.

The *SessionStateStoreData* class is used in the definition of the base state provider class, meaning that you can't entirely replace it. If you don't like it, you can inherit a new class from it, however. To both the session module and state provider, the container of the session items is merely a class that implements the *ISessionStateItemCollection* interface. The real class being used by default is *SessionStateItemCollection*. You can replace this class with your own as long as you implement the aforementioned interface.

> **Tip**   To write a state provider, you might find helpful the methods of the *SessionStateUtility* class. The class contains methods to serialize and deserialize session items to and from the storage medium. Likewise, the class has methods to extract the dictionary of data for a session and add it to the HTTP context and the *Session* property.

Registering a Custom Session-State Provider

To make a custom session-state provider available to an application, you need to register it in the *web.config* file. Suppose you have called the provider class *SampleSessionStateProvider* and compiled it to *MyLib*. Here's what you need to enter:

```
<system.web>
    <sessionState mode="Custom"
```

```
      customProvider="SampleSessionProvider">
      <providers>
        <add name="SampleSessionProvider"
          type="SampleSessionStateProvider, MyLib" />
      </providers>
    </sessionState>
</system.web>
```

The name of the provider is arbitrary but necessary. To force the session-state module to find it, set the *mode* attribute to *Custom*.

Generating a Custom Session ID

To generate the session ID, ASP.NET 2.0 uses a special component named *SessionIDManager*. Technically speaking, the class is neither an HTTP module nor a provider. More simply, it is a class that inherits from *System.Object* and implements the *ISessionIDManager* interface. You can replace this component with a custom component as long as the component implements the same *ISessionIDManager* interface. To help you decide whether you really need a custom session-ID generator, let's review some facts about the default module.

The Default Behavior

The default session-ID module generates a session ID as an array of bytes with a cryptographically strong random sequence of 15 values. The array is then encoded to a string of 24 URL-accepted characters, which is what the system will recognize as the session ID.

The session ID can be round-tripped to the client in either an HTTP cookie or a mangled URL, based on the value of the *cookieless* attribute in the *<sessionState>* configuration section. Note that when cookieless sessions are used, the session-ID module is responsible for adding the ID to the URL and redirecting the browser. The default generator redirects the browser to a fake URL like the following one:

```
http://www.contoso.com/test/(S(session_id))/page.aspx
```

In ASP.NET 1.x, the fake URL is slightly different and doesn't include the *S(...)* delimiters. How can a request for this fake URL be served correctly? In the case of a cookieless session, the session-ID module depends on a small and simple ISAPI filter (*aspnet_filter.dll*, which is also available to ASP.NET 1.x) to dynamically rewrite the real URL to access. The request is served correctly, but the path on the address bar doesn't change. The detected session ID is placed in a request header named *AspFilterSessionId*.

A Homemade Session-ID Manager

Now that we've ascertained that a session-ID manager is a class that implements *ISessionID-Manager*, you have two options: build a new class and implement the interface from the ground up, or inherit a new class from *SessionIDManager* and override a couple of virtual methods to apply some personalization. The first option offers maximum flexibility; the second is simpler and quicker to implement, and it addresses the most compelling reason you might have to build a custom session-ID generator—supply your own session-ID values.

Let's start by reviewing the methods of the *ISessionIDManager* interface, which are shown in Table 13-13.

Table 13-13   Methods of the *ISessionIDManager* Interface

Method	Description
CreateSessionID	Virtual method. It creates a unique session identifier for the session.
Decode	Decodes the session ID using *HttpUtility.UrlDecode*.
Encode	Encodes the session ID using *HttpUtility.UrlEncode*.
Initialize	Invoked by the session state immediately after instantiation; performs one-time initialization of the component.
InitializeRequest	Invoked by the session state when the session state is being acquired for the request.
GetSessionID	Gets the session ID from the current HTTP request.
RemoveSessionID	Deletes the session ID from the cookie or from the URL.
SaveSessionID	Saves a newly created session ID to the HTTP response.
Validate	Confirms that the session ID is valid.

If you plan to roll your own completely custom session-ID generator, bear in mind the following points:

- The algorithm you choose for ID generation is critical. If you don't implement strong cryptographic randomness, a malicious user can guess a valid session ID when the same session is still active, thus accessing some user's data. (This is known as session hijacking.) A good example of a custom session-ID algorithm is one that returns a globally unique identifier (GUID).

- You can choose whether to support cookieless sessions. If you do, you have to endow the component with the ability to extract the session ID from the HTTP request and redirect the browser. You probably need an ISAPI filter or HTTP module to preprocess the request and enter appropriate changes. The algorithm you use to store session IDs without cookies is up to you.

If you are absolutely determined to have the system use your session IDs, you derive a new class from *SessionIDManager* and override two methods: *CreateSessionID* and *Validate*. The former returns a string that contains the session ID. The latter validates a given session ID to ensure that it conforms to the specification you set. Once you have created a custom session-ID module, you register it in the configuration file. Here's how to do it:

```
<sessionState
    sessionIDManagerType="Samples.MyIDManager, MyLib" />
</sessionState>
```

Session-State Performance Best Practices

State management is a necessary evil. By enabling it, you charge your application with an extra burden. The September 2005 issue of *MSDN Magazine* contains an article with the ASP.NET team's coding best practices to reduce the performance impact of session state on Web applications.

The first guideline is disabling session state whenever possible. However, to prevent the session from expiring, the HTTP module still marks the session as active in the data store. For out-of-process state servers, this means that a roundtrip is made. A custom session-ID manager returning a null session ID for requests that are known not to require session state is the best way to work around this issue and avoid the overhead entirely. (Write a class that inherits from *SessionIDManager* and override *GetSessionID*.)

The second guideline entails minimizing contention on session data by avoiding frames and downloadable resources served by session-enabled handlers.

The third guideline regards data serialization and deserialization. You should always use simple types and break complex classes to arrays of simple properties at least as far as session management is concerned. In other words, I'm not suggesting that you factor out your DAL classes—just the way you serialize them into the session store. An alternate approach entails building a custom serialization algorithm that is optimized for session-state storage. Breaking a class into various properties—each stored in a session slot—is advantageous not only because of the simple types being used, but also because the extreme granularity of the solution minimizes the data to save in case of changes. If one property changes, only one slot with a simple type is updated instead of a single slot with a complex type.

The View State of a Page

ASP.NET pages supply the *ViewState* property to let applications build a call context and retain values across two successive requests for the same page. The view state represents the state of the page when it was last processed on the server. The state is persisted—usually, but not necessarily, on the client side—and is restored before the page request is processed.

By default, the view state is maintained as a hidden field added to the page. As such, it travels back and forth with the page itself. Although sent to the client, the view state does not represent, nor does it contain, any information specifically aimed at the client. The information stored in view state is pertinent only to the page and some of its child controls and is not consumed in any way by the browser.

Using the view state has advantages and disadvantages that you might want to carefully balance prior to making your state management decision. First, the view state does not require any server resources and is simple to implement and use. Because it's a physical part of the page, it's fast to retrieve and use. This last point, while in some respects a strong one, turns into a considerable weakness as soon as you consider the page performance from a wider perspective.

Because the view state is packed with the page, it inevitably charges the HTML code transferred over HTTP with a few extra kilobytes of data—useless data, moreover, from the browser's perspective. A complex real-world page, especially if it does not even attempt to optimize and restrict the use of the view state, can easily find 20 KB of extra stuff packed in the HTML code sent out to the browser.

In summary, the view state is one of the most important features of ASP.NET, not so much because of its technical relevance but because it allows most of the magic of the Web Forms model. Used without strict criteria, though, the view state can easily become a burden for pages.

The *StateBag* Class

The *StateBag* class is the class behind the view state that manages the information that ASP.NET pages and controls want to persist across successive posts of the same page instance. The class works like a dictionary and, in addition, implements the *IStateManager* interface. The *Page* and *Control* base classes expose the view state through the *ViewState* property. So you can add or remove items from the *StateBag* class as you would with any dictionary object, as the following code demonstrates:

```
ViewState["FontSize"] = value;
```

You should start writing to the view state only after the *Init* event fires for the page request. You can read from the view state during any stage of the page life cycle, but not after the page enters rendering mode—that is, after the *PreRender* event fires.

View State Properties

Table 13-14 lists all the properties defined in the *StateBag* class.

Table 13-14   Properties of the *StateBag* Class

Property	Description
Count	Gets the number of elements stored in the object.
Item	Indexer property. It gets or sets the value of an item stored in the class.
Keys	Gets a collection object containing the keys defined in the object.
Values	Gets a collection object containing all the values stored in object.

Each item in the *StateBag* class is represented by a *StateItem* object. An instance of the *StateItem* object is implicitly created when you set the *Item* indexer property with a value or when you call the *Add* method. Items added to the *StateBag* object are tracked until the view state is serialized prior to the page rendering. Items serialized are those with the *IsDirty* property set to *true*.

View State Methods

Table 13-15 lists all the methods you can call in the *StateBag* class.

Table 13-15   Methods of the *StateBag* Class

Method	Description
Add	Adds a new *StateItem* object to the collection. If the item already exists, it gets updated.
Clear	Removes all items from the current view state.
GetEnumerator	Returns an object that scrolls over all the elements in the *StateBag*.
IsItemDirty	Indicates whether the element with the specified key has been modified during the request processing.
Remove	Removes the specified object from the *StateBag* object.

The *IsItemDirty* method represents an indirect way to call into the *IsDirty* property of the specified *StateItem* object.

> **Note**   The view state for the page is a cumulative property that results from the contents of the *ViewState* property of the page plus the view state of all the controls hosted in the page.

Common Issues with View State

Architecturally speaking, the importance of the view state cannot be denied, as it is key to setting up the automatic state management feature of ASP.NET. A couple of hot issues are connected to the usage of the view state, however. Most frequently asked questions about the view state are related to security and performance. Can we say that the view state is inherently secure and cannot be tampered with? How will the extra information contained in the view state affect the download time of the page? Let's find out.

Encrypting and Securing

Many developers are doubtful about using view state just because it is stored in a hidden field and left on the client at the mercy of potential intruders. Although the data is stored in a hashed format, there's no absolute guarantee that it cannot be tampered with. The first remark is that the view state as implemented in ASP.NET is inherently more secure than any other hidden fields you might use (and that you were likely using, say, in old classic ASP applications). The second remark is that only data confidentiality is at risk of being disclosed. While this is a problem, it is minor compared to code injection.

Freely accessible in a hidden field named *__VIEWSTATE*, the view state information is, by default, hashed and Base64 encoded. To decode it on the client, a potential attacker must accomplish a number of steps, but the action is definitely possible. Once decoded, though, the view state only reveals its contents—that is, confidentiality is at risk. However, there's no way an attacker can modify the view state to post malicious data. A tampered view state, in fact, is normally detected on the server and an exception is thrown.

For performance reasons, the view state is not encrypted. If needed, though, you can turn the option on by acting on the *web.config* file, as follows:

```
<machineKey validation="3DES" />
```

When the validation attribute is set to 3DES, the view-state validation technique uses 3DES encryption and doesn't hash the contents.

Machine Authentication Check

As mentioned in Chapter 3, the *@Page* directive contains an attribute named *EnableView-StateMac*, whose only purpose is making the view state a bit more secure by detecting any possible attempt at corrupting the original data. When serialized, and if *EnableView-StateMac* is set to *true*, the view state is appended with a validator hash string based on the algorithm and the key defined in the *<machineKey>* section of the configuration file. The resulting array of bytes—the output of the *StateBag*'s binary serialization plus the hash value—is Base64 encoded. By default, the encryption algorithm to calculate the hash is SHA1, and the encryption and decryption keys are auto-generated and stored in the Web server machine's Local Security Authority (LSA) subsystem. The LSA is a protected component of Windows NT, Windows 2000, Windows Server 2003, and Windows XP. It provides security services and maintains information about all aspects of local security on a system.

If *EnableViewStateMac* is *true*, when the page posts back, the hash value is extracted and used to verify that the returned view state has not been tampered with on the client. If it has been, an exception is thrown. The net effect is that you might be able to read the contents of the view state, but to replace it you need the encryption key, which is in the Web server's LSA. The *MAC* in the name of the *EnableViewStateMac* property stands for *Machine Authentication Check*, which is enabled by default. If you disable the attribute, an attacker could alter the view-state information on the client and send a modified version to the server and have ASP.NET bliss-fully use that tampered-with information.

To reinforce the security of the view state, in ASP.NET 1.1 the *ViewStateUserKey* property has been added to the *Page* class. The property evaluates to a user-specific string (typically, the session ID) that is known on the server and hard to guess on the client. ASP.NET uses the content of the property as an input argument to the hash algorithm that generates the MAC code.

Size Thresholds and Page Throughput

My personal opinion is that you should be concerned about the view state, but not for the potential security holes it might open in your code—it can only let hackers exploit existing holes. You should be more concerned about the overall performance and responsiveness of the page. Especially for feature-rich pages that use plenty of controls, the view state can reach a considerable size, measured in KB of data. Such an extra burden taxes all requests, in downloads and uploads, and ends up creating serious overhead for the application as a whole.

What would be a reasonable size for an ASP.NET page? And for the view state of a page? Let's take a sample page that contains a grid control bound to about 100 records (the Customers table in the Northwind database of SQL Server).

```html
<html>
<head runat="server">
    <title>Measure Up Your ViewState (2.0)</title>
</head>
<script language="javascript">
function ShowViewStateSize()
{
    var buf = document.forms[0]["__VIEWSTATE"].value;
    alert("View state is " + buf.length + " bytes");
}
</script>
<body>
    <form id="form1" runat="server">
        <input type="button" value="Show View State Size"
                onclick="ShowViewStateSize()">
        <asp:SqlDataSource ID="SqlDataSource1" runat="server"
                SelectCommand="SELECT companyname, contactname, contacttitle
                                FROM customers"
                ConnectionString="<%$ ConnectionStrings:LocalNWind %>"
        <asp:DataGrid ID="grid" runat="server"
                DataSourceID="SqlDataSource1" />
    </form>
</body>
</html>
```

In ASP.NET 2.0, the total size of the page is about 20 KB. The view state alone, though, takes up about 11 KB. If you port the same page back to ASP.NET 1.x, results are even worse. The whole page amounts to 28 KB, while the view state alone amounts to a burdensome 19 KB. Two conclusions can be drawn from these numbers:

- In ASP.NET 2.0, the view-state field appears to be more compact. (I'll discuss this in more detail later in the chapter.)

- The view state takes up a large share of the downloaded bytes for the page. You won't be too far from the truth if you estimate the view-state size to be about 60 percent of the entire page size.

What can you do about this? First, let's play with some numbers to determine a reasonable goal for view-state size in our applications. You should endeavor to keep a page size around 30 KB, to the extent that this is possible, of course. For example, the Google home page is less than 4 KB. The home page of *http://www.asp.net* amounts to about 50 KB. The Google site is not written with ASP.NET, so nothing can be said about the view state. But what about the view-state size of the home of *http://www.asp.net*? Interestingly enough, that page has only 1 KB of view state. On the other hand, the page *http://www.asp.net/ControlGallery/ default.aspx?Category=7&tabindex=0* is larger than 500 KB, of which 120 KB is view state.

The ideal size for a view state is around 7 KB; it is optimal if you can keep it down to 3 KB or so. In any case, the view state, regardless of its absolute size, should never exceed 30 percent of the page size.

> **Note**   Where do these numbers come from? "From my personal experience," would perhaps be a valid answer, but not necessarily a good and exhaustive one. Let's put it this way: the smallest you can keep a page is the best size. To me, 30 KB looks like a reasonable compromise, because most things can be stuffed into that size. Clearly, if you have 250 items to display, your page size can grow up to 1 MB or so. In the end, having a smaller or larger view state is a design choice and is mostly application-specific. Within these boundaries, though, a few guidelines can be stated. The most important guideline is not so much that view state should be limited to a few KB, but that it should take a minimal percentage of the overall page size. Which percentage? Being the view-state helper, I'd say no more than 25 percent or 30 percent at the most. But here I'm just throwing out numbers using a bit of common sense. If you can disable the view state altogether, do it. At the very least, you should avoid storing the avoidable items, such as a long list of countries, there.

Programming Web Forms Without View State

By default, the view state is enabled for all server controls; however, this doesn't mean that you strictly need it all the time and for all controls. The use of the view-state feature should be carefully monitored because it can hinder your code. View state saves you from a lot of coding and, more important, makes coding simpler and smarter. However, if you find you're paying too much for this feature, drop view state altogether and reinitialize the state of the size-critical controls at every postback. In this case, disabling view state saves processing time and speeds up the download process.

Disabling View State

You can disable the view state for an entire page by using the *EnableViewState* attribute of the *@Page* directive. While this is not generally a recommended option, you should definitely consider it for read-only pages that either don't post back or don't need state to be maintained:

```
<% @Page EnableViewState="false" %>
```

A better approach entails disabling the view state only for some of the controls hosted in the page. To disable it on a per-control basis, set the *EnableViewState* property of the control to *false*, as shown here:

```
<asp:datagrid runat="server" EnableViewState="false">
    ...
</asp:datagrid>
```

While developing the page, you can keep the size of the view state under control by enabling tracing on the page. The tracer doesn't show the total amount of the view state for the page, but it lets you form a precise idea of what each control does. In Figure 13-8, the page contains a relatively simple *DataGrid* control. As you can see, the cells of the grid take up a large part of the view state. The *TableCell* control, in particular, strips the view state of all its user interfaces, including text, column, and row-span style attributes.

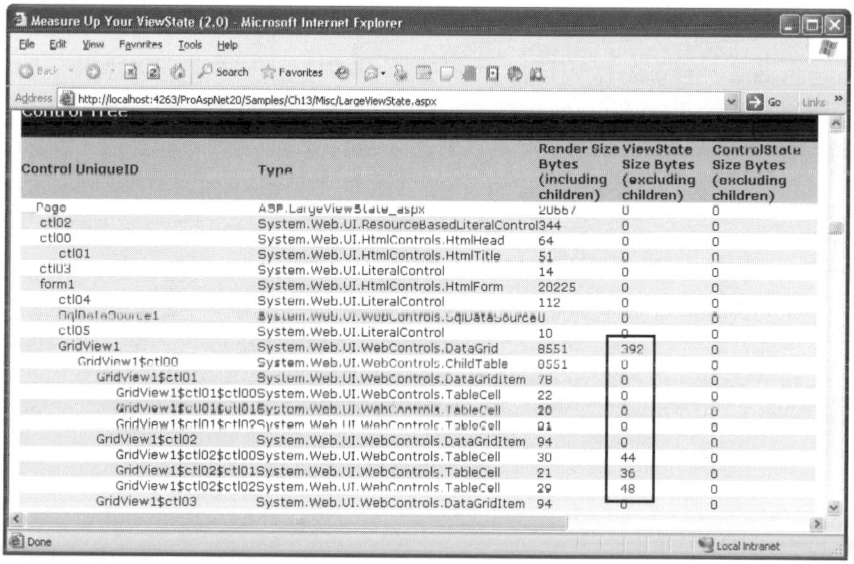

Figure 13-8   All controls, including child controls, contribute to the view-state burden.

> **Note**   Like all other data-bound controls, the *DataGrid* doesn't store its data source in the view state. However, the data source bound to the control has some impact on the view-state size. Each constituent control in the overall data-bound user interface takes up some view state for its settings. The number of child controls (for example, rows and cells in a *DataGrid*) obviously depend on the data source.

Determining When to Disable View State

Let's briefly recap what view state is all about and what you might lose if you ban it from your pages. View state represents the current state of the page and its controls just before the page is rendered to HTML. When the page posts back, the view state—a sort of call context for the page request—is recovered from the hidden field, deserialized, and used to initialize the server controls in the page and the page itself. However, as pointed out in Chapter 3, this is only the first half of the story.

After loading the view state, the page reads client-side posted information and uses those values to override most of the settings for the server controls. Applying posted values overrides some of the settings read from the view state. You understand that in this case, and only for the properties modified by posted values, the view state represents an extra burden.

Let's examine a typical case. Suppose you have a page with a text box server control. What you expect is that when the page posts back, the text box server control is automatically assigned the value set on the client. Well, to meet this rather common requirement, you *don't* need view state. Consider the following page:

```
<% @Page language="c#" %>
<form runat="server">
    <asp:textbox runat="server" enableviewstate="false"
        id="theInput" readonly="false" text="Type here" />
    <asp:checkbox runat="server" enableviewstate="false"
        id="theCheck" text="Check me" />
    <asp:button runat="server" text="Click" onclick="OnPost" />
</form>
```

Apparently, the behavior of the page is stateful even if view state is disabled for a couple of controls. The reason lies in the fact that you are using two server controls—*TextBox* and *CheckBox*—whose key properties—*Text* and *Checked*—are updated according to the values set by the user. For these properties, posted values will override any setting that view state might have set. As a result, as long as you're simply interested in persisting these properties you don't need view state at all.

Likewise, you don't need view state for all control properties that are set at design time in the *.aspx* file and are not expected to change during the session. The following code illustrates this point:

```
<asp:textbox runat="server" id="TextBox1" Text="Some text"
             MaxLength="20" ReadOnly="true" />
```

You don't need view state to keep the *Text* property of a *TextBox* up to date; you do need view state to keep up to date, say, *ReadOnly* or *MaxLength*, as long as these properties have their values changed during the page lifetime. If the two properties are constant during the page lifetime, you don't need view state for them, either.

So when is view state really necessary?

View state is necessary whenever your page requires that accessory control properties (other than those subject to posted values) are updated during the page lifetime. In this context, "updated" means that their original value changes—either the default value or the value you assign to the property at design time. Consider the following form:

```
<script runat="server">
   void Page_Load(object sender, EventArgs e)
   {
      if (!IsPostBack)
         theInput.ReadOnly = true;
   }
</script>

<form id="form1" runat="server">
   <asp:textbox runat="server" id="theInput" text="Am I read-only?" />
   <asp:button ID="Button1" runat="server" text="Click" onclick="OnPost" />
</form>
```

When the page is first loaded, the text box becomes read-only. Next, you click the button to post back. If view state is enabled, the page works as expected and the text box remains read-only. If view state is disabled for the text box, the original setting for the *ReadOnly* property is restored—in this case, *false*.

In general, you can do without view state whenever the state can be deduced either from the client or from the run-time environment. In contrast, doing without view state is hard whenever state information can't be dynamically inferred and you can't ensure that all properties are correctly restored when the page posts back. This is exactly what view state guarantees at the cost of extra bytes when downloading and uploading. To save those bytes, you must provide an alternative approach.

> **Tip**   You can enable and disable the view state programmatically for the page as well as individual controls by using the Boolean *EnableViewState* property.

Disabling the view state can also pose subtler problems that are difficult to diagnose and fix, especially if you're working with third-party controls or, in general, controls for which you have source-code access. Some ASP.NET controls, in fact, might save to the view state not just properties that are officially part of the programming interface (and that can be set accordingly), but also behavioral properties that serve internal purposes and are marked as protected or even private. Unfortunately, for these controls, you do not have the option of disabling the view state. But ASP.NET 2.0 comes to the rescue with *control state*.

Changes in the ASP.NET 2.0 View State

Two important changes occurred to the view-state implementation in ASP.NET 2.0. As a result, two major drawbacks have been fixed, or at least greatly mitigated. The size of the view state is significantly reduced as a result of a new serialization format. The contents of the view state have been split into two states: classic view state and control state. Unlike the classic view state, the control state can't be disabled programmatically and is considered a sort of private view state for a control. This feature is ideal for developers building third-party ASP.NET controls, as it helps them to keep critical persistent properties out of the reach of end page developers.

The Serialization Format

In Figure 13-9, you see the same page running under ASP.NET 1.x and ASP.NET 2.0. A client-side button retrieves the view-state string and calculates its length. The JavaScript code needed is pretty simple:

```javascript
<script language="javascript">
    function ShowViewStateSize() {
        var buf = document.forms[0]["__VIEWSTATE"].value;
        alert("View state is " + buf.length + " bytes");
    }
</script>
```

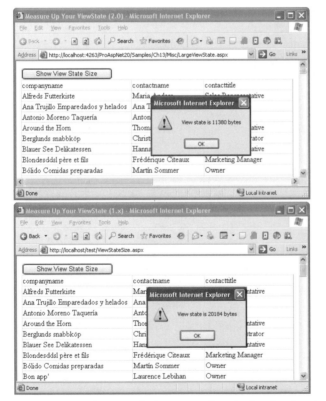

Figure 13-9   The overall view-state size obtained scriptwise.

As you can see, the size of the view state for the same page is quite different, and significantly smaller, in ASP.NET 2.0. Let's see why.

The contents persisted to the view state are ultimately the results of the serialization process applied to an object graph. The object graph results from the hierarchical concatenation of the view state of each individual control participating in the page's construction. The data going to the view state is accumulated in tuples made of special containers such as *Pair* and *Triplet*. *Pair* and *Triplet* are extremely simple classes containing two and three members, respectively, of type *object*. Each object is serialized to the stream according to various rules:

- Simple types such as strings, dates, bytes, characters, Booleans, and all types of numbers are written as is to a binary stream.

- Enum types, and *Color*, *Type*, *Unit* dictionary objects are serialized in a way that is specific to the type.

- All other objects are checked to see whether there's a type converter object to convert them to a string. If there is, the type converter is used.

- Objects that lack a type converter are serialized through the binary formatter. If the type is not serializable, an exception is thrown.

- *Pair*, *Triplet*, and *ArrayList* objects are recursively serialized.

The resulting stream is hashed (or encrypted, based on configuration settings), Base64 encoded, and then persisted to the hidden field. This is more or less what happens already in ASP.NET 1.x. So where's the difference?

The difference is all in a little detail lying in the folds of type serialization. The type of each member being serialized is identified with a byte—specifically, nonprintable characters in the 1 through 50 range. In ASP.NET 1.x, for the same purpose printable characters were used, such as <, >, l, s, I, and a few more. This change brings two benefits—a smaller size and a little more speed in deserialization.

> **Note** The class behind the new serialization format of the ASP.NET 2.0 view state is a new type of formatter object—the *ObjectStateFormatter* class. Specifically designed in ASP.NET 2.0 to serialize and deserialize object graphs to and from a binary writer, the class is a yet another .NET formatter object, as it also implements the *IFormatter* interface. In ASP.NET 2.0, the *ObjectStateFormatter* class replaces the *LosFormatter* class used in ASP.NET 1.x. *LosFormatter* writes to a text writer. This change is not an optimization per se, but it allows a number of other improvements. For example, it allows indexing of strings and more compact storage, as non-string values (such as numbers and Booleans) are written as binaries and take up much less space.

The Control State

It is not uncommon for a server control to persist information across postbacks. For example, consider what happens to a *DataGrid* control modified to support autoreverse sorting. When the user clicks to sort by a column, the control compares the current sort expression and the new sort expression. If the two are equivalent, the sort direction is reversed. How does the *DataGrid* track the current sort direction? If you don't place the sort direction property in the control's view state, it will be lost as soon as the control renders to the browser.

This kind of property is not intended to be used for plain configuration such as pager style or background color. It has an impact on how the control works. What if the control is then used in a page that has the view state disabled? In ASP.NET 1.x, the control feature just stops working. Private or protected properties that are to be persisted across two requests should not be placed in the view state. In ASP.NET 1.x, you can use the session state, the ASP.NET cache, or perhaps another, custom hidden field.

In ASP.NET 2.0, the *control state* is a special data container introduced just to create a sort of protected zone inside the classic view state. It is safer to use the control state than the view state because application-level and page-level settings cannot affect it. If your existing custom control has private or protected properties stored in the view state, you should move all of them to the control state in ASP.NET 2.0. Anything you store in the control state remains there until it is explicitly removed. Also the control state is sent down to the client and uploaded when the page posts back. The more data you pack into it, the more data is moved back and forth between the browser and the Web server. You should use control state in ASP.NET 2.0, but you should do so carefully.

Programming the Control State

The implementation of the control state is left to the programmer, which is both good and bad. It is bad because you have to manually implement serialization and deserialization for your control's state. It is good because you can control exactly how the control works and tweak its code to achieve optimal performance in the context in which you're using it. The page's infrastructure takes care of the actual data encoding and serialization. The control state is processed along with the view state information and undergoes the same treatment as for serialization and Base64 encoding. The control state is also persisted within the same view state's hidden field. The root object serialized to the view state stream is actually a *Pair* object that contains the control state as the first element and the classic view state as the second member.

There's no ready-made dictionary object to hold the items that form the control state. You no longer have to park your objects in a fixed container such as the *ViewState* state bag—you can maintain control-state data in plain private or protected members. Among other things, this means that access to data is faster because it is more direct and is not mediated by a dictionary object. For example, if you need to track the sort direction of a grid, you can do so using the following variable:

```
private int _sortDirection;
```

In ASP.NET 1.x, you have to resort to the following:

```
private int _sortDirection
{
   get {return Parse.Int32(ViewState["SortDirection"]);)
   set {ViewState["SortDirection"] = value;)
}
```

To restore control state, the *Page* class invokes the *LoadControlState* on all controls that have registered with the page object as controls that require control state. The following pseudocode shows the control's typical behavior:

```
private override void LoadControlState(object savedState)
{
    // Make a copy of the saved state.
    // You know what type of object this is because
    // you saved it in the SaveControlState method.
    object[] currentState = (object[]) savedState;
    if (currentState == null)
        return;

    // Initialize any private/protected member you stored
    // in the control state. The values are packed in the same
    // order and format you stored them in the SaveControlState method.
    _myProperty1 = (int) currentState[0];
    _myProperty2 = (string) currentState[1];
    ...
}
```

The *LoadControlState* method receives an object identical to the one you created in *SaveControlState*. As a control developer, you know that type very well and can use this knowledge to extract any information that's useful for restoring the control state. For example, you might want to use an array of objects in which every slot corresponds to a particular property.

The following pseudocode gives an idea of the structure of the *SaveControlState* method:

```
private override object SaveControlState()
{
    // Declare a properly sized array of objects
    object[] stateToSave = new Object[...];

    // Fill the array with local property values
    stateToSave[0] = _myProperty1;
    stateToSave[1] = _myProperty2;
    ...

    // Return the array
    return stateToSave;
}
```

You allocate a new data structure (such as a *Pair*, a *Triplet*, an array, or a custom type) and fill it with the private properties to persist across postbacks. The method terminates, returning this object to the ASP.NET runtime. The object is then serialized and encoded to a Base64 stream. The class that you use to collect the control state properties must be serializable. We'll examine control state in my companion book to this one, *Programming Microsoft ASP.NET 2.0 Applications: Advanced Topics* (Microsoft Press, 2005).

Keeping the View State on the Server

As discussed so far, there's one major reason to keep the view state off the client browser: the more stuff you pack into the view state, the more time the page takes to download and upload because the view state is held in a hidden field. It is important to note that the client-side hidden field is not set in stone, but is simply the default storage medium where the view state information can be stored. Let's see how to proceed to save the view state on the Web server in the sample file.

The *LosFormatter* Class

To design an alternative storage scheme for the view state, we need to put our hands on the string that ASP.NET stores in the hidden field. The string will be saved in a server-side file and read from where the page is being processed. The class that ASP.NET 1.x actually uses to serialize and deserialize the view state is *LosFormatter*.

The *LosFormatter* class has a simple programming interface made of only two publicly callable methods—*Serialize* and *Deserialize*. The *Serialize* method writes the final Base64 representation of the view state to a *Stream* or *TextWriter* object:

```
public void Serialize(Stream stream, object viewState);
public void Serialize(TextWriter output, object viewState);
```

The *Deserialize* method builds an object from a stream, a *TextReader* object, or a plain Base64 string:

```
public object Deserialize(Stream stream);
public object Deserialize(TextReader input);
public object Deserialize(string input);
```

The *LosFormatter* class is the entry point in the view-state internal mechanism. By using it, you can be sure everything will happen exactly as in the default case and, more important, you're shielded from any other details.

The *ObjectStateFormatter* Class

As mentioned, the *LosFormatter* class is replaced by *ObjectStateFormatter* in ASP.NET 2.0. *LosFormatter* is still available for compatibility reasons, however. The new serializer writes to a binary writer, whereas *LosFormatter* writes to a text writer. *LosFormatter* needs to turn everything to a string for storage, while *ObjectStateFormatter* capitalizes on the underlying binary model and writes out just bytes. As a result, *ObjectStateFormatter* serializes the same object graph into roughly half the size, and spends about half as much time in the serialization and deserialization process.

The *Serialize* method of *ObjectStateFormatter* writes the final Base64 representation of the view state to a *Stream* or a string object:

```
public string Serialize(Object graph);
public void Serialize(Stream stream, Object graph);
```

The *Deserialize* method of *ObjectStateFormatter* builds an object from a stream or a plain Base64 string:

```
public object Deserialize(Stream stream);
public object Deserialize(string input);
```

Creating a View-Stateless Page

The *Page* class provides a couple of protected virtual methods that the run time uses when it needs to deserialize or serialize the view state. The methods are named *LoadPageStateFromPersistenceMedium* and *SavePageStateToPersistenceMedium*:

```
protected virtual void SavePageStateToPersistenceMedium(object viewState);
protected virtual object LoadPageStateFromPersistenceMedium();
```

If you override both methods, you can load and save view-state information from and to anything. In particular, you can use a storage medium that is different from the hidden field used by the default implementation. . Because the methods are defined as protected members, the only way to redefine them is by creating a new class and making it inherit from *Page*. The following code just gives you an idea of the default behavior of *LoadPageStateFromPersistenceMedium*:

```
string m_viewState = Request.Form["__VIEWSTATE"];
ObjectStateFormatter m_formatter = new ObjectStateFormatter();
StateBag viewStateBag = m_formatter.Deserialize(m_viewState);
```

The structure of the page we're going to create is as follows:

```
public class ServerViewStatePage : Page
{
    protected override
        object LoadPageStateFromPersistenceMedium()
    { ... }
    protected override
        void SavePageStateToPersistenceMedium(object viewState)
    { ... }
}
```

Saving the View State to a Web Server File

The tasks accomplished by the *SavePageStateToPersistenceMedium* method are easy to explain and understand. The method takes a string as an argument, opens the output stream, and calls into the *LosFormatter* serializer:

```
protected override
void SavePageStateToPersistenceMedium(object viewStateBag)
{
    string file = GetFileName();
    StreamWriter sw = new StreamWriter(file);
    ObjectStateFormatter m_formatter = new ObjectStateFormatter();
```

```
        m_formatter.Serialize(sw, viewStateBag);
        sw.Close();
        return;
    }
```

How should we choose the name of the file to make sure that no conflicts arise? The view state is specific to a page request made within a particular session. So the session ID and the request URL are pieces of information that can be used to associate the request with the right file. Alternatively, you could give the view state file a randomly generated name and persist it in a custom hidden field within the page. Note that in this case you can't rely on the _VIEWSTATE_ hidden field because when overriding the methods, you alter the internal procedure that would have created it.

The *GetFileName* function in the preceding code gives the file a name according to the following pattern:

SessionID_URL`.viewstate`

Notice that for an ASP.NET application to create a local file, you must give the ASP.NET account special permissions on a file or folder. I suggest creating a new subfolder to contain all the view-state files. Deleting files for expired sessions can be a bit tricky, and a Windows service is probably the tool that works best.

Loading the View State from a Web Server File

In our implementation, the *LoadPageStateFromPersistenceMedium* method determines the name of the file to read from, extracts the Base64 string, and calls *LosFormatter* to deserialize:

```
protected override object LoadPageStateFromPersistenceMedium()
{
    object viewStateBag;

    string file = GetFileName();
    try {
        StreamReader sr = new StreamReader(file);
        string m_viewState = sr.ReadToEnd();
        sr.Close();
    }
    catch {
        throw new HttpException("The View State is invalid.");
    }
    LosFormatter m_formatter = new LosFormatter();
    try {
        viewStateBag = m_formatter.Deserialize(m_viewState);
    }
    catch {
        throw new HttpException("The View State is invalid.");
    }
    return viewStateBag;
}
```

To take advantage of this feature to keep view state on the server, you only need to change the parent class of the page code file to inherit from *ServerViewStatePage*:

```
public partial class TestPage : ServerViewStatePage
{
}
```

Figure 13-10 shows the view-state files created in a temporary folder on the Web server machine.

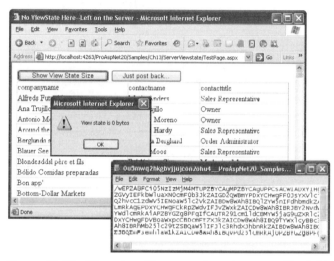

Figure 13-10   View state files created on the server. The folder must grant write permissions to the ASP.NET account.

The page shown in Figure 13-10 enables view state, but no hidden field is present in its client-side code.

Conclusion

Although HTTP is a stateless protocol, Web applications can't just do without certain forms of state. Moreover, state management is a hot topic for all real-world Web applications. Setting up an effective and efficient solution for state management is often the difference between an application being scalable or nonscalable.

One of the most-used forms of state is session state—that is, the state specific to a user and valid as long as that user works with the application. You can store session data in the memory of the ASP.NET worker process as well as in external processes, and even in a SQL Server table or in custom state provider. In spite of the radically different options, the top-level programming interface is identical. More important, the ASP.NET session state can be persisted in a Web farm or Web garden scenario as well.

In the next chapter, we'll deal with another extremely powerful form of state container—the *Cache* object.

Just the Facts

- Compared to the intrinsic *Session* object of classic ASP, the ASP.NET session state is nearly identical in use, but it's significantly richer in functionality and radically different in architecture.

- As of ASP.NET 2.0, there are four possibilities for working with the session state. The session state can be stored locally in the ASP.NET worker process; the session state can be maintained in a remote process; the session state can be managed by SQL Server and stored in an ad hoc database table. Finally, a fourth option is added in ASP.NET 2.0 and allows you to store the sessions in a custom component.

- In ASP.NET 2.0, the session-state subsystem was refactored to allow developers to replace most of the bits and pieces of functionality—a characteristic that is often referred to as session-state pluggability.

- By default, the view state is enabled for all server controls; however, this doesn't mean that you absolutely need it all the time and for all controls. The use of the view-state feature should be carefully monitored because it can hinder your code and unduly bloat your pages.

- In ASP.NET 2.0, the size of the view state is significantly reduced as a result of a new binary serialization format.

- The contents of the view state have been split into two states: classic view state and control state. Unlike the classic view state, the control state can't be disabled programmatically and is considered a sort of private view state for a control.

Chapter 14
ASP.NET Caching

In this chapter:

Caching Application Data. 591

Caching ASP.NET Pages. 624

Conclusion 644

Caching is the system's or the application's ability to save frequently used data to an intermediate storage medium. An intermediate storage medium is any support placed between the application and its primary data source that lets you persist and retrieve data more quickly than with the primary data source. In a typical Web scenario, the canonical intermediate storage medium is the Web server's memory, whereas the data source is the back end data management system. Obviously, you can design caching around the requirements and characteristics of each application, thus using as many layers of caching as needed to reach your performance goals.

In ASP.NET, caching comes in two independent but not exclusive flavors—caching application data, and caching the output of served pages. Page-output caching is the quickest way to take advantage of cache capabilities. You don't need to write code; you just configure it at design time and go. For pages that don't get stale quickly (and also for pages that reclaim "live" data), page-output caching is a kind of free performance booster. To build an application-specific caching subsystem, you use the caching API that lets you store data into a global, system-managed object—the *Cache* object. This approach gives you the greatest flexibility, but you need to learn a few usage patterns to stay on the safe side. Let's tackle application data first.

Caching Application Data

Centered around the *Cache* object, the ASP.NET caching API is much more than simply a container of global data shared by all sessions, like the *Application* object that I briefly discussed in the previous chapter. Preserved for backward compatibility with classic ASP applications, the *Application* intrinsic object presents itself as a global container of data with an indexer property and a user-callable locking mechanism. The *Cache* object is a smarter and thread-safe container that can automatically remove unused items, support various forms of dependencies, and optionally provide removal callbacks and priorities.

The *Application* object is maintained for backward compatibility with legacy applications; new ASP.NET applications should use the *Cache* object.

The *Cache* Class

The *Cache* class is exposed by the *System.Web.Caching* namespace and is a new entry in the set of tools that provide state management in ASP.NET. The *Cache* class works like an application-wide repository for data and objects, but this is the only aspect that it has in common with the *HttpApplicationState* class, as we'll see in a moment.

An instance of the *Cache* class is created on a per-AppDomain basis and remains valid until that AppDomain is up and running. The current instance of the application's ASP.NET cache is returned by the *Cache* property of the *HttpContext* object or the *Cache* property of the *Page* object.

Cache and Other State Objects

In spite of their common goal—to serve as a global data repository for ASP.NET applications—*Cache* and *HttpApplicationState* classes are quite different. *Cache* is a thread-safe object and does not require you to explicitly lock and unlock before access. All critical sections in the internal code are adequately protected using synchronization constructs. Another key difference with the *HttpApplicationState* class is that data stored in *Cache* doesn't necessarily live as long as the application does. The *Cache* object lets you associate a duration as well as a priority with any of the items you store.

Any cached item can be configured to expire after a specified number of seconds, freeing up some memory. By setting a priority on items, you help the *Cache* object to select which items can be safely disposed of in case of memory shortage. Items can be associated with various types of dependencies, such as the timestamp of one or more files and directories, changes on other cached items, database table changes, and external events. When something happens to break the link, the cached item is invalidated and is no longer accessible by the application.

Both *Cache* and *HttpApplicationState* are globally visible classes and span all active sessions. However, neither works in a Web farm or Web garden scenario; in general, they don't work outside the current AppDomain.

> **Note**   When more than one AppDomain is involved (for example, in a Web farm), presumably all AppDomains would contain the same cached data, assuming that the cached information is not dynamic. Unlike with session state, this isn't too troubling because the assumption is that application-wide static values can be read upon initialization and cache timeout. If the cached information is dynamic, that's a different story. In that case, you should consider a global cross-machine container, as we'll discuss shortly.

The *Cache* object is unique in its capability to automatically scavenge the memory and get rid of unused items. Aside from that, it provides the same dictionary-based and familiar programming interface as *Application* and *Session*. Unlike *Session*, the *Cache* class does not store data on a per-user basis. Furthermore, when the session state is managed in-process, all currently running sessions are stored as distinct items in the ASP.NET *Cache*.

> **Note** If you're looking for a global repository object that, like *Session*, works across a Web farm or Web garden architecture, you might become frustrated. No such object exists in the Microsoft .NET Framework. To build a cross-machine container, you need to resort to a shared and remote resource, such as an external service or perhaps an installation of Microsoft SQL Server or another database. This means that each access to data will require serialization and is subject to network latency. In general, this scheme is complex enough to invalidate most of the advantages you get from data caching. As far as caching is involved, the tradeoff to evaluate is accessing ready-made data versus running the query to fetch a fresh copy of desired data. ASP.NET provides an effective infrastructure for caching data locally because that is what you need most of the time. Adding to the infrastructure to cover Web farms is up to you.

Properties of the *Cache* Class

The *Cache* class provides a couple of properties and public fields. The properties let you count and access the various items. The public fields are internal constants used to configure the expiration policy of the cache items. Table 14-1 lists and describes them all.

Table 14-1 *Cache* **Class Properties and Public Fields**

Property	Description
Count	Gets the number of items stored in the cache
Item	An indexer property that provides access to the cache item identified by the specified key
NoAbsoluteExpiration	A static constant that indicates a given item will never expire
NoSlidingExpiration	A static constant that indicates sliding expiration is disabled for a given item

The *NoAbsoluteExpiration* field is of the *DateTime* type and is set to the *DateTime.MaxValue* date—that is, the largest possible date defined in the .NET Framework. The *NoSlidingExpiration* field is of the *TimeSpan* type and is set to *TimeSpan.Zero*, meaning that sliding expiration is disabled. We'll say more about sliding expiration shortly.

The *Item* property is a read/write property that can also be used to add new items to the cache. If the key specified as the argument of the *Item* property does not exist, a new entry is created. Otherwise, the existing entry is overwritten:

```
Cache["MyItem"] = value;
```

The data stored in the cache is generically considered to be of type *object*, whereas the key must be a case-sensitive string. When you insert a new item in the cache using the *Item* property, a number of default attributes are assumed. In particular, the item is given no expiration policy, no remove callback, and a normal priority. As a result, the item will stay in the cache indefinitely, until programmatically removed or until the application terminates. To specify any extra arguments and exercise closer control on the item, use the *Insert* method of the *Cache* class instead.

Methods of the *Cache* Class

The methods of the *Cache* class let you add, remove, and enumerate the items stored. Methods of the *Cache* class are listed and described in Table 14-2.

Table 14-2   *Cache* Class Methods

Method	Description
Add	Adds the specified item to the cache. It allows you to specify dependencies, expiration and priority policies, and a remove callback. The call fails if an item with the same key already exists. The method returns the object that represents the newly added item.
Get	Retrieves the value of the specified *n* item from the cache. The item is identified by key. The method returns *null* if no item with that key is found. (This method is used to implement the *get* accessor of the *Item* property.)
GetEnumerator	Returns a dictionary enumerator object to iterate through all the valid items stored in the cache.
Insert	Inserts the specified item into the cache. *Insert* provides several overloads and allows you to specify dependencies, expiration and priority policies, and a remove callback. The method is void and, unlike *Add*, overwrites an existing item having the same key as the item being inserted. (This method is used to implement the *set* accessor of the *Item* property.)
Remove	Removes the specified item from the cache. The item is identified by the key. The method returns the instance of the object being removed or *null* if no item with that key is found.

Both the *Add* and *Insert* methods don't accept null values as the key or the value of an item to cache. If null values are used, an exception is thrown. You can configure sliding expiration for an item for no longer than one year. Otherwise, an exception will be raised. Finally, bear in mind that you cannot set both sliding and absolute expirations on the same cached item.

> **Note**   *Add* and *Insert* work in much the same way, but a couple of differences make it worthwhile to have both on board. *Add* fails (but no exception is raised) if the item already exists, whereas *Insert* overwrites the existing item. In addition, *Add* has just one signature, while *Insert* provides several different overloads.

An Interior View

The *Cache* class inherits from *Object* and implements the *IEnumerable* interface. It is a wrapper around an internal class that acts as the true container of the stored data. The real class used to implement the ASP.NET cache varies depending on the number of affinitized CPUs. If only one CPU is available, the class is *CacheSingle*; otherwise, it is *CacheMultiple*. In both cases, items are stored in a hashtable and there will be a distinct hashtable for each CPU. It turns out that *CacheMultiple* manages an array of hashtables. Figure 14-1 illustrates the architecture of the *Cache* object.

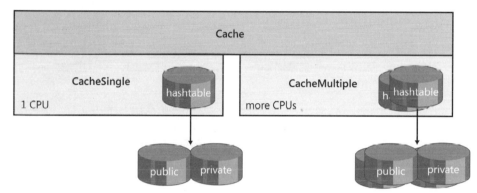

Figure 14-1   The internal structure of the ASP.NET cache.

The hashtable is divided into two parts—public and private elements. In the public portion of the hashtable are placed all items visible to user applications. System-level data, on the other hand, goes in the private section. The cache is a resource extensively used by the ASP.NET runtime itself; system items, though, are neatly separated by application data, and there's no way an application can access a private element on the cache.

The *Cache* object is mostly a way to restrict applications to read from, and write to, the public segment of the data store. Get and set methods on internal cache classes accept a flag to denote the public attribute of the item. When called from the *Cache* class, these internal methods always default to the flag that selects public items.

The hashtable containing data is then enhanced and surrounded by other internal components to provide a rich set of programming features. The list includes the implementation of a least recently used (LRU) algorithm to ensure that items can be removed if the system runs short of memory, dependencies, and removal callbacks.

Caution   On a multiprocessor machine with more than one CPU affinitized with the ASP.NET worker process, each processor ends up getting its own cache object. The various cache objects are not synchronized. In a Web garden configuration, you can't assume that users will return to the same CPU (and worker process) on subsequent requests. So the status of the ASP.NET cache is not guaranteed to be aligned with what the same page did last time.

Working with the ASP.NET *Cache*

An instance of the *Cache* object is associated with each running application and shares the associated application's lifetime. The cache holds references to data and proactively verifies validity and expiration. When the system runs short of memory, the *Cache* object automatically removes some little-used items and frees valuable server resources. Each item—when stored into the cache—can be given special attributes that determine a priority and an expiration policy. All these are system-provided tools to help programmers control the scavenging mechanism of the ASP.NET cache.

Inserting New Items in the Cache

A cache item is characterized by a handful of attributes that can be specified as input arguments of both *Add* and *Insert*. In particular, an item stored in the ASP.NET *Cache* object can have the following properties:

- **Key.** A case-sensitive string, it is the key used to store the item in the internal hashtable the ASP.NET cache relies upon. If this value is null, an exception is thrown. If the key already exists, what happens depends on the particular method you're using: *Add* fails, while *Insert* just overwrites the existing item.

- **Value.** A non-null value of type *Object* that references the information stored in the cache. The value is managed and returned as an *Object* and needs casting to become useful in the application context.

- **Dependencies.** Object of type *CacheDependency*, tracks a physical dependency between the item being added to the cache and files, directories, database tables, or other objects in the application's cache. Whenever any of the monitored sources are modified, the newly added item is marked obsolete and automatically removed.

- **Absolute Expiration Date.** A *DateTime* object that represents the absolute expiration date for the item being added. When this time arrives, the object is automatically removed from the cache. Items not subject to absolute expiration dates must use the *NoAbsoluteExpiration* constants representing the farthest allowable date. The absolute expiration date doesn't change after the item is used in either reading or writing.

- **Sliding Expiration.** A *TimeSpan* object, represents a relative expiration period for the item being added. When you set the parameter to a non-null value, the expiration-date parameter is automatically set to the current time plus the sliding period. If you explicitly set the sliding expiration, you cannot set the absolute expiration date, too. From the user's perspective, these are mutually exclusive parameters. If the item is accessed before its natural expiration time, the sliding period is automatically renewed.

- **Priority.** A value picked out of the *CacheItemPriority* enumeration; it denotes the priority of the item. It is a value ranging from *Low* to *NotRemovable*. The default level of priority is *Normal*. The priority level determines the importance of the item; items with a lower priority are removed first.

- **Removal Callback.** If specified, indicates the function that the ASP.NET *Cache* object calls back when the item will be removed from the cache. In this way, applications can be notified when their own items are removed from the cache no matter what the reason is. As mentioned in Chapter 13, when the session state works in *InProc* mode, a removal callback function is used to fire the *Session_End* event. The delegate type used for this callback is *CacheItemRemoveCallback*.

There are basically three ways to add new items to the ASP.NET *Cache* object—the *set* accessor of *Item* property, the *Add* method, and the *Insert* method. The *Item* property allows you to indicate only the key and the value. The *Add* method has only one signature that includes all the aforementioned arguments. The *Insert* method is the most flexible of all options and provides the following four overloads:

```
public void Insert(string, object);
public void Insert(string, object, CacheDependency);
public void Insert(string, object, CacheDependency, DateTime, TimeSpan);
public void Insert(string, object, CacheDependency, DateTime, TimeSpan,
    CacheItemPriority, CacheItemRemovedCallback);
```

The following code snippet shows the typical call that is performed under the hood when the *Item* set accessor is used:

```
Insert(key, value, null, Cache.NoAbsoluteExpiration,
    Cache.NoSlidingExpiration, CacheItemPriority.Normal, null);
```

If you use the *Add* method to insert an item whose key matches that of an existing item, no exception is raised, nothing happens, and the method returns *null*.

Removing Items from the Cache

All items marked with an expiration policy, or a dependency, are automatically removed from the cache when something happens in the system to invalidate them. To programmatically remove an item, on the other hand, you resort to the *Remove* method. Notice that this method removes any item, including those marked with the highest level of priority (*NotRemovable*). The following code snippet shows how to call the *Remove* method:

```
object oldValue = Cache.Remove("MyItem");
```

Normally, the method returns the value just removed from the cache. However, if the specified key is not found, the method fails and null is returned, but no exception is ever raised.

When items with an associated callback function are removed from the cache, a value from the *CacheItemRemovedReason* enumeration is passed on to the function to justify the operation. The enumeration includes the values listed in Table 14-3.

Table 14-3   The *CacheItemRemovedReason* Enumeration

Reason	Description
DependencyChanged	Removed because the associated dependency changed.
Expired	Removed because expired.
Removed	Programmatically removed from the cache using *Remove*. Notice that a *Removed* event might also be fired if an existing item is replaced either through *Insert* or the *Item* property.
Underused	Removed by the system to free memory.

If the item being removed is associated with a callback, the function is executed immediately after having removed the item.

Tracking Item Dependencies

Items added to the cache through the *Add* or *Insert* method can be linked to an array of files and directories as well as to an array of existing cache items, database tables, or external events. The link between the new item and its cache dependency is maintained using an instance of the *CacheDependency* class. The *CacheDependency* object can represent a single file or directory or an array of files and directories. In addition, it can also represent an array of cache keys—that is, keys of other items stored in the *Cache*—and other custom dependency objects to monitor—for example, database tables or external events.

The *CacheDependency* class has quite a long list of constructors that provide for the possibilities listed in Table 14-4.

Table 14-4   The *CacheDependency* Constructor List

Constructor	Description
String	A file path—that is, a URL to a file or a directory name
String[]	An array of file paths
String, DateTime	A file path monitored starting at the specified time
String[], DateTime	An array of file paths monitored starting at the specified time
String[], String[]	An array of file paths, and an array of cache keys
String[], String[], CacheDependency	An array of file paths, an array of cache keys, and a separate *CacheDependency* object
String[], String[], DateTime	An array of file paths and an array of cache keys monitored starting at the specified time
String[], String[], CacheDependency, DateTime	An array of file paths, an array of cache keys, and a separate instance of the *CacheDependency* class monitored starting at the specified time

Any change in any of the monitored objects invalidates the current item. It's interesting to note that you can set a time to start monitoring for changes. By default, monitoring begins right after the item is stored in the cache. A *CacheDependency* object can be made dependent on another instance of the same class. In this case, any change detected on the items controlled by the separate object results in a broken dependency and the subsequent invalidation of the present item.

> **Note**   Cache dependencies underwent some significant changes and improvements in ASP.NET 2.0. In the previous version, the *CacheDependency* class was sealed and not further inheritable. As a result, the only dependency objects you could work with were those linking to files, directories, or other cached items. In ASP.NET 2.0, the *CacheDependency* class is inheritable and can be used as a base to build custom dependencies. ASP.NET 2.0 comes with a built-in class to monitor database tables for changes. We'll examine custom dependencies shortly.

In the following code snippet, the item is associated with the timestamp of a file. The net effect is that any change made to the file that affects the timestamp invalidates the item, which will then be removed from the cache.

```
CacheDependency dep = new CacheDependency(filename);
Cache.Insert(key, value, dep);
```

Bear in mind that the *CacheDependency* object needs to take file and directory names expressed through absolute file system paths.

Defining a Removal Callback

Item removal is an event independent from the application's behavior and control. The difficulty with item removal is that because the application is oblivious to what has happened, it attempts to access the removed item later and gets only a null value back. To work around this issue, you can either check for the item's existence before access is attempted or, if you think you need to know about removal in a timely manner, register a callback and reload the item if it's invalidated. This approach makes particularly good sense if the cached item just represents the content of a tracked file or query.

The following code-behind class demonstrates how to read the contents of a Web server's file and cache it with a key named *MyData*. The item is inserted with a removal callback. The callback simply re-reads and reloads the file if the removal reason is *DependencyChanged*.

```
void Load_Click(object sender, EventArgs e)
{
    AddFileContentsToCache("data.xml");
}
void Read_Click(object sender, EventArgs e)
{
    object data = Cache["MyData"];
    if (data == null)
    {
        contents.Text = "[No data available]";
        return;
    }
```

```
      contents.Text = (string) data;
}
void AddFileContentsToCache(string fileName)
{
    string file = Server.MapPath(fileName);
    StreamReader reader = new StreamReader(file);
    string buf = reader.ReadToEnd();
    reader.Close();

    // Create and display the contents
    CreateAndCacheItem(buf, file);
    contents.Text = Cache["MyData"].ToString();
}
void CreateAndCacheItem(object buf, string file)
{
    CacheItemRemovedCallback removal;
    removal = new CacheItemRemovedCallback(ReloadItemRemoved);

    CacheDependency dep = new CacheDependency(file);
    Cache.Insert("MyData", buf, dep, Cache.NoAbsoluteExpiration,
        Cache.NoSlidingExpiration, CacheItemPriority.Normal, removal);
}
void ReloadItemRemoved(string key, object value,
        CacheItemRemovedReason reason)
{
    if (reason == CacheItemRemovedReason.DependencyChanged)
    {
        // At this time the item has been removed. We get fresh data and
        // re-insert the item
        if (key == "MyData")
            AddFileContentsToCache("data.xml");

        // This code runs asynchronously with respect to the application,
        // as soon as the dependency gets broken. To test it, add here
        // some code to trace the event
    }
}
void Remove_Click(object sender, EventArgs e)
{
    Cache.Remove("MyData");
}
```

Figure 14-2 shows a sample page to test the behavior of the caching API when dependencies are used. If the underlying file has changed, the dependency-changed event is notified and the new contents are automatically loaded. So the next time you read from the cache you get fresh data. If the cached item is removed, any successive attempt to read returns *null*.

Note that the item removal callback is a piece of code defined by a user page but automatically run by the *Cache* object as soon as the removal event is fired. The code contained in the removal callback runs asynchronously with respect to the page. If the removal event is related to a broken dependency, the *Cache* object will execute the callback as soon as the notification is detected.

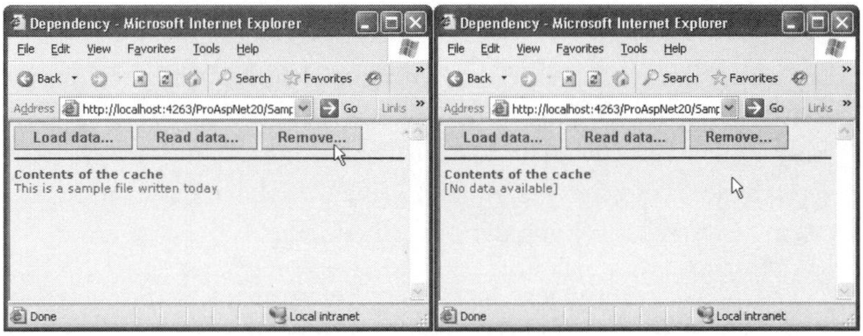

Figure 14-2   A sample page to test the behavior of removal callbacks in the ASP.NET cache.

If you add an object to the *Cache* and make it dependent on a file, directory, or key that doesn't exist, the item is regularly cached and marked with a dependency as usual. If the file, directory, or key is created later, the dependency is broken and the cached item is invalidated. In other words, if the dependency item doesn't exist, it's virtually created with a null timestamp or empty content.

> **Note**   Once an item bound to one or more dependencies is removed from the cache, it stops monitoring for changes. Further changes to, say, the underlying file won't be caught just because the item is no longer in the cache. You can verify this behavior by loading some data, as shown in Figure 14-2. Next, you click *Remove* to dispose of the item and modify the underlying file. Later, if you try to re-read the item, it'll return *null* because the element is no longer in the cache.

To define a removal callback, you first declare a variable of type *CacheRemovedItemCallback*. Next, you instantiate this member with a new delegate object with the right signature:

```
CacheItemRemovedCallback removal;
removal = new CacheItemRemovedCallback(ReloadItemRemoved);
```

The *CacheDependency* object is simply passed the *removal* delegate member, which executes the actual function code for the *Cache* object to call back.

> **Tip**   If you define a removal callback function through a static method, you avoid an instance of the class that contains the method to be kept in memory all the time to support the callback. Static methods (that is, *Shared* methods according to the Microsoft Visual Basic .NET jargon) are callable on a class even when no instance of the class has been created. Note, though, that this choice raises other issues as far as trying to use the callback to re-insert a removed item. In this case, therefore, you reasonably need to access a method on the page class, which is not permitted from within a static member. To work around this issue, you create a static field, say *ThisPage*, and set it to the page object (the *this* keyword in C# or *Me* in Visual Basic .NET) during the *Page_Init* event. You then invoke any object-specific method through the static *ThisPage* member, even from within a static method.

Setting the Items Priority

Each item in the cache is given a priority—that is, a value picked up from the *CacheItemPriority* enumeration. A priority is a value ranging from *Low* (lowest) to *NotRemovable* (highest), with the default set to *Normal*. The priority is supposed to determine the importance of the item for the *Cache* object. The higher the priority is, the more chances the item has to stay in memory even when the system resources are going dangerously down.

If you want to give a particular priority level to an item being added to the cache, you have to use either the *Add* or *Insert* method. The priority can be any value listed in Table 14-5.

Table 14-5   Priority Levels in the *Cache* Object

Priority	Value	Description
Low	1	Items with this level of priority are the first items to be deleted from the cache as the server frees system memory.
BelowNormal	2	Intermediate level of priority between *Normal* and *Low*.
Normal	3	Default priority level. It is assigned to all items added using the *Item* property.
Default	3	Same as *Normal*.
AboveNormal	4	Intermediate level of priority between *Normal* and *High*.
High	5	Items with this level of priority are the last items to be removed from the cache as the server frees memory.
NotRemovable	6	Items with this level of priority are never removed from the cache. Use this level with extreme care.

The *Cache* object is designed with two goals in mind. First, it has to be efficient and built for easy programmatical access to the global repository of application data. Second, it has to be smart enough to detect when the system is running low on memory resources and to clear elements to free memory. This trait clearly differentiates the *Cache* object from *HttpApplicationState*, which maintains its objects until the end of the application (unless the application itself frees those items). The technique used to eliminate low-priority and seldom-used objects is known as *scavenging*.

Controlling Data Expiration

Priority level and changed dependencies are two of the causes that could lead a cached item to be automatically garbage-collected from the *Cache*. Another possible cause for a premature removal from the *Cache* is infrequent use associated with an expiration policy. By default, all items added to the cache have no expiration date, neither absolute nor relative. If you add items by using either the *Add* or *Insert* method, you can choose between two mutually exclusive expiration policies: absolute and sliding expiration.

Absolute expiration is when a cached item is associated with a *DateTime* value and is removed from the cache as the specified time is reached. The *DateTime.MaxValue* field, and its more general alias *NoAbsoluteExpiration*, can be used to indicate the last date value supported by the .NET Framework and to subsequently indicate that the item will never expire.

Sliding expiration implements a sort of relative expiration policy. The idea is that the object expires after a certain interval. In this case, though, the interval is automatically renewed after each access to the item. Sliding expiration is rendered through a *TimeSpan* object—a type that in the .NET Framework represents an interval of time. The *TimeSpan.Zero* field represents the empty interval and is also the value associated with the *NoSlidingExpiration* static field on the *Cache* class. When you cache an item with a sliding expiration of 10 minutes, you use the following code:

```
Insert(key, value, null, Cache.NoAbsoluteExpiration,
    TimeSpan.FromMinutes(10), CacheItemPriority.Normal, null);
```

Internally, the item is cached with an absolute expiration date given by the current time plus the specified *TimeSpan* value. In light of this, the preceding code could have been rewritten as follows:

```
Insert(key, value, null, DateTime.Now.AddMinutes(10),
    Cache.NoSlidingExpiration, CacheItemPriority.Normal, null);
```

However, a subtle difference still exists between the two code snippets. In the former case—that is, when sliding expiration is explicitly turned on—each access to the item resets the absolute expiration date to the time of the last access plus the time span. In the latter case, because sliding expiration is explicitly turned off, any access to the item doesn't change the absolute expiration time.

Statistics About Memory Usage

Immediately after initialization, the *Cache* collects statistical information about the memory in the system and the current status of the system resources. Next, it registers a timer to invoke a callback function at one-second intervals. The callback function periodically updates and reviews the memory statistics and, if needed, activates the scavenging module. Memory statistics are collected using a bunch of Win32 API functions to obtain information about the system's current usage of both physical and virtual memory.

The *Cache* object classifies the status of the system resources in terms of low and high pressure. Each value corresponds to a different percentage of occupied memory. Typically, low pressure is in the range of 15 percent to 40 percent, while high pressure is measured from 45 percent to 65 percent of memory occupation. When the memory pressure exceeds the guard level, seldom-used objects are the first to be removed according to their priority.

Practical Issues

Caching is a critical factor for the success of a Web application. Caching mostly relates to getting quick access to prefetched data that saves you roundtrips, queries, and any other sort of heavy operations. Caching is important also for writing, especially in systems with a high volume of data to be written. By posting requests for writing to a kind of intermediate memory structure, you decouple the main body of the application from the service in charge of writing. Some people call this *batch update*, but in the end it is nothing more than a form of caching for data to write.

The caching API provides you with the necessary tools to build a bulletproof caching strategy. When it comes to this, though, a few practical issues arise.

Should I Cache or Should I Fetch?

There's just one possible answer to this question—it depends. It depends on the characteristics of the application and the expected goals. For an application that must optimize throughput and serve requests in the shortest possible amount of time, caching is essential. The quantity of data you cache and the amount of time you cache it are the two parameters you need to play with to arrive at a good solution.

Caching is about reusing data so data that is not often used in the lifetime of the application is not a good candidate for the cache. In addition to being frequently used, cacheable data is also general-purpose data rather than data specific to a request or a session. If your application manages data with these characteristics, cache them with no fear.

Caching is about memory, and memory is relatively cheap. However, a bad application design can easily drive the application to unpleasant out-of-memory errors regardless of the cost of a memory chip. On the other hand, caching can boost the performance just enough to ease your pain and give you more time to devise a serious refactoring.

Sometimes you face users who claim an absolute need for live data. Sure, data parked in the cache is static, unaffected by concurrent events, and not fully participating in the life of the application. Can your users afford data that has not been updated for a few seconds? With a few exceptions, the answer is, "Sure, they can." In a canonical Web application, there's virtually no data that can't be cached at least for a second or two. No matter what end users claim, caching can realistically be applied to the vast majority of scenarios. Real-time systems and systems with a high degree of concurrency (for example, a booking application) are certainly an exception, but most of the time a slight delay of one or two seconds can make the application run faster under stress conditions without affecting the quality of the service.

In the end, you should be considering caching all the time and filter it out in favor of direct data access only in very special situations. As a practical rule, when users claim they need live data, you should try with a counterexample to prove to them that a few seconds of delay are still acceptable and maximize hardware and software investments.

Fetching to get the real data is an option, but it's usually the most expensive one. If you choose that option, make sure you really need it. Accessing cached data is faster if the data you get in this way makes sense to the application. On the other hand, be aware that caching requires memory. If abused, it can lead to out-of-memory errors and performance hits.

Building a Wrapper Cache Object

As mentioned, no data stored in the ASP.NET cache is guaranteed to stay there when a piece of code attempts to read it. For the safety of the application, you should never rely on the value returned by the *Get* method or the *Item* property. The following pattern keeps you on the safe side:

```
object data = Cache["MyData"];
if (data != null)
{
   // The data is here, process it
   ...
}
```

The code snippet deliberately omits the *else* branch. What should you do if the requested item is *null*? You can abort the ongoing operation and display a friendly message to the user, or you can perhaps reload the data with a new fetch. Whatever approach you opt for, it will unlikely fit for just any piece of data you can have in the cache.

When it comes to building a cache layer, you're better off thinking in a domain-based way. You should avoid caching data as individual elements, with the key being the only clue to retrieve the element later. You can build a helper class with domain-specific properties bound to cache entries. Here's an example:

```
public static class MyCache
{
   protected static class MyCacheEntries
   {
      public const string Customers = "Customers";
   }

   public static CustomerCollection Customers
   {
      get
      {
         object o = HttpContext.Current.Cache[MyCacheEntries.Customers];
         if (o == null)
         {
            HttpContext.Current.Trace.Warn("Empty cache--reloading...");
            LoadCustomers();
         }
         return (CustomerCollection) o;
      }
   }
}
```

```
protected static void LoadCustomers()
{
    // Get data
    CustomerCollection coll = ProAspNet20.DAL.Customers.LoadAll();

    // Set the item (5 seconds duration)
    HttpContext.Current.Cache.Insert(MyCacheEntries.Customers, coll,
        null, DateTime.Now.AddSeconds(5), Cache.NoSlidingExpiration);
    }
}
```

The *MyCache* class defines a property named *Customers* of type *CustomerCollection*. The contents of this property comes from the sample Data Access Layer (DAL) we discussed in Chapter 9, and it's stored in the cache for a duration of 5 seconds. The *Customers* property hides all the details of the cache management and ensures the availability of valid data to host pages. If the cached item is not there because it has expired (or it has been removed), the *get* accessor of the property takes care of reloading the data.

> **Note** If you move the preceding code to a non-code-behind class, you can't access the ASP.NET cache object using the plain *Cache* keyword. Unlike classic ASP, ASP.NET has no intrinsic objects, meaning that all objects you invoke must be public or reachable properties on the current class or its parent. Just as we did in the previous example of the *MyCache* class, you need to qualify the cache using the static property *HttpContext.Current*.

A caller page needs only the following code to populate a grid with the results in the cache:

```
CustomerCollection data = MyCache.Customers;
CustomerList.DataTextField = "CompanyName";
CustomerList.DataValueField = "ID";
CustomerList.DataSource = data;
CustomerList.DataBind();
```

By writing a wrapper class around the specific data you put into the cache, you can more easily implement a safe pattern for data access that prevents null references and treats each piece of data appropriately. In addition, the resulting code is more readable and easy to maintain.

> **Note** This approach is potentially more powerful than using the built-in cache capabilities of data source controls. First and foremost, such a wrapper class encapsulates all the data you need to keep in the cache and not just the data bound to a control. Second, it gives you more control over the implementation—you can set priority and removal callback, implement complex dependencies, and choose the name of the entry. Next, it works with any data and not just with ADO.NET objects, as is the case with *SqlDataSource* and *ObjectDataSource*. You can use this approach instead while building your own DAL so that you come up with a bunch of classes that support caching to bind to data source controls. If your pages are quite simple (for example, some data bound to a grid or other data-bound controls) and you're using only *DataSet* or *DataTable*, the caching infrastructure of data source controls will probably suit your needs.

Enumerating Items in the Cache

Although most of the time you simply access cached items by name, you might find it useful to know how to enumerate the contents of the cache to list all stored public items. As mentioned, the *Cache* class is a sort of collection that is instantiated during the application's startup. Being a collection, its contents can be easily enumerated using a *for..each* statement. The following code shows how to copy the current contents of the ASP.NET cache to a newly created *DataTable* object:

```
private DataTable CacheToDataTable()
{
    DataTable dt = CreateDataTable();
    foreach(DictionaryEntry elem in HttpContext.Current.Cache)
        AddItemToTable(dt, elem);
    return dt;
}
private DataTable CreateDataTable()
{
    DataTable dt = new DataTable();
    dt.Columns.Add("Key", typeof(string));
    dt.Columns.Add("Value", typeof(string));
    return dt;
}
private void AddItemToTable(DataTable dt, DictionaryEntry elem)
{
    DataRow row = dt.NewRow();
    row["Key"] = elem.Key.ToString();
    row["Value"] = elem.Value.ToString();
    dt.Rows.Add(row);
}
```

The *DataTable* contains two columns, one for the key and one for the value of the item stored. The value is rendered using the *ToString* method, meaning that the string and numbers will be loyally rendered but objects will typically be rendered through their class names.

Important   When you enumerate the items in the cache, only two pieces of information are available—the key and the value. From a client page, there's no way to read the priority of a given item or perhaps its expiration policy. When you enumerate the contents of the *Cache* object, a generic *DictionaryEntry* object is returned with no property or method pointing to more specific information. To get more information, you should consider using the .NET *Reflection* API.

Also note that because the *Cache* object stores data internally using a hashtable, the enumerator returns contained items in an apparently weird order that is neither alphabetical nor time-based. The order in which items are returned, instead, is based on the internal hash code used to index items.

Clearing the Cache

The .NET Framework provides no method on the *Cache* class to programmatically clear all the content. The following code snippet shows how to build one:

```
public void Clear()
{
    foreach(DictionaryEntry elem in Cache)
    {
        string s = elem.Key.ToString();
        Cache.Remove(s);
    }
}
```

Even though the ASP.NET cache is implemented to maintain a neat separation between the application's and system's items, it is preferable that you delete items in the cache individually. If you have several items to maintain, you might want to build your own wrapper class and expose one single method to clear all the cached data.

Cache Synchronization

Whenever you read or write an individual cache item, from a threading perspective you're absolutely safe. The ASP.NET *Cache* object guarantees that no other concurrently running threads can ever interfere with what you're doing. If you need to ensure that multiple operations on the *Cache* object occur atomically, that's a different story. Consider the following code snippet:

```
int counter = -1;
object o = Cache["Counter"];
if (o == null)
{
    // Retrieve the last good known value from a database
    // or return a default value
    counter = RetrieveLastKnownValue();
}
else
{
    counter = (int) Cache["Counter"];
    counter ++;
    Cache["Counter"] = counter;
}
```

The *Cache* object is accessed repeatedly in the context of an atomic operation—incrementing a counter. While individual accesses to *Cache* are thread-safe, there's no guarantee that other threads won't kick in between the various calls. If there's potential contention on the cached value, you should consider using additional locking constructs, such as the C# *lock* statement (*SyncLock* in Microsoft Visual Basic .NET).

> **Important**   Where should you put the lock? If you directly lock the *Cache* object, you might run into trouble. ASP.NET uses the *Cache* object extensively, and directly locking the *Cache* object might have a serious impact on the overall performance of the application. However, most of the time ASP.NET doesn't access the cache via the *Cache* object, but rather it accesses the direct data container, that is the *CacheSingle* or *CacheMultiple* class. In this regard, a lock on the *Cache* object probably won't affect many ASP.NET components, but it's a risk that personally I wouldn't like to take. By locking the *Cache* object, you also risk blocking HTTP modules and handlers active in the pipeline, as well as other pages and sessions in the application that need to use cache entries different from the ones you want to serialize access to.
>
> The best way out seems to be using a synchronizer, that is, an intermediate but global object that you lock before entering in a piece of code sensitive to concurrency:
>
> ```
> lock(yourSynchronizer) {
>
>     // Access the cache here. This pattern must be replicated for
>
>     // each access to the cache that requires serialization.
>
> }
> ```
>
> The synchronizer object must be global to the application. For example, it can be a static member defined in the *global.asax* file.

Per-Request Caching

Although you normally tend to cache only global data and data of general interest, to squeeze out every little bit of performance you can also cache per-request data that is long-lived even though it's used only by a particular page. You place this information in the *Cache* object.

Another form of per-request caching is possible to improve performance. Working information shared by all controls and components participating in the processing of a request can be stored in a global container for the duration of the request. In this case, though, you might want to use the *Items* collection on the *HttpContext* class (discussed in Chapter 12) to park the data because it is automatically freed up at the end of the request and doesn't involve implicit or explicit locking like *Cache*.

Designing a Custom Dependency

Let's say it up front: writing a custom cache-dependency object is no picnic. You should have a very good reason to do so, and you should carefully design the new functionality before proceeding. As mentioned, in ASP.NET 2.0 the *CacheDependency* class is inheritable—you can derive your own class from it to implement an external source of events to invalidate cached items.

The base *CacheDependency* class handles all the wiring of the new dependency object to the ASP.NET cache and all the issues surrounding synchronization and disposal. It also saves you from implementing a start-time feature from scratch—you inherit that capability from the base class constructors. (The start-time feature allows you to start tracking dependencies at a particular time.)

Let's start reviewing the limitations of *CacheDependency* in ASP.NET 1.x that have led to removing the *sealed* attribute on the class, making it fully inheritable in ASP.NET 2.0.

What Cache Dependencies Cannot Do in ASP.NET 1.x

In ASP.NET 1.x, a cached item can be subject to four types of dependencies: time, files, other items, and other dependencies. The ASP.NET 1.x *Cache* object addresses many developers' needs and has made building in-memory collections of frequently accessed data much easier and more effective. However, this mechanism is not perfect, nor is it extensible.

Let's briefly consider a real-world scenario. What type of data do you think a distributed data-driven application would place in the ASP.NET *Cache*? In many cases, it would simply be the results of a database query. But unless you code it yourself—which can really be tricky—the object doesn't support database dependency. A database dependency would invalidate a cached result set when a certain database table changes. In ASP.NET 1.x, the *CacheDependency* class is sealed and closed to any form of customization that gives developers a chance to invalidate cached items based on user-defined conditions.

As far as the *Cache* object is concerned, the biggest difference between ASP.NET 1.x and ASP.NET 2.0 is that version 2.0 supports custom dependencies. This was achieved by making the *CacheDependency* class inheritable and providing a made-to-measure *SqlCacheDependency* cache that provides built-in database dependency limited to SQL Server 7.0 and later.

Extensions to the *CacheDependency* Base Class

To fully support derived classes and to facilitate their integration into the ASP.NET caching infrastructure, a bunch of new public and protected members have been added to the *CacheDependency* class. They are summarized in Table 14-6.

Table 14-6   New Members of the *CacheDependency* Class

Member	Description
DependencyDispose	Protected method. It releases the resources used by the class.
GetUniqueID	Public method. It retrieves a unique string identifier for the object.
NotifyDependencyChanged	Protected method. It notifies the base class that the dependency represented by this object has changed.
SetUtcLastModified	Protected method. It marks the time when a dependency last changed.
UtcLastModified	Public read-only property. It gets the time when the dependency was last changed. This property also exists in version 1.x, but it is not publicly accessible.

As mentioned, a custom dependency class relies on its parent for any interaction with the *Cache* object. The *NotifyDependencyChanged* method is called by classes that inherit *Cache-Dependency* to tell the base class that the dependent item has changed. In response, the base class updates the values of the *HasChanged* and *UtcLastModified* properties. Any cleanup code needed when the custom cache dependency object is dismissed should go into the *DependencyDispose* method.

Getting Change Notifications

As you might have noticed, nothing in the public interface of the base *CacheDependency* class allows you to insert code to check whether a given condition—the heart of the dependency—is met. Why is this? The *CacheDependency* class was designed to support only a limited set of well-known dependencies—against changes to files or other items.

To detect file changes, the *CacheDependency* object internally sets up a file monitor object and receives a call from it whenever the monitored file or directory changes. The *CacheDependency* class creates a *FileSystemWatcher* object and passes it an event handler. A similar approach is used to establish a programmatic link between the *CacheDependency* object and the *Cache* object and its items. The *Cache* object invokes a *CacheDependency* internal method when one of the monitored items changes. What does this all mean to the developer?

A custom dependency object must be able to receive notifications from the external data source it is monitoring. In most cases, this is really complicated if you can't bind to existing notification mechanisms (such as file system monitor or SQL Server 2005 notifications). When the notification of a change in the source is detected, the dependency uses the parent's infrastructure to notify the cache of the event. We'll consider a practical example in a moment.

The *AggregateCacheDependency* Class

In ASP.NET 2.0, not only can you create a single dependency on an entry, but you can also aggregate dependencies. For example, you can make a cache entry dependent on both a disk file and a SQL Server table. The following code snippet shows how to create a cache entry named *MyData* that is dependent on two different files:

```
// Creates an array of CacheDependency objects
CacheDependency dep1 = new CacheDependency(fileName1);
CacheDependency dep2 = new CacheDependency(fileName2);
CacheDependency deps[] = {dep1, dep2};

// Creates an aggregate object
AggregateCacheDependency aggDep = new AggregateCacheDependency();
aggDep.Add(deps);
Cache.Insert("MyData", data, aggDep)
```

Any custom cache-dependency object, including *SqlCacheDependency*, inherits *CacheDependency*, so the array of dependencies can contain virtually any type of dependency.

In ASP.NET 2.0, the *AggregateCacheDependency* class is built as a custom cache-dependency object and inherits the base *CacheDependency* class.

A Cache Dependency for XML Data

Suppose your application gets some key data from a custom XML file and you don't want to access the file on disk for every request. So you decide to cache the contents of the XML file, but still you'd love to detect changes to the file that occur while the application is up and running. Is this possible? You bet. You arrange a file dependency and you're done.

In this case, though, any update to the file that modifies the timestamp is perceived as a critical change. As a result, the related entry in the cache is invalidated and you're left with no choice other than re-reading the XML data from the disk. The rub here is that you are forced to re-read everything even if the change is limited to a comment or to a node that is not relevant to your application.

Because you want the cached data to be invalidated only when certain nodes change, you create a made-to-measure cache dependency class to monitor the return value of a given XPath expression on an XML file.

Note   If the target data source provides you with a built-in and totally asynchronous notification mechanism (such as the command notification mechanism of SQL Server 2005), you just use it. Otherwise, to detect changes in the monitored data source, you can only poll the resource at a reasonable rate.

Designing the *XmlDataCacheDependency* Class

To better understand the concept of custom dependencies, think about the following example. You need to cache the inner text of a particular node in an XML file. You can define a custom dependency class that caches the current value upon instantiation and reads the file periodically to detect changes. When a change is detected, the cached item bound to the dependency is invalidated.

Note   Admittedly, polling might not be the right approach for this particular problem. Later on, in fact, I'll briefly discuss a more effective implementation. Be aware, though, that polling is a valid and common technique for custom cache dependencies.

A good way to poll a local or remote resource is through a timer callback. Let's break the procedure into a few steps:

1.   The custom *XmlDataCacheDependency* class gets ready for the overall functionality. It initializes some internal properties and caches the polling rate, file name, and XPath expression to find the subtree to monitor.

2.   After initialization, the dependency object sets up a timer callback to access the file periodically and check contents.

3.   In the callback, the return value of the XPath expression is compared to the previously stored value. If the two values differ, the linked cache item is promptly invalidated.

There's no need for the developer to specify details on how the cache dependency is broken or set up. The *CacheDependency* class in ASP.NET 2.0 takes care of it entirely.

> **Note**   If you're curious to know how the *Cache* detects when a dependency is broken, read on. When an item bound to a custom dependency object is added to the *Cache*, an additional entry is created and linked to the initial item. *NotifyDependencyChanged* simply dirties this additional element which, in turn, invalidates the original cache item. Figure 14-3 illustrates the connections.

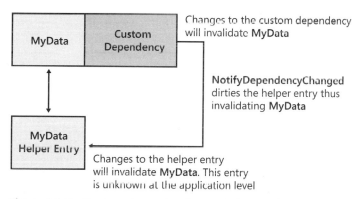

Figure 14-3   Custom dependencies use helper cache entries to invalidate any items under their control.

Implementing the Dependency

The following source code shows the core implementation of the custom *XmlDataCacheDependency* class:

```
public class XmlDataCacheDependency : CacheDependency
{
    // Internal members
    static Timer _timer;
    int _pollSecs = 10;
    string _fileName;
    string _xpathExpression;
    string _currentValue;

    public XmlDataCacheDependency(string file, string xpath, int pollTime)
    {
        // Set internal members
        _fileName = file;
```

```csharp
        _xpathExpression = xpath;
        _pollSecs = pollTime;

        // Get the current value
        _currentValue = CheckFile();

        // Set the timer
        if (_timer == null) {
            int ms = _pollSecs * 1000;
            TimerCallback cb = new TimerCallback(XmlDataCallback);
            _timer = new Timer(cb, this, ms, ms);
        }
    }

    public string CurrentValue
    {
        get { return _currentValue; }
    }

    public void XmlDataCallback(object sender)
    {
        // Get a reference to THIS dependency object
        XmlDataCacheDependency dep = (XmlDataCacheDependency) sender;

        // Check for changes and notify the base class if any are found
        string value = CheckFile();
        if (!String.Equals(_currentValue, value))
            dep.NotifyDependencyChanged(dep, EventArgs.Empty);
    }

    public string CheckFile()
    {
        // Evaluates the XPath expression in the file
        XmlDocument doc = new XmlDocument();
        doc.Load(_fileName);
        XmlNode node = doc.SelectSingleNode(_xpathExpression);

        return node.InnerText;
    }

    protected override void DependencyDispose()
    {
        // Kill the timer and then proceed as usual
        _timer.Dispose();
        _timer = null;
        base.DependencyDispose();
    }
}
```

When the cache dependency is created, the file is parsed and the value of the XPath expression is stored in an internal member. At the same time, a timer is started to repeat the operation at regular intervals. The return value is compared against the value stored in the constructor code. If the two are different, the *NotifyDependencyChanged* method is invoked on the base *CacheDependency* class to invalidate the linked content in the ASP.NET *Cache*.

Testing the Custom Dependency

How can you use this dependency class in a Web application? It's as easy as it seems—you just use it in any scenario where a *CacheDependency* object is acceptable. For example, you create an instance of the class in the *Page_Load* event and pass it to the *Cache.Insert* method:

```
protected const string CacheKeyName = "MyData";
protected void Page_Load(object sender, EventArgs e)
{
    if (!IsPostBack)
    {
        // Create a new entry with a custom dependency
        XmlDataCacheDependency dep = new XmlDataCacheDependency(
            Server.MapPath("employees.xml"),
            "MyDataSet/NorthwindEmployees/Employee[employeeid=3]/lastname",
            1);
        Cache.Insert(CacheKeyName, dep.CurrentValue, dep);
    }

    // Refresh the UI
    Msg.Text = Display();
}
```

You write the rest of the page as usual, paying close attention to accessing the specified *Cache* key. The reason for this is that because of the dependency, the key could be null. Here's an example:

```
protected string Display()
{
    object o = Cache[CacheKeyName];
    if (o == null)
        return "[No data available--dependency broken]";
    else
        return (string) o;
}
```

The *XmlDataCacheDependency* object allows you to control changes that occur on a file and decide which are relevant and might require you to invalidate the cache. The sample dependency uses XPath expressions to identify a subset of nodes to monitor for changes. For simplicity, only the first node of the output of the XPath expression is considered. The sample XPath expression monitors in the sample *employees.xml* file the *lastname* node of the subtree where *employeeid=3*:

```
<MyDataSet>
    <NorthwindEmployees>
        ...
        <Employee>
            <employeeid>3</employeeid>
            <lastname>Leverling</lastname>
            <firstname>Janet</firstname>
            <title>Sales Representative</title>
```

```
        </Employee>
        ...
    </NorthwindEmployees>
</MyDataSet>
```

The XML file, the cache dependency object, and the preceding sample page produce the output shown in Figure 14-4.

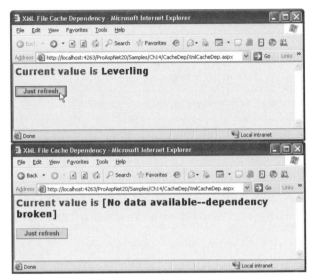

Figure 14-4   The custom dependency object in action in a sample page.

The screen shot at the top is what users see when they first invoke the page. The page at the bottom is what they get when the cached value is invalidated because of a change in the monitored node of the XML file. Note that changes to other nodes, except *lastname* where *employeeid=3*, are blissfully ignored and don't affect the cached value.

> **Note**   I decided to implement polling in this sample custom dependency because polling is a pretty common, often mandatory, approach for custom dependencies. However, in this particular case polling is not the best option. You could set a *FileSystemWatcher* object and watch for changes to the XML file. When a change is detected, you execute the XPath expression to see whether the change is relevant for the dependency. Using an asynchronous notifier, if available, results in much better performance.

SQL Server Cache Dependency

Many ASP.NET applications query some data out of a database, cache it, and then manage to serve a report to the user. Binding the report to the data in the cache will both reduce the time required to load each report and minimize traffic to and from the database. So what's the problem? With a report built from the cache, if the data displayed is modified in the database, users will get an out-of-date report. If updates occur at a known or predictable rate, you can set an appropriate duration for the cached data so that the report gets automatically refreshed at regular intervals. However, this contrivance just doesn't work if serving live data is critical for the application or if changes occur rarely and, worse yet, randomly. In the latter case, whatever duration you set might hit the application in one way or the other. A too-long duration creates the risk of serving outdated reports to end users which, in some cases, could undermine the business; a too-short duration burdens the application with unnecessary queries.

A database dependency is a special case of custom dependency that consists of the automatic invalidation of some cached data when the contents of the source database table changes. Not directly supported by the framework in ASP.NET 1.x, database dependencies are a native feature in ASP.NET 2.0. In ASP.NET 2.0, you find an ad hoc class—*SqlCacheDependency*—that inherits *CacheDependency* and supports dependencies on SQL Server tables. More precisely, the class is compatible with MSDE, SQL Server 7.0, and subsequent SQL Server versions (including SQL Server 2005).

Under the Hood of Database Dependencies

With the notable exception of SQL Server 2005, no database today offers listening features to detect when relevant changes occur. This means that on SQL Server 7.0, SQL Server 2000, and non-SQL Server databases you must create a database-level infrastructure that makes table changes emerge, allows them to be captured, and notifies the ASP.NET cache of the changes.

In the past several years, a few techniques have been investigated by the ASP.NET team and developers in the community. None of the techniques is perfect, but all are worth a look if you plan to implement database cache invalidation in ASP.NET 1.x applications.

A database cache invalidation system is based on two key elements—a mechanism to detect changes on the database, and a mechanism to notify ASP.NET of the changes. To detect changes, triggers are the most commonly used technique. You need to have a trigger active on each table in a database that you want to monitor for changes. The trigger captures insertions, deletions, and updates on a table and does something with them. What exactly it does depends on the second mechanism you implement. Various approaches have been tested over time:

- An extended stored procedure invokes an application-specific HTTP handler (which is simpler than a plain page). The handler receives the key of the cache item that has been invalidated and removes it from the cache.

- An extended stored procedure modifies the timestamp of a disk file that the cached data is dependent upon.

Although some people don't particularly like the use of triggers, as I see things the real issue here is the use of extended stored procedures. They have to be written in C++ and be deployed manually to SQL Server. Furthermore, they require administrative permissions because they run external programs and introduce potentially serious blocking issues. The extended stored procedure can't return until the HTTP call or the file modification is complete. What if the Web server takes a long time to respond? What if the file is locked? In the end, the database will be affected and the flow of information from it or to it might be slowed down. These solutions might work great for small applications with no scalability concerns, but they are not ideal for large, real-world sites.

> **Tip** If you don't like triggers, you might want to try T-SQL checksum functions. The following query returns a value that varies when changes are made to a table record:
>
> ```
> SELECT CHECKSUM_AGG(BINARY_CHECKSUM(*)) FROM Customers
> ```
>
> Checksum functions are reasonably fast but don't work with reference columns such as text and image. The advantage of checksum functions is that all you need to deploy on the database is a stored procedure to wrap the query just shown.

Extended stored procedures implement a push model, where the database backend pushes changes to the ASP.NET application. The reverse approach is also possible—a pull model based on polling—which is the foundation of the ASP.NET 2.0 implementation of database cache invalidation.

The database to be monitored is equipped with triggers and a helper table with one record for each monitored table. Triggers update the helper table whenever the corresponding table is modified. A custom component placed in the ASP.NET cache polls this helper table looking for changes—and because it's a very small table, results are likely to be paged in SQL Server's memory for the fastest performance. When the polling component detects a change in the table, it will invalidate the linked cache item with the data used by the application.

> **Note** To implement database dependencies in ASP.NET 1.x, you start by creating a custom *CacheDependency* class along the lines of the *CacheDependency* class in ASP.NET 2.0. This abstract class will start a timer in the constructor and call an overridable method—for example, *HasChanged*—to check for changes. The user-defined *DatabaseCacheDependency* class inherits from *CacheDependency* and overrides *HasChanged* to query against the helper table of change notifications (or checksums). To insert data in the cache bound to this dependency object, you resort to a helper method that extends the *Insert* method of the native *Cache* object. Basically, your helper insert method will create a pair of cache entries—one for the real data, and one for the dependency object polling for data. The two entries are linked so that changes to the entry with the dependency invalidates the one with real data. Details and sample code are available at *http://msdn.microsoft.com/msdnmag/issues/04/07/CuttingEdge*.

Enabling Database Dependencies in ASP.NET 2.0

In ASP.NET 2.0, database dependencies are implemented through the *SqlCacheDependency* class. The class works with SQL Server 7.0, SQL Server 2000, and the newer SQL Server 2005. To make it work with SQL Server 2005, much less setup work is required. Let's tackle SQL Server 7.0 and SQL Server 2000 first.

For the *SqlCacheDependency* class to work correctly, any tables that you want to monitor for changes must have notifications enabled. Enabling notifications entails administrative changes to the database that must be accomplished before the application is published.

Changes include creating ad hoc triggers and stored procedures to handle any incoming UPDATE, INSERT, or DELETE statements.

You use the command-line tool *aspnet_regsql* to do any required offline work. You first enable notifications on the database, and next do the same on one or more of the database tables. Run the following command to enable notifications on the Northwind database for the local installation of SQL Server:

```
aspnet_regsql.exe -S (local) -U YourUserName -P YourPassword
                  -d Northwind -ed
```

Run the following command to enable notification on the Customers table:

```
aspnet_regsql.exe -S (local) -U YourUserName -P YourPassword
                  -d Northwind -et -t Customers
```

The first command adds a new table to the database whose name is AspNet_SqlCacheTablesForChangeNotification. In addition, a bunch of stored procedures and triggers are added. Note that you need to specify a login with enough permissions to perform all the operations.

The second command adds a trigger to the specified table and a new record to the AspNet_SqlCacheTablesForChangeNotification table that refers to the specified table. Here's the trigger:

```
CREATE TRIGGER dbo.[Customers_AspNet_SqlCacheNotification_Trigger]
ON [Customers]
FOR INSERT, UPDATE, DELETE AS BEGIN
  SET NOCOUNT ON
  EXEC dbo.AspNet_SqlCacheUpdateChangeIdStoredProcedure N'Customers'
END
```

Figure 14-5 provides a view of the structure of the change notification table. This table contains one record for each monitored table.

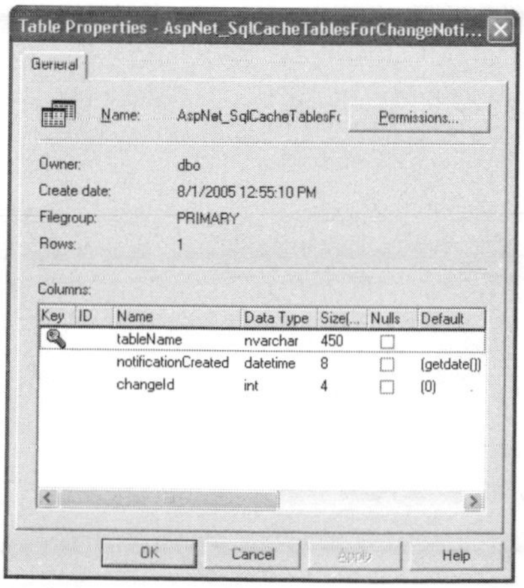

Figure 14-5   The structure of the AspNet_SqlCacheTablesForChangeNotification table.

The trigger executes the following stored procedure whenever a change occurs on the monitored table. As a result, the changeId column for the table is modified.

```
BEGIN
  UPDATE dbo.AspNet_SqlCacheTablesForChangeNotification WITH (ROWLOCK)
    SET changeId = changeId + 1
    WHERE tableName = @tableName
END
```

To finalize the setup of *SqlCacheDependency*, you need to add the following script to the application's *web.config* file:

```
<system.web>
  <caching>
    <sqlCacheDependency enabled="true" pollTime="1000" >
      <databases>
        <add name="Northwind" connectionStringName="LocalNWind" />
      </databases>
    </sqlCacheDependency>
  </caching>
</system.web>
```

The *pollTime* attribute indicates (in milliseconds) the interval of the polling. In the preceding sample, any monitored table will be checked every second. Under the *<databases>* node, you find a reference to monitored databases. The *name* attribute is used only to name the dependency. The *connectionStringName* attribute points to an entry in the *<connectionStrings>* section of the *web.config* file and denotes the connection string to access the database.

> **Note** In addition to using the *aspnet_regsql* command-line tool, you can use a programming interface to create the run-time environment that allows database cache dependencies for SQL Server 7 and SQL Server 2000. The following code enables the Northwind database for notifications:
>
> ```
> SqlCacheDependencyAdmin.EnableNotifications("Northwind");
> ```
>
> You add a table to the list of monitored tables with the following code:
>
> ```
> SqlCacheDependencyAdmin.EnableTableForNotifications(
>     "Northwind", "Employees");
> ```
>
> The *SqlCacheDependencyAdmin* class also counts methods to disable previously enabled dependencies.

Let's see now how to create and use a *SqlCacheDependency* object.

Taking Advantage of SQL Server Dependencies

The *SqlCacheDependency* class has two constructors. The first takes a *SqlCommand* object, and the second accepts two strings—the database name and the table name. The constructor that accepts a *SqlCommand* is intended for use only with SQL Server 2005; the other is designed for dependencies that involve older versions of SQL Server.

The following code creates a SQL Server dependency and binds it to a cache key:

```
protected void AddToCache(object data)
{
    string database = "Northwind";
    string table = "Customers";
    SqlCacheDependency dep = new SqlCacheDependency(database, table);
    Cache.Insert("MyData", data, dep);
}
protected void Page_Load(object sender, EventArgs e)
{
    if (!IsPostBack)
    {
        // Get some data to cache
        CustomerCollection data = Customers.LoadByCountry("USA");

        // Cache with a dependency on Customers
        AddToCache(data);
    }
}
```

The data in the cache can be linked to any data-bound control, as follows:

```
CustomerCollection data = null;
object o = Cache["MyData"];
if (o != null)
    data = (CustomerCollection)o;
else
    Trace.Warn("Null data");

CustomerList.DataTextField = "CompanyName";
CustomerList.DataSource = data;
CustomerList.DataBind();
```

When the database is updated, the *MyData* entry is invalidated and, as for the sample implementation provided here, the listbox displays empty.

> **Important**   You get notification based on changes in the table as a whole. In the preceding code, we're displaying a data set that results from the following:
>
> ```
> SELECT * FROM customers WHERE country='USA'
> ```
>
> If, say, a new record is added to the Customers table, you get a notification no matter what the value in the country column is. The same happens if a record is modified or deleted where the country column is not USA.
>
> SQL Server 2005 offers a finer level of control and can notify applications only of changes to the database that modify the output of a specific command.

Once you are set up for table notifications, pages that use a *SqlDataSource* control can implement a smarter form of caching that monitors the bound table for changes and reloads data in case of changes:

```
<asp:SqlDataSource ID="SqlDataSource1" runat="server"
    ConnectionString="<%$ ConnectionStrings:LocalNWind %>"
    SelectCommand="SELECT * FROM Customers"
    EnableCaching="true"
    SqlCacheDependency="Northwind:Customers">
</asp:SqlDataSource>
```

You set the *SqlCacheDependency* property to a string of the form *Database:Table*. The first token is the name of the database dependency as set in the *<databases>* section. The second token is the name of the table to monitor. You can also define multiple dependencies by separating each pair with a semicolon:

```
<asp:SqlDataSource ID="SqlDataSource1" runat="server"
    EnableCaching="true"
    SqlCacheDependency="Northwind:Customers;Pubs:Authors"
    ...
/>
```

Note that caching must be enabled for the feature to work.

> **Note** Although I've mentioned only *SqlDataSource*, the *SqlCacheDependency* property also works with *ObjectDataSource* as long as *ObjectDataSource* returns data through ADO.NET objects.

Cache Dependencies in SQL Server 2005

As mentioned, the *SqlCacheDependency* class has two constructors, one of which takes a *SqlCommand* object as its sole argument. This constructor is used to create *SqlCacheDependency* objects for SQL Server 2005 databases. Here's how to use it:

```
protected void AddToCache()
{
    SqlConnection conn = new SqlConnection(
        ConfigurationManager.ConnectionStrings["NWind05"].ConnectionString);
    SqlCommand cmd = new SqlCommand(
        "SELECT * FROM Customers WHERE country='USA'",
        conn);

    SqlDataAdapter adapter = new SqlDataAdapter(cmd);
    DataTable data = new DataTable();
    adapter.Fill(data);
```

```
    SqlCacheDependency dep = new SqlCacheDependency(cmd);
    Cache.Insert("MyData", data, dep);
}
```

Note that with SQL Server 2005 no setup work is needed and no external objects must be added to the database. No triggers, stored procedures, and notification tables are needed.

SQL Server 2005 incorporates a made-to-measure component that monitors changes at a finer level than was possible in earlier versions. This component takes a command object and tracks all the ongoing changes to detect whether something happened to modify the result set returned by the command. When this happens, the component pushes new information to the listening object. This mechanism relies on the ADO.NET *SqlDependency* class that we discussed back in Chapter 7.

So when you instantiate a *SqlCacheDependency* object and have it guard a given command, a *SqlDependency* object wraps the command and fires an event when a change is detected. In turn, the *SqlCacheDependency* catches the event and invalidates the cached item. Figure 14-6 illustrates the data flow.

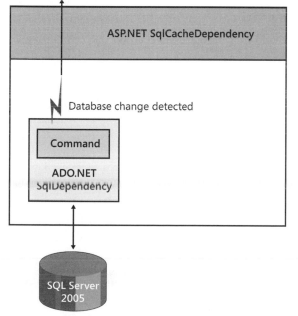

Figure 14-6   The internal implementation of *SqlCacheDependency* when used with SQL Server 2005.

> **Note** The SQL Server 2005 implementation of database cache invalidation is clearly the best possible because it leverages a new infrastructure built in the database. ASP.NET applications receive an asynchronous notification of changes, which is good for performance and poses no blocking issues. Also, no setup is necessary for the feature to work. The SQL Server 7.0 and SQL Server 2000 implementation of the same feature relies on polling and requires some setup work. The ASP.NET team made the SQL dependency setup as smooth as possible, but it still requires an administrative login to get into the database to create triggers, tables, and stored procedures. This might be a problem if you're not allowed full access to the database or if you're working in an ISP scenario. Is polling the best possible option for detecting changes? All things considered, polling is a necessity when there's no built-in notification mechanism in the database. And polling a small table is more efficient than repeatedly running a query. Finally, polling doesn't suffer from blocking issues as do approaches built on extended stored procedures, and it also works great in Web farms and Web gardens. In the end, the ASP.NET team determined that polling was the best option for the broadest number of ASP.NET applications willing to support database cache invalidation.

Caching ASP.NET Pages

In many situations it is acceptable for a page response to be a little stale if this brings significant performance advantages. Want an example? Think of an e-commerce application and its set of pages for the products catalog. These pages are relatively expensive to create because they could require one or more database calls and likely some form of data join. All things considered, a page like this could easily cost you a few million CPU cycles. Why should you regenerate this same page a hundred times per second? Product pages tend to remain the same for weeks and are rarely updated more than once per day. Whatever the refresh rate is for the pages, there's little value in regenerating them on a per-request basis.

A much better strategy is to create the page once, cache it somewhere, and give the page output a maximum duration. Once the cached page becomes stale, the first incoming request will be served in the standard way, running the page's code, and the new page output will be cached for another period until it also becomes stale.

ASP.NET page output caching is the feature that allows you to cache page responses so that following requests can be satisfied without executing the page but instead by simply returning the cached output. Output caching can take place at two levels: entire pages or portions of the page. Page caching is smart enough to let you save distinct output based on the requesting URL, query string or form parameters, and even custom strings.

Easy to set up and terrifically effective, output caching can either be configured declaratively through the @OutputCache directive or programmatically through an API built around the HttpCachePolicy class.

> **Important** Page output caching is simply a way to have the application serve more pages more quickly. It has nothing to do with sophisticated caching strategies or elegant code design. In other words, it will enable your application to serve pages faster, but it won't necessarily make the application more efficient and scalable. With page output caching, you can certainly reduce the workload on the server as pages are cached downstream. Finally, be aware that page output caching works only for anonymous content. Requests for cached pages are served by Internet Information Server (IIS) 6.0 directly or by the ASP.NET worker process under IIS 5.0. In any case, a page request never reaches stages in the ASP.NET pipeline where it can be authenticated, which is a strategy employed to prevent access to protected content.

The @*OutputCache* Directive

Caching the output of a page is as easy as defining an @*OutputCache* directive at the top of the page. The directive accepts a handful of attributes, a couple of which—*Duration* and *VaryBy-Param*—are mandatory. The *Duration* attribute indicates in seconds how long the system should cache the page output. The *VaryByParam* attribute allows you to vary the cached output depending on the *GET* query string or form *POST* parameters. The following declaration will cache the page for one minute regardless of any *GET* or *POST* parameters:

```
<%@ OutputCache Duration="60" VaryByParam="None" %>
```

For frequently requested pages and relatively static pages, the @*OutputCache* directive is a real performance booster. With a shorter duration, even limited to one or two seconds, it provides a way to speed up the entire application.

The @*OutputCache* directive consists of six attributes that indicate the location of the cache, its duration, and the arguments to use to vary page caching. The list of supported attributes is shown in Table 14-7. Note that the directive can be applied to both pages (*.aspx*) and user controls (*.ascx*). Some of the attributes are valid in one case but not the other.

Table 14-7   Attributes of the @*OutputCache* Directive

Attribute	Applies to	Description
CacheProfile	Page	Associates a page with a group of output caching settings specified in the *web.config* file (more on this later). *Not supported in ASP.NET 1.x.*
Duration	Page, User control	The time, in seconds, that the page or user control is cached.
Location	Page	Specifies a valid location to store the output of a page. The attribute takes its value from the *OutputCache-Location* enumeration.
NoStore	Page	Indicates whether to send a *Cache-Control:no-store* header to prevent additional storage of the page output. *Not supported in ASP.NET 1.x.*

Table 14-7 **Attributes of the** *@OutputCache* **Directive**

Attribute	Applies to	Description
Shared	User control	Indicates whether the user control output can be shared with multiple pages. False by default.
SqlDependency	Page, User control	Indicates a dependency on the specified table on a given SQL Server database. Whenever the contents of the table changes, the page output is removed from the cache. *Not supported in ASP.NET 1.x.*
VaryByControl	User control	A semicolon-separated list of strings that represent properties of the user control. Each distinct combination of values for the specified properties will originate a distinct copy of the page in the cache.
VaryByCustom	Page, User control	A semicolon-separated list of strings that lets you maintain distinct cached copies of the page based on the browser type or user-defined strings.
VaryByHeader	Page	A semicolon-separated list of HTTP headers.
VaryByParam	Page, User control	A semicolon-separated list of strings representing query string values sent with *GET* method attributes or parameters sent using the *POST* method.

Note that the *VaryByParam* attribute is mandatory. If you omit it, a run-time exception is always thrown. However, if you don't need to vary by parameters, set the attribute to *None*. The empty string is not an acceptable value for the *VaryByParam* attribute.

Choosing a Duration for the Page Output

When the output caching service is active on a page, the *Duration* attribute indicates the number of seconds that the caching system will maintain an HTML-compiled version of the page. Next, requests for the same page, or for an existing parameterized version of the page, will be serviced while bypassing most of the ASP.NET pipeline. As mentioned, this process has two important repercussions—no authentication is possible and no code is run, meaning that no page events are fired and handled and no state is updated. The implementation of output caching varies with the ASP.NET process model in use. (See Chapter 3 for details on the ASP.NET process models.)

With the IIS 5.0 process model, any request for an ASP.NET page is always handed over to the worker process, assigned to an *HttpApplication* object, and processed by the pipeline. The ASP.NET pipeline includes an HTTP module named *OutputCacheModule* that captures two application-level events related to output caching—*ResolveRequestCache* and *UpdateRequestCache*. In particular, the module uses the *ResolveRequestCache* event handler to short-circuit the processing of requests for pages that have been cached. In the end, the request is hooked by the HTTP module and served by returning the copy of the page stored in the cache. When the page is being generated, *OutputCacheModule* grabs the output of the pages marked with the *@OutputCache* directive and stores it internally for further use. The output of the page is stored in a private slot of the ASP.NET *Cache* object. Setting the *Duration* attribute on a page sets an expiration policy for the HTTP response generated by the ASP.NET runtime. The output is cached by the module for exactly the specified number of seconds. In the meantime, all the incoming requests that hit one of the cached pages are serviced by the module rather than by the ASP.NET pipeline.

With the IIS 6.0 process model, the output caching mechanism is integrated in the Web server, resulting in much better performance and responsiveness, thanks to the IIS 6.0 *kernel caching*. When enabled, this feature makes it possible for IIS to intercept the output of a page generated by ASP.NET. A copy of the page output is then cached by the IIS kernel. Incoming requests for an ASP.NET page are filtered by a kernel-level driver (*http.sys*) and examined to see whether they match cached pages. If so, the output is served to callers directly from kernel-level code without even bothering the worker process and the ASP.NET pipeline. If you have any ASP.NET applications and are still considering an upgrade to IIS 6.0, this is a great reason to do it as soon as possible. Note that this facility in IIS 6.0 is used by ASP.NET since version 1.1 to host the output cache. So, when using the output cache directive in ASP.NET 1.1 and ASP.NET 2.0 applications, your responses are being served from the kernel cache. See the sidebar "Inside IIS 6.0 Kernel Caching" for more performance details.

A fair value for the *Duration* attribute depends on the application, but it normally doesn't exceed 60 seconds. This value usually works great, especially if the page doesn't need to be updated frequently. A short duration (say, 1 second) can be useful for applications that claim live data all the time.

Inside IIS 6.0 Kernel Caching

IIS 6.0 employs an ad hoc component to cache the dynamically generated response to a request in the kernel. This feature has tremendous potential and can dramatically improve the performance of a Web server, as long as enough of the content being served is cacheable. What's the performance gain you can get?

According to the numbers provided with the IIS 6.0 technical documentation, an application using the kernel cache returns a throughput of more than 10 times the throughput you would get in the non-cached case. Additionally, the latency of responses is dramatically better. The following table compares caching in IIS 6.0 kernel mode and user-mode caching as implemented by the ASP.NET runtime in IIS 5.0.

	User Mode	Kernel Mode
Requests / Sec	1,394	15,416
TTFB / TTLB (msec)	70.82 / 70.97	3.39 / 4.02
User Mode CPU %	76.57%	0.78%
Kernel Mode CPU %	22.69%	99.22%
System Calls / Sec	20,110	2,101
Network Util (KB / Sec)	6,153	68,326
Context Switches / Sec	2,621	6,261

Source: *http://www.microsoft.com/technet/prodtechnol/windowsserver2003/technologies/webapp/iis/ iis6perf.mspx*

The numbers in the preceding table provide you with an idea of the results, but the results will vary according to the amount of work and size of the response. The bottom line, though, is that leveraging the kernel cache can make a dramatic difference in the performance of an application. The great news for ASP.NET developers is that no code changes are required to benefit from kernel caching, except for the *@OutputCache* directive.

On a high-volume Web site, an output cache duration of only one second can make a significant difference for the overall throughput of a Web server. There's more to know about kernel caching, though. First and foremost, kernel caching is available only for pages requested through a *GET* verb. No kernel caching is possible on postbacks. Furthermore, pages with *VaryByParam* and *VaryByHeader* attributes set are also not stored in the kernel cache. Finally, note that ASP.NET Request/Cache performance counters will not be updated for pages served by the kernel cache.

Choosing a Location for the Page Output

The output cache can be located in various places, either on the client that originated the request or on the server. It can also be located on an intermediate proxy server. The various options are listed in Table 14-8. They come from the *OutputCacheLocation* enumerated type.

Table 14-8 Output Cache Locations

Location	Cache-Control	Description
Any	*Public*	The HTTP header *Expires* is set according to the duration set in the *@OutputCache* directive. A new item is placed in the ASP.NET *Cache* object representing the output of the page.
Client	*Private*	The output cache is located on the browser where the request originated. The HTTP header *Expires* is set according to the duration set in the *@OutputCache* directive. No item is created in the ASP.NET *Cache* object.
DownStream	*Public*	The output cache can be stored in any HTTP cache-capable devices other than the origin server. This includes proxy servers and the client that made the request. The HTTP header *Expires* is set according to the duration set in the *@OutputCache* directive. No item is created in the ASP.NET *Cache* object.
None	*No-Cache*	The HTTP header *Expires* is not defined. The *Pragma* header is set to *No-Cache*. No item is created in the ASP.NET *Cache* object.
Server	*No-Cache*	The HTTP header *Expires* is not defined. The *Pragma* header is set to *No-Cache*. A new item is placed in the ASP.NET *Cache* object to represent the output of the page.

A page marked with the *@OutputCache* directive also generates a set of HTTP headers, such as *Expires* and *Cache-Control*. Downstream proxy servers such as Microsoft ISA Server understand these headers and cache the page along the way. In this way, for the duration of the output, requests for the page can be satisfied even without reaching the native Web server.

In particular, the *Expires* HTTP header is used to specify the time when a particular page on the server should be updated. Until that time, any new request the browser receives for the resource is served using the local, client-side cache and no server roundtrip is ever made. When specified and not set to *No-Cache*, the *Cache-Control* HTTP header typically takes values such as *public* or *private*. A value of *public* means that both the browser and the proxy servers can cache the page. A value of *private* prevents proxy servers from caching the page; only the browser will cache the page. The *Cache-Control* is part of the HTTP 1.1 specification and is supported only by Microsoft Internet Explorer 5.5 and higher.

If you look at the HTTP headers generated by ASP.NET when output caching is enabled, you'll notice that sometimes the *Pragma* header is used—in particular, when the location is set to *Server*. In this case, the header is assigned a value of *No-Cache*, meaning that client-side caching is totally disabled both on the browser side and the proxy side. As a result, any access to the page is resolved through a connection.

> **Note** To be precise, the *Pragma* header set to *No-Cache* disables caching only over HTTPS channels. If used over nonsecure channels, the page is actually cached but marked as expired.

Let's examine the client and Web server caching configuration when each of the feasible locations is used.

- **Any.** This is the default option. This setting means that the page can be cached everywhere, including in the browser, the server, and any proxies along the way. The *Expires* header is set to the page's absolute expiration time as determined by the *Duration* attribute; the *Cache-Control* header is set to *public*, meaning that the proxies can cache if they want or need to. On the Web server, a new item is placed in the *Cache* object with the HTML output of the page. In summary, with this option the page output is cached everywhere. As a result, if the page is accessed through the browser before it expires, no roundtrip is ever made. If, in the same timeframe, the page is refreshed—meaning that server-side access is made anyway—the overhead is minimal, the request is short-circuited by the output cache module, and no full request processing takes place.

- **Client.** The page is cached only by the browser because the *Cache-Control* header is set to *private*. Neither proxies nor ASP.NET stores a copy of it. The *Expires* header is set according to the value of the *Duration* attribute.

- **DownStream.** The page can be cached both on the client and in the memory of any intermediate proxy. The *Expires* header is set according to the value of the *Duration* attribute, and no copy of the page output is maintained by ASP.NET.

- **None.**   Page output caching is disabled both on the server and on the client. No *Expires* HTTP header is generated, and both the *Cache-Control* and the *Pragma* headers are set to *No-Cache*.

- **Server.**   The page output is exclusively cached on the server, and its raw response is stored in the *Cache* object. The client-side caching is disabled. No *Expires* header is created, and both the *Cache-Control* and *Pragma* headers are set to *No-Cache*.

- **ServerAndClient.**   The output cache can be stored only at the origin server or at the requesting client. Proxy servers are not allowed to cache the response.

Adding a Database Dependency to Page Output

The *SqlDependency* attribute is the *@OutputCache* directive's interface to the *SqlCacheDependency* class that we discussed earlier. When the *SqlDependency* attribute is set to a *Database:Table* string, a SQL Server cache-dependency object is created. When the dependency is broken, the page output is invalidated and the next request will be served by pushing the request through the pipeline as usual. The output generated will be cached again:

```
<% @OutputCache Duration="15" VaryByParam="none"
               SqlDependency="Northwind:Employees" %>
```

A page that contains this code snippet has its output cached for 15 seconds or until a record changes in the Employees table in the Northwind database. Note that the Northwind string here is not the name of a database—it's the name of an entry in the *<databases>* section of the configuration file. That entry contains detailed information about the connection string to use to reach the database. You can specify multiple dependencies by separating multiple *Database:Table* pairs with a semicolon in the value of the *SqlDependency* attribute.

> **Note**   A user control is made cacheable in either of two ways: by using the *@OutputCache* directive or by defining the *PartialCaching* attribute on the user control's class declaration in the code-behind file, as follows:
>
> ```
> [PartialCaching(60)]
>
> public partial class CustomersGrid : UserControl {
>
>    . . .
>
> }
> ```
>
> The *PartialCaching* attribute allows you to specify the duration and values for the *VaryByParam*, *VaryByControl*, and *VaryByCustom* parameters.

The *HttpCachePolicy* Class

The *HttpCachePolicy* class is a programming interface alternative to using the *@OutputCache* directive. It provides direct methods to set cache-related HTTP headers, which you could also control to some extent by using the members of the *HttpResponse* object.

Properties of the *HttpCachePolicy* Class

Table 14-9 shows the properties of the *HttpCachePolicy* class.

Table 14-9   *HttpCachePolicy* Class Properties

Property	Description
VaryByHeaders	Gets an object of type *HttpCacheVaryByHeaders*, representing the list of all HTTP headers that will be used to vary cache output
VaryByParams	Gets an object of type *HttpCacheVaryByParams*, representing the list of parameters received by a *GET* or *POST* request that affect caching

When a cached page has several vary-by headers or parameters, a separate version of the page is available for each HTTP header type or parameter name.

Methods of the *HttpCachePolicy* Class

Table 14-10 shows the methods of the *HttpCachePolicy* class.

Table 14-10   *HttpCachePolicy* Class Methods

Method	Description
AddValidationCallback	Registers a callback function to be used to validate the page output in the server cache before returning it.
AppendCacheExtension	Appends the specified text to the *Cache-Control* HTTP header. The existing text is not overwritten.
SetAllowResponseInBrowserHistory	When true, the response is available in the browser's History cache, regardless of the *HttpCacheability* option set on the server.
SetCacheability	Sets the *Cache-Control* HTTP header to any of the values taken from the *HttpCacheability* enumeration type.
SetETag	Sets the *ETag* header to the specified string. The *ETag* header is a unique identifier for a specific version of a document.
SetETagFromFileDependencies	Sets the *ETag* header to a string built by combining and then hashing the last modified date of all the files upon which the page is dependent.
SetExpires	Sets the *Expires* header to an absolute date and time.
SetLastModified	Sets the *Last-Modified* HTTP header to a particular date and time.
SetLastModifiedFromFileDependencies	Sets the *Last-Modified* HTTP header to the most recent timestamps of the files upon which the page is dependent.
SetMaxAge	Sets the *max-age* attribute on the *Cache-Control* header to the specified value. The sliding period cannot exceed one year.
SetNoServerCaching	Disables server output caching for the current response.

Table 14-10 *HttpCachePolicy* **Class Methods**

Method	Description
SetNoStore	Sets the *Cache-Control: no-store* directive.
SetNoTransforms	Sets the *Cache-Control: no-transforms* directive.
SetOmitVaryStar	If true, causes *HttpCachePolicy* to ignore the * value in *VaryByHeaders. Not supported by ASP.NET 1.x.*
SetProxyMaxAge	Sets the *Cache-Control: s-maxage* header.
SetRevalidation	Sets the *Cache-Control* header to either *must-revalidate* or *proxy-revalidate*.
SetSlidingExpiration	Sets cache expiration to sliding. When cache expiration is set to sliding, the *Cache-Control* header is renewed at each response.
SetValidUntilExpires	Specifies whether the ASP.NET cache should ignore HTTP *Cache-Control* headers sent by some browsers to evict a page from the cache. If set to *true*, the page stays in the cache until it expires.
SetVaryByCustom	Sets the *Vary* HTTP header to the specified text string.

Most methods of the *HttpCachePolicy* class let you control the values of some HTTP headers that relate to the browser cache. The *AddValidationCallback* method, on the other hand, provides a mechanism to programmatically check the validity of page output in the server cache before it is returned from the cache.

Server Cache-Validation Callback

Before the response is served from the ASP.NET cache, all registered handlers are given a chance to verify the validity of the cached page. If at least one handler marks the cached page as invalid, the entry is removed from the cache and the request is served as if it were never cached. The signature of the callback function looks like this:

```
public delegate void HttpCacheValidateHandler(
    HttpContext context,
    object data,
    ref HttpValidationStatus validationStatus
);
```

The first argument denotes the context of the current request, whereas the second argument is any user-defined data the application needs to pass to the handler. Finally, the third argument is a reference to a value from the *HttpValidationStatus* enumeration. The callback sets this value to indicate the result of the validation. Acceptable values are *IgnoreThisRequest*, *Invalid*, and *Valid*. In the case of *IgnoreThisRequest*, the cached resource is not invalidated but the request is served as if no response was ever cached. If the return value is *Invalid*, the cached page is not used and gets invalidated. Finally, if the return value is *Valid*, the cached response is used to serve the request.

Caching Multiple Versions of a Page

Depending on the application context from which a certain page is invoked, the page might generate different results. The same page can be called to operate with different parameters, can be configured using different HTTP headers, can produce different output based on the requesting browser, and so forth.

ASP.NET allows you to cache multiple versions of a page response; you can distinguish versions by *GET* and *POST* parameters, HTTP headers, browser type, custom strings, and control properties.

Vary By Parameters

To vary output caching by parameters, you can use either the *VaryByParam* attribute of the *@OutputCache* directive or the *VaryByParams* property on the *HttpCachePolicy* class. If you proceed declaratively, use the following syntax:

```
<% @OutputCache Duration="60" VaryByParam="employeeID" %>
```

Note that the *VaryByParam* attribute is mandatory; if you don't want to specify a parameter to vary cached content, set the value to *None*. If you want to vary the output by all parameters, set the attribute to *. When the *VaryByParam* attribute is set to multiple parameters, the output cache contains a different version of the requested document for each specified parameter. Multiple parameters are separated by a semicolon. Valid parameters to use are items specified on the *GET* query string or parameters set in the body of a *POST* command.

If you want to use the *HttpCachePolicy* class to define caching parameters, first set the expiration and the cacheability of the page using the *SetExpires* and *SetCacheability* methods. Next, set the *VaryByParams* property as shown here:

```
Response.Cache.SetExpires(DateTime.Now.AddSeconds(60));
Response.Cache.SetCacheability(HttpCacheability.Public);
Response.Cache.VaryByParams["employeeid;lastname"] = true;
```

This code snippet shows how to vary page output based on the employee ID and the last name properties. Note that the *Cache* property on the *HttpResponse* class is just an instance of the *HttpCachePolicy* type.

Dealing with Postback Pages

Most ASP.NET pages do postbacks. The page in Figure 14-7 (*sqldepoutputcache.aspx*) is no exception. The page has two key features: it is dependent on changes to the Customers table in the Northwind database, and it has a cache duration of 30 seconds. Furthermore, the drop-down list (named *Countries*) has auto-postback functionality and places a POST request for the same page whenever you change the selection.

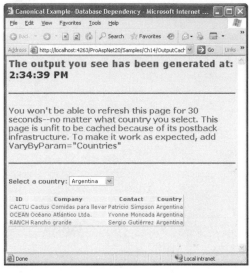

Figure 14-7 To properly cache pages that post back, you need to vary them by one or more parameters.

With *VaryByParam* set to *None*, you'll wait 30 seconds (or whatever the cache duration is) to have your country selection processed. It is a bit frustrating: no matter which selection you make, it is blissfully ignored and the same page is displayed. Worse yet, if you test the page under the Visual Studio .NET Web Development server, after a couple of attempts you get a "page not found" error. If you test the page under IIS, you are repeatedly served the same page response, regardless of the selection made.

Two points clearly emerge from this discussion. First, pages with static content are a better fit for caching than interactive pages. Second, the postback mechanism returns a bunch of form parameters. You need to vary the cached copies of the page by the most critical of them. The sample page in Figure 14-7 has a few hidden fields (try snooping in its HTML source), such as *__VIEWSTATE* and *__LASTFOCUS*, and the drop-down list. Varying by view state makes no sense at all, but varying by the selected countries is exactly what we need:

```
<%@ OutputCache VaryByParam="Countries" Duration="30"
               SqlDependency="Northwind:Customers" %>
```

The directive stores each country-specific page for 30 seconds unless a change occurs in the Customers database. In such a case, all the cached versions of the page will be invalidated.

The bottom line is that enabling page output caching might not be painless for interactive pages. It is free of pain and free of charge for relatively static pages like those describing a product, a customer, or some news.

> **Caution**   A cached ASP.NET page is served more quickly than a processed page, but not as quickly as a static HTML page. However, the response time is nearly identical if the ASP.NET page is kernel-cached in IIS 6.0. Unfortunately, IIS 6.0 doesn't store in its kernel-level cache ASP.NET pages requested via a POST verb and, more importantly, pages with *VaryByParam* or *VaryByHeader*. In the end, postback pages have very few chances to be cached in the IIS kernel. They are cached in the ASP.NET *Cache*, in downstream caching servers, or both.

Vary By Headers

The *VaryByHeader* attribute and the *HttpCachePolicy*'s *VaryByHeaders* property allow you to cache multiple versions of a page, according to the value of one or more HTTP headers that you specify.

If you want to cache pages by multiple headers, include a semicolon delimited list of header names. If you want to cache a different version of the page for each different header value, set the *VaryByHeader* attribute to an asterisk *. For example, the following declaration caches for one-minute pages based on the language accepted by the browser. Each language will have a different cached copy of the page output.

```
<%@ OutputCache Duration="60" VaryByParam="None"
    VaryByHeader="Accept-Language" %>
```

If you opt for a programmatic approach, here's the code to use that leverages the *VaryByHeaders* property of the *HttpCachePolicy* class:

```
Response.Cache.VaryByHeaders["Accept-Language"] = true;
```

If you want to programmatically vary the pages in the cache by all HTTP header names, use the *VaryByUnspecifiedParameters* method of the *HttpCacheVaryByHeaders* class:

```
HttpCacheVaryByHeaders.VaryByUnspecifiedParameters();
```

The preceding code is equivalent to using the asterisk with the *VaryByHeader* attribute.

Vary By Custom Strings

The *VaryByCustom* attribute in the *@OutputCache* directive allows you to vary the versions of page output by the value of a custom string. The string you assign to the *VaryByCustom* attribute simply represents the description of the algorithm employed to vary page outputs. The string is then passed to the *GetVaryByCustomString* method, if any, in the *global.asax* file. The method takes the string and returns another string that is specific to the request. Let's examine a concrete example—varying pages by the type of device that requests the page. You use, say, the string *device* with the *VaryByCustom* attribute:

```
<%@ OutputCache Duration="60" VaryByParam="None" VaryByCustom="device" %>
```

Next, you add your application-specific *GetVaryByCustomString* method in the *global.asax* file. Here's a possible implementation:

```
string GetVaryByCustomString(HttpContext context, string custom)
{
    if (custom == "device")
        return context.Request.Browser.Type;
    return null;
}
```

The output of the page is varied by user agent string. You can use any other custom information as long as the information is available through the *HttpContext* class. You can't use information that is known only when the page is loaded, such as the theme. Custom information gathered by a custom HTTP module might be used if the HTTP module parks the information in the *Items* collection of the *HttpContext* object, and as long as the HTTP module is triggered before the request to resolve the page output cache is made.

Nicely enough, the feature described above—varying pages by user agent strings—is natively available since ASP.NET 1.0. The only difference is that it uses the keyword *browser* instead of *device*. In other words, the following code is perfectly acceptable and leverages the implementation of *GetVaryByCustomString* on the base *HttpApplication* class:

```
<%@ OutputCache Duration="60" VaryByParam="None" VaryByCustom="browser" %>
```

You use the *SetVaryByCustom* method on the *HttpCachePolicy* class if you don't like the declarative approach:

```
Response.Cache.SetVaryByCustom("browser");
```

Caching Portions of ASP.NET Pages

The capability of caching the output of Web pages adds a lot of power to your programming arsenal, but sometimes caching the entire content of a page is not possible or it's just impractical. Some pages, in fact, are made of pieces with radically different features as far as cacheability is concerned. In these situations, being able to cache portions of a page is an incredible added value.

If caching the entire page is impractical, you can always opt for partial caching. Partial caching leverages the concept of ASP.NET user controls—that is, small, nested pages that inherit several features of the page. In particular, user controls can be cached individually based on the browser, *GET* and *POST* parameters, and the value of a particular set of properties.

I cover user controls in detail in my other recent book, *Programming Microsoft ASP.NET 2.0 Applications: Advanced Topics* (Microsoft Press, 2005), but a quick introduction is in order for the purpose of partial caching.

What's a User Control, Anyway?

A user control is a Web form saved to a distinct file with an *.ascx* extension. The similarity between user controls and pages is not coincidental. You create a user control in much the same way you create a Web form, and a user control is made of any combination of server and client controls sewn together with server and client script code. Once created, the user control can be inserted in an ASP.NET page like any other server control. ASP.NET pages see the user control as an atomic, encapsulated component and work with it as with any other built-in Web control.

The internal content of the user control is hidden to the host page. However, the user control can define a public programming interface and filter access to its constituent controls via properties, methods, and events.

User controls and pages have so much in common that transforming a page, or a part of it, into a user control is no big deal. You copy the portion of the page of interest to a new *.ascx* file and make sure the user control does not contain any of the following tags: *<html>*, *<body>*, or *<form>*. You complete the work by associating a code-behind file (or a *<script runat="server">* block) to code the expected behavior of the user control. Finally, you add an *@Control* directive in lieu of the *@Page* directive. Here's an example of a user control:

```
<%@ Control Language="C#" CodeFile="Message.ascx.cs" Inherits="Message" %>
<span style="color:<%= ForeColor%>"><%= Text%></span>
```

Here's the related code-behind class:

```
public partial class Message : System.Web.UI.UserControl
{
    public string ForeColor;
    public string Text;
}
```

To insert a user control into a ASP.NET page, you drag it from the project onto the Web form when in design mode. Visual Studio .NET registers the user control with the page and prepares the environment for you to start adding code:

```
<%@ Page Language="C#" CodeFile="Test.aspx.cs" Inherits="TestUserCtl" %>
<%@ Register Src="Message.ascx" TagName="Message" TagPrefix="uc1" %>
<html><body>
    <form id="form1" runat="server">
        <uc1:Message ID="Message1" runat="server" />
    </form>
</body></html>
```

In the page code-behind class, you work the *Message1* variable as you would with any other server control:

```
protected void Page_Load(object sender, EventArgs e)
{
    Message1.ForeColor = "blue";
    Message1.Text = "Hello world";
}
```

Caching the Output of User Controls

User controls are not only good at modularizing your user interface, but they're also great at caching portions of Web pages. User controls, therefore, fully support the *@OutputCache* directive, although they do so with some differences with ASP.NET pages, as outlined in Table 14-7.

A page that contains some dynamic sections cannot be cached entirely. What if the page also contains sections that are both heavy to compute and seldom updated? In this case, you move static contents to one or more user controls and use the user control's *@OutputCache* directive to set up output caching.

To make a user control cacheable, you declare the *@OutputCache* attribute using almost the same set of attributes we discussed earlier for pages. For example, the following code snippet caches the output of the control that embeds it for one minute:

```
<% @OutputCache Duration="60" VaryByParam="None" %>
```

The *Location* attribute is not supported because all controls in the page share the same location. So if you need to specify the cache location, do that at the page level and it will work for all embedded controls. The same holds true for the *VaryByHeader* attribute.

The output of a user control can vary by custom strings and form parameters. More often, though, you'll want to vary the output of a control by property values. In this case, use the new *VaryByControl* attribute.

Vary By Controls

The *VaryByControl* attribute allows you to vary the cache for each specified control property. For user controls, the property is mandatory unless the *VaryByParam* attribute has been specified. You can indicate both *VaryByParam* and *VaryByControl*, but at least one of them is required.

The following user control displays a grid with all the customers in a given country. The country is specified by the user control's *Country* property.

```
<%@ Control Language="C#" CodeFile="CustomersGrid.ascx.cs"
            Inherits="CustomersGridByCtl" %>
<%@ OutputCache Duration="30" VaryByControl="Country" %>

<h3><%= DateTime.Now.ToString() %></h3>
<asp:ObjectDataSource ID="ObjectDataSource1" runat="server"
    TypeName="ProAspNet20.DAL.Customers"
    SelectMethod="LoadByCountry">
</asp:ObjectDataSource>

<asp:GridView ID="GridView1" runat="server" AutoGenerateColumns="false">
    <Columns>
        <asp:BoundField DataField="ID" HeaderText="ID" />
        <asp:BoundField DataField="CompanyName" HeaderText="Company" />
```

```
            <asp:BoundField DataField="ContactName" HeaderText="Contact" />
            <asp:BoundField DataField="Country" HeaderText="Country" />
        </Columns>
    </asp:GridView>
```

Here is the code file of the user control:

```
public partial class CustomersGridByCtl : System.Web.UI.UserControl
{
    public string Country;

    protected void Page_Load(object sender, EventArgs e)
    {
        if (!String.IsNullOrEmpty(Country))
        {
            ObjectDataSource1.SelectParameters.Add("country", Country);
            GridView1.DataSourceID = "ObjectDataSource1";
        }
    }
}
```

The *@OutputCache* directive caches a different copy of the user control output based on the different values of the *Country* property. Figure 14-8 shows it in action.

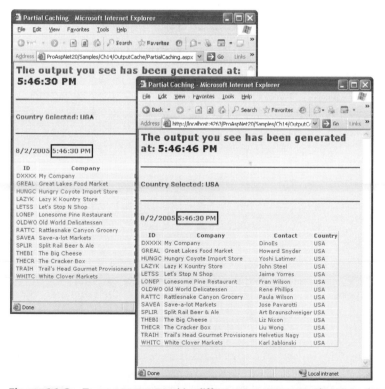

Figure 14-8   Two pages created in different moments use the same user control output, as you can see from the creation time of the grid.

The strings you assign to *VaryByControl* can be properties of the user controls as well as ID property values for contained controls. In this case, you'll get a distinct cached copy for each distinct combination of property values on the specified control.

The *Shared* Attribute

In Figure 14-8, you see two instances of the same page sharing the cached output of a user control. Try the following simple experiment. Make a plain copy of the page (say, *page1.aspx*) and give it another name (say, *page2.aspx*). You should have two distinct pages that generate identical output. In particular, both pages contain an instance of the same cacheable user control. Let's say that the cache duration of the user control is 30 seconds.

As the next step of the experiment, you open both pages at different times while the cache is still valid. Let's say you open the second page ten seconds later than the first. Interestingly enough, the two pages are no longer sharing the same copy of user control output, as Figure 14-9 documents.

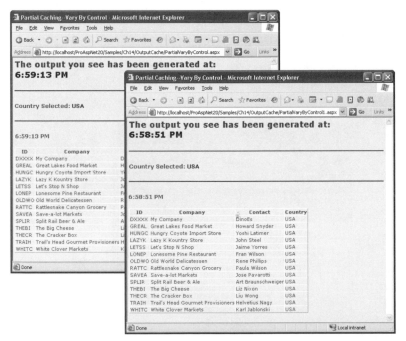

Figure 14-9   Distinct pages don't automatically share the output of the same user control.

By default, distinct pages don't share the output of the same cacheable user control. Each page will maintain its own copy of the user control response instead. Implemented to guarantee total separation and avoid any sort of conflicts, this feature is far more dangerous than one might think at first. It might lead to flooding the Web server memory with copies and copies of the user control responses—one for each varying parameter or control property and one set for each page that uses the control.

To allow distinct pages to share the same output of a common user control, you need to set the *Shared* attribute to *true* in the user control's *@OutputCache* directive:

```
<%@ OutputCache Duration="30" VaryByParam="None" Shared="true" %>
```

> **Tip** To avoid memory problems, you should put a limit on the total amount of memory available to IIS. It is set to 60 percent of the physical memory, but you should keep it under 800 MB per Microsoft recommendations. Setting the IIS 6.0 *Maximum Used Memory* parameter is important especially if output cache is used aggressively. You'll set the parameter on a per-application-pool basis by selecting the IIS 6.0 application pool where your application is configured to run and opening its Properties dialog box.

Fragment Caching in Cacheable Pages

If you plan to cache user controls—that is, you're trying for partial caching—it's probably because you just don't want to, or cannot, cache the entire page. However, a good question to ask is: What happens if user controls are cached within a cacheable page?

Both the page and the controls are cached individually, meaning that both the page's raw response and the control's raw responses are cached. However, if the cache duration is different, the page duration wins and user controls are refreshed only when the page is refreshed.

A cacheable user control can be embedded both in a cacheable page and in a wrapper cacheable user control.

> **Warning** Cacheable user controls should be handled with extreme care in the page's code. Unlike regular controls, a user control marked with the *@OutputCache* directive is not guaranteed to be there when your code tries to access it. If the user control is retrieved from the cache, the property that references it in the code-behind page class is just *null*.
>
> ```
> if (CustomerGrid1 != null)
>
>     CustomerGrid1.Country = "USA";
> ```
>
> To avoid bad surprises, you should always check the control reference against the *null* value before executing any code.

Advanced Features in ASP.NET 2.0

The output caching subsystem has a few new features to offer in ASP.NET 2.0. They are caching profiles and post-cache substitution. In brief, caching profiles let you save a block of output caching-related settings to the configuration file. Post-cache substitution completes the ASP.NET offering as far as output caching is concerned. In addition to saving the entire page or only fragments of the page, you can now also cache the entire page except for a few regions.

Caching Profiles

The *@OutputCache* directive for pages supports the *CacheProfile* string attribute, which references an entry under the *<outputCacheProfiles>* section in the *web.config* file:

```
<caching>
   <outputCacheSettings>
      <outputCacheProfiles>
         <add name="..." enabled="true|false" duration="..."
              location="..." sqlDependency="..."
              varyByCustom="..." varyByControl="..."
              varyByHeader="..." varyByParam="..."
                            noStore=true|false"
         />
      </outputCacheProfiles>
   </outputCacheSettings>
</caching>
```

Basically, by defining a named entry in the *<add>* section you can store in the configuration file all the cache-related settings to be applied to the page. Instead of specifying the same set of parameters for each page over and over again, you can put them in the *web.config* file and reference them by name. In this way, you can also modify settings for a number of pages without touching the source files:

```
<%@ OutputCache CacheProfile="MySettings" %>
```

In the preceding code, the application has a *MySettings* entry in the *<outputCacheProfiles>* section and doesn't need any additional attribute in the *@OutputCache* directive. As you can see, the attributes of the *<add>* node match the attributes of the *@OutputCache* directive.

Post-Cache Substitution

With user controls, you can cache only certain portions of ASP.NET pages. With post-cache substitution, you can cache the whole page except specific regions. For example, using this mechanism, an *AdRotator* control can serve a different advertisement on each request even if the host page is cached.

To use post-cache substitution, you place a new control—the *<asp:substitution>* control—at the page location where content should be substituted, and set the *MethodName* property of the control to a callback method. Here's a quick example:

```
<form id="form1" runat="server">
    <h3>The output you see has been generated at:
        <%=DateTime.Now.ToString() %> and is valid for 30 seconds</h3>
    <hr />
     This content is updated regularly
     <h2><asp:Substitution ID="Substitution1" runat="server"
            MethodName="WriteTimeStamp" /></h2>
    <hr />
```

```
    This is more static and cached content
    <asp:Button runat="server" Text="Refresh" />
</form>
```

Figure 14-10 shows the page in action.

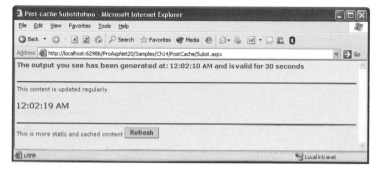

Figure 14-10   The fragment of the page between the two horizontal lines is updated regularly at each postback; the rest of the page is retrieved from the cache.

The *MethodName* property must be set to the name of a static method that can be encapsulated in an *HttpResponseSubstitutionCallback* delegate, as follows:

```
public static string WriteTimeStamp(HttpContext context)
{
    return DateTime.Now.ToString();
}
```

Whatever string the method returns will be rendered out and becomes the output of the *Substitution* control. Note also that the callback method must be static and thread-safe. The *HttpContext* parameter to the method may be used to retrieve request parameters such as query string variables, authentication information, or personalization details.

You can also set up post-cache substitution programmatically through the *WriteSubstitution* method of the *HttpResponse* object:

```
Response.WriteSubstitution(
    new HttpResponseSubstitutionCallback(WriteTimeStamp));
```

The preceding call inserts a sort of placeholder in the response, which will be replaced with the output of the method. This trick allows the *AdRotator* control in ASP.NET 2.0 to automatically display a new banner even on cached pages.

The use of post-cache substitution automatically enables server caching for the page output. If the page is configured for client output caching, the setting is ignored. The reason for this change lies in the fact that markup editing is necessarily a server-side operation. In addition, a page that makes use of post-cache substitution can't rely on IIS 6.0 kernel mode caching because ASP.NET needs to do some work before the page can be served to the user. In light of this, the page can't just be served by IIS without first involving ASP.NET.

> **Note**   The *Substitution* control can also be used in pages that don't use output caching. In this case, the substitution callback will be called at rendering time to contribute to the response. You can think of the *Substitution* control as a server-side control that has the capability of expanding a placeholder to some server-side processed results.

For performance reasons, you should also avoid calling the *Substitution* control from within the callback. If you do so, the callback will maintain a reference to the control and the page containing the control. As a result, the page instance won't be garbage-collected until the cached contents expires.

> **Note**   During the development cycle and until the Beta 2 release disk-based, ASP.NET 2.0 supported a feature known as disk-output caching. In brief, disk output caching was designed to let you store the response of pages on disk as opposed to keeping them in memory and to allow the output cache content to persist across application restarts that always clear the in-memory cache. In the final release of ASP.NET 2.0, though, this feature was removed.

Conclusion

The ability to store in memory chunks of frequently accessed data becomes a winning factor in the building of scalable Web applications that handle significant volumes of data. Instead of continuously connecting to the database server, locking records, and consuming one of the available connection channels, you can simply read the results needed from some block of memory. This scenario delineates caching as an asset for any application. Well, not just any, as we discussed—but certainly for many.

Caching is rather a double-edged sword, and if abused or misused, it can easily morph into an insidious weakness. This typically happens when the quantity of memory-held information grows uncontrolled and beyond a reasonable threshold. Aside from the performance reper-cussions, the theoretical possibility that the data stored in the cache can grow uncontrolled also opens up security concerns. A denial-of-service (DoS) attack, in fact, might succeed in flooding the Web server's memory with useless data if the caching subsystem is not well designed.

Caching is mostly about memory. In the short run, you can perhaps even find that some good caching improves the overall performance enough to appease your customer or your boss. I'm not at all claiming that caching can fix design holes, but caching can sometimes put a patch on nonoptimal performance and allow you time to rethink and refactor the application properly.

Caching is an essential feature to consider for all serious Internet applications. To build high-performance applications, a fundamental guideline is "cache as much as you can." However, be aware that there's a threshold you should never exceed. The more aggressive you are with caching, the more you should be concerned about the invisible memory threshold that suddenly turns good things into bad things.

In ASP.NET, caching comes in two complementary forms—page output caching and the *Cache* object. The former is a relatively quick and simple approach to serve static pages bypassing the ASP.NET pipeline. The latter is the tip of a comprehensive caching API designed to let you place a caching layer inside your business or data tier.

Just the Facts

- Caching is the system's or the application's ability to save frequently used data to an intermediate storage medium. In ASP.NET, caching comes in two independent but not exclusive flavors: caching application data and caching the output of served pages.

- To cache application data, you use the *Cache* object, a global container of data with a dictionary-based API and the capabilities of automatically scavenging the memory and getting rid of unused items.

- Items added to the cache can be linked to an array of files and directories as well as to an array of existing cache items, database tables, or external custom events. Whenever files, folders, existing cache items, and database tables are modified, or whenever the external event fires, the item automatically becomes stale and is removed from memory

- Page output caching is the ability to save the raw HTML of a page to a location on the client, the server, or a downstream proxy server. Cached pages can be given a duration and vary in terms of query and form parameters, HTTP headers, and custom strings.

- When the IIS 6.0 process model is enabled, the output caching mechanism is integrated in the Web server. Incoming requests for an ASP.NET page are filtered by a kernel-level driver and examined to see whether they match cached pages.

- By creating user controls, you can cache only a portion of an ASP.NET page.

- In ASP.NET 2.0, new caching features are available, such as post-cache substitution. Post-cache substitution lets you cache the entire page except for a few regions.

Chapter 15

ASP.NET Security

In this chapter:

Where the Threats Come From 648

The ASP.NET Security Context 648

Using Forms Authentication 660

The Membership and Role Management API 675

Security-Related Controls 691

Conclusion 702

Many developers have learned on their own that security is not a feature that can be added to existing applications or introduced late in the development stage. Security is inherently tied to the functions of an application and should be planned as one of the first features, very early at the design level.

By nature, Web applications are subject to several types of attacks whose damage and impact can vary quite a bit, depending on the characteristics of the application itself. The most secure Web application is the application that actually resists attacks, not the application just designed to do so. Security is a rather intricate puzzle whose solution varies from one application to another. The important thing to remember is that, more often than not, security is manifested through a successful mix of application-level and system-level measures.

ASP.NET simplifies programming secure applications by providing a built-in infrastructure that supplies application-level protection against unauthorized access to Web pages. Be aware, though, that this kind of security is only one side of the coin. A really secure Web site is especially well protected against server attacks, which can sneakily be used to scale the highest protective walls of the application logic.

In this chapter, we will discuss the security context of ASP.NET, including its relationship with server-side Internet Information Server (IIS) authentication mechanisms and best coding practices to fend off Web attacks.

Where the Threats Come From

The concept of security implies the presence of an enemy we're protecting ourselves against. Table 15-1 summarizes the most common types of Web attacks.

Table 15-1   Common Web Attacks

Attack	Description
Cross-site scripting (XSS)	Untrusted user input is echoed to the page.
Denial of service (DoS)	The attacker floods the network with fake requests, overloading the system and blocking regular traffic.
Eavesdropping	The attacker uses a sniffer to read unencrypted network packets as they are transported on the network.
Hidden-field tampering	The attacker compromises unchecked (and trusted) hidden fields stuffed with sensitive data.
One-click	Malicious HTTP posts are sent via script.
Session hijacking	The attacker guesses or steals a valid session ID and connects over another user's session.
SQL injection	The attacker inserts malicious input that the code blissfully concatenates to form dangerous SQL commands.

The bottom line is that whenever you insert any sort of user input into the browser's markup, you potentially expose yourself to a code-injection attack (any variations of SQL injection and XSS). In addition, sensitive data should never be sent across the wire (let alone as clear text) and must be stored safely on the server.

If there's a way to write a bulletproof and tamper-resistant application, it can only consist of the combination of the following measures:

- Coding practices—data validation, type and buffer length checking, and anti-tampering measures

- Data access—strategies using roles to ensure the weakest possible account, and using stored procedures or at least parameterized commands

- Effective storage and administration—no sending of critical data down to the client, using hash codes to detect manipulation, authenticating users and protecting identities, and applying rigorous policies for passwords

As you can see, a secure application can result only from the combined efforts of developers, architects, and administrators. Don't imagine that you can get it right otherwise.

The ASP.NET Security Context

From an application point of view, security is mostly a matter of authenticating users and authorizing actions on the system's resources. ASP.NET provides a range of authentication and authorization mechanisms implemented in conjunction with IIS, the .NET Framework, and the underlying security services of the operating system. The overall security context of an

ASP.NET application is composed of three distinct levels:

- The IIS level associates a valid security token with the sender of the request. The security token is determined according to the current IIS authentication mechanism.

- The ASP.NET worker process level determines the identity of the thread in the ASP.NET worker process serving the request. If enabled, impersonation settings can change the security token associated with the thread. The identity of the process model is determined by settings in the configuration file or the IIS metabase, according to the process model in use.

- The ASP.NET pipeline level gets the credentials of the application-specific user who is using the application. The way this task is accomplished depends on the application settings in the configuration files for authentication and authorization. A common setting for most ASP.NET applications is using Forms authentication.

Among other things, the identity of the ASP.NET worker process influences access to local files, folders, and databases.

Who Really Runs My ASP.NET Application?

When an ASP.NET request arrives at the Web server machine, IIS picks it up and assigns the request to one of its pooled threads. IIS runs under the SYSTEM account—the most powerful account in Microsoft Windows. From this point forward when processing this request, the three security contexts of ASP.NET applications I mentioned execute, one after the other.

IIS Thread Security Context

The thread that physically handles the request impersonates an identity according to the current IIS authentication settings: Basic, Digest, Integrated Windows, or anonymous. If the site is configured for anonymous access, the identity impersonated by the thread is the one you set through the dialog box shown in Figure 15-1. By default, it is named *IUSR_xxx*, where *xxx* stands for the machine name. (The dialog box is the Properties dialog box of the IIS administrative manager application.)

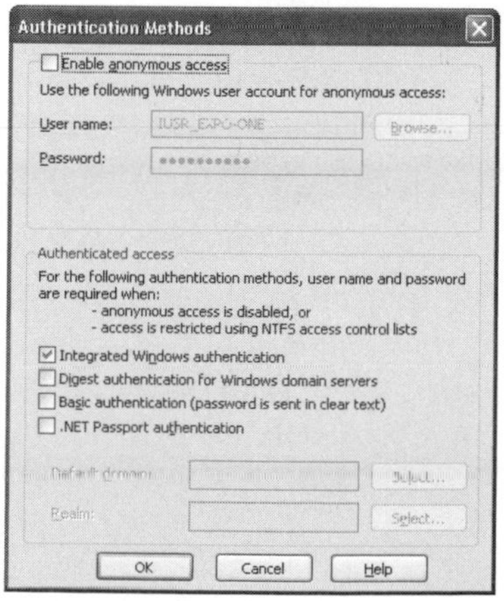

Figure 15-1   Enabling anonymous access and editing authentication methods for the site.

Basic authentication is an HTTP standard supported by virtually any browser. With this type of authentication, a request bounces back with a particular HTTP status code that the browser understands as a demand to display a standard dialog box to request the user's credentials. The information gathered is sent to IIS, which attempts to match it with any of the Web server's accounts. Because credentials are sent out as Base64 encoded text (essentially in clear text) Basic authentication is recommended only for use over HTTPS secure channels.

Digest authentication differs from Basic authentication mostly because it hashes credentials before sending. Digest authentication is an HTTP 1.1 feature and, as such, is not supported by all browsers. In addition, on Windows 2000 it requires the password to be stored on the server with reversible encryption. This is no longer a requirement with Windows Server 2003. Both Basic and Digest authentication work well through firewalls and proxy servers.

Integrated Windows authentication sets up a conversation between the browser and the Web server. The browser passes the credentials of the currently logged-on user, who is not required to type anything. The user needs to have a valid account on the Web server or in a trusted domain to be successfully authenticated. The authentication can take place through the NTLM challenge/response method or by using Kerberos. The technique has limited browser support and is impractical in the presence of firewalls.

> **Note** Yet another type of authentication mode exists and is based on certificates. You can use the Secure Sockets Layer (SSL) security features of IIS and use client certificates to authenticate users requesting information on your Web site. SSL checks the contents of the certificate submitted by the browser for the user during the logon. Users obtain client certificates from a trusted third-party organization. In an intranet scenario, users can also get their certificates from an authority managed by the company itself.

After authentication, the thread dispatches the request to the appropriate external module. For an ASP.NET request, what happens depends on the process model in use within the application.

Worker Process Security Context

In the IIS 5.0 process model, the IIS thread hands the request out to *aspnet_isapi.dll* which, in turn, starts the *aspnet_wp.exe* worker process. In the IIS 6.0 process model, the request is queued to the application pool that hosts the ASP.NET application and picked up by the copy of *w3wp.exe* IIS worker process that serves the application pool. What is the identity of the worker process?

If the IIS 5.0 process model is used, the worker process runs under the guise of the ASPNET account. ASPNET is a local account created when the .NET Framework is installed. It has the least set of privileges required for its role and is far less powerful than the SYSTEM account. You can change the identity to an existing account through the following section in *machine.config*:

```
<processModel userName="..." password="..." />
```

If the IIS 6.0 process model is used, the worker process has the identity of the NETWORK SERVICE account. You can change it through the dialog box shown in Figure 15-2. In the IIS administrative manager, you select the application pool of choice and click to see its properties. NETWORK SERVICE has the same limited set of privileges as ASPNET and is a new built-in account in Windows Server 2003 and Windows XP.

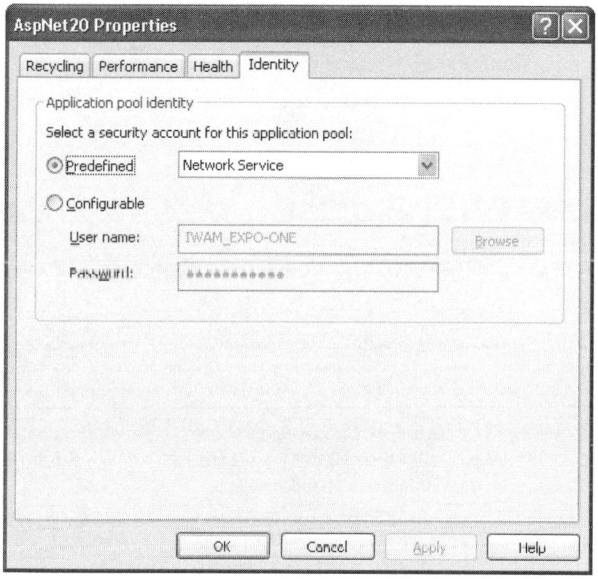

Figure 15-2 Setting the default identity of the worker process serving an application pool in IIS 6.0.

Inside the worker process, a pooled thread will pick up the request to serve it. What's the identity of this thread? If impersonation is disabled in the ASP.NET application, this thread will inherit the identity of the worker process. This is what happens by default. If impersonation is enabled, the worker thread will inherit the security token passed by IIS. You enable impersonation in the *web.config* file as follows:

```
<impersonation enabled="true" />
```

There's more to say about ASP.NET impersonation, particularly about the extended form of impersonation where a fixed identity is specified. We'll discuss this further in a moment.

When impersonation is active, the worker process account doesn't change. The worker process still compiles pages and reads configuration files using the original account. Impersonation is used only with the code executed within the page and not for all the preliminary steps that happen before the request is handed to the page handler. For example, this means that any access to local files or databases occurs using the impersonated account, not the worker process's account.

ASP.NET Pipeline Security Context

The third security context indicates the identity of the user making the request. The point here is authenticating the user and authorizing access to the page and its embedded resources. Obviously, if the requested page is freely available, no further step is performed; the page output is generated and served to the user.

To protect pages against unauthorized access, an ASP.NET application needs to define an authentication policy—Windows, Passport, or Forms. Authentication modules hook up requests for protected pages and manage to obtain the user's credentials. The user is directed to the page only if the credentials are deemed valid and authorize access to the requested resource.

Changing the Identity of the ASP.NET Process

In a situation in which you want to change the default ASP.NET account to give it more privileges, how should you proceed? Is it preferable to create a custom account and use it for the worker process, or should you opt for the worker process to impersonate a fixed identity?

> **Note**   You can hardly create a new, functional account with less than the privileges granted to ASPNET or NETWORK SERVICE. If you give it a try, make sure you pass through a careful testing phase and ensure that it really works for your application.

Setting the Process Account

Using the *<processModel>* section (for the IIS 5.0 process model) or using the dialog box shown in Figure 15-2 (for the IIS 6.0 process model) are the only ways to change the real identity of the ASP.NET process. If you change the process identity, all threads in the process will use this as the base identity and no extra work is needed on thread switches. More important, you should make sure the new account has at least full permissions on the Temporary ASP.NET Files folder. (Review carefully the list of permissions granted to the standard ASP.NET accounts, which you can find in the "Privileges of the ASP.NET Default Account" section.)

Alternately, you could require the worker process to impersonate a fixed identity through the *<identity>* section of the *web.config* file. Note that when fixed impersonation is used, every worker thread processing a request needs to impersonate the specified account. Impersonation must be performed for each thread switch because a thread switch event takes the thread identity back to the process identity.

Impersonating a Fixed Identity

To impersonate a fixed identity, you first define the user account and then add a setting to the *web.config* file. The following snippet shows an example:

```
<identity impersonate="true"
    userName="MyAspNetAccnt" password="ILoveA$p*SinceVer3.0" />
```

As mentioned earlier, impersonation doesn't really change the *physical* identity of the process running ASP.NET. More simply, all threads serving in the context of the ASP.NET worker process will always impersonate a given user for the duration of the application.

Impersonating a fixed identity is different from classic, per-request impersonation such as impersonating the identity of the Windows user making the request. *Per-request impersonation* refers to the situation in which you enable impersonation without specifying a fixed identity. In this case, the security token with identity information is created by IIS and inherited by the worker process. When a fixed identity is involved, the security token must be generated by the ASP.NET worker process. When running under a poorly privileged account, though, the ASP.NET worker process sometimes lacks the permission to do that.

Inside the Fixed Impersonation Feature

A process running under a nonadministrator account cannot impersonate a specific account on Windows 2000 unless you grant it appropriate privileges. Under Windows 2000, a process requires the Act As Part Of The Operating System privilege to impersonate a fixed identity. This is indeed a strong and powerful privilege that, for security reasons, nonadministrator process accounts such as ASPNET and NETWORK SERVICE generally will not have.

The requirement disappears with Windows XP and Windows Server 2003, which will make it possible for processes lacking the Act As Part Of The Operating System privilege to impersonate a given identity.

In ASP.NET 1.1, though, impersonating a fixed identity is possible also under Windows 2000 machines and IIS 5.0. The ASP.NET 1.1 runtime plays some tricks to re-vector the call back to the *aspnet_isapi.dll* module, which is running inside IIS 5.0 and under the SYSTEM account. Basically, the ASP.NET 1.1 ISAPI extension creates the security token and duplicates it in the memory space of the worker process. In this way, ASP.NET 1.1 supports fixed impersonation without requiring the Act As Part Of The Operating System privilege on the worker process account.

In the end, expect to have troubles with fixed impersonation only if you're still running ASP.NET 1.0 applications under Windows 2000. In this case, for the impersonation to work you need to run your ASP.NET applications under the SYSTEM account, with all the security repercussions that this entails.

Impersonating Through the Anonymous Account

A third possibility to change the identity of the ASP.NET worker process is by impersonating through the anonymous account. The idea is that the ASP.NET application grants access to anonymous users, and the anonymous account is configured to be the desired account for the application.

In this case, the application uses per-request impersonation and the ASP.NET code executes as the impersonated account. The process account remains set to ASPNET or NETWORK SERVICE, which means that you don't have to worry about replicating into the new account the minimum set of permissions on folders that allow ASP.NET to work.

Privileges of the ASP.NET Default Account

Of all the possible user-rights assignments, ASPNET and NETWORK SERVICE are granted only the following five:

- Access this computer from the network
- Deny logon locally
- Deny logon through Terminal Services
- Log on as a batch job
- Log on as a service

In addition, the accounts are given some NTFS permissions to operate on certain folders and create temporary files and assemblies. The folders involved are these:

- **.NET Framework Root Folder**   This folder contains some .NET Framework system assemblies that ASP.NET must be able to access. The physical folder is normally *Microsoft.NET\Framework\[version]* and is located under the Windows folder. ASP.NET has only read and list permissions on this folder.

- **Temporary ASP.NET Files**   This folder represents the file system subtree in which all temporary files are generated. ASP.NET is granted full control over the entire subtree.

- **Global Assembly Cache**   ASP.NET needs to gain read permissions on the assemblies in the global assembly cache (GAC). The GAC is located in the *Windows\Assembly\GAC* folder. The GAC folder is not visible in Windows Explorer, but you can view the installed assemblies by opening the *Windows\Assembly* folder.

- **Windows System Folder**   The ASP.NET process needs to access and read the *System32* Windows folder to load any necessary Win32 DLLs.

- **Application Root Folder**   The ASP.NET process needs to access and read the files that make up the Web application. The folder is typically located under *Inetpub\Wwwroot*.

- **Web Site Root**   ASP.NET might have the need to scan the root of the Web server—typically, *Inetpub\Wwwroot*—looking for configuration files to read.

An ASP.NET application running under an account that lacks some of these permissions might fail. Granting at least all these permissions is highly recommended for all accounts used for fixed account impersonation.

The Trust Level of ASP.NET Applications

ASP.NET applications are made of managed code and run inside the common language run-time (CLR). In the CLR, running code is assigned to a security zone based on the evidence it provides about its origin—for example, the originating URL. Each security zone corresponds to a set of permissions. Each set of permissions correspond to a trust level. By default, ASP.NET applications run from the MyComputer zone with full trust. Is this default setting just evil?

An ASP.NET application runs on the Web server and doesn't hurt the user that connects to it via the browser. An ASP.NET application cannot be consumed in other ways than through the browser. So why do several people feel cold shivers down their spine as they think of ASP.NET full trust?

The problem is not with the ASP.NET application itself, but with the fact that it is publicly exposed over the Internet—one of the most hostile environments for computer security you can imagine. Should a fully trusted ASP.NET application be hijacked, a hacker could perform restricted actions from within the worker thread. In other words, a publicly exposed fully trusted application is a potential platform for hackers to launch attacks. The less an application is trusted, the most secure that application happens to be.

The *<trust>* Section

By default, ASP.NET applications run unrestricted and are allowed to do whatever their account is allowed to do. The actual security restrictions that sometimes apply to ASP.NET applications (for example, the inability to write files) are not a sign of partial trust, but more simply the effect of the underprivileged account under which ASP.NET applications normally run.

By tweaking the *<trust>* section in the root *web.config* file, you can configure code access security permissions for a Web application and decide whether it has to run fully or partially trusted:

```
<trust level="Medium" originUrl="" />
```

Table 15-2 describes the levels of trust available.

Table 15-2   Levels Permitted in the *<trust>* Section

Level	Description
Full	Applications run fully trusted and can execute arbitrary native code in the process context in which they run. This is the default setting.
High	Code can use most permissions that support partial trust. This is appropriate for applications you want to run with least privilege to mitigate risks.
Medium	Code can read and write its own application directories and can interact with databases.

Table 15-2   Levels Permitted in the *<trust>* Section

Level	Description
Low	Code can read its own application resources but can't interact with resources located outside of its application space.
Minimal	Code can't interact with any protected resources. Appropriate for nonprofessional hosting sites that simply intend to support generic HTML code and highly isolated business logic.

> **Note**   Web applications and Web services built using .NET Framework version 1.0 always run with unrestricted code access permissions. Configurable levels listed in Table 15-2 do not apply to ASP.NET 1.0 applications.

Admittedly, restricting the set of things an application can do might be painful at first. However, in the long run (in other words, if you don't just give up and deliver the application) it produces better and safer code.

> **Note**   The *<trust>* section supports an attribute named *originUrl*. The attribute is a sort of misnomer. If you set it, the specified URL is granted the permission to access an HTTP resource using either a *Socket* or *WebRequest* class. The permission class involved with this is *WebPermission*. Of course, the Web permission is granted only if the specified *<trust>* level supports that. *Medium* and higher trust levels do.

ASP.NET Permissions

Let's review in more detail the permissions granted to ASP.NET applications when the various trust levels are applied. Key ASP.NET permissions for each trust level are outlined in Table 15-3.

Table 15-3   Main Permissions in ASP.NET Trust Levels

	High	Medium	Low	Minimal
FileIO	Unrestricted	Read/Write to application's space	Read	None
IsolatedStorage	Unrestricted	ByUser	ByUser (maximum of 1 MB)	None
Printing	DefaultPrinting	*Same as High*	None	None
Security	Assertion, Execution, ControlThread, ControlPrincipal	*Same as High*	Execution	Execution
SqlClient	Unrestricted	Unrestricted (no blank password allowed)	None	None

Table 15-3   Main Permissions in ASP.NET Trust Levels

	High	Medium	Low	Minimal
Registry	Unrestricted	None	None	None
Environment	Unrestricted	None	None	None
Reflection	ReflectionEmit	None	None	None
Socket	Unrestricted	None	None	None
Web	Unrestricted	Connect to origin host, if configured	*Same as High*	None

More detailed information about the permissions actually granted to the default trust levels is available in the security configuration files for each level. The name of the file for each level is stored in the *<trustLevel>* section.

In the end, full trust applications run unrestricted. High-trust applications have read/write permission for all the files in their application space. However, the physical access to files is still ruled by the NTFS access control list on the resource. High-trust applications have unrestricted access to Microsoft SQL Server but not, for example, to OLE DB classes. (The *OleDbPermission* and other managed provider permissions are denied to all but fully trusted applications.) Reflection calls are denied with the exception of those directed at classes in the *System.Reflection.Emit* namespace.

Medium applications have unrestricted access to SQL Server, but only as long as they do not use blank passwords for accounts. The *WebPermission* is granted to both medium- and low-trust applications, but it requires that the URL be configured in the *<trust>* section through the *originUrl* attribute. Low-trust applications have read-only permission for files in their application directories. Isolated storage is still permitted but limited to a 1-MB quota.

A rule of thumb is that *Medium* trust should be fine for most ASP.NET applications and applying it shouldn't cause significant headaches, provided that you don't need to access legacy COM objects or databases exposed via OLE DB providers.

Granting Privileges Beyond the Trust Level

What if one of the tasks to perform requires privileges that the trust level doesn't grant? There are two basic approaches. The simplest approach is to customize the policy file for the trust level and add any permissions you need. This solution is easy to implement and doesn't require code changes. It does require administrator rights to edit the security policy files. From a pure security perspective, it is not a great solution, as you're just adding to the whole application the permissions you need for a particular method of a particular page or assembly.

The second approach requires a bit of refactoring but leads to better and safer code. The idea is to sandbox the server-side code and make it delegate to external components (for example, serviced components or command-line programs) the execution of any tasks that exceeds the application's permission set. Obviously, the external component will be configured to have all required permissions.

> **Note** Code sandboxing is the only option you have if your partially trusted ASP.NET application is trying to make calls into an assembly that doesn't include the *AllowPartially-TrustedCallers* attribute. For more information on programming for medium trust, check out the contents at the following URL: *http://msdn.microsoft.com/library/en-us/dnpag2/html/PAGHT000020.asp.*

ASP.NET Authentication Methods

Depending on the type of the requested resource, IIS might or might not be able to handle the request itself. If the resource needs the involvement of ASP.NET (for example, if it is an *.aspx* file), IIS hands the request over to ASP.NET along with the security token of the authenticated, or anonymous, user. What happens next depends on the ASP.NET configuration.

ASP.NET supports three types of authentication methods: Windows, Passport, and Forms. A fourth possibility is None, meaning that ASP.NET does not even attempt to perform its own authentication and completely relies on the authentication already carried out by IIS. In this case, anonymous users can connect and resources are accessed using the default ASP.NET account.

You choose the ASP.NET authentication mechanism using the *<authentication>* section in the root *web.config* file. Child subdirectories inherit the authentication mode chosen for the application. By default, the authentication mode is set to Windows. Let's briefly examine the Windows and Passport authentication and reserve wider coverage for the most commonly used authentication method–Forms authentication.

Windows Authentication

When using Windows authentication, ASP.NET works in conjunction with IIS. The real authentication is performed by IIS, which uses one of its authentication methods: Basic, Digest, or Integrated Windows. When IIS has authenticated the user, it passes the security token on to ASP.NET. When in Windows authentication mode, ASP.NET does not perform any further steps and limits its use of the IIS token to authorizing access to the resources.

Typically, you use the Windows authentication method in intranet scenarios when the users of your application have Windows accounts that only can be authenticated by the Web server. Let's assume that you configured the Web server to work with the Integrated Windows authentication mode and that you disabled anonymous access. The ASP.NET application works in Windows authentication mode. What happens when a user connects to the application? First, IIS authenticates the user (popping up a dialog box if the account of the local user doesn't match any accounts on the Web server or in a trusted domain) and then hands the security token over to ASP.NET.

Using ACLs to Authorize Access

In most cases, Windows authentication is used in conjunction with file authorization—via the *FileAuthorizationModule* HTTP module. User-specific pages in the Web application can be protected from unauthorized access by using access control lists (ACLs) on the file. When ASP.NET is about to access a resource, the *FileAuthorizationModule* HTTP module is called into action. File authorization performs an ACL check on ASP.NET files using the caller's identity. This means that the user Joe will never be able to access an *.aspx* page whose ACL doesn't include an entry for him.

Note, though, that file authorization does not require impersonation at the ASP.NET level and, more important, works regardless of whether the impersonation flag is turned on. There's good news and bad news in this statement. The good news is that once you've set an appropriately configured ACL on an ASP.NET resource, you're pretty much done. Nobody will be able to access the resource without permission. But what about non-ASP.NET resources such as local files?

For example, how can you protect an HTML page from unauthorized access? The first consideration is that an HTML page rarely needs to be protected against access. If you need to protect a page, the page very likely also executes some server-side code. Implementing it as *.aspx* is more useful anyway. That said, by design HTML pages are not protected from unauthorized access because they are not processed by the ASP.NET pipeline. If you want to protect it, the best thing you can do is rename the page to *.aspx* so that it is processed by the ASP.NET runtime.

Note   HTML pages and other resources can still be protected using NTFS permissions. If particular constraints are set on a file using NTFS permissions, there's no way the file can be accessed by anyone lacking proper rights.

Alternately, you can rename the page to a custom extension and write a lightweight Internet Server Application Programming Interface (ISAPI) extension (or a managed HTTP handler) to implement a made-to-measure authorization mechanism. I discuss HTTP handlers in my other recent book, *Programming Microsoft ASP.NET 2.0 Applications: Advanced Topics* (Microsoft Press, 2005).

Note   Windows authentication also works with URL authorization implemented by the HTTP module named *URLAuthorizationModule*. This module allows or denies access to URL resources to certain users and roles. (We'll talk more about URL authorization later while discussing Forms authentication.)

Passport Authentication

Passport authentication is a Microsoft-centralized authentication service. Passport provides a way to authenticate users coming across all the sites that participate in the initiative. Users need to do a single logon and, if successfully authenticated, they can then freely move through all the member sites. In addition to the single logon service, Passport also offers core profile services for member sites.

ASP.NET provides the *PassportAuthenticationModule* HTTP module to set up authentication for Web applications hosted by Passport member sites. When an HTTP request hits a Passport-enabled Web site, the HTTP module verifies whether the request contains a valid Passport ticket. If not, the Web server returns the status code 302 and redirects the client to the Passport logon service. The query string contains properly encrypted information about the original request. The client issues a GET request to the logon server and passes the supplied query string. At this point, the Passport logon server prompts the client with an HTML logon form. After the user has filled out the form, the form is posted back to the logon server over an SSL-secured channel.

The logon server uses the form information to authenticate the user and, if successful, creates a Passport ticket. Next, the user is redirected to the original URL and the ticket is passed, encrypted, in the query string. Finally, the browser follows the redirect instruction and requests again the original Passport protected resource. This time, though, the request contains a valid ticket so that the *PassportAuthenticationModule* will allow the request to pass.

Using Forms Authentication

Both Windows and Passport authentication are seldom practical for real-world Internet applications. Windows authentication is based on Windows accounts and NTFS ACL tokens and, as such, assumes that clients are connecting from Windows-equipped machines. Useful and effective in intranet and possibly in some extranet scenarios, Windows authentication is simply unrealistic in more common situations because the Web application users are required to have Windows accounts in the application's domain. The same conclusion applies to Passport authentication, although for different reasons. Passport is not free, requires the implementation of serious security measures (that are not free and that you don't necessarily need at all sites), and makes sense mostly for e-commerce and co-branded Web sites.

So what is the ideal authentication mechanism for real Web developers? A Web programming best-practice recommends that you place some relatively boilerplated code on top of each nonpublic page and redirect the user to a login page. On the login page, the user is prompted for credentials and redirected to the originally requested page, if successfully authenticated. All this code is not exactly rocket science, but it's still code that you have to write yourself and use over and over again.

Forms authentication is just the ASP.NET built-in infrastructure to implement the aforementioned pattern for login. Forms authentication is the ideal (I would say the only) choice whenever you need to collect user credentials and process them internally—for example, against a database of user accounts. The login pattern implemented by Forms authentication doesn't look radically different from Windows and Passport authentication. The key difference is that with Forms authentication everything happens under the strict control of the application.

You set up an ASP.NET application for Forms authentication by tweaking its root *web.config* file. You enter the following script:

```
<system.web>
    <authentication mode="Forms">
        <forms loginUrl="login.aspx" />
    </authentication>
    <authorization>
        <deny users="?" />
    </authorization>
</system.web>
```

The *<authentication>* section indicates the URL of the user-defined login form. ASP.NET displays the form only to users who have explicitly been denied access in the *<authorization>* section. The *?* symbol indicates any anonymous, unauthenticated users. Note that the anonymous user here is not the IIS anonymous user but simply a user who has not been authenticated through your login form.

All blocked users are redirected to the login page, where they are asked to enter their credentials.

> **Note**   The Forms authentication mechanism protects any ASP.NET resource located in a folder for which Forms authentication and authorization is enabled. Note that only resource types explicitly handled by ASP.NET are protected. The list includes *.aspx*, *.asmx*, and *.ashx* files, but not plain HTML pages or classic ASP pages.

Forms Authentication Control Flow

Form-based authentication is governed by an HTTP module implemented in the *Forms-AuthenticationModule* class. The behavior of the component is driven by the contents of the *web.config* file. When the browser attempts to access a protected resource, the module kicks in and attempts to locate an authentication ticket for the caller. In ASP.NET 1.x, a ticket is merely a cookie with a particular (and configurable) name. In ASP.NET 2.0, it can be configured to be a value embedded in the URL (cookieless Forms authentication).

If no valid ticket is found, the module redirects the request to a login page. Information about the originating page is placed in the query string. The login page is then displayed. The programmer creates this page, which, at a minimum, contains text boxes for the user name and the password and a button for submitting credentials. The handler for the button-click event validates the credentials using an application-specific algorithm and data store. If the credentials are authenticated, the user code redirects the browser to the original URL. The original URL is attached to the query string of the request for the login page, as shown here:

```
http://YourApp/login.aspx?ReturnUrl=original.aspx
```

Authenticating a user means that an authentication ticket is issued and attached to the request. When the browser places its second request for the page, the HTTP module retrieves the authentication ticket and lets the request pass.

Let's see how form-based authentication works in practice and consider a scenario in which users are not allowed to connect anonymously to any pages in the application. The user types the URL of the page—for example, *welcome.aspx*—and goes. As a result, the HTTP module redirects to the login page any users for which an authentication ticket does not exist, as shown in Figure 15-3.

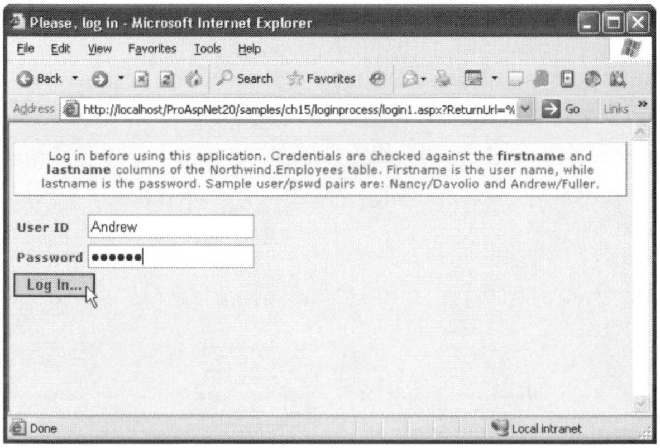

Figure 15-3   The login page of the sample application.

> **Important**   There are inherent security concerns that arise with Forms authentication. Unfortunately, with today's browser technology these potential security concerns can be removed only by resorting to secure channels (HTTPS). I'll return to this topic later in the "General Security Issues" section.

Collecting Credentials Through Login

The layout of a login page is nearly the same—a couple of text boxes for user name and password, a button to confirm, and perhaps a label to display error messages. However, you can make it as complex as needed and add as many graphics as appropriate. The user enters the credentials, typically in a case-sensitive way, and then clicks the button to log on. When the login page posts back, the following code runs:

```
void LogonUser(object sender, EventArgs e)
{
    string user = userName.Text;
    string pswd = password.Text;
```

```
      // Custom authentication
      bool bAuthenticated = AuthenticateUser(user, pswd);
      if (bAuthenticated)
          FormsAuthentication.RedirectFromLoginPage(user, false);
      else
          errorMsg.Text = "Sorry, yours seems not to be a valid account.";
}
```

The event handler retrieves the strings typed in the user name and password fields and calls into a local function named *AuthenticateUser*. The function verifies the supplied credentials and returns a Boolean value. If the user has been successfully authenticated, the code invokes the *RedirectFromLoginPage* static method on the *FormsAuthentication* class to inform the browser that it's time to issue a new request to the original page.

The *RedirectFromLoginPage* method redirects an authenticated user back to the originally requested URL. It has two overloads with the following prototypes:

```
public static void RedirectFromLoginPage(string, bool);
public static void RedirectFromLoginPage(string, bool, string);
```

The first argument is the name of the user to store in the authentication ticket. The second argument is a Boolean value that denotes the duration of the cookie, if any, being created for the authentication ticket. If this argument is *false*, the cookie is given the normal duration— that is, the number of minutes set by the *timeout* attribute (which is 30 minutes by default). If this argument is *true*, the cookie is given a much longer lifetime (50 years). Finally, the third argument optionally specifies the cookie path.

Authenticating the User

The authenticating algorithm—that is, the code inside the *AuthenticateUser* method seen earlier—is entirely up to you. For example, you might want to check the credentials against a database or any other user-defined storage device. The following listing shows a function that compares user name and password against the firstname and lastname columns of the Northwind Employees table in SQL Server 2000:

```
private bool AuthenticateUser(string username, string pswd)
{
    // Performs authentication here
    string connString = "...";
    string cmdText = "SELECT COUNT(*) FROM employees " +
                   "WHERE firstname=@user AND lastname=@pswd";

    int found = 0;
    using(SqlConnection conn = new SqlConnection(connString))
    {
        SqlCommand cmd = new SqlCommand(cmdText, conn);
        cmd.Parameters.Add("@user",
            SqlDbType.VarChar, 10).Value = username;
        cmd.Parameters.Add("@pswd",
            SqlDbType.VarChar, 20).Value = pswd;
        conn.Open();
        found = (int)cmd.ExecuteScalar();
```

```
        conn.Close();
    }
    return (found > 0);
}
```

The query is configured to return an integer that represents the number of rows in the table that match the specified user name and password. Notice the use of typed and sized parameters in the SQL command as a line of defense against possible injection of malicious code. Notice also that the SQL code just shown does not support strong passwords because the = operator doesn't perform case-sensitive comparisons. To make provisions for that, you should rewrite the command as follows:

```
SELECT COUNT(*) FROM employees WHERE
    CAST(RTRIM(firstname) AS VarBinary)=CAST(RTRIM(@user) AS VarBinary)
    AND
    CAST(RTRIM(lastname) AS VarBinary)=CAST(RTRIM(@pswd) AS VarBinary)
```

The *CAST* operator converts the value into its binary representation, while the *RTRIM* operator removes trailing blanks.

Figure 15-4 shows the page of the application once the user has been successfully authenticated.

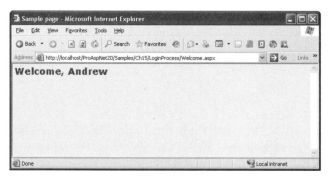

Figure 15-4   The user has been authenticated, and his name shows up in the user interface.

The *welcome.aspx* page has the following, fairly simple, source code:

```
<%@ Page Language="C#" CodeFile="Welcome.aspx.cs" Inherits="Welcome" %>
<html><body>
    <form id="form1" runat="server">
    <h1>Welcome, <%=User.Identity.Name %></h1>
    </form>
</body></html>
```

Signing Out

While an explicit sign-in is always required by Web sites that need authentication, an explicit sign-out is less common but legitimate nonetheless. The Forms authentication module provides an explicit method to sign out. The *SignOut* method on the *FormsAuthentication* class takes no argument and resets the authentication ticket. In particular, when cookies are used, the *SignOut* method removes the current ticket from the *Cookies* collection of the current *HttpResponse* object and replaces it with an empty and expired cookie.

After you call *SignOut*, you might want to redirect the application to another page—for example, the home page. To do this, you don't have to redirect the browser, but as long as the page is publicly accessible, you can use the more efficient *Server.Transfer* method that we described in Chapter 12:

```
void Signout(object sender, EventArgs e)
{
    FormsAuthentication.SignOut();
    Server.Transfer("home.aspx");
}
```

In ASP.NET 2.0, the *FormsAuthentication* class has a new method—*RedirectToLoginPage*— that provides the described functionality, except that it uses *Response.Redirect* instead of *Server.Transfer*.

We've just covered the basics of Forms authentication, but we've not yet covered the programming API we find in ASP.NET 2.0 in any detail. Before we get to this, it is important that you take a look at the methods of the *FormsAuthentication* class and the configurable parameters you find in the *web.config* file. After this, I'll move on to introduce the membership API and role management.

The *FormsAuthentication* Class

The *FormsAuthentication* class supplies some static methods that you can use to manipulate authentication tickets and execute basic authentication operations. You typically use the *RedirectFromLoginPage* method to redirect an authenticated user back to the originally requested URL; likewise, you call *SignOut* to remove the authentication ticket for the current user. Other methods and properties are for manipulating and renewing the ticket and the associated cookie.

Properties of the *FormsAuthentication* Class

Table 15-4 lists the properties of the *FormsAuthentication* class. As you can see, many of them deal with cookie naming and usage and expose the content of configuration attributes in the *<forms>* section. We'll look at the underpinnings of the *<forms>* XML configuration element in the next section. The *FormsAuthentication* class features several new properties in ASP.NET 2.0. All the properties shown in the table are static.

Table 15-4   Properties of the *FormsAuthentication* Class

Property	Description
CookieDomain	Returns the domain set for the authentication ticket. This property is equal to the value of the *domain* attribute in the *<forms>* section. *Not supported in ASP.NET 1.x.*
CookieMode	Indicates whether Forms authentication is implemented with or without cookies. *Not supported in ASP.NET 1.x.*

Table 15-4 Properties of the *FormsAuthentication* Class

Property	Description
CookiesSupported	Returns *true* if the current request supports cookies. *Not supported in ASP.NET 1.x.*
DefaultUrl	Returns the URL for the page to return after a request has been successfully authenticated. Matches the *defaultUrl* attribute in the *<forms>* section. *Not supported in ASP.NET 1.x.*
EnableCrossAppRedirects	Indicates whether redirects can span different Web applications. *Not supported in ASP.NET 1.x.*
FormsCookieName	Returns the configured cookie name used for the current application. The default name is .ASPXAUTH.
FormsCookiePath	Returns the configured cookie path used for the current application. The default is the root path /.
LoginUrl	Returns the configured or default URL for the login page. Matches the *loginUrl* attribute in the *<forms>* section. *Not supported in ASP.NET 1.x.*
RequireSSL	Indicates whether a cookie must be transmitted using only HTTPS.
SlidingExpiration	Indicates whether sliding expiration is enabled.

Most of the properties are initialized with the values read from the *<forms>* configuration section of the *web.config* file when the application starts up.

Methods of the *FormsAuthentication* Class

Table 15-5 details the methods supported by the *FormsAuthentication* class. All the methods listed in the table are static.

Table 15-5 Methods of the *FormsAuthentication* Class

Method	Description
Authenticate	Attempts to validate the supplied credentials against those contained in the configured *<credentials>* section. (I'll say more about this later.)
Decrypt	Given a valid authentication ticket, it returns an instance of the *FormsAuthenticationTicket* class.
Encrypt	Produces a string containing the printable representation of an authentication ticket. The string contains, encoded to URL-compliant characters, the user's credentials optionally hashed and encrypted.
GetAuthCookie	Creates an authentication ticket for a given user name.
GetRedirectUrl	Returns the redirect URL for the original request that caused the redirect to the login page.
HashPasswordForStoringInConfigFile	Given a password and a string identifying the hash type, the method hashes the password for storage in the *web.config* file.
Initialize	Initializes the *FormsAuthentication* class.

Table 15-5   Methods of the *FormsAuthentication* Class

Method	Description
RedirectFromLoginPage	Redirects an authenticated user back to the originally requested URL.
RedirectToLoginPage	Performs a redirect to the configured or default login page. *Not supported in ASP.NET 1.x.*
RenewTicketIfOld	Conditionally updates the sliding expiration on an authentication ticket.
SetAuthCookie	Creates an authentication ticket and attaches it to the outgoing response. It does not redirect to the originally requested URL.
SignOut	Removes the authentication ticket.

The *Initialize* method is called only once in the application's lifetime and initializes the properties in Table 15-4 by reading the configuration file. The method also gets the cookie values and encryption keys to be used for the application.

Not available to ASP.NET 1.x applications, *RedirectToLoginPage* fills a hole in the programming interface of the *FormsAuthentication* class. The method is useful when a user signs out and you want to redirect her to the login page afterwards. When this happens, the method figures out what the login page is and calls *Response.Redirect*.

> **Note**   In spite of their names, in ASP.NET 2.0 both the *GetAuthCookie* method and the *SetAuthCookie* method get and set an authentication ticket, whatever it means to the application. If the application is configured to do Forms authentication in a cookieless manner, the two methods read and write ticket information from and to the URL of the request. They read and write a cookie if the authentication method is configured to use cookies.

Configuration of Forms Authentication

Although ASP.NET Forms authentication is fairly simple to understand, it still provides a rich set of options to deal with to fine-tune the behavior of the authentication mechanism. Most of the settable options revolve around the use of cookies for storing the authentication ticket. All of them find their place in the *<forms>* section under the *<authentication>* section.

The *<forms>* Section

Forms authentication is driven by the contents of the *<forms>* section child of the *<authentication>* section. The overall syntax is shown here:

```
<forms name="cookie"
    loginUrl="url"
    protection="All|None|Encryption|Validation"
    timeout="30"
    requireSSL="true|false"
```

```
      slidingExpiration="true|false"
      path="/"
      enableCrossAppsRedirects="true|false"
      cookieless="UseCookies|UseUri|AutoDetect|UseDeviceProfile"
      defaultUrl="url"
      domain="string">
</forms>
```

The various attributes are described in Table 15-6.

Table 15-6   Attributes for Forms Authentication

Attribute	Description
cookieless	Defines if and how cookies are used for authentication tickets. Feasible values are *UseCookies, UseUri, AutoDetect*, and *UseDeviceProfile. Not supported in ASP.NET 1.x.*
defaultUrl	Defines the default URL to redirect after authentication. The default is *default.aspx. Not supported in ASP.NET 1.x.*
domain	Specifies a domain name to be set on outgoing authentication cookies. (I'll say more about this later.) *Not supported in ASP.NET 1.x.*
enableCrossAppRedirects	Indicates whether users can be authenticated by external applications when authentication is cookieless. The setting is ignored if cookies are enabled. When cookies are enabled, cross-application authentication is always possible. (I'll cover more issues related to this as we go along.) *Not supported in ASP.NET 1.x.*
loginUrl	Specifies the URL to which the request is redirected for login if no valid authentication cookie is found.
name	Specifies the name of the HTTP cookie to use for authentication. The default name is *.ASPXAUTH.*
path	Specifies the path for the authentication cookies issued by the application. The default value is a slash (/). Note that some browsers are case-sensitive and will not send cookies back if there is a path case mismatch.
protection	Indicates how the application intends to protect the authentication cookie. Feasible values are *All, Encryption, Validation*, and *None*. The default is *All*.
requireSSL	Indicates whether an SSL connection is required to transmit the authentication cookie. The default is *false*. If *true*, ASP.NET sets the *Secure* property on the authentication cookie object so that a compliant browser does not return the cookie unless the connection is using SSL. *Not supported in ASP.NET 1.0.*
slidingExpiration	Indicates whether sliding expiration is enabled. The default is *false*, meaning that the cookie expires at a set interval from the time it was originally issued. The interval is determined by the *timeout* attribute. *Not supported in ASP.NET 1.0.*
timeout	Specifies the amount of time, in minutes, after which the authentication cookie expires. The default value is 30.

The *defaultUrl* attribute lets you set the default name of the page to return after a request has been successfully authenticated. This URL is hard-coded to *default.aspx* in ASP.NET 1.x and has been made configurable in ASP.NET 2.0. But isn't the URL of the return page embedded in the query string, in the *ReturnUrl* parameter? So when is *defaultUrl* useful?

If a user is redirected to the login page by the authentication module, the *ReturnUrl* variable is always correctly set and the value of *defaultUrl* is blissfully ignored. However, if your page contains a link to the login page, or if it needs to transfer programmatically to the login page (for example, after the current user has logged off), you are responsible for setting the *ReturnUrl* variable. If it is not set, the URL stored in the *defaultUrl* attribute will be used.

Cookie-Based Forms Authentication

In ASP.NET 1.x, Forms authentication is exclusively based on cookies. The content of the authentication ticket is stored in a cookie named after the value of the *name* attribute in the *<forms>* section. The cookie contains any information that helps to identify the user making the request.

By default, a cookie used for authentication lasts 30 minutes and is protected using both data validation and encryption. Data validation ensures that the contents of the cookie have not been tampered with along the way. Encryption uses the Triple-DES (3DES) algorithm to scramble the content.

When validation is turned on, the cookie is created by concatenating a validation key with the cookie data, computing a message authentication code (MAC) and appending the MAC to the outgoing cookie. The validation key and the hash algorithm to use for the MAC are read out of the *<machineKey>* section in the *web.config* file. The same section also specifies the cryptographic key for when encryption is enabled.

> **Important**   When you create a new ASP.NET application with Microsoft Visual Studio .NET, the default *web.config* file added to the application might not include most of the settings mentioned in this chapter and earlier in the book. It is interesting to note that both the *web.config* file in the application's root and any others you might have in subdirectories override the settings defined in the *machine.config* file. Installed with ASP.NET, *machine.config* contains a default value for each possible section and attribute in the configuration scheme. Therefore, if any given setting is not set (or overridden) in your *web.config* file, that configurable parameter will be set when you run your ASP.NET application using the default value found in *machine.config*.

Cookieless Forms Authentication in ASP.NET 2.0

Using cookies requires some support from the client browser. In ASP.NET 1.x, cookies are mandatory if you want to take advantage of the built-in authentication framework. In ASP.NET 2.0, the core API also supports cookieless semantics. More precisely, the whole API has been reworked to make it expose a nearly identical programming interface but also support dual semantics—cookied and cookieless.

In ASP.NET 2.0, when cookieless authentication is on the ticket it is incorporated into the URL in much the same way as for cookieless sessions. Figure 15-5 provides an example.

Figure 15-5   Cookieless Forms authentication in action.

The URL of the page served to an authenticated user follows the pattern shown here:

```
http://YourApp/(F(XYZ...1234))/samples/default.aspx
```

The ticket, properly encoded to a URL-compliant alphabet, is inserted in the URL right after the server name.

> **Note**   No matter which settings you might have for validation and encryption, or whether your authentication scheme is cookied or cookieless, the information stored in the authentication ticket is encoded so that it is not immediately human-readable. Forms authentication uses a URI-safe derivative of the Base64 encoding that carries six bits of encoding per character.

Cookieless authentication requires an ISAPI filter to intercept the request, extract the ticket, and rewrite the correct path to the application. The filter also exposes the authentication ticket as another request header. The same *aspnet_filter.dll* component that we saw in Chapter 13 for cookieless sessions is used to parse the URL when cookieless authentication is used. To avoid confusion, each extra piece of information stuffed in the URL is wrapped by unique delimiters: *S(...)* for a session ID and *F(...)* for an authentication ticket. The filter extracts the information, removes URL adornments, and places the ticket information in a header named *AspAuthenticationTicket*.

Options for Cookieless Authentication

The *cookieless* attribute in the *<forms>* section specifies if and how cookies are used to store the authentication ticket. The attribute can take any of the values listed in Table 15-7.

Table 15-7   Values for the *cookieless* Attribute

Value	Description
AutoDetect	Uses cookies if the browser has cookie support currently enabled. It uses the cookieless mechanism otherwise.
UseCookie	Always uses cookies, regardless of the browser capabilities.

Table 15-7   Values for the *cookieless* Attribute

Value	Description
UseDeviceProfile	Uses cookies if the browser supports them; uses the cookieless mechanism otherwise. When this option is used, no attempt is made to check whether cookie support is really enabled for the requesting device. This is the default option.
UseUri	Never uses cookies, regardless of the browser capabilities.

There's a subtle difference between *UseDeviceProfile* and *AutoDetect*. Let's make it clear with an example. Imagine a user making a request through Internet Explorer 6.0. The browser does have support for cookies, as reported in the browser capabilities database installed with ASP.NET. However, a particular user might have disabled cookies support for her own browser. *AutoDetect* can correctly handle the latter scenario and opts for cookieless authentication. *UseDeviceProfile* doesn't probe for cookies being enabled and stops at what's reported by the capabilities database. It will wrongly opt for cookied authentication, causing an exception to be thrown.

For compatibility with ASP.NET 1.x, the default value for the *cookieless* attribute is *UseDevice Profile*. You should consider changing it to *AutoDetect*.

Advanced Forms Authentication Features

Let's tackle a few less obvious issues that might arise when working with Forms authentication.

Applications to Share Authentication Cookies

HTTP cookies support a *path* attribute to let you define the application path the cookie is valid within. Pages outside of that path cannot read or use the cookie. If the path is not set explicitly, it defaults to the URL of the page creating the cookie. For authentication cookies, the path defaults to the root of the application so that it is valid for all pages in the application. So far so good.

Already in ASP.NET 1.x, two applications in the same Internet domain can share their own authentication cookies, implementing a sort of single sign-on model. Typically, both applications provide their own login pages and users can log on using any of them and then freely navigate between the pages of both. For this to happen, you only have to ensure that some settings in the root *web.config* files are the same for both applications. In particular, the settings for *name*, *protection*, and *path* attributes in the *<forms>* section must be identical. Moreover, a *<machineKey>* section should be added to both *web.config* files with explicit validation and decryption keys:

```
<machineKey
    validationKey="C50B3C89CB21F4F1422FF158A5B42D0…E"
    decryptionKey="8A9BE8FD67AF6979E7D20198C…D"
    validation="SHA1" />
```

Read Knowledge Base article 312906 (located at *http://support.microsoft.com/default .aspx?scid=kb;en-us;312906*) for suggestions on how to create machine keys. Note that by default, validation and decryption keys are set to *AutoGenerate*. The keyword indicates that a random key has been generated at setup time and stored in the Local Security Authority (LSA). LSA is a Windows service that manages all the security on the local system. If you leave the *AutoGenerate* value, each machine will use distinct keys and no shared cookie can be read.

Applications running in the same domain can share authentication cookies also in ASP.NET 2.0. This happens also between an ASP.NET 1.x and ASP.NET 2.0 application as long as they are hosted in the same domain. Cookie sharing is impossible between ASP.NET 1.0 applications and both ASP.NET 1.1 and ASP.NET 2.0 applications.

Suppose now you run two ASP.NET Web sites named *www.contoso.com* and *blogs.contoso.com*. Each of these sites generates authentication cookies not usable by the other. This is because, by default, authentication cookies are associated with the originating domain. All HTTP cookies, though, support a *domain* attribute, which takes the flexibility of their *path* attribute to the next level. If set, the *domain* attribute indicates the domain for which the cookie is valid. Cookies can be assigned to an entire Internet domain, a subdomain, or even multiple subdomains.

In ASP.NET 2.0, the *Domain* attribute in the *<forms>* section determines the value of the *domain* attribute on the authentication cookie being created:

```
<forms domain="contoso.com" />
```

Add the preceding script to the *web.config* file of the Web sites named *www.contoso.com* and *blogs.contoso.com* and they'll share the authentication cookies (provided the client browser recognizes the *domain* attribute of the cookie, which most modern browsers are bound to do).

The effect of the setting is that the primary domain (*www*) and any other subdomains will be able to handle each other's authentication cookies, always with the proviso that their *web.config* files are synchronized on the machine key values.

> **Note**   Setting the *domain* attribute doesn't cause anything to be emitted into the authentication ticket; it simply forces all Forms authentication methods to properly set the *domain* property on each issued or renewed ticket. The attribute is ignored if cookieless authentication is used. The domain attribute of the *<forms>* section takes precedence over the domain field used in the *<httpCookies>* section and is valid for all cookies created in the ASP.NET application.

External Applications to Authenticate Users

Forms authentication also supports having the login page specified in another application in the same Web site:

```
<forms loginUrl="/anotherAppsamples/login1.aspx" />
```

The two applications must have identical machine keys configured for this to work. If the application is using cookied authentication tickets, no additional work is necessary. The authentication ticket will be stored in a cookie and sent back to the original application. This is possible both in ASP.NET 1.x and ASP.NET 2.0.

In ASP.NET 2.0, if cookieless authentication is used, some extra work is required to enable the external application to authenticate for us. You need to set the *enableCrossAppRedirects* attribute in *<forms>* in the *web.config* file of both applications:

```
<forms … enableCrossAppRedirects="true" />
```

Upon successful authentication, the ticket is generated and attached to a query string parameter to be marshaled back to the original application. Figure 15-6 shows an example.

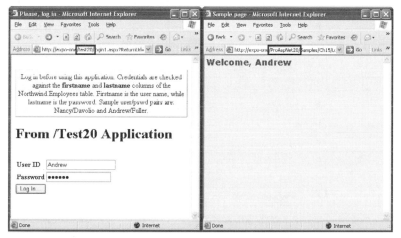

Figure 15-6 Another application performs the authentication and serializes the ticket back.

If the *enableCrossAppRedirects* attribute is missing and cookieless authentication is used, the external application will throw an exception.

Forms Authentication and Secured Sockets

A hacker who manages to steal a valid authentication ticket is in position to perpetrate a replay attack for the lifetime of the ticket—which might be for as long as 50 years if you choose to create ASP.NET persistent tickets! To mitigate the risk of replay attacks, you can perform authentication over a secured socket.

This means that first you must deploy your login page on an HTTPS-capable server, and second you need to set the *requireSSL* attribute to *true* in the *<forms>* section. This setting causes the ASP.NET application to enable the *Secure* attribute on the HTTP cookie being created. When the *Secure* attribute is set, compliant browsers will send back only the cookie containing the ticket over a resource that is protected with SSL. In this way, you can still use a broad cookie scope, such as the whole application ('/'), while providing a reasonable security level for the ticket in transit.

If you don't want to use SSL to protect the ticket, the best you can do to alleviate the risk of replay attacks is set the shortest lifetime for the authentication ticket to a value that is reasonable for the application. Even if the ticket is intercepted, there won't be much time remaining for the attacker to do his or her (bad) things.

Tip What if you don't want to be bound to a fixed time for the ticket expiration, but still don't want to leave perpetual tickets around? You can make the application emit persistent tickets that last as long as 50 years, but change the validation and encryption keys in the *web.config* file when you think it's about time to renew all the tickets. A change in the *web.config* file will restart the application, and the new cryptographic parameters will make issued tickets invalid.

As a final note regarding SSL, consider the following. If *requireSSL* is set and the user attempts to log in on a request not made over SSL, an exception is thrown, as shown in Figure 15-7. If *requireSSL* is set and an authentication cookie (a possibly stolen one at that) is provided over a non-SSL request, no exception is thrown but the cookie is wiped out and a regular login page is displayed through the browser.

Note that if the same happens with cookieless authentication, no protocol check is made, and the request is served to the user—or to the attacker.

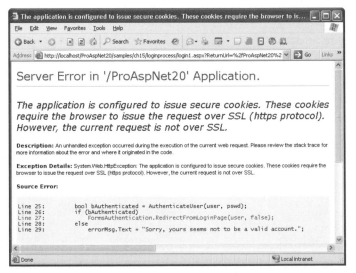

Figure 15-7 An application configured to issue secure cookies can accept requests only over SSL.

General Security Issues

Functionally speaking, Forms authentication is the most appropriate authentication method for Web and ASP.NET applications. However, a few general security issues can't pass unnoticed.

To start with, with Forms authentication credentials are sent out as clear text from the client. (See Figure 15-8.) SSL can be used to protect the communication, but in the end, Forms authentication is as weak as the IIS Basic authentication.

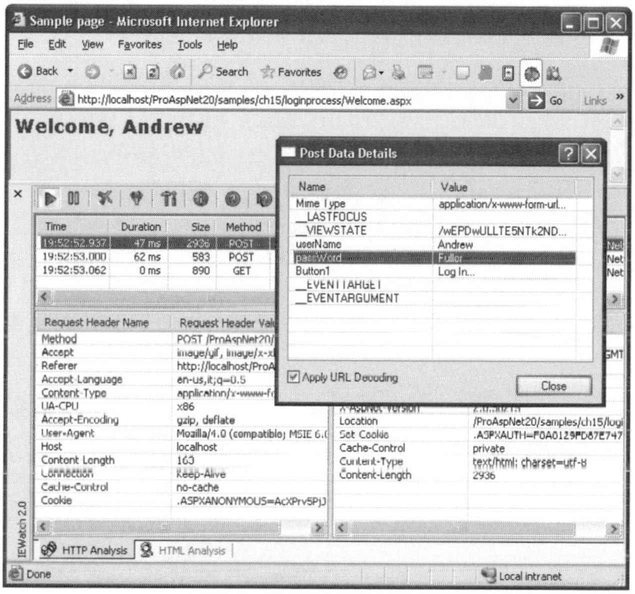

Figure 15-8   Credentials are sent out as clear text.

> **Note**   The tool in the figure—IEWatch 2.0—is a plug-in for Microsoft Internet Explorer that allows you to analyze HTTP/HTTPS requests and the HTML source code. You can get it at *http://www.iewatch.com.*

As mentioned, a stolen authentication cookie can be used to plan replay attacks as long as it is valid. This risk can be partially mitigated by reducing the lifetime of the ticket. Requiring an SSL connection for the cookie transmission resolves the issue if cookied authentication is used, but not if a cookieless solution is employed.

Finally, Forms authentication is based on application code, which is good and bad news at the same time. It is good because you can keep everything under control. It is bad because any bug you leave in your code opens a security hole. A way to mitigate the risk of vulnerabilities stemming from incorrect code is to resort to the newest membership API in ASP.NET 2.0.

The Membership and Role Management API

In ASP.NET 2.0, the core of Forms authentication is the same as in ASP.NET 1.x. Most of the tricks and techniques you have learned remain valid and usable. The most notable change to Forms authentication in ASP.NET 2.0 is the introduction of a complementary API—the membership API. The membership API provides a set of classes to let you manage users and roles.

Partnered with the *FormsAuthentication* class, the new *Membership* and *Roles* classes form a complete security toolkit for ASP.NET developers. The *Membership* class supplies methods to manage user accounts—for adding or deleting a new user and editing any associated user information such as e-mail address and password. The *Roles* class creates and manages associations between users and roles.

What does the expression "managing user accounts" mean exactly? Simply put, it states that the *Membership* class knows how to create a new user or change his or her password. How do you create a user? Typically, you add a new record to some sort of data store. If that's the case, who is in charge of deciding which data store to use and how to actually write the new user information? These tasks represent the core functionality the membership API is designed to provide.

The membership API doesn't bind you to a fixed data store and data scheme. Quite the reverse, I'd say. It leaves you free to choose any data store and scheme you want, but it binds you to a fixed API through which users and roles are managed. The membership API is based on the provider model (discussed in Chapter 1) and delegates to the selected provider the implementation of all the features defined by the API itself.

The *Membership* Class

Centered around the *Membership* static class, the membership API shields you from the details of how the credentials and other user information are retrieved and compared. The *Membership* class contains a few methods that you use to obtain a unique identity for each connected user. This information can also be used with other ASP.NET services, including role-based function enabling and personalization.

Among the members of the class are methods for creating, updating, and deleting users, but not methods for managing roles and programmatically setting what a user can and cannot do. For that you'll have to turn to the *Roles* class, which we'll cover later.

The *Membership* class defaults to a provider that stores user information to a SQL Express database in a predefined format. If you want to use a custom data store (such as a personal database), you can create your own provider and just plug it in.

The Programming Interface of the *Membership* Class

Table 15-8 lists the properties exposed by the *Membership* class.

Table 15-8   Properties of the *Membership* Class

Property	Description
ApplicationName	A string to identify the application. Defaults to the application's root path.
EnablePasswordReset	Returns true if the provider supports password reset.

Table 15-8 Properties of the *Membership* Class

Property	Description
EnablePasswordRetrieval	Returns true if the provider supports password retrieval.
MaxInvalidPasswordAttempts	Returns the maximum number of invalid password attempts allowed before the user is locked out.
MinRequiredNonAlphanumericCharacters	Returns the minimum number of punctuation characters required in the password.
MinRequiredPasswordLength	Returns the minimum required length for a password.
PasswordAttemptWindow	Returns the number of minutes in which a maximum number of invalid password or password answer attempts are allowed before the user is locked out.
PasswordStrengthRegularExpression	Returns the regular expression that the password must comply with.
Provider	Returns an instance of the provider being used.
Providers	Returns the collection of all registered providers.
RequiresQuestionAndAnswer	Returns true if the provider requires a password question/answer when retrieving or resetting the password.
UserIsOnlineTimeWindow	Number of minutes after the last activity for which the user is considered online.

The *Provider* property returns a reference to the membership provider currently in use. As you'll see in a moment, the provider is selected in the configuration file. ASP.NET 2.0 comes with a couple of predefined providers that target MDF files in SQL Server Express and Active Directory. However, many more membership providers are in the works from Microsoft and third-party vendors. You can obtain the list of available providers through the *Providers* collection.

All properties are static and read-only. All of them share a pretty simple implementation. Each property just accesses the corresponding member on the current provider, as shown here:

```
public static int PasswordAttemptWindow
{
   get
   {
      Membership.Initialize();
      return Membership.Provider.PasswordAttemptWindow;
   }
}
```

As the name suggests, the *Initialize* method ensures that the internal structure of the *Membership* class is properly initialized and that a reference to the provider exists.

The class supports fairly advanced functionality, such as estimating the number of users currently using the application. It uses the value assigned to the *UserIsOnlineTimeWindow* property to determine this number. A user is considered online if he has done something with the application during the previous time window. The default value for the *UserIsOnlineTimeWindow* property is 15 minutes. After 15 minutes of inactivity, a user is considered offline.

Table 15-9 details the methods supported by the *Membership* class. This list clarifies the tasks the class accomplishes.

Table 15-9   Methods of the *Membership* Class

Member	Description
CreateUser	Creates a new user and fails if the user already exists. The method returns a *MembershipUser* object representing any available information about the user.
DeleteUser	Deletes the user corresponding to the specified name.
FindUsersByEmail	Returns a collection of *MembershipUser* objects whose e-mail address corresponds to the specified e-mail.
FindUsersByName	Returns a collection of *MembershipUser* objects whose user name matches the specified user name.
GeneratePassword	Generates a random password of the specified length.
GetAllUsers	Returns a collection of all users.
GetNumberOfUsersOnline	Returns the total number of users currently online.
GetUser	Retrieves the *MembershipUser* object associated with the current or specified user.
GetUserNameByEmail	Obtains the user name that corresponds to the specified e-mail. If more users share the same e-mail, the first is retrieved.
UpdateUser	Takes a *MembershipUser* object and updates the information stored for user.
ValidateUser	Authenticates a user by using supplied credentials.

Setting Up Membership Support

To build an authentication layer based on the membership API, you start by choosing the default provider and establishing the data store. In the simplest case, you can stay with the default predefined provider, which saves user information in a local MDF file in SQL Server 2005 Express.

The Web Site Administration Tool (WSAT) in Visual Studio .NET 2005 provides a user interface for creating and administering the registered users of your application. Figure 15-9 provides a glimpse of the user interface.

To add a new user or to edit properties of an existing one, you use the links shown in the figure. When you edit the properties of a new user, you use the page shown in Figure 15-10.

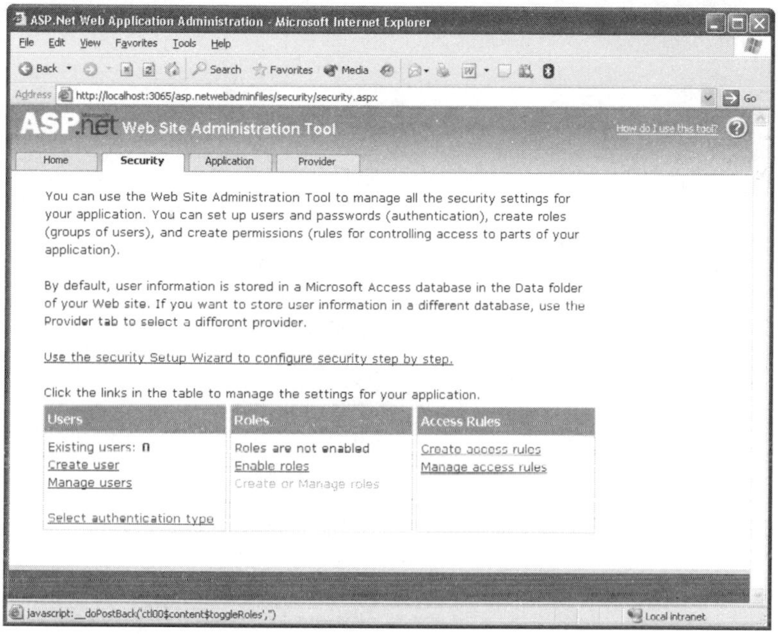

Figure 15-9   WSAT lets you configure the membership data model and manage users offline.

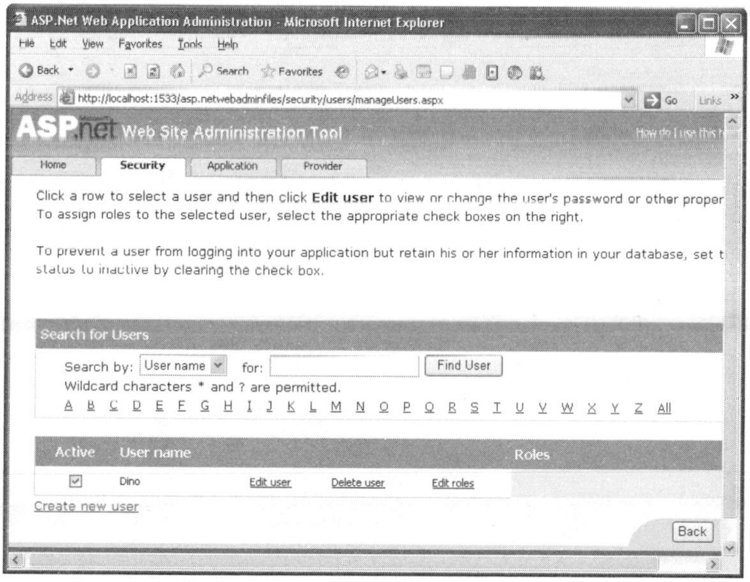

Figure 15-10   Choosing a user to edit or delete through the WSAT tool.

Validating Users

At this point, we're ready to write some code that uses the membership API. Let's start with the most common operation—authenticating credentials. Using the features of the membership subsystem, you can rewrite the code in the login page you saw previously to authenticate a user as follows:

```
void LogonUser(object sender, EventArgs e)
{
    string user = userName.Text;
    string pswd = password.Text;

    if (Membership.ValidateUser(user, pswd))
        FormsAuthentication.RedirectFromLoginPage(user, false);
    else
        errorMsg.Text = "Sorry, yours seems not to be a valid account.";
}
```

This code doesn't look much different from what you would write for an ASP.NET 1.x application, but there's one big difference: the use of the *ValidateUser* built-in function. Here is the pseudocode of this method as it is implemented in the *system.web* assembly:

```
public static bool ValidateUser(string username, string password)
{
    return Membership.Provider.ValidateUser(username, password);
}
```

As you can see, all the core functionality that performs the authentication lives in the provider. What's nice is that the name of the provider is written in the *web.config* file and can be changed without touching the source code of the application. The overall schema is illustrated in Figure 15-11.

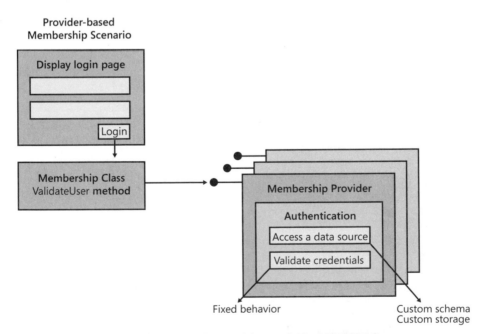

Figure 15-11 Membership using the provider model in ASP.NET 2.0.

Managing Users and Passwords

The *Membership* class provides easy-to-use methods for creating and managing user data. For example, to create a new user programmatically, all you do is place a call to the *CreateUser* method:

```
Membership.CreateUser(userName, pswd);
```

To delete a user, you call the *DeleteUser* method:

```
Membership.DeleteUser(userName);
```

You can just as easily get information about a particular user by using the *GetUser* method. The method takes the user name and returns a *MembershipUser* object:

```
MembershipUser user = Membership.GetUser("DinoE");
```

Once you've got a *MembershipUser* object, you know all you need to know about a particular user, and you can, for example, programmatically change the password (or other user-specific information). An application commonly needs to execute several operations on passwords, including changing the password, sending a user her password, or resetting the password, possibly with a question/answer challenge protocol. Here is the code that changes the password for a user:

```
MembershipUser user = Membership.GetUser("DinoE");
user.ChangePassword(user.GetPassword(), newPswd);
```

To use the *ChangePassword* method, you must pass in the old password. In some cases, you might want to allow users to simply reset their passwords instead of changing them. You do this by using the *ResetPassword* method:

```
MembershipUser user = Membership.GetUser("DinoE");
string newPswd = user.ResetPassword();
```

In this case, the page that calls *ResetPassword* is also in charge of sending the new password to the user—for example, via e-mail. Both the *GetPassword* and *ResetPassword* methods have a second overload that takes a string parameter. If specified, this string represents the answer to the user's "forgot password" question. The underlying membership provider matches the supplied answer against the stored answers; if a user is identified, the password is reset or returned as appropriate.

> **Note**   It goes without saying that the ability to reset the password, as well as support for the password's question/answer challenge protocol, is specific to the provider. You should note that not all the functions exposed by the membership API are necessarily implemented by the underlying provider. If the provider does not support a given feature, an exception is thrown if the method is invoked.

The Membership Provider

The beauty of the membership model lies not merely in the extremely compact code you need to write to validate or manage users but also in the fact that the model is abstract and extensible. For example, if you have an existing data store filled with user information, you can integrate it with the Membership API without much effort. All you have to do is write a custom data provider—that is, a class that inherits from *MembershipProvider*, which, in turn, inherits from *ProviderBase*:

```
public class MyAppMembershipProvider : MembershipProvider
{
    // Implements all abstract members of the class and, if
    // needed, defines custom functionality
    ...
}
```

This approach can be successfully employed to migrate existing ASP.NET 1.x authentication code to ASP.NET 2.0 applications and, perhaps more important, to link a custom and existing data store to the membership API. We'll return to this subject in a moment.

The *ProviderBase* Class

All the providers used in ASP.NET 2.0—not just membership providers—implement a common set of members: the members defined by the *ProviderBase* class. The class comes with one method, *Initialize*, and one property, *Name*. The *Name* property returns the official name of the provider class. The *Initialize* method takes the name of the provider and a name/value collection object packed with the content of the provider's configuration section. The method is supposed to initialize its internal state with the values just read out of the *web.config* file.

The *MembershipProvider* Class

Many of the methods and properties used with the *Membership* class are actually implemented by calling into a corresponding method or property in the underlying provider. It comes as no surprise, then, that many of the methods listed in Table 15-10, which are defined by the *MembershipProvider* base class, support the functions you saw in Table 15-9 that are implemented by the dependent *Membership* class. However, note that although Table 15-9 and Table 15-10 are very similar, they are not identical.

Table 15-10   Methods of the *MembershipProvider* Class

Method	Description
ChangePassword	Takes a user name in addition to the old and new password and changes the user's password.
ChangePasswordQuestionAndAnswer	Takes a user name and password and changes the pair of question/answer challenges that allows reading and changing the password.
CreateUser	Creates a new user account, and returns a *Membership-User*-derived class. The method takes the user name, password, and e-mail address.

Table 15-10   Methods of the *MembershipProvider* Class

Method	Description
DeleteUser	Deletes the record that corresponds to the specified user name.
FindUsersByEmail	Returns a collection of membership users whose e-mail address corresponds to the specified e-mail.
FindUsersByName	Returns a collection of membership users whose user name matches the specified user name.
GetAllUsers	Returns the collection of all users managed by the provider.
GetNumberOfUsersOnline	Returns the number of users that are currently considered to be online.
GetPassword	Takes the user name and the password's answer and returns the current password for the user.
GetUser	Returns the information available about the specified user name.
GetUserNameByEmail	Takes an e-mail address and returns the corresponding user name.
ResetPassword	Takes the user name and the password's answer and resets the user password to an auto-generated password.
UpdateUser	Updates the information available about the specified user.
ValidateUser	Validates the specified credentials against the stored list of users.

All these methods are marked as *abstract virtual* in the class (*must-inherit, overridable* in Visual Basic .NET jargon). The *MembershipProvider* class also features a few properties. They are listed in Table 15-11.

Table 15-11   Properties of the *MembershipProvider* Class

Property	Description
ApplicationName	Returns the provider's nickname
EnablePasswordReset	Indicates whether the provider supports password reset
EnablePasswordRetrieval	Indicates whether the provider supports password retrieval
MaxInvalidPasswordAttempts	Returns the maximum number of invalid password attempts allowed before the user is locked out
MinRequiredNonAlphanumericCharacters	Returns the minimum number of punctuation characters required in the password
MinRequiredPasswordLength	Returns the minimum required length for a password
PasswordAttemptWindow	Returns the number of minutes in which a maximum number of invalid password attempts are allowed before the user is locked out

Table 15-11   Properties of the *MembershipProvider* Class

Property	Description
PasswordStrengthRegularExpression	Returns the regular expression that the password must comply with
RequiresQuestionAndAnswer	Indicates whether the provider requires a question/answer challenge to enable password changes
RequiresUniqueEmail	Indicates whether the provider is configured to require a unique e-mail address for each user name

Extending the Provider's Interface

The provider can also store additional information with each user. For example, you can derive a custom class from *MembershipUser*, add any extra members, and return an instance of that class via the standard *GetUser* method of the membership API.

To use the new class, you cast the object returned by *GetUser* to the proper type, as shown here:

```
MyCompanyUser user = (MyCompanyUser) Membership.GetUser(name);
```

In addition to the members listed in Table 15-10 and Table 15-11, a custom membership provider can add new methods and properties. These are defined outside the official schema of the provider base class and are therefore only available to applications aware of this custom provider:

```
MyCompanyProvider prov = (MyCompanyProvider) Membership.Provider;
```

> **Note**   The *Providers* collection property allows you to use a dynamically selected provider:
>
> ```
> MembershipProvider prov = Membership.Providers["ProviderName"];
> ```
>
> This feature allows applications to support multiple providers simultaneously. For example, you can design your application to support a legacy database of users through a custom provider, while storing new users in a standard SQL Server 2005 table. In this case, you use different membership providers for different users.

A Custom Provider for ASP.NET 1.x Code

Earlier in the chapter, we discussed a few sample pages using the Employees table in the SQL Server 2000 Northwind database as the data store for user accounts. Let's turn this into a membership provider and register it with the WSAT tool:

```
public class MyMembershipProvider : MembershipProvider
{
    public MyMembershipProvider()
    {
```

```
    }
    public override bool ChangePassword(string username,
        string oldPassword, string newPassword)
    {
        // If you don't intend to support a given method
        // just throw an exception
        throw new NotSupportedException();
    }

    ...

    public override bool ValidateUser(string username, string password)
    {
        return AuthenticateUser(username, password);
    }

    private bool AuthenticateUser(string username, string pswd)
    {
        // Place here any analogous code you may have in your
        // ASP.NET 1.x application
    }
}
```

You define a new class derived from *MembershipProvider*. In this class definition, you have to override all the members in Table 15-10 and Table 15-11. If you don't intend to support a given method or property, for that method just throw a *NotSupportedException* exception. For the methods you do plan to support—which for the previous example included only *Validate-User*—you write the supporting code. At this point, nothing prevents you from reusing code from your old application. There are two key benefits with this approach: you reuse most of your code (perhaps with a little bit of refactoring), and your application now embraces the new membership model of ASP.NET 2.0.

Generally speaking, when writing providers there are three key issues to look at: lifetime of the provider, thread-safety, and atomicity. The provider is instantiated as soon as it proves necessary but only once per ASP.NET application. This fact gives the provider the status of a stateful component, but at the price of protecting that state from cross-thread access. A provider is not thread-safe, and it will be your responsibility to guarantee that any critical data is locked before use. Finally, some functions in a provider can be made of multiple steps. Developers are responsible for ensuring atomicity of the operations either through database transactions (whenever possible) or through locks. For more information, refer to the ASP.NET 2.0 Provider Toolkit at *http://msdn.microsoft.com/asp.net/provider*.

Configuring a Membership Provider

You register a new provider through the *<membership>* section of the *web.config* file. The section contains a child *<providers>* element under which additional providers are configured:

```
<membership>
   <providers>
      <add name="MyMembershipProvider"
```

```
            type="ProAspNet20.MyMembershipProvider" />
    <providers>
</membership>
```

You can change the default provider through the *defaultProvider* attribute of the *<membership>* section. Figure 15-12 shows the new provider in WSAT.

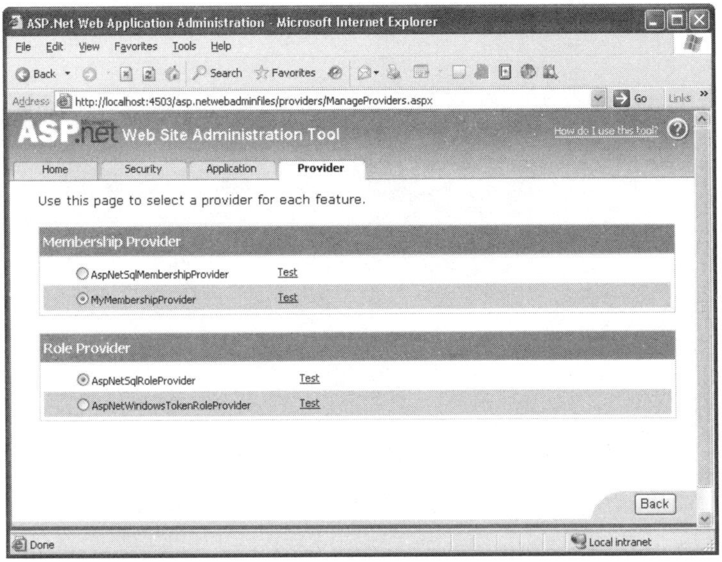

Figure 15-12   WSAT reflects a newly added membership provider.

With the new provider in place, the code to verify credentials reduces to the following code, which is the same as you saw earlier in the chapter:

```
void LogonUser(object sender, EventArgs e)
{
    string user = userName.Text;
    string pswd = password.Text;
    if (Membership.ValidateUser(user, pswd))
        FormsAuthentication.RedirectFromLoginPage(user, false);
    else
        errorMsg.Text = "Sorry, yours seems not to be a valid account.";
}
```

There's more than just this with the membership API. Now a login page has a relatively standard structure and a relatively standard code attached. At least in the simplest scenarios, it can be reduced to a composite control with no binding code. This is exactly what security controls do. Before we get to cover this new family of server controls, though, let's review roles and their provider-based management.

Managing Roles

Roles in ASP.NET simplify the implementation of applications that require authorization. A role is just a logical attribute assigned to a user. An ASP.NET role is a plain string that refers to the logical role the user plays in the context of the application. In terms of configuration, each user can be assigned one or more roles. This information is attached to the identity object, and the application code can check it before the execution of critical operations.

For example, an application might define two roles—Admin and Guest, each representative of a set of application-specific permissions. Users belonging to the Admin role can perform tasks that other users are prohibited from performing.

> **Note** Assigning roles to a user account doesn't add any security restrictions by itself. It is the responsibility of the application to ensure that authorized users perform critical operations only if they are members of a certain role.

In ASP.NET, the role manager feature simply maintains the relationship between users and roles. ASP.NET 1.1 has no built-in support for managing roles. You can attach some role information to an identity, but this involves writing some custom code. Checking roles is easier, but ASP.NET 2.0 makes the whole thing significantly simpler.

> **Note** The Role Management API, although it consists of different methods and properties, works like the Membership API from a mechanical standpoint. Many of the concepts you read in the previous section also apply to role management.

The Role Management API

The role management API lets you define roles as well as specify programmatically which users are in which roles. The easiest way to configure role management, define roles, add users to roles, and create access rules is to use WSAT. (See Figure 15-12.) You enable role management by adding the following script to your application's *web.config* file:

```
<roleManager enabled="true" />
```

You can use roles to establish access rules for pages and folders. The following *<authorization>* block states that only Admin members can access all the pages controlled by the *web.config* file:

```
<configuration>
<system.web>
    <authorization>
        <allow roles="Admin" />
        <deny users="*" />
    </authorization>
</system.web>
<configuration>
```

WSAT provides a visual interface for creating associations between users and roles. If necessary, you can instead perform this task programmatically by calling various role manager methods. The following code snippet demonstrates how to create the Admin and Guest roles and populate them with user names:

```
Roles.CreateRole("Admin");
Roles.AddUsersToRole("DinoE", "Admin");
Roles.CreateRole("Guest");
string[] guests = new string[2];
guests[0] = "JoeUsers";
guests[1] = "Godzilla";
Roles.AddUsersToRole(guests, "Guest")
```

At run time, information about the logged-in user is available through the HTTP context *User* object. The following code demonstrates how to determine whether the current user is in a certain role and subsequently enable specific functions:

```
if (User.IsInRole("Admin"))
{
    // Enable functions specific to the role
 ...
}
```

When role management is enabled, ASP.NET 2.0 looks up the roles for the current user and binds that information to the *User* object. This same feature had to be manually coded in ASP.NET 1.x.

> **Note** In ASP.NET 1.x, you typically cache role information on a per-user basis through a cookie or for all users in a custom *Cache* entry. In both cases, you do this when the application starts by handling the *Application_Start* event in the *global.asax* file. After that, you write a *get* function to read role information from the store and call it wherever required.

The *Roles* Class

When role management is enabled, ASP.NET creates an instance of the *Roles* class and adds it to the current request context—the *HttpContext* object. The *Roles* class features the methods listed in Table 15-12.

Table 15-12 Methods of the *Roles* Class

Method	Description
AddUsersToRole	Adds an array of users to a role.
AddUsersToRoles	Adds an array of users to multiple roles.
AddUserToRole	Adds a user to a role.
AddUserToRoles	Adds a user to multiple roles.
CreateRole	Creates a new role.
DeleteCookie	Deletes the cookie that the role manager used to cache all the role data.

Table 15-12   Methods of the *Roles* Class

Method	Description
DeleteRole	Deletes an existing role.
FindUsersInRole	Retrieves all the user names in the specified role that match the provider user name string. The user names found are returned as a string array.
GetAllRoles	Returns all the available roles.
GetRolesForUser	Returns a string array listing the roles that a particular member belongs to.
GetUsersInRole	Returns a string array listing the users that belong to a particular role.
IsUserInRole	Determines whether the specified user is in a particular role.
RemoveUserFromRole	Removes a user from a role.
RemoveUserFromRoles	Removes a user from multiple roles.
RemoveUsersFromRole	Removes multiple users from a role.
RemoveUsersFromRoles	Removes multiple users from multiple roles.
RoleExists	Returns true if the specified role exists.

Table 15-13 lists the properties available in the *Roles* class. All the properties are static and read-only. They owe their value to the settings in the <*roleManager*> configuration section.

Table 15-13   Properties of the *Roles* Class

Property	Description
ApplicationName	Returns the provider's nickname.
CacheRolesInCookie	Returns *true* if cookie storage for role data is enabled.
CookieName	Specifies the name of the cookie used by the role manager to store the roles. Defaults to .*ASPXROLES*.
CookiePath	Specifies the cookie path.
CookieProtectionValue	Specifies an option for securing the role's cookie. Possible values are *All, Clear, Hashed*, and *Encrypted*.
CookieRequireSSL	Indicates whether the cookie requires SSL.
CookieSlidingExpiration	Indicates whether the cookie has a fixed expiration time or a sliding expiration.
CookieTimeout	Returns the time, in minutes, after which the cookie will expire.
CreatePersistentCookie	Creates a role cookie that survives the current session.
Domain	Indicates the domain of the role cookie.
Enabled	Indicates whether role management is enabled.
MaxCachedResults	Indicates the maximum number of roles that can be stored in a cookie for a user.
Provider	Returns the current role provider.
Providers	Returns a list of all supported role providers.

Some methods in the *Roles* class need to query continuously for the roles associated with a given user, so when possible, the roles for a given user are stored in an encrypted cookie. On each request, ASP.NET checks to see whether the cookie is present; if so, it decrypts the role ticket and attaches any role information to the *User* object. By default, the cookie is a session cookie and expires as soon as the user closes the browser.

Note that the cookie is valid only if the request is for the current user. When you request role information for other users, the information is read from the data store using the configured role provider.

> **Note**   Role management passes through the role manager HTTP module. The module is responsible for adding the appropriate roles to the current identity object, such as the *User* object. The module listens for the *AuthenticateRequest* event and does its job. This is exactly the kind of code you need to write in ASP.NET 1.x.

The Role Provider

For its I/O activity, the role manager uses the provider model and a provider component. The role provider is a class that inherits the *RoleProvider* class. The schema of a role provider is not much different from that of a membership provider. Table 15-14 details the members of the *RoleProvider* class.

Table 15-14   Methods of the *RoleProvider* Class

Method	Description
AddUsersToRoles	Adds an array of users to multiple roles
CreateRole	Creates a new role
DeleteRole	Deletes the specified role
FindUsersInRole	Returns the name of users in a role matching a given user name pattern
GetAllRoles	Returns the list of all available roles
GetRolesForUser	Gets all the roles a user belongs to
GetUsersInRole	Gets all the users who participate in the given role
IsUserInRole	Indicates whether the user belongs to the role
RemoveUsersFromRoles	Removes an array of users from multiple roles
RoleExists	Indicates whether a given role exists

You can see the similarity between some of these methods and the programming interface of the *Roles* class. As we've seen for membership, this is not just coincidental.

ASP.NET 2.0 ships with two built-in role providers—*AspNetSqlRoleProvider* (default) and *AspNetWindowsTokenRoleProvider*. The former stores role information in the same MDF file in SQL Server 2005 Express as the default membership provider. For the latter, role information is obtained based on the settings defined for the Windows domain (or Active Directory) the user is authenticating against. This provider does not allow for adding or removing roles.

Custom role providers can be created deriving from *RoleProvider* and registered using the child *<providers>* section in the *<roleManager>* section. Note that the process for doing so is nearly identical to the process you saw for the custom membership provider we explored previously.

Security-Related Controls

In addition to the membership and role management APIs, ASP.NET 2.0 offers several server controls that make programming security-related aspects of a Web application easier than ever: *Login*, *LoginName*, *LoginStatus*, *LoginView*, *PasswordRecovery*, *ChangePassword*, and *CreateUserWizard*. These are composite controls, and they provide a rich, customizable user interface. They encapsulate a large part of the boilerplate code and markup you would otherwise have to write repeatedly for each Web application you developed. Figure 15-13 offers a comprehensive view of the membership platform and illustrates the role of the login controls.

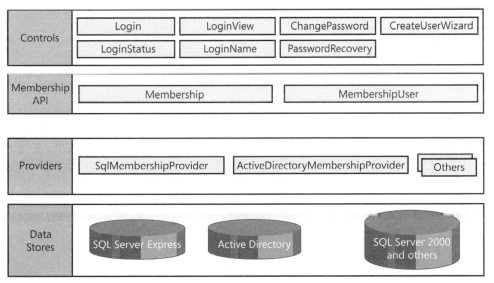

Figure 15-13   The big picture of ASP.NET membership and login controls.

The *Login* Control

An application based on the Forms authentication model always needs a login page. Aside from the quality of the graphics, all login pages look alike. They contain a couple of text boxes (for user name and password), a button to validate credentials, plus perhaps a Remember Me check box, and possibly links to click if the user has forgotten his or her password or needs to create a new account. The *Login* control provides all this for free, including the ability to validate the user against the default membership provider.

Setting Up the *Login* Control

The *Login* control is a composite control that provides all the common user interface elements of a login form. Figure 15-14 shows the default user interface of the control. To use it, you simply drop the control from the toolbox onto the Web form, or you just type the following code:

```
<asp:login runat="server" id="MyLoginForm" />
```

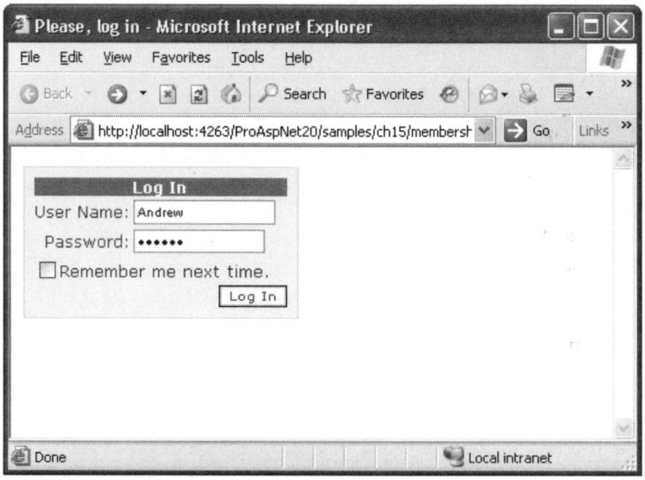

Figure 15-14   The *Login* control in action.

The *Login* control also has optional user interface elements for functions such as password reminder, new user registration, help link, error messages, and a custom action in case of a successful login. When you drop the control onto a Visual Studio .NET 2005 form, the Auto-Format verb lets you choose among a few predefined styles, as in Figure 15-15.

Figure 15-15   The predefined styles of the *Login* control.

The appearance of the control is fully customizable through templates and style settings. All user interface text messages are also customizable through properties of the class.

The Programming Interface of the Control

The control is modularized, and each constituent part can be individually customized. The parts include the Username and Password text boxes, the Submit button, the button to create a new user, the Remember Me check box, and instructions with guidance to the user.

If you don't like the standard user interface of the control, you can define your own template, too:

```
<asp:login runat="server" id="MyLoginForm">
    <layouttemplate>
       ...
    </layouttemplate>
</asp:login>
```

Your template can include new elements, and you can recycle default components. To do the latter, you should use the same ID for the controls as in the default template. To simplify this operation, right-click on the control in the Visual Studio designer, choose Convert To Template, and switch to the Source view. The markup you see is the default template of the control expressed as ASP.NET code. Use it as a starting point for creating your own template.

Events of the Control

The *Login* control fires the server events listed in Table 15-15.

Table 15-15   Events of the *Login* Control

Event	Description
Authenticate	Fires when a user is authenticated.
LoggedIn	Fires when the user logs in to the site after a successful authentication.
LoggingIn	Fires when a user submits login information but before the authentication takes place. At this time, the operation can still be canceled.
LoginError	Fires when a login error is detected.

In most common cases, though, you don't need to handle any of these events, nor will you likely find it necessary to programmatically access any of the numerous properties of the control.

The most common use for the *Login* control is to use it as a single-control page to set up the user interface of the login page for use with Forms authentication. The control relies entirely on the membership API (and the selected provider) to execute standard operations such as validating credentials, displaying error messages, and redirecting to the originally requested page in case of successful login.

If you have a provider with custom capabilities that you want to be reflected by the *Login* control, you need to modify the layout to add new visual elements bound to a code-behind method. In the code-behind method, you invoke the custom method on the custom provider.

The *LoginName* Control

The *LoginName* control is an extremely simple but useful server control. It works like a sort of label control and displays the user's name on a Web page:

```
<asp:loginname runat="server" />
```

The control captures the name of the currently logged-in user from the *User* intrinsic object and outputs it using the current style. Internally, the control builds a dynamic instance of a *Label* control, sets fonts and color accordingly, and displays the text returned by the following expression:

```
string name = HttpContext.Current.User.Identity.Name;
```

The *LoginName* control has a pretty slim programming interface that consists of only one property—*FormatString,* which defines the format of the text to display. It can contain only one placeholder, as shown here:

```
myLogin.FormatString = "Welcome, {0}";
```

If *Dino* is the name of the current user, the code generates a "Welcome, Dino" message.

The *LoginStatus* Control

The *LoginStatus* control indicates the state of the authentication for the current user. Its user interface consists of a link button to log in or log out, depending on the current user logon state. If the user is acting as an anonymous user—that is, he or she never logged in—the control displays a link button to invite the user to log in. Otherwise, if the user successfully passed through the authentication layer, the control displays the logout button.

Setting Up the *LoginStatus* Control

The *LoginStatus* control is often used in conjunction with the *LoginName* control to display the name of the current user (if any), plus a button to let the user log in or out. The style, text, and action associated with the button changes are conveniently based on the authentication state of the user.

The following code creates a table showing the name of the current user and a button to log in or log out:

```
<table width="100%" border="0"><tr>
    <td>
        <asp:loginname runat="server" FormatString="Welcome, {0}" />
    </td>
```

```
    <td align="right">
        <asp:loginstatus runat="server" LogoutText="Log off" />
    </td>
  </tr>
</table>
```

Figure 15-16 shows the results. The first screen shot demonstrates a page that invites a user to log in, while the second shows the *LoginName* and *LoginStatus* controls working together in the case of a logged-in user. To detect whether the current user is authenticated and adapt the user interface, you can use the *IsAuthenticated* property of the *User* object:

```
void Page_Load(object sender, EventArgs e)
{
    if (User.Identity.IsAuthenticated)
        // Adjust the UI by outputting some text to a label
        Msg.Text = "Enjoy more features";
    else
        Msg.Text = "Login to enjoy more features.";
}
```

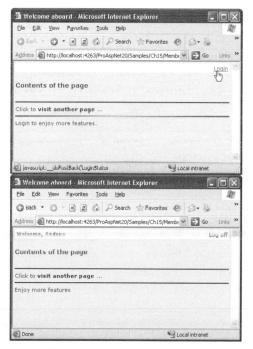

Figure 15-16   The *LoginStatus* control invites a user who is not currently logged in to log in; next, it displays more features reserved to registered users.

The Programming Interface of the Control

Although the *LoginStatus* control is quite useful in its default form, it provides a bunch of properties and events that you can use to configure it. The properties are listed in Table 15-16.

Table 15-16   **Properties of the *LoginStatus* Control**

Property	Description
LoginImageUrl	Gets or sets the URL of the image used for the login link.
LoginText	Gets or sets the text used for the login link.
LogoutAction	Determines the action taken when a user logs out of a Web site. Possible values are *Refresh*, *Redirect*, and *RedirectToLoginPage*. *Refresh* reloads the current page with the user logged out. The other two redirect the user to the logout page or the login page, respectively.
LogoutImageUrl	Gets or sets the URL of the image used for the logout button.
LogoutPageUrl	Gets or sets the URL of the logout page.
LogoutText	Gets or sets the text used for the logout link.

The control also features a couple events—*LoggingOut* and *LoggedOut*. The former fires before the user clicks to log off. The latter is raised immediately after the logout process has completed.

The *LoginView* Control

The *LoginView* control allows you to aggregate the *LoginStatus* and *LoginName* controls to display a custom user interface that takes into account the authentication state of the user as well as the user's role or roles. The control, which is based on templates, simplifies creation of a user interface specific to the anonymous or connected state and particular roles to which they are assigned. In other words, you can create as many templates as you need, one per state or per role.

The Programming Interface of the Control

Table 15-17 lists the properties of the user interface of the *LoginView* control.

Table 15-17   **Properties of the *LoginView* Class**

Property	Description
AnonymousTemplate	Gets or sets the template to display to users who are not logged in to the application.
LoggedInTemplate	Gets or sets the template to display to users who are logged in to the application.
RoleGroups	Returns the collection of templates defined for the supported roles. Templates can be declaratively specified through the *<roleGroups>* child tag.

Note that the *LoggedInTemplate* template is displayed only to logged-in users who are not members of one of the role groups specified in the *RoleGroups* property. The template (if any) specified in the *<roleGroups>* tag always takes precedence.

The *LoginView* control also fires the *ViewChanging* and *ViewChanged* events. The former reaches the application when the control is going to change the view (such as when a user logs in). The latter event fires when the view has changed.

Creating a Login Template

The *LoginView* control lets you define two distinct templates to show to anonymous and logged-in users. You can use the following markup to give your pages a common layout and manage the template to show when the user is logged in:

```
<asp:loginview runat="server">
   <anonymoustemplate>
      <table width="100%" border="0"><tr><td>
         To enjoy more features,
         <asp:loginstatus runat="server">
      </td></tr></table>
   </anonymoustemplate>
   <loggedintemplate>
      <table width="100%" border="0"><tr>
         <td><asp:loginname runat="server" /></td>
         <td align="right"><asp:loginstatus runat="server" /></td>
      </tr></table>
   </loggedintemplate>
</asp:loginview>
```

Basically, the *LoginView* control provides a more flexible, template-based programming interface to distinguish between logged-in and anonymous scenarios, as we did in the previous example by combining *LoginStatus* and *LoginName*.

Creating Role-Based Templates

The *LoginView* control also allows you to define blocks of user interface to display to all logged-in users who belong to a particular role. As mentioned, these templates take precedence over the <*loggedintemplate*> template, if both apply:

```
<asp:loginview runat="server">
   <rolegroups>
      <asp:rolegroup roles="Admin">
         <contenttemplate>
            ...
         </contenttemplate>
      </asp:rolegroup>
      <asp:rolegroup roles="Guest">
         <contenttemplate>
            ...
         </contenttemplate>
      </asp:rolegroup>
   </rolegroups>
</asp:loginview>
```

The content of each *<contenttemplate>* block is displayed only to users whose role matches the value of the *roles* attribute. You can use this feature to create areas in a page whose contents are strictly role-specific. For the *LoginView* control to work fine, role management must be enabled, of course. The control uses the default provider.

The *PasswordRecovery* Control

The *PasswordRecovery* control is another server control that wraps a common piece of Web user interface into an out-of-the-box component. The control represents the form that enables a user to recover or reset a lost password. The user will receive the password through an e-mail message sent to the e-mail address associated with his or her account.

The control supports three views, depending on the user's password recovery stage, as follows. The first view is where the user provides the user name and forces the control to query the membership provider for a corresponding membership user object. The second view is where the user must provide the answer to a predetermined question to obtain or reset the password. Finally, the third view is where the user is informed of the success of the operation.

Requirements for Password Retrieval

For the control to work properly, you must first ensure that the selected membership provider supports password retrieval. The password retrieval also requires that the provider defines a *MembershipUser* object and implements the *GetUser* methods. Remember that the membership provider decides how to store passwords: clear text, hashed, or encrypted.

If passwords are stored as hashed values, the control doesn't work. Hash algorithms are not two-way algorithms. In other words, the hash mechanism is great at encrypting and comparing passwords, but it doesn't retrieve the clear text. If you plan to use the *PasswordRecovery* control, you must ensure that the provider stores password as clear text or encrypted data.

Retrieving a Password

The *PasswordRecovery* control supports a child element named *MailDefinition*:

```
<asp:passwordrecovery runat="server">
    <maildefinition from="admin@contoso.com" />
</asp:passwordrecovery>
```

The *<MailDefinition>* element configures the e-mail message and indicates the sender as well as the format of the body (text or HTML), priority, subject, and carbon-copy (CC). For the same settings, you can also use a bunch of equivalent properties on the associated *Framework* class and set values programmatically.

If the user who has lost the password has a question/answer pair defined, the *PasswordRecovery* control changes its user interface to display the question and ask for the answer before the password is retrieved and sent back. Figure 15-17 demonstrates the behavior of the control.

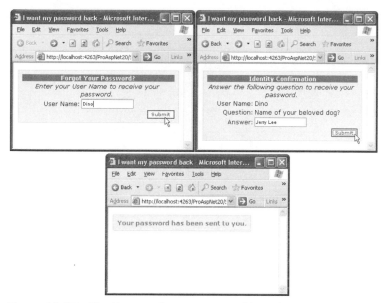

Figure 15-17   The *PasswordRecovery* control in action.

The control first asks the user to provide the user name; next, it retrieves associated information and displays the security question, if any is defined for the user. Finally, if an e-mail address is known, the control sends a message with details, as shown in Figure 15-18.

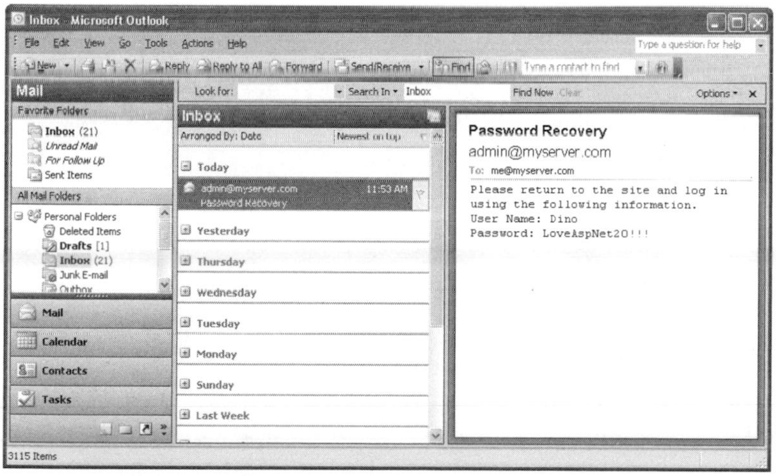

Figure 15-18   The e-mail message with password information.

The *ChangePassword* Control

The *ChangePassword* control provides an out-of-the-box and virtually codeless solution that enables end users to change their password to the site. The control supplies a modifiable and customizable user interface and built-in behaviors to retrieve the old password and save a new one:

```
<asp:ChangePassword ID="ChangePassword1" runat="server" />
```

The underlying API for password management is the same membership API we discussed earlier in this chapter.

User Authentication

The *ChangePassword* control will work in scenarios where a user might or might not be already authenticated. However, note that the User Name text box is optional. If you choose not to display the user name and still permit nonauthenticated users to change their passwords, the control will always fail.

If the user is not authenticated but the User Name text box is displayed, the user will be able to enter his or her user name, current password, and new password at the same time.

Password Change

The change of the password is performed using the *ChangePassword* method on the *MembershipUser* object that represents the user making the attempt. Note that the provider might pose an upper limit to the invalid attempts to change or reset the password. If set, this limit affects the *ChangePassword* control. The control won't work any longer once the limit has been exceeded.

Once the password has been successfully changed, the control might send—if properly configured—a confirmation e-mail to the user, as shown in Figure 15-19.

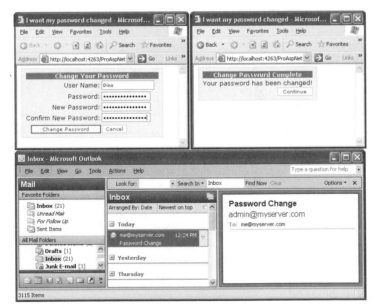

Figure 15-19   The *ChangePassword* control in action.

The e-mail message is configured through the same *<MailDefinition>* element we saw earlier for the *PasswordRecovery* control.

The *Continue* button points the page with the control to a new destination URL to let users continue working. If you don't set the *ContinuePageDestinationUrl* property, clicking the button simply refreshes the current page.

The *CreateUserWizard* Control

The *CreateUserWizard* control is designed to provide a native functionality for creating and configuring a new user using the membership API. The control offers a basic behavior that the developer can extend to send a confirmation e-mail to the new user and add steps to the wizard to collect additional information such as address, phone number, or perhaps roles.

Customization is supported in two ways: by customizing one of the default steps, and by adding more user-defined steps. Figure 15-20 shows the control in action in the Add User page of the WSAT tool.

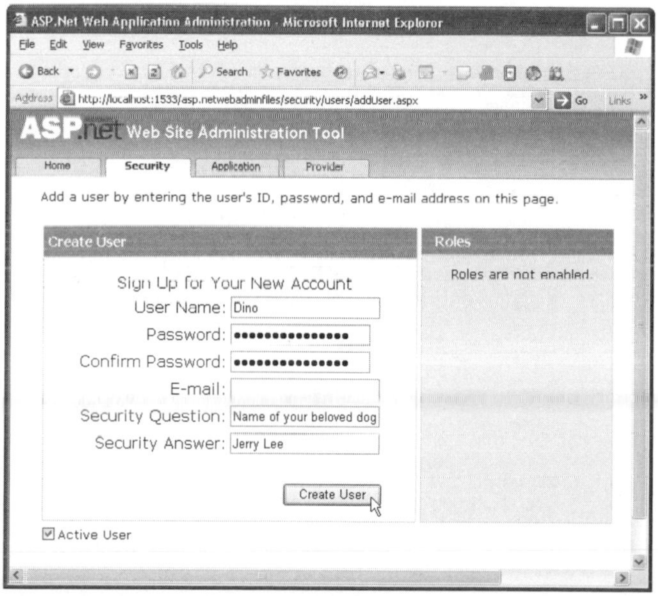

Figure 15-20   The *CreateUserWizard* control in action within WSAT.

The difference between this control and the *CreateUser* method on the membership provider is that the method just adds the user name and password. The wizard provides a user interface and lets you add more information in a single shot.

> **Resources to Write Attack-Resistant Code**
>
> How can we design and code secure ASP.NET applications? First of all, security is strictly related to the application's usage, its popularity, and the type of users who connect to it and work with it. Paradoxically, a poorly secured application that isn't attractive to hackers can be perceived as being much more secure than a well-armored application with just one loophole or two. Successful attacks are possible through holes in the system-level and application-level security apparatus. When it comes to security, don't look for a magic wand to do the job for you. Security is a state of mind, and insecurity is often the result of loose coding styles, if not true programming laziness. Never blindly trust anything regarding Web and ASP.NET security. Always keep in mind that security for Web applications is mostly about raising the bar higher and higher to make it hard for bad guys to jump over.
>
> The following Patterns & Practices links can help you find great information to fend off most common types of attacks and implement effective input validation in ASP.NET 1.x and 2.0 applications:
>
> - **How To—Protect from Injection Attacks in ASPNET**   *http://msdn.microsoft.com/ library/default.asp?url=/library/en-us/dnpag2/html/paght000003.asp*
> - **How To—Use Regular Expressions to Constrain Input in ASP.NET**   *http:// msdn.microsoft.com/library/default.asp?url=/library/en-us/dnpag2/html/ paght000001.asp*
> - **How To—Protect from SQL Injection in ASP.NET**   *http://msdn.microsoft.com/ library/default.asp?url=/library/en-us/dnpag2/html/paght000002.asp*
> - **How To—Prevent Cross-Site Scripting in ASP.NET**   *http://msdn.microsoft.com/ library/default.asp?url=/library/en-us/dnpag2/html/paght000004.asp*

Conclusion

There are three layers of security wrapped around ASP.NET applications: the IIS layer, the ASP.NET worker process layer, and the application layer. As a developer, you can configure parameters in the first two levels, but you are totally responsible for planning and implementing the third one. Forms authentication is the most reasonable approach to protecting pages from unauthorized access in an Internet exposed application. The most reasonable approach for an intranet application is integrated Windows authentication. Although it's not perfect, Forms authentication is broadly used because it is simple to understand and functional. In ASP.NET 2.0, Forms authentication is partnered with the membership API.

The membership API doesn't change the way in which Forms authentication works, it simply adds new and powerful tools for developers. If you're writing a new ASP.NET 2.0 application, there's no reason for not implementing authentication through the membership API and its auxiliary classes and server controls. If you're migrating an existing application, you should try to embrace the newest API by refactoring your code to make it fully reusable.

Is this enough to claim that an ASP.NET application is secure? Unfortunately not. Secure software requires knowledgeable IT personnel, but no software can ever be considered secure if the network is not at least as secure. Likewise, secure software requires knowledgeable developers, because proper administration is useless and ineffective when the code lays itself open to malicious and injurious attacks. Administration is and remains the primary bedrock of security; however, even a wise and restrictive policy can't do much if developers and architects build inherently insecure code.

To achieve security for any piece of software exposed over the Web, you must enforce network and application security. Network threats to guard against include denial of service (DoS), spoofing, and eavesdropping. Bad effects of these attacks include theft of passwords and other critical data, request floods, and an undesired understanding of internal network topologies by potential attackers. Examples of threats aimed at the application include the notorious SQL injection threat and cross-site scripting (XSS). As an ASP.NET developer, you should apply at least one key rule all the time: don't trust user input.

Just the Facts

- The ASP.NET worker process runs under a weak account named ASPNET or NETWORK SERVICE, depending on the process model in use. None of these accounts has administrative privileges.

- You can change the worker process account, but you should at least give the new account full permissions on the folders where the ASP.NET runtime creates temporary files.

- Forms authentication is the most common way of protecting ASP.NET pages and resources from unauthorized access in an Internet application. It works by attaching an authentication ticket to the request to prove the identity of the user; an HTTP module intercepts any requests and checks for that.

- Membership API complements Forms authentication by decoupling the page code and the code that works with user information. This second type of code is isolated in a provider component that can be plugged into and out of the configuration file.

- The role management API provides a rich API to manage roles and an HTTP module that uses a provider to extract role information for the user and that attaches that to the request.

- The membership API is integrated with Visual Studio .NET through the WSAT tool, and it gives administrators a tool to manage users and roles offline.

- The membership API is linked to a new family of controls for common login-related operations, such as password recovery and change, user creation, and login display.

- Secure applications depend on secure coding practices that prevent common attacks. The key rule to apply all the time is, "Don't trust user input." Sanitizing any data the user inserts in the application is key, and validation controls and coded validation rules can raise the security bar much higher for attackers.

Index

A

<A> tag, 16–17, 135, 136. *See also* HtmlAnchor control

Abandon method, 549

AbortTransaction event, 108

AboveNormal priority, 602

Absolute Expiration Date attribute, 596

abstraction layers, HTTP protocol and server-side, 9–10

AcceptChanges method, 334, 341

AcceptChangesDuringFill property, 321, 325

AcceptChangesDuringUpdate property, 321

AcceptTypes property, 531

access control lists (ACLs), 659

Access databases. *See* AccessDataSource control

Access this computer from the network permission, 654

AccessDataSource control, 392–393

  opening Access databases, 393

  overview, 384, 392

  updating Access databases, 393

accessibility check, Visual Studio .NET 2005, 49–50, 153

AccessibleHeaderText property, 435

AccessKey property, 145

accounts. *See also* process identity

  anonymous account impersonation, 653–654

  changing default, for worker process, 652. *See also* ASPNET account; NETWORK SERVICE account

  encryption and, 286

  permissions. *See* permissions

  SQLServer session-state provider hosting identity, 566

ACLs (access control lists), 659

AcquireRequestState event, 505, 506

action attribute, 14

Active Server Pages (ASP), 3, 4, 6, xvii

ActiveStep property, 251

ActiveStepIndex property, 251

ActiveViewChanged event, 252, 257

ActiveX Data Objects (ADO), 263, 264

adapter pattern, 30

Adapter property, 125

adaptive rendering

  development stack and, 21

  server controls and, 125

Add method, 539, 549, 575, 594

<add> tag, 203–204

Add value, 329

AddCacheDependency method, 528

AddCacheItemDependencies method, 528

AddCacheItemDependency method, 528

Added state, 337

AddError method, 516

AddFileDependencies method, 528

AddFileDependency method, 528

AddHeader method, 528

AddNew method, 349

AddUsersToRole method, 688

AddUsersToRoles method, 688

AddUserToRole method, 688

AddUserToRoles method, 688

AddValidationCallback method, 631

AddWithKey value, 329

administration. *See* application administration

administrative permissions, 65, 69

ADO (ActiveX Data Objects), 263, 264

ADO.NET 1.x. *See also* ADO.NET data containers; ADO.NET data providers

  distributed transactions, 312–313

  local transactions, 308–310

ADO.NET 2.0, 275

ADO.NET data containers, 319–352. *See also* ADO.NET data providers

  data adapters. *See* data adapters

  as data-binding data sources, 354–355

  DataRelation objects, 346–348

  DataSet objects, 333–340

  DataTable objects, 340–345

  DataView objects, 348–351

  memory-resident database model and classes of, 332–333

  overview, 319, 351–352

ADO.NET data providers, 263–318. *See also* ADO.NET
    data containers
  command execution. *See* commands, ADO.NET
  components, 265–266
  data source connections. *See* connections, data
    source
  database access technologies, 264
  database-agnostic pages and, 273–274
  enumerating installed, 272–273
  instantiating, 271–272
  interfaces, 266–267
  managed providers and, 265–268
  managed providers vs. OLE DB providers, 267–268
  .NET Framework data access infrastructure,
    264–274
  .NET Framework supported, 268–271
  for ODBC, 271
  for OLE DB providers, 270
  for Oracle, 269–270
  overview, 263, 317–318
  provider factory model, 271–274
  for SQL Server, 268–269
AdRotator control, 155–156
AggregateCacheDependency class, 611–612
algorithms, GridView control paging, 446
AllErrors property, 515
AllKeys property, 539
allowAnonymous attribute, 204
AllowCustomPaging property, 414
allowCustomSqlDatabase attribute, 554
AllowDelete property, 348
AllowEdit property, 348
AllowNew property, 348
AllowPaging property, 414, 428, 469
AllowPartiallyTrustedCallers attribute, 658
AllowRemoteConnection registry entry, 561
AllowSorting property, 414, 428
AlternatingItem item type, 416
AlternatingItemStyle property, 414
AlternatingItemTemplate property, 369, 441
AlternatingRowStyle property, 429, 470
anchor tag. *See* <A> tag; HtmlAnchor control

anomalies, global.asax file, 512–514
anonymous users
  anonymous account impersonation, 653–654
  migrating data for, 212
  user profiles and, 207–208
AnonymousID property, 531
AnonymousIdentification module, 503
AnonymousTemplate property, 696
Any location type, 628, 629
App_Browsers directory, 58
App_Code directory, 54–55, 58, 58–59, 395
App_Data directory, 58
AppDomains, 24, 81, 592
appearance properties
  DetailsView control, 469–470
  GridView control, 430
AppendCacheExtension method, 631
AppendCookie method, 528
AppendDataBoundItems property, 361, 362, 363, 367
AppendHeader method, 528
AppendToLog method, 528
App_GlobalResources directory, 58, 59–62
AppId column, 564
application administration
  editing configuration files, 75–77
  overview, 72–77
  Visual Studio .NET 2005 and, 72–77
  Web Site Administration Tool and, 72–75
application deployment
  Copy Web site feature and, 44
  site precompilation and, 69–72
  Visual Studio .NET 2005 and, 66–72
  XCopy deployment, 66–69
Application Name attribute, 281
Application objects, 100
Application property, 502, 515
Application Root Folder permissions, 654
Application scope, <object> tag, 511
ApplicationInstance property, 515
ApplicationName property, 676, 683, 689
ApplicationPath property, 533

applications
  administration of. *See* application administration
  ADO.NET managed providers vs. OLE DB providers
      and integration of, 267
  application domains, 24, 81, 592
  application factory, 88–89
  configuration of, 25. *See also* configuration;
      web.config files
  data caching. *See* Cache objects; caching
  deployment of. *See* application deployment
  development of. *See* ASP.NET programming; Web
      application development
  directories for, 57–58
  external, to authenticate users, 672–673
  global.asax file directives, 509–510
  initialization of. *See* HttpApplication class
  multilanguage. *See* localization
  restarts, 80, 87, 90–91
  runtime environment and application services,
      25–27. *See also* providers; runtime environment
  to share Forms authentication cookies, 671–672
  state of. *See* HttpApplicationState objects
  Web Site Administration Tool (WSAT) and, 73,
      74–75
Applied XML with the .NET Framework, 379
App_LocalResources directory, 58, 59–62
ApplyAppPathModifier method, 528
ApplyDefaultSort property, 348
ApplyPagePersonalization method, 209
ApplyStyle method, 147
ApplyStyleSheetSkin method, 124, 178
AppName column, 564
<appSettings> section, configuration file, 74
AppSettings:XXX expression, 381
App_Themes directory, 58, 62–63
App_WebReferences directory, 58, 62
.asax file extension, 81
.ascx file extension, 49, 81. *See also* user controls
.ashx file extension, 81
.asmx file extension, 81
ASP (Active Server Pages), 3, 4, 6, xvii
<asp> namespace, 17, 19
AspCompat attribute, 94, 523–524
<asp:Content> tags, 47

ASP.default_aspx class, 84–85, 86
ASP.global.asax class, 89
ASP.NET 1.x. *See also* ASP.NET 2.0; ASP.NET
      programming
  authentication schema, 27–28
  configuration files, 97
  control base classes, 21
  cookieless sessions, 552
  custom membership provider, 684–685
  database cache dependencies, 618
  development of, 3, xvii
  IIS 6.0 process model and, 83
  inadequacies of cache dependencies, 610
  <meta> tag, 134
  page life cycle, 22
  rich pages in, 220–222
  role management, 688
  themes, 236, 243
  user controls, 23
ASP.NET 2.0, 97. *See also* ASP.NET 1.x; ASP.NET
      programming
  adaptive rendering, 125
  AdRotator control, 156
  advantages of, 4, xvii
  application services, 25
  browser-sensitive rendering, 126–127
  cache dependencies, 599
  changes in view state, 581–585
  control adapter architecture, 21
  control state, 128
  cookieless Forms authentication, 669–670
  data-bound controls, 21
  enabling database cache dependencies in, 618–620
  <head> tag and, 18
  input focus, 128–129
  master and content pages, 23
  new features, 125–129
  page life cycle, 22
  page-output caching, 641–644
  protected directories, 57–63
  rich server controls, 21
  themeable controls, 127
  UseSubmitBehavior property, 114

ASPNET account. *See also* accounts; process identity
  SQLServer session-state provider and, 566
  worker processes and, 24, 63
ASP.NET Development Center, 34
ASP.NET programming
  ADO.NET data containers. *See* ADO.NET data
    containers
  ADO.NET data providers. *See* ADO.NET data
    providers
  books about, xvii
  caching. *See* caching
  code samples, xxi. *See also* code
  configuring SQL Server 2005 Express Edition,
    xix–xx
  data binding, 353, 411–412. *See also* data source
    controls; data source-based data binding; data-
    binding expressions
  data-bound grid controls, 413–414, 464–465. *See
    also* DataGrid control; GridView control
  developers and this book about, xviii
  email and postal addresses for questions and
    comments, xxi
  form-based. *See* forms
  HTTP request context. *See* HTTP request context
  languages. *See* languages, programming
  Microsoft Press Technology Updates Web page, xx
  overview, xvii–xxi
  pages. *See* pages
  programming model. *See* programming model
  record-view controls, 467, 497–498. *See also*
    DetailsView control; FormView control
  rich pages, 219–220. *See also* master pages; themes;
    user controls; visual inheritance; Wizard control
  runtime environment. *See* runtime environment
  security. *See* security
  server controls. *See* server controls
  state management. *See* state management
  support for this book about, xxi
  system requirements, xviii–xix
  Visual Studio .NET 2005 Community Technical
    Preview prelease software and, xx
  Web application development history and, xvii–xviii
  Web application development in Visual Studio .NET
    2005. *See* Visual Studio .NET 2005; Web
    application development
ASP.NET projects. *See* projects
ASP.NET Starter Kits, 26

aspnet_compiler tool, 70–71
aspnetdb.mdf database, 73, 203, 207, 214–215
aspnet_isapi.dll, 24, 80–81, 83, 509
aspnet_regiis.exe tool, 285
aspnet_regsql.exe tool, 563
ASP.NETWebAdminFiles directory, 72
aspnet_wp.exe worker process, 24, 63, 81
ASPState database, 563–565
ASPStateTempApplications table, 564
ASPStateTempSessions table, 564–565
.aspx file extension, 11, 39, 42, 45, 84, 92, 93. *See also*
    pages
assemblies
  compilation and, 63. *See also* compilation; site
    precompilation
  default, 96–97
  .NET reflection and, 67
  pages and, 79
  resource, 59–60
@Assembly directive, 91, 96–97
Assistive Technology devices, 416
AssociatedControlID property, 153
Async attribute, 94, 281
asynchronous ADO.NET commands, 303–307
  nonblocking, 303–305
  nonblocking data-driven pages and, 307
  overview, 303
  pages and scenarios for, 305–307
  setting up, 303
  SqlCommand objects and, 296–297
asynchronous notifiers, 612, 616
asynchronous pages, 110
AttachDBFileName attribute, 281
attacks, security, 648, 702
AttributeCollection class, 131
attributes
  <add> tag, 203–204
  Cache objects, 596–597
  connection pooling, 288
  ConnectionString property, 281–282
  <forms> section authentication, 667–669
  HTML, 130–131
  @Master directive, 223–224
  @OutputCache directive, 625–626
  @Page directive, 92–96
  page directives and, 92
  <sessionState> section, 554–555

Attributes collection, 18, 19, 131
Attributes property, 130, 130–131, 145
Authenticate event, 693
Authenticate method, 666
AuthenticateRequest event, 505, 506, 690
AuthenticateUser method, 663–664
authentication, 658–660
   ChangePassword control and, 700
   file authorization and access control lists (ACLs),
     659
   Forms authentication. *See* Forms authentication
   host identity and, 566
   Membership class and, 679–680
   overview, 657–660
   Passport authentication, 660
   provider example, 27–28
   providers and, 28–29
   session state and, 561
   Windows authentication, 658
authorization
   file, 659
   role management and, 686–687
AuthorizeRequest event, 505, 506
Auto property, 253
AutoDetect mode, 552
AutoDetect value, 670
AutoEventWireup attribute, 94
AutoGenerateColumns property, 414, 428
auto generated columns, GridView control, 433
AutoGenerateDeleteButton property, 428, 469
AutoGenerateEditButton property, 428, 469
AutoGenerateInsertButton property, 469
AutoGenerateRows property, 469
AutoGenerateSelectButton property, 428
AutoPostBack property, 150, 362, 363
.axd file extension, 93

B

BackColor property, 145
BackImageUrl property, 414, 430, 469
base classes, providers and, 30, 31–32
Base64 encoding, 670
BaseCompareValidator class, 161
BaseValidator class, 159, 161
batch update, 330–332
   command builders, 331–332
   commands, 322
   data conflicts and optimistic lock, 330–331

BeginExecuteNonQuery method, 295
BeginExecuteReader method, 295
BeginExecuteXmlReader method, 295
BeginInit method, 341, 349
BeginLoadData method, 341
BeginRequest event, 505, 506
BeginTransaction method, 276
behavior properties
   DetailsView control, 469
   GridView control, 428–429
behaviors, command, 300–301
BelowNormal priority, 602
Bin directory, 57, 58, 63, 80, 96
BinaryRead method, 534
BinaryWrite method, 529
Bind method, 380, 496
binding containers, server control, 123
BindingContainer property, 121, 123
blank session items, 570
<body> tag, 17–18
books, 275, xvii, xviii
BorderColor property, 145
BorderStyle property, 145
BorderWidth property, 145
BottomPagerRow property, 430, 471
bound fields, GridView control, 435
BoundColumn column type, 419
BoundField column type, 434
breakpoints, 63, 64. *See also* debugging
.browser file extension, 125, 126, 229
Browser property, 531, 532
<browsercaps> section, configuration file, 229
browsers. *See also* Internet Explorer; Netscape
    Navigator
   adaptive rendering and, 21, 125
   browser-sensitive rendering and, 126–127
   device-specific master pages and, 227–229
   enabling client validation, 170–171
   IDS, 228–229
   mobile browser capabilities, 532
   User-Agent HTTP header, 9
   Visual Studio .NET 2005 target schema validation,
    50–51
Buffer attribute, 94
Buffer property, 524
BufferOutput property, 524
builds. *See* compilation
BulletedList control, 366–368

BulletImageUrl property, 367
BulletStyle property, 367
business classes, 58–59, 396
button columns, DataGrid control, 422
Button control, 114, 148, 149–150
button controls, 149–150
button fields, GridView control, 435–437
button suffixes, Wizard control, 251
<button> tag, 139
ButtonColumn column type, 419
ButtonField column type, 434
ButtonImageUrl button suffix, 251
ButtonText button suffix, 251
ButtonType button suffix, 251

C

C# language, 5
cache dependencies
    custom, 609–612
    page-output caching and database, 630
    SQL Server, 616–624
    tracking, 598–599
    XML, 612–617
Cache objects. *See also* caching
    architecture of, 595
    caching vs. fetching, 604–605
    clearing content of, 608
    controlling data expiration, 602–603
    custom cache dependencies, 609–612
    defining item removal callbacks, 599–601
    deleting items from, 597–598
    enumerating items, 607
    HttpApplicationState objects and memory usage, 541
    inserting new items into, 596–597
    lifetime, visibility, and location of, 538
    memory usage statistics, 603
    methods, 594
    operations with, 596–603
    overview, 591–592
    Page class and, 100
    per-request caching, 609
    practical issues, 604–609
    properties, 593–594
    setting item priority, 602
    SQL Server cache dependencies, 616–624
    state objects and, 592–593
    synchronization and, 608–609

tracking item dependencies, 598–599
    wrapper, 605–606
    XML cache dependencies, 612–617
Cache property, 515, 525
CacheControl property, 525
CacheDependency class, 598–599, 610–611
CacheDuration property, 391, 407
CacheExpirationPolicy property, 391, 407
CacheItemPriority enumeration, 602
CacheItemRemovedReason enumeration, 597–598
CacheKeyDependency property, 391, 408
CacheProfile attribute, 625
CacheRolesInCookie property, 689
caching, 591–645
    application data and page-output, 591, 644–645. *See
        also* Cache objects; page-output caching
    DetailsView control, 480
    fetching vs, 604–605
    If-Modified-Since HTTP header and cache validation,
        9
    ObjectDataSource control, 398–399
    SqlDataSource control, 391–392
    XmlDataSource control, 410
calculations. *See* computations
Calendar control, 156–157
callbacks
    Cache object item removal, 599–601
    custom session-state providers and expiration,
        569–570
    for DetailsView control paging, 477
    for GridView control sorting and paging, 454
    Page class and, 101
    page scripting model and, 22
    server cache-validation, 632
Cancel method, 295, 301
CancelButtonClick event, 252
CancelButtonStyle property, 250
CancelCommand event, 418
CancelSelectOnNullParameter property, 388
CanDelete property, 385
CanInsert property, 385
CanPage property, 385
CanRetrieveTotalRowCount property, 385
CanSort property, 385
CanUpdate property, 385
Caption property, 415, 430, 469
CaptionAlign property, 415, 430, 469

cascading style sheet (CSS) files, 23, 239, 244–245. *See also* themes
CaseSensitive property, 333, 340
Cassini, 40
CausesValidation property, 140, 149
CD-ROM requirements, xix
CellPadding property, 363, 415, 430, 469
CellSpacing property, 364, 415, 430, 470
certificates, client, 650
change notifications, cache dependencies and, 611
ChangeDatabase method, 276
ChangeMode method, 490
ChangePassword control, 699–701
   password change, 700–701
   user authentication, 700
ChangePassword method, 277–278, 682
ChangePasswordQuestionAndAnswer method, 682
Charset property, 525
CheckBox control, 148, 151
CheckBox fields, GridView control, 438
CheckBoxField column type, 434
CheckBoxList control, 363–365
checksum functions, 618
ChildColumns property, 346
ChildKeyConstraints property, 346
ChildRelations property, 340
ChildTable property, 346
Class Library projects, 55
classes. *See also* types
   ADO.NET data provider, 265–266
   ADO.NET data providers vs. OLE DB providers, 267
   App_Code directory and, 58–59
   code-behind. *See* code-behind classes
   collection. *See* collections
   component model and, 15. *See also* component model
   connection string builder, 282–283
   creating sample shared, 55–57
   HTML server control, 129–130
   @Import directive and names for, 97–98
   memory-resident database model and, 332–333
   .NET Framework and, 15. *See also* .NET Framework
   Page. *See* Page class
   partial, 48, 85–86
   proxy, 62
   server control. *See* Control class
   writing helper, 34–35

classic ASP, xvii
ClassName attribute, 92, 223
Clear method, 334, 341, 529, 539, 549, 575
ClearContent method, 529
ClearError method, 516, 518, 557
ClearHeaders method, 529
Client location type, 628, 629
ClientCertificate property, 532
ClientID property, 102, 121, 122
ClientQueryString property, 102
clients. *See also* servers
   client certificates, 650
   client-side cache validation, 9
   client state, 6
   enabling client validation, 170–171
   HttpRequest object client data properties, 532–533
   HttpRequest object client input validation, 535
   HttpSessionState class and state client managers, 543–545
   multiple logical forms and client HTML forms, 179–180
   validation and, 164
   Visual Studio .NET 2005 client targets, 50–51
ClientScript property, 101, 107
ClientScriptManager class, 104
ClientTarget attribute, 95, 171
ClientTarget property, 102
ClientValidationFunction property, 163
Clone method, 334, 341
Close method, 87, 276, 298, 529
CloseConnection parameter, 300
CLR (common language runtime), 313
code
   application restarts and code-access security policy, 91
   attack-resistant, 648, 702
   code-behind classes, 48
      Visual Studio .NET 2005 page design features. *See also* code-behind classes
   code-injection attacks, 648, 702
   code tip windows, 65
   companion content Web page and sample, xxi
   compilation. *See* compilation
   configuration files and, 57. *See also* configuration
   creating sample shared class, 55–57
   defining event handlers, 53–54
   directory, 58–59

code, *continued*
  editing. *See* code editor, Visual Studio .NET 2005
  global.asax file code declaration blocks, 510
  inline. *See* inline code
  overview, 53
  page code section and inline, 11
  page scripting and JavaScript, 22
  providers and reusability of, 30
  sample database, xix, xix–xx
  sample page, 12–14
  sandboxing, 658
  script-related Page class methods, 106–108
  source, 42, 58–59, 69–70
  Source view and, 45
  Visual Studio .NET 2005 and code refactoring,
    51–52
  Visual Studio .NET 2005 projects and, 53–57. *See
    also* projects
  Web applications and, 15
  writing helper classes, 54–55
code-behind classes
  constraints of, 39
  dynamic compilation of, 42
  as partial classes, 86
  Visual Studio .NET 2005 and, 46, 48
code editor, Visual Studio .NET 2005
  special capabilities, 49–51
  toolbox and controls, 49
CodeBehind attribute, 93
CodeFile attribute, 92, 223
codeless paging, GridView control, 443–444
codeless sorting, GridView control, 449–451
CodePage attribute, 95
CodePage property, 548
collections
  as data-binding data sources, 355–357
  HTML server control, 19
  user profiles and, 205
colon symbol (:), 123
columns
  ASPStateTempApplications table, 564
  ASPStateTempSessions table, 564–565
  data adapter column-mapping mechanism
    data adapter, 327–328
  DataColumn objects, 333, 343
  DataGrid control. *See* columns, DataGrid control
  GridView control. *See* columns, GridView control

columns, DataGrid control
  button, 422
  data-bound, 420–421
  hyperlink, 421–422
  sorting, 425–426
  templated, 423
  types of, 419–420
columns, GridView control
  auto-generated, 433
  bound fields, 435
  button fields, 435–437
  CheckBox fields, 438
  configuring, 433–435
  hyperlink fields, 437–438
  image fields, 439–441
  templated fields, 441–442
Columns property, 340, 415, 420, 430
COM objects, 521–523
command builder objects, 331–332
command buttons, HtmlInputButton control,
    139–140
Command object, 266
CommandArgument property, 149
CommandBehavior enumeration, 300–301
CommandBuilder object, 266
CommandField column type, 434
CommandName property, 149
CommandRowStyle property, 470
commands
  ADO.NET. *See* commands, ADO.NET
  GridView control, 460–462
  HTTP request, 9
  submitting forms, 10–11
commands, ADO.NET, 293–317
  asynchronous commands, 303–307
  data readers, 297–302
  multiple active result sets, 315–317
  overview, 293
  SQL notifications and dependencies, 314–315
  SQL Server 2005-specific enhancements, 313–317
  SqlCommand class, 293–297
  support for CLR types, 313
  support for XML as native type, 314
  transactions and, 308–313
CommandText class, 295–296
CommandText property, 294
CommandTimeout property, 294

CommandType property, 294, 294–295
comments, email and postal addresses for, xxi
Commit method, 309
commit model, DataSet object, 337
CommitTransaction event, 108
common language runtime (CLR), 24, 83, 102, 313
Community Technical Preview (CTP) prelease
    software, Visual Studio .NET 2005, xx
companion content Web page, xxi
CompareValidator control, 160, 161, 162–163, 166
compilation
    App_Code directory and, 395
    global.asax file, 508–509
    master page compilation, 229–230
    projects and, 63
    site precompilation. *See* site precompilation
    Visual Studio .NET 2005 and, 42
CompilationMode attribute, 93
CompilerOptions attribute, 93
Complete property, 253
CompletetRequest method, 504
component model
    ASP.NET programming model and, 15–20
    classes. *See* classes
    event-driven programming over HTTP and, 7–8
    .NET Framework and, 15–16
    runat attribute and, 16–19
    server controls and, 19–20
computations
    DataRelation object, 347
    DataTable object, 342–343
Compute method, 341, 342
concurrent data access. *See* locks
.config file extension, 81
configuration
    code and configuration files, 57. *See also*
        machine.config files; web.config files
    connection pooling, 288
    editing web.config files, 75–77
    Forms authentication, 667–671
    GridView control columns, 433–435
    GridView control pagers, 446–448
    HTTP modules and, 25
    membership provider, 685–686
    ObjectDataSource control, 403–404
    predefined providers, 75
    profile providers, 213–214

providers and, 32
runtime environment and, 25. *See also* runtime
    environment
session state, 554–555
SQL Server 2005 Express Edition, xix–xx
SqlDataSource control, 389–390
SQLServer session-state provider, 562–563
StateServer session-state provider, 560–561
tracing, 198–199
<trust> section permissions, 655–656
Visual Studio .NET 2005 and, 39, 669
Web application development and, 20
Web Site Administration Tool (WSAT) and, 74–75
XCopy deployment and, 68–69
conflict detection, SqlDataSource control, 390–391
ConflictDetection property, 388
connection classes, ADO.NET data provider, 266
Connection HTTP header, 9
Connection Lifetime attribute, 288
Connection objects, 266
connection pooling, 287–293
    clearing connection pool, 292–293
    configuring, 288
    detecting connection leaks, 290–291
    getting and releasing objects, 288–290
    managing connection lifetime, 291–292
    overview, 287
connection properties, HttpRequest object, 533–534
Connection property, 294
Connection Reset attribute, 288
connection string builder classes, 282–283
connection strings, 280–287
    configuring properties for, 281–282
    connection string builder classes, 282–283
    overview, 280
    protecting, 285–287
    session-state providers and, 563
    storing and retrieving, 283–285
Connection Timeout attribute, 281
connections, data source, 274–293
    accessing schema information, 278–280
    changing passwords, 277–278
    connection pooling, 287–293
    connection strings, 280–287
    overview, 274–275
    SqlConnection class, 275–280

ConnectionString property, 275, 281–282, 388
ConnectionStrings:XXX expression, 381
ConnectionTimeout property, 275
constraints
    DataTable object, 344–345
    Visual Studio .NET 2005, 38–39
Constraints property, 340
containers. *See* content pages; HTML container
       controls; master pages
    cross-machine, 593
    server control binding containers, 123
    server control naming containers, 122–123
Content control, 226–227
content pages, 225–229. *See also* master pages
    attaching, to master pages, 227
    Content control and, 226–227
    device-specific master pages and, 227–229
    page prototyping and, 23
    processing, 229–233
    setting page titles and, 229
    Visual Studio .NET 2005 and, 46, 47–48
ContentEncoding property, 525, 531
ContentLength property, 531
ContentPlaceholder control, 224
Contents property, 539, 548
ContentType attribute, 95
ContentType property, 525, 531
context, HTTP. *See* HTTP request context
context properties, Page class, 102–103
Context property, 502
ContinueUpdateOnError property, 321
Control attribute, 99
Control class
    events, 124–125
    interfaces, 120–121
    methods, 124
    properties, 121–124
@Control directive, 91, 92
control skins. *See* skins
control state. *See also* state management
    saving, 115
    server control, 128
    ServerChange event and detecting changes, 140–141
    view state and, 583–585
ControlAdapter class, 125
ControlCollection class, 124
ControlParameter type, 389

controls
    categories of, 119–120
    control state. *See* control state
    data-bound. *See* data-bound controls
    design-time vs. run-time, 16
    dynamically created, 113
    generic, 17–18
    input focus and, 128–129
    mobile, 21
    Page class helper methods for, 105–106
    Page class rendering methods for, 103–104
    pages and, 20
    postbacks and detecting control state changes,
       113–114
    server controls. *See* server controls
    skins and, 23
    user controls. *See* user controls
    Visual Studio .NET 2005 IntelliSense and, 44–45
    Visual Studio .NET 2005 toolbox and, 49
    XHTML and, 127
Controls collection, 158
Controls property, 101, 121
ControlStyle property, 145, 146–147
ControlStyleCreated property, 145
ControlToCompare property, 162
ControlToValidate property, 161, 162
ConvertNullToDBNull property, 394
CookieDomain property, 665
cookieless attribute, 554, 668, 670–671
cookieless sessions, 551–554. *See also* cookies
    creating, 551–552
    Forms authentication and, 669–670, 670–671
    issues with, 552–553
    security and, 553–554
CookieMode property, 548, 665
cookieName attribute, 554
CookieName property, 689
CookieParameter type, 389
CookiePath property, 689
CookieProtectionValue property, 689
CookieRequiredSSL property, 689
cookies. *See also* cookieless sessions
    Forms authentication and, 669
    as session IDs, 550–551
    shared Forms authentication, 671–672
Cookies property, 525, 532, 551
CookieSlidingExpiration property, 689

CookiesSupported property, 666
CookieTimeout property, 689
Copy method, 334, 341
Copy Web site feature, Visual Studio .NET 2005, 42–44, 66
CopyBaseAttributes method, 147
CopyFrom method, 147
copying
    applications. *See* application deployment
    files, 66
    Web projects, 42–44
CopyTo method, 349, 549
Count property, 348, 539, 548, 574, 593
CreateCommand method, 271, 276
CreateCommandBuilder method, 271
CreateConnection method, 271
Created column, 564
CreateDataAdapter method, 271
CreateDataReader method, 334, 341
CreateNewStoreData method, 568
CreateObject and CreateObjectFrom Clsid methods, 521–523
CreateObject method, 518
CreateObjectFromClsid method, 518
CreateParameter method, 271, 295
CreatePersistentCookie property, 689
CreateRole method, 688, 690
CreateSessionID method, 572
CreateUninitialized method, 570
CreateUninitializedItem method, 568
CreateUser method, 678, 682
CreateUserWizard control, 701
credentials. *See also* authentication; authorization; passwords; usernames
    ASP.NET 1.x validation of, 28
    login pages and, 662–663
    Membership class and managing, 681
    providers and, 33
cross-machine containers, 593
cross-page postings, 22, 182–187. *See also* postbacks
    detecting, 185
    posting data to other pages, 183–184
    @PreviousPageType directive and, 184
    redirection to other pages, 187
    @Reference directive vs., 99
    validation and, 185–186
    validation groups and, 172

cross-site scripting (XSS) attacks, 648, 702
.cs file extension, 40, 42
.csproj file extension, 81
CSS (cascading style sheet) files, 23, 239, 244–245. *See also* themes
CssClass property, 146
CssStyleCollection class, 146
Culture attribute, 95
Current Language attribute, 281
Current property, 515, 606
CurrentExecutionFilePath property, 531
CurrentHandler property, 515
CurrentMode property, 471
CurrentPageIndex property, 415
custom cache dependencies, 609–612
    AggregateCacheDependency class and, 611–612
    CacheDependency class and, 610–611
    getting change notifications, 611
    inadequacies of ASP.NET 1.x, 610
    overview, 609–610
    SQL Server, 616–624
    XML, 612–617
custom controls, 119
Custom mode, 544
custom session-state providers, 568–571
    default session-state providers, 568
    defining, 568–569
    locking, expiration, and, 569–570
    registering, 570–571
    replaying session data dictionary, 570
<customErrors> section, configuration file, 192–193
customization
    custom ASP.NET 1.x membership provider, 684–685
    custom cache dependencies. *See* custom cache dependencies
    custom error information, 170
    custom error pages, 193–194
    custom profile providers
        profile providers, 215
    custom session ID generators, 571–573
    custom session-state providers. *See* custom session-state providers
    development stack and custom controls, 21
    error pages and custom error messages, 192–193
    GridView control row, 463–464
    page-output caching and custom strings, 635–636

customization, *continued*
  provider classes and, 34
  providers and runtime environment, 30
  themes. *See* customization themes
  user profiles and custom types, 205
customization themes, 238, 240. *See also* themes
customProvider attribute, 554
customProviderData attribute, 204
CustomValidator control, 160, 163–164, 186

D

DAL. *See* Data Access Layer (DAL)
data. *See also* databases
  ADO.NET. *See* ADO.NET data containers; ADO.NET
    data providers
  caching. *See* Cache objects; caching
  data binding, 353, 411–412. *See also* data source
    controls; data source-based data binding; data-
    binding expressions
  data-bound controls. *See* data-bound controls
  DetailsView control operations, 480–489
  migrating anonymous user, 212
  processing posted, 112
  record views. *See* DetailsView control; FormView
    control
  session state data persistence. *See* data persistence,
    session state
  session-state data stores. *See* session-state providers
  types. *See* types
  user profiles and, 203–204, 204–205
  validation. *See* validation
  visualizers, 65
Data Access Layer (DAL)
  business classes and, 396
  data access and, 274
  paging, 444–446
  sorting, 451–452
data adapters, 319–332
  batch update and, 330–332
  filling DataSet objects with, 323–324
  loading options, 324–326
  overview, 319–320
  SqlDataAdapter class, 320–326
  table-mapping mechanism, 326–330
data binding
  DataGrid control, 419–423, 420–421
  DetailsView control, 473, 474–477
  FormView control, 491–494

GridView control. *See* data binding, GridView
    control
  model, 353, 411–412. *See also* data source controls;
    data source-based data binding; data-binding
    expressions
data-binding expressions, 373–382
  Bind method, 380
  creating, 373–375
  DataBinder class, 376–378
  IExpressionsAccessor interface and, 121
  methods, 378–382
  runtime and implementation of, 375–376
  simple data binding, 373–376
  user-defined dynamic, 380–382
  XPath method, 379
  XPathSelect method, 379–380
data binding, GridView control, 432–442
  bound fields, 435
  button fields, 435–437
  CheckBox fields, 438
  configuring columns, 433–435
  empty data sources and auto-generated columns,
    433
  hyperlink fields, 437–438
  image fields, 439–441
  simple, 432–433
  templated fields, 441–442
data-bound controls
  ASP.NET 2.0, 21
  data source controls interaction with, 385–386
  grid controls, 385–386, 413–414, 464–465. *See also*
    DataGrid control; GridView control
  HtmlSelect control, 136
  overview, 119
data dictionary, session, 570
data persistence, session state
  to remote servers, 557–561
  to SQL Server, 562–566
Data property, 408
data readers, 297–302
  accessing multiple result sets, 301–302
  closing, 301
  command behaviors, 300–301
  DataSet objects and, 335–336
  reading data with, 299–300
  SqlDataReader class properties and methods,
    297–299
Data Source attribute, 282

data source-based data binding, 354–373
  feasible data sources, 354–357
  iterative controls, 368–373
  list controls, 362–368
  properties, 357–362
data source controls, 382–411
  AccessDataSource control, 392–393
  caching, 606
  DataGrid control and, 383
  DataSourceView class, 384–385
  GridView control and, 383–384
  hierarchical, 384
  HierarchicalDataSourceView class, 386
  interaction with data-bound controls, 385–386
  internals of, 384–386
  ObjectDataSource control, 393–404
  overview, 382–384
  SiteMapDataSource control, 404–407
  SqlDataSource control, 386–392
  tabular, 384
  XmlDataSource control, 407–411
data sources
  ADO.NET classes, 354–355
  ADO.NET data providers and, 268
  collection-based classes, 355–357
  connections. *See* connections, data source
  data source-based data binding. *See* data source-based data binding
  DataGrid control paging and, 424–425
  DataGrid control rows and, 417–418
  GridView control empty, 433
DataAdapter object, 266
Database attribute, 281
Database property, 275
databases. *See also* data
  Access, 392–393
  cache dependencies and, 616–624
  code samples and, xix, xix–xx
  credentials and, 73–74
  memory-resident database model, 332–333
  Oracle, 269–270
  page-output caching and cache dependencies, 630
  SQL Server. *See* SQL Server
  SQL Server session store, 563–565
  user profile, 206–207, 214–215
  XCopy deployment and, 68
DataBind method, 104, 124, 178, 374
DataBinder class, 376–378

DataBinding event, 108, 124
DataBindings property, 121
DataBoundControl class, 156
DataBoundLiteralControl class, 373
DataColumn objects, 333, 343
DataFile property, 408
DataGrid control, 414–427. *See also* GridView control
  binding data to, 419–423
  button columns, 422
  column types, 419–420
  constituent elements, 416–417
  data-bound columns, 420–421
  data source controls and, 383
  data source rows and displayed rows, 417–418
  editing rows, 426–427
  events, 418–419
  GridView control vs., 419
  hyperlink columns, 421–422
  as iterative control, 372–373
  object model, 414–419
  overview, 413–414, 464–465
  page interaction with, 423–427
  paging through data sources, 424–425
  properties, 414–416
  sorting columns of data, 425–426
  templated columns, 423
  view state and, 579
DataItem property, 471
DataItemCount property, 471
DataItemIndex property, 471
DataKey property, 471
DataKeyField property, 361–362, 415
DataKeyNames property, 403, 431, 462, 471
DataKeys property, 415, 431
DataList control, 368, 370–372
DataMember property, 359, 362, 364, 367, 369, 415, 428, 469
DataNavigateUrlField property, 422
DataNavigateUrlFormatString property, 422
DataObjectTypeName property, 394, 458
DataReader objects, 266
DataRelation objects, 346–348
  as container objects, 333
  creating, 346–347
  performing computations on, 347
  properties, 346
  serialization, 347–348
DataRow objects, 333, 344

DataRowState enumeration, 337
DataSet objects, 333–340
  App_Code directory and, 59
  commit model, 337
  as container objects, 332, 333
  filling, with data adapters, 323–326
  merging, 336
  methods, 334–335
  properties, 333–334
  reading stored data, 335–336
  serialization and remoting format, 339–340
  serializing contents to XML, 337–339
  session state and, 559
DataSet property, 340, 346
DataSetName property, 333
DataSource property, 275, 357–358, 362, 364, 367,
    369, 415, 428, 442, 469
DataSourceID property, 358–359, 362, 364, 367, 369,
    415, 428, 469
DataSourceMode property, 388
DataSourceView class, 384–385
DataTable objects, 340–345
  as container objects, 333
  DataColumn objects and, 343
  DataRow objects and, 344
  performing computations, 342–343
  properties and methods, 340–342
  table constraints, 344–345
DataTextField property, 359–360, 362, 364, 367
DataTextFormatString property, 360, 362, 364, 367
DataValueField property, 360–361, 362, 364, 367
DataView objects, 348–351
  as container objects, 333
  finding rows, 350–351
  methods, 349
  navigation, 349–350
  properties, 348–349
DataViewManager property, 348
DbProviderFactory class, 271
Debug attribute, 93
Debug class, 197
debugging
  options, 196–197. *See also* tracing
  projects, 63–65
  Web Site Administration Tool (WSAT) and, 74
  web.config files and, 63
declarative programming. *See* configuration
Decode method, 572

Decrypt method, 666
default account permissions, 654
default data item retrieval, 378
default error pages, 188–190
default master pagecontent, 225
default names, 48
Default parameter, 300
Default priority, 602
default state providers, 568
DefaultMode property, 469
defaultUrl attribute, 668
DefaultUrl property, 666
defaultValue attribute, 204
DefaultView property, 341
DefaultViewManager property, 333
Delete method, 349, 385
DeleteCommand event, 418
DeleteCommand property, 321, 387
DeleteCommandType property, 387
DeleteCookie method, 688
Deleted state, 337
DeleteItem method, 490
DeleteMethod property, 394
DeleteParameters property, 387, 394
DeleteRole method, 689, 690
deletes
  Cache object, 597–598, 599–601
  DetailsView control, 482–484
  GridView control, 458–459
  ObjectDataSource control, 401–403
DeleteUser method, 678, 683
denial of service (DoS) attacks, 648
Deny logon locally permission, 654
Deny Logon through Terminal Services permission,
    654
dependencies, ADO.NET SQL, 314–315. *See also* cache
    dependencies
Dependencies attribute, 596
DependencyChanged removal reason, 598
DependencyDispose method, 610
deployment. *See* application deployment
Depth property, 297
Description attribute, 94
deserialization, StateServer session-state provider,
    558–559. *See also* serialization
design pattern, provider, 26–27
design-time controls, 16
Design view, Visual Studio .NET 2005, 45, 47, 53

DesignerInitialize method, 105
DestinationPageUrl button suffix, 251
Detached state, 337
DetailsView control, 467–489. *See also* FormView
    control
    binding data to, 474–477
    caching, 480
    controlling displayed fields, 475
    creating master/detail views, 477–480
    data manipulation, 480–489
    deleting records, 482–484
    drilling down into records, 477–479
    editing records, 480–481
    events, 472
    inserting records, 484–485
    overview, 467–468, 497–498
    paging, 475–477
    paging via callbacks, 477
    properties, 468–472
    simple data binding, 473
    templated fields, 485–486
    validation with validation controls, 486–488
    validation without validation controls, 488–489
developers, xviii. *See also* Web application
        development
development stack. *See also* Web application
        development
    application services and, 25–26
    ASP.NET programming model and, 20–27
    component model and, 8
    page framework, 22–23
    presentation layer, 20–21
    runtime environment, 24–27
device-specific master pages, 227–229
DictionaryEntry objects, 607
DiffGram write mode, 338
directives, page. *See* page directives
directories
    application restarts and, 91
    code, 54
    configuration files and, 57
    default account permissions and, 654
    IIS virtual, 40–41, 67
    projects, 45
    protected. *See* protected directories
    web.config files and, 25
Disabled property, 130
disk files. *See* files

Display property, 161
DisplayCancelButton property, 251
DisplayExpression property, 341
DisplayMode property, 367
DisplaySideBar property, 251, 255
Dispose method, 116, 124, 277, 504, 568
Disposed event, 108, 116, 124, 505
Distributed Transaction Coordinator (DTC), 308
distributed transactions, ADO.NET
    in ADO.NET 1.x, 312–313
    local transactions vs., 308
    with TransactionScope object, 311–312
$ (dollar symbol), 122, 123
dollar symbol ($), 122
domain attribute, 668, 672
Domain Name System (DNS), 9
Domain property, 689
DoS (denial of service) attacks, 648
Dotfuscator tool, 70
DownStream location type, 628, 629
DPAPIProtectedConfigurationProvider, 285
drill down, DetailsView control, 477–479
drop-down list boxes, HtmlSelect control, 136
DropDownList control, 362–363
Duration attribute, 625, 626–627
DVD-ROM requirements, xix
dynamic compilation, 79, 90
dynamic data-binding expressions, 380–382
dynamic expressions, 380–382
Dynamic HTML, 160, 170
dynamically changing master pages, 235–236
dynamically created controls, 113
dynamically loading themes, 246–247

E
eavesdropping attacks, 648
edit template, FormView control, 494–495
EditCommand event, 418
EditCommandColumn column type, 419
EditIndex property, 431
editing
    DataGrid control, 426–427
    DetailsView control, 480–481
    FormView control, 494–497
    GridView control. *See* editing, GridView control
    Visual Studio .NET 2005, 44–45, 44–45. *See also*
        code editor, Visual Studio .NET 2005

editing, GridView control, 455–459
  deleting displayed records, 458–459
  in-place, and updates, 455–458
  inserting new records, 459
EditItem item type, 416
EditItemIndex property, 415
EditItemStyle property, 415
EditItemTemplate property, 441
EditItemTemplate template, 490
EditRowStyle property, 429, 470
email
  error messages and, 191
  support addresses, xxi
empty data sources, GridView control, 433
EmptyDataRowStyle property, 429, 470
EmptyDataTemplate property, 430, 471
EmptyDataText property, 430, 470
EnableCaching property, 391, 408, 410
EnableClientScript property, 161
enableCrossAppRedirects attribute, 668
EnableCrossAppRedirects property, 666
Enabled property, 146, 161, 689
EnablePaging property, 394
EnablePagingCallbacks property, 469
EnablePasswordReset property, 676, 683
EnablePasswordRetrieval property, 677, 683
EnableSessionState attribute, 94, 547
EnableSortingAndPagingCallbacks property, 428
EnableTheming property, 102, 121, 127, 243
EnableViewState attribute, 94
EnableViewState property, 102, 121, 581
EnableViewStateMac attribute, 94
EnableViewStateMac property, 102
Encode method, 572
Encrypt attribute, 281
Encrypt method, 666
encryption
  connection strings and, 285–287
  providers, 285
  view state, 575–576
End method, 529
EndExecuteNonQuery method, 295
EndExecuteReader method, 295
EndExecuteXmlReader method, 295
EndInit method, 341, 349
EndLoadData method, 341

EndRequest event, 505, 507
EndRequest method, 568
EnforceConstraints property, 333
Enlist attribute, 288
EnlistDistributedTransaction method, 277, 312–313
EnlistTransaction method, 277
Environment permission, 657
Error event, 108, 190, 196, 505, 512–514
error handling, 188–192
  default error pages, 188–190
  global, 191
  overview, 188
  page-level, 190
  precedence, 196
  robust, 192
error pages, 192–197
  custom, 193–194
  custom error messages and, 192–193
  default, 188–190
  getting information about exceptions, 195–196
  handling common HTTP errors, 194–195
  robust error handling and, 192
  Web Site Administration Tool (WSAT) and, 75
Error property, 515
Error value, 328, 329
ErrorMessage property, 161, 167
ErrorPage attribute, 94
ErrorPage property, 101
errors. *See also* exceptions
  error handling. *See* error handling
  error pages. *See* error pages
  HTTP. *See* HTTP errors
  page. *See* page errors
  tracking global.asax file, 512–514
Eval method, 376–378, 493–494
event-driven programming over HTTP, 6–8
event handlers
  application errors, 512–514
  defining, 53–54
  HtmlAnchor control and, 136
  transition, 254
eventing model
  Page class, 109–110
  single form model and, 109–110
  view state and, 109

events
 Control class, 124–125
 DataGrid control, 418–419
 DataGrid control postback, 423–424
 DetailsView control, 472
 eventing model. *See* eventing model
 GridView control, 431–432
 handling. *See* event handlers
 Login control, 693–694
 LoginStatus control, 696
 LoginView control, 697
 Page class, 22, 108
 page finalization, 114–116
 page setup, 110–113
 personalization, 210–212
 postbacks, 113–114. *See also* postbacks
 session lifetime and, 556
 Wizard control, 252, 255–258
exceptions. *See also* errors
 FormView control and unsupported function,
  477–497
 HtmlException class, 175
 overview, 188
 unhandled. *See* unhandled exceptions
Execute method, 519, 519–521
ExecuteNonQuery method, 295
ExecuteReader method, 295
ExecuteScalar method, 295
ExecuteXmlReader method, 295
execution flow, tracing, 197–199
expiration
 Cache object data, 602–603
 custom session-state providers and callbacks,
  569–570
Expired removal reason, 598
Expires column, 564
Expires property, 525
ExpiresAbsolute property, 525
Explicit attribute, 93, 94
explicit localization, 61–62
export and import of Visual Studio .NET 2005 IDE
  features, 52–53, 52–53
expression builders, 380–382
ExpressionBuilder class, 382
expressions, data-binding. *See* data-binding
  expressions

expressions, regular, 702
ExtendedProperties property, 333, 341, 346
Extensible Stylesheet Language Transformations
  (XSLT), 157, 410
external application login pages, 672–673
external pages, HttpServerUtility class and
  embedding, 519–521

F
factory classes, 271–272
Failover Partner attribute, 281
fetching vs. caching, 604–605
FieldCount property, 297
FieldHeaderStyle property, 470
fields. *See also* properties
 Cache class, 593–594
 code refactoring and, 51–52
 DetailsView control, 475, 485–486
 hidden. *See* hidden fields
 RequiredFieldValidator control and, 166
fields, GridView control
 bound, 435
 button, 435–437
 CheckBox, 438
 hyperlink, 437–438
 image, 439–441
 templated, 441–442
Fields property, 471
file authorization, 659
File Transfer Protocol (FTP), 40, 41, 42, 66
FileAuthorization module, 503
FileAuthorizationModule module, 659
FileIO permission, 656
FilePath property, 531
files
 copying, 66
 file system path Web site access, 40–41
 HtmlInputFile control and uploading, 141–144
 HttpResponse objects and writing large, 530
 loading view state from Web server, 588–589
 saving requests in disk, 534–535
 saving view state to Web server, 587–588
 temporary, 68
 Visual Studio .NET 2005, 39
Files property, 532
FileSystemWatcher objects, 616

FileUpload control, 148, 153–154
Fill method, 322, 323–324
fill operations, data adapter, 323–326
FillLoadOption property, 321, 324
FillSchema method, 322, 329–330
filter expressions, parameters vs., 388
Filter property, 525, 532
FilterExpression property, 387, 394
FilterParameters property, 387, 394
Find method, 349
FindControl method, 105, 124, 178
FindRows method, 349
FindUsersByEmail method, 678, 683
FindUsersByName method, 678, 683
FindUsersInRole method, 689, 690
Finish property, 253
FinishButtonClick event, 252, 258
FinishCompleteButtonStyle property, 250
FinishNavigationTemplate property, 250
FinishPreviousButtonStyle property, 250
Firefox browser, 228, 438
FirstBulletNumber property, 367
fixed identity impersonation, 652–653
Flags column, 565
Flush method, 529
Focus method, 124, 178
folders. *See* directories
Font property, 146
<font> tag, 17
Footer item type, 417
footer rows, FormView control, 491
FooterRow property, 431, 471
FooterStyle property, 415, 420, 429, 435, 470
FooterTemplate property, 369, 441, 471
FooterText property, 420, 435, 470
ForeColor property, 146, 161
ForeignKeyConstraint class, 344–345
Form collection, 11
Form property, 101, 532
<form> tag, 6, 10, 13, 14, 22, 109, 175, 179–182. *See also* HtmlForm class
FormParameter type, 389
forms, 175–217
    ASP.NET tracing, 197–202
    cross-page postings and, 22, 182–188
    debugging options, 196–197

HtmlForm class, 176–178
HTTP protocol and, 10–11
multiple logical forms and, 178–182
overview, 216–217
page errors and. *See* page errors
page personalization with user profiles. *See* user profiles
pages and, 175. *See also* pages
single-form interface (SFI) model and, 176
single form model and, 109–110
Forms authentication, 660–675
authenticating users, 663–664
collecting credentials through login, 662–663
configuration, 667–671
control flow, 661–665
cookie-based, 669
cookieless, in ASP.NET 2.0, 669–670
external application login pages, 672–673
<forms> section attributes, 667–669
FormsAuthentication class, 665–667
options for cookieless, 670–671
overview, 660–661
secured sockets and, 673–674
security issues with, 674–675
shared cookies, 671–672
signing out, 664–665
<forms> section, configuration file, 667–669
FormsAuthentication class, 665–667
    methods, 666–667
    properties, 665–666
FormsAuthentication module, 503
FormsCookieName property, 666
FormsCookiePath property, 666
FormView control, 489–497. *See also* DetailsView control
    Bind method, 496
    binding data to, 491–494
    data display, 492–493
    edit template, 494–495
    editing data, 494–497
    Eval method, 493–494
    header, footer, and pager rows, 491
    insert template, 496
    InsertTemplate property, 442
    members, 489
    methods, 490–491

object model, 489–491
overview, 497–498
templates, 490
unsupported functions and, 477–497
FrontPage Server Extensions, 38
FTP (File Transfer Protocol), 40, 41, 42, 66
Full trust level, 655
fully qualified class names, 97–98

G

GAC (global assembly cache) permissions, 654
GeneratePassword method, 678
generic controls, 17–18, 130
GET command, 9, 10
Get method, 178, 539, 591
GetAllRoles method, 689, 690
GetAllUsers method, 678, 683
GetAppConfig method, 516
GetAuthCookie method, 666, 667
GetBoolean method, 298
GetByte method, 298
GetBytes method, 298, 299
GetCallbackEventReference method, 106
GetChanges method, 334, 342
GetChar method, 298
GetChars method, 298
GetConfig method, 516
GetDataTypeName method, 298
GetDateTime method, 298
GetDecimal method, 298
GetDouble method, 298
GetEnumerator method, 349, 540, 549, 575, 594
GetErrors method, 342
GetFieldType method, 298
GetFillParameters method, 322
GetFloat method, 298
GetGlobalResourceObject method, 516
GetGuid method, 298
GetHistory method, 251
GetInt16 method, 298
GetInt32 method, 298
GetInt64 method, 298
GetItem method, 568
GetItemExclusive method, 569
GetKey method, 540
GetLastError method, 190, 194, 519

GetLocalResourceObject method, 516
GetName method, 298
GetNumberOfUsersOnline method, 678, 683
GetOrdinal method, 298
GetPassword method, 683
GetPostBackClientEvent method, 106
GetPostBackClientHyperlink method, 106
GetPostBackEventReference method, 106
GetRedirectUrl method, 666
GetRolesForUser method, 689, 690
GetSchema method, 277, 278–280
GetSchemaTable method, 298
GetSection method, 516
GetSessionID method, 572
GetString method, 298
GetTypeHashCode method, 105
GetUniqueID method, 610
GetUser method, 678, 683
GetUserNameByEmail method, 678, 683
GetUsersInRole method, 689, 690
GetValidators method, 105
GetValue method, 298
GetValues method, 298
GetVaryByCustomString, 504
GetWebResourceUrl method, 104
GetXml method, 334
GetXmlSchema method, 334
global assembly cache (GAC) permissions, 654
global error handling, 191
global resources, localization and, 61–62
global.asax file, 507–514
    application directives, 509–510
    application restarts and, 91
    code declaration blocks, 510
    compiling, 79, 508–509
    editing, 80
    global error handling, 191
    HttpApplication object and, 89, 90
    overview, 507
    server-side includes, 511
    server-side <object> tags, 510–511
    static properties, 511–512
    syntax of, 509–512
    tracking errors and anomalies, 512–514
graphical DataGrid elements, 416–417
grid pagers. *See* pager rows

GridLines property, 415, 430, 470
GridView control, 427–464. *See also* DataGrid control
  binding data to, 433–442
  bound fields, 435
  button fields, 435–437
  callbacks for paging and sorting, 454
  CheckBox fields, 438
  codeless paging, 443–444
  codeless sorting, 449–451
  configuring columns, 433–435
  configuring pagers, 446–448
  Data Access Layer (DAL) paging, 444–446
  Data Access Layer (DAL) sorting, 451–452
  data source controls and, 383–384
  DataGrid control vs., 419
  deleting displayed records, 458–459
  editing data, 455–459
  empty data sources and auto-generated columns, 433
  events, 431–432
  executing operations on one row, 460–462
  hyperlink fields, 437–438
  image fields, 439–441
  in-place editing and updates, 455–458
  inserting new records, 459
  object model, 428–433
  overview, 413–414, 464–465
  paging algorithms, 446
  paging data, 442–448
  properties, 428–431
  row customization, 463–464
  selecting one row, 462–463
  simple data binding, 432–433
  sorting data, 449–454
  SqlDataSource control vs. ObjectDataSource control and, 454–455
  templated fields, 441–442
  user feedback on sorting, 452–453
<group> tag, 205
grouping properties, user profiles and, 205–206
groups, validation, 171–172

H
handler factory objects, 89, 89–90
Handler property, 515
hardware requirements, xviii–xix
HasChanges method, 334

HasControls method, 105, 124, 178
HasErrors property, 333, 341
HashPasswordForStoringInConfigFile method, 666
HasRows method, 302
HasRows property, 297
<head> tag, 17, 18, 133–135
Header item type, 417
Header property, 101
HeaderImageUrl property, 420, 435
HeaderRow property, 431, 471
headers
  error messages and, 190
  FormView control, 491
  HtmlHead control and, 133–135
  HTTP request, 9
  HTTP response, 9
  page-output caching and, 635
Headers property, 532
HeaderStyle property, 250, 415, 421, 429, 435, 470
HeaderTemplate property, 250, 369, 441, 471
HeaderText property, 251, 421, 435, 470
Height property, 146
help resources
  ASP.NET Development Center, 34
  attack-resistant code resources, 702
  books. *See* books
  code samples, xxi
  email and postal addresses for questions and comments, xxi
  HTTP packet information, 8
  Microsoft Press Technology Updates Web page, xx
  for this book, xxi
  W3C Markup Validation Service, 127
helper classes
  App_Code directory, 58–59
  writing, 54–55
helper methods, Page class, 105–106
hidden-field tampering attacks, 648
hidden fields
  page source code and, 14
  _PREVIOUSPAGE hidden field, 183
  state management and, 6–7
  view state, 112, 115
HiddenField control, 148, 153–154
hierarchical data source controls, 384, 386, 406
HierarchicalDataBoundControl class, 406
HierarchicalDataSourceView class, 386

High priority, 602
High trust level, 655, 656–657
highlights, Visual Studio .NET 2005, 40–45
HorizontalAlign property, 415, 430, 470
hosting identity, SQLServer session-state provider, 566
hostname command, xix
href attribute, 16–17
HTML
    application deployment and, 71
    attributes, 130–131. *See also* attributes
    component model and, 7–8
    container controls. *See* HTML container controls
    Design view, Source view, and, 45
    forms and multiple logical forms, 179–180. *See also*
        forms; HtmlForm class
    HTML server controls. *See* HTML server controls
    HTTP response, 10
    input controls. *See* HTML input controls
    input tags and server controls, 113
    markup code. *See* markup code
    page source code, 14
    tags. *See* tags
    Visual Studio .NET 2005 markup preservation, 50
HTML container controls, 132–138
    HtmlAnchor control and event handling, 136
    HtmlAnchor control and URL navigation, 135
    HtmlHead control and header information, 133–135
    HtmlSelect control and lists, 136
    HtmlTable control and tables, 136–137
    HtmlTextArea control and text boxes, 137–138
    overview, 131, 132–133
HTML input controls, 138–139
    CausesValidation property and controlling
        validation, 140
    ControlToValidate property and associating
        validation controls with, 162
    HtmlImage control and image display, 144
    HtmlInputButton control and command buttons,
        139–140
    HtmlInputFile control and uploading files, 141–144
    overview, 131, 138–139
    ServerChange event and detecting control state
        changes, 140–141
HTML server controls, 129–144
    classes and predefined, 129–130
    hierarchy of, 131–132
    HTML attributes and, 130–131

HTML container controls, 132–138
HTML input controls, 138–139
HtmlControl base class, 130
HtmlImage control, 144
overview, 129
runat attribute and, 17
as server controls, 19
Web server controls vs., 20
HtmlAnchor control, 133, 135, 136
HtmlButton control, 133, 139
HtmlContainerControl class, 132, 176
HtmlControl class, 130
HtmlDecode method, 519
HtmlEncode method, 519
HtmlException class, 175
HtmlForm class, 176–178
    <form> tag and, 175
    methods, 178
    Page class and, 101
    properties, 176–178
    single-form interface (SFI) model, 109–110
HtmlForm control, 133
HtmlGenericControl class, 17–18, 18–19, 19
HtmlGenericControl control, 130, 133
HtmlHead control, 133, 133–135
HtmlImage control, 144
HtmlInputButton control, 138, 139–140
HtmlInputCheckBox control, 138, 140–141, 151
HtmlInputControl class, 13, 138
HtmlInputFile control, 138, 141–144
HtmlInputHidden control, 139
HtmlInputImage control, 139, 140
HtmlInputPassword control, 139
HtmlInputRadioButton control, 139, 151
HtmlInputReset control, 139
HtmlInputSubmit control, 139
HtmlInputText control, 139
HtmlLink control, 135
HtmlMeta control, 134
HtmlSelect control, 133, 136
HtmlTable control, 133, 136–137, 154
HtmlTableCell control, 133
HtmlTableRow control, 133, 137
HtmlTextArea control, 133, 137 138
HTTP errors. *See also* error pages
    getting information about, 195–196
    handling common, 194–195

HTTP protocol, 8–11
  ASP.NET programming and, 5
  ASP.NET programming model and, 3, 8–11
  authorization HTTP handlers, 659
  building server-side abstraction layers, 9–10
  event-driven programming over, 6–8
  HTTP listeners, 83
  HTTP-only session cookie feature, 551
  HTTP pipeline, 86, 649. *See also* runtime
    environment
  HTTP request, 9, 22
  HTTP request context. *See* HTTP request context
  HTTP response, 9–10
  runtime environment modules, 25
  submitting forms, 10–11
  Web Forms model and, 5–6
HTTP request context, 501–536, 501–536
  application initialization and HttpApplication class,
    502–507
  global.asax file, 507–514
  HttpContext class, 514–517
  HttpRequest objects, 530–535
  HttpResponse objects, 524–530
  overview, 501, 535–536
  Server objects and HttpServerUtility class, 518–524
  submitting forms and, 11
HTTP runtime environment. *See* runtime environment
HTTP SessionStateModule module, 543–547
HttpApplication class, 502–507
  events, 504–507
  methods, 503–504
  Modules property and application modules, 503
  overview, 502
  processing requests and, 89
  properties, 502–503
HttpApplicationFactory object, 87, 88–89
HttpApplicationState objects, 538–542
  concurrent data access, locking and, 542
  lifetime, visibility, and location of, 538
  memory occupation and Cache objects, 541
  methods, 539–540
  Page class and, 100
  properties, 539
  state management objects and, 538–539
  state synchronization, 540–541
  tradeoffs of, 541–542

HttpCachePolicy class, 630–632
  methods, 631–632
  properties, 631
  server cache-validation callbacks, 632
HttpContext class, 514–517
  lifetime, visibility, and location of, 538
  loading resources programmatically, 517
  methods, 516–517
  overview, 514
  processing requests, 87
  properties, 515–516
  URL rewriting, 517
HttpCookie objects, 551
HttpCookieMode enumeration, 551–552
<httpHandlers> section, configuration file, 89
HttpMethod property, 531
HttpPostedFile objects, 142–144
HttpRemotingHandlerFactory class, 90
HttpRequest objects, 530–535
  methods, 534–535
  Page class and, 100
  properties, 531–534
HttpResponse objects, 524–530
  methods, 528–530
  output caching features, 529–530
  overview, 524
  Page class and, 100
  properties, 524–527
  setting cache policy, 526
  setting response filter, 526–527
  writing large files, 530
HttpRuntime objects, 87–88
HTTPS, 662, 675
HttpServerUtility class, 518–524
  AspCompat attribute and, 523–524
  creating late-bound COM objects, 521–523
  Execute method and embedding external pages,
    519–521
  methods, 518–524
  Page class and, 100
  properties, 518
  Server objects and, 518
  Transfer method and server-side redirection, 521
HttpSessionState class, 542–549. *See also* session state
    management
  creating objects, 545–546
  HTTP SessionStateModule module and, 543–547

lifetime, visibility, and location of, 538
methods, 549
overview, 542–543
Page class and, 100
properties, 548–549
state client managers and, 543–545
synchronizing session state access, 546–547
http.sys file, 83
HyperLink control, 148, 150
HyperLinkColumn column type, 419
HyperLinkField column type, 434
hyperlinks
    DataGrid control columns, 421–422
    GridView control fields, 437–438
Hypertext Transfer Protocol. See HTTP protocol

I

IButtonControl interface, 149–150, 182
ICallbackContainer and ICallbackEventHandler
        interfaces, 428
ICollection interface, 355
IComponent interface, 120
IControlBuilderAccessor interface, 120
IControlDesignerAccessor interface, 120
ID property, 102, 121
IDataAdapter interface, 266
IDataBindingsAccessor interface, 120
IDataParameter interface, 266
IDataReader interface, 266
IDataSource interface, 407
IDbCommand interface, 266, 293
IDbConnection interface, 266
IDbDataAdapter interface, 266
IDbTransaction interface, 266
IDE, Visual Studio .NET 2005. See also Visual Studio
        .NET 2005
    constraints of, 39
    import and export of features, 52–53
IDictionary interface, 355
IDisposable interface, 120, 277
IDs
    browser, 126, 228–229
    component model and, 15, 16
    server control, 122
    session. See session IDs
IE browser ID, 228
IEditableTextControl interface, 152

IEnumerable interface, 358
IEWatch 2.0 tool, 675
IExpressionsAccessor interface, 121
If-Modified-Since header, HTTP, 9
<iframe> tag, 17
Ignore value, 328, 329
IgnoreSchema write mode, 338
IHierarchicalDataSource interface, 407
IHTTPAsyncHandler interface, 110, 307
IHttpHandler interface, 86, 90, 99
IHttpHandlerFactory interface, 89
IIS. See Internet Information Services (IIS)
IList interface, 355
Image control, 148, 150–151
image fields, GridView control, 439–441
ImageButton control, 148, 149–150, 150–151
ImageField column type, 434
ImageMap control, 148, 150–151
images
    deploying files, 71
    HtmlImage control and displaying, 144
    image button controls and, 150–151
    themes and files, 239
ImageUrl property, 150
<img> tag, 144
impersonation
    anonymous account, 653–654
    fixed identity, 652–653
@Implements directive, 91, 98
implicit localization, 60–62
import and export of Visual Studio .NET 2005 IDE
        features, 52–53
@Import directive, 91, 97–98
ImportRow method, 342
in-place editing, GridView control, 455–458
in-place error information, 169
in-place site precompilation, 70
INamingContainer interface, 99, 100
include files, ASP, 221
includes, global.asax file server-side, 511
indentation, Visual Studio .NET 2005, 50
inetinfo.exe, 83
InferXmlSchema method, 334
inheritance, visual, 221–222
Inherits attribute, 93, 223
Init event, 102, 108, 111, 125, 210
Init method, 304

InitComplete event, 108, 111
Initial Catalog attribute, 281
Initial File Name attribute, 281
initialization, application. *See* HttpApplication class
Initialize method, 31, 32, 569, 572, 666
InitializeRequest method, 569, 572
injection attacks, 648, 702
inline code, 11, 12–13, 48. *See also* code
InnerHtml property, 19
InnerText property, 18, 19
InProc mode, 544
InProc state provider, 568
InProcSessionStateStore class, 568
input controls, HTML. *See* HTML input controls
input focus, server control, 128–129
input steps, WizardStep object, 253–254
<input> tag, 14, 20, 138, 139
input text class, 13
InputStream property, 533
Insert method, 385, 594
insert template, FormView control, 496
InsertCommand property, 321, 387
InsertCommandType property, 387
InsertInvisible property, 435
InsertItem method, 490
InsertItemTemplate template, 490
InsertMethod property, 394
InsertParameters property, 387, 394
InsertRowStyle property, 470
inserts
    Cache object items, 596–597
    DetailsView control, 484–485
    GridView control, 459
InsertTemplate property, 442
Integrated Security attribute, 281
IntelliSense, Visual Studio .NET 2005, 39, 44–45
interfaces
    ADO.NET data provider, 266–267
    Control class, 120–121, 120–121
    data adapter, 320
    @Implements directive and, 98
    providers and, 30, 31–32
internationalization. *See* localization
Internet Explorer
    browser ID, 228
    hyperlink fields and, 438
    IEWatch 2.0 tool, 675

<meta> tag, 134
    testing localization with, 61
    Visual Studio .NET 2005 and, 51
Internet Information Services (IIS)
    IIS 5.0 process model and, 81–82
    IIS 6.0 kernel caching
        page-output caching and, 627–628
    IIS 6.0 process model and, 82–84
    lack of dependency of Visual Studio .NET 2005 on,
        40
    memory limits, 641
    process models and, 24
    system requirements and, 5, xviii
    thread security context, 649, 649–650
    visual configuration editor, 75–77
    Visual Studio .NET 2005 constraints and, 38–56
Internet Server Application Programming Interface.
        See ISAPI extensions; ISAPI filter
intrinsic objects, Page class, 100–101
IPageHeader interface, 101, 133
IParserAccessor interface, 121
IPostBackDataHandler interface, 112, 113, 138, 141
IPostBackEventHandler interface, 114
IPrincipal objects, 100
ISAPI extensions
    ASP, 4
    ASP.NET, 24
    as runtime environment modules, 80–81
    server-side abstraction layers and, 10
ISAPI filter, 58
IsAsync property, 101
IsAuthenticated property, 533
IsCallback property, 101, 111
IsClientConnected property, 525
IsClientScriptBlockRegistered method, 107
IsClosed property, 297
IsCookieless property, 548
IsCrossPagePostBack property, 101, 111, 185
IsCustomErrorEnabled property, 515
IsDbNull method, 298
IsDebuggingEnabled property, 515
IsEnabled property, 199
IsItemDirty method, 575
IsLocal property, 533
IsNewSession property, 548
IsolatedStorage permission, 656
isolation levels, 309–310

IsPostBack property, 101, 111, 112, 185
IsReadOnly property, 548
IsRequestBeingRedirected property, 525
IsReusable property, 86
IsSecureConnection property, 533
IsStartupScriptRegistered method, 107
IsSynchronized property, 548
IsUserInRole method, 689, 690
IsValid property, 101, 159, 161
Item item type, 417
Item property, 297, 349, 539, 548, 574, 593
ItemCommand event, 418, 472
ItemCreated event, 418, 472
ItemDataBound event, 418
ItemDeleted event, 472
ItemDeleting event, 472
ItemInserted event, 472
ItemInserting event, 472
Items property, 362, 364, 367, 369, 415, 515
ItemStyle property, 415, 421, 435
ItemTemplate property, 369, 441
ItemTemplate template, 490
ItemUpdated event, 472
ItemUpdating event, 472
iterative controls
    data source-based data binding, 368–373
    DataGrid control, 372–373
    DataList control, 370–372
    overview, 368
    Repeater control, 368–370
ITextControl interface, 152
ITransaction interface, 312
IUrlResolutionService interface, 121
IValidator interface, 160

J

J# language, 5
Java 2 Enterprise Edition (J2EE), 4
Java language, 4
Java Server Pages (JSP), 4
JavaBeans, 4
JavaScript code, 22, 107–108
JScript .NET, 5
JSP (Java Server Pages), 4

K

kernel caching, page-output caching and, 627–628
Key attribute, 596
KeyInfo parameter, 300
Keys property, 548, 574
keywords. *See also* attributes
    connection pooling, 288
    SQL Server connection string, 281–282

L

Label control, 148, 152–153
LAMP platform, 4
Language attribute, 93
languages, foreign. *See* localization
languages, programming
    ASP.NET programming, 5, 54
    directories and, 59
    JavaScript, 22, 107–108
    Web application development, 4
large files, HttpResponse objects and, 530
late-bound COM objects, 521–523
layout, page, 11, 13
LCID attribute, 95
LCID property, 548
leaks, connection, 290–291
life cycle, page
    events and, 22, 108
    overview, 79, 110
    page finalization, 114–116
    page setup, 110–113
    postbacks, 113–114
    request processing and, 86
lifetime
    connection, 291–292
    session, 555–557
    state management objects, 538
LinkButton control, 148, 149–150
list boxes, HtmlSelect control, 136
list controls
    BulletedList control, 366–368
    CheckBoxList control, 363–365
    data source-based data binding, 362–368
    DropDownList control, 362–363
    ListBox control, 366
    RadioButtonList control, 365–366

ListBox control, 366
listeners, 83, 197
Literal control, 152–153
literal controls, 144, 152–153
LiteralControl objects, 144
Load event, 108, 112, 125
LoadBalanceTimeout property, 292
LoadComplete event, 108, 114
LoadControl method, 105, 106
LoadDataRow method, 342
loading options, data adapter, 324–326
LoadOptions enumeration, 324
LoadPageStateFromPersistenceMedium method, 115
LoadPostData method, 112
LoadTemplate method, 105, 106
LoadViewState method, 112
local resources, localization and, 60–62
local transactions, ADO.NET
    in ADO.NET 1.x, 308–310
    distributed transactions vs., 308
local Web server
    testing and, 65
    Visual Studio .NET 2005, 40
Locale property, 333, 341
localization
    attributes, 96
    local resource files and, 60–62
Location attribute, 625
<location> section, configuration file, 68–69
locations
    page-output caching, 628–630
    state management objects, 538
Lock method, 540
LockCookie column, 565
LockDate column, 565
LockDateLocal column, 565
Locked column, 565
locks
    batch update optimistic, 330–331
    Cache object, 609
    custom session-state providers and, 569–570
    HttpApplicationState objects and, 542
Log on as a batch job permission, 654
Log on as a service permission, 654

LoggedIn event, 693
LoggedInTemplate property, 696
LoggingIn event, 693
logical forms, 178–182
    multiple client HTML forms and, 179–180
    multiple server-side forms and, 180–182
    MultiView and Wizard controls and, 182
Login control, 691–694
    events, 693–694
    programming interface, 693
    setup, 692–693
login pages
    ASP.NET 1.x, 28
    external application, 672–673
    Forms authentication and, 661–662, 662–663
    Login control, 691–694
    LoginName control, 694
    LoginStatus control, 694–696
    LoginView control, 696–698
login templates, LoginView control, 697–698
LoginError event, 693
LoginImageUrl property, 696
LoginName control, 694
LoginStatus control, 694–696
    events, 696
    properties, 695–696
    setup, 694–695
LoginText property, 696
loginUrl attribute, 668
LoginUrl property, 666
LoginView control, 696–698
    events, 697
    login templates, 697
    properties, 696
    role-based login templates, 697–698
LogonUserIdentity property, 533
LogoutAction property, 696
LogoutImageUrl property, 696
LogoutPageUrl property, 696
LogoutText property, 696
LosFormatter class, 583, 586
Low priority, 602
Low trust level, 656, 656–657

M

Machine Authentication Check, view state and, 576
machine-level constraints, Visual Studio .NET 2005, 38–39
machine.config files. *See also* configuration
  application deployment and, 68–69
  application restarts and, 91
  assemblies, 96–97
  authentication settings, 669
  HTTP modules and, 25
  process models and, 81, 82, 84
  system parameters and, 25
  web.config files and, 57. *See also* web.config files
MaintainScrollPositionOnPostback property, 103
managed providers. *See* ADO.NET data providers
MapImageCoordinates method, 534
MapPath method, 105, 519, 534
Mapped value, 330
markup code. *See also* code; HTML
  applications and, 15
  Page class methods, 103–104
  page finalization and generating, 116
  placeholders, 13
  Visual Studio .NET 2005 markup preservation, 50
master/detail views, DetailsView control, 477–480
  caching, 480
  drilling down into records, 477–479
@Master directive, 91, 92, 223–224
master pages, 222–236. *See also* content pages
  attaching content pages to, 227
  compiling, 229–230
  content pages, Content control, and, 226–227
  ContentPlaceholder controls and, 224
  definition of, 222–223
  device-specific, 227–229
  dynamically changing, 235–236
  exposing properties of, 233–234
  invoking properties on, 234
  @Master directive and, 223–224
  @MasterType directive, 235
  nested, 231–233
  page prototyping and, 23
  processing content pages and, 229–233
  programming, 233–236
  rich pages and, 219
  serving, to users, 230
  setting page titles, 229

  specifying default content, 225
  Visual Studio .NET 2005 and, 46, 46–47
  writing, 222–225
  writing content pages for, 225–229
Master property, 101, 236
MasterPageFile attribute, 93, 223, 235–236
MasterPageFile property, 101
@MasterType directive, 235
Max Pool Size attribute, 288
MaxCachedResults property, 689
MaximumRowsParameterName property, 394
MaxInvalidPasswordAttempts property, 677, 683
Medium trust level, 655, 656–657
membership, 675–691
  CreateUserWizard control, 701
  managing usernames and passwords, 681
  Membership class, 676–681
  membership providers and MembershipProvider class, 682–686
  ProviderBase class, 682
  providers and, 27–29
  role management and, 675–676, 686–691. *See also* role management
  setup, 678–679
  validating users, 679–680
  Web Site Administration Tool (WSAT) and, 73–74
Membership class, 676–681
  managing usernames and passwords, 681
  methods, 678
  properties, 676–678
  providers and, 29
  setting membership support, 678–679
  ValidateUser method, 679–680
membership providers, 682–686
  configuring, 685–686
  custom ASP.NET 1.x, 684–685
  extending interfaces of, 684
  ProviderBase and MembershipProvider classes, 682–684
MembershipProvider class, 34, 682–686
  creating custom ASP.NET 1.x provider, 684–685
  extending, 684
  methods, 682–683
  properties, 683–684
  provider configuration, 685–686
  ProviderBase class and, 682

memory
  application restarts and, 90
  Cache object statistics, 603
  HttpApplicationState objects, 541
  memory-resident database model, 332–333
  page-output caching and, 641
Merge method, 334
merges, DataSet object, 336
MergeStyle method, 147
MergeWith method, 147
messages
  error, 167–168, 190, 192
  trace, 199–201
<meta> tag, 134
metabase, IIS, 83–84
Method property, 178
methods
  Cache objects, 594
  CacheDependency class, 610–611
  CommandText class, 295–296
  component model and, 15
  Control class, 124
  data adapter, 322–323
  data-binding expressions, 378–382
  DataSet object, 334–335
  DataSourceView class, 385
  DataTable object, 340–342
  DataView object, 349
  factory classes, 271–272
  FormsAuthentication class, 666–667
  FormView control, 490–491
  HtmlForm class, 178
  HttpApplicationState object, 539–540
  HttpCachePolicy class, 631–632
  HttpContext class, 516–517
  HttpRequest objects, 534–535
  HttpResponse object, 528–530
  HttpServerUtility class, 518–524
  HttpSessionState class, 549
  ISessionIDManager interface, 571–572
  Membership class, 678
  MembershipProvider class, 682–683
  Page class. See methods, Page class
  RoleProvider class, 690–691
  Roles class, 688–689
  SessionStateStoreProviderBase class, 568–569
  SqlCommand class, 295–296
  SqlConnection class, 276–277
  SqlDataReader class, 298–299
  StateBag class, 575
  WebControl class, 147
  Wizard control, 251–252, 251–252
methods, Page class, 103–108
  controls-related methods, 105–106
  rendering methods, 103–104
  script-related methods, 106–108
Microsoft Access databases. See AccessDataSource
    control
Microsoft ASP.NET. See ASP.NET 1.x; ASP.NET 2.0;
    ASP.NET programming
Microsoft ASP.NET 2.0 Step by Step, xviii
Microsoft Data Access Components (MDAC) 2.7, 5
Microsoft Deveopers Network (MSDN), 702
Microsoft FrontPage Server Extensions, 38, 40
Microsoft Internet Explorer. See Internet Explorer
Microsoft Internet Information Services. See Internet
    Information Services (IIS)
Microsoft JScript .NET, 5
Microsoft Knowledge Base articles, xx, xxi
Microsoft Management Console (MMC), 75–77
Microsoft Mouse, xix
Microsoft .NET Framework. See .NET Framework
Microsoft Press support, xx–xxi
Microsoft Press Technology Updates Web page, xx
Microsoft SQL Server. See SQL Server; SQL Server
    2005; SQL Server 2005 Express Edition
Microsoft Visual Basic .NET, 5, 290
Microsoft Visual Basic Scripting Edition (VBScript),
    108
Microsoft Visual Studio .NET 2005. See Visual Studio
    .NET 2005
Microsoft Windows
  Windows 2000, 5, xviii
  Windows Server 2003, 5, 82, xviii
  Windows XP, 5, xviii
Microsoft.Jet.OLEDB.40 provider, 270
MigrateAnonymous event, 212
MIME (Multipurpose Internet Mail Extensions) types,
    10
Min Pool Size attribute, 288
Minimal trust level, 656, 656–657
MinimumCapacity property, 341

MinRequiredNonAlphanumericCharacters property, 677, 683

MinRequiredPasswordLength property, 677, 683

missing mapping actions, data adapter, 328

missing schema actions, data adapter, 329

MissingMappingAction enumeration, 328

MissingMappingAction property, 321, 328

MissingSchemaAction enumeration, 329

MissingSchemaAction property, 321, 329

mobile controls, 21, 119

MobileCapabilities class, 532

MobileControl and MobilePage classes, 21

mode attribute, 554

Mode property, 548

ModeChanged event, 472

ModeChanging event, 472

modes, grid pager, 446–447

Modified state, 337

modules

  application, 503

  ISAPI extensions as. *See* ISAPI extensions

Modules property, 502

mouse requirements, xix

MoveTo method, 251–252

Mozilla browser, 228, 438

Mscorlib.dll, 96

MSDAORA provider, 270

.msi file extension, 67

multilanguage applications. *See* localization

multiline text boxes, HtmlTextArea control, 137–138

multiple ADO.NET result sets, 301–302, 315–317

multiple logical forms. *See* logical forms

MultipleActiveResultSets attribute, 281

Multipurpose Internet Mail Extensions (MIME) types, 10

MultiView control, 148, 158–159, 182. *See also* View control

N

Name attribute, 97, 204

name attribute, 668

Name property, 138, 385

named parameters, 296

names

  code-behind classes, 48

  computer, xix

  directories, 58

@Import directive and, 97–98

  pages and classes, 84

  resource files, 60

Namespace property, 334, 341

namespaces

  linking, 97–98

  managed data providers and, 268

  unknown tags and, 18

naming containers

  Page class, 99

  server control, 122–123

NamingContainer property, 101, 122

navigation

  DataView object, 349–350

  HtmlAnchor control and URL, 135

navigation, Wizard control, 255–258

  canceling navigation events, 257

  filtering navigation with events, 255–257

  finalizing wizard, 258

NavigationButtonStyle property, 250, 255

NavigationStyle property, 250

nested master pages, 231–233

Nested property, 316

Net attribute, 281

.NET Framework

  ASP.NET and, 3, 5

  component model and, 15–16

  root folder permissions, 654

  this book and, xvii

Netscape Navigator, 50, 51, 228

Netscape3 browser ID, 228

Netscape4 browser ID, 228

Netscape6to9 browser ID, 228

Network Library attribute, 281

NETWORK SERVICE account. *See also* accounts; process identity

  encryption and, 286

  SQLServer session-state provider and, 566

  worker processes and, 63

NewRow method, 342

NextButtonClick event, 252, 255

NextPrevious mode, 447

NextPreviousFirstLast mode, 447

NextResult method, 298

NoAbsoluteExpiration property, 593

nonblocking ADO.NET asynchronous commands, 303–305

nonblocking ADO.NET asynchronous data-driven
    pages, 307
None location type, 628, 630
Normal priority, 602
Northwind database, xix, xix–xx
NoSlidingExpiration property, 593
NoStore attribute, 625
Notification property, 294
NotificationAutoEnlist property, 294
notifications and dependencies, ADO.NET SQL,
    314–315
notifiers, asynchronous, 612, 616
NotifyDependencyChanged method, 610
NotRemovable priority, 602
NotSupportedException exception, 477–497
novice developers, xviii
NTFS permissions, 659
Numeric mode, 447
NumericFirstLast mode, 447

O

obfuscation strategy, 70
object model. *See also* classes; methods; properties
    DataGrid control, 414–419
    FormView control, 489–491
    GridView control, 428–433
<object> tags, global.asax file server-side, 510–511
ObjectDataSource control, 384, 393–404
    cache dependencies and, 622
    caching data and object instances, 398–399
    configuring parameters at run time, 403–404
    implementing data retrieval, 395–397
    paging support, 399–400
    programming interface, 394–395
    SelectParameters collection and adding parameters,
        397–398
    SqlDataSource control vs., 454–455, 477
    updating and deleting data, 401–403
objects. *See also* classes
    connection pooling, 288–290
    intrinsic Page class, 100–101
ObjectStateFormatter class, 583, 586–587
ODBC data sources, 264, 268, 317
Off mode, 544
OldValuesParameterFormatString property, 388, 394

OLE DB providers
    as data sources, 264, 268, 317
    tested, 270
one-click attacks, 102, 648
OnInit method, 111
onserverclick attribute, 136
OnServerClick event, 13
Open Database Connectivity. *See* ODBC data sources
Open method, 277
Openwave-powered devices, 228
Opera browser ID, 228
operating system requirements, 5, xviii. *See also*
        Microsoft Windows
Operator property, 163
optimistic lock, batch update, 330–331
Oracle data source, 268, 269–270
originUrl attribute, 656
out-of-process session-state providers. *See* SQLServer
        session-state provider; StateServer session-state
        provider
OutOfProcSessionStateStore class, 568
output filters, HttpResponse object, 526–527
Output property, 525
@OutputCache directive, 625–630
    attributes, 625–626
    database dependencies and, 630
    IIS 6.0 kernel caching and, 627–628
    locations, 628–630
    pages and, 91
    user controls and. *See* user controls
OutputCache module, 503
OutputCacheLocation enumeration, 628
OutputStream property, 525
OverwriteChanges value, 324

P

Packet Size attribute, 281
packets, HTTP, 8. *See also* HTTP protocol
PacketSize property, 276
Page attribute, 99
page behavior attributes, 94–95
Page class. *See also* pages
    compilation, 79
    context properties, 102–103
    controls-related methods, 105–106

eventing model, 109–110
events, 108
<head> tag and, 18
IHttpHandler interface, 86
intrinsic objects, 100–101
methods, 103–108
overview, 99–100
page framework and, 22
properties, 100–103
rendering methods, 103–104
runtime environment and, 84–85
script-related methods, 106–108
tracing properties, 199
Web applications and, 15
worker properties, 101–102
page compilation attributes, 92–94
@Page directive, 46, 91, 92, 92–96
page directives
    @Assembly, 96–97
    global.asax file and, 509–510
    @Implements, 98
    @Import, 97–98
    @Page, 46, 91, 92, 92–96
    pages and, 11
    processing, 91–99
    @Reference, 99
    supported, 91–92
page errors, 188–196. *See also* errors; exceptions
    error handling, 188–192
    error pages, 192–196
    overview, 188
    validation controls and displaying information
        about, 167–168
page factory, 89–90
page finalization, 114–116
    generating markup, 116
    PreRender event, 115
    PreRenderComplete event, 115
    SaveStateComplete event, 115
    Unload event, 116
page layout, 11, 13
page-level error handling, 190
page output attributes, 95–96

page-output caching, 624–644. *See also* caching
    ASP.NET 2.0 features, 641–644
    caching profiles, 641–642
    database dependencies and, 630
    duration, 626–627
    HttpCachePolicy class and, 630–632
    HttpResponse object, 526, 529–530
    IIS 6.0 kernel caching and, 627–628
    locations, 628–630
    of multiple versions of pages and, 633–636
    @OutputCache directive, 625–630
    overview, 624–625
    partial page caching and cacheable pages, 641
    post-cache substitution, 642–644
    postback pages, 633–635
    server cache-validation callbacks, 632
    Shared attribute and, 640–641
    user controls and partial page caching, 636–641
    vary by controls options, 638–640
    vary by custom strings options, 635–636
    vary by headers options, 635
    vary by parameters options, 633
Page property, 101, 122
page setup, 110–113
    handling dynamically created controls, 113
    Init event, 111
    InitComplete event, 111
    Load event, 112
    overview, 110–113
    PreInit event, 111
    PreLoad event, 112
    processing posted data, 112
    view-state restoration, 112
PageAdapter property, 101
PageCount property, 415, 431, 471
PageHandlerFactory class, 89, 90
PageIndex property, 431, 471
PageIndexChanged event, 418, 432, 472
PageIndexChanging event, 432, 472
Pager item type, 417
pager rows. *See also* paging
    FormView control, 491
    GridView control, 446–448
PagerSettings property, 430, 469
PagerStyle property, 415, 429, 470
PagerTemplate property, 430, 471

pages, 79–117
  adding code to. *See* code
  applications and, 15
  ASP.NET programming model and structure of, 11–14
  asynchronous, 110
  caching. *See* page-output caching
  code review, 13–14
  component model and, 8
  controls and, 49
  creating view-stateless, 587
  debugging, 196–197. *See also* debugging
  designing, 45–53
  development stack and, 22–23
  embedding FormView controls, 492–493
  enabling themes on, 241–242
  events, 22
  form-based programming and, 175. *See also* forms
  getting default data item, 378
  HttpServerUtility class and embedding external, 519–521
  interaction with DataGrid control, 423–427
  invoking, 79–99
  linking assemblies to, 97
  login. *See* login pages
  overview, 79, 116–117
  Page class. *See* Page class
  page directives, code, and page layout, 11–12. *See also* page directives; page layout
  page errors. *See* page errors
  page finalization, 114–116. *See also* page finalization
  page life cycle, 110–116. *See also* life cycle, page
  page setup, 110–113. *See also* page setup
  page state, 6
  page throughput, 577–578
  partial page page-output caching and cacheable, 641
  personalization, 23, 202, 206–212. *See also* themes; user profiles
  postbacks, 113–114
  presentation layer and, 20
  processing directives, 91–99
  prototyping, 23
  @Reference directive and, 99
  representing requested, 84–85
  rich. *See* content pages; master pages; themes; user controls; Wizard control
  runtime environment and processing requests, 86–91
  runtime environment, process models, and, 80–86
  sample, 12–13
  scenarios for ADO.NET asynchronous commands, 305–307, 307
  scripting, 22
  site precompilation and, 71
  styling, 23
  supported page directives, 91–92
  test, 48
  tracing. *See* tracing
  view state. *See* view state
  Visual Studio .NET 2005 constraints and, 39
  Visual Studio .NET 2005 page design features, 45–53
  Web application development and, 4, 20
PageSize property, 415, 431
pagewide tags, runat attribute and, 17–18
paging
  DataGrid control, 424–425
  DetailsView control, 475–477, 477
  FormView control, 491
  ObjectDataSource control, 399–400
paging, GridView control, 442–448
  algorithms, 446
  callbacks for, 454
  codeless, 443–444
  configuring pagers, 446–448
  Data Access Layer (DAL), 444–446
Panel control, 148, 152
Parameter object, 266
Parameter type, 389
ParameterCollection class, 389–390
parameters
  aspnet_compiler tool, 71
  filter expressions vs., 388
  named, 296
  ObjectDataSource control, 397–398, 403–404
  page-output caching and, 633
  SqlCommand class, 294
  SqlDataSource control, 389–390
Parameters property, 294
Params property, 533
Parent property, 101, 122
ParentColumns property, 346
ParentKeyConstraint property, 346
ParentRelations property, 341
ParentTable property, 346
ParseControl method, 105, 106

partial classes, 48, 85–86
partial page page-output caching, 636–641
  cacheable pages and
    page-output caching, 641
  Shared attribute
    page-output caching and, 640–641
  user controls and
    page-output caching, 636–638
  vary by controls options
    page-output caching, 638–640
PartialCaching attribute, 630
partitionResolverType attribute, 554
Passport authentication, 660
PassportAuthentication module, 503
PassportAuthorizationModule module, 660
Passthrough value, 328
Password attribute, 281
PasswordAttemptWindow property, 677, 683
PasswordRecovery control, 698–699
passwords. *See also* authentication; authorization;
    credentials; usernames
  ChangePassword control, 699–701
  changing, with ChangePassword method, 277–278
  CreateUserWizard control, 701
  login pages and, 662–663
  Membership class and managing, 681
  PasswordRecovery control
    password retrieval, 698–699
  sample shared class for strong, 55–57
PasswordStrengthRegularExpression property, 677,
  684
path attribute, 668
Path property, 533
PathInfo property, 533
per-request caching, 609
performance
  linking assemblies, 97
  nested master pages, 231
  page-output caching, 635
  session state management best practices, 573
  SQLServer session-state provider, 562
  view state, 577–578
permissions. *See also* accounts; security
  Access databases, 393
  application deployment and, 68, 69
  configuring <trust> section, 655–656
  default account, 654
  granting, beyond trust levels, 657–658

NTFS, 659
  session-state providers and, 563
  trust levels and, 656–657
  Visual Studio .NET 2005 local Web server and, 65
  XCopy deployment and, 67–68
Persist Security Info attribute, 282
persistence, data. *See* data persistence; session state
personalization, 23, 202. *See also* themes; user profiles
personalization events, 210–212
Personalize event, 210–212
PhysicalApplicationPath property, 533
PhysicalPath property, 533
Pics method, 529
pipeline, HTTP, 86, 649. *See also* runtime environment
Pipeline scope, <object> tag, 511
PlaceHolder control, 157
placeholders, 13, 46, 47
policies, cache, 526
polling, 612, 616, 624
Pooling attribute, 288
pooling, connection. *See* connection pooling
pools, application, 83
post-cache substitution, page-output caching, 642–644
POST command, 9, 10
Post method, 178
PostAcquireRequestState event, 505, 507
postal support addresses, xxi
PostAuthenticateRequest event, 505, 506
PostAuthorizeRequest event, 505, 506
postbacks, 113–114. *See also* cross-page postings
  Controls collection and, 158
  DataGrid control, 423–424
  detecting control state changes, 113–114
  executing server-side, 114
  HTML container controls and, 136
  LoadComplete event, 114
  Page class and, 101
  page-output caching and, 633–635
  SelectedIndexChanged event and, 366
  triggering, 150
  view state restoration and, 112
PostBackUrl property, 149, 183–184
posting, cross-page. *See* cross-page postings
PostMapRequestHandler event, 505, 506
PostReleaseRequestState event, 505, 507
PostRequestHandlerExecute event, 505, 507
PostResolveRequestCache event, 505, 506
PostUpdateRequestCache event, 505, 507

precompilation, site. *See* site precompilation
prefilling schemas, 326–327
Prefix property, 334, 341
PreInit event, 108, 111, 210, 243, 246–247
PreLoad event, 108, 112
Prepare method, 295
PreRender event, 108, 115, 125
PreRenderComplete event, 108, 115
PreRequestHandlerExecute event, 505, 507
PreSendRequestContent event, 505
PreSendRequestHeaders event, 505
presentation layer
  adaptive rendering, 21
  custom controls, 21
  development stack and, 20–21
  rich controls, 21
PreserveChanges value, 324
PreviousButtonClick event, 252
PreviousHandler property, 515
_PREVIOUSPAGE hidden field, 187
PreviousPage property, 101, 183–184, 185, 187
@PreviousPageType directive, 184, 187
PrimaryKey property, 341
Printing permission, 656
Priority attribute, 596
priority, Cache object item, 602
priority levels, Cache object, 602
privileges. *See* permissions
process identity, 652–654. *See also* accounts
  anonymous account impersonation, 653–654
  changing default account for, 652
  default account privileges, 654
  fixed identity impersonation, 652–653
process models
  IIS 5.0, 81–82
  IIS 6.0, 82–84
  project compilation and, 63
  runtime environment, 24
<processModel> section, configuration file, 81, 82, 84
processor requirements, xix
ProcessRequest method, 86, 87, 90, 100, 110, 111
Profile module, 503
Profile property, 203, 208–210, 515
profile providers, 212–215
  aspnetdb.mdf structure, 214–215
  configuring, 213–214
  custom, 215
  default, 203
  overview, 212–215

ProfileParameter type, 389
ProfileProvider class, 34
profiles, caching, 641–642. *See also* page-output
    caching
programming. *See* ASP.NET programming
programming languages. *See* languages, programming
Programming Microsoft ADO.NET 2.0
    Applications:Advanced Topics, 275, 659
Programming Microsoft ADO.NET 2.0
    Applications:Core Reference, 275
Programming Microsoft ASP.NET 2.0
    Applications:Advanced Topics, 110, 120, 121,
    141, 220, 287, 307, 358, 368, 378, 382, 454, xvii
programming model, 3–35
  ASP.NET component model and, 15–20
  ASP.NET development stack and, 20–27
  event-driven programming over HTTP and, 6–8
  HTTP protocol and, 8–11
  overview, 34–35
  providers and, 27–34
  structure of ASP.NET pages and, 11–14
  Web application development history and, 3–5
  Web Forms model and, 5–6
projects, 45–65. *See also* Visual Studio .NET 2005
  adding code, 53–57
  Class Library projects, 55
  compilation, 63. *See also* compilation; site
    precompilation
  constraints, 38–39
  copying, 42–44
  debugging, 63–65
  import and export of IDE features and, 52–53
  overview, 45
  page design features, 45–53
  partial classes in, 85–86
  protected directories, 57–63
  setup projects, 67
  solutions vs., 38
  testing, 65
properties
  accessing user profile, 208–210
  BaseValidator class, 161
  Cache objects, 593–594
  CacheDependency class, 610–611
  code refactoring and, 51–52
  component model and, 15
  connection string, 281–282
  Control class, 121–124
  data adapter, 321–322

data source-based data binding. *See* properties, data source-based data binding

DataGrid control, 414–416

DataRelation object, 346

DataSet object, 333–334

DataSourceView class, 384–385

DataTable object, 340–342

DataView object, 348–349

DetailsView control, 468–472

exposing master page, 233–234

FormsAuthentication class, 665–666

global.asax file static, 511–512

GridView control, 428–431

GridView control column, 434–435

HTML server control, 19, 130

HtmlForm class, 176–178

HttpApplicationState object, 539

HttpCachePolicy class, 631

HttpContext class, 515–516

HttpRequest objects, 531–534

HttpResponse object, 524–527

HttpServerUtility class, 518

HttpSessionState class, 548–549

IButtonControl interface, 149–150

invoking master page, 234

LoginStatus control, 695–696

LoginView control, 696

Membership class, 676–678

MembershipProvider class, 683–684

ObjectDataSource control, 394–395

Page class. *See* properties, Page class

Properties window and, 38

Roles class, 689–690

SiteMapDataSource control, 406–407

SqlCommand class, 293–295

SqlConnection class, 275–276

SqlDataReader class, 297–298

SqlDataSource control, 387–389, 391–392

StateBag class, 574–575

user profiles and grouping, 205–206

WebControl class, 145–147

Wizard control, 250, 250–251, 253

XmlDataSource control, 407–408

properties, data source-based data binding, 357–362

AppendDataBoundItems property, 361

DataKeyField property, 361–362

DataMember property, 359

DataSource property, 357–358

DataSourceID property, 358–359

DataTextField property, 359–360

DataValueField property, 360–361

properties, Page class, 100–103

context properties, 102–103

intrinsic objects, 100–101

tracing, 199

worker properties, 101–102

Properties window, 38, 54

property page, visual editor, 76

protected directories. *See also* directories

additional application directories, 57–58

App_Code directory, 58–59

App_LocalResources and App_GlobalResources resource directories, 59–62

linked Web services and App_WebReferences directory, 62

themes and App_Themes directory, 62–63

Visual Studio .NET 2005 projects and, 57–63

protection attribute, 668

prototyping, page, 23

Provider attribute, 204

provider classes

available types of, 33–34

providers and, 26, 27, 30–31

Provider property, 106, 677, 689

provider toolkit, 34

ProviderBase class, 31, 32, 682

ProviderName property, 388

providers

ADO.NET data providers. *See* ADO.NET data providers

application services and, 25–27

ASP.NET implementation, 30–34

ASP.NET programming model and, 27–34

available types of providers, 33–34

benefits of, 30

configuration layer, 32

custom session-state providers. *See* custom session-state providers

default state, 568

encryption, 285

examples, 27–29

interfaces vs. base classes and, 31–32

membership providers. *See* membership providers

out-of-process session-state providers. *See* SQLServer session-state provider; StateServer session-state provider

providers, *continued*
   overview, 213
   provider classes. *See* provider classes
   provider toolkit and, 34
   rationale behind, 27–30
   role providers, 690–691
   selecting and configuring, with Web Site
      Administration Tool (WSAT), 75
   state client managers, 543–545
   storage layer, 33
   strategy pattern and, 27
   Web Site Administration Tool (WSAT) and, 72, 73
Providers property, 677, 684, 689
<providers> section, configuration file, 32–33
proxy classes, 62
pwd attribute, 281

Q
QueryString property, 533
QueryStringParameter type, 389
question mark (?), 296
? (question mark), 296
questions, email and postal addresses for, xxi

R
RadioButton control, 148, 151
RadioButtonList control, 365–366
RaisePostBackEvent method, 114
RaisePostDataChangedEvent method, 113, 138
RAM requirements, xix
RangeValidator control, 160, 161, 165–166
RawUrl property, 533
Read method, 298, 299–300
ReadCommitted isolation level, 309
readOnly attribute, 204
ReadUncommitted isolation level, 309
ReadXml method, 334, 342
ReadXmlSchema method, 334, 342
record-view controls, 467, 497–498. *See also*
      DetailsView control; FormView control
records. *See* rows
RecordsAffected property, 297
Redirect method, 521, 529
RedirectFromLoginPage method, 667
redirection
   cross-page postings and, 187
   HttpServerUtility class and server-side, 521

RedirectLocation property, 525
RedirectToLoginPage method, 667
reentrant forms, 6
refactoring, code, 51–52
@Reference directive, 91
Reflection permission, 657
regenerateExpiredSessionId attribute, 555
Regex object, 165
@Register directive, 17, 19, 91
RegisterArrayDeclaration method, 107
RegisterClientScriptBlock method, 107
RegisterHiddenField method, 107, 153
registering
   assemblies and, 67
   custom session-state providers, 570–571
RegisterOnSubmitStatement method, 107
RegisterRequiresControlState method, 105
RegisterRequiresPostBack method, 105
RegisterRequiresRaiseEvent method, 105
RegisterStartupScript method, 107
RegisterViewStateHandler method, 105
Registry permission, 657
regular expressions, 702
RegularExpressionValidator control, 160, 165
RejectChanges method, 335, 342
RelationName property, 346
relations. *See* DataRelation objects
Relations property, 334
ReleaseItemExclusive method, 569
ReleaseRequestState event, 505, 507
remote servers. *See also* servers
   copying Web projects to, 42–44
   session-state provider. *See* StateServer session-state
      provider
remoting format, DataSet object, 339–340
RemotingFormat property, 334, 341
Removal Callback attribute, 597
Remove method, 540, 549, 575, 594
RemoveAll method, 540, 549
RemoveAt method, 540, 549
Removed removal reason, 598
RemoveItem method, 569
RemoveOutputCacheItem method, 529
RemoveSessionID method, 572
RemoveUserFromRole method, 689
RemoveUserFromRoles method, 689
RemoveUsersFromRole method, 689
RemoveUsersFromRoles method, 689, 690

RenderBeginStyle method, 147
RenderControl method, 104, 124, 178
RenderEndTag method, 147
rendering
    Page class methods, 103–104
    page finalization, 114–116
    presentation layer and adaptive, 21
    server controls and adaptive, 125
    server controls and browser-sensitive, 126–127
RenewTicketIfOld method, 667
RepeatColumns property, 364
RepeatDirection property, 364
RepeatableRead isolation level, 309
Repeater control, 357, 368–370
RepeatLayout property, 364
Request objects
    forms and, 11
    Page class and, 100
Request property, 502, 515
request type properties, HttpRequest object, 531–532
requests, processing. See runtime environment
RequestType property, 531
RequiredFieldValidator control, 160, 162, 166, 172, 185–186
requirements, xviii–xix
RequiresQuestionAndAnswer property, 677, 684
requireSSL attribute, 668, 673–674
RequireSSL property, 666
RequiresUniqueEmail property, 684
Reset method, 147, 335, 342
ResetCommandTimeout method, 295
ResetItemTimeout method, 569
ResetPassword method, 683
ResetStatistics method, 277
ResolveClientUrl method, 124
ResolveRequestCache event, 505, 506
ResolveUrl method, 106, 124
resources
    aspnet_isapi.dll and, 81
    directories for, 58, 59–62
    embedding static, 104
    help. See help resources
    HttpContext class and loading, 517
    Visual Studio .NET 2005 and declarative, 39
Resources: XXX expression, 381
Resources namespace, 62
response filters, HttpResponse object, 526–527

Response objects
    forms and, 11
    Page class and, 100
Response property, 502, 515
ResponseEncoding attribute, 95
restarts, application, 80, 87, 90–91
result sets, multiple ADO.NET, 301–302
.resx file extension, 58. See also resources
RetrieveStatistics method, 277
ReturnProviderSpecificTypes property, 321
reusability, code, 30
RewritePath method, 516
rewriting, HttpContext class and URL, 517
rich controls, 21
rich pages, 219–220, 259–260. See also master pages; themes; user controls; visual inheritance; Wizard control
robustness
    error handling, 192
    SQLServer session-state provider, 562
role management, 686–691
    LoginView control role-based login templates, 697–698
    membership and, 675–676. See also membership
    role providers and RoleProvider class, 690–691
    Roles class, 688–690
    users, authorization, and, 686–687
    Web Site Administration Tool (WSAT) and, 73–74, 687–688
role providers, 690–691
RoleExists method, 689, 690
RoleGroups property, 696
RoleManager module, 503
RoleProvider class, 34, 690–691
Roles class, 688–690
    methods, 688–689
    properties, 689–690
Rollback method, 309
Root Folder permissions
    application, 654
    .NET Framework, 654
    Web site, 654
RowCancelingEdit event, 432
RowCommand event, 432
RowCreated event, 432
RowDataBound event, 432
RowDeleted event, 432

RowDeleting event, 432
RowEditing event, 432
RowFilter property, 349
RowHeaderColumn property, 428
rows. *See also* DataRow objects
   DataGrid control displayed and data source,
      417–418
   DataSet RowState property, 337
   DataView object, 350–351
   editing DataGrid control, 426–427
   FormView control header, footer, and pager, 491
rows, GridView control
   customization, 463–464
   deleting, 458–459
   executing operations on one, 460–462
   inserting new, 459
   selecting one, 462–463
   updating, 455–458
Rows property, 341, 431, 471
RowState property, 337
RowStateFilter property, 349
RowStyle property, 429, 470
RowUpdated event, 432
RowUpdating event, 432
RSA encryption algorithm, 139, 286
RSAProtectedConfigurationProvider, 285
run-time controls, 16
runat attribute
   component model and, 16–19
   Page class methods and, 106
   page code and, 12, 14
   pagewide tags and, 17–18
   server controls and, 11, 16, 16–17, 109
   unknown tags and, 18–19
   Web server controls and, 145
runtime environment
   application configuration and, 25. *See also*
      configuration
   application services and, 25–27
   causes for application restarts, 90–91
   data-binding expressions and, 375–376
   development stack and, 24–27
   HTTP request context. *See* HTTP request context
   HttpApplication class, 89
   HttpApplicationFactory object, 88–89
   HttpRuntime object, 87–88
   IIS 5.0 process model and, 81–82

IIS 6.0 process model and, 82–84
overview, 80–81, 86–87
page factory and handler factory objects, 89–90
pages and, 79, 80–86
partial classes and, 85–86
process models and, 24
processing requests, 86–91
providers and, 30
representing requested pages, 84–85
security context, 649
state management by, 6–7
system HTTP modules and, 25
Web applications and, 15
XCopy deployment and configuring, 68–69

S
sandboxing, code, 658
SaveAs method, 143, 534
SavePageStateToPersistenceMedium method, 115
SaveSessionID method, 572
SaveStateComplete event, 108, 115
SaveViewState method, 115
saving
   requests to disk files, 534–535
   view state, 115, 587–588
scalability, HTTP protocol, 5
SchemaOnly parameter, 300
schemas
   accessing information, with GetSchema method,
      278–280
   App_Code directory and, 59
   prefilling, 329–330
   Visual Studio .NET 2005 and, 44, 50–51
SchemaSerializationMode property, 334
SchemaType enumeration, 329–330
scopes, server-side <object> tag, 511
<script> section, configuration file, 98
<script> tags, 11
scripting. *See also* code
   page, 22
   Page class methods for, 106–108
   Page class script-related methods, 106–108
   script callbacks. *See* callbacks
scrollable panel control, 152
Secure Sockets Layer (SSL), 650, 673–674
secured sockets, Forms authentication and, 673–674

security, 647–703
  anonymous account impersonation, 653–654
  application trust levels, 655–658
  ASP.NET pipeline security context, 652
  ASP.NET process identity, 652–654
  attack-resistant code resources, 702
  authentication methods, 658–660
  configuring <trust> section permissions, 655–656
  cookieless sessions and, 553–554
  default account privileges, 654
  displaying error messages, 190, 192
  file authorization and access control lists (ACLs),
      659
  fixed identity impersonation, 652–653
  Forms authentication. See Forms authentication
  granting permissions beyond trust levels, 657–658
  IIS thread security context, 649–650
  membership and role management. See
      membership; role management
  overview, 647, 702–703
  Passport authentication, 660
  permissions, 656–657. See also permissions
  security context, 648–660
  security context levels, 648–649
  security-related server controls. See server controls,
      security-related
  setting ASP.NET process account, 652
  SQLServer session state provider and, 566
  threats, 648
  view state, 575–576
  ViewStateUserKey property, 102
  Visual Studio .NET 2005 local Web and, 65
  Web Site Administration Tool (WSAT) and, 73,
      73–74
  Windows authentication, 658
  worker process security context, 650–651
Security permission, 656
Select command, 388
Select method, 342, 385
<select> tag, 136
  HtmlSelect control and, 136
SelectCommand property, 321, 387, 444
SelectCommandType property, 387
SelectCountMethod property, 394
SelectedDataKey property, 431
SelectedIndex property, 362, 364, 415, 431

SelectedIndexChanged event, 366, 418, 432
SelectedIndexChanging event, 432
SelectedItem item type, 417
SelectedItem property, 362, 364, 415
SelectedItemStyle property, 415
SelectedRow property, 431
SelectedRowStyle property, 429
SelectedValue property, 362, 364, 431, 471
selection
  GridView control single-row, 462–463
  HtmlSelect control selection boxes, 136
SelectMethod property, 394
SelectParameters collection, 397–398
SelectParameters property, 387, 394
SeparatorTemplate property, 369
SequentialAccess parameter, 300
Serializable isolation level, 309
serialization
  DataRelation object, 347–348
  DataSet object contents to XML, 337–339
  DataSet object formats for, 339–340
  StateServer session-state provider, 558–559
  view state format, 582–583
serializeAs attribute, 204
Server attribute, 282
server controls, 119–173
  adaptive rendering, 125
  binding container, 123
  browser-sensitive rendering, 126–127
  component model and, 7–8, 19–20
  Control class events, 124–125
  Control class interfaces, 120–121
  Control class methods, 124
  Control class properties, 121–124
  control state, 128
  custom controls, 21
  data-bound. See data-bound controls
  HTML server controls, 19. See HTML server controls
  ID properties, 103
  identifying, 122
  input focus assignment, 128–129
  literal controls, 144
  naming container, 122–123
  new features, 125–129
  overview, 119–120, 172–173
  page layout and, 11, 13

server controls, *continued*
  partial classes and, 86
  rich controls, 21
  runat attribute and, 16–17
  security-related. *See* server controls, security-related
  themeable, 127
  themes and, 244
  validation controls. *See* validation controls
  visibility of, 123
  Web applications and, 15
  Web server controls, 20. *See* Web server controls
server controls, security-related, 691–701
  ChangePassword control, 699–701
  CreateUserWizard control, 701
  Login control, 691–694
  LoginName control, 694
  LoginStatus control, 694–696
  LoginView control, 696–698
  PasswordRecovery control, 698–699
Server location type, 628, 630
Server objects
  forms and, 11
  HttpServerUtility class and, 518
  Page class and, 100
Server property, 502, 515
ServerAndClient location type, 630
ServerChange event, 137, 140–141
ServerClick event, 136, 139
servers
  cache-validation callbacks, 632
  copying Web projects to, 42–44
  global.asax file includes, 511
  global.asax file <object> tags, 510–511
  HTTP protocol and abstraction layers, 9–10
  HttpServerUtility class redirection, 521
  keeping view state on, 586–589
  multiple logical forms, 180–182
  postbacks, 114
  server controls. *See* server controls
  session-state providers and remote. *See* StateServer
    session-state provider
  validation and, 164
  Visual Studio .NET 2005 local Web, 40, 65
Server.Transfer method, 187
ServerValidate event, 163
ServerVariables property, 533
ServerVersion property, 276
services, application, 25–27. *See also* providers

servlet applications, 4
session data dictionary, 570
session hijacking attacks, 648
session IDs, 550–555
  configuring session state, 554–555
  cookieless sessions, 551–554
  cookies, 550–551
  custom generators, 571–573
  generating, 550
Session objects, 100
Session property, 502, 515
Session scope, <object> tag, 511
session state management, 549–567
  configuring session state, 554–555
  custom session ID generators, 571–573
  custom session-state providers, 568–571
  customizing, 567–573
  event-driven programming over HTTP and, 6–8
  HttpSessionState class. *See* HttpSessionState class
  loss of session state, 557
  overview, 549–550
  performance best practices, 573
  providers and, 28–29, 34. *See also* session-state
    providers
  session IDs, 550–555. *See also* session IDs
  session lifetime, 555–557
  session state data persistence to remote servers,
    557–561
  session state data persistence to SQL Server,
    562–566
  Web farms, Web gardens, and, 566–567
session-state providers
  custom, 568–571
  default, 568
  out-of-process. *See* SQLServer session-state provider;
    StateServer session-state provider
Session_End event, 556
SessionId column, 564
SessionID property, 548
sessionIDManagerType attribute, 555
SessionItemLong column, 565
SessionItemShort column, 565
SessionParameter type, 389
Session_Start event, 556
SessionState module, 503
<sessionState> section, configuration file, 554–555
SessionStateStoreProviderBase class, 34, 545
SessionStateUtility class, 570

Set method, 540
SetAllowResponseInBrowserHistory method, 631
SetAndReleaseItemExclusive method, 569
SetAuthCookie method, 667
SetCacheability method, 631
SetCookie method, 529
SetETag method, 631
SetETagFromFileDependencies method, 631
SetExpires method, 631
SetFocus method, 107, 128–129
SetFocusOnError property, 161
SetItemExpireCallback method, 569
SetLastModified method, 631
SetLastModifiedFromFileDependencies method, 631
SetMaxAge method, 631
SetNoServerCaching method, 631
SetNoStore method, 632
SetNoTransforms method, 632
SetOmitVaryStar method, 632
SetProxyMaxAge method, 632
SetRenderMethodDelegate method, 124
SetRevalidation method, 632
SetSlidingExpiration method, 632
setup, page, 110–113
setup projects, 67
SetUtcLastModified method, 610
SetValidUntilExpires method, 632
SetVaryByCustom method, 632
Shared attribute, 626, 640–641
sharing
    creating sample shared class, 55–57
    page-output caching Shared attribute, 626, 640–641
    shared Forms authentication cookies, 671–672
ShowFooter property, 415, 430
ShowHeader property, 415, 430, 435
ShowStartingNode property, 406
SideBarButtonClick event, 252, 256
SideBarButtonStyle property, 250
sidebars, Wizard control, 255
SideBarStyle property, 250
SideBarTemplate property, 250
signing out, 664–665
SignOut method, 664–665, 667
simple data binding. *See* data binding
SimpleHandlerFactory class, 90
single-form interface (SFI) model
    eventing model and, 109–110
    form-based programming and, 176. *See also* forms

SingleResult parameter, 300, 301
SingleRow parameter, 300, 301
site maps, providers and, 34
site precompilation, 69–72. *See also* compilation
    for deployment, 70–72
    in-place, 70
    overview, 69–72
Site property, 122
SiteMapDataSource control, 384, 404–407
    displaying site map information, 404–406
    programming interface, 406–407
SiteMapProvider class, 34
SiteMapProvider property, 406
size thresholds, view state, 577–578
SkinID property, 122
skins
    applying, 242–243
    controls and, 23, 127
    themes and, 62, 238, 239. *See also* themes
SkipAuthorization property, 515
SkipLinkText property, 251
Sliding Expiration attribute, 596
slidingExpiration attribute, 668
SlidingExpiration property, 666
SmartNavigation attribute, 95
SmartNavigation property, 103
Socket permission, 657
software requirements, xviii–xix
Solution Explorer window, 42, 72
solutions, 38, 42. *See also* projects
Sort property, 349, 351
SortCommand event, 418
SortDirection property, 429
Sorted event, 432
SortExpression property, 421, 429, 435
sorting, DataGrid control, 425–426
Sorting event, 432, 452
sorting, GridView control, 449–454
    callbacks for, 454
    codeless, 449–451
    Data Access Layer (DAL), 451–452
    user feedback on, 452–453
SortParameterName property, 387, 394
source code, 39, 42, 58–59, 69
Source value, 330
Source view, Visual Studio .NET 2005, 45, 53
<span> tag, 13, 17
SQL injection attacks, 648, 702

SQL Server
  ADO.NET data providers and, 268–269
  custom cache dependency, 616–624
  as data source, 268
  Northwind database of SQL Server 2000, xix
  session-state provider. *See* SQLServer session-state
    provider
  session store, 563–565
  SQL Server 2005. *See* SQL Server 2005
  system requirements and, xviii
SQL Server 2005
  ADO.NET enhancements specific to, 313–317
  ADO.NET multiple active result sets, 315–317
  ADO.NET SQL notifications and dependencies,
    314–315
  ADO.NET support for CLR types, 313
  ADO.NET support for XML as native type, 314
  cache dependencies, 622–624
  database cache invalidation, 624
  system requirements and, xviii
SQL Server 2005 Express Edition
  configuring, xix–xx
  system requirements and, xviii
SqlCacheDependency property, 391, 622
SqlClient permission, 656
SqlCommand class, 293–297
  methods, 295–296, 301
  overview, 293
  properties, 293–295
  synchronous and asynchronous execution, 296–297
SqlCommandBuilder class, 331–332
sqlCommandTimeout attribute, 555
SqlConnection class, 275–280
  accessing schema information, 278–280
  changing passwords, 277–278
  methods, 276–277
  overview, 275
  properties, 275–276
sqlConnectionString attribute, 555
SqlDataAdapter class, 320–326
  filling DataSet objects with, 323–324
  interfaces, 320
  loading options, 324–326
  properties and methods, 321–323
SqlDataReader class, 297–299, 314

SqlDataSource control, 384, 386–392
  caching, 391–392
  conflict detection, 390–391
  declarative parameters, 389–390
  ObjectDataSource control vs., 454–455, 477
  overview, 386–387
  paging and, 444
  programming interface, 387–389
SqlDependency attribute, 626
SqlDependency class, 315
SqlNotificationRequest class, 315
SQLOLEDB provider, 270
SqlParameter class, 294, 296
SQLServer mode, 544
SQLServer session-state provider, 562–566
  configuring, 562–563
  performance and robustness of, 562
  reverting to hosting identity, 566
  storing session data, 563–565
SQLServer state provider, 568
SqlSessionStateStore class, 568
Src attribute, 93, 97
SSL (Secure Sockets Layer), 673–674
Start property, 253
StartFromCurrentNode property, 406
StartingNodeOffset property, 406
StartingNodeUrl property, 406
StartNavigationTemplate property, 250
StartRowIndexParameterName property, 394
StartStepNextButtonStyle property, 250
state management, 537–590
  component model and, 15
  control state. *See* control state
  event-driven programming over HTTP and, 6–8
  HttpApplicationState objects and application state,
    538–542
  objects, 538
  overview, 537, 589–590
  page view state. *See* view state
  session state. *See* HttpSessionState class; session
    state management
  table row state, 337
state objects, Cache object, 592–593

state properties
  DetailsView control, 470–471
  GridView control, 430–431
State property, 276
StateBag class, 574–575
  methods, 575
  overview, 574
  properties, 574–575
stateConnectionString attribute, 555
stateless programming
  event-driven programming over HTTP and, 6–8
  HTTP protocol and, 5
stateNetworkTimeout attribute, 555
StateServer mode, 544
StateServer session-state provider, 557–561
  configuring, 560–561
  overview, 557–558
  state serialization and deserialization for, 558–559
  storing session data, 559–560
StateServer state provider, 568
static properties, global.asax file, 511–512
StaticObjects property, 539, 548
StatisticsEnabled property, 276
status line, HTTP response, 9
Status property, 525
StatusCode property, 525
StatusDescription property, 525
Step property, 253
step styles, Wizard control, 253
StepNavigationTemplate property, 250
StepNextButtonStyle property, 250
StepPreviousButtonStyle property, 250
StepStyle property, 250
StepType property, 253
storage layer, providers and, 33
stored procedures, 294–295, 444, 617–618, 624
StoredProcedure parameter, 294
stores, session-state. *See* session-state providers
strategy pattern, 27, 31
Strict attribute, 93, 94
strings, page-output caching and custom, 635–636
strong passwords sample shared class, 55–57
style properties
  DetailsView control, 470
  GridView control, 429
  Web server control, 146–147
  Wizard control, 250

Style property, 19, 130, 146, 146–147
style sheet themes, 238, 240. *See also* themes
StylesheetTheme attribute, 95
StyleSheetTheme attribute, 242
StyleSheetTheme property, 103
submit buttons, 114
Substitution control, 644
suffixes, Wizard control button, 251
summary error information, 169–170
support. *See* help resources
SuppressContent property, 525
synchronization
  Cache object, 608–609
  Copy Web site feature and, 44, 66
  HttpApplicationState object state, 540–541
  session state access with HttpSessionState class, 546–547
  thread, 305
SyncRoot property, 548
syntax
  global.asax file, 509–512
  syntax-coloring feature, 39, 44
System Folder permissions, 654
system HTTP modules, 25
system requirements, xviii–xix
System.Configuration.dll, 96
System.Data.dll, 96
System.Data.Odbc namespace, 268
System.Data.OleDb namespace, 268
System.Data.OracleClient namespace, 268
System.Data.SqlClient namespace, 268
System.Diagnostics namespace, 197
System.dll, 96
System.Drawing.dll, 96
System.EnterpriseServices.dll, 96
System.Net.Mail namespace, 191
System.Web.dll, 96
System.Web.Mobile.dll, 96
System.Web.Services.dll, 96
System.Web.UI namespace, 99
  overview, 120
System.Web.UI.HtmlControls namespace, 19, 130
System.Web.UI.WebControls namespace, 19, 137, 145
System.Xml.dll, 96

T

T-SQL checksum functions, 618
TabIndex property, 146
table constraints, DataTable object, 344–345
Table control, 137, 148, 154
table-mapping mechanism, data adapter, 326–330
   column-mapping mechanism, 327–328
   missing mapping actions, 328
   missing schema actions, 329
   overview, 326–327
   prefilling schemas, 329–330
Table property, 349
<table> tag, 136–137, 154
TableCell control, 148
TableDirect parameter, 294
TableMappings property, 321
TableName property, 341
TableRow control, 137, 148
tables. *See also* DataTable objects
   HtmlTable control and, 136–137
   Table control and, 154
   table row state, 337
Tables property, 334
tabular data source controls, 384
TagName property, 130
tags. *See also* HTML
   HTML server controls and, 19, 129
   runat attribute and pagewide, 17–18
   runat attribute and unknown, 18–19
   Visual Studio .NET 2005 formatting, 50
Target property, 367
target schema validation, Visual Studio .NET 2005,
   50–51
TCP (Transmission Control Protocol), 8
Technology Updates Web page, xx
template properties
   DetailsView control, 471–472
   Wizard control, 250
TemplateColumn column type, 419
TemplateControl class, 99–100
TemplateControl property, 122
TemplateField column type, 434, 442
templates
   DataGrid control templated columns, 423
   DetailsView control templated fields, 485–486
   FormView control, 490, 494–495, 496
   GridView control templated fields, 441–442
   Login control, 693

LoginView control login, 697–698
master pages as. *See* master pages
themes and, 239
Visual Studio .NET 2005 item, 46
TemplateSourceDirectory property, 101, 122
templating properties, GridView control, 430
Temporary ASP.NET Files directory, 58, 654
temporary files, 68
terminology, themes, 237–238
testing
   pages, 13
   pages with localization, 61
   projects, 65
   test pages, 48
   tested OLE DB providers, 270
   XML cache dependencies, 615–616
text boxes, HtmlTextArea control, 137–138, 137–138
text control, 20
text controls, 152–153
text/html MIME type, 10
Text parameter, 294
Text property, 20, 149, 161
TextAlign property, 364
<textarea> tag, 137–138
TextBox control, 20, 149, 152–153
Theme attribute, 95, 242
Theme property, 103
Themeable attribute, 244
themes, 236–247
   advantages of creating, 244
   applying skins, 242–243
   App_Themes directory, 62–63
   creating, 245–246
   CSS (cascading style sheet) files, 23, 239, 244–245
   customization vs. style sheet, 240
   definition and terminology, 237–238
   directory for, 58
   disabling, 243
   dynamically loading, 246–247
   enabling, on pages, 241–242
   overview, 236–237
   Page class properties and, 102
   page styling with, 23
   personalization and, 202
   rich pages and, 219
   server controls and, 127, 244
   skins and, 62, 238, 239
   structure of, 238–240
   theming pages and controls, 241–244

threads. *See also* asynchronous ADO.NET commands; locks
  AppDomains and, 24
  asynchronous handlers and, 110
threats, security, 648, 702
timeout attribute, 555, 668
Timeout column, 565
Timeout property, 548
Timestamp property, 516
Title property, 103, 135
<title> tag, 135
titles, master page, 229
tlbimp.exe tool, 522
toolbox, Visual Studio .NET 2005, 49
ToolTip property, 146
ToolTips, 135, 150
TopPagerRow property, 431, 471
TotalBytes property, 531
Trace attribute, 93
Trace objects, 100, 197, 200–201
Trace property, 516
trace viewer tool, 201–202
TraceContext class, 100, 199–200
TraceEnabled property, 103, 199
TraceMode attribute, 93
TraceMode property, 199
TraceModeValue property, 103, 199
tracing, 197–202. *See also* debugging
  execution flow, 197–199
  overview, 197
  trace viewer tool and, 201–202
  Web Site Administration Tool (WSAT) and, 74
  writing trace messages, 199–201
Transaction attribute, 95
Transaction object, 266
Transaction property, 294
transactions, ADO.NET, 308–313
  distributed transactions in ADO.NET 1.x, 312–313
  distributed transactions with TransactionScope object, 311–312
  local vs. distributed, 308
  managing ADO.NET 1.x local, 308–310
  TransactionScope object, 310–311
TransactionScope object, 310–312
Transfer method, 187, 519, 521
Transform property, 408
TransformArgumentList property, 408

transformations, XML, 157, 410
TransformFile property, 408
transition event handlers, 254
Transmission Control Protocol (TCP), 8
TransmitFile method, 529, 530
triggers, cache dependency, 617–618
trust levels, 655–658
  configuring <trust> section permissions, 655–656
  granting permissions beyond, 657–658
  overview, 655–658
  permissions, 656–657
<trust> section, configuration file, 655–656
Trusted Connection attribute, 281
try/catch/finally blocks, 192, 290
Type attribute, 204
Type Library Importer tool, 522
Type property, 138
types. *See also* classes
  attributes and, 92
  CLR, 313
  DataGrid columns, 419–420
  DataGrid items, 416–417
  GridView columns, 434
  parameter, 389–390
  request, 531–532
  user profiles and custom, 205
  XML, 314

U
UICulture attribute, 61, 95
uid attribute, 282
Unchanged state, 337
_ (underscore), 122
underscore (_), 122
Underused removal reason, 598
unhandled exceptions. *See also* exceptions
  default error pages and, 188–190
  error pages and, 192–196. *See also* error pages
  overview, 188
  robust error handling and, 192
UniqueConstraint class, 345
UniqueID property, 103, 122, 138
unknown tags, runat attribute and, 18–19
Unload event, 108, 116, 125
UnloadAppDomain method, 87, 91
Unlock method, 540
unsupported function exception, 477–497
Up browser ID, 228

Update method, 322, 385
UpdateBatchSize property, 321
UpdateCommand event, 418
UpdateCommand property, 321, 387
UpdateCommandType property, 387
UpdatedRowSource property, 294
UpdateItem method, 490
UpdateMethod property, 394
UpdateParameters property, 387, 394
UpdateRequestCache event, 505, 507
updates
　GridView control, 455–458
　Microsoft Press Technology Updates Web page, xx
　ObjectDataSource control, 401–403
　site precompilation and, 71–72
UpdateUser method, 678, 683
uploading files, HtmlInputFile control and, 141–144
Upsert value, 324
URL navigation, HtmlAnchor control, 135
Url property, 533
URL rewriting, HttpContext class, 517
UrlAuthorization module, 503
URLAuthorizationModule module, 659
UrlDecode method, 519
UrlEncode method, 519
UrlPathEncode method, 519
UrlReferrer property, 533
UseAccessibleHeader property, 415, 429, 469
UseCookie value, 670
UseCookies mode, 552
UseDeviceProfile mode, 552
UseDeviceProfile value, 671
useHostingIdentity attribute, 555
User-Agent header, HTTP, 9
user controls, 219–222
　benefits of, 220–221
　compiling, 79
　@Control directive and, 92
　disadvantages of, 221
　overview, 119
　page prototyping and, 23
　partial page page-output caching and, 636–641
　@Reference directive and, 99
　rich pages and, 219, 220
　toolbox and, 49

User ID attribute, 282
User objects, 100
user profiles, 202–215, 202–215
　accessing profile properties, 208–210
　anonymous users and, 207–208
　collection types and, 205
　creating, 203–206
　creating profile databases, 206–207
　custom types and, 205
　data model class, 204–205
　data model definition, 203–204
　grouping properties, 205–206
　migrating anonymous data, 212
　overview, 202
　page interaction, 206–212
　personalization and, 202
　personalization events, 210–212
　profile providers and, 212–215
　providers and, 33
User property, 502, 516
UserAgent property, 531
UserHostAddress property, 533
UserHostName property, 533
UserIsOnlineTimeWindow property, 677
UserLanguages property, 533
usernames. *See also* authentication; authorization;
　　　credentials; passwords
　authenticating, 663–664
　CreateUserWizard control, 701
　Membership class and managing, 681
users
　accounts. *See* accounts
　credentials. *See* credentials; usernames
　GridView control sorting and user feedback,
　　　452–453
　providers and user roles, 33
　user-defined dynamic data-binding expressions,
　　　380–382
　user-specific information. *See* personalization; user
　　　profiles
UseSubmitBehavior property, 114, 150
UseUri mode, 552
UseUri value, 671
UtcLastModified property, 610

V

Validate method, 106, 159, 572
ValidateInput method, 534
ValidateRequest attribute, 95
ValidateUser method, 678, 679–680, 683
validation. *See also* validation controls
 CausesValidation property and controlling, 140
 client vs. server, 164
 enabling client, 170–171
 HttpRequest object, 535
 server cache validation callbacks, 632
 user authentication. *See* authentication
 without validation controls for DetailsView control, 488–489
validation controls, 159–172
 BaseValidator class properties, 161
 CompareValidator control, 162–163
 ControlToValidate property and associating input controls with, 162
 cross-page postings and, 185–186
 CustomValidator control, 163–164
 DetailsView control and, 486–488
 displaying error information, 167–168
 enabling client validation, 170–171
 overview, 159–161
 RangeValidator control, 165–166
 RegularExpressionValidator control, 165
 RequiredFieldValidator control, 166
 ValidationGroup property and validation groups, 171–172
 ValidationSummary control, 168–170
ValidationExpression property, 165
ValidationGroup property, 149, 161, 171–172
ValidationProperty attribute, 162
ValidationSummary control, 161, 168–170
Validators property, 101, 159
Value attribute, 596
Value property, 19, 20, 138
Values property, 574
ValueToCompare property, 163
VaryByControl attribute, 626, 638–640
VaryByCustom attribute, 626, 635–636
VaryByHeader attribute, 626, 635
VaryByHeader property, 631
VaryByHeaders property, 635

VaryByParam attribute, 626, 633
VaryByParams property, 631, 633
.vb file extension, 42, 81
.vbproj file extension, 81
VBScript, 108
VerifyRenderingInServerForm method, 104, 175
video requirements, xix
View control, 149, 158–159. *See also* MultiView control
view state, 573–589
 changes in ASP.NET 2.0, 581–585
 common issues with, 575–578
 control state and, 128, 583–585
 creating view-stateless pages, 587
 disabling, 578–581
 encrypting and securing, 575–576
 eventing model and, 109
 keeping, on servers, 586–589
 loading, from Web server files, 588–589
 LosFormatter class and, 586
 machine authentication check, 576
 ObjectStateFormatter class and, 586–587
 overview, 573–574
 Page class events and, 111
 Page class properties and, 102
 postbacks and, 113
 _PREVIOUSPAGE hidden field and, 183
 restoration, 112
 saving, 115
 saving, to Web server files, 587–588
 serialization format, 582–583
 size thresholds and page throughput, 577–578
 StateBag class, 574–575
 ViewStateUserKey property, 102
views, data source controls and, 384–385. *See also* DataView objects; MultiView control; View control
ViewState collection, 111
ViewState dictionary, 115
_VIEWSTATE hidden field, 112, 115
ViewState objects, 538
ViewStateEncryptionMode property, 103
ViewStateUserKey property, 101, 102
virtual directories, IIS, 40–41, 67
VirtualItemCount property, 415

visibility
  server control, 123
  state management objects, 538
Visible property, 103, 122, 123, 149, 421
Visual Basic .NET, 5, 290
visual designers, 38
visual editor, web.config files and, 75–77
visual inheritance, 221–222
Visual Studio .NET 2005, 37–78
  administering applications, 72–77
  application deployment, 66–72
  ASP.NET Web site administration console, 33
  Community Technical Preview (CTP) prelease
    software, xx
  configuration files, 669
  constraints, 38–39
  Copy Web site feature, 42–44
  global.asax file, 191, 507
  highlights, 40–45
  IDE-level constraints, 39
  lack of IIS dependency, 40
  machine-level constraints, 38–39
  master pages and, 232
  Microsoft Press Technology Updates Web page, xx
  overview, 37–38, 77–78
  project compilation, 42
  projects. See projects
  smarter editing with IntelliSense, 44–45
  system requirements and editions of, xviii
  this book and, xviii
  unique IDs and, 16
  Web site access methods, 40–41
visual styles. See themes
visualizers, 64–65
.vssettings file extension, 52

W
W3C Markup Validation Service, 127
w3wp.exe worker process, 24, 63, 83
Warn method, 200
WarningLevel attribute, 93
Watch windows, 64–65
Web Administration Service (WAS), 83

Web application development. See also ASP.NET
  programming
  ASP.NET component model and, 15
  developers and this book about, xviii
  history of, 3–5, xvii–xviii
  in Visual Studio .NET 2005. See Visual Studio .NET
    2005
Web farms
  application deployment and, 68
  session state management and, 566–567
Web Forms. See also forms
  ASP.NET programming and, 5, 5–6
  code and, 53. See also code
  code-behind classes and, 48
  content pages and, 48
  single-form interface (SFI) model, 109–110
  Windows Forms model and, 6–7
Web gardens
  caching and, 595
  session state management and, 566–567
  worker processes and, 81
Web Matrix, 40
Web page help resources. See help resources
Web permission, 657
Web projects. See projects
Web Resource service, 104
Web server controls, 145–159
  AdRotator control, 155–156
  button controls, 149–150
  Calendar control, 156–157
  core, 148–154
  HiddenField and FileUpload controls, 153–154
  HTML server controls vs., 20
  HtmlInputCheckBox and HtmlInputRadioButton
    controls, 151
  HtmlTable and Table controls, 154
  HyperLink control and hyperlinks, 150
  images and image button controls, 150–151
  overview, 145
  Panel control and scrollable panels, 152
  PlaceHolder control, 157
  as server controls, 20
  styling, 146–147

text controls, 152–153
View and MultiView controls, 158–159
WebControl class methods, 147
WebControl class properties, 145–147
Xml control, 157
Web services, App_WebReferences directory and, 62
Web Setup projects, 67
Web site access methods, Visual Studio .NET 2005, 40–41
Web site administration console, Visual Studio .NET 2005, 33
Web Site Administration Tool (WSAT)
application settings management, 74–75
features of, 72–75
membership and role management, 73–74
role management and, 687–688
selecting and configuring providers, 75
Web Site copy feature, 42–44, 66
Web site projects. *See* projects
Web Site Root Folder permissions, 654
web.config files. *See also* configuration
application configuration and, 25
application deployment and, 68–69
application restarts and, 91
application settings management, 74
assemblies, 96–97
authentication settings, 669, 674
custom error messages and, 192–193
debugging and, 63
editing, 80
machine.config files and, 57. *See also* machine.config files
source code directories, 59
visual editor for, 75–77
WebControl class
methods, 147
properties, 145–147
WebPermission class, 656
WebServiceHandlerFactory class, 90
Width property, 146
Windows authentication, 658
Windows Data Protection API (DPAPI), 285
Windows Forms model, 6–7, 72, 355
Windows Installer, 67
Windows operating system. *See* Microsoft Windows

Windows SharePoint Services (WSS), 38
Windows System Folder permissions, 654
WindowsAuthentication module, 503
Wizard control, 247–258
adding steps to, 252–255
canceling navigation events, 257
defining sidebar, 255
filtering navigation with events, 255–257
finalizing, 258
methods, 251–252
multiple logical forms and, 182
MultiView control and, 159
navigating with, 255–258
overview, 248–252
programming interface, 250–252
rich pages and, 219–220
structure of, 248–249
style and template properties, 250
wizards. *See* CreateUserWizard control; Wizard control
WizardStep objects, 252–255
creating input steps, 253–254
defining sidebar, 255
overview, 252–253
StepType property and WizardStepType enumeration, 253
WizardSteps property, 251
WizardStepType enumeration, 253
worker processes
runtime environment and, 24
worker process security context, 649, 650–651
worker properties, Page class, 101–102
Workstation ID attribute, 282
WorkStationId property, 276
wrapper Cache objects, 605–606
Write method, 200, 529
WriteFile method, 529
WriteSchema write mode, 338
WriteSubstitution method, 529
WriteXml method, 335, 337–339, 342
WriteXmlMode enumeration, 338
WriteXmlSchema method, 335, 342
.wsdl file extension, 58, 62

X

XCopy deployment, 66–69
  copying files, 66
  databases and, 68
  directories and, 58
  granting permissions and, 67–68
  overview, 66
  runtime configuration and, 68–69
  Web Setup projects and, 67
XHTML, 126–127
XML
  connection strings and encryption, 285–287
  custom cache dependency, 612–617
  data type, 314
  serialization of DataSet object contents, 337–339
  transformations, 157, 410
  XHTML and, 126–127

Xml control, 157
XML data type, 314
XmlDataSource control, 384, 407–411
  displaying XML data, 408–410
  programming interface, 407–408
  transforming XML data, 410
XmlTextReader objects, 314
XPath method, 379
XPath property, 408
XPathSelect method, 379–380
XSD files, 44, 59
xsd.exe tool, 59
XSLT (Extensible Stylesheet Language
    Transformations), 157, 410
XslTransform class, 157
XSS (cross-site scripting) attacks, 648, 702

About the Author

Dino Esposito is the Microsoft ASP.NET and ADO.NET expert at Solid Quality Learning, a premier training and consulting firm.

Dino writes the "Cutting Edge" column for *MSDN Magazine* and regularly contributes Microsoft .NET Framework articles to the Microsoft ASP.NET and Visual Studio Developer Centers and other magazines, including *asp.netPRO Magazine*, *CoDe Magazine*, and the *Dr. Dobb's ASP.NET-2-The-Max* newsletter. His books include *Programming Microsoft ASP.NET* (Microsoft Press, 2003), *Building Web Solutions with ASP.NET and ADO.NET* (Microsoft Press, 2002), and *Applied XML Programming for Microsoft .NET* (Microsoft Press, 2002). Up-to-date information about Dino's upcoming articles and books can be found in his blog at *http://weblogs.asp.net/despos*.

As a member of the International .NET Association (INETA) team of speakers, Dino is a frequent speaker at local community events, particularly in Europe and the United States.

Before becoming a full-time author, consultant, and trainer, Dino worked for several top consulting companies. Based in Rome, Italy, he pioneered DNA systems in Europe, and in 1994 designed one of the first serious Web applications—an image data bank. These days, you can find Dino at leading conferences such as DevConnections, DevWeek, WinDev, and Microsoft TechEd.

Additional Resources for Visual Basic Developers

Published and Forthcoming Titles from Microsoft Press

Microsoft® Visual Basic® 2005 Express Edition: Build a Program Now!
Patrice Pelland ● ISBN 0-7356-2213-2

Featuring a full working edition of the software, this fun and highly visual guide walks you through a complete programming project—a desktop weather-reporting application—from start to finish. You'll get an introduction to the Microsoft Visual Studio® development environment and learn how to put the lightweight, easy-to-use tools in Visual Basic Express to work right away—creating, compiling, testing, and delivering your first ready-to-use program. You'll get expert tips, coaching, and visual examples each step of the way, along with pointers to additional learning resources.

Microsoft Visual Basic 2005 *Step by Step*
Michael Halvorson ● ISBN 0-7356-2131-4

With enhancements across its visual designers, code editor, language, and debugger that help accelerate the development and deployment of robust, elegant applications across the Web, a business group, or an enterprise, Visual Basic 2005 focuses on enabling developers to rapidly build applications. Now you can teach yourself the essentials of working with Visual Studio 2005 and the new features of the Visual Basic language—one step at a time. Each chapter puts you to work, showing you how, when, and why to use specific features of Visual Basic and guiding as you create actual components and working applications for Microsoft Windows®. You'll also explore data management and Web-based development topics.

Programming Microsoft Visual Basic 2005 *Core Reference*
Francesco Balena ● ISBN 0-7356-2183-7

Get the expert insights, indispensable reference, and practical instruction needed to exploit the core language features and capabilities in Visual Basic 2005. Well-known Visual Basic programming author Francesco Balena expertly guides you through the fundamentals, including modules, keywords, and inheritance, and builds your mastery of more advanced topics such as delegates, assemblies, and My Namespace. Combining in-depth reference with extensive, hands-on code examples and best-practices advice, this *Core Reference* delivers the key resources that you need to develop professional-level programming skills for smart clients and the Web.

Programming Microsoft Visual Basic 2005 Framework Reference
Francesco Balena ● ISBN 0-7356-2175-6

Complementing *Programming Microsoft Visual Basic 2005 Core Reference*, this book covers a wide range of additional topics and information critical to Visual Basic developers, including Windows Forms, working with Microsoft ADO.NET 2.0 and ASP.NET 2.0, Web services, security, remoting, and much more. Packed with sample code and real-world examples, this book will help developers move from understanding to mastery.

Programming Microsoft Windows Forms
Charles Petzold ● ISBN 0-7356-2153-5

Programming Microsoft Web Forms
Douglas J. Reilly ● ISBN 0-7356-2179-9

Debugging, Tuning, and Testing Microsoft .NET 2.0 Applications
John Robbins ● ISBN 0-7356-2202-7

Microsoft ASP.NET 2.0 *Step by Step*
George Shepherd ● ISBN 0-7356-2201-9

Microsoft ADO.NET 2.0 *Step by Step*
Rebecca Riordan ● ISBN 0-7356-2164-0

Programming Microsoft ASP.NET 2.0 *Core Reference*
Dino Esposito ● ISBN 0-7356-2176-4

For more information about Microsoft Press® books and other learning products,
visit: **www.microsoft.com/books** *and* **www.microsoft.com/learning**

Additional Resources for C# Developers

Published and Forthcoming Titles from Microsoft Press

Microsoft® Visual C#® 2005 Express Edition: Build a Program Now!
Patrice Pelland • ISBN 0-7356-2229-9

In this lively, eye-opening, and hands-on book, all you need is a computer and the desire to learn how to program with Visual C# 2005 Express Edition. Featuring a full working edition of the software, this fun and highly visual guide walks you through a complete programming project—a desktop weather-reporting application—from start to finish. You'll get an unintimidating introduction to the Microsoft Visual Studio® development environment and learn how to put the lightweight, easy-to-use tools in Visual C# Express to work right away—creating, compiling, testing, and delivering your first, ready-to-use program. You'll get expert tips, coaching, and visual examples at each step of the way, along with pointers to additional learning resources.

Microsoft Visual C# 2005 *Step by Step*
John Sharp • ISBN 0-7356-2129-2

Visual C#, a feature of Visual Studio 2005, is a modern programming language designed to deliver a productive environment for creating business frameworks and reusable object-oriented components. Now you can teach yourself essential techniques with Visual C#—and start building components and Microsoft Windows®-based applications—one step at a time. With *Step by Step*, you work at your own pace through hands-on, learn-by-doing exercises. Whether you're a beginning programmer or new to this particular language, you'll learn how, when, and why to use specific features of Visual C# 2005. Each chapter puts you to work, building your knowledge of core capabilities and guiding you as you create your first C# based applications for Windows, data management, and the Web.

Programming Microsoft Visual C# 2005 Framework Reference
Francesco Balena • ISBN 0-7356-2182-9

Complementing *Programming Microsoft Visual C# 2005 Core Reference*, this book covers a wide range of additional topics and information critical to Visual C# developers, including Windows Forms, working with Microsoft ADO.NET 2.0 and Microsoft ASP.NET 2.0, Web services, security, remoting, and much more. Packed with sample code and real-world examples, this book will help developers move from understanding to mastery.

Programming Microsoft Visual C# 2005 *Core Reference*
Donis Marshall • ISBN 0-7356-2181-0

Get the in-depth reference and pragmatic, real-world insights you need to exploit the enhanced language features and core capabilities in Visual C# 2005. Programming expert Donis Marshall deftly builds your proficiency with classes, structs, and other fundamentals, and advances your expertise with more advanced topics such as debugging, threading, and memory management. Combining incisive reference with hands-on coding examples and best practices, this *Core Reference* focuses on mastering the C# skills you need to build innovative solutions for smart clients and the Web.

CLR via C#, Second Edition
Jeffrey Richter • ISBN 0-7356-2163-2

In this new edition of Jeffrey Richter's popular book, you get focused, pragmatic guidance on how to exploit the common language runtime (CLR) functionality in Microsoft .NET Framework 2.0 for applications of all types—from Web Forms, Windows Forms, and Web services to solutions for Microsoft SQL Server™, Microsoft code names "Avalon" and "Indigo," consoles, Microsoft Windows NT® Service, and more. Targeted to advanced developers and software designers, this book takes you under the covers of .NET for an in-depth understanding of its structure, functions, and operational components, demonstrating the most practical ways to apply this knowledge to your own development efforts. You'll master fundamental design tenets for .NET and get hands-on insights for creating high-performance applications more easily and efficiently. The book features extensive code examples in Visual C# 2005.

Programming Microsoft Windows Forms
Charles Petzold • ISBN 0-7356-2153-5

CLR via C++
Jeffrey Richter with Stanley B. Lippman
ISBN 0-7356-2248-5

Programming Microsoft Web Forms
Douglas J. Reilly • ISBN 0-7356-2179-9

Debugging, Tuning, and Testing Microsoft .NET 2.0 Applications
John Robbins • ISBN 0-7356-2202-7

For more information about Microsoft Press® books and other learning products,
visit: **www.microsoft.com/books** *and* **www.microsoft.com/learning**

Additional Resources for Web Developers

Published and Forthcoming Titles from Microsoft Press

Microsoft® Visual Web Developer™ 2005 Express Edition: Build a Web Site Now!
Jim Buyens • ISBN 0-7356-2212-4

With this lively, eye-opening, and hands-on book, all you need is a computer and the desire to learn how to create Web pages now using Visual Web Developer Express Edition! Featuring a full working edition of the software, this fun and highly visual guide walks you through a complete Web page project from set-up to launch. You'll get an introduction to the Microsoft Visual Studio® environment and learn how to put the lightweight, easy-to-use tools in Visual Web Developer Express to work right away—building your first, dynamic Web pages with Microsoft ASP.NET 2.0. You'll get expert tips, coaching, and visual examples at each step of the way, along with pointers to additional learning resources.

Microsoft ASP.NET 2.0 Programming
Step by Step
George Shepherd • ISBN 0-7356-2201-9

With dramatic improvements in performance, productivity, and security features, Visual Studio 2005 and ASP.NET 2.0 deliver a simplified, high-performance, and powerful Web development experience. ASP.NET 2.0 features a new set of controls and infrastructure that simplify Web-based data access and include functionality that facilitates code reuse, visual consistency, and aesthetic appeal. Now you can teach yourself the essentials of working with ASP.NET 2.0 in the Visual Studio environment—one step at a time. With *Step by Step*, you work at your own pace through hands-on, learn-by-doing exercises. Whether you're a beginning programmer or new to this version of the technology, you'll understand the core capabilities and fundamental techniques for ASP.NET 2.0. Each chapter puts you to work, showing you how, when, and why to use specific features of the ASP.NET 2.0 rapid application development environment and guiding you as you create actual components and working applications for the Web, including advanced features such as personalization.

Programming Microsoft ASP.NET 2.0
Core Reference
Dino Esposito • ISBN 0-7356-2176-4

Delve into the core topics for ASP.NET 2.0 programming, mastering the essential skills and capabilities needed to build high-performance Web applications successfully. Well-known ASP.NET author Dino Esposito deftly builds your expertise with Web forms, Visual Studio, core controls, master pages, data access, data binding, state management, security services, and other must-know topics—combining definitive reference with practical, hands-on programming instruction. Packed with expert guidance and pragmatic examples, this *Core Reference* delivers the key resources that you need to develop professional-level Web programming skills.

Programming Microsoft ASP.NET 2.0
Applications: *Advanced Topics*
Dino Esposito • ISBN 0-7356-2177-2

Master advanced topics in ASP.NET 2.0 programming—gaining the essential insights and in-depth understanding that you need to build sophisticated, highly functional Web applications successfully. Topics include Web forms, Visual Studio 2005, core controls, master pages, data access, data binding, state management, and security considerations. Developers often discover that the more they use ASP.NET, the 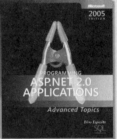 more they need to know. With expert guidance from ASP.NET authority Dino Esposito, you get the in-depth, comprehensive information that leads to full mastery of the technology.

Programming Microsoft Windows® Forms
Charles Petzold • ISBN 0-7356-2153-5

Programming Microsoft Web Forms
Douglas J. Reilly • ISBN 0-7356-2179-9

CLR via C++
Jeffrey Richter with Stanley B. Lippman
ISBN 0-7356-2248-5

Debugging, Tuning, and Testing Microsoft .NET 2.0 Applications
John Robbins • ISBN 0-7356-2202-7

CLR via C#, Second Edition
Jeffrey Richter • ISBN 0-7356-2163-2

For more information about Microsoft Press® books and other learning products, visit: **www.microsoft.com/books** *and* **www.microsoft.com/learning**

Additional Resources for Database Developers
Published and Forthcoming Titles from Microsoft Press

Microsoft® SQL Server™ 2005 Express Edition
Step by Step
Jackie Goldstein • ISBN 0-7356-2184-5

Teach yourself how to get database projects up and running quickly with SQL Server Express Edition—one step at a time! SQL Server Express is a free, easy-to-use database product that is based on SQL Server 2005 technology. It's designed for building simple, dynamic applications, with all the rich functionality of the SQL Server database engine and using the same data access APIs such as Microsoft ADO.NET, SQL Native Client, and T-SQL. With *Step by Step*, you work at your own pace through hands-on, learn-by-doing exercises. Whether you're new to database programming or new to SQL Server, you'll learn how, when, and why to use specific features of this simple but powerful database development environment. Each chapter puts you to work, building your knowledge of core capabilities and guiding you as you create actual components and working applications. You'll also discover how SQL Server Express works seamlessly with the Microsoft Visual Studio® 2005 environment, simplifying the design, development, and deployment of your applications.

Programming Microsoft ADO.NET 2.0
Applications: *Advanced Topics*
Glenn Johnson • ISBN 0-7356-2141-1

Get in-depth coverage and expert insights on advanced ADO.NET programming topics such as optimization, DataView, and large objects (BLOBs and CLOBs). Targeting experienced, professional software developers who design and develop enterprise applications, this book assumes that the reader knows and understands the basic functionality and concepts of ADO.NET 2.0 and that he or she is ready to move to mastering data-manipulation skills in Microsoft Windows. The book, complete with pragmatic and instructive code examples, is structured so that readers can jump in for reference on each topic as needed.

Microsoft ADO.NET 2.0
Step by Step
Rebecca Riordan • ISBN 0-7356-2164-0

In Microsoft .NET Framework 2.0, data access is enhanced not only through the addition of new data access controls, services, and the ability to integrate more seamlessly with SQL Server 2005, but also through improvements to the ADO.NET class libraries themselves. Now you can teach yourself the essentials of working with ADO.NET 2.0 in the Visual Studio environment—one step at a time. With *Step by Step*, you work at your own pace through hands-on, learn-by-doing exercises. Whether you're a beginning programmer or new to this version of the technology, you'll understand the core capabilities and fundamental techniques for ADO.NET 2.0. Each chapter puts you to work, showing you how, when, and why to use specific features of the ADO.NET 2.0 rapid application development environment and guiding as you create actual components and working applications for Microsoft Windows®.

Programming Microsoft ADO.NET 2.0
Core Reference
David Sceppa • ISBN 0-7356-2206-X

This *Core Reference* demonstrates how to use ADO.NET 2.0, a technology within Visual Studio 2005, to access, sort, and manipulate data in standalone, enterprise, and Web-enabled applications. Discover best practices for writing, testing, and debugging database application code using the new tools and wizards in Visual Studio 2005, and put them to work with extensive code samples, tutorials, and insider tips. The book describes the ADO.NET object model, its XML features for Web extensibility, integration with Microsoft SQL Server 2000 and SQL Server 2005, and other core topics.

Programming Microsoft Windows Forms
Charles Petzold • ISBN 0-7356-2153-5

Programming Microsoft Web Forms
Douglas J. Reilly • ISBN 0-7356-2179-9

Inside Microsoft SQL Server 2005: The Storage Engine (Volume 1)
Kalen Delaney • ISBN 0-7356-2105-5

Debugging, Tuning, and Testing Microsoft .NET 2.0 Applications
John Robbins • ISBN 0-7356-2202-7

Microsoft SQL Server 2005 Programming *Step by Step*
Fernando Guerrero • ISBN 0-7356-2207-8

Programming Microsoft SQL Server 2005
Andrew J. Brust, Stephen Forte, and William H. Zack
ISBN 0-7356-1923-9

For more information about Microsoft Press® books and other learning products,
visit: **www.microsoft.com/books** *and* **www.microsoft.com/learning**

What do you think of this book?
We want to hear from you!

Do you have a few minutes to participate in a brief online survey? Microsoft is interested in hearing your feedback about this publication so that we can continually improve our books and learning resources for you.

To participate in our survey, please visit:

www.microsoft.com/learning/booksurvey

And enter this book's ISBN, 0-7356-2176-4. As a thank-you to survey participants in the United States and Canada, each month we'll randomly select five respondents to win one of five $100 gift certificates from a leading online merchant.* At the conclusion of the survey, you can enter the drawing by providing your e-mail address, which will be used for prize notification *only*.

Thanks in advance for your input. Your opinion counts!

Sincerely,

Microsoft Learning

Microsoft | Learning

Learn More. Go Further.